Collier's Conflict of Laws

This reworked version of *Conflict of Laws* introduces a new generation of students to the classic text in the subject. Completely rewritten, it reflects all the recent developments including the increased legislation and case law in the field. The author's teaching experience is reflected in her ability to provide students with a clear statement of rules which sets out a clear framework to the subject, before adding detail and critical analysis. Recognising that the unique procedural aspect of the subject challenges most students, the book explores conflicts of law in its practical context to ensure understanding. Teachers will appreciate the logical structure, which has been reworked to reflect teaching in the field today. Retaining the authority that was the hallmark of the previous edition, this contemporary and comprehensive textbook is essential reading.

Pippa Rogerson is a Senior Lecturer at the University of Cambridge.

Collier's Conflict of Laws

Fourth Edition

PIPPA ROGERSON

CAMBRIDGE
UNIVERSITY PRESS

CAMBRIDGE UNIVERSITY PRESS

Cambridge, New York, Melbourne, Madrid, Cape Town,
Singapore, São Paulo, Delhi, Mexico City

Cambridge University Press
The Edinburgh Building, Cambridge CB2 8RU, UK

Published in the United States of America by
Cambridge University Press, New York

www.cambridge.org
Information on this title: www.cambridge.org/9780521513531

First published 2013

Printed and bound in the United Kingdom by the MPG Books Group

A catalogue record for this publication is available from the British Library

Library of Congress Cataloguing in Publication data

Rogerson, Pippa, author.
  Collier's Conflict of laws. – Fourth edition / Pippa Rogerson.
    pages   cm
  Includes bibliographical references and index.
  ISBN 978-0-521-51353-1 (Hardback) – ISBN 978-0-521-73505-6 (Paperback)
  1. Conflict of laws–England.   I. Collier, John G. (John Greenwood). Conflict of laws.
II. Title.
  KD680.C65 2013
  340.90942–dc23

                                                                    2012040145

ISBN 978-0-521-51353-1 Hardback
ISBN 978-0-521-73505-6 Paperback

To my husband Gerry Fitzsimons
(28 August 1959–22 November 2007)

And our children Olivia, Harriet, Beatrice, Isobel and Amelia

Contents

Preface

John Collier has been a supervisor, mentor, colleague and most importantly friend of mine for over twenty-five years. When he asked if I would like to do a new edition of his 'magic book', I did not hesitate. Although the last edition had been rather overtaken by the outpouring of new cases from the English courts and the CJEU, and the flood of new legislation from the European Union, it remained a book on my shelf to which I often turned for guidance. I hope to have maintained his clarity and brevity of expression as far as possible. I fear I may have failed his high standards in some places. Gender-neutral language has been used as far as possible, though I regret that occasionally that practice makes for less than fluent sentences.

Regrettably, some of the chapters of the old work have had to be jettisoned. Important conflict of laws issues in succession, marriage and family law have been eclipsed in many courses in conflict of laws by the burgeoning and complex questions arising in jurisdiction, in choice of law in contractual and non-contractual obligations, and in property. Not only has there been a great deal of new EU legislation but the cases themselves have become more complicated and need more exposition to make them understandable. Judgments are longer. All of these factors have combined to militate against a shorter book. The interface between public international law and private international law and theoretical considerations in conflict of laws deserve whole books to themselves, which have already been written by people much better versed in the subject than I am. They too had to be excised. The chapter on domicile and habitual residence remains; partly as those concepts remain important in EU legislation and partly due to their inherent interest.

Much of the third edition has been rewritten for this new book: particularly the chapters on domicile and habitual residence, jurisdiction (to include both the Brussels I Regulation and the proposed reforms) including a longer section on restraining orders, enforcement of judgments (also including the reforms to the Brussels I Regulation), choice of law in contractual obligations (to take account of the Rome I Regulation), choice of law in non-contractual obligations (to take account of the Rome II Regulation) and choice of law in property. A new chapter on procedure in the English courts has been included to give readers unfamiliar with the procedural background to international commercial cases insight into the practice behind the decisions. A new chapter on provisional measures covers the important area of freezing injunctions and the particular problems these raise in international litigation. I have discussed more cases in the text. These give illustrations of the factual background to the way the rules are applied, which I hope will aid students' understanding of the subject.

The mythical countries of Ruritania, Utopia and Illyria are used in hypothetical cases. I hope that readers will not then be distracted imagining what the actual rules of law of those countries might be. I assume that readers will know which are the Member States of the EU and so any other country mentioned is a 'third state', i.e., not a Member State of the EU.

Too many people deserve the author's gratitude; many have to remain nameless here but my gratitude to them is nonetheless warm. I thank my editor at CUP, Sinead Moloney, who has stuck with this project and has been very forbearing with my slow progress. She even accepted its increased length and reduced coverage with little demur. My colleagues at Cambridge University with whom I have taught either conflict of laws or international commercial litigation over the years require special mention and thanks: John Collier, Richard Fentiman and Louise Merrett, in particular. Thanks must also go to my many students over the last twenty-five years, you have taught me much more than I suspect I have taught you. All errors are my own fault.

Especial thanks must go to my daughters: Olivia, Harriet, Beatrice, Isobel and Amelia. They have all been a great support and a terrific distraction over the six years this book has been in gestation – but now can have their mother back! Their father and my husband, Gerry Fitzsimons, died shortly after I signed the contract with CUP. He would have been proud to see its completion although he would have been very impatient with the length of time it has taken me to write it. There have been some benefits to the long wait. This book has been able to be completely up-to-date with the recent European legislation. The law is stated at 1 October 2012 but as far as possible changes have been included up to 30 December 2012.

Table of cases

Table of statutes

Statutory instruments

European Legislation

Treaties

Regulations

Decisions

Directives

Treaties and Conventions

1

Introduction

1. The subject matter

The English conflict of laws is a body of rules whose purpose is to assist an English court in deciding a case which contains a foreign element. It consists of three main topics, which concern respectively: (i) the jurisdiction of an English court, in the sense of its competence to hear and determine a case; (ii) the selection of appropriate rules of a system of law, English or foreign, which it should apply in deciding a case over which it has jurisdiction (the rules governing this selection are known as 'choice of law' rules); and (iii) the recognition and enforcement of judgments rendered by foreign courts or awards of foreign arbitrations.

If the case contains no foreign element, the conflict of laws is irrelevant. If an Englishman and woman who are both British citizens, domiciled and resident in England, go through a ceremony of marriage in England and later, when they are both still domiciled and resident here, the wife petitions the English court for a divorce, no foreign element is involved. No problem of jurisdiction arises and any questions about the validity of the marriage or the grounds on which a divorce can be granted, as well as any procedural or evidential matters, are all governed by English law alone. The same is true if two Englishmen in England contract here for the sale and purchase of goods to be delivered from Oxford to Cambridge with payment in sterling in London, and the seller later sues the buyer and serves him with a claim form in England.

But if we vary the facts and suppose in the first example at the time the wife petitions for divorce the husband is domiciled and resident in Utopia, and that the ceremony had taken place in Utopia and the husband argues that it did not comply with the requirements of Utopian law so that there is no marriage to dissolve, the conflict of laws becomes relevant. The husband's absence raises the question of the court's jurisdiction, and his argument raises that of whether Utopian or English law is to determine the validity of the marriage.

Or suppose in the second situation the seller is an Englishman in England who agrees to sell goods in England to a Utopian buyer in Utopia, to be delivered in Utopia and paid for in sterling to an English bank in Utopia. The question arises as to whether the seller can invoke the jurisdiction of the English court against the buyer, who is still in Utopia, if the seller wishes to sue the buyer for breach of contract or for failure to pay the price. The further question may also arise as to which law, English or Utopian, is to be applied to determine the parties' rights and obligations should the English court take jurisdiction.

It will be seen from these examples that a question of jurisdiction and one of choice of law may both be involved in a particular case. But they can arise independently. The court may clearly have jurisdiction, as it has in the divorce case, but it has to answer the choice of law question. Or there may be no question as to what law to apply, as would be the case in the contract example if the parties had stipulated that English law should govern their agreement, but there would be a question whether the English court has jurisdiction.

The third topic of the recognition and enforcement of foreign judgments usually arises independently of questions of the jurisdiction of the English court and does not overlap with choice of law. A foreign judgment on the facts of a case may be raised as a defence to an action on the same facts which is being heard by the courts in England. Alternatively, a person in whose favour a foreign judgment has been awarded seeks to enforce that judgment in England using the summary judgment procedure of the English courts.

These are only examples. A jurisdictional question may arise in any kind of case. There are two broad regimes dealing with the jurisdiction of the English courts in civil and commercial matters. Traditionally, jurisdiction depends upon being able to serve a defendant using the Civil Procedure Rules (CPR). The CPR provide the method of serving a defendant who is physically present within the jurisdiction (the presence providing the basis for jurisdiction under the national rules)[1] and both the grounds for the exercise of jurisdiction and a method for serving the defendant who is not physically present. The alternative Brussels I Regime[2] lays down grounds for the allocation of jurisdiction to the courts in many cases. These European rules are largely triggered by the domicile of the defendant in an EU Member State.[3] In matrimonial cases, both a European regime and statutory rules of jurisdiction exist. For reasons of space, these rules are not covered in this book. There are some occasions on which no jurisdiction exists either because a party is immune from suit[4] or because the subject matter cannot be adjudicated in the English courts.[5] A choice of law problem can arise in any civil law suit. The conflict of laws

---

[1] As opposed to those which apply under the Brussels I Regulation.

[2] The regime includes the Brussels I Regulation and the Lugano Convention on Jurisdiction and Enforcement of Judgments in Civil and Commercial Matters (revised in 2007 [2007] OJ L339/1). The latter came into force on 1 January 2010 in the EU, Norway and Denmark, on 1 January 2011 in Switzerland and on 1 May 2011 in Iceland ([2011] OJ L138/1).

[3] See further Chapter 5.   [4] For example, sovereign or diplomatic immunity.

[5] For example, questions of title to foreign land, *British South Africa Co v Companhia de Moçambique* [1893] AC 602.

is concerned with all of the civil and commercial law but does not deal with criminal, constitutional or administrative cases.[6] It therefore covers the law of obligations (contract, tort and restitution), the law of property (both immovable and movable) whether the question arises between parties who are alive or by way of succession.[7] It is concerned also with family law, including marriage and divorce, civil partnership, and guardianship and the relations of parent and child. Recognition or enforcement of a judgment in some civil or commercial matter may be called for whether it dealt with a breach of contract or a tort (delict) or the ownership of property or concerned status, such as a decree of divorce or nullity of marriage or a custody or adoption order. However, only civil and commercial matters and not those of family law are discussed in this book.

2. The name

Two names for the subject are in common use; however, they are interchangeable. Neither is wholly accurate or properly descriptive. The name 'conflict of laws' is somewhat misleading, since the object of this branch of the law is to eliminate any conflict between two or more systems of law (including English law) which have competing claims to govern the issue which is before the court, rather than to provoke such a conflict, as the words may suggest. However, it was the name given to the subject by A. V. Dicey, when he published his treatise, the first coherent account given by an English lawyer of its rules and principles, in 1896[8] and it has been in use ever since.

Another name is 'private international law', which is in common use in Europe. This is arguably less misleading than 'conflict of laws', and each of its three words requires comment. 'Private' distinguishes the subject from 'public' international law, or international law *simpliciter*. The latter is the name for the body of rules and principles which governs states and international organizations in their mutual relations. It is administered through the International Court of Justice, other international courts and arbitral tribunals, international organizations and foreign offices, although, as part of a state's municipal or domestic law, it is also applied by that state's courts.[9] Its sources are primarily to be found in international treaties, the practice of states in their relations (or custom) and the general principles of municipal legal systems.[10]

---

[6] These are seen as matters falling within the sovereignty and territoriality of each state.

[7] Choice of law rules on succession have been omitted from this book.

[8] The latest edition (14th edn, Sweet & Maxwell, 2006 plus later supplements) of *The Conflict of Laws*, called *Dicey, Morris and Collins* after its more recent editors is still treated as the most authoritative textbook.

[9] The question whether international law is part of English law cannot be pursued here.

[10] Statute of the International Court of Justice, Art. 38. This also states that textbooks on the subject and judicial decisions are subsidiary means for the determination of the rules to be applied by the International Court.

Private international law is concerned with the legal relations between private individuals and corporations, though also with the relations between states and governments so far as their relationships with other entities are governed by municipal law, an example being a government which contracts with individuals and corporations by raising a loan from them.[11] Its sources are the same as any other branch of municipal law, which is to say that English private international law is derived from legislation and the decisions of English courts. A variation on this nomenclature is the Germanic 'international private law' as the title of the subject.

'International' is used to indicate that the subject is concerned not only with the application by English courts of English law but of rules of foreign law also. The word is inapt, however, in so far as it might suggest that it is in some way concerned with the relations between states (it is even more inapt if it suggests 'nations' rather than states).[12]

The word 'law' must be understood in a special sense. The application of the rules of English private international law does not by itself decide a case, unlike that of the rules of the English law of contract or tort. Private international law is not a substantive body of law in this sense, for, as we have seen, it merely provides a set of rules which determine whether the English court has jurisdiction to hear and decide a case, and if it has, what rules of which system of law, English or foreign, will be employed to decide it, or whether a judgment of a foreign court will be recognized and enforced by an English court.

3. Geographical considerations

For the purpose of the English conflict of laws, every country in the world which is not a part of England and Wales[13] is a foreign country and is foreign law. This means that not only totally foreign independent countries such as France or Russia, or independent Commonwealth countries such as India or New Zealand, are foreign countries but also British colonies such as the Falkland Islands. Moreover, the other parts of the United Kingdom – Scotland, Northern Ireland – are foreign countries for present purposes, as are the other British Islands, the Isle of Man, Jersey and Guernsey. It may be that the rules of another system are identical with those of English law, or that they are found in legislation such as the Companies Act 2006 which extends to both England

---

[11] See *R v International Trustee for the Protection of Bondholders A/G* [1937] AC 500, HL, where it was held that certain bonds issued in New York by the British government were governed by New York law.

[12] The rules of private international law apply between, for example, England and Scotland, which are not separate states. The English and the Scots may be regarded as separate nations but that is not why the rules so apply; it is because they have separate legal systems.

[13] Although Wales now has its own legislature, the court system is still unified with that of England and much of the law is the same. Conflict of laws issues between the two countries have yet to arise in abundance.

and Scotland. But if, say, New Zealand or Scots law falls to be applied by an English court, it is nonetheless the rules of New Zealand or Scots law which are being applied, and not English law, even though those are identical.[14]

In the case of foreign countries with a federal constitutional organisation, reference to the foreign country or law is not generally to the state in an international sense, but to one of the component parts thereof, if these are regarded by the constitutional law of that country as being separate entities having separate legal systems.[15] Thus, the reference is not usually to the United States of America, but to a state therein (such as New York or California), or to Canada, but to a province (for example, Ontario or Quebec) or to Australia, but to one of its states (such as Victoria or New South Wales).[16]

4. Glossary

Conflicts lawyers commonly employ some latin terms, which are a convenient shorthand for certain concepts that are in common use. Some of these are:

Forum conveniens – the court which is most appropriate to decide the dispute

Forum non conveniens – a court (usually the English court) which is considered inappropriate to decide the dispute

Lex causae – the law which governs an issue, alternatively the substantive law, the applicable law, the governing law or the proper law

Lex domicilii – the law of a person's domicile

Lex fori – the law of the court hearing the case. English law is the *lex fori* of a case heard in the English court

Lex loci actus – the law of the place where a transaction is concluded; in relation to the conclusion of a contract called *lex loci contractus* and to the celebration of marriage, *lex loci celebrationis*

Lex loci damni – the law of the place where the harm is suffered

Lex loci delicti commissi – the common law concept of law of the place where the tort was committed which can either be the place where the events occurred or where the harm was suffered

Lex loci solutionis – the law of the place of performance (of a contract)

Lex situs – the law of the place where the property is situated

---

[14] Though see *Attorney General for New Zealand v Ortiz* [1984] AC 1, HL, where certain statutes of New Zealand which were in the same terms as English statutes were interpreted by resort to English case law.

[15] For an example of the difficult overlaps in some systems between federal and state law and the problems they cause for conflict of laws see *Adams v Cape Industries plc* [1990] Ch. 433.

[16] However, it is obvious that for the purpose of determining a person's nationality, which is rarely necessary in the conflict of laws, it is the United States, Canada or Australia which must be referred to.

2

Characteristics of the English conflict of laws

1. Late development

Compared with other branches of English law, a systematic body of rules on the conflict of laws only came into being at a comparatively late stage. The earliest cases appear to have concerned the enforcement of foreign judgments.[1] An eighteenth-century case, which is still of binding authority, concerned the validity of a foreign marriage.[2] Lord Mansfield who was pre-eminent in the development of the body of commercial law in the latter half of the eighteenth century, gave judgments concerning foreign contracts,[3] torts,[4] and the duty to give effect to, and sometimes deny effect to, foreign laws.[5]

It can be said with some confidence that the subject began to burgeon in the latter part of the nineteenth century, which at the same time saw the development (after 1857) of family law and the coming into existence of a coherent body of commercial law, since that period witnessed a rapid expansion of international trade and financial transactions. In those years, the courts evolved more sophisticated rules as regards domicile, the validity of marriages and recognition of foreign legitimations, formulated a doctrine of the proper law of a contract, laid down the rules concerning liability for torts committed abroad and adopted clear rules on the recognition and enforcement of foreign judgments. In order to formulate these principles the English courts had to rely more on the writings of jurists than was usual with them; Huber and the American, Story J, are notable examples. These were indeed foreign jurists, as A. V. Dicey did not publish his *Conflict of Laws* until 1896, the first English writer to set down the rules in a systematic fashion and to formulate a theoretical basis for them, extracting a coherent set of principles.

Because of this feature, it is sometimes dangerous to rely on older authorities.[6] Moreover, even decisions of those years or of the early years of the

---

[1] *Wier's* Case (1607) 1 Rolle Ab. 530 K 12.
[2] *Scrimshire v Scrimshire* (1752) 2 Mag. Con. 395, 161 English Rep. 782.
[3] *Robinson v Bland* (1760) 2 Burr. 1077.   [4] *Mostyn v Fabrigas* (1774) 1 Cowp. 161.
[5] *Holman v Johnson* (1775) 1 Cowp. 341.   [6] For example, *Male v Roberts* (1800) 3 Esp. 163.

twentieth century are unreliable or, to our modern eyes, confused. Some questions remain unanswered: for example, what law governs capacity to conclude a commercial contract?[7] Or, does capacity to make a will of movable property depend on the law of the testator's domicile at the time he makes a will or at the time of his death? English cases on the choice of law rules regarding restitution and constructive trusts are sparse and unclear. Other topics are also subject to considerable doubt. Partly this is due to the nature of the subject. Because of the international element in private international law, cases rarely arise on very similar facts and are therefore easily distinguishable and firm precedents are difficult to find. Any student of the subject will need to bear principles in mind to help guide them to acceptable answers in many areas.

It is also worth mentioning that over the last thirty years the emphasis of the subject has changed considerably. Before that time, choice of law questions predominated over the procedural areas of jurisdiction and provisional measures.[8] Matters of jurisdiction, in particular, have become of enormous practical importance and the number of cases has increased greatly. Considerations of the possible enforcement of foreign judgments are also critical to the practice of international commercial litigation as seen in the commercial court in London.[9] There has been a revolution in the traditional rules allocating jurisdiction to the English court and also an influx of EU legislation on jurisdiction. Both these movements have led to uncertainties in the rules which engendered more litigation. It is likely that this period of tremendous change is coming to an end, and questions of choice of law will become more prominent again. However, the rules on choice of law have undergone their own revolution, one imposed by the EU. There are relatively new Regulations providing choice of law rules for contractual and non-contractual obligations.[10] It will be some considerable time before all the uncertainties arising from this new legislation have been determined by the courts, especially by the Court of Justice of the European Union (CJEU).

---

[7] Rome I Regulation (Regulation (EC) 593/2008 [2008] OJ L177/6) on the law applicable to contractual obligations does not apply to capacity (Art. 1(2)(a) without prejudice to Art. 13), see further pp. 320–1 below.

[8] Such as freezing injunctions (also known as *Mareva* injunctions named after the case of *Mareva Compania Naviera SA v International Bulk Carriers SA (The Mareva)* [1975] 2 Lloyd's LR 509); and restraining orders (also known as anti-suit injunctions).

[9] Over 1,300 disputes were commenced in the Commercial Court in 2006. The combined monies in dispute were estimated at £20 billion. A significant percentage of disputes (estimated at over 80 per cent) involved one foreign party. Some 40 per cent involved no English party.

[10] Rome I Regulation and Rome II Regulation (Regulation (EC) 864/2007 on the law applicable to non-contractual obligations [2007] OJ L199/40).

2. Legislation: the increasing role of the EU

Until the latter part of the twentieth century, the English conflict of laws was characterised by a lack of legislative interference; most of the rules were judge-made. A few statutes existed, for example those on the recognition of foreign judgments,[11] but they did not contain any choice of law rules; this was also true of the divorce jurisdiction rules. There were remarkably few Acts which dealt specifically with choice of law rules.[12]

However, this halcyon period[13] is now over. Legislation, national, international and European, has increasingly affected the conflict of laws during the last fifty years. It can safely be said that the common law is supreme in very few areas. National legislation has increasingly taken account of conflict of laws issues.[14] Conventions on specific areas have been incorporated into English law.[15] In particular, the growth in European regulation of conflict of laws is remarkable. This started with the 1968 Brussels Convention[16] by which the six original contracting Member States to the European Economic Community recognised that Article 220 of the original Treaty would need implementation by a Convention determining the jurisdiction of courts and facilitating the reciprocal recognition and enforcement of their judgments. That Convention has been replaced with the Brussels I Regulation.[17] Further Regulations now deal extensively with matters of jurisdiction, recognition and enforcement of judgments in other areas such as insolvency and maintenance.[18] Other Regulations provide for procedural mechanisms such as the

---

[11] Such as the Administration of Justice Act 1920 or the Foreign Judgments (Reciprocal Enforcement) Act 1933.

[12] Examples include the Bills of Exchange Act 1882, s. 72 and the Legitimacy Act 1926, now repealed.

[13] The first edition of *Cheshire and North* referred to conflict of laws being 'relatively free of the paralysing hand of the parliamentary draftsman'.

[14] Recent examples include Companies Act 2006, Gambling Act 2005, Civil Partnership Act 2004, Adoption and Children Act 2002, Employment Rights Act 1996.

[15] For example, the Convention on the Law Applicable to Trusts and their Recognition enacted by the Recognition of Trusts Act 1987.

[16] The Brussels Convention on Jurisdiction and the Enforcement of Judgments in Civil and Commercial Matters was enacted by the Civil Jurisdiction and Judgments Act 1982.

[17] Regulation (EC) 44/2001 on jurisdiction and the enforcement of judgments in civil and commercial matters [2001] OJ L12/1. Originally promulgated under Title IV of the EC Treaty requiring judicial cooperation in maintaining an area of freedom, security and justice for the sound operation of the internal market.

[18] Such as Council Regulation (EC) 1346/2000 on insolvency proceedings [2000] OJ L338/1 (amended [2003] OJ L236/33 and [2005] OJ L100/1); Council Regulation (EC) 2201/2003 concerning jurisdiction and the recognition and enforcement of judgments in matrimonial matters and matters of parental responsibility [2003] OJ L338/1 (amended [2004] OJ L367/1); Regulation (EC) 805/2004 establishing a European Enforcement Order for uncontested claims [2004] OJ L143/15 (amended [2005] OJ L97/64, [2005] OJ L168/50); Regulation (EC) 1896/2006 establishing a European Payment Order [2006] OJ L399/1; Regulation (EC) 861/2007 establishing a European Small Claims Procedure [2007] OJ L199/1.

taking of evidence[19] or service of documents[20] within the EU. In addition, EU Regulations cover choice of law rules in contract,[21] tort,[22] maintenance and parental responsibility,[23] and in succession.[24] All aspects of private international law may be said to be subject to the harmonisation measures adopted under what was Title IV of the EC Treaty. Article 65 EC Treaty expressly permitted measures promoting the compatibility of rules of the Member States concerning conflict of laws and jurisdiction. Although there was a requirement in Article 65 for the measures to be necessary for the proper functioning of the internal market, that has not been carefully tested. It appears to be self-evident that measures to harmonise conflict of laws rules are necessary for the proper functioning of the internal market. Article 81 of the Treaty on the Functioning of the EU (ex Article 65 TEC Treaty) has further watered down this requirement.[25] However, harmonisation of conflict of laws rules within the EU could fall within the general objective of establishing an area of freedom, security and justice in which the free movement of persons is ensured.[26] These provisions are therefore justifiable within the EU.

Apart from family matters, the European Parliament and the Council act jointly under the co-decision procedure to legislate in this area.[27] By Protocol 21 of the Treaty on the Functioning of the European Union (as amended)[28] the United Kingdom is entitled to elect to participate or not in these measures, and so far it has opted in to all Regulations in this area. The EU has exclusive competence over the conclusion of external treaties in relation to rules resolving conflicts of jurisdiction,[29] on the law applicable to contractual and non-contractual obligations and some aspects of family law. It has taken over

---

[19] Regulation (EC) 1206/2001 on cooperation between the courts of the Member States in the taking of evidence in civil or commercial matters [2001] OJ L174/1.

[20] Regulation (EC) 1393/2007 on the service in the Member States of judicial and extrajudicial documents in civil or commercial matters (service of documents), and repealing Council Regulation (EC) 1348/2000 [2007] OJ L324/79.

[21] Rome I Regulation (Regulation (EC) 598/2008 on the law applicable to contractual obligations [2008] OJ L177/6).

[22] Rome II Regulation (Regulation (EC) 864/2007 on the law applicable to non-contractual obligations [2007] OJ L199/40).

[23] Regulation (EC) 4/2009 on jurisdiction, applicable law, recognition and enforcement of decisions and cooperation in matters relating to maintenance obligations [2009] OJ L7/1.

[24] Regulation (EU) 650/2012 of the European Parliament and of the Council on jurisdiction, applicable law, recognition and enforcement of decisions and acceptance and enforcement of authentic instruments in matters of succession and on the creation of a European Certificate of Succession [2012] OJ L201/107.

[25] Article 81 of the Treaty on the Functioning of the European Union refers to such measures 'particularly when necessary' to the functioning of the internal market; this is less powerful than the phrase in the former Art. 65 EC Treaty which is 'in so far as necessary'.

[26] Article 3 of the Treaty on European Union as amended by Lisbon Treaty (ex Article 2 TEU).

[27] Article 81(2) of the Treaty on the Functioning of the European Union.

[28] Ex Art. 69 EC Treaty.

[29] Opinion 1/03 on the competence of the Community to conclude the new Lugano Convention on jurisdiction and the recognition and enforcement of judgments in civil and commercial matters, known as the Lugano Opinion [2006] ECR I-01145.

negotiations with, for example, the Hague Conference on Private International Law which is a global inter-governmental body developing multilateral instruments on private international law.[30] However, the Commission has indicated that it will permit Member States to enter into separate agreements with third countries subject to its prior approval.[31] Even the traditional common law rules concerning the jurisdiction of the English courts over disputes where there is no connection with the EU could have been subsumed into European rules. Lord Goff's carefully crafted towering achievement in the doctrine of *forum conveniens*[32] would then have tottered into obscurity. Fortunately, it appears from the latest proposal that this tragedy has been averted.[33]

---

[30] As a result see Council Decision (EC) of 26 February 2009 on the signing on behalf of the European Community of the Convention on Choice of Court Agreements (2009/397/EC) [2009] OJ L133/1.

[31] Council of Europe press release 10697/09, 5 June 2009.

[32] See further Chapter 6.

[33] Document for discussion by the Council of the European Union on 7 June 2012, 10609/12 ADD 1.

3

Domicile and habitual residence

1. Introduction: personal connecting factor for choice of law and jurisdiction

When the English court is faced with an issue with an international element, it may use a choice of law rule to identify the system of law whose rules will determine the particular issue. Choice of law rules usually have the form of an issue plus a connecting factor.[1] Choice of law rules dealing with personal issues often share a connecting factor. Originally this personal connecting factor was a person's domicile, but in modern times domicile has been replaced in some choice of law rules with residence. In some cases the personal connecting factor is either the domicile or the residence of a person. One can argue that domicile and residence are the same concept but with slightly different rules of attribution. Domicile means 'home' and for choice of law purposes it is a person's permanent home. Residence clearly has the same meaning, particularly when qualified by 'habitual', which is usual for choice of law rules. The intention behind the move towards residence might have been to simplify the identification of the connecting factor. However, identifying either a domicile or a habitual residence can be difficult in any but the most simple cases. Where is a homeless person resident? Where is 'home' for a student who lives at University during the academic year and spends half the rest of the year with each parent who are now divorced? Nevertheless, the identification of the personal connecting factor is critical. It is the law of the domicile which determines, in principle, whether a man or woman has legal capacity to marry, and how the estate of a deceased person is to be distributed.

The personal connecting factor may also determine the jurisdiction of courts to dissolve or annul a marriage, so the English courts have jurisdiction to dissolve a marriage of someone who is domiciled *or* resident in England. Alternatively, the personal connecting factor may provide a ground for recognition of a foreign divorce, such that a divorce decree given by the Ruritanian courts to someone domiciled or resident in Ruritania will be recognised in England. These areas of conflict of laws are not discussed in this book.

---

[1] See Chapter 9.

Apart from the conflict of laws, domicile and residence have significance in other areas of the law, especially revenue law. The courts have shown a willingness to borrow from the interpretation given to the concepts in these other areas when deciding on their use in conflict of laws. There is some strength in the argument that they should be interpreted in the same way, especially when the same words are used in various statutes. However, a note of caution should be sounded. Choice of law rules, in particular, work best when a single law is identified. It matters less that revenue is sought more than once which might result from a person being resident in more than one place.[2] Residence when used for jurisdiction purposes (where again an overlap between two residences is less problematic) will work less well when translated into a choice of law connecting factor.

2. Meaning of domicile

First, we shall focus on identifying a person's domicile at common law, generally for purposes of the personal connecting factor for choice of law. Note that specific definitions of domicile are used in cases of jurisdiction under both the Brussels I Regulation[3] and for the traditional rules under the CPR.[4] Since it is a connecting factor, a person's domicile must be ascertained by applying English law, and not in accordance with the rules of a foreign legal system.

The general meaning of domicile is 'permanent home'. This seems clear enough, but the view expressed by Lord Cranworth V-C in *Whicker v Hume*[5] some 150 years ago that a person's domicile is what he regards as his permanent home is far too simplistic and, indeed, somewhat misleading. It is true that for most people their domicile coincides with their permanent home. However, domicile is a legal concept and one's 'basic' domicile is one's domicile of origin, which is ascribed to you by law at your birth, and is not necessarily the country of your family's permanent home at that time. One's domicile of dependence, whilst you are a minor, is the same as that of one or both of your parents, even though you may have no home with either of them. The ascertainment of a person's domicile of choice does depend on showing that the person intended to establish a permanent home in a particular country, but even so, what the law regards as permanent may not strike the layman as such.

The traditional view is that the rules ascribing domicile to a person are the same regardless of the context, so that one's domicile for taxation purposes would also be one's domicile for choice of law. This has broken down somewhat with specific statutory definitions now in place, for example for jurisdiction.[6] Nevertheless, unless there are clear reasons to suppose that parliament intended a different definition to that generally adopted by the common law rules of

[2] Double tax treaties can resolve the worst aspects of overpayment.
[3] See further pp. 71–3 below.   [4] See further p. 149 below.   [5] (1858) HLC 124 at 160.
[6] Civil Jurisdiction and Judgments Order 2001, SI 2001/3929, Sched. 1 para. 9, see too the Inheritance Tax Act 1984, s. 267.

domicile the common law rules will apply. Where domicile is being used for the purposes of EU legislation[7] there is good reason to suggest that the term should have an autonomous community meaning. Otherwise uniformity and certainty of the operation of the legislation throughout the EU would be prejudiced. However, there is little guidance from the CJEU as to the meaning of habitual residence, and none for the particular purpose of choice of law.

A person must be domiciled in a 'law district'. This coincides with a state such as France if that state possesses one system of law. But this is not so if the state is a federal state or which, like the United Kingdom, contains several different districts, each having its own legal system. Thus, a person must be domiciled in, say, Iowa or California and not in the United States. Likewise a person is domiciled in England or in Scotland but not in the United Kingdom. If an English person goes to the United States intending to stay there permanently but does not settle in any one of the fifty states of the Union, that person continues to be domiciled in England.[8]

When a court is deciding a person's domicile at any time, it makes a very careful evaluation of the facts. Mummery LJ in *Cyganik v Agulian*[9] put it:

> The court must look back at the whole of the deceased's life, at what he had done, at what life had done to him and at what were his inferred intentions in order to decide whether he had acquired a domicile in England by the date of his death. Søren Kierkegaard's aphorism that 'life must be lived forwards, but can only be understood backwards' resonates in the biographical data of domicile disputes.

No person can be without a domicile. A domicile is ascribed to a person by law as the domicile of origin or of dependence. As will be seen, a person keeps such domicile unless and until a domicile of choice is acquired, and if a domicile of choice is abandoned, the domicile of origin revives to be that person's domicile until another domicile of choice is acquired. This inability of anyone to be without a domicile is a feature of English law which makes domicile preferable as a connecting factor for determining personal law to any other, since a person can be without a residence, a home or a nationality. Another advantage is that no one can have more than one domicile, for any one purpose at the same time;[10] a person can, however, have more than one residence, home or nationality.

---

[7] Such as Art. 4 of Rome I Regulation on the law applicable to contractual obligations (Regulation (EC) 593/2008 [2008] OJ L177/6) and Art. 4 of Rome II Regulation on the law applicable to non-contractual obligations (Regulation (EC) 864/2007 [2007] OJ L199/40).

[8] *Gatty v Attorney-General* [1951] P 444. A person whose domicile of origin was Jamaica but who came to Great Britain intending to stay here permanently did not acquire a domicile of choice and lose his Jamaican domicile until he decided to settle in Scotland rather than England: *Bell v Kennedy* (1868) LR 1 Sc. & Div. 307. Australia and Canada are similar to the United States and the United Kingdom in this respect.

[9] [2006] EWCA Civ 129, [2006] 1 FCR 406 at para. 46.

[10] Or probably, for any purpose. But it may be that if, as in Australia, there is a federal divorce law, a person could for the recognition of his divorce be regarded as domiciled in Australia and not, say, in Victoria. Canada also has a federal divorce law.

These general principles were first enunciated by Lord Westbury in *Udny v Udny* in 1869.[11] There are three kinds of domicile: domicile of origin, domicile of choice and domicile of dependence.

3. Domicile of origin

A person's domicile of origin depends on the domicile of one of that person's parents at the time of birth, not on the place of birth, nor on the parents' residence at that time. In *Udny v Udny*,[12] for example, Colonel Udny was born and then lived in Tuscany, where his father resided as British consul. But his father was domiciled in Scotland, so the Colonel's own domicile of origin was Scotland.

The rules for the ascertainment of the domicile of origin are: (i) a legitimate child takes the child's father's domicile, (ii) an illegitimate child and (iii) (possibly) a posthumous child, that is a legitimate child born after the father's death, both take the child's mother's domicile, and (iv) a foundling[13] or one whose parent's domicile is unknown is domiciled in the place where he or she is found or born. In one situation only, (v) the domicile of an adopted child, the domicile of origin can be changed after the child's birth. By statute,[14] an adopted child becomes thereafter for all legal purposes the child of the adoptive parents, so the child takes the parents' domicile[15] as his or her domicile of origin.

A minor's domicile may change after his birth, but any new domicile the minor acquires is a domicile of dependence and not of origin (except where the child is adopted); that remains the domicile the child acquired at birth. This is important as the domicile of origin will revive if the person after majority abandons a domicile of choice without acquiring a new domicile.[16]

4. Domicile of choice

a. Differences from domicile of origin

Domicile of origin and domicile of choice can be distinguished in three ways. First, the domicile of origin is ascribed to a person by law and does not depend on his or her own acts or intentions; a domicile of choice is acquired if a

---

[11] (1869) 1 LR Sc. & Div. 441.   [12] *Ibid.*

[13] There is no English authority. In the Australian case *Re McKenzie* (1951) 51 SR (NSW) 293, an illegitimate child whose mother's domicile was unknown was held to have his domicile of origin where he was born.

[14] Adoption Act 1976, s. 39. This does *not* apply to legitimated children. A legitimated child, whatever domicile of dependence the child may acquire on legitimation, retains the original domicile of origin derived from that of the mother at the child's birth.

[15] Or that of the parent if adopted by only one person. Since 1973 a married woman can have a domicile separate from her husband's. If a child is adopted by parents who have different domiciles, presumably the child takes the new father's domicile.

[16] *Henderson v Henderson* [1967] P 77.

person goes to live in a country with the intention of remaining there permanently. Secondly, it is more tenacious than a domicile of choice. A domicile of origin can only be lost by intentional acquisition of another one, but a domicile of choice can be lost simply by leaving the relevant country intending not to return as an inhabitant. If that should happen, then unless another domicile of choice is acquired, the domicile of origin revives. This, the 'revival' of the domicile of origin, is a third distinguishing feature. It was established by *Udny v Udny* in 1869:[17]

> Colonel Udny was born in Tuscany where his father, then domiciled in Scotland, was the British consul. Thus Scotland was his domicile of origin. He later acquired a domicile of choice in England, but then fled to France to evade his creditors. He thereby abandoned his English domicile but did not acquire one in France.

The House of Lords held that when the Colonel left England, his Scottish domicile of origin automatically revived; he did not need to go and live in Scotland in order to reacquire it.[18]

b. Acquisition

Anyone over the age of 16 can acquire a domicile of choice. Up to that point a minor has either a domicile of origin which continues, or a domicile of dependency following the requisite parent which has supplanted the domicile of origin.[19] A domicile of choice is acquired by a combination of two things, the fact of actual presence or residence in a country, and the requisite intention. The two must coincide. If a person goes to a country and then leaves it, but later wishes to return there for good without actually returning, a domicile of choice is not acquired. However, provided the necessary intention exists, even a stay of a few hours will be enough to gain a domicile of choice.[20]

The chief problems in this area concern the definition of the requisite intention and the proof of its existence in the particular case.

The requisite intention may be defined as that of permanent or indefinite residence;[21] the person must intend, at the relevant time, to reside in a country for good, or at least for an unlimited period.[22] If the person does so, it does not

---

[17] (1869) 1 LR Sc. & Div. 441. See also *Henwood v Barlow Clowes International Ltd (in liquidation)* [2008] EWCA Civ 557, [2008] All ER (D) 330 (May).

[18] The revival of the domicile of origin is one of the most severely criticised rules of the English law of domicile. The criticism is discussed pp. 27–30 below.

[19] See pp. 23–7 below.

[20] As in the celebrated American case of *White v Tennant* (1888) 31 W Va. 790.

[21] *Mark v Mark* [2006] 1 AC 98.

[22] See *Re Fuld (No. 3)* [1968] P 65. For a case in which the requisite intention was not found see *Henwood v Barlow Clowes International Ltd (in liquidation)* [2008] EWCA Civ 557, [2008] All ER (D) 330 (May).

matter that he or she has a later change of mind, so long as the person does not actually cease to reside in the country.

If, however, the person intends to reside in a country for a fixed time, say five years, or for an indefinite time but thinks that he or she will leave some day, then a domicile of choice is not acquired in that country. Also, if a person is only residing in a country for a limited purpose such as employment, or if the intention to remain is conditional,[23] no domicile of choice is acquired. If the possibility of departing is in the person's mind, however, that possibility must be a real and not a fanciful contingency (such as a lottery win), nor one which is too vague. For example, compare *Cyganik v Agulian*[24] with *Lawrence v Lawrence*.[25] In *Cyganik v Agulian*:

> Mr Nathanael had been born in Cyprus but had lived largely in London between 1958 and his death in 2003. Nevertheless, he was found not to have acquired a domicile of choice in England. He had a British passport, substantial businesses in England, owned property here and had children here. On the other hand, he returned regularly to Cyprus and kept money in bank accounts there. He watched Cypriot television and his circle of friends in London were in the Greek Cypriot community.

The Court of Appeal held that he had not intended to live permanently or indefinitely in England.[26] His remaining attachments to Cyprus meant that he had not shaken off his domicile of origin, despite not having lived there or spent more than a few months there in nearly fifty years.[27] In contrast in *Lawrence v Lawrence*:

> Mr Harley was born in Pennsylvania, was a US citizen who had lived in Brazil for over thirty years, first as a US vice-consul and later doing his own business there. He was found to have acquired a domicile of choice in Brazil. Although he had kept his US passport, this was in case there was a revolution in Brazil in which case he would leave.

This eventuality was found by the Court of Appeal to be 'wholly indefinite, unpredictable and indefinable' and therefore too unlikely to prevent his

---

[23] For example in *Cramer v Cramer* [1987] 1 FLR 116. A woman who moved to England intending to live here if she and her lover married did not acquire a domicile of choice. Both he and she were already married to other people and her intention to reside here was conditional upon them both obtaining divorces.

[24] [2006] EWCA Civ 129, [2006] 1 FCR 406.   [25] [1986] Fam. 106.

[26] [2006] EWCA Civ 129, [2006] 1 FCR 406.

[27] Longmore LJ was unenthusiastic about his conclusion, finding it 'surprising that the somewhat antiquated notion of domicile should govern the question whether the estate of a person, who was, on any view, habitually resident in England, should make provision for his dependants'. At para. 58.

acquisition of a domicile of choice.[28] In *Re Furse*[29] an American who lived in England for sixty years also acquired a domicile of choice here as his stated intention to return to the United States if he ceased to be capable of an active life on his farm was found to be too vague and indefinite. As with Mr Harley, Mr Furse had wholly integrated into the community, Mr Nathanael had not.[30]

Re Furse[31] also demonstrates that residence in a country for a particular limited purpose does not in itself create a domicile of choice there. It was argued that Mr Furse had acquired a domicile of dependence in England because, when he was a minor, his father had himself acquired a domicile of choice in England. But his father had only come to England with the children after his wife had died in order to get them away from what he regarded as the undesirable influences of his wife's family, and he had returned to New York, where he died. So the father did not have any intention to remain in England and make his permanent home there, and thus did not acquire an English domicile of choice.

Physical residence and the requisite intention must coincide at the relevant time. If they do not, it is immaterial that the intention can be shown to have been formulated at some subsequent time. In the well-known case of *Bell v Kennedy*:[32]

> Mr Bell left Jamaica, his domicile of origin, as he said 'for good', and went to Scotland intending to reside there. But when he arrived he could not make his mind up as between Scotland and England, though he remained in Scotland. His wife died.

It was held that at that time his, and his wife's, domicile was still in Jamaica. Shortly afterwards he bought an estate in Scotland and settled there, but it was only then that he acquired a domicile of choice in Scotland.

The residence must have the necessary quality of residence 'as an inhabitant'.[33] It does not need to be lengthy,[34] nor need it involve property ownership.[35] However, where a person has more than one residence, the quality of each may need further investigation to determine that person's intention

---

[28] [1985] Fam. 106 at 110.   [29] [1980] 3 All ER 838.

[30] Neither did Mr Winans in *Winans v Attorney General* [1904] AC 287.

[31] [1980] 3 All ER 838.

[32] (1868) LR 1 Sc. & Div. 307. For some obscure reason this case is often thought, especially by students, to be concerned with the revival of the domicile of origin. But it is not; the domicile of origin had been replaced by a domicile of choice. See also *Cramer v Cramer* [1988] 1 FLR 116.

[33] *IRC v Duchess of Portland* [1982] Ch. 314 at 319.

[34] *Bell v Kennedy* (1868) LR 1 Sc. & Div. 307 at 319.

[35] One can be resident in a hotel, *Levene v IRC* [1928] AC 217.

to remain permanently before the person's domicile can be established. So in the more recent case of *Henwood v Barlow Clowes International Ltd (in liquidation):*[36]

> Henwood had an English domicile of origin but had spent years living in the US, the Seychelles and the Bahamas before settling in the Isle of Man for some years and so acquiring a domicile of choice there. He also travelled a great deal and had a house in France where he spent many summer months. Later after apparently leaving the Isle of Man house for his parents-in-law to live in, he bought a further house in Mauritius where he said he intended to stay but because of his work he spent only about three months of each year there.

The Court of Appeal found that he had not acquired a domicile of choice in Mauritius. The character of his residence in Mauritius was not that of his chief or principal residence but of his secondary residence. His chief residence was in France where he had owned a home on which he had expended a great deal of money and time over many years.[37] There may be a tendency to look to the number of days spent in each home as some critical factor. However, the reasons why time is spent in each place are also important. In *F v F (Divorce) (Jurisdiction):*[38]

> A wife who spent many more days each year with her husband in Egypt nevertheless was found to have acquired a domicile of choice in England. She rented a flat here and she travelled around Europe caring for her children and grandchildren, spending less time in England than in any of the other places.

Potter LJ accepted that as a single woman after the marriage started to break down she chose to reside in London on an indefinite basis even though very few days were in fact spent here. She was not found to have acquired a domicile of choice in Egypt despite having lived with her husband there. Their residence in Egypt was precarious as their immigration status was uncertain. Therefore the judge found they could not have intended to remain there indefinitely.

If one's residence is precarious or illegal that may be relevant in determining the intention to reside permanently. The mere fact that one's residence is illegal does not, however, prevent a person from being resident for domicile purposes and so acquiring a domicile of choice.[39]

---

[36] [2008] EWCA Civ 557, [2008] All ER (D) 330 (May).
[37] See too *Plummer v IRC* [1988] 1 WLR 292.   [38] [2009] 2 FLR 1496.
[39] *Mark v Mark* [2006] 1 AC 98.

c. Burden and standard of proof

The burden of proving the acquisition of a domicile of choice rests on the person who alleges it. The standard of proof is that required in ordinary civil cases, that is proof upon a balance of probabilities.[40] However, there is sufficient flexibility in the civil standard of proof to allow for more substantial evidence in some cases than others.[41] It has been said that the doctrine of the revival of the domicile of origin imposes a heavier burden when a domicile has been abandoned and no new one acquired than in cases where a domicile of choice has been acquired after another domicile of choice.[42] However, the better view is that there is no reason for a differential standard in modern times as the domicile of origin no longer necessarily gives such appropriate results.[43]

Some cases, concerning rather unusual people, are often cited in order to show that the burden of proof is extraordinarily difficult to discharge. Thus in *Ramsay v Liverpool Royal Infirmary*:[44]

> George Bowie, a Scotsman born in Glasgow with a Scottish domicile of origin, stopped working when he was thirty-seven and when he was forty-six went to Liverpool to live with (or sponge off) members of his family. He died there aged eighty-seven. He had only left Liverpool on two short trips, and refused to return to Glasgow, even for his mother's funeral. He always took a Glasgow newspaper, and called himself a 'Glasgow man', stating this in his will. He made a will which was formally invalid under English law but valid by Scots law.

The House of Lords held that he died domiciled in Scotland. Though his residence in England was lengthy, it was 'colourless' and motivated only by his attachment to a member of his family who would keep him despite his disinclination to work. The burden of proving his acquisition of a domicile in England had not been discharged. His will was thereby held to be valid.

---

[40] In *Henderson v Henderson* [1967] P 77 it was said that a higher standard was required. However, various courts since then have held that the normal civil standard suffices: *Henwood v Barlow Clowes International Ltd (in liquidation)* [2008] EWCA Civ 557, [2008] All ER (D) 330 (May) at para. 94. Nevertheless, some courts maintain the need for a higher standard, see *Munro v Munro* [2008] 3 FCR 401.

[41] *Henwood v Barlow Clowes International Ltd (in liquidation)* [2008] EWCA Civ 557, [2008] All ER (D) 330 (May) at para. 88.

[42] *Cyganik v Agulian* [2006] EWCA Civ 129, [2006] 1 FCR 406 at para. 56.

[43] See Arden LJ in *Henwood v Barlow Clowes International Ltd (in liquidation)* [2008] EWCA Civ 557, [2008] All ER (D) 330 (May) at paras. 88–96.

[44] [1930] AC 588.

In *Winans v Attorney General*:[45]

> An American, whose domicile of origin was in New Jersey, came to England
> and took tenancies of furnished houses in Brighton, one of which he kept until
> his death there thirty-seven years later. He spent parts of each year in England,
> Germany, Scotland and Russia, but during the last four years of his life, he
> confined himself to Brighton on medical advice. His two abiding preoccupa-
> tions were looking after his health and a project which never came to fruition of
> building 'cigar' or 'spindle' shaped vessels for sale to the United States in order
> to wrest the carrying trade from the British. He acquired part of a waterfront in
> Baltimore to build the ships and talked of returning there to develop the
> scheme. He disliked the English and never mixed with them socially.

The House of Lords held that he did not die domiciled in England; the Crown
had not adduced sufficient evidence of any fixed or determined purpose
positively to acquire a domicile of choice in England, and had not discharged
the burden of proof incumbent upon it.

But these cases, together with *Cyganik v Agulian*,[46] are perhaps on the edge
of the law, and possess somewhat extraordinary features. In other cases, the
burden of proof has not been so difficult to discharge.[47] Two cases can be
contrasted with *Winans v Attorney General*: *Re Furse*,[48] a tax case, and *Brown
v Brown*,[49] a divorce case. In the latter:

> The husband, an American citizen, joined an American company and came to
> England in its employ in 1966. He married here in 1969, and in the same year
> was posted to Rome for three years, but kept his membership of London
> clubs.[50] A child was born in 1971. In 1972 Mr Brown returned to London with
> his family and bought a flat, and the child was entered for an English prep
> school and Eton. In 1977 he was once again posted to Rome for three years, and
> rented the flat to a friend so he could get it back when he wanted it. His wife
> refused to return with him in 1980 and he petitioned for a divorce. She
> challenged the statement in his petition that he was domiciled in England.

It was held by the Court of Appeal that, though he was still a US citizen, he had
spent only forty-eight days out of fifteen years in the United States and that by

---

[45] [1904] AC 287.   [46] [2006] EWCA Civ 129, [2006] 1 FCR 406.

[47] In *Winans v Attorney General* [1904] AC 287, the decision of the House of Lords was by a two-
to-one majority; the majority of all the judges who had heard the case held that he died
domiciled in England.

[48] [1980] 3 All ER 838, see p. 17 above.   [49] [1982] 3 FLR 212.

[50] Including the MCC – membership of that cricket club may be regarded as an unlikely activity
for an American.

his uncontroverted evidence he had succeeded in proving that he had a settled intention to make a permanent home in England.[51]

d. Evidence of intention

Any evidence may be relevant to prove intention. No piece of evidence is necessarily decisive, and evidence which is decisive in one case may be entirely discounted in another. Declarations of the person concerned are viewed warily. For one thing, they may be self-serving.[52] Further, though they are admissible in evidence, they must be scrutinised carefully to ascertain the person to whom, the purpose for which and the circumstances in which they are made. A person who is not a private international lawyer who is asked by, for example, HM Revenue and Customs where he or she is domiciled, may not appreciate what the question means and his answer may not be held against him.[53]

The declaration must be consistent with the person's other behaviour, and must, in any case, be put into effect by conduct. In *Ross v Ross*:[54]

> The question was whether a Scotsman who had no fixed home was domiciled in New York. He told his business associates that he intended to remain there. But he always referred to Scotland as his 'home', and in an affidavit he swore he was a domiciled Scotsman.

The House of Lords held that the statements to his associates were admissible in evidence, but since they were not consistent with the rest of it, a New York domicile was not established.

e. Domicile as a social bond

Domicile denotes a social, not a political, attachment to a particular country. This is shown by cases which concerned persons who became naturalised in a state or persons who were deported or were subject to possible deportation. If a person becomes naturalised in a country this may be evidence of his or her intention to acquire a domicile there,[55] but it may not necessarily be so. That person may want to become a national of a state without wishing altogether to sever social ties with the country of his or her domicile.[56]

An alien who is liable to be deported from England and whose stay may therefore be cut short may nevertheless intend to stay in England and make it his

---

[51] See too *A v L (Divorce) (Jurisdiction)* [2009] EWHC 1448 (Fam), [2009] 2 FLR 1496.
[52] See e.g., *Henwood v Barlow Clowes International Ltd (in liquidation)* [2008] EWCA Civ 557, [2008] All ER (D) 330 (May).
[53] *Buswell v IRC* [1974] 1 WLR 1631.   [54] [1930] AC 1.   [55] *Tee v Tee* [1974] 1 WLR 213.
[56] *Wahl v Attorney General* (1932) 147 LT 382; *Re Fuld (No. 3)* [1968] P 675.

or her permanent home so far as possible.[57] In *Boldrini v Boldrini*,[58] an Italian working in England as a waiter was registered as an alien but liable to deportation. He was nevertheless found to have acquired a domicile here. A person who has become the subject of a deportation order can also acquire a domicile.[59]

A person whose residence is illegal can acquire a domicile of choice in England. Although the illegality may affect a public status such as nationality, the personal law of domicile is not so circumscribed. In *Mark v Mark*,[60] a Nigerian woman who had overstayed her visa had nevertheless resided in England for seven years and acquired a domicile of choice here.

f. Motive and freedom of choice

Motive must be distinguished from intention. The fact that a person has what might be regarded as an unworthy motive in going to a country, for example, to escape payment of taxes, does not prevent the court from holding that the person has formed the necessary intention to reside permanently there.

Generally speaking a person's intention must be the result of a free choice; but all this means is that the fact that, for instance, his or her residence is a result of a flight from justice or from oppression or enemy invasion, may make it perhaps less likely that the requisite intention is formed. However, if there is adequate evidence of such an intention, there is nothing to stop the court from holding that a domicile of choice has been acquired.

Thus, on the one hand, in *Re Lloyd-Evans*[61] a person had a domicile of choice in Belgium. He came to England in 1940 after the German invasion of that country, but he intended to return if and when the Germans were expelled. It was held that he died domiciled in Belgium. On the other hand, in *Re Martin*,[62] a French professor who had committed a crime in France fled to England in 1870 and stayed for twenty years, which was the limitation period for his crime. In 1890, after he could no longer be prosecuted in France, he returned there. Nevertheless, it was held that in 1874 he was domiciled in England.

The point is also illustrated by cases concerning invalids. If a person goes to a country for the temporary purpose of treatment he or she will obviously not acquire a domicile there; nor, it was held in *Re James*,[63] which concerned a sick Welshman who went to South Africa, if a person is told one is mortally ill and goes there to alleviate one's suffering, since the person acts under a kind of compulsion. But if one is not mortally ill, and only believes one has more chance of being well or getting better in another country, as in *Hoskins v Matthews*,[64] that person will be held to have been 'exercising a preference and not acting upon a necessity' and to have acquired a domicile there.

---

[57] *Mark v Mark* [2006] 1 AC 98.   [58] [1932] P 39.   [59] *Cruh v Cruh* [1945] 2 All ER 545.
[60] [2006] 1 AC 98.   [61] [1947] Ch. 695.   [62] [1900] P 211.
[63] (1908) 98 LT 438; see also *Winans v Attorney General* [1904] AC 287.
[64] (1855) 8 De GM&G 13.

A person who is sent to a country for employment there usually does not acquire a domicile there,[65] but may do so.[66] The same is true of a serviceman being posted abroad. In *Donaldson v Donaldson*,[67] an RAF officer stationed in Florida decided to stay there after demobilisation, and brought his wife and child there; he acquired a domicile in Florida. In contrast in *Stone v Stone*,[68] an American serviceman was held to have acquired a domicile in England, where he had been posted.

g. Abandonment of domicile of choice/dependence

In order to abandon a domicile of choice, the requisite intention to do so must be carried into effect and the person must actually leave the country of the domicile of choice. If that is not achieved, the domicile continues to adhere whatever the person's wishes. In *in b Raffenel*,[69] a widow who had a domicile of dependence with her husband in France went on board a cross-channel ferry at Calais intending to sail to England, her domicile of origin, and stay there. Before the ship left France, she fell ill and had to return to land where she died. She died domiciled in France.

Provided, however, a person has actually physically left, that person need not have formed the positive determination never to return; a domicile of choice is lost merely by having no intention to go back to the country.[70]

If no other domicile of choice is acquired, the domicile of origin revives.[71] Thus, had Mrs Raffenel's boat crossed the boundary of French territorial waters, she would have died domiciled in England. This rule is very often severely criticised; it does not represent the law in the United States, where the domicile of choice continues until a new one is established.[72]

5. Domicile of dependence

a. Married women

Until 1 January 1974, as a matter of law, a married woman automatically possessed the domicile of her husband even if he and she lived apart and even though they were judicially separated.[73] Only if their marriage was void or

---

[65] *Attorney General v Rowe* (1862) 1 H&C 31, see too *Tee v Tee* [1974] 1 WLR 213, where an Englishman who had acquired a domicile of choice in the United States did not get one in Germany on being sent there.

[66] *Brown v Brown* [1982] 2 FLR 212.

[67] [1949] P 363, see too the Scots case of *Sellars v Sellars* 1942 SC 206 and *Cruickshanks v Cruickshanks* [1957] 1 WLR 564.

[68] [1958] 1 WLR 1187.   [69] (1863) 3 Sw & Tr 49.

[70] *Re Flynn (No. 1)* [1968] 1 WLR 103 concerning the estate of the late actor, Errol Flynn – Megarry J's judgment may be read for entertainment value alone. It was approved in *Tee v Tee* [1974] 1 WLR 213.

[71] *Udny v Udny* (1869) LR 1 Sc. Div. 441; *Tee v Tee* [1974] 1 WLR 213.

[72] This is discussed further p. 27 *et seq.* below.

[73] *Attorney General for Alberta v Cook* [1926] AC 444 (PC); *Lord Advocate v Jaffrey* [1921] 1 AC 146.

after it had been annulled or dissolved or after her husband's death could she have her own domicile, separate from his.[74]

However, by the Domicile and Matrimonial Proceedings Act 1973,[75] from and after 1 January 1974, the domicile of a married woman is ascertained in the same way as that of an adult male. This rule applied to women who were married either before or after that date. If, immediately before then, a woman was married and had her husband's domicile by dependence, she is to be regarded as retaining that domicile as her domicile of choice, unless and until she acquires another domicile of choice or her domicile of origin revives on or after 1 January 1974. It has been held that her previous domicile of dependence must continue as a 'deemed' domicile of choice until she actually departs from, say, England for another country.[76]

b. Minors

A minor is a person who is aged under eighteen.[77] But a person can, since 1 January 1974, acquire his or her own domicile when that person attains the sixteenth birthday or, below that age, upon marriage.[78]

The domicile of dependence of a legitimate minor is, with the exception discussed below,[79] that of the person's father, and changes automatically if the father changes his own domicile. That will also remain the person's domicile after the father's death until the minor becomes sixteen. It may, however, after the father's death follow that of the person's mother. But if the person's *mother* changes her domicile, the minor's domicile does not necessarily alter. The mother has a power to change the minor's domicile along with her own, but she must positively change it and must not abstain from doing so. If she does exercise this power she must not, it seems, do so fraudulently, that is for a purpose other than for the benefit or welfare of the minor.[80] Thus in *Re Beaumont*:[81]

---

[74] A wife could live in another country from her husband's and if she intended to live there permanently then on his death she would immediately acquire a domicile there, even though she was unaware that she was a widow: *Re Cooke's Trusts* (1887) 56 LJ Ch. 637; *Re Scullard* [1957] Ch. 107; cf. *Re Wallach* [1950] 1 All ER 199.

[75] Domicile and Matrimonial Proceedings Act 1973, s. 1(1). The Act is not retrospective and the common law rules have to be applied to determine the domicile of a married woman before 1 January 1974.

[76] *Ibid.* s. 1(2); *IRC v Duchess of Portland* [1982] Ch. 314. This decision is not, however, free from difficulty: see J. A. Wade (1983) 32 *ICLQ* 1.

[77] Family Law Reform Act 1969, s. 1(1). Before 1 January 1970 it was twenty-one.

[78] Domicile and Matrimonial Proceedings Act 1973, s. 3(1). This does not operate retrospectively. A person can only obtain a new domicile on or after marriage when he or she is below sixteen if that person is domiciled abroad, since someone domiciled here cannot marry until he or she attains the age of sixteen.

[79] See p. 25 below.

[80] Not, for example, to acquire better rights of succession to the child's property, see *Potinger v Wighman* (1817) 3 Mer. 67.

[81] [1893] 3 Ch. 490.

> Mr and Mrs B were domiciled in Scotland. They had several children all of whom had a Scottish domicile of origin and of dependence. The father died and Mrs B then married N. They went to live in England where they acquired a domicile. They took all the children to live with them with the exception of Catherine, who was left in Scotland with her aunt, with whom she had lived since her father's death. Catherine attained her majority and shortly thereafter died in Scotland.

The Court of Appeal held that Catherine died domiciled in Scotland, since her mother had not exercised her power to alter her domicile. It should be observed that Catherine remained with her aunt for all purposes; the case would probably have been different if she had been left in Scotland for a limited and temporary purpose, for example, to remain at school there in order to finish her education.

The domicile of origin of an illegitimate child is, as we have seen, that of his mother when the child is born. Most writers say that *Re Beaumont* applies to an illegitimate child's domicile during that child's minority.[82] It is not clear that this is so. The domicile which Catherine retained was that acquired from her father, that is, her domicile of origin. That which an illegitimate child would retain would be the one derived from her mother. Moreover, Catherine remained in her domicile of origin. Suppose X is born in France and illegitimate, when X's mother is domiciled in New Zealand. If X's mother acquires a domicile in England leaving X in France, then if X's domicile does not automatically change, X will remain domiciled in New Zealand, a country in which X has never set foot, until X is sixteen at least. This does not look very sensible. The alternative, that X acquires an English domicile, could also be unattractive.

Re Beaumont does not seem a very satisfactory decision in modern times, when men and women are equal in law (although it had good reasons behind it when it was decided).[83] The situation should have been properly dealt with in 1973, when reforms, about to be discussed, were made by statute, in respect of a minor's domicile.

If, as is thought, a legitimated child acquires a domicile of dependence upon the father when the child is legitimated, the child's domicile will thereafter be ascertained as if the child were legitimate. The same must be true of a child who is adopted by a man and wife, since the child takes the adoptive parents' (presumably the father's) domicile as the domicile of origin.[84]

---

[82] See e.g., *Dicey, Morris and Collins, The Conflict of Laws* (14th edn, Sweet & Maxwell, London, 2006) p. 158.

[83] Until 31 December 1973, a married woman's domicile automatically changed with that of her husband. So if N had left his wife and acquired a domicile in Ruritania, her domicile and that of her children, including Catherine, would have become Ruritanian. But the unity of domicile of husband and wife was, as has been said (see p. 23 above), abolished as from 1 January 1974.

[84] See Adoption Act 1976, s. 39. The same problem arises in the case of a child who is adopted by a woman alone as in the case of the illegitimate child just discussed.

One problem was dealt with in a not very lucid manner in the Domicile and Matrimonial Proceedings Act 1973. It concerned the domicile of a minor whose parents had been divorced before 1 January 1974 or after that date separated, and lived in different countries and acquired different domiciles, and who lived exclusively with the mother. The Act provides[85] that where the parents of a child, including an adopted child under sixteen, are alive but live apart, the child's domicile of dependence is that of the father. But if the child has a home with the mother and none with the father, the domicile of the child is that of the mother. Once the child acquires the mother's domicile under this provision the child retains it until he or she is sixteen even if the child ceases to have a home with her, unless the child has at any time a home with the father.[86]

Two questions arise out of this. First, the statutory rules appear to apply only to the domicile of dependence since they envisage the child's domicile of origin being that of the father. Suppose the child is legitimate but the parents separate before the child's birth. Presumably, the domicile of dependence is that of the mother but the domicile of origin is that of the father, in which case the domicile changes immediately after birth. This seems very artificial.

Second, suppose the child acquires a domicile with his or her mother under the 1973 Act, then goes to live with the father on 1 February and the father dies on 2 February. The child reacquires the domicile of the father. Thereafter, the statutory rule ceases to govern, and the common law rules, including *Re Beaumont*,[87] apply. Moreover, since the 1973 Act is concerned with a situation where the parents are alive, it may be that *Re Beaumont* will apply after the father dies, even though the child has not reacquired a home with him. None of this seems satisfactory; it would have been better if Parliament had made it clear that the 1973 Act continued to apply, or better still had abolished the common law rule in *Re Beaumont* altogether.

c. Mental patients

It appears that the domicile of a mentally disordered person cannot be changed by the person's own act since he or she is incapable of forming the requisite intention,[88] and thus that person retains the domicile he or she had on becoming insane.[89] Although the Mental Health Act 1983 and the Mental Capacity Act 2005 make provisions for dealing with the residence, property and affairs of someone with a mental disorder, there are none dealing with changing that person's domicile.

---

[85] Domicile and Matrimonial Proceedings Act 1973, s. 4(1).
[86] *Ibid.* s. 4(2). The common law continues to apply in order to ascertain the minor's domicile at any time *before* 1 January 1974. By s. 4(4) and (5) the statutory rule does not apply to illegitimate children. But if the child is illegitimate the child has the mother's domicile anyway.
[87] [1893] 3 Ch. 490.   [88] *Urquhart v Butterfield* (1887) 37 Ch. D 357.
[89] *Crumpton's Judicial Factor v Finch-Noyes* 1918 SC 378.

There is authority for the proposition that if a person becomes insane during that person's minority and the insanity continues, the domicile of dependence can be changed by an alteration of the domicile of the parent upon whom that person is dependent, even if this takes place after he or she attains majority.[90] However, if that person becomes insane after he or she attains majority, the domicile cannot be changed.[91]

6. Criticism and reform

a. General

Some features of the law of domicile have long been criticised. The rules were, for the most part, laid down by judges in Victorian times, and it is argued that, though they may have been quite satisfactory as reflecting social factors then in existence, they are nowadays artificial or inadequate.

The only reform of the law has been the Domicile and Matrimonial Proceedings Act 1973. As we have seen, this discarded the common law unity of domicile between married persons and made some limited reforms in relation to the domicile of minors.[92]

Two frequently voiced complaints remain. The first concerns the alleged difficulty, which arises from the presumption of the continuance of the domicile of origin, in establishing the acquisition of a domicile of choice.[93] The other concerns the revival of the domicile of origin.[94]

These are sometimes unfavourably compared with the corresponding rules in US law. They demonstrate the tenaciousness of the domicile of origin; the American rules do not. But the contrast can be explained. When the rules were being formulated England was not a country of immigration as was the United States, and it was more a country of emigration. But many Englishmen went abroad for particular, temporary purposes, such as governing the Empire, especially India, or to make their fortune, intending to return home. The courts would be slow to hold that such people had acquired a domicile in the country to which they had gone.[95] But US courts could not possibly have presumed that immigrants from, say, Poland or Italy or Ireland were still domiciled there; especially if they had come to America to escape from persecution or hardship in Europe and did, in fact, intend to make a new life in the New World.

---

[90] i.e., when under the age of sixteen: Domicile and Matrimonial Proceedings Act 1973, s. 3(1).

[91] *Sharpe v Crispin* (1869) LR 1 P&C 611 at 618. This is aptly stigmatised as 'irrational' by J. Fawcett and J. Carruthers in *Cheshire, North and Fawcett, Private International Law* (14th edn, Oxford University Press, 2008) p. 177.

[92] Whether this exercise in law reform has been completely successful is perhaps open to doubt.

[93] See p. 19 above.   [94] See p. 23 above.

[95] The concept of an 'Anglo Indian' domicile which found favour at one time was rejected in *Casdagli v Casdagli* [1919] AC 145. No such place as 'Anglo India' ever existed.

The same considerations underlie the doctrine of the domicile of origin and explain its absence from US law. If an Englishman did acquire a domicile abroad, in New Zealand, for example, and then decided to leave that country, it was probable that he intended to return home. The law reflected what usually happened. Such a doctrine could not have been contemplated by US courts. If an Italian had settled in Illinois and then decided to go west to California to seek his fortune, but having set off met his death in an accident somewhere between the two states, it would have been irrational to hold that he died domiciled in Italy.

Attempts were made in the 1950s to abolish the presumption of the continuance of the domicile of origin and replace it with a presumption that a person is domiciled in that person's country of residence, but Bills[96] introduced into the House of Lords for this purpose were lost or withdrawn in consequence, it appears, of representations from American businessmen resident and working in England, who saw that if the burden of proving that they were not domiciled here was placed on them, it would be much more likely that the Revenue would successfully claim that they had acquired a domicile and that they would, therefore, be liable to pay more by way of UK taxes. Similar considerations may still be in play today despite the recent changes to taxation of 'non-domiciled' residents which may have made the rules on domicile less acute in taxation matters. It might be argued that the difficulty of proving the acquisition of a domicile of choice is not, in practice, as great as is often suggested.[97] However, recent cases such as *Cyganik v Agulian*[98] and *Henwood v Barlow Clowes*[99] both show the tenacity even in modern times of the domicile of origin in English law.

As to the revival of the domicile of origin,[100] neither the English nor the opposed American principle that a domicile of choice continues until another is acquired is entirely unobjectionable. In the American case *Re Jones's Estate*:[101]

> Jones was born in Wales with an English domicile of origin. He fathered an illegitimate daughter. To escape paying for this sin, he went in 1883 to the United States, married there, amassed a fortune, and became an American citizen. By Iowa law he acquired a domicile in Iowa. In May 1914 his wife died. He decided to leave Iowa and return to live out his days with his sister in Wales. In May 1915 he sailed in the *Lusitania* from New York but it was sunk in the Atlantic off Ireland by a German submarine. By Iowa law his illegitimate daughter succeeded to his estate but by English law it went to his brothers and sisters.

96 Domicile Bills 1958 and 1959.   97 See the earlier editions of this work.
98 [2006] EWCA Civ 129, [2006] 1 FCR 406.
99 [2008] EWCA Civ 557, [2008] All ER (D) 330 (May).
100 See p. 23 above.   101 192 Iowa 78 (1921).

The Supreme Court of Iowa held that, since his domicile of choice continued until he acquired another and because he never got to England, he died domiciled in Iowa.

This is hardly satisfactory in that it frustrated Jones's intentions, which were to reacquire his connection with English law and to avoid having any responsibility for his illegitimate daughter. It is also just as artificial as the revival of the domicile of origin, since it makes the devolution of a person's estate depend on the law of a country which that person has left, wishing never to return to it.

The best solution in such a case might be to deem a person to be domiciled in the country to which he or she intended to go. This would be reasonable in a case with facts such as *Re Jones's Estate* but it might not always be safe to rely on unfulfilled expectations. If the submarine had not sunk the *Lusitania*, Jones would have reached England. But suppose it had been scheduled to call at Cherbourg? We do not know that if it had done so and Jones had still been alive he would have remained on board; he might have disembarked and stayed in France.

In addition, the rules on the changing of a domicile of dependence for minors are not satisfactory. Where children are living in more complex arrangements with time spent at each parent or in an alternative household, identifying the domicile of the child with one parent may become far removed from the realities of the child's life.

Also, the law of domicile does not seem to have developed rules for identifying the domicile of children of same sex relationships. A solution might be that a child of such a relationship will be treated analogously to an illegitimate child. Therefore, the child will take the domicile of the 'mother' identified on the birth certificate as the child's domicile of origin. The child's domicile of dependence will follow that parent's domicile as it changes. This solution will not suffice when there is a child of a male-male partnership. In addition, what if the relationship breaks down and the child then lives with the other parent? A domicile of dependence which more accurately reflected a close connection between the child and a country, rather than a possibly absent parent, would be preferable.

Possible solutions to these problems in the law of domicile, if they really are serious problems, are either to regard the law as beyond redemption and abandon it as a connecting factor or make another connecting factor as an alternative to domicile. Nationality is, in general, both artificial, insufficiently personal and unsatisfactory despite its general use by civilian law countries. Citizenship is a matter of political will of a state, can be withheld or withdrawn, and a person may have no citizenship or many citizenships. Added to that, which law district is identified by American citizenship? Successive Hague Conventions on Private International Law and much European legislation[102]

---

[102] See e.g., Hague Convention on the Civil Aspects of International Child Abduction 1980; Hague Convention on Jurisdiction, Applicable Law, Recognition, Enforcement and Co-operation in respect of Parental Responsibility and Measures for the Protection of Children (1996); Wills

have resulted in a compromise between those systems which adopt domicile in our sense and those which adopt a different test and have produced 'habitual residence'[103] which has similarities to our domicile without (yet) some of the technicalities.

b. Law Commission's proposals (1987)

The Law Commission considered the law of domicile and, in 1987,[104] made proposals for far-reaching reforms. It had earlier[105] rejected the possibility of abandoning domicile as a connecting factor in favour of habitual residence. It included in its Report a Draft Bill.

It proposed that the domicile of origin should be discarded. Instead it put forward rules for determining the domicile of children at birth and until their sixteenth birthday. The domicile of such a person should be determined as follows:

(i) he or she should be domiciled in the country with which he or she is, for the time being, most closely connected;

(ii) where the child's parents are domiciled in the same country and the child has his or her home with either or both of them, it would be presumed, unless the contrary be shown, that the child is most closely connected with that country;

(iii) where the parents are not domiciled in the same country and the child has a home with one and not with the other, it would be presumed, unless the contrary be shown, that the child is most closely connected with the country in which the parent with whom the child has his or her home is domiciled.

No person or court could override or abrogate these rules.

No special rule is required for a person who marries or becomes a parent when under the age of sixteen.

The normal civil standard of proof on a balance of probabilities would apply in all disputes about domicile.

As to the acquisition of a domicile of choice, a person of sixteen or over would be able to acquire one if he or she is present in a country with the requisite intention and no higher or different quality of intention should be required if the alleged change of domicile is from one acquired at birth than from any other domicile. The requisite intention would be merely to settle in a

---

Act 1963; Family Law Act 1986; Brussels II*bis* Regulation (EC) 2201/2003 concerning jurisdiction and the recognition and enforcement of judgments in matrimonial matters and matters of parental responsibility, Art. 4. Rome I Regulation, and Art. 4 of Rome II Regulation.

[103] See p. 32 below.

[104] Law Commission Report 168 (1987). For comment see P. B. Carter, 'Domicile: the Case for Radical Reform' (1987) 36 *ICLQ* 713.

[105] Law Commission Working Paper no. 88 (1984).

country for an indefinite period and should be determined without reference to any presumption. The revival of the domicile at birth would be replaced by the continuance of the existing domicile until another is acquired.

If enacted, these recommendations would have brought about great simplification and improvement in the law of domicile. However, they have not been put into legislation.

7. Ordinary residence

A person's residence is where he or she lives. It is a question of fact. For the purpose of statutory provisions in which it is found 'ordinary residence' appears to differ from 'residence *simpliciter*'[106] although there is no difference with 'habitual residence'.[107] For the purpose of taxing statutes it has been held to mean 'residence' in a place with some degree of continuity and apart from accidental or temporary absence.[108] The residence must be adopted voluntarily and for settled purposes, although those purposes might be limited, for example for employment.[109] In *IRC v Lysaght* it was held, in a case concerning a person who lived in Ireland but spent about a week in each month in England living in hotels when on business there, that a person can have an ordinary residence in each of two places, and so, surprisingly perhaps, that person was ordinarily resident in England as well as in Ireland.

A person can continue to be ordinarily resident in country A though he or she spends more time in another residence elsewhere, so long as that person continues to maintain a home in country A.[110] It has been held that a minor who usually lived in England with one parent continued to be ordinarily resident there, though the child had been removed abroad by the other parent and had resided with that other parent in the other country for some time.[111]

Where someone is resident in England unlawfully, having outstayed their visa for example, they may not be ordinarily resident in England.[112] However, this depends on the interpretation of the particular statute.[113]

---

[106] *R v Barnet LBC, ex parte Nilish Shah* [1983] 2 AC 309 (determining ordinary residence for eligibility for a grant for further education).

[107] See p. 32 *et seq.* below.   [108] *Levene v IRC* [1928] AC 217.

[109] *R v Barnet LBC, ex parte Nilish Shah* [1983] 2 AC 309.

[110] This is illustrated by cases concerning the ordinary residence of a wife under statutory provisions which gave the English court jurisdiction to grant her a divorce if her husband was domiciled abroad: *Hopkins v Hopkins* [1951] P 116; *Stransky v Stransky* [1954] P 428; *Lewis v Lewis* [1956] 1 WLR 200. These provisions were repealed by the Domicile and Matrimonial Proceedings Act 1973. See more recently *Ikimi v Ikimi* [2001] 3 WLR 672.

[111] *Re P (GE) (An Infant)* [1965] Ch. 568. Thus the English court had jurisdiction to make a custody order in respect of him. This case would now be decided under the Child Abduction Act 1985.

[112] *R v Barnet LBC, ex parte Nilish Shah* [1983] 2 AC 309.

[113] *Mark v Mark* [2005] UKHL 42 at para. 31, [2006] 1 AC 98 (residence for the purpose of acquiring domicile).

8. Habitual residence

This connecting factor has been employed in several statutes, some of which are based upon international conventions which use the term either in addition to, or in place of, domicile. It is the connecting factor of choice for many European instruments. Thus, habitual residence is used by itself to determine the jurisdiction of the English courts to grant decrees of divorce, judicial separation and nullity of marriage,[114] and as an alternative to domicile in respect of the law governing the formal validity of wills.[115] It is used as an alternative to domicile and nationality as a basis for the jurisdiction of a non-EU Member State's court when recognition of an overseas divorce is in issue.[116] It has relevance in the choice of law rules for contract[117] and tort.[118] It also plays a part in the laws of taxation, immigration and social security. It has become a critically important concept in the context of child abduction.[119] The meaning of habitual residence is not necessarily the same for all these purposes as occasionally a specific definition will be given by the legislation. In particular, where the concept is used in EU legislation, it must be autonomously defined. That means that habitual residence must have the same meaning across Europe and that meaning is independent of domestic law.[120] Nonetheless, in cases which do not depend on EU legislation, where no definition has been given, the concept is to be determined in a similar way for every purpose of domestic law.[121] Much of the discussion and case law above regarding domicile can usefully be reconsidered to give examples of areas of likely difficulty with habitual residence. For example, where is a person habitually resident when they go abroad for employment or study? How long does it take to establish habitual residence? Where is a child habitually resident? What if one has residences in and connections with more than one country?

[114] Article 3(1) of Regulation (EC) 2201/2003 concerning jurisdiction and the recognition and enforcement of judgments in matrimonial matters and the matters of parental responsibility (Brussels II*bis*).

[115] Wills Act 1963, s. 1.

[116] Family Law Act 1986, s. 46(1). For the recognition of divorces granted by an EU Member State's court, see Art. 21 of Brussels II*bis*.

[117] For example, Art. 4 of Regulation (EC) 593/2008 on the law applicable to contractual obligations (Rome I).

[118] For example, Art. 4(2) of Regulation (EC) 864/2007 on the law applicable to non-contractual obligations (Rome II).

[119] Child Abduction and Custody Act 1985 enacting the Hague Convention on the Civil Aspects of International Child Abduction (1980) and the Council of Europe Convention on Recognition and Enforcement of Decisions concerning Custody of Children and on the Restoration of Custody of Children (1980). The Brussels II*bis* Regulation where it applies takes precedence over these two Conventions.

[120] *Hagen v Einfuhr- und Vorratsstelle Getreide* Case C-49/71 [1972] ECR 23 at para. 6 and cases following.

[121] *Ikimi v Ikimi* [2001] 3 WLR 672 at para. 31 but compare *Nessa v Chief Adjudication Officer* [1999] 1 WLR 1937 at 1941.

In *Cruse v Chittum*,[122] an early case which concerned the recognition of an overseas divorce, habitual residence was said to denote 'regular physical presence which must endure for some time'. In several cases, the courts have said that it is a question of fact; this has turned out to be over-optimistic and, unavoidably perhaps, legal rules have developed.

Some principles were stated by Lord Brandon in *Re J (A Minor: Abduction)*.[123] Habitual residence must be understood in the natural and ordinary meaning of those words and is a question of fact to be decided in the light of the circumstances of the case.[124] Unlike domicile it cannot be acquired in a single day, since 'an appreciable period of time and a settled intention to reside on a long-term basis'[125] are necessary. It appears from the cases that habitual residence is always found where a person has resided in a country for over a year.[126] The objective fact of residence is conclusive in these cases even if the person clearly does not want to live in that country in the longer term.[127] For periods of time shorter than a year, the residence must be sufficient to be 'habitual'. In *Nessa v Chief Adjudication Officer*,[128] a person who had only arrived in England four days earlier did not acquire habitual residence despite her intention to remain there permanently. On the other hand, the residence need not be very long. In *Re S (Custody: Habitual Residence)*,[129] habitual residence was established within a month. What is important is the quality of the residence and the intention of the person residing rather than a mere counting up of days of residence.[130] The critical factor was the person had definitely decided to settle in England. So in a case where there was no settled intention to reside, eight months' stay was insufficient to establish a habitual residence.[131] Residence does not require unbroken physical presence. A person is still habitually resident in a country despite absences for holidays, employment or to attempt a reconciliation with a spouse.[132] The absences may be quite lengthy.[133] Each case depends on a factual inquiry. It may well be easier to regain a habitual residence in a country in which one has already been established and left, than to establish a habitual residence in place in which one has not lived previously.[134]

---

[122] [1974] 2 All ER 940.
[123] [1990] 2 AC 562, a case on the Child Abduction and Custody Act 1985, *Mark v Mark* [2005] UKHL 42, [2006] 1 AC 98. See too Rogerson [2000] *ICLQ* 87, Shuz [1995] *ICLQ* 771.
[124] *Nessa v Chief Adjudication Officer* [1999] 1 WLR 1937.
[125] Habitual residence can change quite quickly: *Re S (A Minor) (Custody: Habitual Residence)* [1998] AC 750; *V v B (A Minor) (Abduction) (No. 2)* [1991] 2 FLR 992.
[126] See Clive [1997] Jur. Rev. 137.
[127] *M v M (Abduction: England and Scotland)* [1997] 2 FLR 263.
[128] [1999] 1 WLR 1937.   [129] [1998] AC 750.
[130] *Armstrong v Armstrong* [2003] EWHC 777, [2003] 2 FLR 375.
[131] *A v A (Child Abduction)* [1993] 2 FLR 225.
[132] *Re B (Child Abduction: Habitual Residence)* [1994] 2 FLR 915.
[133] See e.g., *Ikimi v Ikimi* [2001] 3 WLR 672 in which the person was absent for 204 days in a year. In *Re H (Abduction: Habitual Residence: Consent)* [2000] 2 FLR 294, a student was away on a one year course and kept her habitual residence.
[134] *Nessa v Chief Adjudication Officer* [1999] 1 WLR 1937.

The 'settled intention' need not be an intention to stay in the country permanently or indefinitely.[135] It can be an intention to remain for employment, even on a short-term contract for six months.[136] The Court of Appeal in *M v M (Abduction: England and Scotland)*[137] regarded the intention to reside as 'part of the regular order of his life for the time being, whether of short or of long duration'.[138] The person must adopt the residence voluntarily[139] but can voluntarily reside in a country despite being posted there for employment.[140] Like domicile, habitual residence is immediately lost by leaving the country with a settled intention not to return. The burden of proving a change of habitual residence is on the person seeking to show that change.[141] Unlike domicile, it is possible to have more than one habitual residence[142] or none.[143] Thus, it is less attractive as a connecting factor in choice of law rules, where a unique solution is preferable. It is also different from domicile in other ways. It is not ascribed to a person at birth; the intention required for its acquisition is different and there is no doctrine of revival. Once a person leaves his or her habitual residence, it is lost and that person is without a habitual residence until another is acquired. Nevertheless, the House of Lords has held that it may be important to ensure that there is no gap in habitual residence for some legislation to be effective.[144]

As regards the habitual residence of children, the fact that a child may be without one may deprive that child of the protection of various legislation, particularly if the child is abducted. Many of the reported cases about habitual residence have been decided under that legislation. A child's habitual residence is influenced by the parent or carer who has responsibility for and is exercising lawful rights of custody for that child. The habitual residence of the child is a matter of fact, so the child must actually be resident where the habitual residence is alleged.[145] If the child's parents are living together and the child lives there as well, the child has his or her parents' habitual residence.[146] Where the parents have joint parental responsibility, neither can change the

---

[135] *Re B (Minors) (Abduction) (No. 2)* [1993] 1 FLR 993; *M v M (Abduction) (England and Scotland)* [1997] 2 FLR 263; *Mark v Mark* [2005] UKHL 42, [2006] 1 AC 98.
[136] *Re R (Abduction: Habitual Residence)* [2003] EWCH 1968 (Fam), [2004] 1 FLR 216.
[137] [1997] 2 FLR 263.   [138] *Ibid.* 267.
[139] So not by kidnapping or imprisonment.
[140] *Re A (Minors) (Abduction: Habitual Residence)* [1996] 1 WLR 25 at 32–3.
[141] *F v S (Wardship: Jurisdiction)* [1993] 2 FLR 686.
[142] In *Ikimi v Ikimi* [2001] 3 WLR 672 and *Mark v Mark* [2005] UKHL 42, [2006] 1 AC 98, the two habitual residences were concurrent. Compare with *R v Barnet LBC, ex parte Nilish Shah* [1983] 2 AC 309, where a person living for part of the year in one country and the remainder in another had consecutive rather than concurrent habitual residences. However, note that in EU legislation a person can probably only have one habitual residence at a time: *Marinos v Marinos* [2007] EWCH 2047 (Fam), [2007] 2 FLR 1018.
[143] *Re J (A Minor: Abduction)* [1990] 2 AC 562; *Mark v Mark* [2006] 1 AC 98 at para. 37.
[144] *Nessa v Chief Adjudication Officer* [1999] 1 WLR 1937.
[145] *Re M (Abduction: Habitual Residence)* [1996] 1 FLR 887 at 895.
[146] *Re A (Minors) (Abduction: Habitual Residence)* [1996] 1 WLR 25.

child's habitual residence by wrongfully removing or retaining the child in breach of the other parent's rights[147] as both parents must consent.[148] If one parent has lawful custody, that parent's habitual residence is also that of the child.[149] One parent can acquiesce to the change of the child's domicile either where there is agreement or where that parent takes no steps to challenge a child's change of home for a period of time.[150] A court order may change the child's habitual residence.[151] Where there is only one parent with parental rights (for example, where the father has no parental rights), that parent can change a child's habitual residence. If that parent dies, so that the child has no one with parental rights, the habitual residence of the child cannot be changed by the person who takes care of the child.[152] A child's habitual residence can be changed to one different from that of its parents. Although sending a child away to school is insufficient to change the child's habitual residence,[153] the child's habitual residence may change when the child goes abroad to live with the child's grandparents.[154] However, the burden of proof on the parent wishing to establish that the child's habitual residence is different from their own is 'strong'.[155] On the other hand, a parent cannot unilaterally decide to change a child's habitual residence without a change in the child's physical presence. In *K (A Minor: Habitual Residence)*:

> The parents were habitually resident in England and decided to send their child to India to be brought up by the grandparents until he was an adult. A year later, the mother (who by then had sole parental responsibility) changed her mind and sought to have the child returned to England. This depended on whether the child was habitually resident in England. She failed. The child's habitual residence could not be changed without an actual change of residence.[156]

The habitual residence of a child probably ceases at the age of sixteen, when the child can acquire his or her own habitual residence.

147 *Re M (Abduction: Habitual Residence)* [1996] 1 FLR 887.
148 *Re K (Abduction: Consent: Forum Conveniens)* [1995] 2 FLR 211.
149 *Re J (A Minor) (Abduction: Custody Rights)* [1990] 2 AC 562.
150 *Re F (A Minor: Child Abduction)* [1992] 1 FLR 548.
151 *Re F (A Minor: Child Abduction)* [1992] 1 FLR 548. If a child is a ward of court, the court's consent is needed to change the child's habitual residence: *Re B-M (Wardship Jurisdiction)* [1993] 1 FLR 495.
152 *Re S (A Minor: Abduction: European Convention)* [1998] AC 750.
153 *Re A (Wardship: Jurisdiction)* [1995] 1 FLR 767.
154 *Re M (Residence Order: Jurisdiction)* [1993] 1 FLR 495, where a mother sent her children to live with their grandparents for at least a year and the children acquired a habitual residence in Scotland with their grandparents.
155 *Re A (Wardship: Jurisdiction)* [1995] 1 FLR 767.
156 *Re KM (A Minor: Habitual Residence)* [1996] 1 FLR 887.

9. Habitual residence in EU legislation

There are several CJEU cases which lay down particular rules to define habitual residence for the purposes of EU legislation. Terms in EU legislation have to be given an autonomous meaning if there is no explicit reference to national law.[157] The definition of habitual residence laid down in the following cases therefore applies in Brussels II*bis* Regulation, Rome I and Rome II Regulations, and the Insolvency Regulation but not the Brussels I Regulation.[158] Habitual residence is 'the place where the person had established, on a fixed basis, his permanent or habitual centre of interests, with all the relevant facts being taken into account for the purpose of determining such residence'.[159] This is a similar test to that outlined in the paragraphs above and the cases may not distinguish between the different sources.[160] However, sometimes the concept of habitual residence in EU legislation operates slightly differently. The overarching purpose of some EU legislation is to facilitate free movement of persons and to remove barriers to that free movement. Habitual residence after someone moves country for employment is therefore possibly more easily established. A person can be resident in one place and habitually resident in another. Also, the context in which the concept is used may affect the weight of various factors. If the EU legislation is concerned with the entitlement of a worker to social security, the place of employment is important. In family matters the place where the family lives, as a family, is more important.[161] In *Swaddling v Adjudication Officer*,[162] the CJEU held that 'account should be taken in particular of the employed person's family situation; the reasons which have led him to move; the length and continuity of his residence; the fact (where this is the case) that he is in stable employment; and his intention as it appears from all the circumstances'. However, length of residence of itself is not to be intrinsic to the concept. It has been said that the European authorities demonstrate far less emphasis on the length of time before a person has established habitual residence.[163] A child's habitual residence must reflect some degree of social integration by the child in a social and family environment. In *Mercredi v Chaffe*:

---

[157] *Mercredi v Chaffe* Case C-497/10 [2010] ECR I-14309, [2011] 1 FLR 1293.

[158] The domicile of an individual is a matter of the law of the Member State whose courts are seised of the matter (Brussels I Regulation, Art. 59).

[159] *Silvana di Paulo v Office national de l'emploi* Case C-76/76 [1977] ECR 315; *Rigsadvokaten v Ryborg* Case C-297/89 [1991] ECR I-1943; *Knoch v Bundesanstalt für Arbeit* Case C-102/91 [1992] ECR I-4341; *Pedro Magdalena Fernández v Commission* Case C-452/93P [1994] ECR I-4295; and *Swaddling v Adjudication Officer* Case C-90/97 [1999] ECR 1–01075.

[160] See e.g., *In re P-J (Children) (Abduction: Consent)* [2009] EWCA Civ 588, [2010] 1 WLR 1237, which raised questions both under the Child Abduction Convention and Brussels II*bis* Regulation. The determination of habitual residence was the same for both.

[161] *Marinos v Marinos* [2007] EWHC 2047 (Fam), [2007] 2 FLR 1018 at para. 34.

[162] Case C-90/97 [1999] ECR 1–01075.

[163] See *L-K v K (No. 2)* [2006] EWHC 3280 (Fam) at para. 36.

> A child who was registered as a French national had been born to an English father and a French mother in 2009. The parents had separated very soon after the birth of the child. The mother took the baby to Réunion, a French territory, without informing the father. The child's habitual residence up to that point was in England.[164]

Had the child obtained a habitual residence in Réunion, by staying with her mother there for a few days? The CJEU held that it was up to the national court (here England) to decide where the child was habitually resident. The national court establishing the habitual residence of the child must take all circumstances into account, including the reasons for a child's stay in a Member State, its nationality, how old the child is, and whether its presence in a Member State is temporary or permanent. A transfer of a child's habitual residence can be indicated where a parent with parental responsibility has taken tangible steps to settle permanently, such as buying or renting accommodation. If the child is very young, particularly if it is an infant, then the mother's geographic and family and social connections are also important to aid the identification of the child's habitual residence by integration in a family and social environment. In the event, the English court decided that the child was still habitually resident in England at the point that the English court was seised of the action which had been only four days after the child had been taken to Réunion.[165]

10. Corporations

a. Status and domicile

The personal law of a corporation[166] is that of its domicile, which means the law of the place of its incorporation.[167] This is contrasted with the domicile of a corporation for the purposes of jurisdiction, which is discussed in Chapter 5.[168] The company owes its existence to the law of incorporation, and that law also governs its dissolution[169] and its capacity to contract. The law of the place of incorporation dictates who can sue (or cause it to sue) and be sued on its behalf,[170] and governs the extent to which a member can be personally liable for its debts.[171]

---

[164] Case C-497/10 [2010] ECR I-14309, [2011] 1 FLR 1293.   [165] [2011] EWCA Civ 272.

[166] 'Corporation' includes clubs, associations, and other legal persons as well as companies. For an example where the status to sue of an Indian Hindu Temple was in dispute, see *Bumper Development Corporation v Commissioner of the Police for the Metropolis* [1991] 1 WLR 1362.

[167] *Gasque v IRC* [1940] 2 KB 80. A company registered in England, Wales or Scotland cannot change its domicile since it cannot alter the country of the place of registration.

[168] See further pp. 73–5 below.   [169] *Lazard Bros v Midland Bank* [1933] AC 289.

[170] *Bank of Ethiopia v National Bank of Egypt and Liguori* [1937] Ch. 413; *Banco de Bilbao v Sancha* [1938] 2 KB 176; *Carl Zeiss Stiftung v Rayner & Keeler Ltd (No. 2)* [1967] 1 AC 853.

[171] *Risdon Iron and Locomotive Works v Furness* [1906] 1 KB 49.

The law of incorporation also governs the effect of mergers or takeovers of the company on its shareholders, creditors and assets. In *National Bank of Greece and Athens SA v Metliss*:[172]

> Sterling mortgage bonds governed by English law were issued by a Greek bank in 1927 and guaranteed by the National Bank of Greece, a Greek bank. In 1941 payment of interest on the bonds ceased. In 1949 the Greek government passed a moratorium extinguishing liability on the bonds. In 1953 another Greek decree amalgamated the National Bank with the Bank of Athens into a new bank, the National Bank of Greece and Athens, which the decree declared to be the 'universal successor' of the two banks. In 1955 a bondholder claimed arrears of interest from the new bank.

The House of Lords held that he could do so, since the status of the new bank and the effects thereof were governed by Greek law. The moratorium law was said not to have affected the old bank's liability since that was a matter for the proper law of the contract, English law. Subsequently, a decree provided that this status should not carry with it liability under the bonds. But the House of Lords held that this affected the obligations thereunder, and since these were governed by English law the new Greek law was irrelevant. (It was also said that if it had affected status, it would be disregarded in so far as it was meant to have retrospective effect.)[173]

Other countries, especially some in the European Union, prefer to use the 'real seat' of the company to govern its status. Although this may be also called its 'domicile', these countries refer such questions to the principal place of business of the company, not the place of its incorporation. The principal place of business is often much easier to alter than the law under which the company was incorporated.

b. Residence

The residence of a company is chiefly important for tax purposes and is determined not by the place of incorporation, but by where its 'central management and control' is exercised.[174]

---

[172] [1958] AC 509, see too *Siemens Schweiz AG v Thorn Security Ltd* [2008] EWCA Civ 1161, [2009] RPC 3 at para. 78.

[173] *Adams v National Bank of Greece and Athens SA* [1961] AC 255.

[174] *Cesena Sulphur Co. v Nicholson* (1876) 1 Ex. D 428. A company incorporated in the United Kingdom is also treated as resident in the United Kingdom (Corporation Tax Act 2009, s. 14).

Thus in *De Beers Consolidated Mines v Howe:*[175]

> A diamond company was incorporated in South Africa and had a head office there. A board of directors there handled day-to-day administrative matters. Another board in London, which joined with that of South Africa in making major policy decisions, in fact controlled those decisions because most of the directors lived in London. Meetings of members and mining operations and sales of diamonds all took place in South Africa.

The House of Lords held that the company should be assessed for tax as resident in the United Kingdom, since the central management and control was exercised there, where it 'kept house and did business'. In *Egyptian Delta Land & Investment Co. v Todd,*[176] where the company simply maintained in England an office, a register of members and a local secretary to comply with minimum legal requirements, but its active secretary, directors, seals, books and bank account were all in Cairo, it was held to be resident in Egypt. It is, for this purpose, also irrelevant where the central management and control should be exercised under the company's constitution, if it is, in fact, exercised elsewhere, as in the case of foreign subsidiaries who were held to be resident in England since they were wholly controlled by their English holding company which usurped the powers of the subsidiaries' boards.[177]

If the test is 'central management and control' it is difficult to see how this can be in more than one country. But such was held to be the case in *Swedish Central Railway Co. Ltd v Thompson,*[178] and Lord Radcliffe said in *Unit Construction Co. Ltd v Bullock*[179] that this might be true where it is impossible to identify one country or the control is 'peripatetic'.

It should be noted that the test of residence may be different for a different purpose, for example, enemy character, and the test stated above is not the test of residence for jurisdictional purposes.[180]

Nationality of a company is determined according to the law of incorporation.[181]

---

[175] [1906] AC 455.   [176] [1929] AC 1.
[177] *Union Construction Co. Ltd v Bullock* [1960] AC 351; *Wood v Holden* [2006] EWCA Civ 26, [2006] 1 WLR 1393.
[178] [1925] AC 295.   [179] [1960] AC 351.   [180] See pp. 71–3 below.
[181] Nationality is unimportant in the conflict of laws. The law of the place of incorporation is the national law of a company for the purposes of public international law. See *Barcelona Traction Power & Light Co.* [1970] ICJ Rep. 3.

4

Selected aspects of procedure of the English court

1. Introduction

Disputes in the English court are presented and decided in accordance with the rules of procedure in that court.[1] The Civil Procedure Rules[2] were laid down following the Woolf Report. They state that the overriding objective of the rules is to 'deal with cases justly'. Among other things, 'justly' includes ensuring the parties are on an equal footing, saving expense, dealing with the case in ways that are proportionate to its complexity and value, speed and fairness and ensuring a proper allocation of court resources.[3] The CPR make special provision for aspects of conflict of laws, particularly with regard to the service of documents and the determination of jurisdictional disputes.

It is difficult to understand many aspects of the conflict of laws without an overview of the procedure of cases in the English court. Most cases concerning conflict of laws are decided in the Commercial Court of the Queen's Bench Division.[4] The statistics of cases from that court[5] show that of over 1,300 disputes commenced, an estimate of over 80 per cent involved one foreign party and some 40 per cent had no English party. The minimum value of the claim is £25,000 and many run into several million pounds. Litigation in the Commercial Court is not cheap. The usual costs rule is that the loser pays about three-quarters of the winner's total costs of the litigation. The best barristers command around £10,000 fees per day in court each, and City solicitors charge over £600 per hour for a partner's time, and every party will have at least one barrister and one solicitor

---

[1] See generally N. Andrews, *English Civil Procedure* (Oxford University Press, 2003).

[2] The Civil Procedure Rules are most easily available at www.justice.gov.uk/civil/procrules_fin/index.htm. The rules are updated frequently.

[3] CPR r. 1.1.

[4] Specialised rules of procedure for the Commercial Court are laid down in CPR r. 58 (to the extent that they differ from the usual CPR).

[5] The most recent are available at www.judiciary.gov.uk/docs/annual_report_comm_admiralty_ct_0506.pdf.

present. Much expensive work is done by each party before trial, particularly in discovering evidence. Therefore, costs also run to millions of pounds in a large case. International litigation adds considerably to the balance of payments.

Litigation in England is, in principle and largely in practice, adversarial. Each party makes its own case and the judge is relatively passive. Judges do not investigate the facts and generally take the law as it is presented by each party. Parties have to prove the facts in issue by finding and presenting their own evidence, and the usual rule is that facts are proved by oral evidence and examination of witnesses in court. However, factual evidence is often largely agreed and 'disclosure' of relevant documents by each side to the other is an important stage of proceedings. Where evidence is in issue, each party can produce their own witness to be examined and cross-examined in order that the judge may ascertain the truth. Finding, disclosing and proving evidence is time-consuming and expensive. This is particularly so of finding and proving foreign law in conflict of laws cases.

Party autonomy in running litigation in the Commercial Court is preserved. If a party does not wish to make a particular argument and the other side do not force them to do so, the judge does not intervene. In principle, each party must bring its whole case against the other to be decided at one time (the rule in *Henderson v Henderson*[6] supports this). English statements of claim and defence are therefore long and cover many possible, often alternative, claims and defences. However, before trial, many matters will be agreed between the parties, leaving only those issues and facts which are in dispute to be decided before the judge.

2. Outline of a case

a. Issue of claim form

A case is officially commenced when the court issues the claim form at the request of the claimant, but often the parties will have had extensive negotiations beforehand.[7] The claim form will lay out the claim being made against the defendant, including the amount in dispute where it is a debt.[8] However, more detailed particulars of claim may be served later, within fourteen days of the service of the claim.[9]

---

[6] (1843) 3 Hare 100.

[7] Pre Action Protocols require the parties (on pain of losing costs) to endeavour to settle their dispute without litigation prior to issuing a claim form.

[8] CPR r. 7.4.   [9] CPR r. 7.4.

b. Service of claim form

In the Commercial Court the claimant usually serves the claim form on the defendant rather than leaving that to the court.[10] The defendant then has a short time[11] from receiving the claim form to give notice of the defendant's intention to defend the claim or to challenge the jurisdiction of the court.

Service of the claim form is essential to give notice of the commencement of the proceedings to the defendant. Under the traditional rules of jurisdiction, service on a defendant within the territorial jurisdiction is both the basis of and the exercise of that power to adjudicate. Within the European regime,[12] the basis for jurisdiction is contained in the rules of the Brussels I Regulation. However, service of the claim form is still necessary and is achieved either within the jurisdiction using domestic rules of procedure contained in the CPR or on a defendant elsewhere using either the Service Regulation[13] or, where permitted by the foreign law, the CPR.

Between them, the claimant and defendant must produce a 'statement of case', laying out the specific grounds of the dispute. Claims in the Commercial Court are generally allocated to the multi-track process. The parties then commence preparing the case to go to trial. Meanwhile, negotiations will be continuing with a view to settle their dispute without incurring large expenses.

c. Case management

Case management by a judge aims to encourage the parties to settle before going to full trial of the dispute. Its purpose is to identify the real issues in dispute and minimise the time necessary for trial. The judge will have had the opportunity to read papers prepared by the parties such as an agreed description of what the case is about, what is common ground, what are the parties' proposals for dealing with documentary evidence and disclosure of it, expert witnesses and an estimate of the likely length of trial. It is often at this stage that the parties settle or they may be encouraged to an alternative method of dispute resolution.[14] One of the issues raising concerns at this stage will be the jurisdiction of the court. The judge may direct that there is a separate, relatively quick, initial trial of the issue of jurisdiction or other preliminary questions. Also, the judge will make directions as to the way in which

---

[10] Service must be effected within four months if within the territory of England and Wales or within six months if without the jurisdiction (CPR r. 7.5).
[11] Depending on the country in which service has been effected, it may be up to thirty-one days (CPR PD 6 para. 7.2).
[12] Brussels I Regulation (Regulation (EC) 44/2001 on jurisdiction and enforcement of judgments in civil and commercial matters).
[13] Regulation (EC) 1393/2007 on the service in the Member States of judicial and extrajudicial documents in civil or commercial matters [2007] OJ L324/79.
[14] Mediation, conciliation or other form of alternative dispute resolution.

documentary evidence is to be exchanged and set a timetable for trial. The judge also has power to stay[15] the proceedings to permit the parties to negotiate further towards settlement. Case management powers are quite wide-ranging and the judges use them proactively.

d. Interlocutory hearing on jurisdiction

Questions of the jurisdiction of the court are decided in England at a relatively early stage in proceedings.[16] That is not to say that these issues are not central, indeed they are often the only real matter in dispute between the parties. Once they know which court will hear their case, the parties will prefer to settle in the better knowledge of what the outcome in that court is likely to be. Essentially the question whether the case will proceed to full trial in England is determined after the statement of case[17] has been served on the defendant but before full disclosure of the evidence by each side. Indeed, the defendant may not even have to lay out the defence to the claim at this stage.[18] Parties do have to make a declaration that the facts in the claim or defence are true,[19] but the truth has yet to be tested and verified by a full trial. The court therefore has to decide on its jurisdiction without proper knowledge of the facts of the dispute. This interlocutory hearing on jurisdiction is also usually only on the basis of written evidence. It is meant to be speedy and lead to rough and ready conclusions. The court is careful to avoid the wastefulness of taking too much time and trouble (both of the parties and by the court) over such a preliminary issue as jurisdiction, especially if it may decide that it does not have or should not take jurisdiction. The court therefore has to make certain assumptions in order to reach a decision. These assumptions may be wrong but once made can be utilised by a party, perhaps especially a claimant, to its own advantage. The risk of a penalty

---

[15] Which may be described as a judicially imposed pause in the litigation.

[16] So early that in some cases (where the claimant is unsuccessful in persuading a master to grant permission to the claimant to serve the claim form out of the jurisdiction), the defendant may not even be aware of a possible claim. These cases are rare in practice though the requirement of seeking permission remains important to prevent claimants from making speculative claims to jurisdiction to force a potential defendant into settlement of a nuisance claim.

[17] This is an important document which may run to many pages, outlining the facts (not the law) of the claimant's cause of action against the defendant. The claimant has to include in the statement of claim *all* matters on which the claimant intends to rely in the dispute, and the claimant will be prevented from raising any issue which is not included in that statement of claim.

[18] CPR r. 11(9). In practice, the statement of defence is often drawn up and served on the claimant by the time of the interlocutory hearing.

[19] The consequences of making an untrue statement are outlined in CPR r. 32.14. However, a claimant only has to make disclosure of points that are relevant to its case and those which it should anticipate will be raised by the other side (*Konamaneni v Rolls Royce Industrial Power (India) Ltd* [2002] 1 WLR 1269 at para. 180).

costs order should prevent a claimant from making an unsubstantiated claim to jurisdiction and also from making less than full and frank disclosure of the facts. Nevertheless, a defendant faced with a speculative claim still has to go to the trouble of challenging the jurisdiction and establishing that the claimant has behaved improperly.

The English court inevitably adopts a pragmatic solution to both the possible improper exercise of jurisdiction and to the balance between careful consideration and excessive wasted expenditure. It requires the party which has the burden of proving some jurisdictional aspect of the case to do so to the standard of a 'good arguable case'. These are fine words, but it can be difficult to decide their precise meaning.[20]

e. Disclosure

Disclosure used to be known as discovery. It is the requirement on each party to a case to find and show documentary evidence to the other. Often it is at this point that the real merits of each party's case becomes clear. There is a wide array of further powers to aid parties to gain access to material information relevant to their case.[21] Parties are required to disclose to each other everything which is relevant to their own case *or* to the other party's case, i.e., documents which are adverse to your own case and supportive of the other party's case must be disclosed. Documents both within the territorial jurisdiction of the court and those found abroad must be disclosed. Initially, each party prepares a list of such documents, the party is then under a duty to preserve the documents and permit inspection of them by the other party. Only disclosed documents can be relied upon at trial. The real purpose of disclosure is to prevent surprise at trial and to inform each party of the strength of the other party's case, both encourage settlement. Complying with the disclosure requirements is very expensive in large cases. Do not be fooled by reference to 'documents' into thinking that it is only paper that must be disclosed. Documents are defined as 'anything in which information of any description is recorded'.[22] Increasingly sophisticated electronic search methods are needed to scour computers and databases to locate the necessary information. There are exceptions from the duty to disclose, for example, where the document is privileged such as legal advice in contemplation of trial, offers to the other party made 'without prejudice' or self-incriminatory material.

---

[20] The test was described as 'flexible' in *Canada Trust Co. v Stolzenberg (No. 2)* [1998] 1 WLR 547 at 558, per Waller LJ, which was approved by Lord Steyn in the House of Lords [2002] 1 AC 1 at 10. See further pp. 55–6 below.

[21] For example, letters of request made of a foreign court (*First American Corp. v Zayed* [1999] 1 WLR 1154) or inspection of property (CPR r. 25.5).

[22] CPR r. 31.4.

f. Trial: a substantive hearing on merits

Although many cases never get to trial, the final hearing of the merits of the case and a decision of the dispute by a judge is the purpose of the process thus far explained. It is possible to obtain earlier judgment, for example, in default of the defendant appearing to defend the claim[23] or by summary judgment where either the claim or defence has no real prospect of success.[24]

Civil cases in the High Court are decided by a judge of considerable skill and experience[25] who sits alone, without a jury. At trial the claimant makes the claimant's case before the defendant replies with the defence. In conclusion, the order is reversed, so that the claimant makes the final submissions. Other than agreed documentary and factual evidence, proof of disputed matters is done via oral examination. Witnesses are called to give evidence, examined by a barrister for one party and then cross-examined by the other side's barrister. It is a long and gruelling process and very expensive.

At the end of the trial or after some time for reflection, the judge will give judgment. This may be done orally or handed down in a written form. Often the judge will indicate the result with written reasons to follow.

g. Enforcement of judgments

A judgment is only a piece of paper. If a losing party does not pay the award, the winner (a judgment creditor) will need the aid of the court to enforce the judgment. Usually this is done by means of a charging order[26] or a third party debt order.[27] The latter are particularly useful: a judgment creditor can obtain an order of the court to require someone else owing money to the judgment debtor to pay the judgment creditor directly. Banks are often the best subjects of a third party debt order. Enforcement remedies are also available to enforce a recognisable foreign judgment.[28] A judgment creditor may not know where the judgment debtor holds bank accounts, either in England or abroad. The worldwide freezing order[29] is obtainable in some cases to ensure that assets are available to satisfy the judgment and the ancillary disclosure orders may force a judgment debtor to identify where the assets are to be found.

---

[23] CPR r. 12.1.   [24] CPR r. 24.2.

[25] Despite changes to widen the pool of applicants, judges are normally appointed to the High Court after at least fifteen years of experience as a barrister. Solicitors, academics, women and people in the ethnic minorities of the population remain rare.

[26] Under CPR r. 73.   [27] Under CPR r. 72.   [28] See further Chapter 8.

[29] Previously known as a *Mareva* injunction (*Mareva Cia Naviera SA v International Bulkcarriers SA* [1975] 2 Lloyd's LR 509. The order is made under CPR r. 25.

h. *Res judicata*: the binding effect of a judgment

English law places a heavy emphasis on the principle that there should be an end to litigation.[30] There are strong public policy reasons for preventing parties from re-opening issues which have already been the subject of a decision. The doctrine of *res judicata* prevents successive litigation between the parties over the same issues. The doctrine in England prevents both the claim and individual issues from being re-opened. It also operates where a recognisable foreign judgment has been obtained to prevent the parties starting again in the English court. *Res judicata* encompasses the more limited doctrines of cause of action estoppel and issue estoppel. Cause of action estoppel means that the material facts supporting the legal ground of the claim cannot be challenged. Issue estoppel prevents particular issues being raised in a case on a different cause of action. Both cause of action and issue estoppel are subject to exceptions but these are not very extensive. For example, issue estoppel may be relaxed where there has been a change in the law or significant new evidence which was not available with reasonable diligence at the time of the first proceedings comes to light.[31] In addition, English law requires a party to bring all issues relevant to the action before the court.[32] The court then opposes any later action to relitigate what could have been decided in the case, as it would be an abuse of process to do so. It is different from cause of action estoppel or issue estoppel as this rule covers issues which were not subject to specific decision but which should have been raised by the parties in the earlier case. This argument also applies to foreign judgments.

3. Pleading and proof of foreign law

a. Foreign law as fact

A question of the content of foreign law may arise either at the jurisdictional or the substantive stage of proceedings.[33] Under the national rules on jurisdiction, a party may be arguing that a foreign law applies to the contract and that therefore England is not the proper forum for the dispute.[34] Under the Brussels I Regulation rules on jurisdiction, a question of foreign law may rarely arise under Article 5(1)(a). If the place of performance of the obligation in question is not clearly expressed in the contract rules, the foreign applicable law will supply the place of performance and so identify the court with

---

[30] See e.g., Lord Woolf in *Taylor v Lawrence* [2002] 3 WLR 640 at para. 6.
[31] *Smith v Linskills* [1996] 1 WLR 763 at 771.   [32] *Henderson v Henderson* (1843) 3 Hare 100.
[33] See generally R. Fentiman, *Foreign Law in the English Courts* (Oxford University Press, 1998) and R. Fentiman, *International Commercial Litigation* (Oxford University Press, 2010) ch. 6.
[34] See further pp. 168–9 below.

jurisdiction.[35] Alternatively, and more obviously, a party may be relying on foreign law to determine the outcome of the litigation as a matter of substance once the choice of law rule has identified the system of law to be applied, so, for example, where a tort has been committed resulting in personal injury suffered abroad; or where the applicable law of the contract to decide whether it has been breached or whether a party is discharged from the obligation is a foreign law; or where the law determining the ownership of an oil rig, between two parties claiming it, is not English law.

In any case, a party who relies on the rules of a foreign system of law must plead and prove those rules. The traditional view is that foreign law is treated as a fact,[36] much like any other. The application of the foreign law must be therefore pleaded in the statement of claim. Importantly, the content of the foreign law – what effect that foreign law would have on the dispute – must also be proved to the satisfaction of the judge at the point at which the case is heard. Because foreign law is a matter of fact, judicial notice[37] is not taken of foreign law but it must be proved each time.[38] The high point of treating foreign law as fact in the usual sense came in *Bumper Development Corp. Ltd v Metropolitan Commissioner of Police*.[39] There the first instance judge was not permitted to reject the evidence of the experts and form his own opinion from his own researches of the foreign law unless the expert witness was clearly unreliable or the evidence preposterous.[40] But foreign law is not treated exactly as a fact. An appeal on a matter of foreign law is permitted. So in *MCC Proceeds v Bishopsgate Investment Trust plc*,[41] the Court of Appeal took an independent view of provisions of New York law from that decided by the trial judge. However, generally the Court of Appeal is reluctant to disturb the trial judge's findings. Secondly, a judge in deciding a matter of interpretation of foreign law will inevitably look at the evidence in a particular way by employing legal skills and experience to resolve the issue.[42] In contrast, rules of public international law have the status of rules of law in an English court, because it is part of the law of England.[43]

---

[35] See further pp. 82–6 below. To complicate matters further, if the law to govern the contract has not been expressly chosen, the applicable law will have to be determined using the Rome I Regulation. Note that Art. 5(1)(b) should not raise similar questions as the place of delivery or of provision of services is essentially a factual exercise. See further pp. 79–82 below.

[36] *Bumper Development Corp. Ltd v Metropolitan Commissioner of Police* [1991] 1 WLR 1362 at 1368 *et seq.*

[37] By which judges are assumed to have knowledge of English law and only of certain 'notorious' facts.

[38] However, see the suggestion in *Morgan Grenfell v SACE* [2001] EWCA Civ 1932 at para. 53. The Civil Evidence Act 1972, s. 4 also makes it possible in certain circumstances to rely on a decision on foreign law made by another English court as admissible evidence unless the contrary is proved.

[39] [1991] 1 WLR 1362.

[40] *Grupo Torras SA v Sheikh Mohammed Al-Sabah* [1996] 1 Lloyd's LR 7.   [41] [1999] CLC 417.

[42] *Morgan Grenfell v SACE* [2001] EWCA Civ 1932 at para. 19.

[43] *Trendtex Trading Corp. v Central Bank of Nigeria* [1977] QB 529.

b. Method of proof

If the content of the foreign rules is not disputed by either party,[44] the English court will merely apply the foreign rule on which the parties have agreed. However, where the parties dispute the content or interpretation of foreign law each party appoints an expert to give the court an objective opinion on the foreign law. The expert's role is to 'predict the likely decision of the foreign court and not to press upon the English judge the witness's personal views as to what the foreign law might be'.[45] These experts give testimony either by a statement of truth or by oral testimony which is examined and cross-examined at the hearing. Who is an expert is not easy to state. Ideally, it should be a judge or lawyer qualified to practise in the relevant foreign country but that is not an exclusive requirement. Often, the experts are academics from the foreign legal system. The Civil Evidence Act 1972 provides 'it is hereby declared that in civil proceedings a person who is suitably qualified to do so on account of his knowledge or experience is competent to give expert evidence as to [foreign law] ... irrespective of whether he has acted or is entitled to act as a legal practitioner there'.[46] In practice, particularly given the possibility of cross-examination, the expert's fluency in English is considered more essential than the highest level of legal expertise. It is therefore possible for an expert on foreign law to be an English lawyer who has some experience of the foreign system. Indeed even a non-lawyer can be considered an expert.[47] The expert is not to press the expert's personal view as to what the foreign law might be but to predict the likely decision of the foreign court. The approach has inherent difficulties in trying to decide as a foreign court would, but not being as knowledgeable as a foreign judge. Sometimes this difficulty is spotted at the early stage of deciding whether the English court should hear a case, and on occasion the English court has declined to hear a case which raises intractable questions of foreign law.[48]

c. Duty of the English court

If the expert's evidence is uncontradicted or if the experts are agreed, the judge cannot reject the evidence and form his or her own opinion from independent judicial research.[49] But the evidence does not have to be accepted if the witness is obviously unreliable or the evidence is preposterous.[50] The court has to

---

[44] For example, the parties have agreed what the foreign law lays down and are disputing only whether foreign law applies.

[45] *MCC Proceeds v Bishopsgate Investment Trust plc* [1999] CLC 417 at para. 23.

[46] Civil Evidence Act 1972, s. 4(1).

[47] See Fentiman, *International Commercial Litigation*, para. 6.47.

[48] *Royal Sun Alliance Insurance plc and another v MK Digital FZE (Cyprus) Ltd and others* [2006] 2 All ER (Comm) 145.

[49] *Bumper Development Corp. Ltd v Metropolitan Commissioner of Police* [1991] 1 WLR 1362, CA.

[50] *Grupo Torras SA v Sheikh Fahad Mohammed Al-Sabah* [1996] 1 Lloyd's LR 7, CA.

approach conflicting evidence on foreign law in the same way as any other conflicting evidence. This is very difficult, as the English judge is required to conclude what a foreign judge would decide in applying the foreign judge's own law to the facts of the case.[51]

d. Party autonomy

The parties may choose not to plead the application of foreign law.[52] A famous example is *Suisse Atlantique Societe d'Armement Maritime SA v Rotterdamsche Kolen Centrale*,[53] in which the contract clearly expressed a choice of Swiss law but the case was eventually decided in the House of Lords on an important issue of English contract law. The parties may alternatively choose not to go to the bother of proving the content of the foreign law. The traditional view is that English law applies in both cases. Because of the way in which pleading is done, if *either* party wishes to rely on foreign law, that issue will be raised. If the claimant wants to rely only on English law, then the claimant does not plead the application of foreign law. However, the claimant alternatively may wish to rely on foreign law as the basis of the claim, in which case it is raised even if the defendant pleads a defence under English law. If it is the defendant who wishes to rely on foreign law (usually because no claim is possible under that law or because a defence is available under it) then the defendant can plead the foreign law. By doing so the defendant raises foreign law as an issue for determination. Therefore, English law will decide the dispute only if neither party raises foreign law. In effect, the parties can be said to have agreed to the application of English law by failing to raise foreign law as an issue.

When the parties failed to plead or alternatively failed to prove the content of the foreign law, the judge is faced with a problem. In the case of failing to plead foreign law, the court may be unaware of the possible application of foreign law except by careful reading of the facts. As with other arguments the parties might have, but have not, made, the judge is in difficulty. The parties have, in effect, chosen not to plead the application of foreign law. That is not a point in dispute. English law therefore applies by default. In the second case of failing to prove the content of the foreign law, the judge is also left in a quandary. The statement of claim refers to the application of foreign law but the court has not been given the content of the foreign law to apply. The English court has no mechanism and no power to indulge in a fact-finding mission on the parties' behalf. More importantly, English courts consider that

---

[51] English judges have been very aware of the artificiality of this process, see, for example, Rix J in *The Spirit of Independence* [1999] 1 Lloyd's LR 43 at 66.

[52] For example in *Romalpa Aluminium Industrie Vaasen BV v Romalpa Aluminium Ltd* [1976] 1 WLR 676.

[53] [1967] 1 AC 361.

it is for the parties to decide what their case should be about, and how best to make their individual arguments – whether on fact or law. One explanation is that the conduct of litigation in England is voluntary, it is entirely up to the parties to make their case as they see it. If they choose to ignore a foreign law, it is probably for good reason. Proving a foreign law is expensive, the outcome can be uncertain and, where the foreign law would lead to the same result, unnecessary. As with the decision to plead or not to plead the application of foreign law, the parties can be said to have chosen not to prove the content of the foreign law. Different solutions to this problem could be adopted. In *Bumper Development Corp. Ltd v Metropolitan Commissioner of Police*,[54] the judge formed his own view of the primary evidence, which was criticised by the Court of Appeal. The Australian courts have treated the application of a foreign rule as a matter of construction which is a question for the *lex fori*.[55] Maybe 'general principles of law' could be used.[56] In principle, English law applies by default as with a failure to plead foreign law. It has been said that the application of English law operates via a presumption that the foreign law is the same as English law but this is not very appealing. In *Shaker v Al Bedrawi*,[57] the Court of Appeal concluded that there could be no presumption of identity between foreign law and English law, nor could English law necessarily apply automatically by default. Indeed in that case, English law did not apply at all, despite the failure to plead foreign law, as the accounting provisions of the English Companies Act 1985 were found to be inapplicable to a company incorporated abroad.[58] As Fentiman argues, it would be better for the English court to consider first whether it is appropriate for English law to apply before merely assuming the foreign law to be the same as English law or that it applies by default. However, he posits that even if English law is to apply by default it is subject to three exceptions: (a) where English law is inapplicable by default;[59] (b) where the application of foreign law is mandatory;[60] and (c) where strict proof of foreign law is required.[61] Also, claimants should not be able to make assertions about foreign law without proving the content of that law necessary in order to make out their claim.[62] Therefore the party who pleads the foreign rule must prove it and only the other party can rely on the default rule.[63]

[54] [1991] 1 WLR 1362, CA.
[55] *Neilson v Overseas Projects Corporation of Victoria Ltd* [2005] HCA 54.
[56] *The Spirit of Independence* [1999] 1 Lloyd's LR 43.
[57] [2002] EWCA Civ 1452, [2003] Ch. 350.
[58] An alternative explanation could be that the English law by its own terms did not extend to foreign companies.
[59] For example, if the applicable English statute is territorially limited see Fentiman, *International Commercial Litigation*, para. 6.118–6.124.
[60] *Ibid.* para. 6.125. This is controversial.   [61] *Ibid.* para. 6.126–6.127.
[62] *Global Multimedia International Ltd v ARA Media Services* [2007] 1 All ER (Comm) 1160.
[63] Fentiman, *International Commercial Litigation*, para. 6.128 *et seq.*

Suppose that a contract in dispute expressly states that it should be governed by the law of Ruritania. This raises a more focussed question. Can the parties, by deciding not to plead that the law of Ruritania applies,[64] evade the choice of law rule (say that imposed by Article 3 of the Rome I Regulation[65]) and merely rely on domestic English rules? Both the Rome I Regulation and the Rome II Regulation[66] use mandatory language. For example, in Article 3 of the Rome I Regulation 'a contract shall be governed by the law chosen by the parties'. In the pre-Rome II Regulation case of *Parker v Tui UK Ltd,*[67] the Court of Appeal refused to require the application of foreign law under the Private International Law (Miscellaneous Provisions) Act 1995 where the parties had not pleaded it. This was partly on the grounds that even if the parties were required to have foreign law applied they could evade it by failing to prove the content of the foreign law. It is unclear whether the EU legislation is in more mandatory terms than the law contained in the English statute.

The manner of proof of foreign law can be criticised for leading to unacceptably uncertain results. There are decisions on foreign law which may well be unrecognisable to lawyers of the foreign legal system. Proving foreign law is also extremely expensive as it may involve many days of cross-examining each party's expert legal witnesses. In contrast, a judge in the German legal system has the possibility of obtaining an independent report on the application of a foreign law from an expert (often from the Max Planck Institute). Although in theory this looks a very attractive alternative to the English system, adopting it wholesale would undermine central principles of party autonomy in pleading and proof, and of the adversarial nature of the English judicial process. Funding for an English equivalent of the Max Planck Institute would be impossible in the present economic climate.[68] Nor have other mechanisms, such as obtaining a report from single joint expert[69] or referring to the relevant foreign legal system,[70] apparently been used.[71]

Pleading and proving foreign law may raise particularly difficulties in some cases which are only deciding matters of jurisdiction, for example, cases where the application of foreign law makes England not the proper forum in which to hear the dispute.[72] These cases on jurisdiction are decided at an interlocutory hearing at which the taking of expert evidence is rarely permitted in an effort to keep costs and wastage of time to a minimum. A complicating factor is that the content of foreign law may be unclear. If the court does not have the advantage of hearing from foreign law experts there is a risk that these jurisdictional cases are not properly and carefully decided.

---

[64] Or by not proving the content of that law.
[65] Regulation (EC) 593/2008 on the law applicable to contractual obligations [2008] OJ L177/6.
[66] Regulation (EC) 864/2007 [2007] OJ L199/40.   [67] [2009] EWCA Civ 1261.
[68] Despite it being of possible considerable benefit for legal academics!
[69] As permitted by CPR r. 35.7.
[70] As permitted by the London Convention on Information on Foreign Law 1968.
[71] No reported case uses either method.   [72] Under CPR r. 6.36 and PD 6B.

5

Jurisdiction of the English courts

1. Introduction

'Jurisdiction' is a word capable of several meanings but is here used to denote the power of the English courts to hear and decide cases brought before them. The rules on jurisdiction include both whether there is power and how that power should be exercised. For the purpose of determining the jurisdiction of the English courts, actions are of two kinds:

(1) actions *in personam*: these are actions brought to compel a defendant to do or to refrain from doing something or to pay damages. Jurisdiction over such actions depends primarily, though not exclusively, on some connection between the parties (usually the defendant), the subject matter of the dispute and England; or the parties may have chosen to submit to the determination by the English court. This chapter is mainly concerned with actions *in personam*;
(2) actions *in rem*: these are actions against land, ships and aircraft when jurisdiction depends upon the presence of the land, ship or aircraft in England.

It should be added that, in some cases, such as divorce or nullity of marriage, sometimes called 'actions *quasi in rem*' since they involve determination of personal status, jurisdiction is entirely statutory. These are not dealt with in this work.

Along with rules which permit cases to be heard in England, there are also rules for declining to exercise jurisdiction, usually so that the case is heard in a foreign court. Various principles may underly both the exercise of and the refusal to exercise jurisdiction. These should be fair to both claimants and defendants. The notion of fairness here is a complicated matter. A claimant must have access to a forum to ventilate the dispute as a matter of human rights under Article 6 of the European Convention on Human Rights.[1] However, it can be seen as unfair that a defendant is surprised by an action in a court where the claimant is likely to have unwarranted advantage. On the

---

[1] Implemented by the Human Rights Act 1998.

other hand, a claimant may legitimately desire to use the local courts where the claimant has best knowledge of and faith in the procedures available. The English courts are viewed by many people internationally as being neutral, with experienced judges and lawyers. The English language is often an attractive factor. The interim or provisional measures available in the English court[2] favour the claimant, as do the rules on disclosure of evidence. The English court has experience of class actions[3] and many complex financial disputes.[4] However, proceedings in England are very expensive in terms of the cost of lawyers, if not in the court fees.[5] Other factors to consider include the principle that any judgment should be enforceable and England may be the place where the defendant resides and has substantial assets. England may be the forum which the parties can expect to sue and be sued because of its connections with the subject matter of the dispute (for example, a tort which is committed against property in England). Where the parties have articulated a choice of place to sue and be sued, their agreement should be upheld. Where the defendant has taken part in proceedings in a court, the defendant should be bound by the decision of that court. There may also be concerns about administrative convenience, such as the cost of proceedings, possible delays, and the location of witnesses or evidence. Having two sets of proceedings over the same subject matter in two different courts is obviously wasteful and can lead to conflicting judgments. Therefore duplicate proceedings should be avoided.

Jurisdiction is an interlocutory matter. That means it is to be determined at a very early stage of proceedings before all the evidence is obtained in discovery. Only once the court decides it has jurisdiction is discovery ordered. Eventually a full trial of the substance (also known as the merits) of the dispute is heard and judgment reached. It makes sense to decide questions of jurisdiction quickly and efficiently without running up the huge costs associated with a full trial.[6] Many cases settle after the question of jurisdiction is established. Once it is clear which court will hear the case, the outcome on the merits is predictable and the parties would prefer to settle than go to a full trial. The court has a difficult balance to strike between properly hearing the jurisdictional case which is the major area of dispute and preventing costs on an interlocutory matter from becoming disproportionately high. It also has to consider whether there is sufficient evidence to decide the jurisdictional case

---

[2] Such as freezing orders (protecting the assets available for enforcement) and the ancillary orders for disclosure of the defendant's assets. See further Chapter 7.

[3] Which are very useful for personal injury claims against manufacturers or employers.

[4] Such as fraud, banking, insurance and reinsurance cases.

[5] Many people are surprised at the expense of pursuing proceedings in England. A conservative estimate of the total cost of lawyers *per day* of High Court proceedings is £25,000. That does not include any preparation work which often takes many months.

[6] Many continental civilian countries try issues of jurisdiction only immediately before the full merits. Therefore parties must prepare for a full trial in case they lose the argument on jurisdiction.

fairly for both claimant and defendant. Although the onus is on the party who alleges a fact to prove it, interlocutory matters are decided assuming the allegations to be true in order to keep costs to a minimum. These are usually the allegations of the claimant who is seeking to establish jurisdiction in England. There is a risk that a defendant will be dragged to England unfairly to challenge the jurisdiction of the English court merely because the claimant makes a plausible, but ultimately weak, case. It is true that a defendant who succeeds in establishing that the case should not be heard in England will have costs awarded to the defendant.[7] However, these will not be on an indemnity basis and the pain of challenging a claim is not merely financial so the defendant will still have paid a high price.

There are two broad regimes covering the jurisdiction of the English courts. Primarily, one must ask whether the dispute falls within the rules of the Brussels I Regulation[8] or of its sister convention, the Lugano Convention.[9] These are paramount. Therefore it is essential to ask the question, does the Brussels regime apply to a case? If the answer is (yes), then those rules of jurisdiction must operate. Only where those regimes do not apply do the national (i.e., the traditional common law) rules on jurisdiction residually operate. This work will focus on the Brussels I Regulation and refer only to the Lugano Convention where necessary.[10] The Brussels I Regulation engages when the dispute is a civil and commercial matter[11] and:

(a) where the defendant is domiciled in a Member State;[12] or
(b) (whether or not the defendant is domiciled in a Member State):
    (i) there is a jurisdiction agreement in favour of a Member State;[13] or
    (ii) there are proceedings in another Member State;[14] or
    (iii) the subject matter of the dispute comes within the exclusive jurisdiction provisions of Article 22.[15]

In the residual cases, under the national rules, the jurisdiction of the English court depends on the service of the claim form on the defendant. This can be achieved either by serving a defendant who is present in England or by

---

[7] A successful defendant can expect to receive at most three-quarters of the cost of defence.
[8] Regulation (EC) 44/2001 on jurisdiction and the recognition and enforcement of judgments in civil and commercial matters [2001] OJ L12/1, binding all Member States apart from Denmark. There is a parallel but separate regime for Denmark. In relation to jurisdiction within the United Kingdom, similar rules to those in the Brussels I Regulation apply by virtue of Civil Jurisdiction and Judgments Act 1982, Sched. 4.
[9] A new Lugano Convention between the EU and EFTA was concluded in 2007, replacing the original 1988 Lugano Convention. It covers the EU countries (including Denmark), Iceland, Norway and Switzerland.
[10] The two regimes are substantially similar.
[11] Article 1, see further pp. 59–68 below on the meaning of civil and commercial matters and the exclusions in Art. 1.
[12] Article 2.   [13] Articles 4 and 23.
[14] *Overseas Union Insurance Ltd v New Hampshire Insurance Co.* Case C-351/89 [1992] 1 QB 434.
[15] Articles 4 and 22.

obtaining the permission of the court to serve the claim form on the defendant abroad.[16] In either case, the defendant may ask the court to exercise its discretion not to hear the case using the doctrine of *forum conveniens*.[17] The two regimes are completely different in approach. The purpose of the Brussels I Regulation is largely to unify rules of jurisdiction primarily so that judgments within the EU can be easily recognised and enforced. It emphasises certainty and uniformity and mutual trust and confidence in the courts of Member States. The national rules are flexible, discretionary and aim to achieve justice to the parties in the light of a 'jungle'[18] of overlapping and competing jurisdictional rules.

2. Preliminary matters: a good arguable case and a serious issue to be tried

English courts have developed a highly sophisticated approach to resolve the difficulties of determining jurisdictional questions at the early interlocutory stage of proceedings. Note that at the time at which the jurisdiction of the court has to be established, there has been no full disclosure of the evidence between the parties. Indeed, there has been little more than allegations made in the statement of claim and no statement of defence might yet have been made. In attempting to balance the rights of the claimant to have the case decided in the English court and those of the defendant who may not wish to suffer the costs of English litigation, the claimant has to show issues of contested jurisdictional fact or law to the standard of a 'good arguable case'. This phrase is not capable of very precise definition[19] but the onus is on the claimant to satisfy the court that it is right to take jurisdiction in the circumstances alleged. At the point at which both parties are before the court to dispute jurisdiction the claimant has to have 'a much better argument' on the material available than the defendant.[20] This does not mean that the claimant has to prove on the balance of probabilities that the claimant's view of the court's jurisdiction is the correct one. So a 'good arguable case' is not as strong as one which would satisfy the balance of probabilities. Nevertheless, the court should be mindful not to permit a claimant to bully a defendant into the English court. It ought to be ready to penalise improper behaviour if it were to find that at trial of the merits the claimant has not satisfactorily made out the case on the facts on the balance of probabilities.

In contrast, the claimant does not have to establish the facts on the merits of the case to a high standard at all at this early jurisdictional stage. However, the claimant does have to show that there is a case between the claimant and defendant to be heard in the English courts. Otherwise the claimant could

---

[16] See further pp. 139–64 below.   [17] See further pp. 164–77 below.

[18] Lord Goff of Chieveley in *Airbus Industrie GIE v Patel* [1999] 1 AC 119 at 132.

[19] *Cube Lighting v Afcon Electra* [2011] EWHC 2565 (Ch).

[20] *Canada Trust Co. Ltd v Stolzenberg* [1998] 1 WLR 547 at 555; *Bols Distilleries (t/a Bols Royal Distilleries) v Superior Yacht Services Ltd* [2006] UKPC 45, [2007] 1 WLR 12 at paras. 26–28; *AK Investment CJSC v Kyrgyz Mobil Tel Ltd* [2011] UKPC 7.

make spurious allegations and force the defendant to England to show that there is no case to answer. The standard is that of the 'serious issue to be tried'.[21] The claimant must show that there a real (as opposed to a fanciful) prospect of success.[22] The test is only just above the level at which a defendant would be successful with a plea to strike out the proceedings as showing no cause of action.[23] This is the same test as for summary judgment.[24] Although it is not a very high hurdle it is still important to remember that if the case is bound to fail it would be improper for the English court to require the defendant to come to England to argue that case.[25]

3. Brussels I Regulation

a. History

The Brussels I Regulation[26] came into force on 1 March 2002. As a Regulation it applies directly to all Member States except Denmark, although Denmark has now entered into a parallel agreement.[27] The Brussels I Regulation replaced the Brussels Convention of 1968 which was agreed between the original six members of the European Economic Community.[28] There were four subsequent amending Accession Conventions.[29] When the United Kingdom joined the European Community it acceded to the Brussels Convention, which was implemented in the Civil Jurisdiction and Judgments Act 1982. Like Denmark and Ireland, the United Kingdom had the power not to opt into the Brussels I Regulation but, in the event, decided to do so. The Commission instituted a review of the Brussels I Regulation in accordance with Article 73, publishing a Green Paper and Report in February 2009.[30] The proposals culminated in the Brussels I Regulation (recast) which will apply from 10 January 2015.[31]

---

[21] *Seaconsar Far East v Bank Markazi* [1993] 3 WLR 756.

[22] Lord Collins in *AK Investment CJSC v Kyrgyz Mobil Tel Ltd* [2011] UKPC 7 at para. 71.

[23] *Carvill America Inc. v Camperdown UK Ltd* [2005] EWCA Civ 645, [2005] 2 Lloyd's LR 457.

[24] *AK Investment CJSC v Kyrgyz Mobil Tel Ltd* [2011] UKPC 7 at para. 82.

[25] *Barings Plc and another v Coopers & Lybrand* [1997] ILPr. 12 at para. 38.

[26] Regulation (EC) 44/2001 on jurisdiction and the recognition and enforcement of judgments in civil and commercial matters [2001] OJ L12/1.

[27] Council Decision (EC) 790/2005 [2005] OJ L299/61.

[28] Convention on Jurisdiction and the Enforcement of Judgments in Civil and Commercial Matters 1968. The text and that of the Protocol on Interpretation of 1971 can be found at [1978] OJ L304/77 and 97.

[29] A consolidated version of the Brussels Convention as amended can be found at [1998] OJ C27/1.

[30] Those followed extremely useful studies on the Brussels I Regulation by B. Hess, T. Pfeiffer and P. Schlosser (available at http://ec.europa.eu/justice_home/doc_centre/civil/studies/doc_civil_studies_en.htm), and by Nuyts (available at http://ec.europa.eu/justice_home/doc_centre/civil/studies/doc_civil_studies_en.htm).

[31] Regulation (EU) 1215/2012 on the jurisdiction and enforcement of judgments in civil and commercial matters (recast) [2012] OJ L351/1.

b. Interpretation and purpose

Article 220 of the original EC Treaty obliged the then members of the European Community to enter into negotiations to secure for their nationals simplification of formalities governing the recognition and enforcement of judgments, but the framers of the 1968 Convention went further and laid down rules of jurisdiction as well. It was taken as self-evident that lack of rules permitting easy enforcement of judgments was a barrier to the internal market. After the Treaty on European Union[32] community competence was established for private international law. Along with other measures necessary for the sound operation of the internal market, the Brussels I Regulation is part of a wider objective of establishing an area of freedom, security and justice ensuring the free movement of persons.[33]

Article 267 of the Treaty on Functioning of the European Union permits *any* court of a Member State to seek a ruling from the Court of Justice of the European Union (CJEU) if the court considers 'that a decision on the question is necessary to enable it to give judgment'.[34] Matters of interpretation have been rather rarely referred in practice to the CJEU from English courts. It is generally a party to a dispute which asks for the reference rather than the court and English lawyers seem unwilling to do so. Partly this may be due to the rule on costs which follow the domestic rules that the loser pays and a reference to the CJEU is likely to be very expensive. Partly it might be that the consequence of a reference to the CJEU on the interpretation of the Brussels I Regulation can be unpredictable. However, now that lower courts should be more aware that they may refer matters to the CJEU it is possible that more cases will be taken there.

An English court wishing to determine the meaning of the Brussels Convention was permitted to look at the official Reports on the Convention and the modifying Accession Conventions.[35] Both the English courts and the CJEU have referred to these Reports as aids to interpretation. Recital 19 of the Brussels I Regulation requires continuity between the Brussels Convention and the Regulation and so the Regulation should be decided in principle consistently with the previous case law.[36] The Brussels I Regulation took many concepts over from the Brussels Convention and therefore the Reports on the

---

[32] The Amsterdam Treaty, now amended by the Lisbon Treaty.

[33] Article 67(4) (ex Art. 61(c) TEC) and Art. 81 (ex Art. 65 TEC) of the Treaty on Functioning of the European Union.

[34] Courts from which there is no further judicial remedy *must* seek rulings from the CJEU, i.e., the Supreme Court (previously the House of Lords) or the Court of Appeal in some circumstances, but lower courts may also do so. The previous limitation on references to the CJEU contained in ex Art. 68(1) EC has gone.

[35] Civil Jurisdiction and Judgments Act 1982, 5.3(3). These reports are the Jenard Report [1979] OJ C59/1, Schlosser Report [1979] OJ C59/71, Evrigenis and Kerameus Report [1986] OJ C298/1, Almeida Cruz, Desantes Real, Jenard Report [1990] OJ C189/6.

[36] *Ilsinger* Case C-180/06 [2009] ECR I 3961 at para. 41.

Brussels Convention and cases decided on it will still be relevant to the Regulation. However, there are changes to the wording and some of those are substantial. Also, the CJEU has expanded the purposes of the Brussels I Regulation over the years. Therefore, care has to be taken in using older cases and materials. The Brussels I Regulation was accompanied by an Explanatory Memorandum from the Commission which is very brief and less useful than the previous Reports. Careful reference should be made to the recitals to the Regulation which are extensive in outlining the background and purposes of the Regulation.

The CJEU has laid out some principles of interpretation of the Brussels Convention and Brussels I Regulation. First and most importantly, the purpose of a provision is critical to its interpretation rather than its literal meaning.[37] This teleological interpretation is used both with a view to the particular purpose of the provision in question and to the general purposes of the Brussels I Regulation. The primary purpose of the Regulation is to promote the internal market by harmonising the rules of jurisdiction and simplifying the recognition and enforcement of judgments. However, there are also subsidiary purposes such as the prevention of irreconcilable judgments, protection of vulnerable parties and supporting party autonomy. Secondly, the Brussels I Regulation is to be interpreted as uniformly as possible. The uniform application of the Brussels I Regulation itself serves the objective of the internal market. Therefore many of the concepts of the Regulation are given an autonomous, community-wide definition which is not dependent on local domestic national law. In addition, the EU has claimed exclusive competence over matters of civil jurisdiction.[38] Thirdly, the Brussels I Regulation is part of the new area of EU policy, that of the Area of Freedom, Justice and Security, which requires judicial cooperation in civil matters having cross-border implications.[39] So it must be interpreted in such a way as to give effect to the policy of greater integration. Regard may be had to the interpretation of cognate European legislation.[40] It is also universal in its application. Fourthly, the principle of mutual trust requires the Brussels I Regulation to be interpreted in a manner which assumes all courts are equally competent. Interplay between these principles can reveal conflicting purposes. In such cases some purposes are shown to be of greater hierarchical value than others.

The recitals to the Brussels I Regulation are very helpful to aid interpretation of various provisions.

---

[37] See e.g., *Somafer SA v Saar Ferngas AG* Case C-33/78 [1978] ECR 2183; *Overseas Union Insurance Ltd v New Hampshire Insurance Co.* Case C-351/89 [1991] ECR I 3317; and more recently *Ilsinger* Case C-180/06 [2009] ECR I 3961 at para. 44.

[38] Lugano Opinion (Opinion 1/03) [2006] ECR I 1145.

[39] COM(1997)609 final [1998] OJ C33, 31 January 1998 and Tampere Summit.

[40] *Geemente Steenbergen v Baten* Case C-271/100 [2002] ECR I-10489 and *Lechouritou v Greece* Case C-292/05 [2007] ECR I-1519 at para. 45.

c. Scope

The Brussels I Regulation applies 'whatever the nature of court or tribunal', this includes not just the High Court and County Courts but also, for example, the Employment Appeals Tribunal. European systems of law will have a wider variety of tribunals which do not necessarily appear to have a judicial input, for example, the Tribunal de Commerce in France which has a panel of commercial people to decide disputes before it. Nonetheless, the Regulation applies to judgments from such tribunals so long as they are exercising the judicial functions of the state.[41]

The Regulation applies only to cases which concern 'civil and commercial matters'. This concept has an autonomous meaning. Although continental civilian systems draw a clear distinction between public and private law issues, they do not all draw that line in the same place. Common law legal systems do not clearly draw such a distinction at all. For the avoidance of doubt the Regulation specifies that 'civil and commercial matters' do not include 'revenue, customs or administrative matters'.[42] Actions arising out of a sovereign's exercise of public powers are excluded, even if the claim is made in private law.[43] In contrast, where a case overall concerns a relationship between private parties but raises some issue of tax, it is not excluded from the Regulation. Cases imposing the punishment of the state for breach of the criminal law are excluded, although ancillary actions for damages brought by private parties[44] within the criminal courts are included. Litigation between private parties usually falls within the scope of the Brussels I Regulation but actions in which a state or public body such as a local authority is a party may also do so. So long as the public authority was acting in a private law capacity rather than in accordance with public law powers, a claim can be made within the Regulation's rules or a judgment recognised. So in *Sonntag v Waidmann*:

> An Italian judgment against a German teacher found negligently liable for the death of a pupil on a school trip was held by the CJEU to come within civil and commercial matters. Although the teacher had been employed in a publicly funded school and could be argued to be acting in some sense on behalf of the state, the right to compensation for criminally culpable conduct 'is generally recognised as being a civil law right'. In addition, the teacher's exercise of the powers were only those 'existing under the rules applicable to relations between private individuals', which would be the same whether the school was a state-funded or private school.[45]

---

[41] *Solo Kleinmotoren GmbH v Boch* Case C-414/92 [1994] ECR I-2237 at para. 17.
[42] Article 1.
[43] *Lechouritou v Greece* Case C-292/05 [2007] ECR I-1519.
[44] For example, a *partie civil* action.
[45] *Volker Sonntag v Hans Waidmann* Case C-172/91 [1993] ECR I-1963.

Whereas in *LTU v Eurocontrol*:

> Eurocontrol, a body formed under public law, obtained a judgment in Belgium against a German company for payment of various charges. Eurocontrol sought enforcement of that judgment in Germany and the German court referred the question of whether the definition of a civil and commercial matter was to be determined according to German or Belgian law. The CJEU held an autonomous definition had to be applied to the scope of the Brussels Convention rather than either domestic law interpretation. In this case, Eurocontrol was acting in accordance with public law powers, despite the charges appearing to be of a private law nature. The public law nature of the relationship was found as 'the use of equipment and services, provided by such body ... [was] obligatory and exclusive' and also because of the unilateral nature of the relationship. The judgment was therefore not within the scope of the Convention.[46]

It is the nature of the legal relationship between the public authority and the other party which is crucial. The nature of the relationship is autonomously defined.[47] In *Verein Für Konsumenteninformation v Henkel*,[48] a consumer protection organisation brought an action on behalf of the consuming public against a trader. The CJEU found this to be within the Brussels I Regulation as any private person could have brought the action.

Actions regarding environmental matters and other types of private law enforcement are beginning to raise concerns as to whether they are civil and commercial matters or not.[49] Characterisation of these mixed public-private law actions vary in the Member States. For example, the regulation of gambling is not uniformly regarded by Member States as a civil law matter. At least some aspects are regarded as deriving from public or administrative law.[50] Likewise, an imposition of liability for misleading information in a prospectus for the issue of shares is not necessarily wholly a private law matter. Although many of these actions have a private law form, as for example an injunction to prevent the escape of ionising radiation from a power plant in another state,[51] they raise issues of policy and public law which need careful consideration.

---

[46] *LTU Lufttransportunternehmen GmbH & Co. KG v Eurocontrol* Case C-29/76 [1976] ECR 1541.
[47] *Préservatrice foncière TIARD SA v Staat der Nederlanden* Case C-266/01 [2003] ECR I-4867.
[48] Case C-167/00 [2002] ECR I-8111.
[49] See B. Hess, T. Pfeiffer and P. Schlosser *Report on the Application of Regulation Brussels I in the Member States*, Study JLS/C4/2005/03, paras. 75–8.
[50] See in France *GIE Pari Mutuel Urbain v Zeturf Ltd*, Cour de Cassation, Chambre Commerciale, Financière et Économique, Arrêt No. 1023 du 10 juillet 2007, and in Malta, Civil Court (First Hall) Application 82/2007, 2 March 2007.
[51] See, e.g., *Land Oberösterreich v ČEZ as* Case C-343/04 [2006] ECR I-4557, where such an action was excluded from Art. 16. However, the prior question of whether the Brussels I Regulation applied was not taken. An implicit assumption of the application of the Regulation had been made by all concerned.

Whether to include such cases within 'civil and commercial matters' and bring them within the scope of the Regulation is a political question, which would more properly be answered by amendment of the Regulation than piecemeal by the CJEU. In addition, some actions in these areas are commenced to impose criminal penalties, which are not within civil and commercial matters[52] although an ancillary civil damages remedy would be a civil and commercial law matter. The nature of the legal relationships and the subject matter of the dispute is what is critical. A criminal action in which the state is exercising public law powers is not a civil and commercial matter. On the other hand, if private rights are being enforced and the action did not involve the exercise of public powers, the matter is within the Brussels I Regulation. So in *Realchemie Nederland BV v Bayer CropScience AG*:

> A civil court in Germany imposed a fine to enforce the Dutch defendant's compliance with an order of that court to provide details of its business in the chemicals and transfer stock to the possession of the German court. The German claimant sought to enforce the fine in Holland, though the fine was payable to the German state. The CJEU held this was a civil and commercial matter and within the Brussels I Regulation. Although the fine was not payable to a private party, the matter was nonetheless characterised by the nature of the legal relationships between the parties and the subject matter of the action. Interim measures of this kind are characterised according to the substantive rights which are being protected.[53]

i. Excluded matters generally

The Brussels I Regulation specifically excludes some civil and commercial matters. The CJEU decided in *Préservatrice Foncière TIARD SA v Netherlands State*[54] that the Regulation nevertheless applies to cases which involve excluded matters which arise in the disputes only as preliminary issues. This is a contrary conclusion to the one the court came to in two other cases where it held that if the substance of the dispute was an excluded matter, then even if some preliminary matters could have been thought to be determinable within the Regulation, the Regulation was not invoked.[55] The two views may be

---

[52] For example, if a penalty is imposed by the state authorities against an unregulated provider of gambling services. The state penalty may be contrary to freedom of establishment under EU law (see *Gambelli* Case C-243/01 [2003] ECR I-13031) but the penalty would not be a 'civil and commercial matter' within the Regulation. The penalty is therefore not enforceable under the Regulation.

[53] Case C-406/09 [2012] IL Pr. I.   [54] Case C-266/01 [2003] ECR I-4867.

[55] *Marc Rich & Co. AG v Società Italiana Impianti PA* Case C-190/89 [1991] ECR I-3855 at para. 26 *et seq.*; *Owens Bank Ltd v Fulvio Bracco and Bracco Industria Chimica SpA* Case C-129/92 [1994] ECR I-117 at para. 34.

reconcilable by identifying the substance of the dispute. If the substance is an excluded matter, the whole dispute is excluded. Where, however, the substance is not excluded, but some preliminary, ancillary or incidental issue is raised which is without the scope of the Regulation by virtue of Article 1, then the whole dispute falls within it.[56] This is not very satisfactory. Whether a dispute 'in substance' raises an excluded matter is often dependent on national law rules of procedure (such as pleading) and on which party raises the claim or defence. Such distinctions do the law no service. In addition, the CJEU has interpreted the exclusions narrowly where possible in order to give the greatest effect to the Brussels I Regulation.[57]

ii. Expressed exclusions

(a) The status or legal capacity of natural persons, rights in property arising out of a matrimonial relationship, wills and succession. Thus cases principally concerning the voidability of marriages, dissolution of marriages, whether someone is considered to have died, and the custody or adoption of children are all excluded. So too are disputes over property where the ownership is affected by a marriage, such as disputes over community property regimes. Recognition and enforcement of judgments from Member States relating to divorce and parental responsibility fall within Brussels II*bis*.[58] Cases which determine questions of maintenance[59] in family matters are now completely excluded from the Brussels I Regulation by the Maintenance Regulation for all cases commenced after 18 June 2011.[60] These Regulations should make the exclusion in Article 1(2) clearer.[61] However, it is only property rights arising out of a 'matrimonial relationship' which are excluded from the Brussels I Regulation, proceedings which concern property of individuals who happen to be married to one another may fall within the Regulation.[62] England does not have a community property regime affecting property held under a matrimonial relationship but civilian law countries may take a different view.

---

[56] See too *Allianz SpA, Generali Assicurazioni Generali Spa v West Tankers Inc. (The Front Comor)* Case C-185/07 [2009] ECR I-663 at para. 26.

[57] *Préservatrice foncière TIARD SA v. Staat der Nederlanden* Case C-266/01 [2003] ECR I-4867.

[58] Council Regulation (EC) 2201/2003 of 27 November 2003 concerning jurisdiction and the recognition and enforcement of judgments in matrimonial matters and matters of parental responsibility.

[59] For a definition of maintenance see *Van den Boogaard v Laumen* Case C-220/95 [1997] ECR I-1147.

[60] Regulation (EC) 4/2009 on jurisdiction, applicable law, recognition and enforcement of decisions and cooperation in matters relating to maintenance obligations, Recital 44 and Art. 76. Previously, some maintenance judgments were enforceable via the Brussels I Regulation with concomitant jurisdiction provisions (see Art. 5(2)).

[61] For the previous difficulties see *De Cavel v De Cavel (No. 1)* Case C-143/78 [1979] ECR 1055; *De Cavel v De Cavel (No. 2)* Case C-120/79 [1980] ECR 731; *CHW v GJH* Case C-25/81 [1982] ECR 1189.

[62] *De Cavel v De Cavel (No. 2)* Case C-120/79 [1980] ECR 731.

In addition, the definition of matrimonial relationship is unclear.[63] Many Member States have quasi-matrimonial regimes which the EU recognises as marriage for some purposes. Would the determination of possible constructive trust over property bought after a civil partnership has been celebrated fall within or without the Regulation? An English court would view the case as being essentially the same whether or not there is a state-sanctioned relationship between the parties and therefore would decide the case within the Brussels I Regulation. A civilian European court might take a different view that this is a case concerning (quasi-) matrimonial property and therefore excluded. The CJEU has not determined this issue and it is uncertain that a reference to the 'general principles which stem from the corpus of the national legal systems'[64] to find an autonomous definition will greatly help.

Proceedings concerning wills and succession are also excluded by this paragraph. So are disputes as to the interpretation or validity of a will or codicil, or claims to testate or intestate succession to property, and the appointment and removal of trustees or administrators to administer the succession are excluded from the scope of the Regulation. However, the matter may fall within the Regulation where the dispute is between a trustee or administrator and someone other than a beneficiary, such as a debtor to the estate.[65] A very difficult question might arise in such cases where the debtor seeks as a matter of defence to assert that the trustee does not have power as the will is invalid. The main subject matter of the proceedings would be within the Regulation, but the defence directly raises an excluded matter.[66] Proceedings relating to gifts *inter vivos* are within the Regulation as are disputes over some trusts.[67]

(b) Bankruptcy, proceedings relating to the winding-up of insolvent companies or other legal persons, judicial arrangements, compositions and analogous proceedings. The Brussels I Regulation must be read with the Insolvency Regulation,[68] as the two Regulations must be interpreted so that proceedings fall within one or the other, without any gap.[69] Not all insolvency issues are covered by the Insolvency Regulation, which can lead to problems. The CJEU in *Gourdain v Nadler*[70] decided that an order of the French court requiring a *de facto* manager of an insolvent company to contribute to the company's

---

[63] In contrast, the Maintenance Regulation covers 'maintenance obligations arising from a family relationship, parentage, marriage or affinity' (Art. 1).

[64] *LTU Lufttransportunternehmen GmbH & Co. KG v Eurocontrol* Case C-29/76 [1976] ECR 1541, 1550 at para. 3.

[65] Schlosser Report, para. 52.

[66] The mere possibility of defences does not generally exclude the claim from the scope, see *Préservatrice foncière TIARD SA v Staat der Nederlanden* Case C-266/01 [2003] ECR I-4867.

[67] Jenard Report, p. 11 and Art. 5(6).

[68] Regulation (EC) 1346/2000 on insolvency proceedings.

[69] Jenard Report, p. 12.   [70] Case C-133/78 [1979] ECR 733.

assets was within the exclusion. It held that the exclusion had to be given an autonomous definition, not merely decided by reference to national law:

> The French court order derived directly from the bankruptcy[71] and was closely connected to the *'liquidation des biens'*. This was due to the application for the order only being made to the court making the *liquidation des biens*, the order could only be made by that court (or by the manager of the liquidation), the period of limitation ran from a date when the final list of claims was drawn up and the reimbursement from the manager was for the benefit of all creditors rather than any individual creditor being able to take this action for itself.

On the other hand, an action by a liquidator to recover debts due to the company comes within the Brussels I Regulation, not the exclusion. Such an action does not derive directly from the winding up, but is drawn from the general law.[72] Therefore, in *German Graphics Graphische Maschinen GmbH v Alice van de Schee*:[73]

> The German seller had obtained a German judgment based upon a reservation of title clause. The Dutch liquidator of the Dutch purchaser challenged the enforcement under the Brussels I Regulation of the German judgment. The CJEU held that the scope of the Insolvency Regulation was to be interpreted narrowly compared with that of the Brussels I Regulation. In order for the German judgment to be excluded from recognition on the grounds of being related to the winding up of an insolvent company, there would have to be a sufficiently direct and close link between the proceedings and the insolvency. In this case the action on the reservation of title clause was an independent claim, not based upon the law of the insolvency proceedings and did not require the involvement of a liquidator. It therefore fell within the Brussels I Regulation and was to be enforced in the Netherlands, even though a liquidator had been appointed there and the company was insolvent.

Actiones paulianae are a civil law action by which a creditor can obtain a remedy against a third party once an asset has passed from the debtor; it is somewhat comparable to an action to enforce a security interest. These actions

---

[71] See too Jenard Report, p. 12.

[72] In *Powell Duffryn Plc v Wolfgang Petereit* Case C-214/89 [1992] ECR I-1745, the liquidator brought an action to recover calls on shares and improperly paid dividends from a shareholder. This action would be within the scope of the Regulation. Two English cases are to similar effect, *In Re Hayward dec'd* [1997] Ch. 45 and *Ashurst v Pollard* [2001] Ch. 595, CA, in neither case did the liquidator's action derive directly from the bankruptcy and were actions the bankrupt could have taken himself.

[73] Case C-292/08 [2009] ECR I-8421.

can arise during or before the debtor's bankruptcy or even more generally, if the transaction between the debtor and third party can be impeached by the debtor's intention (for example, to improperly transfer the asset to defeat creditors). *Actiones paulianae* therefore might fall within the Insolvency Regulation or the Brussels I Regulation. Those which arise directly from the debtor's bankruptcy are excluded from the Brussels I Regulation.[74] Those which derive from the general law, where the power to obtain the remedy is in an individual creditor rather than the liquidator, are within the Brussels I Regulation.[75]

(c) Social security. This also has an autonomous definition. The Jenard Report noted that this exclusion was to be limited to disputes between the administrative authorities and employers or employees.[76] In *Gemeente Steenbergen v Baten*,[77] the CJEU noted that other legislation[78] lays down certain rules regarding social security so the concept must be uniformly interpreted in all community law. However, public authorities' actions against third parties or in subrogation to the rights of an injured party fall within the Regulation. Therefore, where the public body which has paid out benefits to an assisted person has a right of recourse against a third person, the proceedings for recourse will be within the Brussels I Regulation. It is important that the third person has an obligation under private law to maintain the assisted person as it is this private law foundation which gives rise to the 'civil and commercial' nature of the claim.[79]

(d) Arbitration. There are considerable difficulties in determining the exact boundaries of the exclusion of arbitration from the Brussels I Regulation. The intention of the original framers of the Brussels Convention 1968 was to exclude arbitration matters entirely as there were international agreements on arbitration to which the contracting states were parties. At that time, it had been hoped that there might be a separate European agreement for a uniform law of arbitration, which has never come to fruition. The Jenard Report noted that the Brussels Convention did not apply to the recognition and enforcement of arbitral awards, nor to the jurisdiction of the courts in respect of litigation relating to arbitration (such as proceedings to set aside arbitral awards) nor to judgments of those proceedings.[80] A wide definition of arbitration was taken in *Marc Rich v Società Italiana Impianti*:[81]

---

[74] *Seagon v Deko Marty Belgium NV* Case C-339/07 [2009] ECR I-767.

[75] *Reichert and Kockler v Dresdner Bank* Case C-115/88 [1990] ECR I-27 and *Reichert and Kockler* Case C-261/90 [1992] ECR I-2149, as explained by AG Ruiz-Jarabo Colomer in *Seagon v Deko Marty NV* Case C-339/07 [2009] ECR I-767.

[76] Jenard Report, p. 13.

[77] *Gemeente Steenbergen v Luc Baten* Case C-271/00 [2002] ECR I-10489.

[78] For example, Regulation (EC) 1408/71 now replaced by Regulation (EC) 883/2004.

[79] *Gemeente Steenbergen v Luc Baten* Case C-271/00 [2002] ECR I-10489 at paras. 46, 48. See too Regulation (EC) 883/2004, recital 36, Art. 1(z) and Annex 1.

[80] Jenard Report, p. 13.

[81] Also known as *The Atlantic Emperor* Case C-190/89 [1991] ECR I-3855.

Proceedings were started in England between a Swiss claimant and an Italian defendant. The Swiss claimant asked the English court to appoint an arbitrator under an agreement allegedly requiring arbitration of substantive contractual disputes between the parties in England. The Italian defendants had already commenced proceedings in Italy for a declaration that they were not liable to the claimants. The defendants disputed the validity of the arbitration agreement in the English proceedings and the claimants relied on the arbitration agreement in the Italian proceedings to challenge the jurisdiction of the Italian courts. The English Court of Appeal referred the question whether the English proceedings were within or without the scope of the Brussels Convention to the CJEU. The CJEU held that the intention was 'to exclude arbitration in its entirety'. Particularly, ancillary proceedings such as these proceedings for the appointment of arbitrators fell outside the scope of the Convention.

This would be so even if in such proceedings a national court would have to determine the validity of the arbitration agreement as a preliminary issue.[82] This apparently answered the English court's question to the CJEU's satisfaction but its exact effect is rather unclear. Some Member States take the view that the courts can determine the validity of any arbitration agreement, its scope and effect, even if the arbitral seat is in another Member State. Others, such as England, regard jurisdiction to determine those questions as exclusively a matter for the courts of the Member State at the seat of the arbitration. The Schlosser Report identified divisions between the views of Member States on the matter but the wording of the text was unchanged when the Brussels Convention was replaced by the Brussels I Regulation.

Where the proceedings in a national court are principally for the purpose of appointing or removing an arbitrator, or for fixing the place of the arbitration, enforcing or setting aside an arbitral award, or are declaratory proceedings as to the validity and effect of the arbitration agreement,[83] or answer some point of law raised in an arbitration, then those proceedings fall outside the Regulation.[84] In such a case the Member State's court can assume jurisdiction under its national rules, ignore any proceedings continuing in another Member State on the same issue and use its national rules to determine whether to refuse to recognise or enforce any judgment ordered by another Member State's court

---

[82] *Marc Rich & Co. AG v Società Italiana Impianti PA* Case C-190/89 [1991] ECR I-3855 at para. 26.

[83] The CJEU in *Allianz SpA, Generali Assicurazioni Generali Spa v West Tankers Inc. (The Front Comor)* Case C-185/07 [2009] ECR I-663, decided that an anti-suit injunction to support the arbitration agreement was impermissible but the proceedings by which the injunction was granted were outside the scope of the Regulation; these proceedings included a request for a declaration as to the effect of the arbitration agreement binding the insurer (para. 23).

[84] Schlosser Report, para. 65; *Marc Rich & Co. AG v Società Italiana Impianti PA* Case C-190/89 [1991] ECR I-3855 at para. 26.

on the same issue. However, the less clear cases include: proceedings in which the arbitration agreement is used to challenge jurisdiction;[85] proceedings for damages for breach of the arbitration agreement; proceedings to require the taking of evidence or the protection of evidence; proceedings as to awards of costs or security in arbitration; and proceedings to recognise or enforce a judgment which has been given in violation of an arbitration agreement (whether the validity of the arbitration agreement was decided in that judgment or not).

Until the CJEU decision in *Allianz SpA Assicurazioni Generali Spa v West Tankers*,[86] the prevailing view of English lawyers was that the arbitration exception should be given a wide interpretation to ensure that all these cases would likewise fall outside the scope of the Brussels I Regulation.[87] In *West Tankers*:

> The English courts were requested to grant a restraining order (an anti-suit injunction) to restrain an insurer from continuing proceedings in Italy. The insurer in the Italian proceedings sought by way of subrogation to recover amounts from the applicant which the insurer had already paid to an insured for damage allegedly caused by the applicant. Those Italian proceedings were allegedly in breach of an arbitration agreement between the defendant in Italy (the applicant in the English proceedings) and the insured. Arbitration on the matter of liability between the applicant and the insured was continuing in England. The English proceedings were also declaratory as to the effect of the arbitration agreement and its breach by the Italian proceedings.[88]

The CJEU found the English proceedings to fall outside the scope of the Regulation as their subject matter was the right to arbitrate. However, the Italian proceedings fell within the Brussels I Regulation as the validity and effect of the arbitration agreement was only a preliminary matter in that dispute. The Italian proceedings primarily concerned the substance of the case, the liability for the original damage. The Italian court could therefore establish jurisdiction for the case about liability under the rules of the Regulation. As a consequence, the English court could not grant an anti-suit injunction over the Italian proceedings as to do so would interfere with the Italian court's determination of its own jurisdiction under the Regulation.

---

[85] This might be seen as an incidental question, which could be argued to be within the Regulation as the primary purpose of the proceedings is not the arbitration agreement.

[86] *Allianz SpA, Generali Assicurazioni Generali Spa v West Tankers Inc. (The Front Comor)* Case C-185/07 [2009] ECR I-663.

[87] Cf. P. Schlosser, 'The 1968 Brussels Covention and Arbitration' (1991) 7 *Arb. Int.* 227, who argued that only arbitral proceedings themselves come within the exception.

[88] *West Tankers Inc. v Allianz SpA (formerly RAS Riunione Adriatica di Sicurtà SpA) and another* Case C-185/07 [2008] ECR I-663.

This solution, however compatible with other CJEU cases which uphold mutual trust and confidence and apply *effet utile*,[89] has very unfortunate consequences. As we shall see below, the English proceedings, even if commenced first, are not within Articles 27 and 28,[90] so inevitably there will be the risk of irreconcilable decisions on the validity and effect of the arbitration agreement as well as the expense of two sets of proceedings in which the same matter is in issue. Also, the judgment of the Italian court on the substance of the proceedings is enforceable within the Regulation throughout the EU. An irreconcilable decision of the English court is not within the Regulation, although the Italian judgment would not be recognised or enforced in England.[91] The judgment of the Italian court will compete with the arbitration award, necessarily, but there will also be competing judgments on the effect of the arbitration agreement. The case undermines the effectiveness of arbitration agreements. In a later case in England, a decision of a Spanish court as to the interpretation of an arbitration agreement as a preliminary question in a case which was substantially about liability had to be recognised in England in accordance with the Brussels I Regulation.[92] The arbitration agreement purportedly for arbitration in England was therefore robbed of effect. The Spanish court had decided that the arbitration agreement did not cover the dispute in question, therefore the English court could not uphold the arbitration agreement, even though under English law it bound the parties to arbitrate their dispute.

d. Outline

The Brussels I Regulation contains a hierarchy of jurisdictional rules. The strongest rule is that of exclusive jurisdiction found in Article 22. Under Article 22, a court of a Member State has jurisdiction over cases with specified subject matters irrespective of the defendant's domicile (either within or without the EU). In addition, any judgment brought in another court is unenforceable. Also, a defendant's submission to a court other than that specified does not even grant that court jurisdiction.[93] Second in the hierarchy come the particular rules of jurisdiction which apply to consumers, employees and insureds to control the jurisdiction of courts in those cases.[94] Judgments brought in breach of those rules (except those for employees) do not have to be recognised or enforced in other Member States.[95] Jurisdiction agreements are only permissible in certain instances under those rules.[96] The third level is the submission of the defendant to a court by appearance in the court to argue the

[89] *Turner v Grovit* Case C-159/02 [2004] ECR I-3565; *Van Uden Maritime BV, trading as Van Uden Africa Line v Kommanditgesellschaft in Firma Deco-Line* Case C-391/95 [1998] ECR I-7091; *Erich Gasser GmbH v MISAT Srl* Case C-116/02 [2003] ECR I-14693.
[90] See pp. 120–32 below.   [91] Article 34(3).
[92] *National Navigacion v Endesa* [2009] EWCA Civ 1397, [2010] 1 Lloyd's LR 193, noted R. Fentiman [2010] *CLJ* 242.
[93] Article 24.   [94] Articles 8–21.   [95] Article 35(1).   [96] See pp. 100–5 below.

merits of the case,[97] which gives jurisdiction to that court in any case other than one falling within Article 22. Fourthly, under Article 23(1) where there is an exclusive jurisdiction agreement, that chosen court has exclusive jurisdiction.[98] However, another court may decide to hear the case and override the jurisdiction agreement because, for example, the agreement is invalid in accordance with Article 23.[99] A judgment obtained in breach of a jurisdiction agreement, even if exclusive, has to be recognised and enforced in other Member States. Fifthly, the general and special rules of jurisdiction are of equal validity and a claimant can choose between them freely. These include the grounds of jurisdiction based upon the defendant's domicile, upon the performance of a contract, upon the commission of a tort, in multi-party cases, and on a non-exclusive jurisdiction agreement, *inter alia*.

Nevertheless, the structure of the Brussels I Regulation rules appears to give prominence to the domicile of the defendant. It is important to understand the manner in which the Regulation operates. Article 2 provides that a defendant shall be sued in the courts of his domicile. Article 3 then provides that a defendant may only be sued in another Member State's courts if sections 2 to 7 of Chapter 1 apply.[100] Article 4 finally provides that if the defendant is not domiciled in a Member State then the national rules of jurisdiction apply subject to Articles 22 and 23. It can appear then, that the Brussels I Regulation is only triggered by the domicile of the defendant in the EU. However, the way in which Article 27 has been interpreted by the CJEU is a trap for the unwary. The effect of Article 27 is that where proceedings have been commenced first in another Member State on the same cause of action and between the same parties the English court cannot hear the dispute. This is true even if neither party comes from the EU[101] and even if the dispute has no connection with the EU.[102] It is only once the other proceedings have ceased, for example, if the other court considers it has no jurisdiction, that the English court can hear the case.

In conclusion, faced with an issue of jurisdiction before the English court, one should ask:

(1) Is there a matter of exclusive jurisdiction under Article 22? If so, then unless the English court is the specified jurisdiction, the case cannot go ahead here.

---

[97] Article 24.
[98] Cf. non-exclusive jurisdiction agreements under Art. 23, which merely confer jurisdiction upon a court, see p. 117 below.
[99] See p. 113 below.
[100] Presuming the dispute does not fall within Art. 22 due to its subject matter, or within the particular rules for consumers, insureds and employees, the English court may take jurisdiction either under Arts. 2, or Art. 23 or Art. 5–7.
[101] *Overseas Union Insurance Ltd v New Hampshire Insurance Co.* Case C-351/89 [1991] ECR I-3317.
[102] See pp. 120–9 below.

(2) Are there proceedings continuing in another Member State between the same parties and on the same cause of action? If so, then the English court cannot take jurisdiction.[103]

(3) Is there a particular rule of jurisdiction involving a consumer, insured or employee? If so, the English court may only take jurisdiction under those rules.[104]

(4) Will the defendant submit to the jurisdiction of the English courts (i.e., will not contest jurisdiction under CPR r. 11)? If so, the English courts will have jurisdiction unless the matter is one of exclusive jurisdiction under Article 22.[105]

(5) Is there a jurisdiction agreement? If there is one (either exclusive or non-exclusive) in favour of England, the English courts can take jurisdiction.[106] If there is an exclusive jurisdiction agreement in favour of another Member State's courts, then the English court cannot take jurisdiction unless the jurisdiction agreement can be attacked.[107] If there is a non-exclusive jurisdiction agreement in favour of another Member State's court, then the English court may take jurisdiction on another permitted ground.

(6) Is the defendant domiciled in England? If so the English court can hear the case.[108]

(7) Or is the defendant domiciled in another Member State and one of the grounds in Articles 5–7 apply? If so the English court can hear the case.[109]

e. General rule: defendant's domicile

Article 2 provides the general rule of jurisdiction: a defendant shall be sued in the courts of the Member State of the defendant's domicile, whatever the nationality of the defendant.[110] Article 2 does not determine the manner by which jurisdiction is to be effected within Member States as that is a procedural matter.[111] Domicile is a different concept to nationality and the concept of domicile used in the Brussels I Regulation is completely different from that used as a connecting factor for choice of law purposes.[112] A defendant cannot complain or be surprised that the courts of the place of the defendant's domicile have jurisdiction to hear any dispute raised against the defendant,

---

[103] Article 27 and see further pp. 120–9 below.   [104] Articles 8–21 and see further pp. 105–9 below.
[105] Article 24.   [106] Article 23(1) and (3). See further pp. 111–18 below.
[107] See p. 118 below.   [108] Article 2.   [109] Article 3.
[110] Jurisdiction over persons who are not nationals of the Member State in which they are domiciled is to be established by the rules of jurisdiction applicable to nationals of that state, Art. 2. How jurisdiction is allocated to courts within a Member State is left to the national procedural law.
[111] Therefore in England, the service rules in CPR r. 6 provide the method of service. Confusingly, at common law, those rules also provide the basis for jurisdiction.
[112] See Chapters 9–13.

whoever is the claimant and whatever the subject matter.[113] It is irrelevant to the Brussels I Regulation that the claimant comes from outside the EU.[114] There is no further connection between the facts of the dispute and the court necessary.[115] Both claimants and defendants have a clear, predictable forum in which disputes can be ventilated. As a corollary, the courts of the defendant's domicile must hear the case and cannot stay their proceedings in favour of another Member State or third state[116] except in accordance with the provisions of the Brussels I Regulation.[117]

Certain bases of jurisdiction which are used by courts of Member States are specifically suppressed as against persons domiciled in other Member States. These include arrest of assets, as was the case in Scotland; nationality, as in France; presence of assets, as was the case in Germany; and casual presence, as in England.[118] However, they may still be used against persons domiciled in third states. Judgments granted against such persons and obtained using those outlawed bases of jurisdiction are automatically enforceable throughout the EU. Therefore a casual visitor to England from the United States can be subject to English jurisdiction under the rules in CPR r. 6 and any, even a default, judgment can be enforced throughout the EU.[119] Equally, a judgment from a Polish court obtained against the same US citizen is enforceable whatever ground of jurisdiction the Polish court used.

i. Definition: domicile of natural persons

The rules on domicile differ depending on whether the defendant is a natural person (an individual) or a legal person (a corporation, partnership,[120] association, company or other legal entity). It is determined at the time the proceedings commence.[121] The domicile of an individual is determined according to the internal law of the Member State in which the case is continuing.[122] Therefore the English court applies English rules to decide if an individual is domiciled in England for the purposes of cases before it. If an individual is domiciled in England the court has jurisdiction under Article 2.

---

[113] Clearly apart from cases the subject matter of which falls within Art. 22.

[114] *Group Josi Reinsurance Co. SA v Universal General Insurance Co.* Case C-142/98 [2000] ECR I-5925.

[115] *Owusu v Jackson* Case C-281/02 [2004] ECR I-1383. Compare with the doctrine under the national rules, see further p. 164 *et seq*. below.

[116] I.e., one which is not a Member State of the EU.

[117] *Owusu v Jackson* Case C-281/02 [2004] ECR I-1383.   [118] Article 3 and Annex 1.

[119] If a treaty exists obliging the United Kingdom not to enforce judgments of other EU countries obtained on a ground of jurisdiction outlawed by Annex 1, then the judgment need not be enforced (Brussels Convention Art. 59). The power to enter into such treaties was not included in the Brussels I Regulation. Two Conventions exist between the United Kingdom and Canada concluded in 1984 (Cmnd 9337) and Australia concluded in 1991 (Cmnd 1394).

[120] *Phillips v Symes* [2002] 1 WLR 853.

[121] *Canada Trust Co. v Stolzenberg (No. 2)* [2000] UKHL 51, [2002] 1 AC 1.

[122] Article 59.

The English rules are found in Civil Jurisdiction and Judgments Order (CJJO) 2001.[123] The structure of the CJJO 2001 is somewhat complicated. First, we have to decide whether an individual is resident in the United Kingdom and the nature and circumstances of that residence indicate that he or she has a substantial connection with the United Kingdom. Then, we have to decide whether an individual is domiciled in a part of the United Kingdom, for example, England, as it is the English courts, rather than say Scots, which are determining jurisdiction. An individual is domiciled in the part of the United Kingdom if he or she is resident in that part and has a substantial connection with that part. Finally, an individual is domiciled in a place in the United Kingdom if he or she is domiciled in the part where the place is located and has a residence in that place.

Residence in the United Kingdom (or a part or place) is accorded the usual statutory meaning which is that of the defendant's settled or usual place of abode.[124] It is possible to be resident in more than one place and therefore to be domiciled in more than one Member State. Residence can be established in merely one day but the additional requirement of a substantial connection imposes a strong association with that place before an individual obtains a domicile there. Although a substantial connection can be presumed if an individual has been resident in the United Kingdom (or at a particular place) for three months leading up to the commencement of proceedings, that presumption can be rebutted. This qualitative test can be quite fine-textured.

In *Yugraneft v Abramovich*:[125]

> the claimants alleged that the defendant Mr Abramovich was resident in England so that Article 2 applied to require proceedings to continue in England. Despite owning residences here, being in the United Kingdom for nearly ninety days a year, having many business interests in England (including ownership of Chelsea Football Club) and having his children in English boarding schools, the court found the defendant was not resident here. Mr Abramovich is a very rich man who has a global business and lives an unsettled life.

Christopher Clarke J was impatient with any numerical approach based on the number of days a year the defendant spent at his properties in England, preferring to look for Mr Abramovich's 'home'. Not only did he spend more days there, but the quality of the time spent in Russia showed that Russia was the real focus of his life.

However, if a defendant is not domiciled in England that is not the end of the matter. The English court may also have to decide whether the defendant is domiciled in another Member State, in which case the court cannot take

---

[123] SI 2001/3929.   [124] See further p. 31 *et seq.* above.   [125] [2008] EWHC 2613 (Comm).

jurisdiction over him or her unless another permitted ground is available, for example, under Article 5. In order to determine whether a defendant is domiciled in another Member State, the court has to apply the law of that other Member State. A defendant challenging the jurisdiction of the English court may successfully show that he or she is domiciled under the law of another Member State to evade the English court. For example, in *Haji Ioannu v Frangos*:[126]

> The defendant was resident in Monaco (not a Member State) but had a special business domicile in Greece under Greek law due to his business interests there. He was found to be domiciled in another Member State under that state's law. The English court could not therefore use its national rules to take jurisdiction and as there was no alternative ground under the Brussels I Regulation it could not hear the case. The claimant would have to sue in Greece.

ii. Definition: domicile of legal persons

The domicile of legal entities is governed by the uniform rules imposed by Article 60. A 'company or other legal person or association of natural or legal persons' is domiciled where it has its:

(a) statutory seat; or
(b) central administration; or
(c) principal place of business.

Each of these is a true alternative for the others and it is possible for a corporation to be domiciled in more than one of these places. The Brussels I Regulation rules on domicile of corporations satisfies both broad company law traditions around Europe: (a) is a nod to those states, as England, which adopt a *lex incorporationis* approach; (b) and (c) permit domicile to be based on *siège réel* notions. All Member States should interpret this article uniformly, but it is likely that the particular rules identifying the central administration or principal place of business vary from Member State to Member State. Note that this provision does not apply to those cases in which the seat of a company has to be located for Article 22 (exclusive jurisdiction over specified matters such as the validity of the company's constitution). For that Article, each Member State's courts use their private international law rules to identify the seat of a company.[127]

A corporation may have a specified statutory seat under the law of its incorporation. However, for the purposes of the United Kingdom and Ireland, Article 60 provides that the 'statutory seat' means 'the registered office of the corporation or, where there is no such place anywhere, the place of incorporation

---

[126] [1999] 2 Lloyd's LR 337.
[127] Article 22(2). The English rules are in SI 2001/3929, Sched. 1 para. 10.

or, where there is no such place anywhere, the place under the law of which the formation took place'. These decline in order of importance, so that it is only possible to identify the domicile of a corporation at its place of incorporation if there is no registered office. English companies are required to have a registered office the address of which is publicly available via the companies register. However, partnerships, clubs and so on do not have to have registered offices. For these and foreign companies the courts would have to look to see where the registered office is to be found; if there is none then to the place of incorporation; if there is no such place, then to the place under the law of which the formation took place.

The central administration or principal place of business of a company is not its central management and control,[128] which is a tax concept much fortified by case law. There is an overlap between the factual matrices behind the company's central administration and principal place of business but the two concepts are distinct. English courts have not been entirely clear in dealing with them. *The Rewia*[129] was a pre-Brussels Convention case in which the principal place of business of a company had to be identified to interpret a jurisdiction agreement. It has been followed subsequently. The Court of Appeal held that 'principal' did not mean largest in terms of volume of business but rather meant the most important, the centre from which instructions were given and ultimate control exercised. This was explained in *Ministry of Defence of Iran v Faz Aviation*[130] as the place where the corporate authority was to be found and policy determined, rather than where the day-to-day activities were carried out. However, 'central administration' has something of the 'back office' about it. This is where the policy is executed. Therefore, in *889457 Alberta Inc v Katanga Mining Ltd*:

> The company was incorporated in Bermuda, listed on the Toronto Stock Exchange and resident there for tax purposes. However, it was in London that the entirety of the administration of the company (which was a holding company with a subsidiary owning shares in mines in DRC) was carried out. Also, all the directors resided here, even if the meetings were carefully held in Canada for the purposes of tax domicile. Arguably, the principal place of business was in Canada.[131]

The court adopted Prof. Briggs' test that the company's central administration is where those who hold serious responsibilities in the company have their place of work, i.e., in London. A similar result was reached in *King v Crown Energy Trading AG*:

---

[128] *889457 Alberta Inc. v Katanga Mining Ltd* [2008] EWHC 2679 (Comm), [2009] 1 BCLC 189.
[129] [1991] 2 Lloyd's LR 325.   [130] [2007] EWHC 1042 (Comm), [2008] 1 BCLC 599.
[131] [2008] EWHC 2679 (Comm), [2009] 1 BCLC 189.

> a company incorporated in Switzerland conducted its business at its Head Office there and at branches in London and Gibraltar. The London branch was a 'service agent' for the Head Office and the Gibraltar branch. However, the London office had seventy employees, by comparison with the forty employed in Crown's other offices. More importantly, the principal executive and operational staff were employed in London, including the Chairman, Chief Executive Officer and Chief Operating Officer, and the heads of each of the firm's main departments. Both its central administration and principal place of business was therefore in London.[132]

It is unlikely that continental civilian courts would adopt the same tests, so uniformity will not be achieved.

Remember that the national rules on service on a company at a place of business will provide a method of service for a company domiciled in a Member State but do not provide the ground of jurisdiction (unlike under the national rules). Therefore, a company which is incorporated with a registered office in France cannot be sued here unless either its central administration or principal place of business is here or some other ground of jurisdiction under the Brussels I Regulation is available, for example, Article 5(5).[133] If there is some permissible ground, then service can be effected at the place of business of the company in England under CPR r. 6.9.

If a defendant is found to be domiciled in more than one Member State, the claimant has a free choice to sue the defendant anywhere he, she or it is domiciled. The defendant cannot argue that the defendant would prefer to be sued in another court and there is no discretion by which the court can refuse to exercise jurisdiction established by means of the defendant's domicile.[134] Article 27 operates to prevent parallel proceedings in more than one Member State and is the mechanism for denying a court's jurisdiction.

iii. Domicile of trusts

Faced with a question of a trust, the court must apply its private international law rules to determine its domicile.[135] A trust is domiciled in England if English law is that with which it has its closest and most real connection. The parties can make an express choice of English law in the trust deed, which is then effective to make the trust domiciled in England for questions of jurisdiction, as well as for English law to govern matters of substance.[136]

---

[132] [2003] EWHC 163 (Comm), [2003] ILPr. 28. See A. Briggs and P. Rees, *Civil Jurisdiction and Judgments* (4th edn, LLP, 2005) para. 2.115.

[133] See p. 87 *et seq.* below.   [134] *Owusu v Jackson* Case C-281/02 [2004] ECR I-1383.

[135] Article 60(3). The English rules are found in Civil Jurisdiction and Judgments Order 2001, SI 2001/3929, Art. 3 and Sched. 1 para. 12.

[136] See also *Gomez v Gomez-Monche-Vives* [2008] EWCA Civ 1065, [2009] Ch. 245.

f. Special rules of jurisdiction: generally

The special rules of jurisdiction in Articles 5–7 permit a defendant domiciled in another Member State to be sued in England. Broadly, these rules provide for jurisdiction at a court with a particularly close relationship to the events or the case which justifies an alternative forum, for example, the place where the harmful events occurred in cases regarding tort claims.[137] The courts in that place are especially well placed to make factual determinations of the events, as much of the evidence will be located there.[138] This is an attenuated form of *forum conveniens* as a specified connecting factor is identified rather than a more open-textured approach taking many factors into account. These rules are to be restrictively interpreted as they derogate from the general rule of the defendant's domicile.[139] In particular, the rules are to be interpreted in such a way as to enable a reasonably well-informed defendant to be able to foresee where he, she or it might also be sued.[140] However, an excessively narrow interpretation is only necessary when the meaning of the article derogating from domicile is unclear. Where the meaning is clear, the article is to be followed, even if the court identified by the connecting factor is not especially well placed to decide the case in fact.[141] A predictable and certain interpretation is preferred over one which is flexible.[142] The CJEU has also been unwilling to interpret these special rules in favour of the claimant's domicile.[143]

Note that the claimant has a free choice under the principle of mutual trust between the general basis of jurisdiction based on the defendant's domicile and the special bases in Articles 5–7.[144]

g. Article 5(1) contract

Article 5(1) provides special jurisdictional rules for 'matters relating to a contract'. Note that there are other special rules for employment contracts,[145] contracts of insurance[146] and consumer contracts.[147]

---

[137] Article 5(3). [138] Recitals 11 and 12.
[139] *Kalfelis v Bankhaus Schröder, Munchmeyer, Hengst and Co.* Case C-189/87 [1988] ECR 5565 at para. 19 and *Freeport Plc v Arnoldsson* Case C-98/06 [2007] ECR I-8319 at paras. 35 and 36.
[140] *Reisch Montage AG v Kiesel Baumaschinen Handels GmbH* Case C-103/05 [2006] ECR I-6827.
[141] *Custom Made Commercial v Stawa Metallbau GmbH* Case C-288/92 [1994] ECR I-2913.
[142] Recent cases emphasising the importance of predictability in these special rules of jurisdiction include *Zuid Chemie v Philippos Mineralenfabriek* Case C-18/08 [2009] ECR I-6917; *Falco Privatstiftung* Case C-533/07 [2009] ECR I-3327; and *eDate Advertising GmbH v X, Martinez v MGN* Joined Cases C-509/09 and C-161/10 [2012] QB 654.
[143] *Kronhofer v Maier* Case C-168/02 [2004] ECR I-6009 at paras. 19–20.
[144] *Besix SA v Wassereinigungsbau Alfred Kretschmar GmbH & Co. KG and another* Case C-256/00 [2002] ECR I-1699.
[145] See further pp. 103–5 below. [146] See further pp. 100–1 below.
[147] See further pp. 101–3 below.

i. 'Matters relating to a contract' has an autonomous meaning

The CJEU decided that 'matters relating to a contract' has to have an autonomous, Community-wide definition.[148] Different legal systems take different views as to what claims relate to a contract, and which ones might fall in, say, restitution or even in tort. The problem can be illustrated by *Jacob Handte and Co. GmbH v Traitements Mecano-chemiques*:[149]

> An action by a buyer against the manufacturer rather than the seller of defective products was not within Article 5(1). It did not 'relate to' a contract, even though there was a contract between seller and buyer and the French law at that time treated this claim as a contractual one. There was no privity between the manufacturer and the eventual buyer so the CJEU held that this was a non-contractual claim (tortious) and therefore had to be treated within Article 5(3) rather than Article 5(1).

In *Réunion Européenne SA v Spliethoff's Bevrachtingskantoor BV*,[150] the CJEU expanded on this reasoning. A matter relating to a contract requires at least some relationship freely entered into between the parties but that is not necessarily straightforwardly a contractual relationship:

> This case involved a claim on a bill of lading. The party to litigation was not party to the original bill but became a holder of it. The CJEU held that there was room for the conflict of laws rules of the court seised of the matter to decide if parties not apparently bound by a contract are bound by it in law. If so a matter arising on that bill of lading would be a matter relating to a contract within the Community meaning. In this case, however, there was no contractual relationship between the parties to the dispute.[151]

On the other hand, the duty to negotiate in good faith, which some countries consider a precontractual duty, is not within Article 5(1) as it is not an obligation which is freely assumed.[152] Any other liability falling outside

---

[148] *SPRL Arcado v Haviland* Case C-9/87 [1988] ECR 1539.
[149] Case C-26/91 [1992] ECR I-3967.   [150] Case C-51/97 [1998] ECR I-6511.
[151] See too *Petra Engler v Janus Versand GmbH* Case C-27/02 [2005] ECR I-481 (contractual relationship found); cf. *Frahuil SA v Assitalia SpA* Case C-265/02 [2004] ECR I-1543 (no obligation freely assumed).
[152] *Fonderie Officine Meccaniche Tacconi SpA v Heinrich Wagner Sinto Maschinenfabrik GmbH* Case C-334/00 [2002] ECR I-7357. See too the House of Lords view that a restitutionary claim arising out of a void contract fell outside Art. 5(1) as it did not relate to a contract: *Kleinwort Benson Ltd v Glasgow City Council* [2001] 1 AC 223. cf. a claim arising out of an allegedly (but not yet found to be) void contract, which does fall within Art. 5(1), *Agnew v Lansforsaksringsbolaget* [2001] 1 AC 223.

Article 5(1) falls within Article 5(3).[153] The court which has jurisdiction by virtue of Article 5(1) can only take jurisdiction over claims falling within Article 5(1), it cannot also take jurisdiction over matters which fall outside Article 5(1) and within Article 5(3).[154]

ii. Disputes about the existence of a contract

Is it possible to evade Article 5(1) special jurisdiction by alleging that there is no contract? To put it another way, does the claim have to relate to a valid contract in order to fall within Article 5(1)? Or is it sufficient that a breach of contract is merely alleged in order to trigger Article 5(1) jurisdiction? The English courts have a particular difficulty in that because jurisdiction is dealt with at such an early stage of proceedings, the true facts of what has happened may still be unclear. There has to be a balance between a claimant merely alleging a contract to force the defendant to England and a defendant merely challenging the validity of the contract in order to evade that jurisdiction. In principle, Article 5(1) may still apply even if there is a real dispute about the existence of a contract. The CJEU held in *Effer v Kantner*[155] that even if there was a challenge to the existence of a contract, by the defendant alleging as a defence that it is invalid, the case still fell within Article 5(1). However, the House of Lords in *Kleinwort Benson Ltd v Glasgow City Council*[156] seems to have decided that if the sole object of the case is the determination of the validity of the contract, then it falls outside Article 5(1). This can probably be criticised as *obiter*, the invalidity of the contract in that case was not in question at all. The case dealt solely with the consequences of an arrangement of a type already found to be void as a contract.[157] A case where the claimant was seeking a declaration that the claimant was not liable as the contract was invalid was found to fall under Article 5(1).[158]

Note that in order to obtain jurisdiction the English court requires the claimant to satisfy the procedural requirement of a 'good arguable case'[159] on any question of jurisdiction. In addition, a claimant must show a 'serious issue to be tried' on the merits of the case. A mere allegation is insufficient. Those tests are aimed at striking a balance in matters of jurisdiction between the claimant and the defendant. In these cases under Article 5(1), the claimant would have to show to the standard of a good arguable case that the claim is related to a contract and then that the required connecting factor (performance of the principal obligation or the delivery or the provision of services) is to be in England. The claimant would also have to show on the merits of the

---

[153] See p. 87 *et seq.* below.
[154] *Kalfelis v Bankhaus Schröder, Munchmeyer, Hengst and Co.* Case C-189/87 [1988] ECR 5565.
[155] Case C-38/81 [1982] ECR 825.
[156] [1999] 1 AC 153. cf. *Agnew v Lansforsaksringsbolaget* [2001] 1 AC 223 in which an action on an *allegedly* voidable contract was within Art. 5(1).
[157] See too A. Briggs, 'Jurisdiction over Restitutionary Claims' [1992] *LMCLQ* 283.
[158] *Boss Group v Boss Group France* [1997] 1 WLR 351.   [159] See further pp. 55–6 above.

claim that there was sufficient evidence of a serious issue to be tried. If the claimant fails in that, perhaps because the defendant has shown that there are flaws in the argument on jurisdiction or that the evidence is too weak to support a claim, the case will not go ahead in England.

iii. Structure of Article 5(1)

Article 5(1) requires a division of contracts into different types to allocate jurisdiction. There are three possiblilities:

(a) Article 5(1)(a) (for contracts that do not fall within Article 5(1)(b)): 'the courts of the place of performance of the obligation in question' have jurisdiction;

(b) Article 5(1)(b) (first indent) for sale of goods contracts: the courts of 'the place in a Member State where, under the contract, the goods were delivered or should have been delivered' have jurisdiction (unless otherwise agreed);

(c) Article 5(1)(b) (second indent) for provision of services contracts: the courts of 'the place in a Member State where, under the contract, the services were provided or should have been provided' have jurisdiction (unless otherwise agreed).

If neither of the provisions in Article 5(1)(b) apply then the case falls under Article 5(1)(a).[160]

The original Article 5(1) in the Brussels Convention has now become Article 5(1)(a) in the Brussels I Regulation. The English court was particularly adept in locating the obligation in question in England in order to obtain jurisdiction. Article 5(1)(b) was inserted into the Regulation to provide a more strict rule. Case law decided under Article 5(1) of the Brussels Convention must now be confined to cases which fall within Article 5(1)(a).[161] It is a residual article, with specific rules adopted for sale of goods contracts and provision of services contracts. However, it is to be determined exactly as Article 5(1) used to be.[162]

iv. Sale of goods contracts

The first indent gives the court of the place of delivery in a sale of goods contract jurisdiction over all claims arising out of that contract. So, whether the issue is non-delivery, interpretation of a term, non-payment, breach of warranty or failure of consideration, and whether the action is by way of damages or negative declaration, all matters are referred to the courts of the place of delivery or provision of services.[163] That place is the autonomous linking factor with a close link between the contract and that place. It is

---

[160] Article 5(1)(c).
[161] *Peter Rehder v Air Baltic Corporation* Case C-204/08 [2009] ECR I-6073 at para. 37.
[162] *Falco Privatstiftung* Case C-533/07 [2009] ECR I-3327.
[163] *Color Drack GmbH v Lexx International Vertriebs GmbH* Case C-386/05 [2007] ECR I-3699 at paras. 24, 26, 38 and 39.

referable neither to the national law nor to its conflict of laws rules. The CJEU added another justification to that of the courts of that place being particularly well placed to determine factual matters. Those courts are also certain and predictable. Certainty and predictability are becoming very important concerns in allocating jurisdiction under the Brussels I Regulation. Sadly, the first indent of Article 5(1)(b) is not as certain and predictable as might at first appear.

The CJEU has held that an express place of delivery is decisive of the place of performance.[164] Therefore, if the contract provides that the goods are to be delivered to London, the English courts will have jurisdiction. However, what if the place of delivery has not been specified in the contract? The Brussels Convention case law referred to the private international law rules of the forum in order to identify the applicable law of the contract whose rules of domestic contract law would fill the gap with an implied term.[165] The CJEU has rejected this solution for Article 5(1)(b).[166] The definition of the place of delivery is to be autonomously determined, which precludes an application of the private international law rules of the forum.[167] The place of delivery is to be 'based on a purely factual criterion'.[168] In a case where the sale included carriage of the goods, that is where they 'were physically transferred or should have been physically transferred to the purchaser at their final destination'.[169] Factual performance of the contract can be relied on, but note only so far as that is consistent with the parties' intentions.[170]

Those conclusions do not resolve the problems where the goods have not been transferred, so giving rise to claims for non-performance. If the contract is silent or if performance is at the option of one of the parties, how is the place of delivery or provision of services to be identified? It is possible that in such a case Article 5(1)(b) does not apply as no factual, autonomous definition of the place of delivery is possible. If that is right, perhaps Article 5(1)(a) fills the gap to apply the previous case law, including the rule in *Tessili*.[171] Alternatively, and preferably, Article 5 may be altogether inapplicable as it is to be restrictively interpreted and where it cannot be precisely applied, it does not operate.[172] In that case the claimant can only sue the defendant under Article 2 at the defendant's domicile.

A further difficulty arises if there is more than one place where the goods were or were to have been delivered. Where these are all in one Member State

---

[164] *Car Trim GmbH v KeySafety Systems Srl* Case C-381/08 [2010] ECR I-1255.

[165] *Tessili v Dunlop* Case C-12/76 [1976] ECR 1473.

[166] *Car Trim GmbH v KeySafety Systems Srl* Case C-381/08 [2010] ECR I-1255.

[167] *Color Drack GmbH v Lexx International Vertriebs GmbH* Case C-386/05 [2007] ECR I-3699.

[168] *Ibid.* para. 52.   [169] *Ibid.* para. 60.

[170] *Wood Floor Solutions Andreas Doomberger GmbH v Silva Trade SA* Case C-19/09 [2010] ECR I-2121 and *Color Drack GmbH v Lexx International Vertriebs GmbH* Case C-386/05 [2007] ECR I-3699 at para. 40.

[171] *Tessili v Dunlop AG* Case C-12/76 [1976] ECR 1473, see further pp. 82–6 below.

[172] *Besix SA v Kretschmar* Case C-256/00 [2002] ECR I-1699.

the CJEU in *Color Drack* held that the court at the 'place of the principal delivery' determined by 'economic criteria' is the one which has sole jurisdiction. This 'principal delivery' test was developed to cover contracts to be delivered to more than one Member State.[173] One might argue that the 'principal delivery' is the one with the largest number of units if all the deliveries involve the same goods. However, it might be more difficult to identify a principal place if different goods of differing values are to be delivered each time. Using the alternative description of the 'main' place of delivery does not necessarily make matters clearer. Where there is no one main or principal place, the CJEU held that the claimant can choose one of the places of delivery in which to sue for all the claims arising. This is different to the Brussels Convention case law under which the claimant also has a choice in these circumstances, but can only sue for the part of the obligation which was performed in that place, not all the issues arising under the contract.[174] That solution does not survive for Article 5(1)(b) contracts.[175]

Another question can be posed. What do the words 'unless otherwise agreed' mean in Article 5(1)(b)? It might be argued that the parties can agree a place of performance, for example, of the place of payment, and therefore circumvent the place of delivery rule;[176] or a variant on that argument might be offered, that the parties can specify an obligation (and therefore its place of performance) other than that of delivery. Neither of these appear to be possible after *Car Trim GmbH v KeySafety Systems Srl*,[177] in which the CJEU accepted that an express place of delivery would be decisive for Article 5(1)(b) as it provides 'unless otherwise agreed ... the place in a Member State where, *under the contract*, the goods were delivered'. Linking the two parts of the indent together in that way appears to rule out identifying another obligation, such as the place of payment. Nevertheless, either one or other part of the indent then becomes redundant.

v. Provision of services contracts
Many of the points made above in relation to the first indent of Article 5(1)(b) can also be made in relation to the indent for the provision of services. The CJEU has emphasized that both indents of Article 5(1)(b) are to be interpreted

---

[173] *Wood Floor Solutions Andreas Doomberger GmbH v Silva Trade SA* Case C-19/09 [2010] ECR I-3699.

[174] See pp. 82–6 below. In *Leathertex v Bodetex* Case C-420/97[1999] ECR I-6747, which lead to a *dépeçage* of the proceedings, and the possibility of irreconcilable judgments: neither is appealing.

[175] *Peter Rehder v Air Baltic Corporation* Case C-204/08 [2009] ECR I-6073 at para. 37.

[176] J. Fawcett and J. Carruthers, *Cheshire, North and Fawcett, Private International Law* (14th edn, Oxford University Press, 2008) pp. 242–3. So long as the place of performance identified is a practical place at which something of the contract is performed, see the Brussels Convention case of *MSG v Les Gravières Rhénanes* Case C-106/95 [1997] ECR I-911.

[177] Case C-381/08 [2010] ECR I-1255.

similarly.[178] If the parties express a place at which the services are to be provided, the courts of that place will have jurisdiction. It is quite common that the services are to be provided in more than one place, and again, the solution is to identify the principal place. In *Wood Floor Solutions Andreas Doomberger GmbH v Silva Trade SA*:[179]

> The claimant sought damages for termination of a commercial agency contract. It had provided the agency services (negotiating and concluding contracts, communicating with the principal and complying with instructions) in a number of states, but its business activity was largely conducted in Austria. The CJEU identified the place of provision of services as 'the place of the main provision of services by the agent'. This place must be deduced from the provisions of the contract itself, or if that is not possible, by the actual performance of the contract.

The same problem as analysed above in relation to an unperformed contract with no specified place where the services were to be provided is possible. The solutions suggested above can be similarly considered. However, contracts to provide services can raise specific difficulties. Where the contract can be described as having one indivisible obligation, such as a contract to fly a passenger from one country to another, then neither place is principal.[180] A party can choose to sue for all breaches in either place, so a claimant passenger suing for compensation for a cancelled flight can choose the place of take-off or of landing. A provider of flights suing a passenger for non-payment can presumably likewise choose, although it is doubtful that the passenger defendant would have expected to be sued in those places.

vi. Article 5(1)(a) contracts

If the contract falls within Article 5(1)(a), the previous Brussels Convention case law applies. This is not entirely straightforward. First, one must identify the obligation in question to establish jurisdiction. That is the obligation which is placed upon the defendant, of which the claimant is claiming non-performance.[181] This is easy enough when the claimant is only complaining about one breach. Where a range of breaches of contract are alleged (perhaps in the alternative as is common in England), the principal obligation for which

---

[178] *Peter Rehder v Air Baltic Corporation* Case C-204/08 [2009] ECR I-6073.
[179] *Wood Floor Solutions Andreas Doomberger GmbH v Silva Trade SA* Case C-19/09 [2010] ECR I-3699.
[180] *Peter Rehder v Air Baltic Corporation* Case C-204/08 [2009] ECR I-6073.
[181] *De Bloos v. Bouyer* Case C-14/76 [1976] ECR 1497; *Tessili v Dunlop AG* Case C-12/76 [1976] ECR 1473; *Custom Made Commercial Ltd v Stawa Metalbau GmbH* Case C-288/92 [1994] ECR I-2913.

the claimant seeks a remedy must be found.[182] This has been described as the 'fundamental' obligation on which the claim is based.[183] When that principal obligation has been identified, other ancillary claims can also be brought in for adjudication by that court.[184] The English courts have permitted claimants a good deal of leeway in structuring their claim such that the English courts have jurisdiction. For example, in *Medway Packaging v Meurer*:

> A dispute arose concerning the termination of an exclusive distribution agreement. The German defendants had entered into a contract with English claimants and then broke it by allowing someone else to distribute the goods in England. The English court found that the principal obligation in question was the failure to terminate the distributorship properly with notice and that was to be performed in England. All the other claims were also to be determined by the English court.[185]

However, if neither obligation is principal to the other, the claims must be split up. In such a case, the claimant can only sue for each breach of the equally important obligation in the court of the place of performance of that obligation. So in *Leathertex SpA v Bodetex BVBA*:

> The Belgian agent Bodetex alleged that Leathertex had reneged on their contract and so Bodetex treated it as terminated. Bodetex claimed first for non-payment of commission and secondly for damages for failing to give proper notice of termination of the contract. The CJEU held that the second claim could be brought in Belgium under what is now Article 5(1)(a) but that the first, which was equally important, could not. If Bodetex wished to sue for both claims it could do so in Leathertex's domicile, Italy.[186]

---

[182] *Shenavai v Kreischer* Case C-26/85 [1987] ECR 239.

[183] *PRS Prodotti Siderugici SRL v The Sea Maas* [2000] 1 All ER 536 at 541 (a bill of lading claim where the fundamental obligation was to exercise due diligence in respect of the goods, not to keep and return them).

[184] *Shenavai v Kreischer* Case C-26/85 [1987] ECR 239.

[185] [1990] 2 Lloyd's LR 112. See also *Source Ltd v TUV Rheinland Holding AG* [1998] QB 54 (the principal obligation was to take reasonable care in presenting reports on the quality of the goods, rather than their obligations to inspect the goods, to refer the defective goods and make the report); *AIG Europe UK Ltd v The Ethniki* [2000] 2 All ER 566 (the principal obligation under a reinsurance contract was the claims control clause requiring the defendant to notify a claim, not the obligation on the defendant to ascertain the loss in good time); *Credit Agricole Indosuez v Chailease Finance Corp.* [2000] 1 Lloyd's LR 348 (the principal obligation in a letter of credit claim is that of the bank to pay rather than its obligation to receive the documents presented); *Viskase Ltd v Paul Kiefel GmbH* [2000] ILPr. 29 (the principal obligation was to deliver machines of the specification implied by the applicable law).

[186] Case C-420/97 [1999] ECR I-6747.

The *dépeçage* (splitting up) of the contractual claims is alien to English procedure which prefers to hear all the claims between the parties in one court in one dispute. The possibilities of incongruent, if not necessarily irreconcilable, decisions are obvious.[187] In contrast, all claims in contracts falling under Article 5(1)(b) are brought together in one place.

Once the obligation has been identified, its place of performance must be determined as it is the courts of the Member State of that place which have jurisdiction under Article 5(1)(a). Locating the place of performance of the obligation in question is relatively easy where the parties have expressly specified where the obligation is to be performed.[188] Note that the parties cannot choose a place of performance which is impossible or is out of line with the reality of the contract in order to give the courts of that place jurisdiction.[189]

If the parties have not expressly provided a place of performance of the obligation in question, then the conflict of laws rules of the Member State whose courts are seised of the matter operate to fill the gap (the *Tessili* doctrine).[190] The conflict of laws rules identify the applicable law of the contract, which may be via an express choice of law,[191] and the substantive rules of contract of that law will determine where the place of performance of that obligation is located. For example, if the applicable law is English law, the place of payment is inferred to be that of the creditor's residence under the domestic rules of contract.[192]

The previous case law on Article 5(1) of the Brussels Convention indicates that Article 5(1)(a) can be unpredictable with multiple obligations. Identifying and locating the principal obligation in these cases is not straightforward.[193] There are also difficulties when the claimant asks the court for a negative declaration. In such cases, the 'obligation' for which the claimant wishes to be declared not liable is both flexible and hard to locate.[194]

One might conclude that there are few contracts that are neither sales of goods nor provision of services. However, sales of land, shares or debts; third party guarantees; licensing and distribution agreements; joint venture agreements; agreements not to do something; and agreements to be performed in a non-Member State would all fall outside Article 5(1)(b) and within

---

[187] See further pp. 122–9 and 232 below.

[188] *Custom Made Commercial Ltd v Stawa Metalbau GmbH* Case C-288/92 [1994] ECR I-2913.

[189] *MSG v Les Gravières Rhénanes SARL* Case C-106/95 [1997] ECR I-911.

[190] *Tessili v Dunlop AG* Case C-12/76 [1976] ECR 1473. The choice of law rules are found in the Rome I Regulation (Regulation (EC) 593/2008 on the law applicable to contractual obligations).

[191] *Zelger v Salinitri* Case C-129/83 [1984] ECR 2937 and as to choice of law in contract see further Chapter 9.

[192] For a different example, see *Definitely Maybe Touring Ltd v Marek Lieberberg GmbH* [2001] 1 WLR 1745, in which the English court had to apply German law to locate a place of performance.

[193] See e.g., *Union Transport plc v Continental Lines SA* [1992] 1 WLR 15.

[194] See e.g., *Boss Group Ltd v Boss Group France SA* [1997] 1 WLR 351.

Article 5(1)(a).[195] For example, a claim under a contract for the use of intellectual property is neither a sale of goods nor a provision of services.[196] As we have seen there are substantial differences in operation between Article 5(1)(b) and Article 5(1)(a). First, the obligation which locates the jurisdiction is the one placed upon the defendant. Secondly, ancillary claims can be brought in the same court. Thirdly, the *Tessili* doctrine applies to fill the gap if the parties do not specify a place of performance. Therefore it is important to characterise the contract in dispute to identify which of the two subparagraphs applies. Would a contract of sale which contains some continuing obligation on the supplier (for example, to maintain the goods sold) fall within Article 5(1)(b) and if so, within which indent? Or would it fall within Article 5(1)(a)?

It is possible to argue that Article 5(1)(b) was inserted to cover only simple contracts and provide a clear and predictable rule for them. This is a narrow view of Article 5(1)(b). That narrow view can be contrasted with an argument that Article 5(1)(b) should cover most contracts and Article 5(1)(a) with its complexities should be left to truly complicated arrangements only. The CJEU appears to take a narrow view of Article 5(1)(b).[197] It has noted that each indent of Article 5(1)(b) identifies the characteristic obligation of the particular type of contract (delivery or provision of services). Therefore in order to decide within which indent a contract falls, the court held that one must determine the characteristic obligation of the contract. In *Car Trim GmbH v KeySafety Systems Srl*:[198]

> The German claimant agreed to produce some airbag components for the Italian defendants who made airbags for car manufacturers. The components had to satisfy various conditions imposed by the defendants. Was this a sale of goods or a provision of services? The CJEU decided this was a sale of goods as the characteristic obligation was the provision of the components. Secondly, where the purchaser has supplied materials the contract is more likely to fall within the second indent than the first. Thirdly, if the seller bears the responsibility for the quality of the goods then it is more likely to be a contract for the sale of goods.

These factors do not easily help the classification of any but the most straightforward contract. The last factor in particular appears to need reference to some domestic system of law to determine on whom responsibility lies. This is inconsistent with its other conclusion that the place of delivery or

---

[195] Article 5(1)(c).   [196] *Falco Privatstiftung* Case C-533/07 [2009] ECR I-3327.
[197] *Falco Privatstiftung* Case C-533/07 [2009] ECR I-3327.
[198] Case C-381/08 [2010] ECR I-1255.

provision of services is to have an autonomous, factual determination. Returning to our example on a contract of sale with some continuing obligation to maintain: if the characteristic obligation is that of maintenance then the contract falls within the second indent, if the characteristic obligation is sale it will fall within the first indent. It is easy to argue that neither obligation is characteristic in such a case. As the contract cannot fall completely within a single indent of Article 5(1)(b) it must fall into Article 5(1)(a) by virtue of Article 5(1)(c).

Negative obligations, i.e., ones which impose a requirement on a party not to perform some act, are often difficult to locate at a particular place. In *Besix SA v Wasserreinigungsbau Kretzschmar GmbH & Co KG*:[199]

> the contract contained a covenant by Belgian and German companies to act exclusively together and not commit themselves to other partners. The German defendants sought to join with another consortium and the Belgian companies sued for breach of the covenant. The CJEU held that there was no particular place where the obligation was performable as the German companies could act in breach anywhere in the EU. In such a case Article 5(1) does not apply but the claimant has to seek the adjudication of the Article 2 court, at the defendant's domicile.

h. Special rules: Article 5(2) maintenance

Cases in which the principal subject matter is that of the status of legal persons or the rights in property arising out of a matrimonial relationship fall outside the Brussels I Regulation rules.[200] Matters of maintenance in family cases are now completely excluded from the Brussels I Regulation for all cases commenced after 18 June 2011.[201] In cases which were commenced before that date, the courts of the Member State in which the maintenance creditor is domiciled or is habitually resident have jurisdiction. Where the maintenance issue is ancillary to the proceedings concerning the status of someone, the Member State's court which has jurisdiction over those proceedings has jurisdiction over the maintenance issue.[202] Maintenance proceedings have been difficult to define. It is clear that this concept has an autonomous definition. In *De Cavel v De Cavel (No. 2)*:

---

[199] Case C-256/00 [2002] ECR I-1699.
[200] Article 1(2)(a).
[201] Regulation 4/2009 on jurisdiction, applicable law, recognition and enforcement of decisions and cooperation in matters relating to maintenance obligations, Recital 44 and Art. 76.
[202] Unless the jurisdiction over the status proceedings is based solely on the nationality of one of the parties (Art. 5(2)).

> A French divorce court had awarded an interim compensatory allowance to Mrs De Cavel. She wished to enforce that order in Germany. The CJEU held, without much elaboration, that compensatory payments which are fixed on the basis of the parties' respective needs and resources are in the nature of maintenance.[203]

A maintenance creditor includes a person who is bringing a maintenance action for the first time.[204]

i. Special rules: Article 5(3) tort

i. Autonomous definition of tort

In matters relating to tort, jurisdiction is given to the courts for the place where the harmful event occurred or may occur. Tort expressly includes delicts and quasi-delicts. In addition, the CJEU has held that claims for all liability which is not contractual falls within Article 5(3).[205] That is probably too wide a definition, as liability for maintenance is non-contractual but cannot be said to be analogous to tortious liability. There is a similar distinction to be drawn between obligations falling within the Rome I Regulation[206] and those within the Rome II Regulation.[207] Fault is not necessary as strict liability torts must fall within Article 5(3). As with contract, Article 5(3) is not to be interpreted any more widely than necessary for the fulfilment of its objectives. The courts for the place where the harmful event occurred are likely to be well placed to determine the evidence.[208] Again, like contractual jurisdiction, tort is given an autonomous meaning. This is less straightforward than for contractual claims. There is wide agreement across the Member States as to the basis of consensual liability but much less agreement on whether substantive non-contractual liability arises and how that liability is characterised for domestic law. The negligence of a surgeon would be included, but what of equitable claims, infringement of intellectual property rights or any right to reclaim losses due to breaches of securities regulations?[209] It could be argued that those latter claims are not tortious or delictual but *sui generis*. Article 5(3) itself appears to require a harmful event in order to work, although the CJEU has reiterated that Article 5(3) covers all liability which is not contractual and has not taken this particular point.[210]

---

[203] Case C-120/79 [1980] ECR 731.   [204] *Farrell v Long* Case C-295/95 [1997] ECR I-1683.

[205] *Kalfelis v Bankhaus Schröder, Munchmeyer, Hengst and Co.* Case C-189/87 [1988] ECR 5565 at para. 17.

[206] Regulation (EC) 593/2008 on the law applicable to contractual obligations.

[207] Regulation (EC) 864/2007 on the law applicable to non-contractual obligations, see further pp. 339–40 below.

[208] Recitals 11 and 12 and *Kronhofer v Maier* Case C-168/02 [2004] ECR I-6009.

[209] Which might be characterised as misrepresentation in English law but as some administrative law failure under other systems where the losses are sought from a regulator.

[210] *Rudolf Gabriel* Case C-96/00 [2002] ECR I-6367 at para. 33.

Where a court does not consider the event as harmful, recognises no substantive liability under its own law and therefore does not characterise the conduct as tortious to provide a remedy, it can be difficult for that court to provide a remedy. However, this is to confuse choice of law with jurisdiction. The claim in such a case must be pleaded as arising under an applicable law which does provide a remedy for harmful events and that law might be foreign. The question of whether the court has jurisdiction over such a claim is a separate matter. The alleged foreign law claim so pleaded has to be characterised for jurisdictional purposes as a non-contractual one and therefore falling within Article 5(3), partly by elimination (it is not a contractual claim within Article 5(1)) and partly by the autonomous definition required by the CJEU. The dispute on the merits as to whether the defendant is ultimately liable requires the identification of the applicable law by application of English choice of law rules.[211] The claim may fail at this point but that is a matter of substance not of jurisdiction. The twin procedural requirements of a serious issue to be tried on the merits and a good arguable case on jurisdiction serve to protect the defendant against weak claims and poor arguments on jurisdiction. The English court has considered infringement of a foreign copyright to fall within Article 5(3).[212] An equitable claim for dishonest assistance has also been accepted as within Article 5(3).[213] In another case:

> A claim for precontractual liability which was based on the Italian Civil Code requiring good faith in the negotiation and formation of a contract was not within Article 5(1) as the basis of the claim could not be contractual as the duty to negotiate existed whether or not the contract was eventually concluded. It fell instead within Article 5(3).[214]

The operation of Article 5(3) can be more problematic when as a matter of substance (for example, with many instances of unjust enrichment in English domestic law) there is no harmful event giving rise to liability. There is then no place at which the harmful event occurred to locate jurisdiction. In such cases, by analogy with equivalent cases under Article 5(1),[215] the special jurisdiction in Article 5(3) may not apply and the claimant is left with jurisdiction under Article 2.

---

[211] Now contained in the Rome II Regulation (Regulation (EC) 864/2007 on the law applicable to non-contractual obligations).

[212] *Pearce v Ove Arup Partnership Ltd* [1997] Ch. 293, reversed by the Court of Appeal but not on this point [2000] Ch. 403. However, if invalidity of the intellectual property is alleged as a defence the claim will fall within Art. 22(3), *Gesellschaft für Antriebstechnik mbH & Co KG v Luk Lamellen und Kupplungsbau Beteiligungs KG* Case C-4/03 [2006] ECR I-6509.

[213] *Casio Computer Co. Ltd v Sayo (No. 3)* [2001] ILPr. 43.

[214] *Fonderie Officine Meccaniche Tacconi SpA v Heinrich Wagner Sinto Maschinenfabrik GmbH* Case C-334/00 [2002] ECR I-7357.

[215] *Besix SA v Wasserreinigungsbau Kretzschmar GmbH & Co. KG* Case C-256/00 [2002] ECR I-1699.

It does not matter that the person bringing the claim has not suffered the particular harm but is acting for others who may do so. The CJEU has held that Article 5(3) operates to provide jurisdiction over a claim made by a consumer organisation which had not itself suffered damage but was alleging breaches of consumer protection law.[216]

ii. Threatened wrongs

These are now explicitly covered by Article 5(3), following the change of wording in the Brussels I Regulation. Therefore actions for an injunction to prevent a wrong which has not yet occurred fall within Article 5(3).

iii. Concurrent actions in tort and contract

Concurrent actions in tort and contract can be difficult to classify for jurisdictional purposes. As we have seen, a court with jurisdiction over a claim in contract cannot also take jurisdiction over a concurrent claim in tort unless the connecting factors (place of delivery and place of harmful event) coincide in the Member State of the court.[217] The English court has had difficulties with claims which arise under the duty to take reasonable care in the performance of a contract. For example, in *Source Ltd v TUV Rheinland Holding AG*:

> The German defendants agreed with the English claimants to inspect goods in the Far East and send a report to the claimants in England where the monies were to be released to pay for the goods. The claimants argued that the defendants had not taken reasonable care in the production of the reports. The Court of Appeal held that it did not have jurisdiction. The contractual claim was to be performed in the Far East.[218] The tortious claim related to the contract, despite the fact that a contract did not have to be pleaded for it to exist. It therefore fell within Article 5(1) not Article 5(3).[219]

That decision is correct when the contractual claim is pleaded and the tortious claim is clearly linked to it and is overlapping. Where both are brought together in the alternative, the claimant will only recover under one head. However, under English procedural law the claimant has a free choice to make the case and may choose to make the claim solely in tort.[220] In that case, the defendant could argue by way of defence to the jurisdiction that the claim is related to a contract rather than merely tortious. If there is no contractual

---

[216] *Verein Für Konsumenteninformation v K. H. Henkel* Case C-167/00 [2002] ECR I-8111.
[217] *Kalfelis v Bankhaus Schröder, Munchmeyer, Hengst and Co.* Case C-189/87 [1988] ECR 5565 at para. 19.
[218] This was a Brussels Convention case, so fell under the previous Art. 5(1), now Art. 5(1)(a).
[219] [1998] QB 54.
[220] See too A. Briggs, 'Jurisdiction over Restitutionary Claims' [2003] *LMCLQ* 12.

obligation to locate performance then Article 5(1) does not operate.[221] In circumstances where the two claims are not linked and even are premised on opposite lines of argument the claims are treated separately for jurisdictional purposes.[222]

The restrictive interpretation of Article 5(3) is consistent with its status as a special jurisdiction derogating from the general rule of suing a defendant in the defendant's domicile. However, dépeçage of the dispute into different but overlapping claims in contract and in tort leads to a waste of court resources and the parties' time and expense, as well as the likelihood of irreconcilable or contradictory judgments. The basic problem in these cases is that the Brussels I Regulation does not permit, and indeed actively dissuades, bringing together related claims into one jurisdiction except under Article 2. That can be compared with the permission to bring one case against several defendants.[223]

iv. Place where the harmful event occurred

Article 5(3) gives jurisdiction over non-contractual claims to the courts of the Member State in which the harmful event occurred or may occur. This place therefore has to be identified. The CJEU has appeared to give an autonomous meaning to the place where the harmful event occurred in the case of libel.[224] However, it is hard to see what this exactly means beyond a factual determination of where the events occurred unless a reference to the CJEU is to be made in any complex case. It is not difficult when all the elements of the tort and all the damage suffered happened in one place, as that place must be where the harmful event occurred. In more complex cases, however, the location of the harmful event becomes more interesting. In *Bier v Mines de Potasse d'Alsace SA:*[225]

> French defendants polluted the waters of the Rhine in France but the poisoned water did damage to flower growers in Holland. The Dutch claimants wanted to sue in Holland where they said the harmful event occurred. The CJEU gave the place where the harmful event occurred an autonomous meaning. That could be either where the events which gave rise to the damage happened (France) or where the damage occurred (Holland).

This interpretation multiplies the courts with jurisdiction. Nevertheless both the courts of the place where the events happened and those where the damage occurred are in an equally good position to determine particular issues (either the facts giving rise to the damage or the extent of the damage itself), neither

---

[221] *Kleinwort Benson Ltd v Glasgow City Council* [1999] 1 AC 153.

[222] *Domicrest v Swiss Bank Corp.* [1999] QB 548.   [223] See Art. 6(1) and (3).

[224] *Shevill v Press Alliance SA* Case C-68/93 [1995] ECR I-415, see too *Cheshire, North and Fawcett,* p. 254.

[225] Case C-21/76 [1976] ECR 1735.

being better than the other.[226] The claimant has a free choice between these two alternatives. Note that if the interpretation of Article 5(3) is unclear, the court should not interpret it in favour of the claimant's domicile,[227] nor the defendant's domicile as it is meant to derogate from Article 2.[228] So in *Zuid Chemie v Philippos Mineralenfabriek*:

A Dutch claimant bought ingredients for fertiliser it was making from another company. That company subcontracted the manufacture of the ingredients to the Belgian defendant who had a factory in Belgium from where the claimant collected the ingredients. The fertiliser was then made in Holland and sold all over Europe. The ingredients manufactured by the defendant were faulty. The claimants wanted to sue in tort in Holland but the Dutch court declined jurisdiction on the ground that the harmful event occurred in Belgium where the faulty ingredients were collected.

The CJEU accepted that the place where the events giving rise to the damage occurred was Belgium. However, it interpreted the place where the damage occurred narrowly. This was where the damage caused by the defective product actually manifested itself, i.e., at the factory in Holland where the faulty ingredients were combined into fertiliser.[229]

In the case of libel, the place where the events giving rise to the damage occurred has been found to be the place where the libel originated from, i.e., where it was originally published.[230] The claimant can sue for all damage in that place.

Identifying the place where the damage occurred may be even less straight-forward, particularly if the damage is economic or appears over a longer period (such as psychiatric damage). It is clear that the court where any indirect damage is suffered does not have jurisdiction. So in *Marinari v Lloyds Bank plc*:

A claimant brought an action in Italy for the wrongful sequestration of prom-issory notes in London. He alleged that his financial loss and the damage to his reputation were suffered in Italy where he was domiciled.[231]

---

[226] *Bier v Mines de Potasse d'Alsace* Case C-21/76 [1976] ECR 1735 at para. 17.

[227] *Kronhofer v Maier* Case C-168/02 [2004] ECR I-6009. Although very often the place where the damage occurred coincides with the domicile of the claimant.

[228] *Zuid Chemie v Philippos Mineralenfabriek* Case C-18/08 [2009] ECR I-6917. Nevertheless the place where the events giving rise to the damage occurred are likely to be the same as the defendant's domicile.

[229] Case C-18/08 [2009] ECR I-6917 at para. 31.

[230] *Shevill v Press Alliance SA* Case C-68/93 [1995] ECR I-415. Likewise with negligent misstatement, the place where the harmful event occurs is where the misstatement originates from (*Domicrest Ltd v Swiss Bank Corp.* [1999] QB 548).

[231] Case C-364/93 [1995] ECR I-2719.

The CJEU held that the initial damage was suffered in London and that the consequential financial loss was indirect. He could not sue in Italy under Article 5(3) but would have been able to sue in London. Therefore any financial loss must be directly suffered. An example of indirect financial loss is *Dumez France SA and Tracoba SARL v Hessische Landesbank*:

> A French parent company argued it had suffered loss on its balance sheet due to the liquidation of a German subsidiary in Germany.[232]

The CJEU here decided that the company could not sue the German banks which had caused the liquidation in France. Otherwise, the jurisdiction under this head would be so extensive as to cover any place where the adverse consequences of the events were felt.

Note that suffering financial harm directly at one's place of business should fall within this part of Article 5(3). In *Henderson v Jaouen*:

> The French court had granted a judgment for damages but French law permitted a claimant to return to court for a further award if the original injuries worsened. The claimant lived in England and argued that he had suffered further loss here when his condition deteriorated.[233]

The Court of Appeal denied it had jurisdiction over the claim for increased damages. It held that the further claim was part of the harmful event and must be brought in France. That was a rare example of the English court restricting its jurisdiction, more commonly the court has allowed claimants to be inventive in locating where the damage occurred. So in *Dolphin Maritime & Aviation Services Ltd v Sveriges Angartygs Assurans Forening*,[234] the claimant was suing to recover damages alleging that the defendant had induced a breach of contract between the claimant and another. Clarke J agreed with the claimant's argument that it had not received US $8.5million into its London bank account as required under the contract and therefore London was where the harm was suffered.

In *Shevill v Presse Alliance SA*,[235] the CJEU limited the jurisdiction under this interpretation of the place where the harmful event occurred to that damage which was sustained in the particular territory of the court. This has been described as the 'mosaic principle'. It is possible to argue that the mosaic principle is limited to libel and slander, in which both the act of publication

---

[232] Case C-220/88 [1990] ECR I-49.   [233] [2002] EWCA Civ 75, [2007] 1 WLR 2971.
[234] [2009] EWHC 716 (Comm), [2009] 2 Lloyd's LR 123.
[235] Case C-68/93 [1995] ECR I-415.

damaging the claimant's reputation and the reputation so damaged occur in the same jurisdiction (as otherwise there is no tort committed). It could by analogy also apply to actions for the infringement of intellectual property rights which are territorial. The mosaic principle does not apply to the jurisdiction founded upon the place of the events giving rise to the harm but only to jurisdiction based on the place where the harm was suffered.

The CJEU has recently identified three places where a claim based on an Internet libel can be made. So in *eDate Advertising GmbH v X* and *Martinez v MGN*:

> The actor Oliver Martinez complained that his privacy was infringed when the *Sunday Mirror* published a picture and story about his alleged affair with Kylie Minogue on its website which was hosted in England. He sued in France, where such a right of privacy exists. The court held that unlike with physical publication, the Internet is universal and that there are technical difficulties with assessing the distribution of the content of the webpage.[236]

The CJEU adopted a new test for jurisdiction, i.e., the place where the alleged victim has his centre of interests, which will generally be his or her habitual residence.[237] The publisher is taken to know the centres of interests of the people about whom the publication is made. The claimant in alleged infringement of personality rights online may therefore sue for *all* damage caused either at the defendant's domicile or at the place of the centre of the claimant's interests. It appears that this latter place is additional to the place where the events occurred or where the harm is suffered under the mosaic principle. The CJEU held that it is also possible to sue in a third Member State only in respect of the damage caused in the territory of that particular Member State using *Shevill*.

A related difficulty occurs when there is damage to goods in transit. Identifying the place where the events occurred or the harm suffered can be impossible. The CJEU has preferred the place where the carrier was to deliver the goods, rather than the place of actual delivery or the place where the damage was discovered.[238]

Note that if the place where the events giving rise to the damage or where the damage was suffered is impossible to locate or is outside the EU, no Member State's court has jurisdiction under Article 5(3). In such a case the claimant will have to rely on locating a place in the EU where the damage occurred or on another ground of jurisdiction.[239]

[236] Joined Cases C-509/09 and C-161/10 [2012] QB 654.
[237] The court accepted that it is also possible to have a close link with another state, for example by pursuing a professional activity there (at para. 49).
[238] *Réunion européene SA v Spliethoff's Bevrachtingskantoor BV* Case C-51/97 [1998] ECR I-6511.
[239] *Anton Durbeck GmbH v Den Norske Bank ASA* [2003] 2 WLR 1296, where the direct damage was to the cargo of a ship arrested in the Caribbean.

j. Special rules: Article 5(4) criminal proceedings

A civil claim can be made in criminal proceedings in many continental European countries, by way of *partie civil*. That claim for restitution or damages based on an act which has given rise to criminal proceedings may be brought in the court seised of the criminal proceedings in so far as the law of that court permits such claims. The jurisdiction of the court seised of the criminal case may be on very much wider grounds than is permitted under the Brussels I Regulation. See for a striking example, *Krombach v Bamberski*:

> Mr Krombach allegedly killed Mr Bamberski's daughter in Germany by administering too much of a lethal drug, but the German criminal court discontinued criminal proceedings. The French court was seised of the criminal proceedings by virtue of the victim's French nationality. Her father made a successful claim as a *partie civil* for damages for loss of her affection. Mr Krombach did not enter a plea to that case and remained in Germany out of the physical reach of the French criminal jurisdiction (this was before the European Arrest Warrant).[240]

k. Special rules: Article 5(5) branches

Article 5(5) provides a further ground of special jurisdiction. A defendant domiciled in another Member State may be sued in England if the dispute arises out of the operations of a branch, agency or other establishment of the defendant situated in England.

i. Definition of branch, etc.

What is a branch, agency or other establishment? Legal or natural persons may choose to do business in other countries around the EU in a variety of ways. They may open a branch office in the other Member State, rent premises there and directly employ local staff. They may employ a local representative or agent (which may be a company or a natural person). They may incorporate a local subsidiary to do the business (which may itself be an agent). They may enter into a joint venture arrangement with a local business either by incorporating a new company or by joining in partnership. Or they may merely send out an employee to do the business of the company abroad, without renting premises or establishing a location for that employee. For Article 5(5), however, the concept must be interpreted uniformly throughout the EU, therefore

---

[240] Case C-7/98 [2000] ECR I-1935. The French judgment for damages was sought to be enforced in Germany, but failed on the ground of public policy (see further pp. 225–9 below). The case had an astonishing dénouement as Mr Krombach was found tied up and beaten outside a police station in France in 2011. He was finally sentenced to fifteen years' imprisonment by the French court for the death of Mr Bamberski's daughter.

it needs an autonomous definition. Branch, agency and establishment are to be identified by their common characteristics.[241] The CJEU has identified three characteristics of a branch, agency or other establishment:

(i) a permanent place of business in a fixed, identifiable place.[242] This is the 'appearance of permanency' test. The purpose of this exceptional ground of jurisdiction is that third parties who deal with the branch, agency or other establishment can transact with the local office knowing that there is a legal link with the foreign parent but do not have to deal directly with that foreign parent. A mere travelling representative is not sufficiently permanent unless there is a fixed place of business;[243]

(ii) the agent to be subject to the direction and control of the parent.[244] It is important that the branch, agency or other establishment is part of the parent's business, rather than, say, a commercial representative doing his own business which includes representing the foreign principal. If the agent is able to arrange his or her own work and may represent several firms, the agent is not under the control of the parent and is not a branch, agency or other establishment.[245] An exclusive distributor for the foreign company may nonetheless not be a branch, agency or other establishment of that company unless it controls the distributor.[246] A certain autonomy is possible, for example with subsidiary companies which may as a matter of domestic company law be independent entities. Where a subsidiary appears to third parties to be acting as an extension of the parent company it may be a branch, agency or other establishment;[247]

(iii) the branch, agent or other establishment is able to act on behalf of the parent. Therefore in the case where the alleged representative did not have power to contract on behalf of his or her principal (the defendant company), there was no branch, agency or other establishment.[248]

The emphasis in applying these rules seems to be on the outlook of a person dealing with the branch, agency or other establishment. Would someone dealing with the office have concluded that the office is conducting the business of the parent?

ii. Operations of the branch, etc.

When does the dispute arise out of the operations of that branch, agency or other establishment? In *Somafer SA v Saar Ferngas AG*, operations included the management of the agency, branch or other establishment itself (such as

---

[241] *De Bloos SPRL v Société en Commandite par Actions Bouyer* Case C-14/76 [1976] ECR 1497.
[242] *Somafer SA v Saar Ferngas AG* Case C-33/78 [1978] ECR 2183.   [243] *Ibid.*
[244] *De Bloos SPRL v Société en Commandite par Actions Bouyer* Case C-14/76 [1976] ECR 1497.
[245] *Blanckaert and Willems PVBA v Trost* Case C-139/80 [1981] ECR 819.
[246] *De Bloos SPRL v Société en Commandite par Actions Bouyer* Case C-14/76 [1976] ECR 1497.
[247] *SAR Schotte GmbH v Parfums Rothschild SARL* Case C-218/86 [1987] ECR 4905.
[248] *Somafer SA v Saar Ferngas AG* Case C-33/78 [1978] ECR 2183.

the employment of staff) and also the contracts entered into and torts committed by that agency, branch or other establishment.[249] If the claim is contractual, it is enough that the contract was entered into by the branch, agency or other establishment. It does not also need to be performed at that place of business. In *Lloyd's Register of Shipping v Société Campenon Bernard*:

> A French branch of the English corporation Lloyds Register entered into a contract for the Spanish branch to survey some containers in Spain. The survey was not properly carried out, and the CJEU held that Lloyds Register could be sued in France.[250]

If the claim is tortious, the actual damage does not need to be done at the branch. Therefore in *Anton Durbeck GmbH v Den Norske ASA*:

> The London branch of a Norwegian bank with a branch in London negotiated a loan over a vessel. The owners defaulted on the repayments and the London branch gave instructions to arrest the vessel in Panama. The cargo of bananas carried on the ship went bad and the German cargo owners could sue the Norwegian bank in London as the dispute arose out of the operations of the London branch. There was a sufficient connection between the events and the activities of the London branch.[251]

However, it is important that the contract entered into or the tortious liability incurred is the defendant parent's not the agent's own business.

I. Special rules: Article 5(6) trusts

The English court would have jurisdiction over a defendant domiciled in another Member State in certain matters to do with trusts.[252] (1) The trust must be created by operation of statute or by writing.[253] English constructive and resulting trusts do not generally arise in this way and are therefore not covered by this article. (2) The claim can only be made against a settlor, trustee or beneficiary. (3) The trust must be domiciled in England.

If the trust is created in writing, it is also possible for the instrument to contain an English jurisdiction clause, which would then confer jurisdiction on the English court. The domicile of a trust is not always easy to ascertain. The Brussels I Regulation provides that a Member State's court must apply its

---

[249] *Ibid.* para. 13.   [250] Case C-439/93 [1995] ECR I-961.   [251] [2003] QB 1160, CA.
[252] Note also the exclusive jurisdiction over some matters of trust in Art. 22. Jurisdiction over matters which fall within Art. 22 can only be established under that article and not Art. 5(6).
[253] Either by a written instrument, or if created orally, evidenced in writing.

own private international law rules to determine where a trust is domiciled.[254] The English rules are that a trust is domiciled in England only if English law is the system of law with which it has its closest and most real connection.[255] The trust instrument may have an express choice of law.[256] That will usually be definitive as to the closest and most real connection and will therefore identify the domicile of the trust. In *Gomez v Gomez-Monche Vives*:

> A trust created by a father in favour of his wife and children was administered in Liechtenstein, where all decisions relating to the trust and all the bank accounts and trust documents were kept. The trust had professional trustees, mostly operating in Switzerland and Liechtenstein. There was no connection with England except that the trust was expressly governed by English law. Some of the beneficiaries complained about the administration of the trust and overpayment to the widow who was one of the defendants. She was domiciled in Spain and argued she could not be sued in London.[257]

The Court of Appeal held that the trust was domiciled in England by virtue of the express choice of law. Therefore the English court had jurisdiction.

m. Special rules: Article 6 co-defendants, third parties and counterclaims

i. Article 6(1) co-defendants

Article 6(1) provides that jurisdiction in England may be established against a person domiciled in another Member State where that person is one of a number of defendants, one of whom is domiciled in England. The claimant has an unrestricted choice between jurisdiction based upon Article 2, Article 5 or Article 6. There are obvious procedural efficiencies when several defendants are sued together in one court and irreconcilable competing judgments are thereby avoided. However, the jurisdiction is very expansive and open to abuse. A claimant may search for an anchor defendant who is domiciled in England, but who is not absolutely central to the claim, in order to drag in all other possible (and more wealthy) defendants from around the EU. As a safeguard, Article 6(1) requires that the claims between the various defendants must be so closely connected that 'it is expedient to hear and determine them together so as to avoid the risk of irreconcilable judgments'.

It is difficult to define what might be irreconcilable judgments with any precision. First, because at the stage of the opening of proceedings, the claims

---

[254] Article 60(3).

[255] Civil Jurisdiction and Judgments Order 2001, SI 2001/3929, Sched. 1 para. 12(1).

[256] Article 6 of the Hague Convention on the Law Applicable to Trusts and on their Recognition 1985, enacted in the Recognition of Trusts Act 1987.

[257] [2009] Ch. 245.

and defences might be unclear. Secondly, it is not obvious that 'irreconcilable' in this article necessarily has the same meanings as in Article 28[258] or Article 34(3).[259] A wide construction of 'irreconcilable' would permit proceedings leading to any possible contradictory judicial findings to ground jurisdiction under this Article 6(1). A narrow construction which requires a congruence of the facts and rules of law relied upon in each proceedings such that the two judgments could not be logically executed would constrict the availability of this jurisdiction. One might argue that it is better that 'irreconcilable' is not interpreted in the same way in all of Article 6(1), Article 28 or Article 34(3) as the word performs a different function in each Article. Here, as an exceptional ground of jurisdiction, it arguably should be narrowly interpreted. Nevertheless, some of the wording of Article 6(1) and Article 28 is the same, which suggests they should be interpreted similarly. The CJEU did not shine much light on this issue in *Freeport Plc v Arnoldsson*:

> The claimant wished to sue in Sweden an English company in contract and its Swedish subsidiary in tort. The English company complained that the two disputes would not necessarily lead to irreconcilable judgments as the actions had different legal bases although they arose out of the same facts. The judgments might not be irreconcilable if one made the Swedish company not liable in tort and the other made the English company liable in contract.[260]

The CJEU disagreed. The legal context and the factual situation do not have to be identical.[261] There is a risk of irreconcilable judgments if (1) there is some divergence in the possible outcomes of the disputes but which (2) arise out of *same* situation of law and fact.[262] However, ultimately it was for the Swedish court to determine the risk, presumably applying its national law.

The English Court of Appeal in *Gascoigne v Pyrah* has also held that it had jurisdiction in a case against an insurer and another against a reinsurer for the same loss:

---

[258] The *lis pendens* rules in related actions are triggered if they give rise to contradictory judicial findings, see further p. 129 *et seq.* below.

[259] Another Member State's judgment can be refused enforcement on the grounds that the two judgments cannot logically be executed simultaneously, see further p. 232 below.

[260] Case C-98/06 [2007] ECR I-8319. The CJEU noted that the dicta in *Réunion Européenne SA v Spliethoff's Bevrachtingskantoor BV* Case C-51/97 [1998] ECR I-6511 at para. 50 (that an action brought under Art. 5(1) in contract cannot be regarded as connected with one brought under Art. 5(3) in tort) did not apply to Art. 6(1).

[261] *Roche Nederland BV v Primus* Case C-539/03 [2006] ECR I-2535.

[262] *Ibid.* para. 26. Irreconcilable judgments were not a risk in this case as although the cases involved similar patents taken out under each national law, it was possible that the identical activity did not infringe the particular patent in dispute.

A claim in contract was made against Pyrah, a bloodstock agent domiciled in England. That was used to found jurisdiction over a linked-in tort against a German vet who had advised Pyrah. At the heart of both claims was the issue of the soundness of the horse.[263]

The English court requires the claimant to show a good arguable case[264] that the 'anchor' defendant is domiciled in England at the time of the issue of the claim form.[265] The same standard of good arguable case must apply to the questions whether the claims arise out of the same situation, of the expediency of hearing the claims together and also to assessing the risk of irreconcilable judgments. On the other hand, the claimant only has to show that there is a serious issue to be tried on the substance of the case against the anchor defendant and the joined defendants. This is not a high threshold.[266] It is not necessary any longer to show that the English proceedings were not started with the object of removing the defendant from the Member State's courts which would otherwise have jurisdiction.[267]

ii. Article 6(2) third parties

If the English court has jurisdiction over proceedings by virtue of some provision of the Brussels I Regulation, it can also take jurisdiction over third parties[268] to those proceedings domiciled in another Member State.[269] This includes actions on a warranty or guarantee as well as more general third party actions. However, unlike the previous subparagraph, Article 6(2) is expressly restricted. The English court cannot take jurisdiction if the original proceedings were instituted solely with the object of removing the third party from the court which would otherwise have jurisdiction. It would be unfair for this derived jurisdiction to be too widely available and so there must be some real connection between the original and third party proceedings. The English court determines whether there is sufficient connection to make the defendant a third party, presumably under its national law.[270] Actions between insurers for indemnity arising out of the same loss has an inherent connection.[271] It is probably not necessary for jurisdiction over the original defendant to have been founded under the Brussels I Regulation. English national procedural law may deny that a third party action is available, thus denying jurisdiction under

---

[263] [1994] ILPr. 82.   [264] See further pp. 55–6 above.

[265] *Canada Trust Co. v Stolzenberg (No. 2)* [2002] 1 AC 1; rather than at the time the claim form is served on the first defendant or at the time that the additional defendants were joined or served.

[266] See further pp. 55–6 above.

[267] That test was imposed by *Kalfelis v Bankhaus Schroder, Munchmeyer, Hengst and Co.* Case C-189/87 [1988] ECR 5565, but limited to Art. 6(2) (where it is now expressed) by *Roche Nederland BV v Primus* Case C-539/03 [2006] ECR I-2535.

[268] Now known in English procedure as Part 20 defendants (CPR PD 20).   [269] Article 6(2).

[270] *GIE Réunion Européene v Zurich España* Case C-77/04 [2005] ECR I-4509.   [271] *Ibid.*

this article.[272] The English court has a wide discretion to dismiss or strike out third party proceedings under CPR Part 20. However, the English court must be careful not to impair the operation of the Brussels I Regulation by applying its procedural law.[273]

iii. Article 6(3) counterclaims

Article 6(3) allows the English court also to take jurisdiction over counterclaims arising from the same contract or facts on which the original claim was based. The need to prevent incompatible judgments and strong efficiency arguments support this type of jurisdiction. However, the availability of counterclaims varies greatly around the EU. The Jenard Report envisaged a counterclaim as a claim which could have been brought in distinct proceedings which could survive even if the claimant stops the original proceedings. It could lead to a separate judgment.[274] On the other hand, a claim brought by way of pure defence is not a counterclaim and can be raised as a defence in the ordinary way in the court seised by the claimant.[275]

It is likely that an English court faced with an exclusive jurisdiction agreement in favour of the courts of another Member State or of a non-Member State would decline to join the party in breach of that jurisdiction agreement despite ostensibly having jurisdiction under Article 6.[276] Generally there is no discretion in the Brussels I Regulation and the court does not have power to decline jurisdiction except in specified circumstances (such as Articles 27 and 28). However, it is possible to argue that the necessary connection between the anchor defendant and the co-defendant or third party is non-existent or to say that the counterclaim is not available.[277] In contrast, if the English court only has jurisdiction by virtue of a jurisdiction agreement it is still able to take jurisdiction over a defendant domiciled in another Member State under Article 6(2) or 6(3) but not Article 6(1).

n. Special rules: Articles 8–14 insurers

There are special rules for matters relating to insurance.[278] Unfortunately, the Brussels I Regulation does not define insurance. The CJEU has held that the rules of this section do not apply to disputes between insurers and reinsurers

---

[272] *Kongress Agentur Hagen GmbH v Zeehaghe BV* Case C-365/88 [1990] ECR I-1845.

[273] *West Tankers Inc. v Allianz SpA (formerly RAS Riunione Adriatica di Sicurtà SpA) and another* Case C-185/07 [2008] ECR I-663 para. at 36.

[274] Jenard Report, p. 28.

[275] *Danavaern Production A/S v Schuhfabriken Otterbeck GmbH & Co.* Case C-341/93 [1995] ECR I-2053.

[276] See further p. 111 *et seq.* below on jurisdiction agreements. But cf. *Citi-March Ltd v Neptune Orient Lines Ltd* [1996] 1 WLR 1367.

[277] See in relation to Member States and Art. 6(1), *GIE Réunion Européene v Zurich España* Case C-77/04 [2005] ECR I-4509.

[278] Brussels I Regulation, Section 3 of Chapter II.

as neither are the weaker party.[279] The purpose of the provisions is to protect the weaker party in insurance contracts.[280] These provisions apply to the exclusion of other rules of jurisdiction in the Regulation except in so far as this section permits.[281] They generally provide that the insurer as a defendant can be sued in the domicile of the insured, policy-holder or beneficiary as well as in the insurer's domicile.[282] The rules apply to defendant insurers whether domiciled in a Member State or where the defendant insurer has established a branch agency or other establishment in a Member State. If the latter, the insurer is deemed to be domiciled in that Member State and subject to the rules of this section.[283] However, if the insurer is claimant, the defendant (whether policy-holder, beneficiary or insured) can only be sued in the defendant's domicile.[284] It is possible to enter into a jurisdiction agreement in some circumstances.[285] The agreement must be entered into after the dispute arose, or the parties must agree a Member State's jurisdiction different from those permitted under this section, or the insurer and policy-holder must have their domicile or habitual residence in the same Member State and the agreement confers jurisdiction on that state (where that is allowed by the law of that state), or where the policy-holder is not domiciled in a Member State (except if insurance is compulsory or relates to immovable property in a Member State), or where the contract of insurance covers a risk set out in Article 14.[286] Any agreement probably must comply with the requirements of Article 23 in addition. Any jurisdiction agreement contrary to Article 13 is void.[287] A judgment of a Member State's court which has taken jurisdiction in violation of this section will not be recognised and enforced in other Member States.[288] Parties can opt out of the regime by incorporating an arbitration clause in their insurance contract.

o. Special rules: Articles 15–17 consumers

As with the provisions on insurance, Section 4 provides protection for consumers and applies in matters relating to a contract[289] concluded by a consumer. The rules are exclusive, so it is not possible to fall back on the general rules, for example, Article 2 or Article 5. A consumer is a person

---

[279] *Group Josi Reinsurance Company SA v Universal General Insurance Company* Case C-412/98 [2000] ECR I-5925.

[280] Recital 13.   [281] Article 8, jurisdiction based upon Art. 4 and Art. 5(5) is also permitted.

[282] Article 9(1)(a) and (b).   [283] Article 9(2).

[284] Except if Art. 11(3) applies, Art. 12.   [285] Article 13.

[286] These are generally risks of operating shipping and aircraft, and those covering goods in transit and 'large risks' as defined in Council Directive 73/239/EEC, as amended by Council Directives 88/357/EEC and 90/618/EEC.

[287] Article 23(5).   [288] Articles 35(1) and 45(1).

[289] A matter relating to a contract is to be construed in the same way as in Art. 5(1) because Art. 15 is a specialised version of a contract (*Rudolf Gabriel* Case C-96/00 [2002] ECR I-6367, I-6399 at para. 36).

entering into the contract 'for a purpose which can be regarded as being outside his trade or profession'. The concept of a consumer is to be restrictively interpreted.[290] In addition, the contract must be one which:

(1) is for the sale of goods on instalment credit terms; or
(2) is for a loan repayable by instalments, or for any other form of credit, made to finance the sale of goods; or
(3) (in all other cases) 'has been concluded with a person who pursues commercial or professional activities in the Member State of the consumer's domicile or, by any means, directs such activities to that Member State or to several States including that Member State, and the contract falls within the scope of such activities'.[291] Unlike the Brussels Convention, this latter subparagraph covers not just contracts for the sale of goods or provision of services but any contract such as a licence to buy software. The use of 'activities' widens the possible interactions between the consumer and the other party beyond specific advertising which was required under the Brussels Convention. Activities are not defined but must involve some proactive conduct by the seller, such as an email or television advertising.[292]

Contracts for transport, other than all-inclusive 'package holidays', are excluded from this section.[293] The rules apply to defendants whether domiciled in a Member State or where the defendant has established a branch, agency or other establishment in a Member State. If the latter, the other party defendant is deemed to be domiciled in that Member State and subject to the rules of this section but only in respect of disputes arising out of the operation of that branch, agency or other establishment.[294] The consumer may sue the other party either in the consumer's domicile or the domicile of the other party, i.e., at the place of the branch, agency or other establishment.[295] So in *Rudolf Gabriel*:

> An Austrian consumer sued a German company which had sent the consumer several personalised letters informing him that he had won a prize if he ordered a minimum value of goods. He ordered the goods and sued the company when he did not receive the prize.[296]

---

[290] A contract between two commercial parties is not a consumer contract, *Société Betrand v Paul Ott KG* Case C-150/77 [1978] ECR 1431. If a contract is partly a professional and partly a private contract, it will not fall within these rules unless the part of the contract for professional purposes is negligible (*Johann Gruber v Bay Wa AG* Case C-464/01 [2005] ECR I-439).

[291] Article 15(1).

[292] Including a website accessible from the consumer's domicile, see the Explanatory Memorandum in the Proposal for a Council Regulation COM(1999)348 final, p. 16. It has been suggested that websites in English are directed at any country in the EU because of the ubiquity of the language, on the other hand, a website in Swedish might not be an activity directed at Spain.

[293] Article 15(3).   [294] Article 15(2).   [295] Article 16(1).

[296] Case C-96/00 [2002] ECR I-6367.

The CJEU held this was a matter relating to a contract and that the contract was a consumer contract. The company could therefore be sued in Austria. On the other hand, the consumer may only be sued in the consumer's domicile.[297]

As with insurance contracts, a jurisdiction agreement can be entered into only in limited circumstances: (1) if it was entered into after the dispute arose;[298] or (2) if it permits the consumer to bring proceedings in other Member States than those identified in these provisions[299] (i.e., where the agreement is not restrictive or exclusive); or (3) if it was 'entered into by the consumer and the other party to the contract, both of whom are at the time of conclusion of the contract domiciled or habitually resident in the same Member State, and which confers jurisdiction on the courts of that Member State'.[300] Therefore, an exclusive jurisdiction agreement conferring jurisdiction on the English courts between a company with its principal office in England and a consumer habitually resident in England would be permitted. As with insurance contracts, jurisdiction agreements with consumers should conform to the requirements of Article 23. A judgment from a Member State which does not have jurisdiction under one of the provisions of this section can be refused recognition and enforcement in other Member States.[301]

p. Special rules: Articles 18–21 employees

Employment law matters fall within the Brussels I Regulation despite them being considered public law issues in some EU countries.[302] The previous Brussels Convention did not deal with employment disputes separately from the usual rules. As with insurance and consumer contracts, the rules in this Section 5 are exclusive of the general rules except in so far as the section permits.[303] Likewise, an employer who is not domiciled in a Member State is treated as domiciled where it has a branch, agency or other establishment in a Member State, but only in respect of disputes arising out of the operation of that branch, agency or establishment.[304] The section applies to individual contracts of employment and seeks to protect the employee as the weaker party in the contract. Although there is no express definition of an individual contract of employment it should have an autonomous interpretation. Contracts of employment can be difficult to distinguish from a contract for the provision of work or services (e.g., a self-employed contractor) but the CJEU has identified two characteristics (1) a lasting bond with the worker and (2) the worker being within the organisational framework of the business.[305]

---

[297] Article 16(2).   [298] Article 17(1).   [299] Article 17(2).
[300] Provided that such an agreement is not contrary to the law of that Member State (Art. 17(3)).
[301] Articles 35(1) and 45(1).   [302] *Sanicentral v Collin* Case C-25/79 [1979] ECR 3423.
[303] Article 18(1).   [304] Article 18(2).
[305] *Shenavai v Kreischer* Case C-266/85 [1987] ECR 239; *Mulox IBC Ltd v Geels* Case C-125/92 [1993] ECR I-4075.

The employer may be sued in the courts of the Member State of the employer's domicile[306] or in the Member State in which the employee habitually carries out his or her work.[307] The latter place is considered to be well connected with the dispute and the cheapest place for the employee to bring litigation. It is also likely that the law governing the dispute will be that where the employee habitually carried out his or her work.[308] The place where the employee habitually carries out his or her work has an autonomous definition.[309] It is identified as the place 'where or from which the employee principally discharges his obligations towards his employer'.[310] The CJEU is concerned not to multiply the possible jurisdictions in which a case can be brought, but at the same time the rules are to protect the employee. It has also been described as the place where the employee had established the effective centre of his or her working activities. An illustration is *Rutten v Cross Medical*:

> A Dutchman lived in the Netherlands and worked from an office at home, he also spent one-third of his time in the United Kingdom, Belgium, Germany and the United States.[311]

The CJEU held that the Dutch courts had jurisdiction as that was the place where the employee spent most of his time.[312] It appears that it is the quality of what is done at that place as well as the quantity of time which is important.

If the employee did not habitually carry out his or her work in any one country, then the employer can be sued in the courts of the place where the business which engaged the employee is situated.[313] It can be tricky to identify the business which engaged the employee – is it the employer alone or is some other business envisaged? For example, can an Italian company which seconds a worker to one of its associated companies in Germany be sued in Italy as well as in Germany where the employee now carries out his or her activities? Can a French company which uses an English employment agency to find workers for oil rigs be sued in England? The Posted Workers Directive[314] also imposes minimum standards for international jurisdiction for workers temporarily posted abroad and permits such a worker to sue in the courts of the Member State in whose territory he or she is posted.[315]

---

[306] Article 19(1).   [307] Article 19(2)(a).

[308] Rome I Regulation, Art. 8, though the parties may have expressly chosen another law.

[309] *Mulox IBC Ltd v Geels* Case C-125/92 [1993] ECR I-4075.   [310] *Ibid.*

[311] Case C-383/05 [1997] ECR I-57.

[312] See too *Weber v Universal Ogden Services Ltd* Case C-37/00 [2002] ECR I-2013. A cook worked on several platforms located at sea, doing the same job at each. The number of days worked was used as the criterion to establish the place where he habitually carried out his work.

[313] Article 19(2)(b).

[314] Directive 96/71/EC of the European Parliament and of the Council of 16 December [1997] OJ L18/1.

[315] Directive 96/71/EC, Art. 6.

The employer can only bring proceedings against the employee in the courts of the Member State in which the employee is domiciled. As an employee is a natural person, this would be determined in accordance with Article 59.

It is possible to enter into a jurisdiction agreement in individual contracts of employment only (1) if it is entered into after the dispute has arisen, or (2) if it permits the employee to bring proceedings in courts other than those indicated by these rules (i.e., is not restrictive or exclusive).[316] The agreement must conform to the requirements of Article 23. A judgment from a Member State which does not have jurisdiction under one of the provisions of this section can be refused recognition and enforcement in other Member States.[317]

q. Exclusive jurisdiction: Article 22

Article 22 of the Brussels I Regulation provides for exclusive jurisdiction to the courts of Member States in particular matters. It is the most powerful article in the hierarchy: (1) it applies irrespective of the defendant's domicile whether within or without the EU;[318] (2) a defendant cannot confer jurisdiction on a different court either by submission to that court[319] or by a jurisdiction agreement;[320] (3) any other court must of its own motion decline jurisdiction (it is not therefore subject to the rules on *lis pendens* in Articles 27 and 28); and (4) a judgment obtained in a court other than that identified in Article 22 need not be recognised or enforced.[321] The parties are deprived of the normal rules of jurisdiction because of the particular subject matter of these disputes and their exclusive connection with the identified Member State. Those require cases to be heard by the courts of that state for the sound administration of justice. As such, the rules are to be restrictively interpreted and not given any wider interpretation than is necessary to attain the objective of the article.[322] Article 22 is only engaged if the principal subject matter of the proceedings falls within the article. If the exclusive subject matter is raised only as an ancillary or incidental question, then the normal rules of jurisdiction are applied.[323] If, in a rare case, a matter falls within the exclusive jurisdiction of the courts of more than one Member State, then any court other than the one first seised must decline jurisdiction.[324]

i. Rights *in rem* in immovable property

Proceedings which have as their object rights *in rem* in or tenancies of immovable property can only be brought in the courts of the Member State where the property is situated, irrespective of the domicile of the

---

[316] Brussels I Regulation, Art. 21.   [317] Articles 35(1) and 45(1).

[318] Article 4, therefore even if the defendant is domiciled in a third state jurisdiction is established under Art. 22.

[319] Article 24.   [320] Jenard Report, p. 34.   [321] Articles 35(1) and 45(1).

[322] *Sanders v Van der Putte* [1977] ECR 2383 at para. 18; *Reichert v Dresdner Bank* Case C-115/88 [1990] ECR I-27 at para. 9.

[323] *Land Oberösterreich v ČEZ as* Case C-343/04 [2006] ECR I-4557.   [324] Article 29.

defendant.[325] Where the principal subject matter of the dispute concerns rights *in rem* in immovable property located in England, clearly the English courts are best placed to decide the case. Not only is English law almost certain to be applied,[326] but also if the judgment is to be enforced, English bailiffs and ultimately even the police will be used to clear any occupation of the land. English courts will be closest to the physical evidence on the ground. Likewise if the land is situated in another Member State, those courts have exclusive jurisdiction. Immovable property includes land, buildings fixed to land, and probably also other rights which attach to the land (such as the right to hunt, collect wood, fish or easements to pass over the land).[327] First, the proceedings must have 'as their object' the rights *in rem*. This is given an autonomous meaning. They are proceedings which 'seek to determine the extent, content, ownership or possession of immovable property or the existence of other rights *in rem* therein and to provide the holders of those rights with the protection of the powers which attach to their interest'.[328] The rule can be seen from *Sanders v Van der Putte*:

> A florist's business was sold by a Dutch seller to a Dutch buyer, however, the shop itself was in Germany. There was a dispute over the agreement. The part of the dispute about the interpretation of the lease fell within Article 22(1) but the remainder of the proceedings, concerning how the business was being run from the premises, fell outside.[329]

The CJEU decided that the proceedings had to be split up, with the part on the lease going to Germany and the remainder being heard in the Netherlands.

Secondly, 'rights *in rem*' need to be defined. These are rights which are enforceable not just against a particular person (such as a right arising out of a contract or a tort) but are available against all the world. *Webb v Webb* shows how difficult it is to place equitable interests in this binary analysis:

> A father claimed that a constructive or resulting trust arose in his favour over a flat in Antibes which was in the legal name of his son. The CJEU held that this was not a dispute which had as its object rights *in rem* in immovable property as the equitable interest under a constructive trust was not good against all the world.[330]

---

[325] Article 22(1).   [326] See further Chapter 9.

[327] Opinion of AG Maduro that easements are within Art. 22, *Land Oberösterreich v ČEZ as* Case C-343/04 [2006] ECR I-4557 at para. 82.

[328] *Reichert v Dresdner Bank* Case C-115/88 [1990] ECR I-27.

[329] Case C-73/77 [1977] ECR 2383.

[330] *Webb v Webb* Case C-294/92 [1994] ECR I-1707.

This is not straightforward. Were the father to seek to enforce any judgment in Antibes, he would need an amendment of the register of land ownership, and he was also asking for this remedy as part of the proceedings. That would certainly be an issue *in rem*. Indeed, the English court has accepted that equitable interests are part of the law of property and can be described as operating *in rem* for some purposes.[331] Nevertheless, *Webb v Webb* was followed in *Ashurst v Pollard*[332] in which proceedings by a trustee in bankruptcy to order the sale of a villa in Portugal were outside Article 22. In that case the trustee did not need to perfect the title to the land, which was not in dispute. Disputes on contracts for the sale of land are not within Article 22.[333] Nor are disputes to set aside a gift of immovable property by a defendant allegedly to defraud his creditors.[334] Actions to prevent a continuing nuisance emanating from the land are also outside Article 22(1).[335]

Disputes relating to tenancies will often fall within Article 22(1). However, there is a proviso that disputes concerning private short-term tenancies, where the tenant is a natural person and domiciled in the same Member State as the landlord, can also be heard in the Member State of the tenant's domicile.[336] This is an additional jurisdiction to that of Article 22(1) for tenancies of less than six months' duration. There have been cases on the rental of holiday homes[337] and it may well be that even this paragraph's relaxation of the strict rules is too inflexible.[338]

ii. Corporations and legal persons

For certain matters, exclusive jurisdiction is given to the courts of the Member State in which a company, a legal person or association or natural or legal persons has its seat.[339] These are proceedings which have as their object the validity of the constitution, the nullity or the dissolution of such a company, etc., and the decisions of their organs. The seat of a company, etc., is to be determined according to the private international law rules of the courts of the Member State which are seised of the matter.[340] Partnerships, clubs and other corporations (such as colleges) fall within this article. Their organs would

---

[331] *Tinsley v Milligan* [1994] AC 340 at 371.   [332] [2001] Ch. 595.
[333] *Gaillard v Chekili* Case C-518/99 [2001] ECR I-2771.
[334] *Reichert v Dresdner Bank* Case C-115/88 [1990] ECR I-27.
[335] *Land Oberösterreich v ČEZ as* Case C-343/04 [2006] ECR I-4557.
[336] Article 22(1) second para.
[337] *Rösler v Rottwinkel* Case C-241/83 [1985] ECR 99; *Hacker v Euro-Relais GmbH* Case C-280/90 [1992] ECR I-1111 (dispute with travel agent about letting of accommodation not within Art. 22(1)); *Jarrett v Barclays Bank Plc* [1999] QB 1 (dispute with bank as part of a timeshare not within Art. 22(1)); *Dansommer A/S v Götz* Case C-8/98 [2000] ECR I-393 (dispute with tour operator who was subrogated to accommodation's owner and rented flat to the claimant was within Art. 22(1)).
[338] Hess, Pfeiffer and Schlosser Report, paras 879–80.   [339] Article 22(2).
[340] Article 22(2). The English private international law rules are to be found in Civil Jurisdiction and Judgments Order 2001, SI 2001/3929, Sched. 1 para. 10. Broadly, a company has its seat where it is incorporated or from where its central management and control is exercised.

include boards, committees and even single administrators who have been required to administer the company's affairs.[341] The purpose of Article 22(2) is to give exclusive jurisdiction to the courts whose law is most likely to apply to determine such questions as members' liability, capacity of the company, the powers of the directors, and formalities and procedures by which those powers are executed.[342] As with rights *in rem* in immovable property, this paragraph is to be interpreted narrowly. Therefore the principal object of the proceedings must concern the excluded subject matter.[343] So in *Hassett v South Eastern Health Board*:

> Some doctors complained about the refusal of the defendant Medical Defence Union to indemnify their contribution to monies paid out in negligence cases. The defendants were incorporated under English law with a registered office in England. The claimants sued in Ireland but the defendants argued that they could only be sued in England under Article 22(2) as the proceedings concerned the decisions of the boards of management.[344]

The CJEU disagreed. These disputes were about the manner in which decisions were made rather than the validity of the decisions under the rules of the applicable company law. There was no challenge to the authority of the board to make the decisions, merely to the outcome. Otherwise any challenge to a decision of the board would fall within Article 22(2).

Recently the courts have had to face a number of cases which appear to fall within this article after the financial crash of 2008. For example, *Berliner Verkehrsbetriebe (BVG), Anstalt des öffentlichen Rechts v JP Morgan Chase Bank NA*:

> A company argued that it must be sued in Germany, where it had its seat, rather than in England under an exclusive jurisdiction agreement. It had raised by way of defence in the English proceedings that its directors lacked capacity to enter into a 'swaps' contract. Did Article 22(2) apply to prevent the English court from hearing the case or did Article 23 apply to prevent the German court from hearing the case?[345]

On a reference from the German court the CJEU held that the issues raised on the validity of the directors' decisions to enter into the contract was collateral to the principal issue, that of the validity, interpretation or enforceability of

---

[341] Irish case of *Papanicolaou v Thielen* [1997] ILPr. 37.

[342] *Grupo Torras SA v Sheikh Fahad Mohammed al Sabah* [1995] ILPr. 667.

[343] *Berliner Verkehrsbetriebe (BVG), Anstalt des öffentlichen Rechts v JP Morgan Chase Bank NA* Case C-144/10 [2011] 1 WLR 2087.

[344] Case C-372/07 [2008] ECR I-7403.   [345] Case C-144/10 [2011] 1 WLR 2087 at para. 38.

the contract itself. This is a surprising conclusion. The fundamental dispute was whether the company had power to enter into this type of contract, which is an argument central to the validity of the contract. It is not easy to distinguish between an argument that the contract is invalid and the reason it is invalid. The English Court of Appeal had already decided that the proceedings in England did not 'principally concern' a matter falling within Article 22(2). Although the defence raised the invalidity of the contract as being *ultra vires* the powers of the German company, the court must make an overall classification of the proceedings. Otherwise, raising any issue which falls within Article 22(2) would prevent the whole claim from being heard. This is a difficult balance to strike. It seems that it is possible under the English court's view to have proceedings which on an overall classification principally concern the validity of the decisions of an organ of the company. A well-informed potential defendant would immediately commence declaratory proceedings in the courts of its seat. Those proceedings would have as their object the validity of the directors' powers to enter into the contract and should fall within Article 22(2). That is what the German company attempted to do in this case and failed. It now appears that only actions which directly attack the constitution of a company will fall within Article 22(2).[346]

iii. Entries in public registers

If the proceedings have as their object the validity of entries in public registers, the courts of the Member State in which the registers are kept have exclusive jurisdiction.[347] This is obvious. Only the courts of the place where the registers are kept have jurisdiction to amend or interfere with the register. The register is a matter of public record within the sovereign powers of the state. Examples would include the land register and the companies register.

iv. Registration or validity of intellectual property rights

Proceedings which have as their object 'the registration or validity of patents, trademarks, designs or other similar rights required to be deposited or registered' can only be brought in the courts of the Member State in which the deposit or registration is made irrespective of the domicile of the defendant.[348] The exclusive jurisdiction also covers any European patent granted for that state, without prejudice to the jurisdiction of the European Patent Office which can also make decisions on validity or registration of European patents. Whether proceedings concern the registration or validity of such intellectual

---

[346] In which case *Speed Investments Ltd v Formula One Holdings Ltd (No. 2)* [2005] 1 WLR 1936 would probably not be decided the same way today.

[347] Article 22(3).

[348] Or has been applied for or is deemed to have taken place under some international Convention or Community instrument (Art. 22(4)).

property is autonomously defined.[349] The exclusive jurisdiction is justified by the territoriality of the protection given to intellectual property, particularly of the registered patents and trademarks covered by Article 22(4). The law applicable to questions of validity and registration will be the law of the place where the intellectual property is protected[350] and the courts of the place of registration and infringement will be especially well placed to decide factual matters. As with the other provisions in Article 22, this paragraph is to be narrowly interpreted. It is limited to proceedings which principally concern matters of validity or registration and not ones which only raise the question of validity incidentally. Therefore actions for infringements of intellectual property rights and proceedings in relation to licensing of those rights are not covered by the exclusive jurisdiction of Article 22(4).[351] As with the other paragraphs of Article 22 there are problems with delineating the principal object of the proceedings, in particular when a defendant raises the invalidity of the patent, trademark or other intellectual property as a defence to the action.

In two English cases, the defendant claimed the invalidity of the patent as a defence to a patent infringement action.[352] The court held that these proceedings 'principally concerned' the issue of the validity of the patent. In effect that there was only one issue, whether raised by way of claim or defence.[353] The CJEU has also held that it did not matter whether the excluded matter was raised by way of claim or defence, an infringement action where the validity of the patent, etc., is in issue is excluded from any court other than that where the patent, etc., is registered.[354] That conclusion is at odds with the court's findings in relation to other paragraphs of Article 22[355] and with the analogous difficulties of determining the substance of the action in Article 2.[356] The interpretation of this article has given rise to a good deal of academic criticism[357] but the Brussels I Regulation (recast)[358]

---

[349] *Duijnstee v Golderbauer* Case C-288/82 [1983] ECR 3663.

[350] Rome II Regulation (Regulation (EC) 864/2007 on the law applicable to non-contractual obligations), Art. 8.

[351] *Mölnlycke AB v Procter & Gamble Ltd* [1992] 1 WLR 1112.

[352] *Coin Controls Ltd v Suzo International (UK) Ltd* [1999] Ch. 33; *Fort Dodge Animal Health Ltd v Akzo Nobel NV* [1998] FSR 222.

[353] As explained in the English proceedings in *JP Morgan Chase Bank NA v Berliner Verkehrsbetriebe* [2010] ILPr. 28 at para. 69.

[354] *Gesellschaft fur Antriebstechnik mbH & Co. KG (GAT) v Lamellen und Kupplungsbau Beteiligungs KG (LuK)* Case C-4/03 [2006] ECR I-6509.

[355] Such as *Berliner Verkehrsbetriebe (BVG), Anstalt des öffentlichen Rechts v JP Morgan Chase Bank NA* Case C-144/10 [2011] 1 WLR 2087.

[356] See e.g., *Préservatrice foncière TIARD SA v. Staat der Nederlanden*, Case C-266/01 [2003] ECR I-4867; *Allianz SpA Assicurazioni Generali Spa v West Tankers* Case C-185/07 [2009] ECR I-663.

[357] See Hess, Pfeiffer and Schlosser Report, paras. 791 *et seq.*

[358] Regulation (EU) 1215/2012 (Brussels I Regulation (recast)), Art. 24(4), applying from 10 January 2015.

explicitly makes Article 24 (ex Article 22) apply to the validity of a patent whether raised by way of claim or by way of defence.

r. Jurisdiction agreements: Article 23

The Brussels I Regulation permits prorogated jurisdiction in Article 23. If the parties have entered into an agreement by which the courts of a Member State are to have jurisdiction, that agreement will generally be effective.[359] The Regulation upholds the principle of party autonomy by which the parties are considered best placed to decide in which courts their disputes are to be litigated.[360] However, English law accords greater effect to jurisdiction agreements than some other systems of law and these differences in attitude have led to criticisms of the Brussels I Regulation.[361] Jurisdiction agreements raise three broad questions. First, what effect does a court give to the agreement as a matter of its own procedure? Does the clause confer or deny jurisdiction? As a corollary, does the clause affect the jurisdiction of other Member State's courts? Secondly, is the clause valid? Generally, a valid jurisdiction agreement will be given effect to but the law governing these two questions is different. The first is procedural and a matter for the *lex fori*. The second is substantive and may be answered by the substantive law governing the agreement.[362] Thirdly, how is the jurisdiction agreement to be interpreted? Does it cover the dispute in question? Some jurisdiction agreements may be ambiguous as to their scope or difficult to construe. This is probably a matter for the substantive law of the agreement but is often swept into the question of the effect to be given to the agreement and treated as a procedural question.

One might consider that jurisdiction agreements are straightforward. Indeed they can be very simple, for example, 'the parties agree to the exclusive jurisdiction of the English courts'. That clause purports to do two things: (1) confer jurisdiction on the English courts (or confirm that it has jurisdiction if there is any doubt), and (2) exclude jurisdiction from any other court which might otherwise have power to adjudicate the dispute. In practice, jurisdiction agreements between businesses are often lengthy and complicated. The clause may confer jurisdiction on a number of courts at the choice of one party, it

---

[359] Subject to the formal requirements in Art. 23(1).   [360] Recitals 11 and 14.

[361] See, e.g., *JP Morgan Europe Ltd v Primacom AG* [2006] ILPr. 11. Note that even English law has limited the effect of jurisdiction agreements in order to protect consumers and employees. These groups are subject to special rules under the Brussels I Regulation (see further p. 101 *et seq.* above).

[362] This issue of choice of law may not be straightforwardly answered. It is likely that rules the same as those in the Rome I Regulation should apply to decide which law governs the agreement despite agreements on jurisdiction being excluded from that Regulation (Art. 1). It is also probable that the jurisdiction agreement can be severed from the contract where the validity of the whole contract is in dispute (*Deutsche Bank AG v Asia Pacific Broadband Wireless Communications Inc.* [2008] EWCA Civ 1091, [2008] 2 Lloyd's LR 619). Generally, however, the cases appear to assume that the law governing the whole contract and that governing the jurisdiction agreement are the same.

may provide an address at which service of documents can be effected, and it may also prevent the other party from suing anywhere other than in a specified court. It may even purport to prevent a party from challenging the validity or effectiveness of the jurisdiction agreement by explicitly agreeing in advance to waive such arguments. Some clauses go further and require an indemnity from a party which breaches the agreement by suing other than where specified. Where one party is commercially stronger, that party often forces a jurisdiction agreement which is more favourable to it on the other party. Alternatively, a 'battle of the forms' can ensue when one party agrees to contract on its terms (including a jurisdiction agreement) and the other party accepts the contract on its terms (with a conflicting jurisdiction agreement). Those complexities have to be dealt with under the Brussels I Regulation.

Article 23 operates in two distinct situations. Article 23(1) applies if one of the parties (not necessarily the defendant) to the agreement is domiciled in a Member State and jurisdiction is conferred on the courts of a Member State. Article 23(3) applies if neither party is domiciled in a Member State but jurisdiction is conferred on the courts of a Member State. Note that the article says nothing about jurisdiction agreements conferring jurisdiction on a third state.[363] Like other special rules of jurisdiction derogating from the general rule of the defendant's domicile, Article 23 is to be strictly construed.[364]

i. Article 23(1)

An agreement which complies with Article 23(1) gives the Member State's court jurisdiction.[365] Unlike under the national rules, the English court must accept jurisdiction and hear the case where there is such an agreement.[366] The parties can freely choose a neutral forum in a Member State which has no connection with either the parties or the events.[367] The Article expressly makes such jurisdiction exclusive unless the parties have agreed otherwise. Therefore if the parties to a contract have identified the English court as having jurisdiction, only that court should hear the case.[368] However, Article 23 says nothing explicitly about the effect of agreements in which the parties have expressly agreed for more than one Member State's court, or for a Member State's court to have non-exclusive jurisdiction. Such agreements should confer jurisdiction on the courts chosen but other courts may also have jurisdiction under the usual rules of the Brussels I Regulation. In those cases a party is free

---

[363] See further p. 188 *et seq.* below.

[364] *Estasis Salotti di Colzani Aimo e Gianmario Colzani Snc v Rüwa Polstereimaschinen GmbH* Case C-24/76 [1976] ECR 1831.

[365] Subject to Art. 22 and 24.

[366] This follows from *Owusu v Jackson* Case C-281/02 [2005] ECR I-1383, cf. the old view of the English court in *Eli Lilly & Co. v Novo Nordisk A/S* [2000] ILPr. 73.

[367] *Zelger v Salinitri* Case C-56/79 [1980] ECR 89 at para. 4.

[368] This is somewhat different to the English court's interpretation of jurisdiction agreements under the traditional rules, see further below p. 181 *et seq.* below.

to commence proceedings in another court (ignoring the jurisdiction agreement). The chosen court cannot then decide the dispute as it would be the court second seised.[369] Even where the parties have agreed to the exclusive jurisdiction of the English court, another Member State's court may be first seised of proceedings and can determine the validity, scope and effect of the exclusive English jurisdiction agreement.[370] That has been heavily criticised as being contrary to the concept (common in arbitration) of *competence-competence* by which only the courts chosen should be deciding the validity, scope and effect of a jurisdiction agreement. There are proposals for the reform of the Brussels I Regulation which attempt to modify that result.[371]

ii. Validity of agreement: consensus and form

The validity of a jurisdiction agreement is tested autonomously in accordance with the formal requirements laid out in Article 23(1).[372] These have been expanded such that jurisdiction agreements:

(1) in writing or evidenced in writing;[373]
(2) in a form which accords with a practice which the parties have agreed between themselves; or
(3) in international trade or commerce, in a form which accords with a usage of which the parties are or ought to have been aware and which in such trade or commerce is widely known to, and regularly observed by, parties to contracts of the type involved in the particular trade or commerce

are all valid. National law is not permitted to expand on the requirements contained in Article 23 so English courts cannot require any extra formal steps in order for a jurisdiction clause to be effective.[374] In the early cases the CJEU insisted on the parties coming to a consensus on jurisdiction which appeared to impose a separate requirement of validity. The purpose of the formal requirements was said to be to establish the parties' consent to the clause.[375] Nevertheless, in the more recent cases of *Benincasa v Dentalkit Srl*[376] and *Trasporti Castelletti Spedizioni Internationali SpA v Hugo Trumpy SpA*,[377] it has held that a jurisdiction agreement which complies with the rules on form contained in Article 23(1) is presumed to be valid. These later cases leave no apparent role for the national law, nor its conflict of laws rules, to determine questions of the validity of the jurisdiction agreement. Some commentators have criticised this conclusion as a jurisdiction 'agreement' arrived at by use of undue

---

[369] Article 27, unlike under the traditional rules.
[370] *Erich Gasser v MISAT* Case C-116/02 [2003] ECR I-14693.
[371] See further p. 133 *et seq.* below.
[372] *Benincasa v Dentalkit Srl* Case C-269/95 [1997] ECR I-3767.
[373] An oral contract subject to general terms later confirmed by writing is one which is evidenced in writing, *Galeries Segoura Sprl v Firma Rahim Bonakdarian* Case C-25/76 [1976] ECR 1851.
[374] *Elefanten Schuh v Pierre Jacqmain* Case C-150/80 [1981] ECR 1671 at para. 26.
[375] *F. Berghoefer GmbH & Co. KG v ASA SA* Case C-221/84 [1985] ECR 2699.
[376] Case C-269/95 [1997] ECR I-3767.   [377] Case C-159/97 [1999] ECR I-1597.

influence or fraud may well apparently be in writing.[378] These commentators would argue that any court should be able to decide on the question whether the agreement itself is effective as an exclusive jurisdiction agreement, not only the court apparently identified in the agreement and that the jurisdiction of those courts is unaffected by the (to their eyes) invalid agreement. That argument does not conform to ideas of *competence-competence* by which only the court identified in the agreement has power to decide questions of effectiveness of the jurisdiction agreement. Fentiman argues that it might be possible to use a community concept of good faith as a means to prevent the effectiveness of jurisdiction agreements affected by duress or fraud.[379]

A jurisdiction agreement can be in writing if there is a written contract between the parties which expressly refers, for example, to standard terms and conditions which contain the jurisdiction clause. Article 23(5) also permits communication by electronic means which provides a durable record of the agreement to be the equivalent of writing.

An example of (2) above is when the parties have negotiated contracts between themselves in the past which have referred to a standard form containing a jurisdiction clause.[380] However, in *Lafarge Plasterboard Ltd v Fritz Peters & Co. KG*:

Lafarge Plasterboard was an English company. It ordered some lining paper from Fritz Peters, a German company. On the reverse of a 'European Purchase Order' issued by Lafarge Plasterboard were its terms and conditions, including a jurisdiction agreement giving exclusive jurisdiction to the English court but nothing on the front of the order indicated the terms. A consignment note had different terms and conditions with no jurisdiction agreement. There was some dispute about whether the European Purchase Order was ever seen by the seller. Fritz Peters delivered the goods with a confirmation fax containing its own terms and conditions. There were some thirty-eight orders but in one the lining paper was defective and Lafarge Plasterboard sued for breach of contract. Fritz Peters challenged the jurisdiction of the English court.[381] Was there an agreement evidenced in writing?

The CJEU in *Galeries Segoura Sprl v Firma Rahim Bonakdarian*[382] had accepted that an Article 23(1) jurisdiction agreement could be found in a

---

[378] A. Briggs and P. Rees, *Civil Jurisdiction and Judgments* (4th edn, LLP, London, 2005) para. 2.105; cf. Merrett, 'Article 23 of the Brussels I Regulation: a Comprehensive Code for Jurisdiction Agreements?' [2009] *ICLQ* 545, who argues that there is no role for national law even in such cases.

[379] R. Fentiman, *Principles of International Commercial Litigation* (Oxford University Press, 2010) paras. 2.46–2.50.

[380] *Lafi Office and International Business Sl v Meriden Animal Health Ltd* [2000] 1 Lloyd's LR 51.

[381] [2000] 2 Lloyd's LR 689.   [382] Case C-25/76 [1976] ECR 1851.

continuing trading relationship where the confirming party's general conditions contained a jurisdiction agreement which was not challenged by the other party. The English court in *Lafarge Plasterboard Ltd v Fritz Peters & Co. KG* held that that case was different. Both parties had their own terms and conditions and there was no actual agreement to either. Therefore the English court did not have jurisdiction.

Another explanation for *Galeries Segoura Sprl v Firma Rahim Bonakdarian*[383] is to note that the party who did not have notice of the jurisdiction clause (for example, because the clause is in general terms and conditions) can challenge it by arguing that the formalities have not been complied with. However, the other party should be bound by it despite the possible lack of formalities on the basis of good faith or estoppel.

The relaxation of the formal requirements to include (3) above may raise more difficulties. In *Trasporti Castelletti Spedizioni Internationali SpA v Hugo Trumpy SpA*:

> Castelletti brought an action against Trumpy in Italy for damage to goods delivered under bills of lading issued by the shippers in Buenos Aires. Trumpy was the agent for the carrier and therefore not a party to the bill of lading. Trumpy argued that the Italian court did not have jurisdiction as the bill of lading contained an exclusive jurisdiction agreement in favour of the English courts. The agreement to jurisdiction was in small type on the reverse of the bills of lading so Castelletti argued that the shipper had only signed and accepted the particulars on the front of the bill.[384]

The CJEU held Castelletti and Trumpy were presumed to have consented to the jurisdiction agreement if their conduct was consistent with a usage governing the particular area of international trade.

In order to comply with (3) above, the agreement must be in a form which accorded with practices in that trade or commerce of which the parties are or ought to have been aware. This appears to be a factual matter. It is to be determined by the national court. Was this international trade? Should the parties have been aware of the practice regarding the form of jurisdiction agreements in this particular international trade? A practice exists if there is a particular course of conduct generally and regularly followed by operators in that area of international trade when concluding the type of contract in question.[385] So where it is not usual in international insurance to incorporate the jurisdiction agreement from an insurance contract into the reinsurance

---

[383] Case C-25/76 [1976] ECR 1851 and also *Colzani v Rüwa* Case C-24/76 [1976] ECR 1831.
[384] Case C-159/97 [1999] ECR I-1597.
[385] *Mainschiffahrts-Genossenschaft eG (MSG) v Les Gravières Rhénanes* Case C-106/95 [1997] ECR I-911.

contract there is no agreement for Article 23(1).[386] That is an example of incorporation of terms from one contract into another contract. It is easier to establish that standard *terms* containing a jurisdiction agreement have been incorporated into the contract.[387]

Although generally such contracts are concluded in writing, contracts such as those completed in commodity exchanges are most likely to be oral. However, the practice of contracting subject to the general terms of the market will often include a jurisdiction agreement. Parties should have been aware of the particular practice if they had previously had relations with each other or with other parties in the sector, or if the practice is generally and regularly followed such that is well known to those operating in that sector.[388]

In contrast to questions of material validity of a jurisdiction agreement, questions of its interpretation are ones for the national law.[389] Whether this is done according to the applicable law governing the jurisdiction agreement itself or the law of the forum chosen may be less clear.[390] The better approach is for the interpretation to be a matter of the applicable law of the agreement to determine whether, for example, an exclusive jurisdiction agreement covers within its scope disputes between the parties arising in tort as well as those arising out of the contract. English courts interpreting English jurisdiction agreements tend to take an expansive view, arguing that the parties as rational businessmen are to be assumed to have intended all disputes to be covered by an exclusive jurisdiction clause.[391]

Jurisdiction agreements are severable from their host contract. Therefore they can survive an allegation that the contract containing the agreement is invalid.[392]

Any question of the validity or scope of the jurisdiction agreement must be proved to the usual standard in matters of jurisdiction, that of the good arguable case. If there is no agreement in fact, for example because a jurisdiction clause contained in a draft of the contract does not form part of the final terms, then the party seeking to rely on the clause has not satisfied that standard.[393]

---

[386] *AIG Europe (UK) Ltd v Ethniki* [2000] 2 All ER 566, CA and *Africa Express Line Ltd v Socofi SA* [2009] EWHC 3223 (Comm) [2010] 2 Lloyd's LR 181.

[387] *7E Communications Ltd v Vertex Antennentechnik GmbH* [2007] 1 WLR 2175.

[388] *Mainschiffahrts-Genossenschaft eG (MSG) v Les Gravières Rhénanes* Case C-106/95 [1997] ECR I-911 at para. 43.

[389] *Powell Duffryn Plc v Petereit* Case C-214/89 [1992] ECR I-1745.

[390] The applicable law of the agreement is likely to be the applicable law of the whole contract, especially where the parties have made an express choice of law. The applicable law was applied in *Provimi Ltd v Aventis Animal Nutrition* [2003] EWHC 961 (Comm), [2003] 2 All ER (Comm) 683, but the Court of Appeal did not make a distinction between the law of the forum and the law of the agreement in *UBS AG v HSH Nordbank AG* [2009] EWCA Civ 585, [2009] 2 Lloyd's LR 272.

[391] Following the practice in arbitration agreements, *Fiona Trust & Holding Corp. v Privalov* [2007] UKHL 40, [2007] 4 All ER 951.

[392] For example, because the contract was made beyond the authority of the agent concluding it (*Deutsche Bank AG v Asia Pacific Broadband Wireless Communications Inc.* [2008] EWCA Civ 1091, [2008] 2 Lloyd's LR 619; Merrett, 'Article 23 of the Brussels I Regulation'.

[393] *Bols Distilleries v Superior Yacht Services Ltd* [2007] 1 WLR 12.

iii. Article 23(3)

Article 23(3) is in a somewhat different form. It applies where neither party to the agreement is domiciled in a Member State but the contract specifies that a Member State's court is to have jurisdiction. Article 23(3) refers to 'such an agreement', which must impose the formal requirements of Article 23(1) on these jurisdiction agreements between parties not domiciled in Member States. Unlike Article 23(1), the article explicitly states that no other Member State's court shall have jurisdiction over the dispute unless the chosen court has declined jurisdiction. Therefore, Article 23(3) is concerned with the preclusive effect of the jurisdiction agreement on the jurisdiction of the Member State's courts which have not been chosen. However, the extent and exercise of jurisdiction which is conferred on the chosen court by virtue of the jurisdiction agreement is a matter for the national rules of that Member State. The effect of the jurisdiction agreement on the jurisdiction of the Member State's court is probably also a question for the procedural law of that court. The English court might then in its discretion stay its proceedings despite a jurisdiction agreement between a Ruritanian bank and a Utopian borrower referring disputes to the English court.[394] Matters of interpretation of the clause are also for the national rules of the Member State, whether those are considered to be for the *lex fori* or, the better view, for the applicable law.

iv. Interpretation of jurisdiction agreements

Article 23(1) provides that a jurisdiction agreement conferring jurisdiction on a Member State's court is to be exclusive unless the parties have agreed otherwise. This permits parties to a contract to enter into a non-exclusive jurisdiction agreement which does confer jurisdiction under that article. The article also covers an agreement specifying that each party can only sue the other in the other's courts.[395] It is probably also correct that the parties can specify the exclusive jurisdiction of two Member States' courts, thus conferring jurisdiction on those two courts and excluding the jurisdiction of any other Member States' court.[396] Other than what the article itself provides, the interpretation of a jurisdiction agreement is a matter for national law. The English court tends to use English law to determine whether a jurisdiction agreement is exclusive or non-exclusive, as often it is interpreting a jurisdiction agreement which purports to confer jurisdiction on the English courts. In principle, however, if the English court has to interpret a jurisdiction agreement in favour of the French courts, then French law should be applied to decide whether the clause is exclusive or

---

[394] Although the English court rarely declines jurisdiction in such cases, it retains the power under its traditional rules to do so, see pp. 171, 178 *et seq.* below.

[395] *Meeth v GlacetalSarl* Case C-23/78 [1978] ECR 2133.

[396] *Kurz v Stella Musical Veranstaltungs GmbH* [1992] Ch. 196.

non-exclusive or whether the dispute falls within the scope of the clause.[397] The matter might be complicated if the jurisdiction agreement is contained in a contract governed expressly by another law, say German law. Either the jurisdiction agreement is treated as totally severable and to be interpreted according to its own law, presumably French law. Or it is recognised that the agreement is merely part of a whole contract and should be interpreted according to the law of the whole contract. English law requires a jurisdiction agreement to be an express choice of the parties.[398] In construing jurisdiction agreements the court will determine the parties' intentions.[399] Using the word 'exclusive' is a clear indication of what the parties intended. However, this has a much less sophisticated effect than under the national rules of jurisdiction.[400] Once the court has decided that the jurisdiction agreement confers jurisdiction (whether exclusive or non-exclusive) and includes the particular dispute within its scope, the English court must take jurisdiction over that dispute. There is no room for the exercise of discretion. Any parallel proceedings are dealt with by Article 29, if there are two courts with exclusive jurisdiction, or Article 27; in both cases the court first seised of the action has priority.[401]

v. Limitations on Article 23

Matters which fall within Article 22 exclusive jurisdiction[402] cannot be made subject to a jurisdiction agreement, either before or after the dispute has arisen.[403] Jurisdiction agreements contrary to the special rules on insurance, consumers and employees[404] likewise are denied legal force. By submitting to a different court, the defendant overrides any previous jurisdiction agreement that the defendant has entered into.[405]

s. Submission – (Article 24)

The English court has jurisdiction in a case where the defendant has submitted to its adjudication by voluntarily appearing in the case to contest the merits of the claim.[406] If a defendant appears merely to contest jurisdiction (but not the substance of the case), the defendant has not submitted. In *Elefanten Schuh v Pierre Jacqmain*,[407] the CJEU held that a defendant who pleads both as to jurisdiction and the merits has not necessarily submitted voluntarily. This is because the procedural law of some Member States requires that a defendant

---

[397] *British Sugar Plc v Fratelli Babbini di Lionello Babbini & Co. SAS* [2004] EWHC 2560 (TCC), [2005] 1 Lloyd's LR 332.

[398] *New Hampshire Insurance Co. v Strabag Bau AG* [1992] 1 Lloyd's LR 361 at 371.

[399] *Satyam Computer Services Ltd v Upaid Systems Ltd* [2008] EWCA Civ 487, [2008] 2 All ER (Comm) 465 at para. 93.

[400] See further p. 182 *et seq.* below.   [401] See further p. 122 *et seq.* below.

[402] Immovable property and so on, see pp. 105–11 above.   [403] Article 23(5).

[404] Articles 13, 17 or 21.

[405] *Elefanten Schuh v Pierre Jacqmain* Case C-150/80 [1981] ECR 1671.   [406] Article 24.

[407] Case C-150/80 [1981] ECR 1671 and *Rohr v Ossberger* Case C-27/81 [1981] ECR 2431.

must plead the whole of the defendant's case (both as to jurisdiction and as to substance) in order to make any argument, even only as to jurisdiction. So long as the defendant is only pleading as to the merits for the purpose of challenging jurisdiction, and the purpose is clear to the parties, the defendant has not submitted.[408] Nevertheless, once the defendant has voluntarily taken steps to defend the proceedings the defendant is taken to have submitted. In England, the jurisdiction of the court is determined at a particularly early stage of the proceedings, well before the case on the merits is developed by disclosure of evidence. It is therefore reasonably clear whether a defendant has submitted on the merits or not.[409] This is not the situation in many continental European countries, which decide the case on the merits immediately after determining that the court has jurisdiction. A defendant in such a court should be advised to prepare the whole case, even if in the end the defendant succeeds in establishing that the court has no jurisdiction and the work done on the merits is wasted. Submission by contesting the merits will not confer jurisdiction in a case falling within Article 22 but will do so in any other case, including overriding a jurisdiction agreement.

Defendants are generally careful not to submit to the jurisdiction unless they are going to accept the decision of the court. However, this is of less importance in the Brussels I Regulation regime than it is under the national rules. A judgment given by a Member State's court will be recognised and enforced in all but the most limited of circumstances.[410] In particular, a judgment debtor is not given opportunity to challenge the grounds of jurisdiction at the recognition or enforcement stage except in cases which should have been decided under Article 22, or for insurance or consumer contracts.[411] Once judgment has been given, there are extremely limited circumstances in which the merits of the judgment can be questioned,[412] except by appeal in the court giving the judgment. Therefore, a defendant who wishes to contest the merits of a claim is probably best advised do so as well as challenging jurisdiction of the court first seised.

t. Examination of jurisdiction

The English court is adversarial. That practice requires the parties to make their own case and present it to the court. However, the Brussels I Regulation imposes a requirement on the court to examine its own jurisdiction where

---

[408] See the analogous case under the traditional rules, *Marc Rich & Co. AG v Società Italiana Impianti PA (The Atlantic Emperor) (No. 2)* [1992] 1 Lloyd's LR 624.

[409] The defendant challenges jurisdiction under CPR Part 11. The defendant must challenge the jurisdiction within fourteen days of receipt of the claim form, or will be treated as having submitted under English domestic law (CPR Part 11 r. 11(5)). However, it is doubtful that the English approach of submitting by failing to challenge jurisdiction can be treated as voluntary appearance for Art. 24 (see Fentiman, *International Commercial Litigation*, p. 372).

[410] See further p. 225 *et seq.* below.

[411] Article 35(3). Note there is not similar protection for employees.   [412] Articles 34 and 36.

the defendant is domiciled in another Member State and does not enter an appearance. If the court does not have jurisdiction under the Regulation, it must declare of its own motion that it does not.[413]

u. *Lis pendens* – (Articles 27 and 28)

The Brussels I Regulation permits various Member States' courts to have jurisdiction in many cases. Apart from Article 22 and other special cases such as exclusive jurisdiction agreements, insureds, consumers and employees, generally a claimant is given a free choice in which to commence proceedings. However, one of the major purposes of the Brussels I Regulation is to avoid irreconcilable judgments. It is also aimed at unifying the rules of jurisdiction and making them more certain. It would frustrate these objectives if proceedings on the same dispute were continuing in two Member States simultaneously. In addition, that would lead not only to a waste of the courts' and the parties' time and resources but also to a possible race to judgment. So there are three mechanisms to avoid duplication of proceedings. First, a Member State's court cannot reject hearing the dispute where it has jurisdiction under the Regulation on the ground that another Member State's court is better placed.[414] The principle of mutual trust and confidence means that each Member State's court is as good as any other, so long as the rules of jurisdiction are complied with. Secondly, the Regulation provides that a judgment shall not be recognised if it conflicts with a judgment given either in the recognising Member State[415] or with a previously granted judgment on the same cause of action and between the same parties in another Member State.[416] This provision removes much incentive to pursue two actions. Thirdly, the Regulation additionally has strict rules to deal with proceedings pending in more than one Member State (*lis pendens*). These strict rules apply only where the dispute falls within the scope of the Brussels I Regulation. So where proceedings are continuing in England the principal object of which is arbitration, these are not prevented from continuing by Article 27 despite prior proceedings in Italy.[417] However, a judgment from a court in Spain which decides a matter of the scope of the arbitration agreement as an ancillary question to the substance of the dispute will have to be recognised in the English proceedings. The Spanish decision is within the scope of the Brussels I Regulation.[418]

Where the proceedings are between the same parties and involve the same cause of action, Article 27 prevents any court other than the court first seised

---

[413] Article 26(1). But there is no mechanism in the English procedural rules for this to happen unless the defendant appears and objects to the jurisdiction.

[414] *Boss Group Ltd v Boss Group France SA* [1997] 1 WLR 351 at 358.   [415] Article 34(3).

[416] Article 34(4).

[417] *Allianz SpA Assicurazioni Generali Spa v West Tankers* Case C-185/07 [2009] ECR I-663.

[418] *National Navigation Co. v Endesa Generacion SA (The Wadi Sudr)* [2010] ILPr. 10.

from continuing with the action until the court first seised has decided on its jurisdiction. The court second seised must do this of its own motion.[419] If the court first seised determines that it has jurisdiction, then the court second seised must decline jurisdiction.

In *Overseas Union Insurance Ltd v New Hampshire Insurance Co.*[420] the CJEU applied Article 27 to proceedings in which neither of the parties was domiciled in the EU. Therefore the English court had no jurisdiction to hear any case in which there were proceedings between the same parties on the same cause of action already continuing in another Member State. The only exception is if the case concerns a matter falling within the exclusive jurisdiction rules in Article 22.[421] In any other case, including where the parties have entered into a jurisdiction agreement, or if the case falls within the protective rules for consumers, insureds and employees, any court other than that first seised must stay its proceedings. The strength of Article 27 is most powerfully illustrated by *Erich Gasser v MISAT Srl*:

> Gasser, an Austrian company, sold children's clothes to MISAT, an Italian company. MISAT brought proceedings in Italy against Gasser for wrongful termination of the contract. Gasser later brought an action against MISAT in Austria for payment of outstanding invoices. It contended that the invoices all contained a jurisdiction agreement in favour of the Austrian courts. Mostly, it was concerned at the considerable delays in the Italian courts, meaning that judgment on the merits of the dispute was unlikely for several years.[422]

The CJEU held that despite the jurisdiction agreement, the Italian courts were first seised and the Austrian courts must therefore stay their proceedings to await the outcome of the Italian case. The Austrian courts could not investigate the grounds of jurisdiction of the Italian court. The court second seised must never challenge the exercise of jurisdiction of the court first seised. Under the principle of mutual trust and confidence the Italian courts were as capable as the Austrian courts of determining the validity and effect of the jurisdiction agreement. This case has been heavily criticised for preferring the Regulation's twin objectives of mutual trust and confidence, and certainty, over the objective of party autonomy. It has permitted parties to escape an agreement which they have made as to the courts in which their dispute is to be ventilated. The CJEU decided that it was irrelevant that the party commencing litigation in a forum other than that chosen was doing so in bad faith. The result is that *Erich Gasser v MISAT Srl* encourages tactical litigation in slow

---

[419] Article 27(1).　　[420] Case C-351/89 [1991] ECR I-3317.

[421] *Overseas Union Insurance Ltd v New Hampshire Insurance Co.* Case C-351/89 [1991] ECR I-3317.

[422] Case C-116/02 [2003] ECR I-14693.

courts. Some commentators[423] have argued that the state of the court second seised which does not hear the dispute when the court first seised is so slow as to amount to a breach of Article 6 of the European Convention on Human Rights, might also be in breach of Article 6.

Where the proceedings are related, Article 28 of the Brussels I Regulation provides a discretion for any court other than that first seised to stay its proceedings and await the outcome of the case in the court first seised.

Note that neither Article 27 nor Article 28 says anything about proceedings continuing in a third state. The rules on *lis pendens* between a dispute being heard in the English court and one being heard in a Ruritanian court are dealt with under the national rules.[424] However, in so far as the Brussels I Regulation is engaged (for example, where the defendant is domiciled in England), it is possible to argue that there is no power for the English court to stay proceedings in accordance with those rules.[425]

Article 30 lays out when a court is deemed to be seised. Unlike the Brussels Convention, seisin is now autonomously defined. Article 30 provides two alternative definitions to cover the various rules adopted in the domestic procedural law of the Member States. English law is covered by Article 30(1). It provides that a court shall be deemed to be seised 'at the time when the document instituting the proceedings or an equivalent document is lodged with the court, provided that the plaintiff has not subsequently failed to take the steps he was required to take to have service effected on the defendant'. The English court is seised at the instant when the claim form is issued by ('lodged with' in the terminology of the article) the court. Although the form must later be served on the defendant, it is the time of issue which is critical. Article 30(2) provides for the alternative, that a court shall be deemed to be seised 'if the document has to be served before being lodged with the court, at the time when it is received by the authority responsible for service, provided that the plaintiff has not subsequently failed to take the steps he was required to take to have the document lodged with the court'. An English court may have to determine when another Member State's court is seised using this rule if that Member State's law requires service of the document instituting proceedings on the defendant before it has to be lodged with the court.

i. Article 27: same cause of action and same parties

Article 27 only engages if the two sets of proceedings involve the same cause of action and the same parties. As we have seen, it is a strict rule which prevents a court, other than that first seised, from hearing the case. In no circumstances, other than if the matter concerns Article 22 exclusive jurisdiction, can the

---

[423] T. Hartley in J. Nafziger and S. Symeonides (ed.), *Law and Justice in a Multistate World* (Martinus Nijhoff, 2002) p. 73. See too on *Erich Gasser v MISAT* and human rights generally R. Fentiman in U. Magnus and P. Mankowski (ed.), *Brussels I Regulation* (Sellier, 2007) p. 490 *et seq.*

[424] See further pp. 169–70 below.   [425] See further pp. 188–94 below.

court second seised investigate the jurisdiction of the court first seised, even if the court first seised is in error as to the operation of the Brussels I Regulation.[426] Only if the court first seised has declined jurisdiction can the other court hear the dispute. It is essential, therefore, to be able to identify when the same cause of action and the same parties are involved. Unfortunately, this is not entirely straightforward. Two things are clear. First, the same cause of action has an autonomous meaning. Secondly, Article 27 is aimed at preventing conflicting judgments which may compete for enforcement.[427] In *Gubisch Maschinenfabrik KG v Giulio Palumbo*:

> Palumbo, an Italian, brought proceedings in Italy against Gubisch, a German company. He alleged that the contract was never made because he revoked his offer before it reached Gubisch, alternatively he claimed that the contract should be set aside for lack of his consent or alternatively that it was discharged due to Gubisch's failure to deliver. Gubisch had already commenced proceedings in Germany against Palumbo to enforce the payment obligation of the contract.[428]

The CJEU held it was necessary to satisfy both that the cause of action and that the subject matter of the disputes were the same. However, it was not necessary for the two actions to take identical form. In this case the causes of action were the same as they arose out of the same contract. The subject matter of the causes of action was the same. One was to enforce the contract and the other was to seek its recission or discharge. At the heart of the two actions lay the question of whether the contract was binding. The court pointed out that a decision in one set of proceedings as to whether the contract was binding could be incompatible with a decision to enforce it. This is a relatively wide interpretation of same cause of action. It is irrelevant whether the first action is positive for damages or negative, asking for a declaration of non-liability.[429] The CJEU took a similarly wide view in *The Tatry*:

> Some soybean oil owned by a number of cargo owners was shipped on *The Tatry* from Brazil to Hamburg and Rotterdam. The ship was owned by a Polish ship-owner. The cargo owners complained that the soybean oil had become contaminated. The ship-owner sued some cargo owners in the Netherlands asking for a declaration of non-liability. Later the ship-owner sought to limit its

---

[426] *Erich Gasser GmbH v. MISAT Srl* Case C-116/02 [2003] ECR I-14693. The only exception is if the matter falls within Art. 22.

[427] Fentiman, *International Commercial Litigation*, para. 11.30 *et seq.*

[428] *Gubisch Maschinenfabrik KG v Giulio Palumbo* Case C-144/86 [1987] ECR 4861.

[429] *Owners of the Cargo lately Laden on Board the Ship Tatry v Owners of the Ship Maciej Rataj* Case C-406/92 [1994] ECR I-5439.

liability in proceedings in the Netherlands. Some of the cargo owners sued the ship-owner for damages in England.[430]

It decided that the cause of action includes both the subject of the action and its object. The object of the action is the 'end the action has in view', to put that another way: its legal objective. The legal objective in both sets of cases was to establish the ship-owner's liability in damages. That is the 'facts and rules of law relied on as the basis of the action'.[431] Likewise an action for a declaration of non-liability for negligence for personal injury has been found to be the same as a statutory claim for wrongful death.[432]

The English court has held that in order to determine the legal objective of the various proceedings, it must take a view of the object of the proceedings as a whole and identify the 'central or essential' issue in each.[433] This can be a complex matter. A single contract could give rise to several different claims (or causes of action). For example:

A and B enter into a contract for A to sell and deliver paper to B monthly. The contract provides for termination on 12 months' notice. B complains about the lateness of delivery in February and the poor quality of the paper when delivered. A sues in France for non-payment of invoices for January and February. B's defence is the lateness of delivery in February and the poor quality of the paper delivered in January.

What is the cause of the French action? If one simply looks at the claim, it appears to be a breach of the contractual obligation to pay. Turning to the object, is it the enforceability of the contract generally or of the particular obligation? Were B to sue later in England for damages for lost profit from the two deliveries as B has to source the paper from elsewhere, how should Article 27 operate? A's defence to that action is that the paper was not late and the quality of the paper delivered was satisfactory. Simply looking at the claim to identify the cause suggests that it is the breach of an obligation to provide goods of a suitable quality. However, the object could be broadly defined as the enforceability of the contract. There are certain issues common to both actions: was the delivery late, giving B a defence and a claim? Was the paper not of contract quality, giving B a defence and a claim? The issues concern the same contractual rules of law (what is the term of the contract about payment, timing of delivery and quality) and factual (what happened in fact).

---

[430] *Ibid.* para. 41.   [431] *Ibid.* para. 39.   [432] *Kinnear v Falcon Films NV* [1996] 2 WLR 920.
[433] *The Underwriting Members of Lloyd's Syndicate 980 for the 1999, 2000, 2001, 2002, 2003, 2004 and 2005 Underwriting Years of Account as Managed by Limit Underwriting Ltd v Sinco SA* [2008] ILPr. 49 at para. 51.

Res judicata would encompass both the facts and the rules of law.[434] But each allegation is possibly independent, particularly those concerning the quality and the timing of delivery. A broad interpretation of Article 27 should lead to the conclusion that the actions are likely to result in irreconcilable judgments and that the English action should be stayed to await the outcome of the French proceedings. The obligation to pay only arises if the delivery obligation has been properly fulfilled. If B is not liable to pay A, because the defence succeeds, then B is also able to recover losses. If A can recover the payments then B has not satisfactorily proved its claim for poor quality and late delivery.

If one action seeks to rescind the whole contract and the other seeks damages for some part of that contract, both would have the same subject matter and the same object. However, if one action seeks breach of, say, a payment clause and the other seeks damages for early termination, the legal objectives of each arguably differ. In *Maersk Olie & Gas A/S v Firma M. de Haan en W. de Boer*,[435] an action to establish liability and another to seek to limit liability if any arose were found not to involve the same cause of action as the actions do not share a common legal objective. Also, in *Mecklermedia Corp. v DC Congress GmbH*,[436] an action for the tort of passing off was not the same cause of action as one in another Member State for the infringement of a trademark. These cases appear to suggest a narrower meaning for 'same cause of action'.

The CJEU has held that only the claim in each action is to be taken into account, not any possible defences, in order to promote the twin aims of certainty and uniformity to ensure the proper administration of justice.[437] Nevertheless, as we have seen in the above example, irreconcilable judgments may easily result from the defence to the claim in the first court being the basis of the claim in the second court. Article 27 cannot therefore completely eradicate any risk of irreconcilable judgments.

In addition to the causes of action being the same, Article 27 only operates if the parties to the action are the same. Therefore in *The Tatry*:

> Proceedings had already been commenced in the Netherlands between the ship-owner of *The Tatry* and some of the cargo owners for a declaration of non-liability. Some of the cargo owners then used *in rem* jurisdiction over the ship-owner by arresting a sister ship in the same ownership (*The Maciej Rataj*) in England. The ship-owner then agreed to submit to the jurisdiction of the English courts in order to release *The Maciej Rataj*.[438]

---

[434] English rules on *res judicata* are surprisingly wide. Therefore in England a conflicting judgment may be much more widely interpreted than in a country with a civil law tradition. See further Chapter 7.

[435] Case C-39/02 [2004] ECR I-9657.   [436] [1998] Ch. 40.

[437] *Gantner Electronic GmbH v Basch Exploitatie Maatschappij BV* Case C-111/01 [2003] ECR I-4207.

[438] *Owners of the Cargo lately Laden on Board the Ship Tatry v Owners of the Ship Maciej Rataj* Case C-406/92 [1994] ECR I-5439.

The CJEU held that as between the identical parties, Article 27 operated to prevent proceedings in the later seised court, England. So one has to identify the particular ship-owner and each of the cargo owners in each set of proceedings in order to determine which must be stayed. There was some overlap between the parties in the various courts but not a complete overlap. Where the parties were not identical, the proceedings in the other court could go ahead. Although the English proceedings were commenced in the form of *in rem* actions those proceedings had become *in personam* once the ship-owner had submitted.

The CJEU in *The Tatry*[439] also decided that the definition of parties had to be autonomous and independent of national law. However, in *Drouot Assurances SA v Consolidated Metallurgical Industries*,[440] this was interpreted as requiring some reference to national law to determine the issue on the facts before the national court. Whether the parties were the same depended upon whether a decision against one of them would have the force of *res judicata* against the other. In this case, the question before the court was whether an insurer was the same party as the insured and the CJEU held that an insurer would normally be the same party as its insured as their respective interests in the dispute were 'indissociable'. Nevertheless, on the facts of this particular case, the insurers were suing cargo owners for a contribution to salvage in France. The cargo owners were suing the insured ship-owner for a declaration of non-liability to contribute in the Netherlands. The insurers' interest in the salvage of the vessel was found to be different to that of the ship-owner's interest, those interests were thus dissociable and they were not the same parties.

Other difficulties have arisen in identifying what amounts to the same parties. For example, where the parties involved a majority shareholder in a company, English company law treats a company as entirely separate from its majority shareholder but that is not necessarily the case in other Member States. In *Turner v Grovit*,[441] the English court decided that a company was the same party as its majority shareholder for the purposes of Article 27. This conclusion may partly be explained as the majority shareholder was using the company in bad faith to commence proceedings in Spain to harass the claimant in English proceedings which is a recognised exception to the English company law rule.[442] Lifting the veil of incorporation in this way should have the effect of rendering a judgment against the shareholder *res judicata* against the company. There are similar difficulties where the parties involve assignees as in *Kolden Holdings Ltd v Rodette Commerce Ltd*:

---

[439] *Ibid.*   [440] Case C-351/96 [1998] ECR I-3075.

[441] [2000] 1 QB 345, point not considered in House of Lords decision reported at [2002] 1 WLR 107 nor in the decision of the CJEU Case C-159/02 [2004] ECR I-3565.

[442] The decision in *Berkeley Administration Inc. v McClelland* [1995] ILPr. 201 is not so easily explained. A French wholly-owned subsidiary was found to be the same party as its English holding company without any explanation in complicated proceedings.

A case was commenced in England by some assignors against the defendants Rodette Commerce for a declaration that Rodette was to transfer some shares. Later, an action was commenced in Cyprus by Rodette Commerce against Kolden for a declaration of non-liability under the contract of sale and purchase of the shares. The assignors had transferred their rights under the contract, including the cause of action in the English proceedings, to Kolden. The parties agreed that the causes of action were the same but argued in the English court that Article 27 prevented the English proceedings as the parties were the same in the Cypriot proceedings which were first seised as between those parties.[443]

The Court of Appeal held that an assignor of a cause of action was the same party as the assignee, as a judgment given against one of them would be *res judicata* against the other. Therefore the English proceedings were commenced first between Kolden (in place of the assignors) and Rodette. In fact, Rodette were not prejudiced by this. Rodette had had notice of the assignment of the English cause of action to Kolden before commencing the Cypriot proceedings, even though Kolden had not been formally named as a party in the English action until a few days after the Cypriot case had started. The Court of Appeal decided that in determining identity of interest it should look to the substance of the claim, not the form.[444] Similar complexities arise with holders of bills of lading and the original consignees of the cargo, guarantors and the person whose performance is guaranteed, and other indemnity actions.

Commentators have criticised Article 27 for permitting forum shopping. First, a court is seised of proceedings before it has decided upon its own jurisdiction which encourages a race to the court, even to one which is likely to decline jurisdiction. The court first seised may properly decide that it has no jurisdiction but meanwhile the defendant has had to defend proceedings on jurisdiction and, under some Member State's procedural law, also bring forward a case on the merits which will never be heard. That is wasteful and may force an unwarranted settlement. An important example is *JP Morgan Europe Ltd v Primacom AG*:

JP Morgan were the lead bank of a syndicate of banks which had lent money to Primacom, a German company. The loan agreements contained exclusive jurisdiction clauses in favour of the English courts. Primacom was on the verge of bankruptcy and JP Morgan commenced proceedings to protect the banks'

---

[443] [2008] EWCA Civ 10, [2008] ILPr. 20.

[444] Therefore, in *Mecklermedia Corp v DC Congress GmbH* [1998] Ch. 40 and *Mölnlycke Health Care AB v BSN Medical Ltd* [2010] ILPr. 171, the interests of a licensee were found to be not identical to the licensor (i.e., not indissociable). In the former case the defence of each against the single claimant was different and in the latter the licensee had an additional, not merely assigned, right.

position in the English court under the jurisdiction agreement. Some days before these proceedings were issued Primacom had commenced proceedings in the German courts for a declaration of non-liability for repayment and challenging the interest clause.[445]

Cooke J found that he had to stay the English proceedings to await the outcome of the decision of the German courts. Under German procedural law, the question of jurisdiction is decided immediately before the decision on the merits of the case. Therefore JP Morgan and the banks had to prepare for a full trial in case they lost on the jurisdiction aspect. In the event, some four months later, the German courts declined jurisdiction in the face of the jurisdiction agreements. The case could therefore go ahead in England on the merits. This was a pyrrhic victory for the banks. Not only had they wasted the expense of preparing for trial in Germany but meanwhile Primacom's financial state had worsened such that the English proceedings aimed at protecting the banks' position were worthless. In these circumstances the operation of Article 27 had robbed the jurisdiction clause of much of its effect.[446]

Secondly, Article 27 operates to prevent proceedings continuing in any court other than that first seised even if the proceedings in the first seised court are for a declaration of non-liability.[447] That allows well-advised likely defendants to pre-empt an action and commence one in a preferred forum. For example, in *Bank of Tokyo-Mitsubishi Ltd v Baskan Gida Sanayi Pazarlama AS*:

Complicated proceedings in England and Italy arose out of a financing arrangement granted by Bank of Tokyo (and others) to Baskan Gida. The financing was to help Baskan Gida with its cash flow difficulties during sales to Ferrero. Baskan Gida agreed to assign its rights under sales contracts to the banks who would give notice to Ferrero and an advance would then be made to Baskan Gida by way of a letter of credit. Baskan Gida did not repay the advance and it became clear that the signatures of Ferrero were forgeries. Ferrero sued the banks and Baskan Gida in Italy, seeking a negative declaration as to Ferrero's liability to the banks. The banks commenced later proceedings in England against Baskan Gida and other individuals and companies. These proceedings

---

[445] *JP Morgan Europe Ltd v Primacom AG* [2006] ILPr. 11.

[446] Note that the English court was prevented from hearing the case only in relation to the same causes of action to be decided in the German courts. The related proceedings were permitted to go ahead in England. However, the clever framing of the German causes of action meant that the banks lost most of their ability to protect themselves.

[447] *Owners of the Cargo lately Laden on Board the Ship Tatry v Owners of the Ship Maciej Rataj* Case C-406/92 [1994] ECR I-5439.

> included a claim for repayment of the advance credit based on contract and
> claims based in fraud. Ferrero was joined to these proceedings as assignees of
> Baskan Gida's rights and because of the alleged involvement of a Ferrero
> employee in the fraud.[448]

Lawrence Collins J (as he then was) held that the contractual part of the two
proceedings involved the same cause of action. Both were about Ferrero's
liability to pay the banks as a result of the assignments and undertakings. It is
noteworthy that the Italian proceedings were very widely framed (seeking to
establish no liability for whatever reason arising out of the contracts)[449] and
encompassed the more detailed English claims. The pre-emptive strike in Italy
succeeded in preventing the continuation of English proceedings. However,
the fraud claims were found not to be the same cause of action.

The forum shopping argument can be countered. There are limited fora
available under the Brussels I Regulation, and X (a potential claimant) turned
into a defendant by this action can hardly complain at being sued in X's own
domicile. However, jurisdiction may be available in other courts and X's
choice of forum is usurped by Y's (the real defendant's) action for a negative
declaration. In particular, it is in Y's interest to start proceedings in a forum
which takes a long time to come to judgment. In addition, the way in which
the cause of action is interpreted permits Y to frame the declaration extremely
widely, so catching all possible claims. That puts unwarranted pressure on X,
who has been turned into an actual defendant by Y's action, to settle at a
reduced rate. Money paid now in settlement is more valuable than money
ordered by the court many years later. The principle of mutual trust and
confidence makes this point unarguable although many practitioners agree
that the tactic is widely adopted.

Thirdly, the strict application of Article 27 may encourage the action to be
split up (*depéçage*) with part being heard in one court and part in another,
rather than a consolidation in one court. This is inefficient and encourages
tactical litigation. It compares unfavourably with the general trend under the
national rules.[450]

ii. Article 28: related causes of action

Article 28 is triggered when the related actions are 'pending' at first instance
before two Member States' courts. Article 28(1) provides a discretion for the
court second seised of a related cause of action to stay its proceedings to await
the outcome of the court first seised. The court second seised does not have to

---

[448] [2004] 2 Lloyd's LR 395.
[449] *Bank of Tokyo-Mitsubishi Ltd v Baskan Gida Sanayi Pazarlama AS* [2004] 2 Lloyd's LR 395 at para. 207.
[450] See further pp. 169–71 below.

stay its proceedings but is permitted to do so. In addition, Article 28(2) permits the court second seised to decline jurisdiction in favour of the court first seised where that court has jurisdiction over the related action and the actions can be consolidated. Note that neither Article 28(1) nor 28(2) provides a ground for jurisdiction in related actions.[451] In the case of Article 28, the causes of action do not have to be the same but actions are 'deemed related where they are so closely connected that it is expedient to hear them together to avoid the risk of irreconcilable judgments'.[452] In *The Tatry* (see above) the actions between the various cargo owners and the ship-owner arose out of separate but identical contracts. As such the judgments would not conflict, though they may be inconsistent as to their reasoning. The CJEU held that those were 'related actions' as the concept must be broadly interpreted.[453] That case was followed by the House of Lords in *Sarrio SA v Kuwait Investment Authority*:

> Sarrio had sold its paper business in Spain. It brought actions against KIA in Spain claiming damages for amounts unpaid under a put option relating to the sale. It also brought actions against KIA in England for damages for negligent misrepresentation which had allegedly been made during the course of the sale. KIA asked the English court to stay its proceedings in favour of those going ahead in Spain.[454]

The House of Lords stayed the English action, holding that a broad common-sense view of the two sets of proceedings was to be taken to determine that these two proceedings were related. The case is relatively unusual as the claimant brought proceedings in two courts on different aspects of the case. More usually, a claimant in one court is the defendant in another and therefore it might be more difficult to identify whether the proceedings are related. Both essential and other issues necessary to establish the cause of action could be taken into account. 'Irreconcilable' therefore has a wider meaning than the same word in Article 34(3) dealing with conflicting judgments. So, causes of action are related when the legal issues are the same but the legal object of the two sets of proceedings is different.[455] In *Research in Motion UK Ltd v Visto Corporation*:

> Research in Motion had commenced proceedings in England for revocation and a declaration of non-infringement of a UK patent, and similarly in Italy for revocation and non-infringement of corresponding Italian, German, Spanish,

---

[451] Article 6(1) and (3) may do so for some actions.   [452] Article 28(3).

[453] *Owners of the Cargo lately Laden on Board the Ship Tatry v Owners of the Ship Maciej Rataj* Case C-406/92 [1994] ECR I-5439.

[454] [1999] 1 AC 32.   [455] Fentiman, *International Commercial Litigation*, para. 11.44 *et seq.*

> Dutch and Belgian patents. Visto counterclaimed in the English proceedings, alleging that Research in Motion was abusing the process of the English and Italian courts by bringing the action in Italy.[456]

The Court of Appeal held that merely because irreconcilable judgments were possible, the proceedings were not necessarily related. The court did not stay the English proceedings. The irreconcilability of the judgments would have been at a factual rather than a legal level (as each of the patents and infringements were governed by different laws). The case is also explicable on the ground that the court would not exercise its discretion to stay as it was not entirely appropriate to hear all the claims in one court. In *FKI Engineering v Stribog Ltd*,[457] the Court of Appeal reiterated that a broad common-sense approach 'free of over-sophisticated analysis or encouragement to satellite, interlocutory, litigation' was required to determine if proceedings were related. In that case the court decided that the two proceedings became related after an amendment to the German claim. Even so, the court exercised its discretion to stay the English proceedings.

Article 28 may also operate even when the parties to the two sets of proceedings are not the same. It applies, therefore, when there is no risk of conflicting judgments competing for enforcement, but the two judgments might be inconsistent as being incompatible at the level of judicial decision on legal issues or facts.

How is the discretion to stay the proceedings in the court second seised to be exercised? Are the national rules on *lis pendens* adopted or is there a modification to those rules in the context of the Brussels I Regulation? There are good reasons of efficiency and justice to encourage courts to avoid parallel litigation. As we shall see, the national rules take a variety of factors into account (such as the likely time to trial in each country, the appropriateness of the other forum, and so on). There are several arguments in favour of more actively staying proceedings in favour of another Member State's court. The Brussels I Regulation is a mutual recognition and enforcement of judgments regime founded on mutual trust which would be undermined if the discretion to stay was only rarely exercised. Generally, the CJEU mistrusts the discretionary exercise of jurisdiction in the *forum conveniens* doctrine and prefers a more certain approach.[458] There are limited grounds on which jurisdiction can be allocated under the Regulation and so a party should not be surprised nor can the party readily complain about the exercise of jurisdiction by the other Member State. However, Advocate-General Lenz in *Owens Bank Ltd v Fulvio Bracco*[459] suggested using wider factors that mirror rather closely

---

[456] [2008] ILPr. 34.   [457] [2011] EWCA Civ 622, [2011] 1 WLR 3264.
[458] See e.g., *Owusu v Jackson* Case C-281/02 [2004] ECR I-1383.
[459] Case C-129/92 [1994] ECR I-117.

the *forum conveniens* ones under the national rules. He argued that the possible irreconcilability of the judgments was not the only factor in the exercise of the discretion. He considered that the relatedness of the proceedings to the respective countries, the stage at which each set of proceedings had reached and the connection between the proceedings and the countries should be taken into account. This approach has been followed by the English court.[460]

In principle, it appears that the English court should generally lean more in favour of a stay of its own proceedings than it might under the national rules.[461] However, the justifications for a stay have less force in cases in which the English court has jurisdiction via an exclusive jurisdiction agreement and the other Member State's court has taken jurisdiction in breach of that agreement. In such cases, the English court has stayed its own proceedings in so far as the causes of action and parties are the same, as required by Article 27, but has refused to do so under Article 28 for related actions falling within the jurisdiction agreement.[462] In effect, the court privileges the parties' expression of their preferred forum in the jurisdiction agreement to any wider concerns of mutual trust and efficient administration of justice.

v. Provisional measures

Article 31 permits the English court to grant provisional or protective measures even when the courts of another Member State have jurisdiction under the Brussels I Regulation. These would include freezing injunctions,[463] ancillary disclosure orders to those injunctions and other interim relief which may be made in support of proceedings on the substance of the dispute continuing in another Member State.[464] The orders are usually aimed at preserving the status quo of the parties or their assets pending trial. The CJEU defines such orders as those which are intended to maintain a legal or factual situation in order to safeguard rights.[465] The French order of *saisie conservatoire* and the Dutch *kort geding* would also be covered. If the English court has jurisdiction over the substance of the action by some provision of the Regulation then the court can grant its own interim relief as widely as it would like. There is no territorial restriction in such a case, so a worldwide freezing order would be

---

[460] *Grupo Torras v Al Sabah* [1995] 1 Lloyd's LR 374, point not taken on appeal [1996] 1 Lloyd's LR 7; *Cooper Tire & Rubber Co. Europe Ltd v Dow Deutschland Inc.* [2010] EWCA Civ 864, [2010] 2 CLC 104.

[461] As it did in *Sarrio SA v Kuwait Investment Authority* [1999] 1 AC 32.

[462] *JP Morgan Europe Ltd v Primacom AG* [2006] ILPr. 11 and *Seven Licensing Co. Sarl v FFG-Platinum SA* [2011] EWHC 2967 (Comm).

[463] Previously known as *Mareva* injunctions.

[464] Civil Jurisdiction and Judgments Act 1982 (Interim Relief) Order 1997, SI 1997/302.

[465] *Mario Reichert and Kockler v Dresdner Bank AG* Case C-261/90 [1992] ECR I-2149 and *St Paul Dairy Industries NV v Unibel Exser BVBA* Case C-104/03 [2005] ECR 1-3481.

permissible.[466] On the other hand, where another Member State's court is hearing the merits of the dispute, there are limitations on what provisional measures can be made by the English court. First, if any payment of money is ordered, the defendant must be guaranteed to be repaid if the claim is unsuccessful. It is essential that the provisional measure is truly provisional.[467] Secondly, and importantly, there must be some 'real connecting link' between the territory of the English court and subject matter of the measures.[468] Commentators have different views as to the extent of the territorial limitation. Some argue that the measure can only extend to assets within the jurisdiction of the court.[469] Others point out that in two cases[470] the CJEU appeared to acknowledge that orders made under this article could be enforced in another Member State.[471] English worldwide freezing injunctions pose difficulties as the orders do not attempt to freeze the assets abroad directly but indirectly do so through the use of contempt orders against the person who misapplies the assets subject to the order.[472] It would be more certain if Article 31 was restricted to assets within the territory of the English court. It is open to any claimant to seek similar interim measures from the courts of the Member State in whose territory other assets are found, for which Article 31 would provide a ground of jurisdiction. That would avoid overlapping and inconsistent orders.

An English order made under Article 31 jurisdiction would be enforceable in other Member States under two conditions: first, so long as the requirements of notice to the defendant are met. Often freezing injunctions are made without notice to the defendant. In that case, the order would not be recognisable until the defendant had been given notice.[473] Secondly, so long as the order complied with Article 31.[474]

w. Brussels I Regulation (recast)

The European Commission has proposed alterations to the Brussels I Regulation. The Commission's latest Report to the Parliament, the Council and the European Social and Economic Committee on the Brussels I

---

[466] However, in a case where the substance of the dispute is excluded from the Brussels I Regulation as a matter of arbitration, then the court does not have jurisdiction to make such orders except under Art. 31 in which case there are restrictions (*Van Uden Maritime BV v Kommanditgesellschaft in Firma Deco-Line* Case C-391/95 [1998] ECR I-7091).

[467] *Van Uden Maritime BV v Kommanditgesellschaft in Firma Deco-Line* Case C-391/95 [1998] ECR I-7091.

[468] *Ibid.*   [469] For example, *Cheshire, North and Fawcett*, p. 317.

[470] *Denilauler v SNC Couchet Frères* Case C-125/79 [1980] ECR I-1553 and *Mietz v Intership Yachting Sneek BV* Case C-99/96 [1999] ECR I-2277.

[471] Marta Pertegas Sender in U. Magnus and P. Mankowski (eds.), *Brussels I Regulation* (Sellier, 2007) p. 532.

[472] See Fentiman, *International Commercial Litigation*, para. 17.143 *et seq.*   [473] Article 34(2).

[474] *Mietz v Intership Yachting Sneek BV* Case C-99/96 [1999] ECR I-2277.

Regulation[475] was required by Article 73 of the Regulation. Two reports had been commissioned; one general from Profs. Hess, Pfeiffer and Schlosser,[476] and one specifically on residual jurisdiction from Prof. Nuyts.[477] Proposals for reform have also come from the European Parliament,[478] and a previous one from the European Commission.[479] The proposals made wide-ranging and controversial changes to the Brussels I Regulation. These have culminated in the Brussels I Regulation (recast) which will apply to actions commencing after 10 January 2015. The reforms cover four broad areas: (1) abolishing the step of *exequatur* in enforcing judgments from other Member States (which will be dealt with in Chapter 8 on the recognition and enforcement of judgments);[480] (2) reforming the rules on parallel proceedings where the proceedings are continuing in another Member State, particularly with regard to giving more effect to jurisdiction agreements; (3) providing rules on *lis pendens* where the proceedings are continuing in a third state;[481] (4) dealing with some of the concerns surrounding the exclusion of arbitration from the scope of the Regulation. In addition, the recitals would be recast to explain the Regulation further. The proposals to extend the rules of jurisdiction to defendants domiciled in third states, providing new grounds for jurisdiction based on forum necessitatis and on the presence of movable property were dropped in the recast Regulation as enacted.

i. Extending jurisdiction to defendants domiciled in third states

The original proposal from the Commission planned to extend the rules of jurisdiction under the Brussels I Regulation to defendants domiciled in third states. Article 4 was to have been abolished so the English court would no longer have been able to use the national rules of jurisdiction based upon service of the claim form including the doctrine of *forum conveniens*. The Commission had argued that EU-domiciled defendants may be discriminated against when they can be

---

[475] Regulation (EU) 1215/2012 on jurisdiction and the recognition and enforcement of judgments in civil and commercial matters [2012] OJ L351/1 (Brussels I Regulation (recast)). The UK government has indicated that it will opt into any amended Regulation.

[476] *General Study on the Practical Application of the Regulation*, available at http://ec.europa.eu/justice_home/doc_centre/civil/studies/doc_civil_studies_en.htm.

[477] *Study on Residual Jurisdiction, General Report* (6 July 2007), available at http://ec.europa.eu/justice_home/doc_centre/civil/studies/doc_civil_studies_en.htm.

[478] Green Paper, available at www.europarl.europa.eu/sides/getDoc.do?pubRef=-//EP//NONSGML+COMPARL+PE-430.865+01+DOC+PDF+V0//EN&language=EN); Draft Report 2009/2140(INI), available at www.europarl.europa.eu/sides/getDoc.do?pubRef=-//EP//NONSGML+COMPARL+PE-439.997+01+DOC+PDF+V0//EN&language=EN and amendments, available at www.europarl.europa.eu/sides/getDoc.do?pubRef=-//EP//NONSGML+COMPARL+PE-441.266+01+DOC+PDF+V0//EN&language=EN.

[479] Green Paper on the review of the Brussels I Regulation, COM 2009/0175 (21 April 2009). The latest proposal by the European Council dated 1 June 2012 (doc. 10609/12) is available at http://register.consilium.europa.eu/pdf/en/12/st10/st10609-ad01.en12.pdf.

[480] See further pp. 234–5 below.   [481] See further pp. 136–7 below.

easily sued in various courts in the EU whilst their competitors might not be so easily sued within the EU. Several authors criticised the reforms of the Brussels I Regulation in this area.[482] Even the Commission recognised that its proposed rules were 'mildly exorbitant'.[483] The proposals have sensibly been dropped in the recast Regulation.

The European Commission proposed two new grounds for jurisdiction in a Member State. First, new Article 25 provides that if there is no court of a Member State which has jurisdiction under the usual rules of Articles 2 to 24[484] then the court of the Member State in which property belonging to the defendant is found is to have jurisdiction. Therefore the English court could take jurisdiction over a defendant where the defendant owns property in England. Necessarily, the defendant must be domiciled in a third state, otherwise jurisdiction can be obtained under Article 2 in the Member State of the defendant's domicile. Secondly, new Article 26 permitted the courts of a Member State to take exceptional jurisdiction if the right to a fair trial or the right to access to justice requires it (a *forum necessitatis*). This was only available if no other Member State's court has jurisdiction and the dispute has a sufficient connection with the Member State taking jurisdiction. Both these proposals have been dropped from the Brussels I Regulation (recast).

ii. Parallel proceedings in other Member States

The Brussels I Regulation amends Articles 27 and 28. They will be replaced with new Articles 29 and 30. New Article 29(2) is inserted to require the court first seised to establish its own jurisdiction 'without delay'. There appears to be no consequences if the court first seised fails to comply with this provision.

New Article 31(2) attempts to resolve the difficulties after *Erich Gasser v MISAT*.[485] As we have seen, an exclusive jurisdiction agreement is given no priority in the present Article 27, so that a court other than that chosen may determine the validity of the agreement and the substance of the case if it is first seised. The party with the benefit of the agreement is left having to defend it in any court in which the other party has started proceedings. Although that court may decline jurisdiction, it may still be harmful.[486] New Article 31(2) provides that where an exclusive jurisdiction agreement has been concluded, and the courts of the Member State identified by the agreement are seised of

---

[482] See R. Fentiman, 'Brussels I and Third States: Future Imperfect' [2011] *Cambridge YB Eur. L* 66; A. Dickinson, 'Surveying the Proposed Brussels I bis Regulation: Solid Foundations but Resovation Needed' [2010] *YB Priv. Int. Law* 247.

[483] See the Commission's Impact Assessment, SEC(2010)1547 and 1548 final pp. 24 and 27.

[484] Those corresponding to Arts. 2 to 24 in the present Brussels I Regulation.

[485] Case C-116/02 [2003] ECR I-14693.

[486] See *JP Morgan Europe Ltd v Primacom AG* [2006] ILPr. 11 (discussed pp. 127–8 above).

an action, and any other Member State's court shall stay its proceedings until the agreed courts have declined jurisdiction. The jurisdiction agreement will have to be in the form required by the new Article 25(1).[487] Under new Article 25 an agreement is exclusive unless agreed otherwise. It is open to the courts of the Member State identified by the agreement to decline jurisdiction, if the agreement is null and void under its own law.[488]

iii. Parallel proceedings in third states

New Articles 33 and 34 of the Brussels I Regulation (recast) allow the staying of actions commenced in a Member State in favour of proceedings in third states. Article 33 permits the staying of proceedings commenced earlier on the same cause of action in a third state, where the stay is necessary for the proper administration of justice. A recognisable (and enforceable, where appropriate) judgment of the courts of the third state must be expected. This change is beneficial. First, it avoids the worst excesses of the decision in *Owusu v Jackson*.[489] Secondly, it is not quite the mechanical rule that the existing Article 27 contains. The Member State's court second seised may continue proceedings if (1) the proceedings in the first court are stayed or discontinued; (2) the proceedings in the court first seised are unlikely to be concluded within a reasonable time; or (3) the proper administration of justice requires it.[490] A foreign judgment which will take many years to obtain is not worth very much except to a party who wishes to avoid judgment. One that is not enforceable is worthless. Article 34 provides for actions to be stayed in favour of related proceedings in third states. Like the present Article 28 (new Article 30) it must be 'expedient to hear and determine the related proceedings together to avoid the risk of irreconcilable judgments'. The stay must also be necessary for the proper administration of justice. The Member State's court may continue proceedings for the same reasons as under new Article 33(2), as well as if the risk of irreconcilable judgments no longer appears.

There are some difficulties with these new provisions. It is unclear what is 'necessary for the proper administration of justice'. Great uncertainty will result. There is no explicit requirement or power to stay an action in a Member State where there is a jurisdiction agreement in favour of the courts of the third state, if proceedings have not yet been commenced in the third state. That is an encouragement to rush to a Member State's court to frustrate the jurisdiction agreement. Party autonomy[491] and the protection of jurisdiction and arbitration

---

[487] Which compresses the current Art. 23(1), (3). The formal and consensual requirements remain the same as at present.

[488] By insertion of words into new Art. 25(1). See also recitals 20 and 22.

[489] Case C-281/02 [2004] ECR I-1383. See further pp. 188–93 below.

[490] New Art. 34(3).

[491] See new recital 19.

agreements from forum shopping are strengthened in other changes to the Regulation.[492] Not carrying this through to third state jurisdiction agreements is unfair on the party whose agreement is not being upheld and is euro-centric. New recital 24 mentions 'consideration' of exclusive jurisdiction in circumstances where a Member State would have exclusive jurisdiction. This is not particularly strong. The Hague Choice of Court Convention,[493] once ratified and brought into force in the European Union, will address some aspects of this. It requires courts, other than that chosen, to suspend or dismiss proceedings except in certain circumstances, such as where the jurisdiction agreement is deemed to be void.[494] However, it only covers exclusive jurisdiction agreements conferring jurisdiction on the courts of other contracting states. If the parties have entered into a non-exclusive jurisdiction agreement, they have expressed a willingness to entertain proceedings in that court. A stay would be justified, particularly where there is little or no connection with the Member State's court. The Hague Convention also excludes certain claims.[495] Nor are arbitration agreements with a seat in a third state protected by the possibility of a stay of a Member State's court action. Arbitration remains excluded from the Brussels I Regulation (recast).[496] It is to be hoped that Member States' courts can continue to stay proceedings in favour of arbitration in a third state, as they are required to do by the New York Convention.[497]

Similarly, there is no requirement of a stay of a Member State's court proceedings in respect of a matter concerning exclusive jurisdiction in a third state. The Regulation specifically refers some matters to the exclusive jurisdiction of Member States' courts in new Article 24. In the current Brussels I Regulation, this is strengthened by the non-recognition of judgments obtained in other Member States in breach of Article 22.[498] In relation to proceedings in England dealing with a US patent, there are very strong arguments that an English court should not hear that dispute, leaving the case to go ahead in the US federal courts.[499] Public international law notions of sovereignty may preclude a national court from deciding such matters. These are not limited to matters of exclusive jurisdiction of the Member States *inter se*. Recital 24 mentioned above does not go far enough to resolve this problem.

---

[492] For example, in new Art. 31, restricted to jurisdiction agreements in favour of Member States.

[493] Hague Convention of 30 June 2005 on Choice of Court Agreements (signed by the European Union on 1 April 2009 but not yet in force). Only Mexico has ratified the Convention. See further p. 186 *et seq.* below.

[494] Article 6.   [495] Such as personal injury, Art. 2.   [496] Article 1(1)(d).

[497] Article II(3) of the New York Convention on the Recognition and Enforcement of Foreign Arbitral Awards 1958.

[498] Article 34(3).

[499] See *Lucasfilm v Ainsworth* [2010] Ch. 503, but cf. the same case in the House of Lords [2011] 3 WLR 487. The copyright dispute was found not to fall within the exclusive jurisdiction of the United States and could therefore be heard in England. Lord Collins accepted that disputes concerning the validity of patents should not be heard in England, at para. 106.

iv. Arbitration

Although the Brussels I Regulation excludes arbitration from its scope, we have seen that this is not an absolute exception.[500] The Commission proposed to deal with arbitration in several ways. However, these were all deleted in the recast Brussels I Regulation. Article 73(2) provides explicitly that the Brussels I Regulation 'shall not affect' the application of the New York Convention, along with an extensive new recital to make matters clearer. That recital is confusing. It says that the ruling by a Member State's court that the arbitration agreement is void or ineffective, whether as a principal or as an incidental question, does not have to be recognised by another Member State's court,[501] although it may be. Presumably it is up to the recognising court to decide, but uniformity throughout the EU is unlikely. There is no proposal to deal with the case in which the arbitral award and a judgment conflict.

v. Jurisdiction agreements

Article 25 of the Brussels I Regulation (recast) makes Article 23(1) apply to all parties wherever domiciled.[502] Jurisdiction agreements in which the parties have agreed that the courts of a member state are to have jurisdiction shall give jurisdiction to those courts. However, other Member States' courts can hear the case if the agreement is null and void as to its substantive validity according to the law of the chosen Member State. A new recital confirms that it is the law of the chosen court including its conflict of laws rules[503] which is to apply to determine the substantial validity of the jurisdiction agreement. Proposed new Article 25(5) provides that the jurisdiction agreement is independent of the contract and that its validity cannot be contested solely on the grounds that the contract containing the jurisdiction agreement is invalid. This is the case under the English national rules.[504]

vi. Examination of a court's jurisdiction

Brussels I Regulation (recast) makes it more clear that a court which has no jurisdiction under the Brussels I Regulation must declare of its own motion that it has no jurisdiction.[505] A Member State's court must stay its proceedings where a defendant has not entered an appearance unless it is shown that the defendant has been able to have notice of the proceedings in time to enable the defendant to arrange for a defence.[506]

---

[500] See e.g., *Allianz SpA, Generali Assicurazioni Generali Spa v West Tankers Inc. (The Front Comor)* Case C-185/07 [2009] ECR I-663.

[501] So the decision in *National Navigacion v Endesa* [2009] EWCA Civ 1397, [2010] 1 Lloyd's LR 193 would be different.

[502] Present Art. 23(3) is deleted.   [503] I.e., a *renvoi*.   [504] See further p. 178 *et seq.* below.

[505] New Art. 27 (amended ex Art. 25).   [506] New Art. 28(2) (amended ex Art. 26).

6

National rules of jurisdiction

1. Jurisdiction under national law (including staying of proceedings)

a. Introduction

The traditional English rules of jurisdiction were originally based directly on notions of territorial sovereignty. Once a person was within the territorial jurisdiction of the English court that person had impliedly accepted that he or she was subject to the adjudication of the English courts in the same way as he or she would be subject to criminal jurisdiction of the state. The person could be served here with notice of the proceedings and that was sufficient to give the English courts jurisdiction. This form of jurisdiction remains and the rules by which defendants can be personally served within the territory of the English courts are now contained in rule 6.3 of the Civil Procedure Rules. Obviously, there were difficulties when a defendant left the territorial jurisdiction, having run up debts or committed torts here. Over the course of the nineteenth century, therefore, the Rules of the Supreme Court extended the ways in which the English court would hear a case even when the defendant was not present within the territorial jurisdiction to be served with the writ. These originally were known as 'Order 11' rules, but more recently have been updated and are found in rules 6.36 and 6.37 and Practice Direction 6B (which is annexed to rule 6 of the Civil Procedure Rules). These 'service out' rules were always subject to the discretion of the English court. The court realises that in some way they are exorbitant, risking dragging a defendant to England to defend an action which might not be as strong as the claimant alleges and which might not have a sufficient connection with England to justify the English court hearing the case. Nevertheless, the House of Lords has restated its view that 'the jurisdiction of the English courts can be extended over persons abroad to cover new causes of actions and situations'.[1] Jurisdiction based on the presence of the defendant has also been criticised as exorbitant. It requires no more than mere physical

---

[1] *Masri v Consolidated Contractors International Co SAL* [2009] UKHL 43 [2010] 1 AC 90 at para. 14. This aspect of the case was concerned with requiring the disclosure of assets to satisfy a judgment debt. Nevertheless the statement was broadly couched in terms of rule-making powers.

presence of the defendant to be served with the claim form, without any further connection between the parties, the subject matter and the English court.[2] This form of jurisdiction has been specifically outlawed as a ground under the Brussels I Regulation.[3] Additionally, a defendant may consent to be brought before the English courts, either by submitting to the jurisdiction in an agreement, or by turning up to proceedings and arguing the defendant's case, or by counterclaiming in proceedings brought.

The rules on jurisdiction are discretionary. The English court may decide not to exercise its jurisdiction over a case in the interest of justice. One of the concerns might be to prevent forum shopping. As Lord Goff of Chieveley in *Airbus Industrie GIE v Patel* noted:

> There is, so to speak, a jungle of separate, broadly based, jurisdictions all over the world. In England, for example, jurisdiction is founded on the presence of the defendant within the jurisdiction, and in certain specified (but widely drawn) circumstances on a power to serve the defendant with process outside the jurisdiction. But the potential excesses of common-law jurisdictions are generally curtailed by the adoption of the principle of *forum non conveniens* – a self-denying ordinance under which the court will stay (or dismiss) proceedings in favour of another clearly more appropriate forum.[4]

'Forum shopping' has pejorative overtones.[5] However, it can be explained as simply that the parties have a choice where to bring their dispute. It is only where the case is going ahead in a forum (or venue as the Americans would describe it) which is not anticipated by the parties and to the substantial advantage of one of them that the choice of forum could be said to be unjust. The advantage to one is a disadvantage to the other. Vying for advantage is a very normal part of litigation. However, a party seeking out an unconnected forum merely to gain advantage can be considered an abusive forum shopper. Perhaps the parties could not have anticipated disputes between them being heard in English courts due to a lack of substantial connections with England. As stated by Sopinka J in the powerful Canadian case of *Amchem Products Inc. v British Columbia (Workers' Compensation Board)*:

---

[2] For a notable example, see *Maharanee of Baroda v Wildenstein* [1972] 2 QB 283.
[3] Article 3(2) and Annex 1.   [4] [1999] 1 AC 119 at 132.
[5] Cf. Lord Denning's comment in *McShannon v Rockware Glass (The Atlantic Star)* [1972] QB 364 at 381: 'No one who comes to these courts asking for justice should come in vain ... This right to come here is not confined to Englishmen. It extends to any friendly foreigner. He can seek the aid of our courts if he desires to do so. You may call this "forum shopping" if you please, but if the forum is England, it is a good place to shop in, both for the quality of the goods and the speed of service.' To which Lord Reid replied in the same case in the House of Lords 'My Lords, with all respect, that seems to me to recall the good old days, the passing of which many may regret, when inhabitants of this island felt an innate superiority over those unfortunate enough to belong to other races.' [1974] AC 436 at 453.

The weight to be given to juridical advantage is very much a function of the parties' connection to the particular jurisdiction in question. If a party seeks out a jurisdiction simply to gain a juridical advantage rather than by reason of a real and substantial connection of the case to the jurisdiction, that is ordinarily condemned as 'forum shopping'. On the other hand, a party whose case has a real and substantial connection with a forum has a legitimate claim to the advantages that that forum provides. The legitimacy of this claim is based on a reasonable expectation that in the event of litigation arising out of the transaction in question, those advantages will be available.[6]

Sometimes the parties have articulated where their disputes should be heard in a jurisdiction or arbitration agreement. This is an expression of their expectations and litigation in their chosen court is made fair despite any lack of connection with that court or any advantage to one party or the other.

The English law mostly focuses on the defendant and the defendant's expectations as to where the case should be heard. The claimant's connections are often ignored, partly because the choice is with the claimant who is more likely to choose a court with which the claimant is familiar (and therefore connected). However, the court should be alert to inappropriate proceedings being heard in England. It can be seen to be to the advantage of English lawyers and the UK economy that cases are heard here, but there is a risk of unfairness to defendants. In particular, as English court proceedings are relatively very expensive, there is a real possibility that an unscrupulous claimant might seek an unwarranted advantage by commencing proceedings in England to force a defendant into settlement rather than fight. Too wide a use of the English courts might also be a breach of international norms of appropriate use of adjudicatory jurisdiction.[7] The English courts recognise that service abroad is an incursion into foreign territorial sovereignty[8] but regularly accept jurisdiction in cases in which there is no real connection with England.[9]

The English court has developed a very sophisticated doctrine of *forum conveniens* to decide whether or not to exercise its own jurisdiction. These discretionary rules operate both where the defendant was present to be served and where the court has granted permission to serve out of the jurisdiction. There are some differences between the two strands, such as the burden of proof,

---

[6] (1993) 102 DLR (4th) 96 at 110–11.

[7] There is very little in international law on the proper boundaries of a state's adjudicatory jurisdiction. Concern in the 1970s over the US courts enforcing US legislation on anti-trust and alien torts so-called 'effects-based' jurisdiction seems to have died down.

[8] See e.g., *Cecil v Byat* [2011] EWCA Civ 135, [2011] 1 WLR 3086 at paras 63, 64.

[9] See e.g., *Sharab v Prince Al-Waleed Bin Tala Bin Abdal-Aziz-Al-Saud* [2009] EWCA Civ 353, [2009] 2 Lloyd's LR 160.

but they have now coalesced into one.[10] In practice, and in the reported cases, the dispute about jurisdiction is heard in CPR r. 11 proceedings at which the claimant is arguing that England is the proper forum for trial of the substance of the dispute and the defendant is arguing that another court is more appropriate. At that point the determination of the proper forum for the dispute is most clearly articulated, whether the original jurisdiction was exercised by service on the defendant within or without the territory. The exercise of discretion is subject to principles, which are not often articulated very clearly in the cases. A student of this area of the law has to read many cases to gain an understanding of the way in which the discretion is likely to be exercised in any particular case.

There are distinctions to be drawn between the method of service, the grounds for service and the defendant's challenge to the jurisdiction of the English court. Depending upon the circumstances, a defendant might argue either (1) that service was not properly effected within CPR r. 6; or (2) that the grounds for service in CPR rr. 36 and 37 and PD 6B para. 3 are not available; or (3) that in any event the jurisdiction of the English court should not be exercised against the defendant. A defendant could also argue that the claim is an abuse of process of the English court where the claim is weak.[11] This 'striking out' power is rather rarely used and relates to the abusive nature of the claim rather than the lack of connection between the dispute and England.[12]

b. Service on defendant present within the jurisdiction

Serving the defendant with the claim form initiating an action within the territorial jurisdiction of the English court is known as service 'as of right' for all cases not falling within the Brussels I Regulation. Generally, therefore a defendant domiciled in a Member State (including a defendant domiciled in England) can be served under the rules laid out below but the jurisdiction of the English court is determined by the Brussels I Regulation. By serving the defendant within the territory the claimant places the burden of challenging the exercise of the English jurisdiction onto the defendant. Once properly served, the defendant has to prove that there is another clearly more appropriate forum in which justice can be done in order for proceedings in England to be stayed to await the outcome of those proceedings abroad.[13]

i. Natural persons

The most straightforward method of service of claim form is to leave it with an individual.[14] As we have seen, an individual domiciled in a Member State (including in England) can be served using these rules but the English court's

---

[10] Most recently reasserted in *AK Investment CJSC v Kyrgyz Mobil Tel Ltd* [2011] UKPC 7, [2011] 4 All ER 1027; *Cherney v Deripaska* [2009] EWCA Civ 849, [2009] CLC 408.
[11] CPR r. 3.4.   [12] *Maharanee of Baroda v Wildenstein* [1972] 2 QB 283.   [13] CPR r. 11.
[14] CPR r. 6.5(3)(a).

jurisdiction is dependent upon the Brussels I Regulation.[15] Whether an individual is or is not actually present in the territorial jurisdiction and personally served with the claim form is usually clearcut. Service on an individual present in England would be good service even if the individual defendant were only here for a very short time. So in *Maharanee of Baroda v Wildenstein*:

> The Maharanee wished to sue Wildenstein over the provenance of a painting she had bought from him in Paris. She served the claim form on Wildenstein in the Royal Enclosure at Ascot where he had come to watch the horse-racing. Both parties and the dispute had much stronger connections with France. Nevertheless, Wildenstein had been properly served.[16]

In the past, there have been suggestions that a defendant would not be present if the defendant's presence was fraudulently brought about (say if the defendant was tricked into coming to England by the claimant) or was fortuitous (perhaps in transit at Heathrow). Jurisdiction based on presence within the territory in principle requires a voluntary acceptance of the power of the state. These concerns are now somewhat ameliorated by the possibility of the defendant's challenge to jurisdiction under CPR Part 11 on the grounds that there is another clearly more appropriate forum than England.

The Civil Procedure Rules also permit service by post at the last known address of the individual defendant.[17] The Court of Appeal in *City & Country Properties v Kamali*[18] held that service at the residence of the defendant is good service notwithstanding that the defendant had not been present in the jurisdiction at the time of service.[19] That case is best understood as allowing such service to be good notwithstanding a temporary absence of the defendant. A defendant who had ceased to reside in England and was not present should not be subject to the jurisdiction.[20] As above, the individual defendant is able to challenge the jurisdiction of the court on the basis that there is another clearly more appropriate forum.[21]

ii. Legal persons

Companies and other legal persons do not have a single physical manifestation but are the creatures of law. Law also provides rules to identify their presence. The English rules are somewhat complex. There are two overlapping regimes,

---

[15] So if, for example, the dispute is already being heard in another Member State, the English court will not have jurisdiction (Art 27).

[16] *Maharanee of Baroda v Wildenstein* [1972] 2 QB 283.   [17] CPR r. 6.9(2)1.

[18] [2007] 1 WLR 1219.

[19] Cf. Lawrence Collins J in *Chellaram v Chellaram (No. 2)* [2002] 3 All ER 17, who held that presence is a fundamental part of the rule.

[20] Jurisdiction could be exercised against such a defendant using the service out rules in CPR r. 6.36 and PD 6B subject to the control in r. 6.37 (see p. 147 *et seq.* below on service out).

[21] Using CPR Part 11.

under the Companies Act 2006 and under the CPR r. 6. These are true alternatives, so claimants can take advantage of whichever is more attractive.[22] Note that a company which has its seat[23] in a Member State is domiciled in that Member State and therefore the rules of jurisdiction of the Brussels I Regulation would apply.[24] The rules outlined below simply provide a means for service on such a company within the jurisdiction. For companies without a seat in a Member State, such as a company incorporated in Ruritania, the following rules provide both a means of service and jurisdiction over it. (1) Under the Companies Act 2006, a company incorporated in England can be served at its registered address.[25] A foreign company which establishes a place of business here is required under the Companies Act 2006 to register names and addresses of its officers on which it can be served.[26] The foreign company can then be served by post at the registered address of an officer.[27] The advantage of establishing jurisdiction using the Companies Act 2006 is that the place of service is certain and easily determined. If the foreign company has not registered the claimant may rely on the CPR rules. (2) Under CPR r. 6.5(3)(b) a company incorporated in England can be served by leaving the document with a person holding a senior position[28] in the company. However, a foreign company cannot be served using this method by service on one of its officers merely being present in England.[29] Under CPR r. 6.9, a company incorporated in England[30] can be served at 'the principal office of the corporation or any place within the jurisdiction where the corporation carries on its activities and which has a real connection with the claim'. A foreign company can be served at 'any place within the jurisdiction where the corporation carries on its activities or any place of business of the company within the jurisdiction' (CPR r. 6.9).

A foreign company establishing a place of business in England is therefore equivalent to a natural person's presence here. It is similarly based on a voluntary acceptance of the court's power to adjudicate disputes against the company. There is no statutory definition of establishing a place of business. Companies may carry on their business in England in a number of ways. A company could send an employee out temporarily from their main location

---

[22] CPR r. 6.3(2). In fact, the Overseas Companies Regulations 2009, SI 2009/1801 made consequent to the Companies Act 2000 mirror much more closely the CPR r. 6.9, therefore the old debate as to priority between these regimes (resolved in *Sea Assets Ltd v PT Garuda* [2000] 4 All ER 371 and *Saab v Saudi Bank* [1999] 1 WLR 1861) is now otiose.

[23] Brussels I Regulation, Art. 60.   [24] See Chapter 5.

[25] Companies Act 2006, s. 1139. A company incorporated in England is required to maintain an up-to-date registered office at which it can be served (Companies Act 2006, ss. 86 and 87). The actual address is publicly available via the Companies Registry.

[26] Companies Act 2006, s. 1046, and Overseas Companies Regulations 2009, SI 2009/1801, reg. 7.

[27] Companies Act 2006, s. 1139.

[28] Defined as a director, treasurer, secretary, chief executive, manager or other officer in CPR PD 6A para. 6.2.

[29] *SSL International Plc v TTK LIG Ltd and others* [2011] EWCA Civ 1170, [2012] 1 WLR 1842.

[30] CPR 6.9 uses the words 'a company registered in England and Wales'. These were held to mean a company incorporated in England in *Sea Assets Ltd v PT Garuda* [2000] 4 All ER 371.

to England to make contracts (for example, a sales manager). It might rent local premises and employ local people (a branch office). Alternatively, it could set up a local subsidiary to do business (in which case that subsidiary is a different legal person). It could also enter into a joint venture or partnership with a local person. Lastly, the company could employ a local representative who is a natural or legal person. Only in the branch office case is the company necessarily establishing a place of business. In order to establish a place of business, there must be (1) a fixed and reasonably permanent place,[31] (2) at which the company's business is done,[32] and (3) an agent of the company at that place who can bind the company contractually.[33] If there is no such agent it is difficult to say that it is the company's business which is being conducted from that place. In the old case of *Dunlop Pneumatic Tyre Co. Ltd v Cudell & Co.*:

> The defendant German tyre company had hired a stand at an exhibition at Crystal Palace. It exhibited at the show at a stand for nine days. It had exclusive use of the stand and the name of the company was prominently displayed. During that time two agents of the company took orders and explained the working of the exhibits. The Court of Appeal held that the company had established a place of business in England at the stand such that service on an officer there was good service.[34]

Note that the place of business in that case was rather temporary but still sufficient. Under CPR r. 6.9 the dispute does not necessarily have to have a connection with that place of business.[35] Business does not have to mean actual trade, it can include any activities of the company such as marketing.[36] A subsidiary company may operate as the agent for the holding company principal or may be doing the holding company's business, but generally it is not.[37] An employee who rents premises for the company may establish a place of business for the company. A commercial representative who works

---

[31] It must be a specific location: *Re Oriel Ltd* [1985] 1 WLR 180 (CA). That place must be identifiable as a place at which the foreign company's business is being done. That was proved in *Cleveland Museum of Art v Capricorn* [1990] 2 Lloyd's LR 166, by evidence of drivers who regularly dropped off clients and artworks at the home of one of the directors of company dealing in art.

[32] *Lakah v Al-Jazeera* [2003] EWCA Civ 1287, [2004] BCC 703, which shows that a subsidiary company is not necessarily doing the business of the parent company defendant. Service on the subsidiary was therefore ineffective.

[33] *Rakusens v Baser Ambulaj* [2001] EWCA Civ 1820, [2001] 1 BCLC 104.

[34] [1902] 1 KB 342.

[35] Cf. Brussels I Regulation, Art. 5(5) jurisdiction taken against a branch, office or other establishment (see pp. 94–6 above).

[36] *South India Shipping Corp. v Export-Import Bank of Korea* [1985] 1 WLR 585.

[37] It would if as a matter of fact there is a contract of agency between the companies or the subsidiary can contract for the holding company. In most cases, the holding company will carefully avoid this situation.

exclusively for the foreign company and can bind it to contracts is probably doing the company's business and so the foreign company will have established a place of business. The cases on jurisdiction based on establishing a place of business in England overlap substantially with those on the enforcement of foreign judgments under the national rules[38] in which the establishment of a place of business is also critical.[39] It is arguable that they can be used interchangeably.[40]

c. Service on agent of defendant

Where the claim relates to a contract which was entered into by an agent within the jurisdiction, the foreign principal can be served via that agent so long as the agent still has the authority of the defendant and the court has granted permission.[41] Generally, the court prefers service on the principal overseas using one of the service out gateways discussed below.[42]

d. Submission of defendant

i. Defendant argues merits of case or counterclaims

Once the defendant comes to the English court and argues the case for the defendant on its merits it is too late afterwards to contest the jurisdiction of the court. First, it is unfair for a defendant to put the claimant to the full cost of trial of the dispute only to argue the issue of jurisdiction once the defendant is unsuccessful on the merits. Secondly, there must be an end to litigation. Arguing as to the merits of the case is an implied submission to the court's power. A defendant who voluntarily takes a step in the proceedings has recognised the court's jurisdiction.[43] However, merely challenging the jurisdiction of the English court, using CPR Part 11, is not a submission on the merits despite the possibility that some issue of the substance of the case (such as the breach of the contract) will be raised and adjudicated upon in that challenge. The interlocutory decision on jurisdiction is not binding on the court which will later try the merits of the dispute. Merely acknowledging service of the claim form is not a submission so long as a timely application under CPR Part 11 is made.[44] A defendant submits to the jurisdiction by taking some step 'which is only necessary or only useful if the objection to the

---

[38] I.e., under the common law, not the Brussels I Regulation.

[39] See e.g., *Adams v Cape Industries plc* [1990] Ch. 433.

[40] *Rakusens Limited (a Company) v Baser Ambalaj Plastik Sanayi Ticaret AS* [2001] EWCA Civ 1820, [2002] 1 BCLC 104 at paras 40–41. See further pp. 240–44 below.

[41] CPR r. 6.12.

[42] See in relation to agents CPR PD 6B para. 3.5(b) and see further p. 147 *et seq.* below.

[43] *The Messiniaki Tolmi* [1984] 1 Lloyd's LR 266 per Lord Goff at 270.

[44] CPR r. 11(3) and (5).

jurisdiction has been waived'.[45] So long as the defendant makes it very clear that they are objecting to the jurisdiction, the defendant can ask for a stay of the English proceedings without submitting. However, a defendant who has applied to strike out only part of a claim[46] or served a defence[47] has submitted.

By bringing an action in England the claimant submits for any counterclaim made by a defendant.[48] On the other hand, a defendant who counterclaims in the same or for a related matter in the same proceedings is submitting to the jurisdiction.[49] However, a defendant counterclaiming in a totally unrelated matter may not necessarily be submitting in the first action.[50]

ii. Providing an address for service within the jurisdiction

CPR r. 6.11 permits service in accordance with an agreed method or at a place specified in the contract so long as the claim is solely in respect of that contract. It is commonplace for complex contracts to provide an address for service within England so that a ground for jurisdiction is clearly established and service is easily effected. A defendant can still challenge the jurisdiction utilising CPR Part 11. However, the English courts may treat such an expression of a place for service similarly to a jurisdiction agreement, as by making such a place for service available the parties have agreed that the English courts should have jurisdiction. Instructing a solicitor to accept service for the defendant also provides a means of service.[51]

e. Service on defendant out of the jurisdiction

The English court may take jurisdiction over a defendant who cannot be served within the territorial jurisdiction in cases not falling within the Brussels I Regulation. This jurisdiction is colloquially known as 'service out' jurisdiction. The rules do not have to be used as a means of service in a case subject to the Brussels I Regulation. In those cases the basis of jurisdiction is dependent on the Brussels I Regulation, and CPR r. 6.33 permits service out of the jurisdiction without seeking the permission of the court. The claimant must file a notice with the court along with the claim form that there are no proceedings continuing in another Member State and grounds by which the English court has jurisdiction under the Brussels I Regulation. Therefore, for example, jurisdiction can only be taken in a dispute relating to a contract if

---

[45] *Williams & Glyns Bank v Astro Dinamico* [1984] 1 WLR 438.
[46] *The Messiniaki Tolmi* [1984] 1 Lloyd's LR 266 (CA).
[47] *Sage v Double A Hydraulics Ltd* (Official Transcript, 26 March 1992) (CA) cited in *Ngcobo v Thor Chemicals Holdings Ltd, Times*, 10 October 1995 (CA).
[48] *Derby & Co. v Larsson* [1976] 1 WLR 202.
[49] *Glencore International AG v Metro Trading International Inc. (No. 3)* [2002] CLC 1090.
[50] *India High Commissioner v Ghosh* [1960] 1 QB 134 (CA), where the plaintiff sovereign was not taken to have submitted to the jurisdiction for all counterclaims but only related counterclaims.
[51] CPR r. 6.7(b).

England is the place of performance of the contract under Article 5(1), not if English law is the applicable law which is a gateway at common law discussed below.

Service out is effected under CPR rr. 36 and 37 and PD 6B.[52] Initially, the court's permission must be sought to serve out of the jurisdiction on the defendant. This permission is at first obtained without notice to the defendant. Therefore the court only has the claimant's allegations and arguments. Because of the danger of dragging an unsuspecting defendant to England to challenge jurisdiction, the burden to prove matters is placed on the claimant.[53] Full and frank disclosure must be made of all material facts,[54] even those detrimental to the claimant's case.[55] In outline, the claimant must show that:

(1) there is a serious issue to be tried on the merits of the claim;
(2) that there is an available gateway in CPR PD 6B para. 3[56] to the standard of a good arguable case:[57] and also
(3) that England is the proper place for trial to the standard of a good arguable case.[58]

In addition, any dispute about the interpretation of a gateway should be resolved in the defendant's favour as the defendant is being brought into the jurisdiction.[59] The claimant must limit the claim to the gateway alleged.[60] Therefore, if a claimant is asking the English court to exercise its jurisdiction and hear a case based upon breach of a contract committed within the territory,[61] then the claimant cannot add further and alternative claims in relation to breach of contract outside the territory or claims in tort;[62] or if the claimant had been permitted to serve out of the jurisdiction on the basis of a contract made within the jurisdiction the permission does not extend to a claim for a quantum meruit.[63] If further claims are to be added then a fresh application for service out in respect of those claims must be made.[64] Some of

---

[52] These replace the previous CPR r. 6.20 and the original RSC Order 11.
[53] *Spiliada Maritime Corp. v Cansulex Ltd (The Spiliada)* [1987] AC 460.
[54] *MRG (Japan) Ltd v Englehard Metals Japan Ltd* [2003] EWHC 3418 (Comm), [2004] 1 Lloyd's LR 731.
[55] *ABCI v Banque Franco-Tunisienne* [1996] 1 Lloyd's LR 485 at 489.
[56] Previously known as a 'ground' of jurisdiction under CPR r. 6.20 or as a 'head' of jurisdiction under Order 11 of the previous Rules of the Supreme Court.
[57] As to which see p. 55 above.   [58] CPR r. 6.37.   [59] *The Hagen* [1908] P 189 at 201.
[60] *Bas Capital Funding v Medfinco* [2003] EWHC 1798 (Ch), [2004] ILPr. 16.
[61] CPR PD 6B para. 3.1(7).   [62] Which would fall within CPR PD 6B para. 3.1(9).
[63] *Sharaab v Prince Waleed bin Talal bin Abdul-Aziz Al-Saud* [2012] EWHC 1798 (Ch).
[64] *Parker v Schuller* (1901) 17 TLR 299 (CA); *ED & F Man Sugar Ltd v Lendoudis* [2007] 2 Lloyd's LR 579. Although *Parker v Schuller* was disapproved of *obiter* by the Supreme Court in *NML Capital Ltd v Argentina* [2011] 2 AC 495, Lord Collins appeared to reiterate what is said above, noting (at para 132) 'it is a rule that the court must decide an application for permission to serve out of the jurisdiction on the basis of the cause or causes of action expressly mentioned in the pleadings and the claimant will not be allowed to rely on an alternative cause of action which he seeks to spell out of [*sic*] the facts pleaded if it has not been mentioned'. Cf. *VTB Capital PLC v Nutritek International Corp.* [2011] EWHC 3107 (Ch), in which the parties appeared to

the gateways are wide enough to permit a broad range of claims.[65] A claimant who has used one of these gateways is more likely to be able to bring all the claims through it, or to amend the statement of claim later.

Once permission is obtained and the claim form served upon the defendant abroad, the defendant may seek to have the permission set aside by challenging the jurisdiction of the English court using CPR r. 11. At that point the hearing is between the parties. Nevertheless, the burden remains on the claimant to satisfy the court of the three requirements above.

i. Gateways
1. Defendant domiciled within the jurisdiction
In cases outwith the Brussels I Regulation, the court can grant permission for service of the claim form abroad on a defendant domiciled in England but who is not present within the territory to be served.[66] This is a very wide ground for service out, although the jurisdictional effect is curtailed by the Brussels I Regulation. If the case falls within the Brussels I Regulation, service out of the jurisdiction on an individual or legal person domiciled in England must be made as of right and not through this gateway.[67] Any claim can be brought through this gateway. The defendant's domicile (whether a natural or legal person) is determined according to the rules in the Civil Jurisdiction and Judgments Order 2001.[68]

2. Claim for an injunction ordering the defendant to do or refrain from doing something within the jurisdiction
Under the national rules a claimant may seek the jurisdiction of the English court to claim for an injunction which orders the defendant to do or refrain from doing something in England.[69] This gateway covers a wider ground than that in Article 5(3) of the Brussels I Regulation. Only substantive claims for injunctions can be brought through this gateway.[70] Therefore, it can be used where a claimant is seeking an injunction from the English court to prevent a nuisance in England. It does not cover interim injunctions such as those

---

concede that the rule in *Parker v Schuller* had been overturned by the decision in *NML Capital v Argentina*. However, no new claims were added in that case. The amended claims arose out of the same pleaded facts.

[65] Such as CPR PD 6B 3.1(6)(a) claims in respect of a contract made within the jurisdiction, which would cover all contractual claims not merely for breach of contract.

[66] CPR PD 6B para. 3.1(1).

[67] CPR r. 6.33. However, remember that is not the case if, for example, proceedings are already continuing in another Member State: Brussels I Regulation, Art. 27, see further p. 68 above.

[68] SI 2001/3929, Sched. 1 para. 9 in relation to individuals (see pp. 70–5 above) and para. 10 in relation to corporations.

[69] CPR PD 6B para. 3.1(2).

[70] *Siskina (Owners of Cargo Lately Laden Onboard) v Distos Compania Naviera SA* [1979] AC 210.

restraining a defendant from continuing proceedings abroad[71] or freezing orders[72] which fall within a different gateway.[73]

3. Claims against necessary and proper parties and third parties

The gateway allows a claimant who has made a claim against a defendant who has been or will be served (otherwise than in reliance on this gateway) to serve another party who is a necessary and proper party to the claim, so long as there is a real issue which is reasonable for the court to try between the claimant and the first defendant (known as the anchor defendant).[74] A claimant may often wish to bring proceedings in one court against several parties in order to obtain judgment against one or all of them. This is common in commercial cases with many parties to a contract, or a claim against a manufacturer and a seller of defective goods, or against the shipper, ship-owner and charterer in the case of goods found to be damaged on arrival. A single set of proceedings leading to one judgment on all the issues has obvious advantages of efficiency and convenience. Within the Brussels I Regulation, this could be achieved using the basis for jurisdiction in Article 6. However, the gateway at common law is extraordinarily wide as it does not require any connection between the parties, in particular the defendant to be joined, and England. It is open to abuse and its use must be subject to careful scrutiny.[75] A claimant might find a weak case against a nominal anchor defendant in order to drag the real defendants into proceedings in England.

This gateway can be illustrated by *AK Investment CJSC v Kyrgyz Mobil Tel Ltd*[76] before the Privy Council on appeal from the Isle of Man:

> This was a very complex dispute between two Russian groups concerning a telecommunications business in Kyrgyzstan. One of the parties attempted to enforce a Kyrgyz judgment in the Isle of Man and the judgment debtor sought to counterclaim in that proceeding. The judgment debtor wanted to join additional defendants to the counterclaim who were incorporated in other jurisdictions such as the British Virgin Islands and Russia. Permission to serve out was granted against the defendants. There were no connections with the Isle of Man except that the judgment debtor was incorporated there.

Lord Collins gave the opinion of the Privy Council asking a series of questions. First, had an action been or would it be 'properly brought' against an 'anchor defendant' in the jurisdiction? A claimant may still get permission

---

[71] Also known as anti-suit injunctions.
[72] Also known as *Mareva* injunctions after the initial case of *Mareva Cia Naviera SA v International Bulk Carriers SA* [1980] 1 All ER 213 (CA).
[73] CPR PD 6B para. 3.1(5).   [74] CPR PD 6B para. 3.1(3).
[75] *The Brabo* [1949] AC 326 at 338.   [76] [2011] UKPC 7.

to serve out on any defendant to be joined even if the motive of the claimant in suing the anchor defendant is merely to bring the defendant to be joined into the jurisdiction. If there is no serious issue to be tried in the action against the anchor defendant (or it is bound to fail)[77] then the 'necessary or proper party' ground of jurisdiction is not available against the defendant to be joined. However, so long as there is a good arguable case against the anchor defendant, the claimant's motive is merely a factor in the exercise of the discretion to serve out. Secondly, is the defendant to be joined a 'necessary or proper party' to that action? This is answered if there is a serious issue to be tried against that defendant. Thirdly, a connection between the anchor defendant and the defendant to be joined is necessary to make the latter a 'proper party'. The necessary connection is established if there is 'one investigation' against both defendants or the claims are 'closely bound up' with one another. In the event, permission was granted to serve out because there was no expectation that the case would be heard in Kyrgyzstan.[78]

Third parties, such as those who might be called upon to contribute or indemnify the defendant, can be joined to a dispute in England using CPR Part 20 which also covers counterclaims by the defendant. It is possible to obtain jurisdiction over third parties who are out of the territorial jurisdiction so long as the third party is a necessary and proper party (in the sense outlined above).[79]

4. Claims for interim remedies

Civil Jurisdiction and Judgments Act (CJJA) 1982, s. 25 gives the English court powers to make interim remedies in support of substantive proceedings on the merits of the dispute abroad. These are commonly freezing orders,[80] restraining orders[81] and orders for disclosure of evidence.[82] The House of Lords in *The Siskina*[83] and the Privy Council in *Mercedes Benz AG v Leiduck*[84] had held that there was no power in the English court to permit service out of the jurisdiction for these orders where there were no substantive proceedings in England. The effect of these decisions was reversed by CJJA 1982, s. 25(3) for proceedings both in Member States and, later, in third states.[85] However, in principle the claimant must still show that England is the proper place for trial.[86] This might be satisfied if there are assets in England[87] or an English

---

[77] The case against the anchor defendant was bound to fail in *Multinational Gas v Multinational Gas Services* [1983] Ch. 258 (CA).
[78] See p. 179 below.   [79] CPR PD 6B para. 3.1(4).
[80] Otherwise known as *Mareva* injunctions, see p. 207 *et seq.* below.
[81] Also known as anti-suit injunctions, see p. 194 *et seq.* below.
[82] *Anton Piller* orders, *Norwich Pharmacal* orders, and the like.
[83] *The Siskina v Distos Compania Naviera* [1979] AC 210.   [84] [1996] AC 284.
[85] I.e., not Member States of the EU.   [86] CPR r. 6.37.
[87] See the discussion below on *Credit Suisse* and *Refco*.

jurisdiction or arbitration agreement to be upheld.[88] The court may refuse to grant a freezing order if it is inexpedient to grant it due to the lack of jurisdiction over the substance of the case.[89] The English court should not be 'the policeman of the world'[90] and its interim remedies should not be available without a sufficient connection with England, either by having territorial jurisdiction or some interest to protect. Article 31 provides a similar ground of jurisdiction within the Brussels I Regulation.[91]

5. Claims over contracts

There are six ways[92] in which claims over a contract can be brought in England using the service out rules. These are much broader than the equivalent rules in Article 5(1) of the Brussels I Regulation. As with any of the gateways the claimant must show that the claimant has a good arguable case that the dispute falls within this ground of jurisdiction. Unlike some of the other gateways, this one may raise questions of the substance of the dispute in order to determine jurisdiction. So, if the claim is in respect of a breach of contract committed within the jurisdiction, the claimant must show that there is a contract, which has been breached, and that the breach was committed within the jurisdiction. All of these must be shown to the standard of the good arguable case.[93] If, on the other hand, the claimant is relying on the gateway that the contract was made within the jurisdiction, all that has to be shown is that there was a contract which was made here to the level of the good arguable case.[94] The actual merits of the dispute, such as whether there was a breach of that contract, only have to be shown to the lower standard of a serious issue to be tried. As we have seen,[95] that is not a particularly high standard.

Four of these gateways cover claims 'in respect of' a contract. They are not necessarily limited to claims arising from the terms of the contract itself. For example, they can be relied upon by an assignee of the contract suing for breach of it.[96] Claims in frustration[97] and declarations of no liability for breach of contract also come within this gateway.[98] However, a claim in the

---

[88] See the discussion below on restraining orders. Note that a jurisdiction agreement alone does not give service as of right, it should also include an address for service within the jurisdiction.

[89] *Credit Suisse Fides Trust SA v Cuoghi* [1998] QB 818 (CA).

[90] *Airbus Industrie GIE v Patel* [1999] 1 AC 119 at 131.

[91] See further Chapter 6.

[92] The sixth contractual gateway, where the contract contains a jurisdiction agreement, is discussed further p. 178 *et seq.* below.

[93] *Seaconsar Far East Ltd v Bank Markazi Jomhouri Islami Iran* [1994] AC 438.

[94] For examples of cases showing how wide this gateway can be see *Cherney v Deripaska* [2009] EWCA Civ 849, [2009] CLC 408 and *Sharab v Prince Al-Waleed Bin Tala Bin Abdal-Aziz-Al-Saud* [2009] EWCA Civ 353, [2009] 2 Lloyd's LR 160.

[95] See p. 55 above.

[96] *DR Insurance Co. v Central National Insurance Co. of Omaha* [1996] 1 Lloyd's LR 74.

[97] *BP Exploration Co. (Libya) Ltd v Hunt* [1976] 1 WLR 788.

[98] *Hogg Insurance Brokers Ltd v Guardian Insurance Co. Inc.* [1997] 1 Lloyd's LR 412.

alternative for a quantum meruit does not fall within the gateway.[99] It is not enough that the contract relied upon for jurisdiction merely forms part of the background matrix, the claim must relate directly to that contract. Related contracts, such as guarantees and reinsurance contracts can raise difficulties. In *Global 5000 Ltd v Wadhawan*:

> The claimant brought an action on a guarantee and needed to serve the claim form out of the jurisdiction. The guarantee did not contain an express choice of English law but the contract which contained the obligations which were to be guaranteed did have that express choice. The claimant therefore wanted to rely on the gateway that its claim was in respect of the contract governed by English law, even though its actual claim was based on the separate contract of guarantee. A further difficulty arose because it was not clear that the claim on the contract of guarantee could be proved to the standard of the good arguable case and in the event it failed even to satisfy the lower standard of the serious issue to be tried.[100]

After considering the extensive previous case law, Rix LJ in the Court of Appeal gave his opinion on the question whether such a claim could be 'in respect of a contract'. He concluded that a claim could only be in respect of a contract if it was sufficiently legally connected to the contract. In a 'one contract' case, this was relatively straightforward. So long as the claim was connected to the contract, it did not matter that the claim as pleaded was not framed in contract. However, in a case such as this where there were two contracts, the claimant had to rely on the contract in relation to which the claim was raised as the gateway for jurisdiction. He noted 'the need for the clear establishment, to the standard of a good arguable case, of the necessary link between the defendant to be brought to face trial in England and this jurisdiction'. Such a necessary link can be found where the claim is closely related to a contract which complies with the requirements of the gateway.[101] Note that the exercise of jurisdiction remains discretionary so that mere fulfilment of those requirements does not necessarily mean that the English court will hear the case. The exercise of discretion will take into account how closely related are the claim and contract.

---

[99] *Sharaab v Prince Waleed bin Talal bin Abdul-Aziz Al-Saud* [2009] EWCA Civ 353, [2009] 2 Lloyd's LR 160.

[100] [2012] EWCA Civ 13, [2012] 1 Lloyd's LR 239.

[101] *Ibid.* para. 64. See too *Cecil v Byat* [2010] EWHC 641; point not taken on appeal [2011] EWCA Civ 135 (a two contract case, no jurisdiction over person not party to the contract used for the gateway); *Albon v Naza Motor Trading Sdn Bhd* [2007] 1 WLR 2489 (a restitutionary claim under an agency contract was in respect of the contract); *Green Wood & McLean LLP v Templeton Insurance* [2009] 1 WLR 2013 (a one contract case in which a claim for contribution by an insurer to claims paid out under a contract between the insurer and the payees was in respect of the contract even if the claimants were not party to it).

The court may grant permission to serve on a defendant out of the jurisdiction if the claimant makes a claim:

(a) in relation to a contract 'made within the jurisdiction'.[102]

A claimant wishing to utilise this gateway must show to the level of a good arguable case that the contract was concluded in England. There are English domestic rules of contract determining where a contract is made which in principle apply to determine where a contract is made for the purpose of jurisdiction.[103] As jurisdiction is a question for the *lex fori* the domestic rules of law are applied. Therefore, a contract made by letter is made where the acceptance of the offer is posted, a contract made by telephone or telex is made where the notice of acceptance is received, but there is as yet no direct case law on where a contract made by email or the Internet is made. In *Chunilal v Merrill Lynch International Inc.*, Burton J accepted that the case law[104] all agreed that contracts entered into by instantaneous communication were made when and where the acceptance is received.[105] There is one case which assumes that a contract governed by a foreign law is made in the place determined according to those foreign rules.[106] However, there is no explanation for this assumption and it could be considered *per incuriam*.

It does not matter if the contract is made in several places so long as the contract has been substantially made here.[107] In an age where travel and communications were difficult, the place where a contract was made was clearly a very important factor. It was not a fortuitous or haphazard place, as contracting parties would have to make an effort to consider where to meet and contract. There would have been a connection with England and also the parties would have expected that the English court should exercise its adjudicatory power over them and the contract. It is much more difficult to justify the English court exercising its adjudicatory power based on this gateway in the modern era. A contract may be concluded here for no better reason than that Heathrow is a hub for the travelling businessman or where he opened his laptop to send an email. This is therefore a rather wide gateway of jurisdiction. The courts should be alert to abuse where a contract has been made rather fortuitously in England, where there may be very little connection between the dispute and England.[108] The parties to such a contract could not have expected

---

[102] CPR PD 6B para. 3.1(6)(a).
[103] *Entores v Miles Far East Corp.* [1955] 2 QB 327 (CA).
[104] Both English and Commonwealth cases had been cited to him.
[105] [2010] EWHC 1467 (Comm) at para. 8.
[106] *Marconi v PT Pan Indonesia Bank Ltd TBK* [2005] EWCA Civ 422, [2005] 2 All ER (Comm) 325, [2007] 2 Lloyd's LR 72.
[107] *Apple Corp. Ltd v Apple Computer Inc.* [2004] EWHC 768 (Ch), [1004] ILPr. 34, for example, if several counterparts are signed in different countries.
[108] For somewhat egregious examples of the use of this gateway see *Sharab v Prince Al-Waleed Bin Tala Bin Abdal-Aziz-Al-Saud* [2009] EWCA Civ 353, [2009] 2 Lloyd's LR 160 and *Cherney v Deripaska* [2009] EWCA Civ 849, [2009] CLC 408.

that any dispute arising on it should be heard in England. The lack of real connection should be taken into account in deciding upon the exercise of the court's discretion.[109]

(b) in relation to a contract which was 'made by or through an agent trading or residing in the jurisdiction'.[110]

A claim on a contract concluded by an agent in England for a principal outside the territory could be served either on the agent (under CPR r. 6.12) in some circumstances[111] or on the principal abroad through this gateway. The permission of the court is required in both cases, but the claimant here must also show that England is the proper place for trial. This gateway can be quite wide, as in *National Mortgage and Agency Co. of New Zealand Ltd v Gosselin*,[112] where the principal was served abroad notwithstanding that the agent had no authority to conclude contracts. Nevertheless, the contract was made through the agent who had obtained the order and sent information to the claimant. As with the previous gateway, the court should be careful to avoid taking jurisdiction over a dispute where there is very little connection with England merely because the agent happens to be found within the jurisdiction. Any excess of jurisdiction should be dealt with by the discretionary exercise of jurisdiction.[113]

(c) in relation to a contract which is 'governed by English law'.[114]

Unlike the Brussels I Regulation, a dispute which is in respect of a contract merely governed by English law can come within this gateway. A contract is commonly in practice explicitly governed by English law. However, the gateway is also available when the contract is only governed by English law as a result of English choice of law rules in the absence of an express choice of English law.[115] In modern choice of law parlance English law must be the applicable law of the contract. A determination of the applicable law of the contract can involve a long and extensive hearing and appeals.[116] The court at the interlocutory hearing on jurisdiction has to make a decision on an issue which might be critical to resolving the dispute on its substance. The claimant must therefore show that the contract is governed by English law only to the level of a good arguable case.[117] Sometimes, the court considers it has sufficient uncontested evidence to be able to determine the matter of the applicable law.[118]

---

[109] CPR r. 3.37.   [110] CPR PD 6B para. 3.1(6)(b).   [111] See p. 146 above.
[112] (1922) 38 TLR 832 (CA).   [113] CPR r. 3.37.   [114] CPR PD 6B para. 3.1(6)(c).
[115] *Bank of Baroda v Vysya Bank Ltd* [1994] 2 Lloyd's LR 87. As to the detailed choice of law rules, see further Chapter 10. For contracts entered into after 17 December 2009, these are found in the Rome I Regulation (Regulation (EC) 593/2008 on the choice of law in contractual matters [2008] OJ L1776/9).
[116] See e.g., *Amin Rasheed Shipping Corp. v Kuwait Insurance Co.* [1984] AC 50 and more recently *Cherney v Deripaska* [2009] EWCA Civ 849, [2009] CLC 408.
[117] See further p. 55 above.   [118] *The Elli 2* [1985] 1 Lloyd's LR 107 at 114.

On other occasions it does not and accepts that its decision as to the applicable law may be decided differently at trial on the substance.[119] As we shall see, the fact that a contract is governed by English law can be an important factor in the exercise of the court's discretion such that the case will be heard in England. It might be argued to be quite unsatisfactory that the English court takes jurisdiction where the applicable law of the contract is disputed. There may have to be a lengthy hearing and ultimately an indeterminate decision. That is a waste of resources when in the end at the hearing on the substance the court decides that it was wrong at the interlocutory stage. The gateway is open to abuse. A claimant can make a weak case that English law should apply to a contract to force a defendant into an unwarranted settlement rather than have to fight even this issue (let alone the subject matter of the dispute) before a court with very little connection with the facts and the parties. Therefore this writer argues that this gateway should be restricted to an express choice of English law. In such a case the parties have at least made some intentional choice of a connection with England. Where there has been no such express choice, the connection with England and the parties' expectations of the English court's adjudication are possibly weak. Indirectly, the choice of law rules in the Rome I Regulation would make English law the applicable law if there is a 'close connection' with England.[120] That may satisfy the first element of connection but not that of the parties' expectations. As with the previous gateways, the discretionary exercise of jurisdiction should take the lack of connection into account.[121]

(d) in relation to a contract 'containing a term to the effect that the court shall have jurisdiction to determine any claim in respect of the contract'.[122]

This gateway raises very specific rules. The parties have clearly indicated in advance of the case that they wish their dispute to be resolved in the English courts. The exercise of the court's adjudicatory power is therefore proper. The jurisdiction agreement both provides a strong connection with England and evidence of the parties' intentions and expectations. It will be discussed further below.[123]

(e) in respect of a 'breach of contract committed within the jurisdiction'.[124]

This gateway has its analogy in Article 5(1) of the Brussels I Regulation. If a contract has been breached within the jurisdiction, there is very likely to be a connection with England which justifies the exercise of the court's adjudicatory power. Certainly the factual evidence of the performance, of the breach of

---

[119] *Cherney v Deripaska* [2009] EWCA Civ 849, [2009] CLC 408 at para. 67.
[120] This is the exceptional rule, the general rules may have less connection with England, see further p. 307 *et seq.* below.
[121] CPR r. 6.37.   [122] CPR PD 6B para. 3.1(6)(d).   [123] See p. 178 *et seq.* below.
[124] CPR PD 6B para. 3.1(7).

the contract and probably also of the damage suffered by the breach, is quite likely to be located in England. Also the parties should have expected the English court to have an interest in a dispute arising out of the non-performance of a contract in England. To come within this gateway the claimant must show to the level of a good arguable case that there was a contract, that there was a breach and that the breach took place in England. These are also matters to be decided at trial of the substance of the dispute and the court should be careful not to give the impression of pre-trying the issues.[125] Where the contract was to be performed partly in England and partly abroad, a claimant can use this gateway so long as it was the part to be performed in England that forms the basis of the dispute.[126] It is important that England is the place of performance of the contract, not merely a possible place for performance.[127] If the contract states that performance is to be in England, that is sufficient. It is more difficult if no express place of perform-ance is given. This could be resolved by an application of English domestic contract law rules, because procedure is a matter for the *lex fori*. There are cases which appear to follow this in which the court has attempted to divine the intention of the parties from the surrounding circumstances,[128] or fallen back on the English rule that a debtor should seek out his creditor.[129] Alternatively, by analogy with Article 5(1)(a) of the Brussels I Regulation, it could be argued that the place of performance of the contract should be identified by the applicable law of the contract where there is no place of performance expressed in it.[130] This would be inconsistent with what has been done in relation to the first gateway above.[131]

(f) for a declaration 'that no contract exists where, if the contract was found to exist, it would comply with the conditions set out above (a)–(d)'.[132]

This gateway permits a claimant to bring a claim in England for a declaration that the alleged contract is invalid.[133] This permits a party who would other-wise have to wait for a claim to be brought to pre-empt and commence proceedings in England. The claimant must show to the level of a good arguable case that were the contract to have existed it would have been made in England, been made by an agent in England, been governed by English law or contained an English jurisdiction agreement.

---

[125] *Canada Trust Co. v Stolzenberg (No. 2)* [2002] 1 AC 1 at 13.
[126] *Rein v Stein* [1892] 1 QB 753 (CA).   [127] *Comber v Leyland* [1898] AC 524.
[128] For example, *Rein v Stein* [1892] 1 QB 753.   [129] *The Eider* [1893] P 119 (CA).
[130] See *Vitkovice Horner A Huntni Tezirstvo v Korner* [1951] AC 869 to determine the place for payment. See too R. Fentiman, *International Commercial Litigation* (Oxford University Press, 2010) para. 9.62.
[131] CPR PD 6B para. 3.1(6)(a).   [132] *Ibid.* para. 3.1(8).
[133] Reversing the effect of *Finnish Marine Insurance Co. v Protective National Insurance Co.* [1990] 1 QB 1078.

6. Claims in tort

CPR PD 6B para. 3.1(9) permits a claimant to bring a case in England where the claim is made in tort and the damage was sustained in England or the damage resulted from an act committed in England. This gateway is analogous to Article 5(3) of the Brussels I Regulation and provides an obvious connection with England to justify the court's exercise of its adjudicatory power. The parties can clearly have expected that the action and the consequences of acting can be decided in either the place where the damage was sustained or where the act took place. The courts in those places are also well positioned to deal with factual matters. In addition, when it comes to trial of the substantial dispute the law applicable to the tort will often be the law of one of those places.[134] The alternative between the place of acting and the place where the damage was sustained appears to expand the gateway to encompass more international torts. However, in order to come within this gateway the claimant must show that there is a tort. The claimant should have to show that the defendant is liable in damages for some tortious act and that the claimant has suffered loss. There may be several, slightly different, problems. First the classification of the claim for jurisdictional purposes. What is the relevance of the applicable law? Conduct which gives rise to a tort in English *or* foreign law should come within this gateway but that has not always been clear in the past. It would be too chauvinistic and unfair if only conduct which is classified as giving rise to a claim in tort in English domestic law can come within this gateway. The difficulty is that, unlike in contract, the definitions of wrongful conduct vary in different legal systems.[135] Some of the less than completely recent cases may not be entirely relevant. The wording of the gateway has widened and also the applicable law rules have changed significantly. Secondly, at this interlocutory stage, how much must the claimant prove to show that there has been a tort committed? The following can be said.

(1) If the conduct and damage are classified as tortious under English law, the claimant can use this gateway, even if the applicable law is not English law so long as the claimant can show to the level of a good arguable case that there is liability under that foreign applicable law.[136]

(2) Where the conduct is not classified as tortious in England but does give rise to tortious liability under an applicable foreign law the exercise of jurisdiction is more problematic.[137] (a) The liability may be classified under some other wrongful conduct characterisation in England. The gateway does not

---

[134] As to the rules determining the applicable law of a tort, see further Chapter 11 on the Rome II Regulation (Regulation (EC) 864/2007 on the law applicable to non-contractual obligations).

[135] For example, infringement of intellectual property rights, protection of privacy, undue influence on a contract, breach of trust may or may not be classified as torts.

[136] *Metall und Rohstoff AG v Donaldson, Lufkin & Jenrette Inc.* [1990] 1 QB 391 (CA).

[137] Such as a breach of privacy under Ruritanian law, which currently does not provide an action in England. Where the conduct occurred in England, but the damage was sustained in Ruritania, this gateway may not be available.

cover claims brought using English concepts of restitution[138] or breach of trust[139] which come within different jurisdictional gateways.[140] Arguably other claims for wrongs should now be covered by some gateway, if not this one. There is no specific gateway for infringement of intellectual property or for breach of confidence, for example. (b) In the alternative, the conduct may not be classified as wrongful under English law but the conduct may give rise to tortious liability under the foreign applicable law. The claimant has possibly insurmountable difficulties. In principle, if the claimant has a claim under the applicable foreign law classified by that law as tortious, the English court should hear the claim using this gateway, but only so long as England is the proper place for trial and there is a good arguable case that there is a tort under the foreign applicable law. This might be quite difficult to show. In any event, in the case where no liability is likely under the applicable law (whether English or foreign) the English court should not take jurisdiction as there is no legal basis for making the defendant liable.[141]

(3) A different concern arises if there is a dispute about the applicable law and the likelihood of liability or damage. How should the court resolve these questions at this interlocutory stage? It is not clear whether these are matters which go to the substance of the dispute and therefore only have to be shown to the level of a serious issue to be tried, or if alternatively they are matters of jurisdiction which have to be shown to the level of a good arguable case. The latter interpretation is probably the correct one. The gateway is analogous to that of breach of contract within the jurisdiction and therefore should be subject to the same level of proof at this stage. Neither all the damage nor all the events have to happen within the jurisdiction. It is enough that significant damage occurs here or results from substantial and efficacious acts done here, even if substantial and efficacious acts are done outside the territory.[142] The courts should look to the case law on Article 5(3) of the Brussels I Regulation in order to decide where the damage was sustained or where the acts were committed, as the altered wording of this gateway reflects that Article. Claims are limited to direct damage or loss suffered in England.[143] However, the claimant can still frame the claim carefully to obtain jurisdiction in England. For example, in *Cooley v Ramsay*,[144] the court was prepared to accept that damage was suffered here in a claim by a man injured in a road

---

[138] *ISC Technologies Ltd v Guerin* [1991] 2 Lloyd's LR 430.
[139] *Metall und Rohstoff AG v Donaldson, Lufkin & Jenrette Inc.* [1990] 1 QB 391 (CA). However a claim in negligence against the trustees is within this gateway: *Langlands v SG Hambros Trust Co. (Jersey) Ltd* [2007] EWHC 627 (Ch).
[140] See p. 161 *et seq.* below.
[141] *OT Africa Line Ltd v Magic Sportswear Corp.* [2004] EWHC 2441 (Comm), [2005] 1 Lloyd's LR 252, point not taken on appeal.
[142] *Metall und Rohstoff AG v Donaldson, Lufkin & Jenrette Inc.* [1990] 1 QB 391 at 437 (CA).
[143] *ABCI v Banque Franco Tunisienne* [2003] EWCA Civ 205, [2003] 2 Lloyd's LR 146 at para. 44.
[144] [2008] EWHC 129.

accident in Australia. The claim had been drafted to cover increased expenditure on adapting a home here. Although not inconsistent with some of the Article 5(3) cases, this case is at the outer limit of the rule. Many of the cases concern libel[145] and the Internet. If the claimant has a reputation in England and the libel is published in England by download here the claimant can use this gateway (irrespective of wherever the server or upload may be found).[146] It is important to remember that the court must be satisfied that England is the proper place for trial. In cases where there is no significant reputation to protect in England, or very little publication in England, or where the applicable law is a foreign law, it is quite likely that England is not the proper place for trial of the tort.[147]

7. Enforcement

Permission of the court to grant service of the claim form out of the jurisdiction can be given for a claim which is made 'to enforce any judgment or arbitral award'.[148] The foreign judgment or arbitral award forms the basis of the claim.[149] The claimant must show (a) that there is a good arguable case the judgment will be recognised and enforced in England, and (b) that the claimant is likely to obtain a benefit from enforcing the foreign judgment (which does not mean that assets have to be available in England).[150]

8. Property

This gateway allows the service out of a claim form where 'the whole subject matter of a claim relates to property located within the jurisdiction'.[151] This is quite a wide gateway as it covers not just claims such as ownership but also, for example, transfers of property or even damages for breach of contract relating to property.[152] It covers all types of property, immovable,[153] tangible and intangible. Note that this gateway provides *in personam* not *in rem* jurisdiction. Clearly if the claim relates to real property in England (land or leases on land), there is no difficulty in identifying whether the property is in England.[154] Similarly, tangible property is easily located at any particular time.

---

[145] For example, *Berezovsky v Forbes Inc.* [2000] 1 WLR 1004 (SC); *King v Lewis* [2005] ILPr. 16; *Dow Jones Inc. v Jameel* [2005] EWCA Civ 75, [2005] QB 946.

[146] *Dow Jones Inc. v Jameel* [2005] EWCA Civ 75, [2005] QB 946 at paras 48–9.

[147] *Berezovsky v Forbes Inc.* [2000] 1 WLR 1004 (SC). And see further p. 167 below.

[148] CPR PD 6B para. 3.1(10).

[149] A party is now prevented from bringing a wholly new action on the events giving rise to the cause of action (Civil Jurisdiction and Judgments Act 1982, s. 34).

[150] *Demirel v Tasarruff* [2007] EWCA Civ 799, [2007] 1 WLR 2058 at paras 10–25.

[151] CPR PD 6B para. 3.1(11).

[152] *Re Banco Nacional de Cuba* [2001] 1 WLR 2039 and J. Fawcett and J. Carruthers, *Cheshire, North and Fawcett Private International Law* (14th edn, Oxford University Press, 2008) p. 392.

[153] Real property in a domestic law sense.

[154] Indeed, the English courts are probably the only courts with jurisdiction over the dispute.

Intangible property, such as confidential information,[155] a debt, or shares,[156] is much less easily provided with a location.[157] As usual in service out cases, the English court must be the proper place for trial. This is self-evidently so in cases regarding ownership of land in England but less so if the case concerns a breach of a contract of sale of shares in a company incorporated here but which has all other connections with another country.[158]

9. Trusts and restitution

There are several gateways in relation to claims about trusts. Permission to serve the claim form out of the jurisdiction may be obtained if the claim is for a remedy to execute a written trust where 'the trusts ought to be executed according to English law; and the person on whom the claim form is to be served is a trustee of the trusts'.[159] Permission can also be given if the claim is for a remedy 'in proceedings for the administration of the estate of a person who died domiciled within the jurisdiction'[160] or a claim in probate or a claim for rectification of a will.[161] So too can permission be obtained if the claim is for 'a remedy against the defendant as constructive trustee where the defendant's alleged liability arises out of acts committed within the jurisdiction'.[162] The domestic concept of constructive trust is quite wide, covering fraudulent breach of trust, equitable proprietary claims and also imposition of liability for dishonest assistance and knowing receipt of trust property. The recovery of bribes also comes within this gateway.[163] It is possible that not all the acts have to be committed within the jurisdiction[164] so long as substantial and efficacious acts have been committed here.[165] Finally, the English court can grant permission to serve the claim form out of the jurisdiction where the claim is made 'for restitution where the defendant's alleged liability arises out of acts committed within the jurisdiction'.[166] This gateway appears to cover not merely claims in restitution but any claim for restitution, whatever the cause of action. Therefore an equitable proprietary claim also comes within this gateway.[167] So too does a breach of confidence.[168] It is probably the case, as with torts and constructive trusts, that substantial and efficacious acts were

---

[155] *Ashton Investments Ltd v OJSC Russian Aluminium RUSAL* [2006] EWHC 2545 (Comm), [2007] 1 Lloyd's LR 311.

[156] *Walanpatrias Stiftung v Lehman Brothers International (Europe)* [2006] EWHC 3034 (Comm).

[157] See further p. 398 *et seq.* below.   [158] *Re Banco Nacional de Cuba* [2001] 1 WLR 2039.

[159] CPR PD 6B para. 3.1(12).   [160] *Ibid.* para. 3.1(13).   [161] *Ibid.* para. 3.1(14).

[162] *Ibid.* para. 3.1(15).

[163] *Republic of Pakistan v Zardari* [2007] EWCA Civ 134, [2006] 2 CLC 667.

[164] *ISC v Guerin* [1992] 2 Lloyd's LR 430.

[165] *Metall und Rohstoff AG v Donaldson, Lufkin and Jenrette Inc.* [1990] 1 QB 391.

[166] CPR PD 6B para. 3.1(16).

[167] *NABB Brothers Ltd v Lloyds Bank International (Guernsey) Ltd* [2005] EWHC 405 (Ch), [2005] ILPr. 37.

[168] *Douglas v Hello! Ltd (No. 2)* [2003] EWCA Civ 139 at para. 36.

done in England even if other acts were done abroad. Additionally, of course, the claimant has to show that England is the proper place for trial.

ii. Procedure

As we have seen, the claimant must first seek the permission of the court to serve the defendant out of the jurisdiction and there are various requirements placed upon the claimant to ensure that the defendant is not unnecessarily dragged to England.[169] The claimant must make an application for permission supported by written evidence (a) of the gateway relied upon, (b) of the reasonable prospect of success of the claim and (c) of the defendant's address.[170] In addition, and importantly, the court will not give its permission unless England is the proper place for trial of the claim. In practice, permission is readily granted, but by placing an onus on the claimant, the rules probably weed out potentially improperly brought cases before permission is sought. Once served, the defendant may either submit to the jurisdiction and the case continues to trial of the substance of the dispute; alternatively, the defendant may challenge the jurisdiction of the English court using CPR Part 11. At this point there is a hearing at which both parties will make argument and allege facts before the court makes a determination of its jurisdiction. In these cases of service out, the onus is on the claimant. This is a discretionary exercise and the decisions in the cases, particularly at first instance, are very dependent upon their facts. However, the exercise of discretion must be subject to principles. The court has to strike a balance between the choice of the English court by the claimant and the defendant's preference for another court.

In *AK Investments v Kyrgyz Mobil Tel Ltd.*[171] Lord Collins laid down the general principles governing service out of the jurisdiction. He held that the claimant had to satisfy the three requirements (1) 'that there is a serious issue to be tried on the merits, i.e. a substantial question of fact or law, or both'; (2) 'the claimant must satisfy the court that there is a good arguable case that the claim falls within one or more classes of case in which permission to serve out may be given'; and (3) 'the claimant must satisfy the court that in all the circumstances England is clearly or distinctly the appropriate forum for the trial of the dispute, and that in all the circumstances the court ought to exercise its discretion to permit service of the proceedings out of the jurisdiction'. This means that the court has to identify the forum in which the case can be suitably tried for the interests of all the parties and for the ends of justice. In service out cases the burden is on the claimant to persuade the court that England is clearly the appropriate forum. Difficulties may arise when there is a question of law or fact which has to be determined in order to decide upon the court's jurisdiction which at the same time may be a crucial matter in the substance of the dispute. The decision on jurisdiction is taken at an

---

[169] See p. 147 *et seq.* above.   [170] CPR r. 3.37(1).   [171] [2011] UKPC 7.

interlocutory stage before full disclosure of the evidence. On the one hand, the court is anxious not to pre-try the matter before a full trial.[172] On the other, the question of venue for the ventilation of the dispute might be the only real issue between the parties and is therefore to be decided carefully. The court is also keen to ensure that the costs of and time taken for interlocutory hearings are minimised. Therefore, evidence is not examined orally and experts are rarely to be used. The decision must be taken in 'hours not days'.[173] The trial judge's decision should only rarely be upset.[174] Nor should lengthy case law be cited to the judge. On the other hand, if the question is one of law which only goes to the existence of jurisdiction, the court will normally want to decide it, rather than treating it as a question of whether there is a good arguable case.[175] This may require much more extensive argument and a careful assessment of what evidence there may be.

iii. Possible alternative claims

A claimant may have overlapping claims or alternative claims in, for example, contract and tort or in restitution and contract. The claimant in principle can elect to sue on whatever classification of claim is most beneficial.[176] A claimant can also sue in the alternative or additionally for every claim. However, permission should only be given for each claim to be pursued in the English courts which satisfies the requirements of the jurisdictional gateway relied upon, that there is a serious issue to be tried and that England is the proper place for trial. Those rules must also be applied stringently to any later amendment of the claim form to include other claims falling within a different gateway.

iv. Effecting service abroad

It is much easier to effect service in England using CPR r. 3 than to effect service abroad. Not only does a claimant have to obtain the court's prior permission to serve the claim form out of the jurisdiction, but a claimant must also follow the various foreign procedures for local service of the English claim form. Within the EU, the claimant must use the Service Regulation[177] and the defendant cannot be served by an alternative method such as by service on an

---

[172] *Canada Trust v Stolzenberg (No. 2)* [1998] 1 WLR 547 at 555.

[173] Lord Templeman in *Spiliada Maritime Corp. v Cansulex Ltd (The Spiliada)* [1987] AC 460 at 465.

[174] This is a vain hope to prevent too many appeals. However, it is often used by appeal courts as a reason not to disturb the findings of the first instance judges, see e.g., *Limit (No. 3) Ltd v PDV Insurance Co. Ltd* [2005] EWCA Civ 383, [2005] 2 All ER (Comm) 347.

[175] *EF Hutton & Co. (London) Ltd v Mofarrij* [1989] 1 WLR 488 at 495 (CA).

[176] *Matthews v Kuwait Bechtel Corp.* [1952] 2 QB 57 (CA).

[177] Regulation (EC) 1393/2007 on the service in Member States of judicial and extrajudicial documents in civil and commercial matters.

agent within the jurisdiction.[178] Where that Regulation is inapplicable the claimant often requires the assistance of foreign judicial or other administrative officers.[179] In some countries, the Hague Service Convention can be used.[180]

f. Defendant's challenge to jurisdiction

i. Stays of proceedings on *forum non conveniens* grounds

A defendant who has been served within the territory of the English court 'as of right' may challenge the exercise of the jurisdiction.[181] In this case, the defendant is requesting that the proceedings against the defendant are stayed in favour of another clearly more appropriate forum.[182] The onus is here on the defendant to show that there is another available forum in which the trial of the dispute can be achieved in the interests of the parties and the ends of justice. The foreign forum must be 'available', which means that the defendant can be sued there.[183] A foreign court may not be available if the claimant is prevented from bringing the dispute in that forum because of the political and judicial culture which prevents substantial justice being achieved in this dispute.[184] However, a claimant who wishes to use that argument to prevent a stay of English proceedings must have cogent evidence for the lack of substantial justice.[185]

ii. Challenges to permission to serve out

A defendant who has been served with the claim form out of the territory of the English court may dispute the exercise of the jurisdiction.[186] The defendant may argue that there is no gateway of jurisdiction (by challenging the claimant's allegations of law or fact which support the alleged gateway), that there is no serious issue to be tried between them, or that England is not the proper place for trial. By doing so, the defendant is not submitting to the jurisdiction but is asking that the permission to serve the claim form out of the jurisdiction on the defendant be set aside.[187] The onus remains on the claimant to show that England is the proper forum, and so on. If the proper place for trial is found to be the foreign court, the permission to serve out of

---

[178] *Knauf UK v British Gypsum Ltd* [2001] EWCA Civ 1570, [2002] 1 Lloyd's LR 199 at para. 47.

[179] CPR rr. 6.42 and 6.43.

[180] Hague Convention on the Service Abroad of Judicial and Extrajudicial Documents in Civil or Commercial Matters.

[181] Senior Courts Act 1982, s. 49; CPR r. 11.

[182] *Spiliada Maritime Corp. v Cansulex Ltd (The Spiliada)* [1987] AC 460.

[183] *Hondocha v Gheewala* [2003] UKPC 77. So the defendant must offer to submit to that court if the defendant has not already done so (for example, *Lubbe v Cape Plc* [2000] 1 WLR 1545).

[184] *Cherney v Deripaska* [2009] EWCA Civ 849, [2009] CLC 408.

[185] *Mohammed v Bank of Kuwait and Middle East KSC* [1996] WLR 1483 (CA).

[186] CPR r. 11.

[187] The older cases use a slightly different terminology, 'setting aside leave' to serve out.

the jurisdiction will normally be set aside. However, where the claimant can show that substantial justice will not be done in that foreign forum, the permission will stand and the case will go ahead in England.

g. Natural or proper forum: *forum conveniens*

Faced with the defendant's challenge to its jurisdiction, either in an application to stay its proceedings or in a service out case, the English court has to decide whether it or the alternative forum is the proper one. The identification of the best venue for ventilation of the dispute is central to this decision. The idea of the best venue appears in a number of different guises in the case law: as the 'natural forum', the 'proper forum' and the 'appropriate forum'. It has been described as the forum 'in which the case may be tried more suitably for the interests of all the parties and the ends of justice'.[188] Depending on whether it is a service out or stays case the onus on who has to prove which is the best venue varies. However, in principle, if England is the best venue then the case will go ahead here, if the foreign court is the best venue then it will go ahead abroad. In searching for the best venue, the English courts have generally followed a two-stage approach. At the first stage the natural forum is identified, followed in some cases by a second stage in which the natural forum is usurped by England as the proper forum. However, particularly at first instance where most of the cases are decided, these two stages are not distinct. The court comes to an overall decision as to the best venue taking all the factors into account.

i. Most real and substantial connection

The early cases place emphasis on the natural forum (which was said to be synonymous with the appropriate forum),[189] which is ascertained by searching for the country with which the action has its most real and substantial connection. In the seminal case of *The Spiliada*, Lord Goff of Chieveley identified the natural forum as one with which the action has its 'most real and substantial connection'.[190] The connection is established through the connecting factors such as the place where the parties reside or carry on business, the nature of the dispute, the place where the events occurred (as it will be more convenient and cheaper to decide a case close to where the witnesses are found), or the governing law of the claim.[191] Lord Wilberforce in *Amin Rasheed v Kuwait Insurance Co.* said that to identify the natural forum 'the court must take into account the nature of the dispute, the legal and

---

[188] *Spiliada Maritime Corp. v Cansulex Ltd (The Spiliada)* [1987] AC 460 at 476.

[189] *European Asian Bank AG v Punjab and Sind Bank* [1982] 2 Lloyd's LR 356 at 364.

[190] *Spiliada Maritime Corp. v Cansulex Ltd (The Spiliada)* [1987] AC 460 at 477–8.

[191] This is particularly strong in tort claims see *Berezovsky v Forbes Inc.* [2000] 1 WLR 1004 and see further p. 169 below.

practical issues involved, such questions as local knowledge, availability of witnesses and their evidence, and expense'.[192]

The purpose of identifying the natural forum in this manner is because usually cases are most conveniently[193] and practicably tried close to the events which give rise to them. It is justified as being a cost-effective result.[194] It is also true that the parties may have expectations[195] that the court with the closest and most substantial connection with the dispute should hear the case, and the defendant should not be surprised at that court's jurisdiction.

Lubbe v Cape Plc[196] is an example of how the natural forum is identified:

> Over 3,000 claimants commenced proceedings in England against Cape Plc as the holding company of South African asbestos mining and processing companies for asbestosis. Most of the claims were against the claimants' employers, the South African subsidiary companies, which were unlikely to have sufficient funds to pay out for these personal injury claims. Cape Plc is a multinational company incorporated in England with a Head Office in London. As a holding company it controlled the subsidiaries and made profits out of them. It was served with the claim forms here. Cape Plc asked for a stay of proceedings in favour of South Africa and undertook to submit to that jurisdiction.[197] The mining and processing had taken place there, the claimants' illnesses discovered there, the claimants lived there and their doctors worked there. The company employing them was there. Therefore, all the witnesses and documentary evidence of the events, their employment, their damage and loss was in South Africa. It was also quite likely that South African law would apply to the claims. The claimants could have expected to bring their claims in South Africa and the defendants could have expected to be sued there.[198] It was obviously a proper forum for this dispute. On the other hand, the claimants had carefully framed their claims on the basis of failure of health and safety advice coming from

---

[192]   [1984] AC 50 at 72.

[193]   The Latin word 'conveniens' does not mean convenient but appropriate. However, the convenience of trying facts close to where they occurred is an advantage to both parties and keeps the cost of proceedings down.

[194]   See Fentiman, *International Commercial Litigation*, para. 12.64.

[195]   The parties' expectations perhaps reached their zenith as a factor in Lord Hoffmann's powerful dissent in *Connelly v RTZ Corp.* [1998] AC 854 at 876.

[196]   The Court of Appeal decision shows the working of the test most clearly, [2000] 1 Lloyd's LR 139. The parties did not appeal the Court of Appeal's decision that South Africa was the natural forum so the House of Lords decision turned on the second stage. Note that the availability of legal aid in England was withdrawn and replaced with a conditional fee arrangement by the time the case reached the House of Lords, [2000] 1 WLR 1545.

[197]   The reasons why it operated through locally incorporated subsidiaries and was carefully not subject to South African jurisdiction is clear from *Adams v Cape Industries Plc* [1990] Ch 433. See further p. 240 *et seq.* below.

[198]   See Lord Hoffmann's dissent in a similar foreign personal injury case against the holding company of the subsidiary defendant employer, *Connelly v RTZ Corporation Plc* [1998] AC 854 at 876.

> London such that documentary evidence was here and not in South Africa. It was possible that English law would apply to the dispute but the choice of law at this interlocutory stage was unclear. The best expert medical evidence was in London although there were experts in South Africa. Solicitors and courts who were very competent at managing large class actions of this type were in London. Although South African courts were willing to undertake a class action there was less experience of such complex actions.

The natural forum for these claims was South Africa. The claims relating to the causation of the injuries and their quantum could most efficiently be heard in South Africa. That was where the witnesses were found, that was where most of the documentary evidence was found, that was where the strongest connections with the events and the dispute occurred. Nonetheless, as we shall see, England was found to be the proper court for trial in that case after the second stage.[199] A somewhat more evenly balanced example of identifying the natural forum is *The Spiliada* itself:

> The claimants were a Liberian company which owned a ship, *The Spiliada*. The defendants were from British Columbia in Canada and shipped sulphur from Vancouver to India. The claimants alleged that the sulphur had been loaded wet in Vancouver, and therefore caused damage to the cargo holds of their ship. They claimed for breach of contract. The contract of carriage was found to be governed by English law and the claim form was permitted to be served out of the jurisdiction. There was no dispute about the legal effect or terms of the contract. The real issues between the parties were the evidential ones of whether the cargo was improperly loaded and the scientific evidence of the causes and consequences of the wet sulphur. Witnesses to the loading were in British Columbia, but witnesses of the damage done were elsewhere. Either could relatively easily come to England or their testimony be dealt with by sworn statement of fact[200] rather than oral cross-examination. Importantly, the expert witnesses to the effect of the damage were around the world and their evidence could most easily be heard in England. The availability of extensive expertise in a very similar case between very similar parties which had only just been settled in England, *The Cambridgeshire*, meant that a trial of *The Spiliada* in England could be done more effectively than in Canada.[201]

In conclusion, their Lordships decided that England was the natural forum. There were good reasons of efficiency in hearing the case here. The decision

---

[199] See p. 174 *et seq.* below.   [200] What used to be called an affidavit.
[201] [1987] AC 460. There was a complication in that the action was time-barred in British Columbia but this is an example of a second stage factor, see below.

rested on a number of factors, not merely those mentioned above, but the reasoning shows that efficiency and keeping down the administrative costs of trial, are important drivers in locating the natural forum.

ii. Particular factors

There are several factors which may play a critical role in determining the natural forum. No one factor is conclusive, and what may be central in a particular case can be less relevant in another as much depends on the whole situation giving rise to the dispute. For example, if the witness evidence can be taken by video-link[202] or by a sworn statement, then where the witnesses physically are likely to be found may not be at all relevant to the natural forum. If the case will turn on long cross-examination of a witness, then where that witness can most easily be heard will be likely to be the natural forum. It will be cheaper for the parties and less inconvenient for the witness if the dispute is decided close to that witness's location. So, for example, in *Amin Rasheed v Kuwait Insurance Co.*:[203]

> The central issue was one of fact, whether the crew had been involved in smuggling when they were arrested in Saudi Arabia. Although the contract was governed by English law, there was no real dispute about the terms of the contract.

The court held that the factual matters were better decided in the foreign forum, Kuwait. Kuwait is closer to Saudi Arabia and to the Indian sub-continent (where the witnesses in the crew came from).

1. Applicable law

The first of these factors to be discussed is that of the applicable law in a dispute. The applicable law can be very important. It is clearly better to decide a difficult question of domestic contract law in the court whose law it is. Not only will it be cheaper to avoid having evidence from foreign experts, it will also lead to an accurate result as the judge will be expert in that law. Therefore, if the dispute is over the interpretation of a particular term of English law then England tends to be the natural forum for that dispute. Alternatively, if the dispute is over the defendant's liability under Ruritanian law of unjust enrichment, the Ruritanian courts should be the natural forum. This is said to be particularly true of claims in tort.[204] Note that often in tort cases the applicable

---

[202] As in *Stonebridge Underwriting Ltd and others v Ontario Municipal Insurance Exchange* [2010] EWHC 2279 (Comm).

[203] [1984] AC 50.

[204] *Metall und Rohstoff v Donaldson, Lufkin & Jenrette* [1990] 1 QB 391; *Berezovsky v Forbes* [2000] 1 WLR 1004 (HL).

law and either the place where the events which give rise to the tort or, more likely, the place where the damage is suffered will coincide.[205] It might be said that there is a presumption that the place where the tort occurred will be the appropriate forum[206] so this could be argued not to be specifically a matter of the factor of the applicable law. Cases in which the particular disputed question of law is especially difficult are especially well decided in the courts whose law will apply. So in *EI Pont de Nemours v Agnew*,[207] a challenging question of the application of English public policy was in issue and that factor made England the natural forum.[208] However, the importance of this factor should not be overemphasised. Where the disputed issues in the case are more about fact than law, and the foreign court is able to apply English law, then the other closer connections with the foreign forum will mean it remains the natural forum.[209] In the case where the foreign court is not able to apply English law, especially where it has been expressly chosen by the parties, England remains the natural forum.[210] This case is probably better understood as an example of a second stage decision.[211]

2. *Lis pendens*

Proceedings continuing abroad (*lis pendens*) may be an important factor in determining the natural forum. Senior Court Act 1981, s. 49(2) imposes a requirement that the court must 'so exercise its jurisdiction in every cause or matter before it as to secure that, as far as possible, all matters in dispute between the parties are completely and finally determined, and all multiplicity of legal proceedings with respect to any of those matters is avoided'. This is usually considered important in domestic cases but is also relevant to ones with a foreign element. Where a case is already being litigated in another country, which is an appropriate forum, whose judgment is enforceable in England, and in which there is no real concern about the propriety of the decision, it is unjust for the English court also to exercise its discretion and take jurisdiction over the same dispute. Even if England is a natural forum, there is no justification for the additional expense of proceedings in England, the possibility of an 'unseemly race to judgment', and the difficulties of conflicting judgments.[212] It would be unfair to put a defendant to the extra expense and trouble of two sets of proceedings. As Lord Diplock noted in *The Abidin Daver*,[213] 'The policy of the law must nonetheless be to favour the

---

[205] See further Chapter 11.
[206] *The Albaforth* [1984] 2 Lloyd's LR 91 but note *Lewis v King* [2004] EWCA Civ 1329, [2005] ILPr. 16, this is only an initial presumption and will be weaker if the connection with the place where the tort was committed is tenuous.
[207] [1987] 2 Lloyd's LR 585.   [208] See too *BP Exploration (Libya) Ltd v Hunt* [1976] 1 WLR 786.
[209] *Amin Rasheed v Kuwait Insurance Co.* [1984] AC 50.
[210] *Banco Atlantico v British Bank of Middle East* [1990] 2 Lloyd's LR 504.
[211] See p. 174 below.   [212] *The Abidin Daver* [1984] AC 398 at 411–412.
[213] *The Abidin Daver* [1984] AC 398 at 423.

litigation of issues once only, in the most appropriate forum'. These '*lis pendens*' cases might be considered a separate strand of the doctrine of *forum conveniens*. Certainly, it was easier to stay English proceedings on the ground that foreign proceedings were continuing before the more general doctrine developed.[214] However, this factor is also more sophisticated than it might appear, particularly in comparison with Articles 27 and 28 which are the equivalent provisions in the Brussels I Regulation.

If the claimant is suing the defendant both in Ruritania and in England, the defendant can ask the claimant to elect where to continue in challenging the English court's jurisdiction or under its case management powers.[215] Where the situation is more complex and the parties are suing each other, maybe with other parties, in more than one jurisdiction, then the court will exercise its discretion. In some circumstances, permitting the case to go ahead in two jurisdictions is the result. It is important to notice that the English court does not refuse to entertain proceedings merely because there are proceedings already commenced in a foreign forum.[216] It is only where the foreign proceedings are well advanced that the English court will refuse to take jurisdiction in proceedings here. This is a flexible test. A case which has advanced to lengthy pre-trial discovery of evidence was not found to be very well advanced.[217] On the other hand, a case which had come to a hearing of the substance was considered well advanced.[218] The English court has been reluctant to refuse to take jurisdiction in cases where the foreign proceedings are commenced for 'tactical' reasons.[219] Also, if the claimant would be denied access to justice in the foreign proceedings the English court will nonetheless take jurisdiction and hear the case.[220]

3. Consolidating actions

The English court has a pronounced preference for consolidating actions in one court.[221] Therefore, the natural forum is likely to be the one in which all the claims between the claimants and defendants arising out of a dispute can be decided. This factor can be so strong as to override an exclusive jurisdiction

---

[214] *The Atlantic Star* [1974] AC 436.

[215] Under the CPR the court has power actively to manage its own proceedings in order to deal with cases justly (CPR rr. 1.1(1) and 1.4). An example, where the English court required the claimant to elect which proceedings to continue to judgment first, is *Racy v Hawila* [2004] EWCA Civ 209 at para. 63.

[216] *Cleveland Museum of Art v Capricorn Art SA* [1990] 2 Lloyd's LR 166.

[217] *Société Nationale Industrielle Aérospatiale v Lee Kui Jak* [1987] AC 871.

[218] *Spiliada Maritime Corp. v Cansulex Ltd (The Spiliada)* [1987] AC 460.

[219] For example, *Arkwright Mutual Insurance Co. v Bryanston Insurance* [1990] 2 QB 649.

[220] Where, for example, the foreign court would not apply English law as expressly chosen by the parties or where it could not properly determine difficult questions of English law (see e.g., *E I Du Pont de Nemours & Co. v Agnew* [1987] 2 Lloyd's LR 585).

[221] As required by Senior Courts Act 1981, s. 49(2).

agreement.[222] Apparently, the overwhelming justice of consolidating all the actions in one court outweighs the injustice of not holding some of the parties to a jurisdiction agreement to their bargain.[223] It would be unfair on those parties not bound by the jurisdiction agreement to risk inconsistent decisions.

4. Jurisdiction and arbitration agreements

The existence of a jurisdiction or arbitration agreement is generally a critically important factor in the determination of the natural forum, so much so that these agreements form a somewhat separate doctrine. There are occasional statements by a judge and even fewer decisions that a jurisdiction agreement is only a factor which can be overcome by other factors,[224] but in practice the existence of a jurisdiction agreement (even a non-exclusive jurisdiction agreement) is a very strong indication of the natural forum. Therefore, if there is a jurisdiction agreement in favour of the English courts, the parties are taken to have expected that the English courts will be the most appropriate forum for their dispute even where there is no other connection with England. The parties may have chosen the English courts as a venue for the very reasons that those courts are neutral and have experienced judges and practitioners. If the parties have entered into an exclusive jurisdiction agreement in favour of a foreign court that foreign court is the appropriate forum. Be careful to note the interrelationship with the Brussels I Regulation. We will discuss this and the effect of jurisdiction and arbitration clauses on the English court's exercise of discretion in more detail below.[225]

5. Practical advantages

Practical advantages available in England which are to the benefit of both parties may make England the natural forum. So, for example, in *The Spiliada* as discussed above, the lawyers and experts in the case had all developed extensive expertise in the scientific evidence in a very similar case between some of the parties to *The Spiliada*. It was to the advantage of all parties that the case be heard in England where this expertise could be efficiently relied upon. This factor may be difficult to justify without appearing chauvinistic. Taken to extremes it encourages claimants to seek adjudication in England. Lord Diplock in *The Abidin Daver* noted that 'judicial chauvinism has been replaced by judicial comity'[226] and several cases have held that it is improper for the English court to undertake a comparison of the quality of justice

---

[222] See e.g., *Donohue v Armco Inc.* [2001] UKHL 64, [2002] 1 All ER 749; *Citi March Ltd v Neptune Orient Lines Ltd* [1996] 1 WLR 1367; and *Bouygues Offshore SA v Caspian Shipping Co.* [1998] 2 Lloyd's LR 461.

[223] *The MC Pearl* [1997] 1 Lloyd's LR 566 at 569.

[224] For example, *The El Amria* [1981] 2 Lloyd's LR 119. For a case in which an exclusive jurisdiction agreement in favour of England was set aside in favour of proceedings abroad see *Donohue v Armco Inc.* [2001] UKHL 64, [2002] 1 All ER 749.

[225] See further p. 178 below.   [226] [1984] AC 398 at 411.

obtained abroad.[227] Expert judges and well-qualified lawyers or experts in England should not, of themselves, be the reason why cases must be heard in England, particularly if there is little other connection with England; otherwise there is a risk of abusive forum shopping and dragging a defendant to England to defend expensive proceedings in an unexpected court. It may be better to consider this factor as relevant at the second stage. Where justice cannot be done in the foreign forum due to a lack of expertise available there but available in the English court then there may be a justification for the hearing of the dispute by the English court.[228]

iii. Treatment of advantages

Generally, following these earlier cases, once the natural forum is identified the claimant should take the forum as it is found.[229] So if the natural forum is abroad, even if the claimant does not have particular advantages in that forum that would be available to the claimant in England, it is not necessarily unjust to stay the English proceedings and have the case go ahead abroad.[230] This is an important control on unjust forum shopping – the case should go ahead in the natural forum which conforms to the parties' expectations. A claimant should not be permitted to seek litigation advantages in England which are also equal and opposite disadvantages to the defendant. Examples of advantages available in England which should be insufficient to outweigh the natural forum include:

(1) a more wide-ranging procedure for discovery of evidence available in England.[231] In *The Spiliada*, Lord Goff said that it was not unjust if the parties were compelled to accept a system of procedure in a well-recognised foreign system of law.[232] This should also be true of other procedural advantages, such as a more generous regime for security of costs,[233] or ancillary relief, or of costs awards;

(2) a more generous limitation period available in England;[234] although where the claimant has acted reasonably in not commencing and pursuing

---

[227] Notably *The Abidin Daver* [1984] AC 398 at 410; *Amin Rasheed v Kuwait Insurance Co.* [1984] AC 50 at 67.

[228] This reasoning would better explain the decision in *Lubbe v Cape Plc* [2000] 1 WLR 1545; *Connelly v RTZ Corp.* [1998] AC 854.

[229] *Connelly v RTZ Corp.* [1998] AC 854 at 872.

[230] See e.g., *The Abidin Daver* [1984] AC 398 and *Amin Rasheed Shipping Co. v Kuwait Insurance Co.* [1984] AC 50.

[231] *Connelly v RTZ Corp.* [1998] AC 854 at 873.

[232] *Spiliada Maritime Corp. v Cansulex Ltd (The Spiliada)* [1987] AC 460 at 482–3.

[233] But compare with the judgment of Lord Goff who saw nothing wrong in permitting a claimant to retain security obtained by commencing proceedings in England (*The Spiliada* [1987] AC 460 at 483). See also Civil Jurisdiction and Judgments Act 1982, s. 26, which permits stays to be granted conditional on a retention of security.

[234] *The Pioneer Container* [1994] 2 AC 324 (PC).

proceedings abroad and so the time period has passed there, the English court may decide to hear the case;[235]

(3) a more expeditious trial in England.[236] In *Chellaram v Chellaram (No. 2)*,[237] Collins J noted that there are delays in every system. Delays of even up to ten years or more were not necessarily due to the court or only to one party but both could be dragging the matter out. However, where the delays in the foreign system are so extensive as to amount to a denial of justice, the English court may decide to hear the case;[238]

(4) higher damages available in England.[239] This is the most obvious example of abusive forum shopping. Nevertheless, where the damages which might be obtained in the foreign forum are so substantially less[240] or totally used up by the costs award[241] such that justice is not going to be done abroad, the case may be permitted to continue in England;

(5) ease of enforcement in England. If the foreign proceedings continue to judgment, that judgment will be enforceable in England and so there is no advantage. Nevertheless, the English court has held that it would be unjust to deprive a claimant of an English judgment which is freely enforceable throughout the EU where a third state judgment would not be.[242]

Allowing any of these factors to outweigh the foreign natural forum would obviously encourage forum shopping. A claimant would be seeking the decision of the English court merely because the claimant gained some advantage in England that is a disadvantage to the defendant and which is not available in the natural forum. However, if England is *an* appropriate forum then it may be argued that a claimant is not acting improperly by seeking such an advantage. An explanation for the decision in *Lubbe v Cape plc*[243] might be that England was entirely *an* appropriate forum in which to pursue the action.[244] South Africa was a natural forum as that was where the claimants were resident, and where the factories which had caused the damage were found. The court at the first stage and at appeal decided that South Africa was the natural forum for the dispute, which left the appeal turning only on the exceptional second stage factors which meant that England was the best venue. Nevertheless, the defendant was a multinational company which had chosen to incorporate in England and to have its headquarters in London. There were

---

[235] *Citi March Ltd v Neptune Orient Lines Ltd* [1996] 1 WLR 1367.

[236] *Radhakrishna Hospitality Service Private Ltd v EIH Ltd* [1999] 2 Lloyd's LR 249.

[237] [2002] EWHC 632.   [238] *The Vishva Ajay* [1989] 2 Lloyd's LR 558.

[239] *Spiliada Maritime Corp. v Cansulex Ltd (The Spiliada)* [1987] AC 460 at 482.

[240] *The Vishva Abha* [1990] 2 Lloyd's LR 312.

[241] *Roneleigh Ltd v MII Exports Ltd* [1989] 1 WLR 619 (CA).

[242] *International Credit and Investment Co. (Overseas) Ltd v Adham* [1999] ILPr. 302 (CA).

[243] [2000] 1 WLR 1545 (SC).

[244] That case would now have to be decided differently after *Owusu v Jackson* Case C-281/02 [2004] ECR I-1383, as the defendant was domiciled in England and therefore the English court now has no power to stay its proceedings in favour of a third state. See further pp. 188–93 above.

advantages to it of being located in England (such as ready access to a well-developed financial market and a stable political system) and it should be taken to have expected to be sued here. After all, the entirely acceptable general rule in the Brussels I Regulation is to sue a defendant at the domicile of the defendant. However, the rigid operation of a *forum conveniens* doctrine which seeks to identify a single appropriate forum imposes this problem. By searching for a single 'natural forum' the connections which may justify the exercise of the English court's jurisdiction are obscured.

We can compare the English doctrine with the Canadian operation of *forum conveniens* which is more flexible and does not seek to establish a single best venue. In the leading case of *Amchem Products Inc. v British Columbia (Workers' Compensation Board)*,[245] Sopinka J noted that taking the benefit of better advantages in a natural forum in which the parties expected to ventilate their disputes is not abusive forum shopping.

An alternative explanation for the exceptional cases where the factors have outweighed the foreign natural forum is that they were examples of the operation of the second stage of *The Spiliada* test. The importance of the distinction lies in the imposition of the burden of proof. The claimant has to prove the facts giving rise to the exception if the factor falls into the second stage, whereas if it is part of the first stage that may not be true.[246]

h. Second stage: the test of substantial justice

We have seen that the identification of the natural forum is the first stage in *The Spiliada* test. Lord Goff went on to hold that even if the natural forum was abroad, at the second stage the claimant could continue with the case in England where the claimant could show that substantial justice would not be done abroad. It does not matter whether the case was a stays or a service out case. In either case the burden falls onto the claimant to show that substantial justice could not be done in the natural forum.[247] Many of the cases heard in the appeal courts appear to turn on this second stage.

Examples of cases in which substantial justice was found not to be obtainable abroad[248] include the following.

(1) Where the foreign court will not come to a fair decision due to racial or political motivation. As Lord Diplock remarked in *The Abidin Daver*:

---

[245] [1993] 1 SCR 897.

[246] See *AK Investment CJSC v Kyrgyz Mobil Tel Ltd* [2011] UKPC 7, [2011] 4 All ER 1027.

[247] See e.g., *Lubbe v Cape Plc* [2000] 1 WLR 1545; *Connelly v RTZ Corp.* [1998] AC 854.

[248] Occasionally, these cases overlap with the requirement at the first stage of a case where the defendant is seeking a stay of English proceedings that the foreign forum is 'available'. Substantial justice cannot be done if the foreign forum is unavailable, see e.g., *Mohammed v Bank of Kuwait and the Middle East KSC* [1996] 1 WLR 1269.

The possibility cannot be excluded that there are still some countries in whose courts there is a risk that justice will not be obtained by a foreign litigant in particular kinds of suits whether for ideological or political reasons.[249]

A party who is alleging that justice will not be obtained abroad cannot merely make allegations, the party must give cogent and credible evidence to support the argument.[250] An example is *Cherney v Deripaska*:

> The claimant alleged he had been in partnership with the defendant in an aluminium business in Siberia, Russia. Both parties were from Russia but Cherney had become unpopular with the Russian regime and had fled the country. He was fearful of returning there, arguing that his life was at risk. Deripaska was well connected to the regime which came to power in Russia. Russia was clearly the natural forum but Cherney alleged that he would not obtain justice in Russia.[251]

The Court of Appeal gave permission for service out of the jurisdiction on Deripaska. There was sufficient evidence that Cherney was at risk of his life if he returned to Russia and without his testimony substantial justice would not be obtained there.

On the other hand, if the evidence is insufficiently strong, this factor will not displace the natural forum.[252] In *AK Investment CJSC v Kyrgyz Mobil Tel Ltd*,[253] the Privy Council opined that there was substantial evidence of specific irregularities, breach of principles of natural justice and irrational conclusions by the Kyrgyzstan courts. At this interlocutory stage, however, that evidence only has to show a 'real risk that justice will not be obtained by reason of incompetence or lack of judicial independence or corruption'[254] in that natural forum rather than having to be proved on the balance of probabilities. This factor operates consistently with what are perceived to be the obligations on the United Kingdom under Article 6 of the European Convention on Human Rights. In many of the cases a very slight connection with England is found, such as the alleged making of a contract here or English law being the alleged applicable law of the contract.[255] Nevertheless, taken to its logical conclusion, a claimant from anywhere in the world can commence and continue

---

[249] *The Abidin Daver* [1984] AC 398 at 411.   [250] *Ibid.*

[251] [2009] EWCA Civ 849. See also *Oppenheimer v Louis Rosenthal* [1937] 1 All ER 23 and *Mohammed v Bank of Kuwait and Middle East KSC* [1996] 1 WLR 1483.

[252] See e.g., *Askin v Absa Bank* [1999] ILPr. 471 and *Pacific International Sports Clubs Ltd v Igor Surkis and others* [2010] EWCA Civ 753.

[253] [2011] UKPC 7, [2011] 4 All ER 1027.   [254] Lord Collins at para. 95.

[255] See e.g., *Cherney v Deripaska* [2009] EWCA Civ 849 and *Sharab v Prince Al-Waleed Bin Tala Bin Abdal-Aziz-Al-Saud* [2009] EWCA Civ 353, [2009] 2 Lloyd's LR 160.

proceedings in England irrespective of a complete lack of connection between the parties, the events and England.[256]

(2) Inexperienced foreign court: where the foreign court has insufficient experience of complex commercial cases the English court may continue with proceedings despite the foreign court being the natural forum.[257]

(3) Nature and complexity of the case: the English court will continue to hear a dispute in a very complex case which would not be fairly dealt with by a court with insufficiently developed rules to deal with the particular procedural, factual or legal issues raised in that case.[258]

The notion of substantial justice is fraught with difficulties. First, it requires the court to evaluate the claimant's argument that justice will be denied in the foreign court. This necessarily leads the court into comparing the quality of justice which is obtainable in each forum. The English court by doing so sets itself up as an arbiter of the foreign judiciary. The court recognises that that raises serious concerns of comity and even of justiciability of that issue. However, the Privy Council has swept aside such concerns in *AK Investment CJSC v Kyrgyz Mobil Tel Ltd*, holding that there is no rule of act of state or comity which prevents the court from assessing the evidence of such matters as endemic corruption or bias.[259] Secondly, it should be a truly exceptional exercise of the jurisdiction which requires careful consideration of extensive evidence. This is inconsistent with the requirement that interlocutory proceedings such as those on jurisdiction are to be decided in 'hours not days'[260] and without cross-examination of experts.

Some of the more recent cases seek for the proper forum which is also described as the appropriate forum.[261] This version of the best venue for the dispute also takes its origins from *The Spiliada*. The court, in ascertaining the proper forum for trial, appears to take all issues into account and then comes to a decision of the proper forum, rather than starting with some objective identification of a natural forum. There is therefore much less emphasis on the parties' expectations and little heed paid to the possible exorbitant exercise of jurisdiction over foreign defendants. Matters such as efficiency of a one-stop dispute resolution[262] or the application of English law[263] can be given great weight. The risk in these cases is that the wide gateways for

---

[256] A new gateway of jurisdiction will need to be developed to cover these cases.

[257] See e.g., *Limit (No. 3) Ltd v PDV Insurance Co.* [2005] Lloyd's LR IR 552 at para. 66.

[258] *Lubbe v Cape Plc* [2000] 1 WLR 1545 and *Connelly v RTZ Corp.* [1998] AC 854.

[259] [2011] UKPC 7, [2011] 4 All ER 1027 at para. 101.

[260] Lord Templeman in *Spiliada Maritime Corp. v Cansulex Ltd (The Spiliada)* [1987] AC 460.

[261] See the discussion on this in *Cherney v Deripaska* [2009] EWCA Civ 849 at paras 19–20.

[262] See e.g., *The Abidin Daver* [1984] AC 398 at 423.

[263] See e.g., *Stonebridge Underwriting Ltd v Ontario Municipal Insurance Exchange* [2010] EWHC 2799 (Comm).

jurisdiction permit a claimant to start an action in the English court which then forces a defendant into an unwarranted settlement rather than expend large sums to mount a defence both as to jurisdiction and on the merits. This risk is exacerbated, as the test of a serious issue to be tried on the merits is not particularly robust.

i. Criticism of *forum conveniens*

The doctrine of *forum conveniens* might be argued to lead to the most sophisticated, flexible and careful determination of the best venue for the parties' dispute. The court is charged with considering and balancing a wide range of factors to come to a conclusion to resolve complex international cases where international rules on jurisdiction overlap and compete. It is in stark contrast to the more clearcut rules which apply under the Brussels I Regulation. However, it can also be said to be uncertain and unpredictable and that it encourages rather than discourages forum shopping, not necessarily in the sense that the choice of litigation in England is improper as being completely unjustified, but because the doctrine gives an incentive for a well-funded claimant to make a speculative application. The exhortations from the appeal courts that the decisions of first instance judges should not be overturned, that these jurisdictional decisions should be speedy and not incurring great cost, appear to be in vain given the huge number of appealed cases. The conclusion that the English court is too willing to accept jurisdiction over cases that have very little connection with England is perhaps inescapable.[264] Some of those cases are explicable on the ground that the case might never be heard if it is not heard in England. Nevertheless, the English court has been dragged into making some uncomfortable decisions about the quality of justice done in foreign courts, some of which are controversial.[265] One might also argue that a search for a single best venue is illusory. Cases will have various connections to a number of jurisdictions and each of those places could have some legitimate claim to being a good court in which to hear the dispute. Nevertheless, the structure of the service out rules does appear to require that England is *the* (singular) proper place for trial. The doctrine on stays requires that there must be another *clearly* more appropriate forum, which forces the defendant into an identification of a single alternative best venue for trial. It would be better if the rules simply required the claimant to show that England was sufficiently connected with the dispute to make it a proper place for trial.

---

[264] As the recent cases arising out of disputes which have their strongest connections with the old Soviet republics illustrate.

[265] For example, *Lubbe v Cape Plc* [2000] 1 WLR 1545 was hotly debated in South Africa, where the reaction of some newspapers was that the decision was an example of judicial colonialism.

j. Jurisdiction and arbitration agreements

The English court's decision on jurisdiction under the national rules can be very different to the discussion above if the parties have entered into a jurisdiction or arbitration agreement. Such clauses in contracts are evidence that the parties have agreed that their disputes are to be resolved in a particular way. They have articulated their expectations of the best venue for any dispute. Upholding these agreements is justified on the basis of party autonomy. The parties to an agreement are taken to know their own interests best and those interests should not be overridden.[266] In the case of arbitration, the court's jurisdiction is controlled by s. 9 of the Arbitration Act 1996. The court must stay proceedings where there is a valid, performable arbitration agreement. The whole point of arbitration is to remove the dispute from the jurisdiction of the courts. A party to litigation who wishes to escape from an arbitration agreement will seek to deny the validity of the agreement or to argue that the dispute does not fall within the scope of the agreement or that they are not party to the agreement.

As we have seen,[267] jurisdiction agreements often operate in a less singular manner. It is possible to have jurisdiction agreements which choose a single court, excluding the jurisdiction of any other. However, many jurisdiction agreements are more complicated. Where the English court is presented with a jurisdiction agreement in favour of England, whether exclusive or non-exclusive, if one party is domiciled in a Member State, the Brussels I Regulation applies so long as the formal requirements have been fulfilled.[268] This includes the operation of Article 27, so that if proceedings are continuing in another Member State, the English court must stay its own proceedings until the jurisdiction of that other court is established irrespective of the existence of an English jurisdiction agreement.[269] There is no room for the national rules to operate, although the cases have sometimes overlooked the operation of Article 23(1). Where a party is domiciled in a Member State and there is a jurisdiction agreement in favour of another Member State, the English court must also apply the Brussels I Regulation.

Article 23(3) applies if no party to the litigation is domiciled in a Member State and the parties have 'entered into such an agreement'. However, the Article provides merely that in the case of an agreement which complies with the formal requirements of Article 23(1), no other Member State's court can take jurisdiction over the dispute. Article 23(3) does not make provision for the jurisdiction of the court identified in the jurisdiction agreement and therefore the national rules do probably operate to determine that court's

---

[266] This argument is most forceful in contracts between equally strong parties. Inequality of bargaining power may have to be dealt with by limiting the stronger party's choice of court, as for example with consumers and employees.

[267] See p. 111 *et seq.* above.   [268] Article 23(1).

[269] *Eric Gasser v MISAT srl* Case C-116/02 [2003] ECR I-14693.

jurisdiction.[270] Article 23 does not apply to jurisdiction agreements which purport to confer jurisdiction on a third state. The effect of these agreements on the English court's jurisdiction should be determined by the national rules. However, where a party to the proceedings is domiciled in a Member State, the Brussels I Regulation apparently applies. The Regulation makes no explicit provision for jurisdiction agreements in favour of third states. After *Owusu v Jackson*,[271] it is possible to argue that even an exclusive jurisdiction agreement in favour of Ruritania should be ignored and only the Brussels I Regulation rules applied to determine the jurisdiction of the English courts.[272] That is clearly very unsatisfactory. Further guidance must be obtained from the CJEU or the Brussels I Regulation has to be amended. Once the Hague Convention on choice of court agreements has been implemented, exclusive jurisdiction agreements must be given effect to under that Convention, to which the EU is a party as well as all the Member States.[273]

An English court should be able to use its national rules to decide whether it should hear a case between a Ruritanian bank and a Utopian borrower where a contract provides for the jurisdiction of the English court, including the discretionary element of those national rules. The national rules certainly apply to determine whether the English court can hear such a case where their contract provides for the jurisdiction of a third state's court and neither party is domiciled in a Member State. The case law is very extensive but it is clear that the English court regards the exercise of its jurisdiction in both these cases as discretionary. The English court does not automatically follow the will of the parties expressed in their agreement on jurisdiction but takes into account a range of other factors.[274] However, the jurisdiction agreement, especially if expressly exclusive, will almost always be upheld.

i. Validity

A party who wishes to escape a jurisdiction agreement might argue that it is invalid. It could be materially invalid, formally invalid or entered into under conditions which make it ineffective to bind the party. Material invalidity could be due to the contract being entered into under duress or undue influence or fraud or it may suffer from illegality. Formal invalidity may be a concern where jurisdiction agreements have to be made in a particular form,

---

[270] After *Owusu v Jackson* Case C-281/02 [2004] ECR I-1383, it remains unclear whether the English court retains the discretion to stay proceedings in favour of a third state. On the one hand, the national rules of jurisdiction under a jurisdiction agreement are founded upon the possibility of a discretionary stay. On the other hand, the exercise of discretion to stay proceedings appears to be completely outlawed by the judgment in *Owusu v Jackson*.

[271] Case C-281/02 [2004] ECR I-1383.   [272] See further p. 188 *et seq.* below.

[273] See further p. 186 *et seq.* below.

[274] On foreign jurisdiction agreements see *The El Amria* [1981] 2 Lloyd's LR 119 and *The Sennar (No. 2)* [1985] 1 WLR 490 at 500; on English jurisdiction agreements see *Donohue v Armco Inc.* [2001] UKHL 64, [2002] 1 All ER 749 at para. 24.

such as in writing, in order to be valid. The jurisdiction clause might be argued to be ineffective if the contract containing it was allegedly made without authority or if the clause has to be incorporated from some other contract. In principle, note that it is not necessarily English law which should apply to answer these questions. In practice, partly because the clause is usually governed by English law and often because these issues are muddled up with the effect of a jurisdiction agreement, English law is usually applied without discussion. However, where the jurisdiction agreement is contained in a contract expressly governed by Ruritanian law and provides for the jurisdiction of the Ruritanian courts, one might argue that Ruritanian law should apply to determine the validity of the jurisdiction agreement.[275] English law would still apply to the effect of the agreement on the decision of the English court as to its own jurisdiction.[276]

The courts have held that a jurisdiction agreement can be severed from the remainder of the contract so that it may be effective to grant jurisdiction even if one party argues that it is not bound by the contract which was made without authority.[277] It may be possible to attack the jurisdiction agreement on some specific argument that the agent lacked authority to enter into the jurisdiction agreement itself or probably where the entire agreement is materially invalid due to fraud, for example.[278] Otherwise a party might be obliged to pursue a case to declare a contract void for fraud in the courts imposed into the agreement by the other party. The argument that the court allegedly chosen is the only court which should determine whether or not it has jurisdiction is known as the *competence-competence* argument. It is often used in relation to arbitration clauses. Even there it has its limitations where there is reasonably strong evidence that the arbitration clause has been entered into under fraud or duress.[279]

The question of whether a jurisdiction agreement has been incorporated from one contract into another, say from a charterparty to a bill of lading or from an insurance contract to the contract of reinsurance, has vexed the English court recently.[280] The contract which contains the jurisdiction agreement is governed by one law, the second contract into which the jurisdiction

---

[275] Although the Rome I Regulation on choice of law in contractual matters expressly does not apply to jurisdiction agreements, it is probable that the same rules will be applied to determine the applicable law of such agreements as it makes little sense to subject a jurisdiction agreement to different choice of law rules to those applied to the contract of which it is a part. But cf. *Cheshire, North and Fawcett*, p. 449 note 239.

[276] See e.g., *Mackender v Feldia AG* [1967] 2 QB 590.

[277] *Deutsche Bank AG v Asia Pacific Broadband Wireless Communications Inc.* [2008] EWCA Civ 1091, [2008] 2 Lloyd's LR 619, a case under the Brussels I Regulation but noting that this rule is as much one of English as European law (at para. 24).

[278] Dicta of Lord Denning in *Mackender v Feldia AG* [1967] 2 QB 590.

[279] See e.g., *Dallah Real Estate and Tourism Holding Co. v Government of Pakistan* [2010] UKSC 46, [2011] 1 AC 763.

[280] See e.g., *SSL International plc v TTK LIG Ltd* [2011] EWCA Civ 1170.

agreement from the first contract is allegedly to be incorporated may be governed by a different law. Again, it is common to apply English law to resolve the matter of possible incorporation of an English jurisdiction agreement. This will turn on the interpretation of the parties' intentions, which can be determined by looking at the factual matrix of the whole agreement.[281]

ii. Interpretation

The jurisdiction agreement may need to be interpreted to determine its meaning. Interpretation may cover whether the agreement is intended to confer jurisdiction or to confirm jurisdiction (and whether to do so exclusively or non-exclusively). The clause may need interpreting to decide whether it is intended to exclude jurisdiction, and also to decide what disputes fall within its scope. In principle, these are questions to be referred to the law governing the jurisdiction agreement. However, the question of interpretation is often taken with the matter of the effect to be given to the jurisdiction agreement. The latter is a matter of English law as the *lex fori*.[282] Alternatively, if the jurisdiction agreement is an English jurisdiction agreement English law is likely to apply as the applicable law of the agreement.[283] Nevertheless, if the English court is deciding the meaning of a clause conferring non-exclusive jurisdiction on Ruritanian courts in an agreement governed by Utopian law, Utopian or Ruritanian law should be applied.[284] Between those two on balance, it should be Utopian law as that governing the whole contract, including the jurisdiction agreement.

The English court has interpreted jurisdiction agreements which confer jurisdiction on the English courts in a very sophisticated manner. If an agreement on jurisdiction is expressly exclusive, that is clear. However, one which is not expressly exclusive, such as an agreement that 'the English courts have jurisdiction' may be interpreted as an exclusive jurisdiction agreement. In *British Aerospace plc v Dee Howard Co.,*[285] the contract provided:

> This agreement shall be governed by and construed and take effect according to English law and the parties hereto agree that the courts of law in England shall have jurisdiction to entertain any action in respect hereof.

The court held that the agreement in terms conferred jurisdiction on the English court. The court could also have jurisdiction under the choice of English law gateway. Some further effect had to be added to the apparently

---

[281] *Satyam Computer Services Ltd v Upaid Systems Ltd* [2008] EWCA Civ 487, [2008] 2 All ER (Comm) 465 at para. 93.

[282] See further p. 182 below.

[283] See in the context of the Brussels I Regulation, *Powell Duffryn plc v Wolfgang Petereit* Case C-214/89 [1982] ECR I-1745 at para. 36, which refers the interpretation of the clause to national law, but does not distinguish whether this includes the conflict of laws rules of the national law.

[284] See e.g., *Roche Products Ltd v Provimi Ltd* [2003] All ER (Comm) 683.

[285] [1993] 1 Lloyd's LR 368.

non-exclusive jurisdiction agreement by the parties' choice of English law. The language of the clause was transitive as it submitted the disputes rather than simply the parties to the jurisdiction of the courts and the purpose of doing that was to give the English courts exclusive jurisdiction. The clause additionally required the parties to provide an address for service in England. Also the use of the word 'shall' imposed an obligation as to jurisdiction. Taking these factors together, Waller J held that this was an exclusive jurisdiction agreement. It is a little unclear whether any of these factors taken on their own is sufficient. The better advice is for the parties to make their intentions clear by using words such as exclusive or non-exclusive.

iii. Effect

The effect of a jurisdiction agreement can be argued to be a contractual matter and so a question for the law governing the parties' contract. Alternatively, the effect is a procedural matter and so governed by English law as the *lex fori*.[286] Ultimately, the effect of an agreement on the English court's jurisdiction must be procedural, but one cannot deny the contractual aspects (such as the validity and interpretation of the jurisdiction agreement). In general, a jurisdiction agreement will be upheld and the parties held to their bargain. So an agreement in favour of England will give the English court jurisdiction and the English court will usually exercise that jurisdiction either by permitting service out or refusing a stay of proceedings.[287] The corollary that the English court will not take jurisdiction over a case where there is a jurisdiction agreement in favour of a third state's court is usually also true, especially if the agreement is exclusive. Nevertheless the English court has a discretion, even in the case of a jurisdiction agreement, whether or not to take jurisdiction.[288] It is up to the party who wishes to avoid the effect of the jurisdiction agreement in either case to show 'strong cause' why it should not be followed.[289] The strong cause must be shown to the level of a 'good arguable case'.[290]

This has a subtle but clear effect on the determination of the *forum conveniens*. By entering into even a non-exclusive jurisdiction agreement a party accepts that the chosen court is appropriate. That party can no longer challenge the jurisdiction chosen on the ground that it is expensive, inconvenient, or not well-connected with the events and the parties. That leaves rather little room for the party to argue that a court other than one identified in the jurisdiction agreement is a more appropriate court. An exclusive jurisdiction

---

[286] See Fentiman, *International Commercial Litigation*, para. 2.71.
[287] See e.g., *Deutsche Bank AG v Highland Crusader Offshore Partners LP* [2009] EWCA Civ 725, [2010] 1 WLR 1023.
[288] *The El Amria* [1981] 2 Lloyd's LR 119; Brandon LJ laid down the principles at 123–4.
[289] *Unterweser Rederei GmbH v Zapata Off-shore Co. (The Chaparral)* [1968] 2 Lloyd's LR 158; *Bas Capital Funding Corp. v Medfinco* [2004] 1 Lloyd's LR 652 at 678.
[290] *Dornoch Inc. v Mauritius Union Assurance Co. Ltd* [2006] EWCA Civ 389, [2006] 2 Lloyd's LR 475 at para. 18.

agreement is particularly difficult to escape from as pursuing proceedings in another jurisdiction than that chosen is a breach of contract.[291] The 'strong cause' has to be one which the parties did not reasonably foresee at the time of entering into the contract.[292] Therefore, the location of documents or witnesses far away from the English court is not a factor to take into account.

There are three possibilities where a strong cause has been shown:

(1) where proceedings are continuing abroad: the strength of this factor is reduced to nothing with a non-exclusive jurisdiction agreement as the parties have accepted the possibility of parallel proceedings;[293]

(2) where third parties are involved: there are cases in which the dispute has arisen between many parties, some of which were not bound by the agreement. In those cases, the preference for a single venue to consolidate the dispute into one judgment may be a justification for ignoring the jurisdiction agreement. However, where it was reasonably likely that third parties would be brought into the action at the time of entering into the contract, such as a charterparty, the involvement of third parties has been no excuse not to uphold the jurisdiction agreement;[294]

(3) where the chosen court cannot do justice: the courts have taken jurisdiction in the face of a foreign jurisdiction agreement in cases where the political situation in the country whose courts have been chosen had drastically changed since the time the contract was entered into.[295]

1. English jurisdiction agreements

In almost all cases an exclusive jurisdiction agreement in favour of the English courts is given the fullest effect. The English courts will take jurisdiction either by giving permission to serve out of the jurisdiction or by refusing a stay of proceedings commenced in England. England is the proper forum by virtue of the agreement without more. In addition, the court will grant a restraining order (an anti-suit injunction) to prevent proceedings being continued abroad in breach of the exclusive English jurisdiction agreement.[296] In effect, there is a presumption in favour of enforcing an English exclusive jurisdiction agreement which can only be rebutted by the strongest reasons. An example of a case in which the English courts have stayed English proceedings commenced under an exclusive jurisdiction agreement conferring jurisdiction on the English court is *Donohue v Armco*:

---

[291] Which can be supported by an anti-suit injunction and possibly an action for damages.

[292] *Antec International Ltd v Biosafety USA Inc.* [2006] EWHC 47 (Comm).

[293] *Royal Bank of Canada v Cooperatieve Centrale Raiffeisen-Boerenleenbank BA* [2004] EWCA Civ 7, [2004] 1 Lloyd's LR 471.

[294] *Konkola Copper Mines plc v Coromin Ltd (No. 2)* [2006] EWHC 1093 (Comm).

[295] See e.g., *Carvalho v Hull Blyth (Angola) Ltd* [1979] 1 WLR 228.

[296] See further p. 194 *et seq.* below.

> The claimants in English proceedings were some of many defendants in New York proceedings. The dispute partly arose out of a management buy out under a contract containing an exclusive English jurisdiction agreement. The New York proceedings included claims in conspiracy, fraud and also claims under the Racketeer Influenced and Corrupt Organizations (RICO) Act. These latter claims could not be advanced in an English court.[297]

The House of Lords held that the proceedings in England should be stayed. Although the claimants' contractual rights to enforce the jurisdiction clause would normally be upheld, there was a strong reason in this case not to do so. The defendants in England had successfully commenced litigation in New York against the English claimants and other parties not bound by the jurisdiction agreement. Proceedings would go ahead in New York in any event between those parties. The English court could not enable a single action to dispose of all the issues but a single judgment could be achieved in the New York courts, so the interests of justice required the staying of the English proceedings.[298]

Lord Bingham considered that damages might be available for the breach of contract. This is difficult territory. How are damages to be assessed?[299] What is the loss suffered by failing to proceed in England and proceeding abroad? There is both the risk that the result would be different and the cost of the proceedings. In theory the English court could have a trial to see how it would have decided the case but that would merely incur more costs and is inconsistent with the estoppels arising out of a foreign judgment. If the foreign court comes to the same conclusion as the English court would, but at a lower cost, in theory there is no loss suffered. If the foreign court comes to a different conclusion at a higher cost, does the party obtain all the damages paid and the cost of proceeding abroad?[300] It might be easier to assess damages if the foreign court declines jurisdiction (as the loss would be the wasted costs of the jurisdiction hearing)[301] or if the claimant there loses (again the loss would be the costs of the hearing).[302]

---

[297] [2001] UKHL 64, [2002] 1 All ER 749.

[298] The anti-suit injunction was also refused. A similar result was reached in *Bouygues Offshore SA v Caspian Shipping Co.* [1998] 2 Lloyd's LR 461.

[299] See on costs as damages generally L. Merrett, 'The Enforcement of Jurisdiction Agreements within the Brussels Regime' [2006] *ICLQ* 315. As she suggests, the costs of the foreign action could be recovered (as an exception to the general rule) under a separate cause of action from the damages arising on the substance of the case. That cause of action is due to the breach of the jurisdiction agreement.

[300] There might here be a problem of estoppel arising out of the foreign judgment. See further on recognition of judgments Chapter 8.

[301] See *Union Discount Co. Ltd v Zoller* [2001] EWCA Civ 1755, [2002] 1 WLR 1517.

[302] An estoppel on the foreign judgment might arise here as well.

A non-exclusive jurisdiction agreement in favour of the English courts will also be given wide effect by the English court. The court will grant permission to serve out of jurisdiction and refuse a stay of proceedings on the ground that England is the appropriate forum by virtue of the clause.[303] One might think that the non-exclusive agreement should be less powerful than an expressly exclusive agreement. The parties have entered into an agreement that does not appear to contemplate a single venue for their dispute. The non-exclusive jurisdiction agreement confers jurisdiction but does not remove jurisdiction from other courts. There is no necessary breach of contract by commencing proceedings in another court.[304] Nevertheless, as a matter of the English court's exercise of its own jurisdiction, there seems to be little difference between the treatment of an exclusive and a non-exclusive jurisdiction agreement. The English court is appropriate by virtue of the agreement despite any lack of connection with the events and despite any inconvenience. A party seeking to escape from it still has to show strong cause and can only rely on factors which were unforeseeable at the time the contract was concluded.[305]

2. Foreign jurisdiction agreements

In principle, jurisdiction agreements in favour of foreign courts should be accorded the same respect and treatment as those in favour of English courts. The court has agreed that both should be treated in the same way.[306] Therefore the approach as a matter of the exercise of discretion should be the same. The foreign court is an appropriate forum despite any lack of connection with that court and despite the court being inconvenient or expensive. A party wishing to commence proceedings in England must explain why it objects to the jurisdiction of the foreign court even where there is merely a non-exclusive jurisdiction agreement in favour of that court.[307] However, there are more reported cases in which a foreign exclusive jurisdiction agreement has been overridden in favour of proceedings in England than examples of overriding an English jurisdiction agreement.[308] One could conclude that there is uneven treatment of foreign jurisdiction agreements. Alternatively, this might be more due to another factor. The English court is ready to consolidate actions between many parties, which makes England the venue in which justice between all the parties can more effectively be done despite a foriegn

---

[303] *British Aerospace plc v Dee Howard Co.* [1993] 1 Lloyd's LR 368.

[304] So commencing proceedings in another court is not necessarily a basis for an anti-suit injunction: *Royal Bank of Canada v Cooperatieve Centrale Raiffeisen-Boerenleenbank BA* [2004] EWCA Civ 7, [2004] 1 Lloyd's LR 471.

[305] *Antec International Ltd v Biosafety USA Inc.* [2006] EWHC 47 (Comm).

[306] See e.g., *Akai Pty Ltd v People's Insurance Co. Ltd* [1998] 1 Lloyd's LR 90 at 104.

[307] *BP plc v National Union Fire Insurance Co.* [2004] EWHC 1132 (Comm).

[308] For example, *The Fehmarn (Cargo Owners) v Fehmarn (Owners)* [1958] 1 WLR 159; *Aratra Potato Co. Ltd v Egyptian Navigation Co. (The El Amria)* [1981] 2 Lloyd's LR 119; *Citi-March Ltd v Neptune Orient Lines Ltd* [1996] 1 WLR 1367.

jurisdiction agreement between a few parties. Added to which it is relatively easy to obtain jurisdiction over other parties to the dispute which are not party to the jurisdiction agreement.

2. Hague Convention on Choice of Court Agreements

The Hague Conference on private international law drafted a convention on jurisdiction, recognition and enforcement of judgments to operate across all countries in a similar manner to the Brussels Convention (now the Brussels I Regulation). However, agreement proved impossible to reach. A more limited Convention on choice of court agreements was concluded in 2005.[309] The name is perhaps misleading as the Convention applies largely to exclusive jurisdiction agreements in civil and commercial matters.[310] The EC became a member of the Hague Conference and ratification of the Convention is to be done by the Community rather than by the individual states.[311] The Convention has been signed by the United States and the EC, Mexico has also acceded to it. It will enter into force in those states which have ratified or acceded on the first day of the month following the expiration of three months after the deposit of the second instrument of ratification, acceptance, approval or accession.[312] It appears that there is little impetus for bringing this Convention into operation despite the original air of optimism at having agreed it.

This Convention will prevail over the Brussels I Regulation only if one of the parties to the jurisdiction agreement is resident in a contracting state to the Convention which is not a Member State. It does not apply to jurisdiction agreements between residents in two Member States which remain subject to the Brussels I Regulation.[313] Nor does it apply to jurisdiction agreements which are not international.[314] Nor does it apply to agreements to which a consumer or an employee is a party.[315] Other exclusions include claims for personal injury and rights *in rem* against immovable property, as well as anti-trust matters and claims for environmental pollution.[316] Exclusive jurisdiction agreements are defined in Article 3. Agreements must be in writing or 'by any

---

[309] For the Hague Convention on Choice of Court Agreements, see www.hcch.net.

[310] Article 1. A contracting state may declare that it will recognise and enforce judgments of another contracting state which have been given pursuant to a non-exclusive jurisdiction agreement under Art. 22 but this is optional.

[311] After Lugano Opinion (Opinion 1/03) [2006] ECR I-1145, it is clear that the EU has external competence over matters which affect its internal competence, such as jurisdiction in civil and commercial matters. See A. Schulz, 'The Accession of the European Community to the Hague Conference on Private International Law' [2007] *ICLQ* 915.

[312] Article 31.   [313] Article 26(6)(a).

[314] I.e., to agreements between two residents of the same state where all the elements apart from the jurisdiction clause are connected to that state (Art. 1(2)). The parties agreement to confer exclusive jurisdiction on the courts of another state is not covered by the Hague Convention.

[315] Article 2(1).   [316] See the full list at Art. 2(2).

other means of communication which renders information accessible so as to be usable for subsequent reference'.[317] The agreement must designate one or more courts of a contracting state to the exclusion of the jurisdiction of any other court.[318] Therefore, the Hague Convention largely only covers exclusive jurisdiction agreements.[319] The agreement is to be treated independently of the rest of the contract and its validity is not to be contested solely on the ground that the contract is invalid.[320]

The Convention has four consequences. (1) Jurisdiction is conferred on the named court of a contracting state unless the agreement is invalid under the law of the state whose courts are identified.[321] (2) The agreed court cannot decline to exercise its jurisdiction on the basis that the dispute should be decided in another court.[322] (3) Courts of a contracting state other than those identified in the agreement must usually decline jurisdiction.[323] There are exceptions such as the invalidity of the agreement, the incapacity of one of the parties to it, where giving effect to the agreement would lead to manifest injustice or would be manifestly contrary to the public policy of the state, where the agreement cannot be performed,[324] and where the chosen court has decided not to hear the case. (4) Other contracting states' courts must recognise and enforce the judgment of the court of the contracting state chosen by the clause.[325] The judgment recognising court must not review the decision of the judgment granting court on its merits, but may postpone recognition and enforcement if a review of the judgment granting court is outstanding.[326] The Convention does make some changes to the existing position in England but it is not very extensive. It is restricted to a limited range of exclusive jurisdiction agreements and necessarily requires a wide ratification by contracting states. A party seeking to escape from a jurisdiction agreement may still argue that the agreement is void, or that to enforce it would lead to manifest injustice, or would be contrary to public policy. These arguments might cover the situations in which the English courts currently exercise their discretion to stay proceedings.

The Hess, Pfeiffer and Schlosser Report on the Brussels I Regulation advises that Article 23 will need some amendment if the EU wishes to conform to the Hague Convention, in particular on the relationship between *lis pendens* and

---

[317] Article 3(c).

[318] Article 3(a). An agreement shall be deemed to be exclusive unless the parties have expressly agreed otherwise (Art. 3(b)).

[319] A contracting state may declare that it will recognise and enforce judgments of another contracting state which have been given pursuant to a non-exclusive jurisdiction agreement under Art. 22 but this is optional.

[320] Article 3(d).   [321] Article 5(1).   [322] Article 5(2).   [323] Article 6.

[324] Only exceptionally and where that is beyond the control of the parties to the agreement.

[325] Article 8. So long as the judgment of the judgment granting court is effective and enforceable in the judgment granting state.

[326] Article 8(4).

jurisdiction agreements.[327] The Hague Convention will resolve the present problem that jurisdiction agreements in favour of third states may not be upheld as a basis for refusing to exercise jurisdiction over a party domiciled in a Member State.[328]

3. Relationship between Brussels I Regulation and national rules of jurisdiction

Although so far we have considered the two principal regimes for jurisdiction separately, their relationship to each other is a matter of some importance. The Brussels I Regulation is largely, although not wholly, engaged when the defendant has a domicile in a Member State.[329] Generally, the jurisdiction of the English court is determined by its national traditional common law rules where the defendant is not domiciled in a Member State (and Articles 22, 23 and 27 do not apply).[330] The two regimes are very different: one with clear and limited grounds of jurisdiction without any discretion as to their application, the other a flexible, discretionary regime with the aim of achieving a just and efficient result in particular cases. However, what is to happen if there are proceedings in a third state but the defendant is domiciled in a Member State?[331] How should a Member State's court deal with a jurisdiction agreement in favour of a third state? What if the subject matter of the dispute concerns a right *in rem* in immovable property in a third state? What if the matter is excluded from the Brussels I Regulation but proceedings are continuing in another Member State?[332] There are no express provisions in the Brussels I Regulation which deal with these issues. It does not provide a means of allocating jurisdiction between third states and Member States or of recognising and enforcing judgments of third states. That is not so surprising. The original purpose of the Brussels I Regulation was to support the single market by providing accepted rules of jurisdiction between Member States in order to have free movement of judgments. Nevertheless, the purposes of the Brussels I Regulation have expanded to include establishing an area of freedom, security and justice so as to further the free movement of persons.[333]

---

[327] B. Hess, T. Pfeiffer and P. Schlosser, *General Study on the Practical Application of the Regulation* (2007), para. 884, available at http://ec.europa.eu/justice_home/doc_centre/civil/studies/doc_civil_studies_en.htm.

[328] See further p. 190 *et seq.* below.   [329] Article 2.

[330] Article 4. The Brussels I Regulation has some relevance even in these cases, such that the national law rules are perhaps not completely free of the principles underlying the regime. See Fentiman, *International Commercial Litigation*, para. 11.77 *et seq.*

[331] I.e., one which is not a member of the EU.

[332] In *Allianz SpA, Generali Assicurazioni Generali Spa v West Tankers Inc. (The Front Comor)* Case C-185/07 [2009] ECR I-663, it is clear that the Brussels I Regulation operates to some extent. Articles 27 and 28 apply and anti-suit injunctions over proceedings in another Member State are prohibited.

[333] Article 67(4) (ex Art. 61(c)) and Art. 81 (ex Art. 65) of the Treaty on the Functioning of the European Union.

The CJEU in *Group Josi Reinsurance Co. SA v Universal General Insurance Co.*,[334] clearly held that the Brussels I Regulation rules applied to a case in which the defendant was domiciled in a Member State but the claimant was from a third state. The connections of the case to third states were not to be taken into account in determining jurisdiction. What then of the English doctrine of *forum conveniens*? Does it have any application when the defendant is domiciled in England but the appropriate forum is a third state? In *Owusu v Jackson*:

> The claimant had an accident when diving into the sea while holidaying in Jamaica and was paraplegic. He sued the villa owner who was domiciled in England for breach of contractual term to provide a safe beach. He also sought to bring an action in tort against the Jamaican owners of the club which provided access to the beach and other Jamaican defendants. The defendants all challenged the jurisdiction of the English courts. There had been a similar accident previously and an action was continuing in the Jamaican courts to establish liability in that case. It would be most efficient and in the interests of justice for this case to be stayed to await the outcome of that case in the natural forum for this dispute, Jamaica. Any judgment from Jamaica would be enforceable in England. The claimant argued that the English court had jurisdiction under Article 2 as the defendant was domiciled in England and that it could not decline to exercise the jurisdiction on the grounds of *forum conveniens*.[335]

The CJEU agreed. First, Article 2 of the Brussels I Regulation is a mandatory provision engaged by the defendant's domicile in a Member State and there is no need for any further connection between the events, the parties and a Member State. The Regulation is applicable when there are connections with third states, such as if the claimant is from a third state, or if the matter concerns immovable property in a Member State but the parties are from third states. Secondly, the *forum conveniens* doctrine was held to be incompatible with the principle of legal certainty which is one of the objectives of the Regulation. In particular, it is important that a defendant can predict where the defendant will be sued. The CJEU held that an objective[336] of the Regulation is the uniform application of jurisdictional rules. That objective would not be promoted if *forum conveniens* were permitted as only a few Member States have a *forum conveniens* doctrine. The court concluded that a Member State's courts are only permitted to decline to exercise jurisdiction under Article 2

---

[334] Case C-142/98 [2000] ECR I-5925.   [335] Case C-281/02 [2004] ECR I-1383.

[336] Perhaps the primary objective of the Brussels I Regulation, but this does not conform to the recitals of the Regulation or Art. 293 of the EC Treaty, see Fentiman, *International Commercial Litigation*, paras 11.86–11.87.

where there is express provision in the Regulation.[337] The English court cannot decline to exercise its jurisdiction over a defendant domiciled in England and stay its proceedings on the grounds of *forum conveniens*.

a. Criticism of *Owusu*

The decision in *Owusu* dismayed many English lawyers and has been subject to considerable criticism.[338] The reasoning deployed by the CJEU was not entirely satisfactory. The argument that Article 2 is to protect the defendant looks weak as it is the defendant who requests a stay under the *forum conveniens* doctrine. Taken literally, the argument that there must be some reason expressly in the Brussels I Regulation not to exercise jurisdiction mandated by Article 2 (such as Article 22) means that a Member State's court must take jurisdiction over a case which, for example, concerns rights *in rem* in immovable property in a third state. The argument that the internal market is necessarily served by the mandatory rule of jurisdiction in Article 2 absent any other connection with the EU needs more elucidation. The apparent prohibition on the use of discretion of any kind is inflexible and overlooks the provision for discretion in the Brussels I Regulation itself.[339] The more pertinent question asked by the English Court of Appeal in the reference to the CJEU was unanswered. The extent of *Owusu* is therefore unclear. For example, can the English court stay its proceedings on the ground of *forum conveniens* when the case concerns a question of rights *in rem* in immovable property in a third state? Or where a jurisdiction agreement in favour of the courts of a third state exists?[340] Or where proceedings are continuing in a third state?

b. Outstanding questions

It might be possible to argue that *Owusu* is so flawed that the CJEU must be encouraged to overrule it. This is unlikely. Critics of the decision would limit it to its narrowest scope. On this basis, it applies only when Article 2 is the ground of jurisdiction and when the reason for the stay of English proceedings is *forum conveniens*. Limiting *Owusu* to its narrowest scope might also open an argument that it does not apply when the ground of jurisdiction for the

[337] Case C-281/02 [2004] ECR I-1383 at para. 37.
[338] See e.g., A. Briggs, 'The Death of *Harrods*: *forum non conveniens* and the European Court' [2005] *LQR* 535 and '*Forum non conveniens* and Ideal Europeans' [2005] *LCMLQ* 378; E. Peel, '*Forum non conveniens* and European Ideals' [2005] *LCMLQ* 363; J. Harris, 'Stays of Proceedings and the Brussels Convention' [2005] *ICLQ* 933; R. Fentiman, 'Civil Jurisdiction and Third States: *Owusu* and After' (2006) 43 *CMLR* 705; J. Mance, 'Is Europe Aiming to Civilise the Common Law?' [2007] *EBL Rev.* 77; C. Knight, '*Owusu* and *Turner*: The Shark in the Water?' [2007] *CLJ* 288.
[339] In Article 28.
[340] In *Coreck Maritime GmbH v Handelsveem BV* Case C-387/98 [2000] ECR I-9337, the CJEU suggested that a stay in these circumstances was possible.

English court is Article 5 or 6 or 23, for example. This is a weak argument. The special and prorogated grounds of jurisdiction are of equal hierarchy to the general ground in Article 2 and so *Owusu* applies to prevent a stay of English proceedings.[341]

A slightly broader interpretation of *Owusu* would leave open the possibility of a stay due to *lis pendens* in the third state, a jurisdiction agreement in favour of the courts of the third state or immovable property in the third state. A stay on one of these grounds has been described as reflecting the effect of similar provisions in the Brussels I Regulation.[342] This reflective effect may be (a) direct, because the English court is declining jurisdiction *pursuant to* and consistent with the terms of the Regulation itself, or (b) indirect, where the national law rules apply but only if they are consistent with the Regulation. It is unclear whether the rules have to replicate the Brussels I Regulation exactly. So, for example, if a stay is sought due to a *lis pendens* in the third state, those proceedings must be between the same parties, in relation to the same cause of action and commenced first; or if a stay is on the basis of a jurisdiction agreement, it must conform to the formal requirements of Article 23(1). Alternatively, it may be sufficient for the rules merely to be consistent with the specific or more broad objectives of the Regulation. For example, the operation of *lis pendens* in *forum conveniens* doctrine is aimed at similar objectives of preventing parallel proceedings and competing judgments.

Some questions therefore remain as to the scope of *Owusu*. We have seen that the case applies to prevent a stay on *forum conveniens* grounds of a case commenced before the English court when the defendant is domiciled in a Member State where the more appropriate forum is a third state. The unclear examples are the following.

(1) Where the subject matter of the dispute falls within Article 22 but the location is a third state. English national rules of jurisdiction do not permit jurisdiction over a question concerning title to foreign land.[343] The Supreme Court in *Lucasfilm Ltd v Ainsworth*[344] held that a case alleging the infringement of a US copyright does not fall within that exclusion, partly because it would not fall within Article 22. Therefore, it could exercise jurisdiction over the defendant for breach of that US copyright. It did not answer the question whether, had the action fallen within Article 22, the court could or must refuse to exercise jurisdiction over the defendant who was domiciled in England in favour of the US courts.[345] More recently, in *Ferrexpo AG v Gilson Investments*

---

[341] *Gomez v Gomez-Monche Vives* [2008] 3 WLR 309 at para. 112.

[342] Also known as *effet réflexe*.

[343] *British South Africa Co. v Cia de Moçambique* [1893] AC 602.

[344] [2011] UKSC 39, [2012] 1 AC 208.

[345] Jacob LJ in the Court of Appeal [2009] EWCA Civ 1328, [2010] Ch. 503, held without much explanation that Art. 2 did not confer jurisdiction where the subject matter was intellectual property situate abroad.

Ltd,[346] Andrew Clarke J held that the English court retained the power to stay proceedings falling within Article 22 commenced against a defendant domiciled in England in favour of a third state's court:

> A long running dispute between Mr Babakov and Mr Zhevago had been carried on over the ownership of a Ukrainian mining company, OJSC. As part of the dispute, proceedings had been commenced in Ukraine by Mr Babakov for a declaration that the shares were ultimately owned by him. Mr Zhevago commenced proceedings in England against English companies owned by Mr Babakov for transfer of the shares in OJSC to him.

The dispute was found to fall within Article 22(2) or (3). It was therefore exclusively a matter for the courts of the company's domicile and where the registries were kept, i.e., Ukraine. Although this is a third state, Andrew Clarke J held that most countries recognised the legal principles underlying these rules of jurisdiction. Therefore a well-informed defendant would expect that court to have jurisdiction over the dispute. There was no uncertainty which the CJEU in *Owusu* was so keen to avoid. However, he did then hold that the power to stay the proceedings was discretionary: first, because there was no reason of principle or policy to adopt a strict reflexive approach; secondly, because if a strict approach was adopted the court might be required to stay proceedings in favour of a court in which justice could not be done,[347] thirdly, because the English court's machinery for granting a stay is 'inherently discretionary'. Only the second of these is persuasive. It is quite likely that the CJEU faced with this issue would decide that the exclusive jurisdiction in Article 22 should also be a ground for declining jurisdiction where the location of the immovable property was in a third state.

(2) Where there is a jurisdiction agreement in favour of a third state. In *Masri v Consolidated Contractors International (UK) Ltd*, Collins LJ said it would be 'odd' if the Regulation did not permit a stay in such cases.[348] The CJEU has suggested that a Member State's court has power to give effect to a jurisdiction agreement in favour of a third state.[349] The validity of that agreement is a matter for national law, and so should be the effect to be given to it. That effect would include the exercise of discretion in the English national law.[350]

(3) Where there are proceedings continuing in a third state. Here the English court has not provided a consistent answer. In *Lucasfilm Ltd v*

---

[346] [2012] EWHC 721 (Comm).

[347] I.e., in which Art. 6 of the European Convention on Human Rights might be infringed.

[348] [2009] QB 485 at paras 125–6. See too *Konkola Copper Mines Plc v Coromin Ltd* [2005] EWHC 896 (Comm) (point unaffected by appeal [2006] EWCA Civ 5, [2006] 1 Lloyd's LR 410) and *Winnetka Trading Corp. v Julius Baer International Ltd* [2009] 2 All ER (Comm) 735.

[349] *Coreck Maritime GmbH v Handelsveem BV* Case C-387/98 [2000] ECR I-9337 at para. 19.

[350] See Fentiman, *International Commercial Litigation*, para. 11.107 *et seq.*

Ainsworth,[351] Jacob LJ would permit a stay of English proceedings. On the other hand, in *Catalyst Investment Group Ltd v Lewinsohn*,[352] Barling J refused a stay arguing that the English rules on *lis pendens* were part of the discretionary doctrine of *forum conveniens* outlawed by *Owusu v Jackson*. Andrew Clarke J in *Ferrexpo AG v Gilson Investments Ltd*[353] disapproved *Catalyst* to hold that a stay was permissible as a reflexive interpretation of Article 28. A stay would uphold important policy concerns of the Brussels I Regulation such as the prevention of irreconcilable judgments.

(4) Where the parties have agreed to the exclusive jurisdiction of the English courts but the defendant argues that a third state is more appropriate.[354] As we have seen, it is likely that jurisdiction taken under Article 23(1) will be treated in the same way as that under Article 2. There is probably no discretion to stay in this case.[355] In a case where neither party is domiciled in a Member State then Article 23(3) applies to prevent other Member States' courts from taking jurisdiction but does not itself confer jurisdiction. In such cases, there is an argument that the English national rules on jurisdiction contain a discretion which can still be exercised.

(5) Where the parties have agreed to *non*-exclusive jurisdiction of the English courts it is possible that *Owusu* also removes the ability of the English courts to decline jurisdiction on discretionary grounds once an action has been commenced in England.[356] However, if neither of the parties are domiciled in a Member State then the argument above might operate to retain the discretion.

c. Proposals for alterations to the Brussels I Regulation after *Owusu*[357]

As we have seen,[358] the recast Brussels I Regulation make provision for staying actions in a Member State in favour of proceedings in third states. New Article 33 does not exactly mirror the flexibility or sophistication of the rules on *forum conveniens*, but follows the current Article 27 in applying to proceedings between the same parties on the same cause of action commenced first in a third state. All the criticisms of Article 27 can be deployed against this article. However, new Article 34 mirrors present Article 28 and so is slightly more flexible. Additionally, and most importantly, there is nothing expressly in Articles 33 and 34 to require[359] a Member State's court to stay

---

[351]   [2009] EWCA Civ 1328, [2010] Ch. 503, point unaffected by appeal [2011] UKSC 39, [2012] 1 AC 208.

[352]   [2009] EWHC 1964 (Ch), [2010] Ch. 218.   [353]   [2012] EWHC 721 (Comm).

[354]   As was successful in *Donohue v Armco Inc.* [2001] UKHL 64, [2002] 1 All ER 749.

[355]   *Equitas Ltd v Allstate Insurance Co.* [2008] EWHC 1671 (Comm), [2009] 1 All ER (Comm) 1137; *Skype Technologies SA v Joltid Ltd* [2009] EWHC 2783 (Ch), [2011] ILPr. 8.

[356]   See *Antec International Ltd v Biosafety USA Inc.* [2006] EWHC 11 (Comm) in which Gloster J raised this question but did not answer it.

[357]   See too R. Fentiman [2011] *C Yb Eur. Law* 66 on proposals for reform of Brussels I Regulation. See Brussels I Regulation (recast) 1215/2012 [2012] OJ L351/1.

[358]   See p. 133 *et seq.* above.   [359]   Recital 24 is insufficiently strong to achieve this.

proceedings in favour of a third state due to an exclusive jurisdiction agreement for the courts of that state or where the case concerns, say, rights *in rem* in immovable property located in a third state.

4. Restraining foreign proceedings (anti-suit injunctions)

a. Introduction

The English court has a wide statutory power to grant an injunction[360] 'in all cases in which it appears to the court to be just and convenient to do so'.[361] It has granted injunctions to restrain someone who is subject to its jurisdiction from proceeding with litigation in another country for many years.[362] Colloquially, the injunction is called an 'anti-suit' injunction which is the terminology used in the United States. One party, the applicant, applies for the injunction and the other party, the respondent, defends that application. Confusingly, in the cases, the respondent is often called the defendant. However, the applicant for an injunction is usually a defendant in substantive proceedings in the foreign proceedings so it is clearer to use applicant and respondent to the injunction.

The exercise of the power to grant an injunction to restrain foreign proceedings appears to infringe the foreign court's sovereignty to decide its own cases and outrages some civilian lawyers.[363] However, the English court has routinely granted these injunctions in order to do justice and denies that their grant necessarily breaches comity.[364] The power to grant the injunction depends upon the court having personal jurisdiction over the respondent. As with all injunctive relief that power is exercised over the conscience of the respondent, not directly on the foreign court. The respondent may decide not to obey the terms of the injunction and continue proceedings abroad. By doing so, the respondent is at risk of contempt of court proceedings initiated by the applicant. The court may penalise the contempt by fining the respondent, preventing the respondent from taking any further step in the proceedings,[365]

---

[360] See generally Thomas Raphael, *The Anti-Suit Injunction* (2nd edn, Oxford University Press, 2010).

[361] Senior Courts Act 1981, s. 37.

[362] *Bushby v Munday* (1821) 5 Madd 297 and *Portarlington v Soulby* (1834) 3 My & K 104 are two of the earliest authorities.

[363] See the German court's response to *Phillip Alexander Securities and Futures Ltd v Bamberger* [1997] ILPr. 73; *Re the Enforcement of an English Anti-suit Injunction* [1997] ILPr. 320. Orders to restrain the continuance of foreign proceedings have been held by the CJEU to be incompatible with the Brussels I Regulation (*Turner v Grovit* Case C-159/02 [2004] ECR I-3565).

[364] But cf. the recent case of *Star Reefers Pool Inc. v JFC Group Co. Ltd* [2012] EWCA Civ 14, [2012] 1 Lloyd's LR 376, in which the Court of Appeal expressly noted the importance of not infringing comity.

[365] Which puts the respondent, if a defendant in substantive proceedings, at risk of a summary judgment. That summary judgment would be enforceable both in England and throughout the EU (see further Chapter 8).

requisitioning the respondent's property in England or ultimately imprisoning the respondent. In this way, the injunction does give the impression that it is an exercise of quasi-criminal power which has an indirect effect on the foreign court. Therefore, the power to grant the restraining order should be exercised with caution.[366] On occasion, the practical purpose of the injunction is to ensure that the foreign proceedings, even if pursued to judgment, cannot be enforced in England or elsewhere.[367]

The respondent can attempt to avoid the grant of an injunction by giving an undertaking to the English court not to make certain arguments in the foreign court which might amount to the injustice which the injunction would otherwise prevent.[368] Conversely, the injunction is more likely to be granted if the applicant undertakes to make advantages to the respondent in the foreign court available in England.[369] Proceedings brought abroad in breach of an exclusive jurisdiction or arbitration agreement are the most obvious examples when an injunction will be granted. The injustice of permitting proceedings in breach of contract is clear. However, there are further grounds for granting the injunction to restrain continuance of foreign proceedings where the respondent is seeking unfair advantages in the foreign court such that injustice is done to the applicant.

Note that the English court cannot grant an injunction restraining a respondent from continuing proceedings falling within the Brussels I Regulation in another Member State.[370]

b. Basis for injunction

i. Jurisdiction over respondent

In order to grant an injunction to restrain the respondent from continuing proceedings in a foreign court the English court must have jurisdiction over the respondent. Where the respondent is not domiciled in a Member State, the national rules of jurisdiction may be utilised to take jurisdiction. That includes service on the respondent within the jurisdiction and where the court has given permission for the notice of the proceedings to be served on the respondent out of the jurisdiction. Where the respondent is domiciled in a Member State, the rules of the Brussels I Regulation must be followed.

---

[366] *Airbus Industrie GIE v Patel* [1999] AC 119.

[367] *Masri v Consolidated Contractors International (UK) Ltd (No. 3)* [2009] 2 WLR 669.

[368] *Société Nationale Industrielle Aérospatiale v Lee Kui Jak* [1987] AC 871 at 896–7. The respondent undertook to pursue the claim in Texas under Brunei law (so avoiding the Texas strict liability regime and the possibility of punitive damages) and for a judge alone to hear the case not a jury trial. In the event, these were insufficient to prevent the grant of the injunction.

[369] In *Société Nationale Industrielle Aérospatiale v Lee Kui Jak* [1987] AC 871, the applicant offered to make evidence from the Texan action available in England.

[370] *Turner v Grovit* Case C-159/02 [2004] ECR I-3565.

In most cases, an injunction is granted while proceedings are continuing in England on a substantive dispute. The jurisdiction of the English court over the parties to that substantive dispute then is the foundation of the jurisdiction to grant an injunction. The injunction in those cases is ancillary to the substantive dispute[371] and needs no separate decision on the exercise of the court's power over the respondent (nor indeed on the interest of the court). These cases will turn exclusively on the exercise of the discretion.

It is exceptionally possible to obtain an injunction restraining the continuance of proceedings in another country without substantive proceedings continuing in England, or indeed where such proceedings are impossible.[372] These are known as the single forum cases, where the claim is only possible in a single forum which is not England, as for example a claim based on the RICO Act in the United States. The injunction therefore prevents any possible recovery or even a ventilation of the alleged claim. In these cases the court must be especially careful to ensure that it has jurisdiction over the respondent. In both cases in which a single forum injunction was discussed,[373] the respondent was a company incorporated in England so there was no question that the respondent was subject to the jurisdiction. If a respondent can be served within the jurisdiction then the respondent may wish to argue that England is not the proper place to hear the application. Alternatively, if the respondent has to be served out of the jurisdiction the applicant would have to show that England is the proper place for trial which is problematic where the trial of the substance is to take place elsewhere. However, any decision on jurisdiction would probably be subsumed into the decision on the merits of the application.[374] It is clear that England being the appropriate forum is insufficient to grant the injunction, as both injustice and a sufficient interest in the dispute is also necessary.[375] However, it is less clear that England must be the single natural forum in order to have jurisdiction to grant the injunction in these single forum cases or whether being *a* natural forum (coupled with injustice and sufficient interest) would be sufficient.[376] Where the defendant is domiciled in a Member State, the jurisdiction must be established under the Brussels I Regulation. There is no difficulty if the defendant is domiciled in England or there is a jurisdiction agreement in favour of the English courts. It is difficult to establish jurisdiction in any other case.[377]

---

[371] *Masri v Consolidated Contractors International (UK) Ltd (No. 3)* [2008] EWCA Civ 625, [2009] 2 WLR 669 (CA). In that case the English case had already come to trial and a judgment obtained. Nevertheless, the injunction was given to protect those substantive proceedings.

[372] The only reported example is *Midland Bank Plc v Laker Airways Ltd* [1986] QB 689 (CA).

[373] *British Airways Board v Laker Airways Ltd* [1985] AC 58 (HL); *Midland Bank Plc v Laker Airways Ltd* [1986] QB 689 (CA).

[374] See p. 198 *et seq.* below.   [375] *Airbus Industrie GIE v Patel* [1999] AC 119.

[376] In a single forum case, there is an argument that the foreign forum in which the claim can be ventilated (because it can only be made there) must be the natural forum, rather than England where the claim cannot be made, *ex hypothesi.*

[377] Article 31 would only apply where there are proceedings in another Member State. Note that the proceedings to be enjoined must be continuing in a third state.

ii. A 'sufficient interest' in the dispute

The English court must have an interest in the dispute to justify the grant of the injunction. This requirement goes some way towards defending the argument that the injunction is contrary to the principle of comity. As Lord Goff of Chieveley noted 'comity requires that the English forum should have a sufficient interest in, or connection with, the matter in question to justify the indirect interference with the foreign court which an anti-suit injunction entails'.[378] The question arose in *Airbus Industrie GIE v Patel*:[379]

Following an aircraft crash in India, the respondents commenced proceedings in India against the pilots' employers which was largely settled after the court found the cause of the accident to be pilot error. The aircraft had been designed and produced in France by the applicants who were a French company. The respondents then commenced proceedings in Texas against the applicants. The Texas court had many advantages to the respondents such as greater total damages, strict liability, wider discovery, contingency fees and the expertise to obtain and understand the complex scientific evidence. However, the respondents would be unable to claim contribution from other possible tortfeasors in the Texas court and there was no connection between this dispute and Texas. The Texas court was taking jurisdiction on the basis of the applicants 'doing business' in Texas. The Indian court made an order restraining the respondents from pursuing the Texas proceedings which was ineffective as the respondents had no assets in India and lived in London. The applicants sought to enforce this judgment in England but were unsuccessful.[380] They then applied for an injunction from the English court to restrain the proceedings in Texas.

The House of Lords refused to grant the injunction. Although England was a natural forum for this dispute, that of itself was insufficient to justify the injunction. Neither was the finding that Texas was inappropriate sufficient. Merely suing in an inappropriate forum is not a good enough reason to grant the injunction. India was *the* natural forum but was unable to grant effective relief. Lord Goff argued that the English courts should not act as international policemen patrolling the boundaries of appropriate exercise of jurisdiction.

Where substantive proceedings are continuing between the parties in England, the injunction is ancillary to those proceedings and there is a sufficient interest. Where the English court is restraining foreign proceedings in breach of an English arbitration clause[381] or exclusive jurisdiction agreement,[382] it also has a sufficient interest despite the lack of substantive English proceedings.

---

[378] [1999] AC 119 at 138.   [379] [1999] AC 119.

[380] As a judgment is only enforceable under the national rules if it is a debt, which obviously an injunction is not. See further p. 249 *et seq.* below.

[381] *AES Ust-Kamenogorsk Hydropower Plant LLC v Ust-Kamenogorsk Hydropower Plant JSC* [2011] EWCA Civ 647.

[382] *Donohue v Armco Inc.* [2001] UKHL 64, [2002] 1 All ER 749.

A completely free-standing injunction,[383] such as the single forum case, requires more consideration. Lord Goff explicitly excluded the single forum cases from his decision in *Airbus Industrie GIE v Patel*. He noted that the English court could grant an injunction in these cases where 'the relevant transaction was overwhelmingly English in character' or perhaps 'that the injunction is necessary to protect the policies of the English forum'.[384] For example, where both parties were English and acted in England under a contract governed by English law there is a sufficient interest that the English court must protect from proceedings in the United States.

iii. Injustice

The basis for any injunction is to prevent injustice. 'Injustice' is necessarily a flexible concept and the courts appear unwilling to categorise the flexibility with precise definition.[385] Note that it is not necessarily unjust for proceedings to be continuing in two courts.[386] Something more is needed. There are three examples of injustice which have resulted in the grant of an injunction[387] but these often overlap:[388] (1) the respondent's conduct is in breach of contract; (2) the respondent's conduct in pursuing proceedings abroad is unconscionable; (3) the applicant is being vexed or oppressed by the proceedings abroad.

1. Proceedings in breach of a jurisdiction or arbitration agreement

This is the strongest ground for the grant of a restraining injunction. A party who has entered into a valid exclusive jurisdiction or arbitration agreement will be in breach of contract by seeking the adjudication of a court other than that agreed to. In these cases, the injunction will ordinarily be granted. The English court in these cases has no real concerns of comity.[389] This is somewhat disingenuous despite arguments based on *competence-competence*.[390] A foreign court may entirely properly come to a different decision as to the validity, scope or effect of an English jurisdiction or arbitration clause and it does not infringe comity by making that decision

---

[383] I.e., where there are no substantive proceedings and no English jurisdiction or arbitration clause (with or without litigation going on under the jurisdiction or arbitration clause).

[384] However, in *Turner v Grovit* [2002] 1 WLR 107 at para. 24, it was said that policy considerations go to the exercise of the discretion rather than the existence of the power to make the order. See Fentiman, *International Commercial Litigation*, para. 15.18.

[385] *Castanho v Brown & Root Ltd* [1981] AC 557 at 553.

[386] *Société Nationale Industrielle Aérospatiale v Lee Kui Jak* [1987] AC 871.

[387] *Airbus Industrie GIE v Patel* [1999] AC 119 at 135.

[388] Note Fentiman, *International Commercial Litigation*, para. 15.26 *et seq.* who would categorise the injustice differently into (1) enforcing the applicant's rights, (2) preventing illegitimate parallel proceedings, and (3) preventing legitimate parallel proceedings where applicant would be denied justice in the foreign court.

[389] *The Angelic Grace* [1995] 1 Lloyd's LR 87 (CA).

[390] I.e., that the court identified in the jurisdiction agreement should be the only court to determine the validity, scope or effect of the jurisdiction or arbitration agreement.

itself. In reverse, the English court has decided on the validity and effect of a foreign jurisdiction agreement with no suggestion that it is acting improperly.[391] In cases of an exclusive jurisdiction agreement the onus is placed on the respondent to show why the injunction should not be granted.[392] The factors taken into account in determining whether to grant the injunction or not include those which operate when the court is deciding whether or not to grant a stay of proceedings where the court has jurisdiction by virtue of an exclusive jurisdiction agreement. Also the respondent has to show this by reference to factors which were unforeseeable at the time the contract was entered into.[393] The injunction may not be granted where the applicant has not acted quickly or where third parties would be prejudiced by the enforcement of the agreement or where the respondent would suffer injustice, for example, by being deprived of security.[394]

Note that the breach of contract is only clear when the parties have entered into a valid, binding, exclusive jurisdiction or arbitration agreement. A respondent might seek to prevent the injunction by arguing that such jurisdiction or arbitration agreement is invalid, or not binding, or does not cover the dispute in question, or that it is not exclusive.[395] In the case of an expressly non-exclusive jurisdiction agreement, the applicant should have to show injustice beyond the respondent commencing proceedings in a foreign court. The parties have contemplated the possibility of proceedings elsewhere than in England because of the non-exclusive nature of the jurisdiction agreement. With a non-exclusive jurisdiction agreement the respondent is not limited to matters which were unforeseeable at the time the contract was entered into. Therefore, in *Deutsche Bank AG v Highland Crusader Offshore Partners LP*,[396] although England was the court identified in the non-exclusive jurisdiction agreement and English law governed the contract there was no other connection with England. There were connections with the United States, although not particularly strongly with the state of Texas where the proceedings were continuing. The restraining order was not granted.[397]

---

[391] For example in *The El Amria* [1981] 2 Lloyd's LR 119 and *The Sennar (No. 2)* [1985] 1 WLR 490.

[392] *Donohue v Armco Inc.* [2001] UKHL 64, [2002] 1 All ER 749.

[393] *Sebastian Holdings Inc. v Deutsche Bank AG* [2010] EWCA Civ 998, [2010] ILPr. 52 at para. 78 approving Gloster J in *Antec International Ltd v Biosafety USA Inc.* [2006] EWHC 47 (Comm).

[394] *Welex AG v Rosa Maritime* [2003] 2 Lloyd's LR 509; usually the applicant will give an undertaking to provide equivalent security in the English court and so the injunction can be awarded.

[395] On the interpretation of jurisdiction agreements as exclusive or not, see further pp. 181–2 below.

[396] [2009] EWCA Civ 725, [2010] 1 WLR 1023.

[397] cf. *Sabah Shipyard (Pakistan) Ltd v Pakistan* [2002] EWCA Civ 1643, [2003] 2 Lloyd's LR 571, in which a differently phrased non-exclusive jurisdiction agreement was upheld by an anti-suit injunction. That case probably turns on its special circumstances that the commencement of proceedings in Pakistan included an anti-suit injunction against English proceedings continuing here under the non-exclusive jurisdiction agreement.

2. Unconscionable conduct

Injunctions to restrain a party from continuing proceedings in another country may be granted on the general ground that the party is acting unconscionably in pursuing those proceedings. It could be said that the other grounds are encompassed by this one but the cases appear to distinguish them. In *Société Nationale Industrielle Aerospatiale v Lee Kui Jak*:

> The widow of a Brunei businessman brought an action in Texas against the manufacturer of a helicopter after her husband had been killed when the helicopter crashed in Brunei. The Texas court could take jurisdiction over this dispute despite the lack of connections between the events and Texas on the basis that the manufacturer did business in Texas. The advantages to the widow of proceeding in Texas included a wider system of discovery, strict liability under Texas law, conditional fees, and the possibility of punitive damages. There were also proceedings continuing in Brunei between the widow and the manufacturers to which the operators of the helicopter were joined as possible contributors in the event that the manufacturers were liable. The Texas proceedings were fairly well advanced but the operator refused to submit to the Texas jurisdiction. The manufacturer applied for an injunction restraining the widow from continuing the Texas proceedings. The case was appealed to the Privy Council from Brunei.

Lord Goff of Chieveley gave the opinion of the Board. Brunei was the natural forum. The proceedings in Texas were not in an appropriate or natural forum but it was not necessarily unjust for the respondent to pursue advantages available there.[398] However, on the facts, serious injustice would be done if the respondent were to be permitted to continue proceedings in Texas. The injustice was that the operators would not be subject to the Texas proceedings. Therefore the manufacturer would be unjustly deprived of an advantage in the natural forum as the claim for contribution could not be pursued in the same court that was deciding on liability. He held that the injunction should be granted. This was not a case in which the respondent was acting vexatiously or oppressively by continuing proceedings in Texas, however, it would be unconscionable for those proceedings to continue given the overwhelming disadvantage to the applicant.

3. Vexation or oppression of the applicant

A powerful example of vexatious or oppressive conduct can be seen in *Turner v Grovit*. Although it would no longer be possible to enjoin proceedings in another Member State as was done here, the decision is still applicable to cases in which the proceedings to be enjoined are continuing in a third state:

---

[398] The respondent gave undertakings not to pursue certain of the advantages, such as strict liability in an attempt to stave off the injunction. In reply the applicant gave undertakings to make some of the advantages in Texas, such as the fruits of wider discovery, available in Brunei in an attempt to make it just to continue in Brunei not Texas.

The respondent commenced proceedings in Spain against the applicant who had already started a case against the respondent in England which was well advanced.[399] The purpose of the Spanish proceedings was to harass the English applicant into dropping his action in the English employment tribunal.[400]

Laws LJ in the Court of Appeal had no hesitation in granting the injunction. The Spanish proceedings were commenced in bad faith and were vexatious. Indeed, he considered them 'abusive as a matter of elementary principle'.[401] Lord Hobhouse in the House of Lords also had no hesitation but said that the injunction could only be founded on the wrongful conduct of the respondent which the applicant has a legitimate interest in seeking to prevent. Thus, he saw the case as one falling under the previous heading. He noted that a party has no right not to be sued in a particular forum except where some specific factor gives the party that right, such as a jurisdiction clause. In this case, there was a clear interest of the applicant to protect the English proceedings.

Turner v Grovit is probably an extreme example of vexation and oppression of the applicant. Another example is *Glencore AG v Metro Trading International Inc. (No. 3)*,[402] where the respondent ship-owners were prevented from pursuing some of their claims against the applicants in Georgia. The respondents had claimed and counterclaimed in earlier litigation in England and there was no legitimate reason for the Georgian proceedings which were part of a strategy to wear down the applicants who had to fight in various courts. These Georgian proceedings were therefore vexatious and oppressive. In modern international litigation, parallel proceedings are not uncommon as parties jostle for the advantage. When the English court is deciding on its own jurisdiction it uses the doctrine of *forum conveniens* to determine whether or not it should hear the case. Initially, the anti-suit injunction cases utilised some aspects of *forum conveniens* in deciding to grant the injunction.[403] However, merely commencing proceedings in a forum that is not a natural forum is not sufficient to be vexatious and oppressive conduct. Nor does the decision that England is the natural forum make proceedings abroad vexatious and oppressive of themselves.

Proceedings abroad which are bound to fail or are inherently weak may also be enjoined as being vexatious and oppressive where there is litigation between the parties going ahead in England.[404] However, it can be difficult to assess

---

[399] The Spanish proceedings may not have been prevented by what is now Art. 27 of the Brussels I Regulation as the parties were not exactly the same and the cause of action different (although the Court of Appeal, as the court first seised, took a different view).

[400] [2000] QB 345 (CA), [2001] UKHL 65, [2002] 1 WLR 107 (HL).

[401] [2000] QB 345 (CA) at 362.   [402] [2002] EWCA Civ 528, [2002] 2 All ER (Comm) 1.

[403] See e.g., *Société Nationale Industrielle Aérospatiale v Lee Kui Jak* [1987] AC 871.

[404] *Elektrim SA v Vivendi Holdings 1 Corp.* [2008] EWCA Civ 1178, [2009] 1 Lloyd's LR 59.

whether the foreign proceedings are bound to fail and the English court should not set itself up as an arbiter of the dispute in the foreign court.[405]

In general, the English court must respect considerations of comity and not permit the restraining order merely because of the existence of parallel proceedings. So in *Star Reefers Pool Inc. v JFC Group Co. Ltd*:

> JFC (a Russian charterer) had given guarantees to Star (a Cayman ship-owner). JFC had commenced proceedings in Russia for a declaration that the guarantees were invalid under Russian law. Star then sued JFC in England for payment of the guarantees under English law and sought an anti-suit injunction against the Russian proceedings.[406]

Rix LJ in the Court of Appeal was clear that JFC merely commencing and continuing proceedings in Russia was not inherently vexatious and oppressive even if England was the natural forum for the dispute. Although the applicants would have an advantage in the English court which was unavailable to them in the Russian court,[407] he was concerned that the grant of an anti-suit injunction would infringe comity unless the party had agreed not to be sued in the foreign forum. Absent an English jurisdiction or arbitration clause it might now be more difficult to obtain an anti-suit injunction. This case illustrates rather well that anti-suit injunctions are to prevent injustice and not merely police the tactics of international litigation.

At one time the English court appeared to consider that anti-suit injunctions were an appropriate way of controlling the exorbitant exercise of power by other courts, particularly the US courts in personal injury cases and anti-trust actions.[408] Lately, injunctions for these cases do not seem to have been applied for, or granted. That may be due to a more circumspect exercise of jurisdiction by the US courts, particularly in Texas. Also, the use of undertakings by the applicants and respondents to annul advantages in competing jurisdictions has probably led to more settlements, thus obviating the need for injunctions restraining foreign proceedings.

c. Article 6 of the European Convention on Human Rights

Article 6(1) of the ECHR confers a right of access to justice on the respondent. If a restraining order is granted, is that right infringed as the respondent will be unable to ventilate the dispute in a court of the respondent's choosing? The

---

[405] *Midland Bank plc v Laker Airways Ltd* [1986] QB 689 at 700.

[406] [2012] EWCA Civ 14, [2012] 1 Lloyd's LR 376.

[407] The guarantees would be likely to be valid under English law and not under Russian law. The point of the Russian proceedings was largely therefore to make any English judgment unenforceable in Russia.

[408] See e.g., *Société Nationale Industrielle Aérospatiale v Lee Kui Jak* [1987] AC 871 and *Midland Bank Plc v Laker Airways Ltd* [1986] QB 689 (CA).

English court has held that Article 6 rights are not infringed by anti-suit injunctions so long as there is an alternative forum.[409] That would apparently outlaw anti-suit injunctions in single forum cases. The international effect of the ECHR requires more analysis. Why should a claimant be permitted to bring a speculative action in a court anywhere in the world in which recovery might be possible irrespective of connections of the parties with that state? What about the injustice to the defendant who never expected to be subject to that state's law or jurisdiction? What if the claimant is acting in bad faith or is infringing the defendant's rights not to be sued in that state? The Brussels I Regulation limits a claimant's ability to sue in any court. Presumably, that Regulation does not infringe the ECHR. So some control on the claimant's access to courts is apparently permissible. In *Al-Adsani v United Kingdom*,[410] the European Court of Human Rights held that Article 6(1) applied notwithstanding a plea of sovereign immunity. However, the better view is that a limitation on jurisdiction is possible so long as it is proportionate and is in pursuit of a legitimate aim. It might be argued that a restraining order promotes the legitimate aim of preventing abusive forum shopping.

d. Restraining proceedings in another Member State

Articles 27 and 28 of the Brussels I Regulation deal with parallel proceedings within the Member States. In theory there is no need for restraining orders to control proceedings continuing in another Member State's courts. The English court will not even be able to take jurisdiction over a case where proceedings are already commenced in another Member State, even where there is an exclusive jurisdiction agreement in favour of the English court.[411] There may nonetheless be examples of injustice which the English court would wish to prevent with an injunction against the continuance of proceedings in another Member State, for example, if the respondent has commenced proceedings in bad faith in another Member State after continuing proceedings in England or to protect an agreement requiring arbitration in England.

The CJEU in a pair of cases, *Turner v Grovit*[412] and *Allianz SpA, Generali Assicurazioni Generali SpA v West Tankers Inc. (The Front Comor)*,[413] has decided that restraining orders over proceedings in another Member State are not allowed within the Brussels I Regulation regime. We have seen that the facts in the first case were quite exceptional but nevertheless, the CJEU held that the important principle of mutual trust required that Member States did not question the exercise of jurisdiction by other Member States' courts. The Spanish courts had to be allowed to decide on their own jurisdiction under the

---

[409] *OT Africa Line Ltd v Hijazy (The Kribi)* [2002] ILPr. 18.
[410] Judgment of 21 November 2001, (2001) 34 EHRR 273 at para. 52.
[411] *Eric Gasser v MISAT srl* Case C-116/02 [2003] ECR I-14693.
[412] Case C-159/02 [2004] ECR I-3565.   [413] Case C-185/07 [2009] ECR I-663.

Brussels I Regulation and that decision was not to be usurped by another Member State. The court was unimpressed with the argument that an injunction only acts *in personam* on the respondent's conduct. It reiterated that national procedural rules were not permitted to impair the operation of the Regulation. The width of the decision in *Turner v Grovit* can be seen in the *West Tankers* case:[414]

> A ship owned by West Tankers crashed into a jetty in Italy and caused damage to the charterer's jetty. The charterparty was governed by English law and contained an agreement for arbitration in England. The charterers claimed under their insurance and sought to claim in arbitration against the ship-owners for the excess. The insurers having paid out to the charterers then brought a subrogated action against the ship-owners in Italy. The ship-owners brought an action in England for a declaration that the insurers' action was to be settled by arbitration and also for an anti-suit injunction over the Italian proceedings.

We have seen that the arbitration proceedings in England were not within the scope of the Brussels I Regulation. The proceedings in Italy on the substance of the dispute were, however, within the Regulation despite the existence of the arbitration agreement being raised as a defence to jurisdiction. The issue of the arbitration agreement was only a preliminary matter which was only ancillary to the primary question of the liability for damages. Under the principle of mutual trust the Italian court's decision on its own jurisdiction could not be questioned by the English court. The Italian court must be permitted to come to its own conclusion on the existence, validity and scope of the arbitration agreement. The CJEU argued that otherwise the jurisdiction of a Member State's court might be usurped merely by an allegation of the existence of an arbitration agreement.

These cases have been subject to criticism, particularly *West Tankers*.[415] Arbitration agreements may be easily undermined when a party commences proceedings in the courts of a Member State other than those identified in the arbitration agreement.[416] The entire point of an arbitration agreement is to take the dispute away from the realm of the courts. Difficult questions as to the recognition and enforcement of the other Member State's judgment can arise.[417] However, they are entirely consistent with

---

[414] Also discussed p. 62 *et seq.* above in relation to the scope of the Brussels I Regulation.

[415] Hare [2004] *CLJ* 570; Fentiman [2010] *CLJ* 242, [2009] *CLJ* 278; Peel [2009] *LQR* 365. The proposed changes to the Brussels I Regulation do not entirely resolve the difficulties over arbitration. See Benedetelli [2011] *Arb. Int.* 583.

[416] See e.g., *National Navigacion v Endesa* [2010] 1 Lloyd's LR 193 and L. Radicati di Brazolo [2011] *Jo. Priv. Int. Law* 423.

[417] See *National Navigacion v Endesa* [2009] EWCA Civ 1397, [2010] 1 Lloyd's LR 193.

other cases on the operation of the Brussels I Regulation, such as *Eric Gasser v MISAT srl*[418] and *Owusu v Jackson,*[419] which uphold the strict applicability of the Regulation.

It appears that the English court will still restrain proceedings in a third state even if the respondent is domiciled in a Member State.[420]

---

[418] Case C-116/02 [2003] ECR I-14693.
[419] Case C-281/02 [2004] ECR I-1383. See further below p. 188 *et seq.* below.
[420] *Skype Technologies SA v Joltid Ltd* [2009] EWHC 2783 (Ch), [2011] ILPr. 8. cf. Knight [2007] *CLJ* 288.

7

Provisional measures

1. Introduction

The English court has inherent powers as well as wide powers under s. 37 of the Senior Courts Act 1981 to make orders in support of its own proceedings. These provisional measures or interim remedies commonly include freezing injunctions,[1] orders for the retention of property, restraining orders,[2] and orders for the disclosure of evidence.[3] The purpose of these orders is often to prevent the interests of the applicant (usually the claimant) from being irreparably harmed while the case is continuing and before judgment has been obtained and enforced. A party must be stopped from hiding or destroying evidence or dissipating assets which would make that party 'judgment-proof'. Such orders may have implications in international litigation, for example, if the assets to be frozen are located abroad or the evidence is found in a foreign country. An order to do or refrain from doing something abroad has obvious extraterritorial implications and may raise issues of infringement of a foreign sovereign's power.[4] The English courts are alert to those concerns but are also aware of the importance of being able to grant these orders in an increasingly globalised world. In particular, money can be so easily moved out of one jurisdiction and into another, where ownership is less transparent, and frustrating the later English judgment.[5]

Civil Jurisdiction and Judgments Act 1982, s. 25 gives the English court powers to make interim remedies in support of foreign proceedings. Therefore, if substantive proceedings are continuing abroad on the merits of the

---

[1] Otherwise known as *Mareva* injunctions after *Mareva Cia Naviera SA v International Bulkcarriers SA* [1975] 2 Lloyd's LR 509.

[2] Also known as anti-suit injunctions, discussed in relation to jurisdiction see pp. 151–2 above.

[3] *Anton Piller* orders, *Norwich Pharmacal* orders, and the like. See generally CPR r. 25 for a list of interim remedies. Orders to restrain proceedings abroad are also provisional measures and were discussed in Chapter 5.

[4] See Lawrence Collins LJ in *Masri v Consolidated Contractors International (UK) Ltd and others (No. 3)* [2008] EWCA Civ 625, [2009] QB 503 at para. 35.

[5] As Sir John Donaldson MR put it in *DST v Rakoil* [1990] 1 AC 295 at 307, money can be moved by the 'twinkling of a telex', in more modern practice by the blink of a cursor.

dispute, the English court can aid the foreign court by granting similar orders as it would in support of substantive proceedings in England. The application for such an order usually comes from one of the parties to the foreign proceedings (the applicant). Jurisdiction over the respondent to the application has to be established and the court has a discretion whether or not to grant the order. These orders too raise interesting questions in international litigation.

The court must balance the interests of the applicant in ensuring that there are assets against which a possible judgment can be enforced with those of the respondent who may succeed in defence. In particular, the freezing injunction is known as a 'nuclear weapon' as it so limits the respondent's ability to deal with assets that the respondent is likely to capitulate rather than risk a lengthy trial during which assets up to the full value of the claim are, in effect, frozen. Interim remedies also assist in the efficient administration of justice and ensure the integrity of the legal process.[6]

2. Freezing injunctions

a. Introduction

Freezing injunctions can be granted before or after judgment. They are often granted before trial and indeed before the issue of the claim form. Those applications made before issue of the claim form are made without notice to the respondent[7] but must be supported by a statement of truth,[8] and draft claim form and order. The power of surprise ensures that assets can be kept safe from dissipation. However, the applicant must undertake to issue and serve the claim form on the respondent defendant as soon as possible. The applicant must also make full and frank disclosure of all material matters, including the likely defence of the respondent.

CPR r. 25 lays out the procedure for granting interim remedies. It provides that the court may grant a 'freezing injunction' restraining a party from removing from the jurisdiction assets located there or restraining a party from dealing with any assets whether located within the jurisdiction or not. However, the freezing injunction does not actually freeze the assets but prevents the party from dealing with that party's assets (except in the normal course of business) below a sum sufficient to cover the claim. In addition, usual living expenses and legal fees can be paid without breaching the injunction.[9] So, if

---

[6] R. Fentiman, *International Commercial Litigation* (Oxford University Press, 2010) para. 17.02.

[7] I.e., *ex parte*.

[8] Statements of truth are also called affidavits and attest to the evidence on which the order is based.

[9] See *JSC BTA Bank v Ablyazov* [2012] EWHC 1819 (Comm) for a very wide-ranging order requiring the respondent to inform the applicant before expending sums on legal advice.

the claim is for £1m and the respondent has assets of £1m, the respondent may only expend usual living expenses, legal fees and normal business transactions. It is assumed that normal business transactions do not too adversely affect the assets of the respondent. A respondent cannot, however, give assets away or transfer them below market value to escape enforcement. The paralysing effect of a freezing injunction lies in the uncertainty of what would be a transaction in the 'normal course of business' coupled with the severe penalties for breaching the order. Assets can include cash, accounts held in banks and other financial intermediaries, shares and securities, movables (such as a ship) and perhaps even goodwill.[10]

In addition to the freezing injunction, the court may grant an order to direct a party to provide information about assets or their location. This disclosure order is often more important than the freezing order as it enables the applicant to identify and locate assets (often abroad) against which local measures can be taken. The disclosure order can only be ancillary to the freezing injunction; it is not a free-standing remedy.[11]

Both the freezing injunction and the disclosure order are enforced by use of contempt of court remedies. The consequences of breach of a freezing injunction therefore include striking out of the defence (leaving the way open to summary judgment for the claim); preventing participation in further hearings on the claim; fines or requisition of assets; and ultimately committal to prison for contempt. Note that not only the respondent but also any other person given notice of the injunction by being named in it (even though not a party to the substantive proceedings) will be subject to contempt for allowing breach of the order. Usually, therefore, the respondent's bank will be named in the order as a third party.[12] Cautious institutions are very likely to comply with the order and refuse to permit the respondent to remove assets from the accounts. Those institutions are also rather likely to disclose the whereabouts of the respondent's accounts at other branches, possibly abroad. Note that banks can also be defendants to the substantive proceedings where the claimants allege that the bank has been assisting in a fraud, receiving trust property or is subject to a proprietary tracing claim. In those cases, a tracing order directly against the defendant bank is more appropriate.[13]

The power to grant the injunction originates in equity and is therefore discretionary. The original case is *Mareva Cia Naviera SA v International Bulkcarriers SA*:

---

[10] *Rasu Maritima SA v Perusahaan Pertambangan* [1978] QB 644 (CA).
[11] *Parker v CS Structured Credit Fund Ltd* [2003] EWHC 391 (Ch), [2003] 1 WLR 1680.
[12] See e.g., *Babanaft International SA v Bassatne* [1990] Ch. 13 (CA), where a foreign bank was made subject to a freezing order against one of its account holders because it had a branch in London.
[13] *A v C* [1981] QB 956n.

> The ship *Mareva* had been chartered by the defendants from the claimant owners. The defendants had then subchartered the ship to a company which paid the hire in advance into an account in London. The defendants did not pay the claimants the hire due under the charter and repudiated the agreement. The claimants claimed the outstanding hire and were fearful that the money already paid by the subcharterers would be removed from London and transferred abroad. The charterer, a 'one ship' company, would then be liquidated leaving no assets against which judgment could be enforced. The claimants therefore sought an injunction to restrain the disposal of the sums in the account.[14]

Lord Denning in a robust judgment granted the order. He avoided the decision in *Lister v Stubbs* in which the Court of Appeal had held that it had no power to grant an injunction unless the applicant had a legal or equitable right to protect. Roskill LJ also agreed that the court should intervene to protect the ship-owner's rights to payment of the hire although the nature of their rights had yet to be determined. The case has been widely followed[15] and upheld as a useful practice.[16] Note that these were not claims for tracing to recover money embezzled but a contractual claim to damages.[17] The freezing injunction is therefore not limited to fraudsters and claims to recover embezzled funds which demand such extreme measures. The injunction is also available in fairly standard commercial litigation where there is evidence that the respondent has the capacity to move assets around different countries. However, a freezing injunction is more freely given in the case of claims relating to fraud, claims to trace assets embezzled,[18] and in the case of a post-judgment freezing order. The English court can be remarkably supportive of applicants in the face of dishonest respondents. For example, in *Masri v Consolidated Contractors International Co. SAL*,[19] the Court of Appeal granted a post-judgment worldwide freezing order against future foreign debts (the prospective revenues from a concession in Yemen) where the judgment debtors had deliberately escaped execution of the English judgment.

There are three aspects of a freezing injunction which need to be separated. First, does the court have jurisdiction over the respondent? This is important

---

[14] [1975] 2 Lloyd's LR 509.

[15] The Court of Appeal granted a similar injunction in *Nippon Yusen Kaisha v Karageorgis* [1975] 1 WLR 1093 and in *Rasu Maritima SA v Perusahaan Pertambangan Minyak Dan Gas Bumi Negara* [1978] QB 644.

[16] See e.g., *Owners of Cargo Lately Laden on Board the Siskina v Distos Compania Naviera* [1979] AC 210 at 216, 229, 261.

[17] Tracing claims are distinguishable from freezing injunctions and interim orders made in a tracing claim would assert a proprietary interest in the asset (*A v C* [1981] QB 956n).

[18] Except against a bank whose business might be threatened if its assets are subject to a freezing injunction, see *Polly Peck International Plc v Nadir (No. 2)* [1992] 4 All ER 769.

[19] [2008] EWCA Civ 303, [2009] QB 450.

because equity acts *in personam*. The injunction is to prevent injustice to the applicant by the respondent's conduct and imposes a personal obligation on the respondent.[20] Secondly, does the court have jurisdiction to grant the order? The power in s. 37 of the Senior Courts Act 1981 is extremely widely drawn but there are limits to its exercise. The respondent must demonstrate a good arguable case on the substantive merits of the claim.[21] Notably, there must be a real risk of dissipation or removal of the assets.[22] Modern commercial practice makes the possibility of removing assets from one jurisdiction to another relatively easy so it is unclear what more than having an international business is needed to satisfy this test. The applicant must also identify assets against which judgment could be enforced. Thirdly, should the court exercise its discretion and grant the order? That question is particularly acute in the case of a worldwide freezing injunction, which raises concerns of extraterritoriality. These aspects are often commingled, particularly when the respondent challenges the grant of the original order which has been made without notice. Often the respondent will offer security for the amount claimed so that the injunction is lifted.

Freezing injunctions raise two particular concerns in the conflict of laws: first, where the substantive proceedings are foreign, and secondly, where the assets are abroad.

b. Foreign proceedings: jurisdiction over the respondent

As we have seen, equity acts *in personam*. The English court must have jurisdiction over the respondent in order to grant a freezing injunction. Where substantive proceedings are already continuing in England, the jurisdiction over the respondent is established by the exercise of jurisdiction in the substantive proceedings. This can be achieved either under the Brussels I Regulation (for example, if the defendant respondent is domiciled here or via another permitted ground of jurisdiction) or under the national rules (if the claim form has been served in England or out of the jurisdiction with permission of the court). Where there are no substantive proceedings and the freezing injunction is sought in aid of foreign proceedings, the jurisdiction of the English court over the respondent has to be established independently.

---

[20] Importantly, the freezing injunction does not grant a proprietary interest in the respondent's assets (*Bekhor Ltd v Bilton* [1981] QB 923), unlike a tracing claim whereby a claimant alleges that the claimant has a proprietary interest in the property.

[21] A good arguable case is 'one which is more than barely capable of serious argument, but not necessarily one which the judge considers would have a better than 50% chance of success': *Ninemia Maritime Corp. v Trave KG* at first instance [1984] 1 All ER 398 at 404.

[22] *Ninemia Maritime Corp. v Trave KG* [1983] 1 WLR 1412 (CA) at 1422.

i. National law

The House of Lords in *The Siskina*[23] and the Privy Council in *Mercedes Benz AG v Leiduck*[24] had held that there was no power in the English court to permit service out of the jurisdiction for these orders where there were no substantive proceedings in England. The effect of these decisions was reversed by s. 25(3) of the Civil Jurisdiction and Judgments Act (CJJA) 1982 for proceedings both in Member States and, later, in third states. However, in principle the claimant must still show that England is the proper place for trial if jurisdiction can only be established under national law.[25] This has not been properly tested, but it seems that this question is swept into the broader one of the proper exercise of the discretion to grant the injunction. The requirement might be satisfied if there are assets in England[26] or the contract contains an English jurisdiction or arbitration agreement.[27]

ii. Brussels I Regulation

Article 31 provides a similar ground of jurisdiction within the Brussels I Regulation as that in CJJA 1982, s. 25. An applicant can request provisional measures from the English court even if there are proceedings in another Member State's court. The CJEU has described provisional measures as being those which 'are intended to preserve a factual or legal situation so as to safeguard rights'.[28] A freezing injunction can be a provisional measure. It is important that the court granting the provisional measure takes into consideration 'the need to impose conditions or stipulations such as to guarantee their provisional or protective character'.[29] It is likely that the provisional measure should be limited to assets located within the territory of the Member State whose court is granting the measure.[30] In *Van Uden Maritime BV v Firma Deco-Line*, the CJEU made the grant of the provisional measure conditional upon a 'real connecting link between the subject-matter of the measures sought and the territorial jurisdiction' of the Member State whose court makes the order.[31] So in *Banco Nacional de Commercio Exterior SNC v Empresa Telecomunicaciones de Cuba SA*,[32] only a domestic freezing injunction was granted not a worldwide freezing injunction. Note that if proceedings are

---

[23] *Owners of Cargo Lately Laden on Board the Siskina v Distos Compania Naviera* [1979] AC 210.

[24] [1996] AC 284.   [25] CPR r. 6.37.

[26] See the discussion below on *Credit Suisse Fides Trust SA v Cuoghi* [1998] QB 818 (CA) and *Refco Inc. v Eastern Trading Co.* [1999] 1 Lloyd's LR 159.

[27] See the discussion at p. 195 *et seq.* above on restraining orders (anti-suit injunctions). Note that a jurisdiction agreement alone does not give service as of right, it should also include an address for service within the jurisdiction.

[28] *Reichert v Dresdner Bank (No. 2)* Case C-261/90 [1992] ECR I-2149 at para. 34.

[29] *Van Uden Maritime BV v Firma Deco-Line* Case C-391/95 [1998] ECR I-7091 at para. 41.

[30] As to worldwide freezing orders, see p. 213 *et seq.* below.

[31] *Van Uden Maritime BV v Firma Deco-Line* Case C-391/95 [1998] ECR I-7091 at para. 40. See L. Merrett, 'Worldwide Freezing Orders in Europe' [2008] *LCMLQ* 71.

[32] [2007] EWCA Civ 662, [2008] 1 WLR 1936.

continuing in England, there is no need to use Article 31 in order to have jurisdiction to make the order so there is no requirement to limit the scope of the order to assets within the jurisdiction.

c. Exercise of discretion in support of foreign proceedings

Subject to the limitations in using Article 31 of the Brussels I Regulation, if proceedings are continuing on the substance in another Member State, the English court may grant a freezing injunction in support of proceedings in a foreign country by virtue of CJJA 1982, s. 25. The order is discretionary. The court may refuse to grant a freezing order in support of foreign proceedings if it is inexpedient to grant it due to the lack of jurisdiction over the substance of the case. Should the English court be granting interim or provisional orders, such as a freezing injunction, which are not available in the foreign court? It appears from *Credit Suisse Fides Trust SA v Cuoghi*[33] that the English court is prepared to make wider remedies available than in the court considering the substance of the case. This practice can be criticised. It may upset the balance which a foreign court strikes between the parties in its own proceedings. It may infringe comity, usurp the subordinate position of the English court to the foreign court where proceedings are continuing on the substance, and create inconsistent or overlapping orders. The English court should not be 'the policeman of the world'[34] and s. 25 should not be used where it would interfere with comity, procedural justice and procedural efficiency.[35] Limitations on s. 25 have been accepted by the English court. It will grant a freezing order only where there is sufficient connection with England to justify the order. So in *Motorola Credit Corp. v Uzan (No. 2)*,[36] the Court of Appeal held that there was a sufficient connection with England in the case of a respondent domiciled and resident here, and also in the case of a respondent who had assets here, but not in the case of the respondents who had neither residence nor assets in England. The Court said that in exercising its discretion to grant a freezing injunction in support of foreign proceedings the court must bear in mind (a) whether the making of the order would interfere with the management of the case in the primary court; (b) whether it was the policy in the primary jurisdiction not itself to grant the relief sought; (c) whether there was a danger that the orders made would give rise to disharmony or confusion and/or risk of conflicting, inconsistent or overlapping orders in other jurisdictions; (d) whether at the time the order was sought there was likely to be a potential conflict as to jurisdiction; and (e) whether, in a case

---

[33] [1998] QB 818 (CA).

[34] See Lord Goff's remarks on the analogous restraining order in *Airbus Industrie GIE v Patel* [1999] 1 AC 119 at 131.

[35] See Fentiman, *International Commercial Litigation*, para. 17.83 *et seq.*

[36] [2003] EWCA Civ 752, [2004] 1 WLR 113.

where jurisdiction was resisted and disobedience to be expected, the court would be making an order which it could not enforce.

d. Worldwide freezing injunctions

It was originally thought that freezing injunctions should not be granted over assets overseas.[37] Worldwide freezing orders can be considered to infringe comity by seeking to control assets extraterritorially. It would be better if the claimant sought a local order from the court where the respondent's assets are found. However, CPR r. 25.1(f) expressly permits the English court to grant freezing injunctions over assets overseas. Indeed, the English court does not regard this as an extraterritorial use of its powers. *In personam* jurisdiction over the respondent is required and that is seen as only operating intraterritorially. Nevertheless, the court must be careful not to exceed the limits imposed on its jurisdiction by the principles of public international law. In *Masri v Consolidated Contractors International (UK) Ltd (No. 2)*,[38] Lawrence Collins LJ explained that despite personal jurisdiction over the party, the court must also have 'subject matter jurisdiction' as otherwise the order might be contrary to international law.[39] This he defined as jurisdiction (i.e., power) to regulate the conduct of that party.[40] He therefore said:

> In deciding whether an order exceeds the permissible territorial limits it is important to consider: (a) the connection of the person who is the subject of the order with the English jurisdiction; (b) whether what they are ordered to do is exorbitant in terms of jurisdiction; and (c) whether the order has impermissible effects on foreign parties.

However, unlike a third party debt order,[41] a freezing injunction does not purport to affect title to the asset and can be granted in more wide-ranging circumstances. Nevertheless, worldwide freezing injunctions should be ordered only if there are insufficient English assets to satisfy the claim. The English court has also ordered the transfer of assets from abroad into England or another country where the English judgment will be recognised.[42] Worldwide freezing orders can cause problems for the respondent and third parties. The order is therefore made subject to provisos and undertakings.[43]

---

[37] *Ashtiani v Kashi* [1987] QB 688.   [38] [2008] EWCA Civ 303, [2009] QB 450.
[39] *Masri v Consolidated Contractors International (UK) Ltd (No. 2)* [2008] EWCA Civ 303, [2009] QB 450 at para. 35.
[40] Citing Hoffmann J in *Mackinnon v Donaldson, Lufkin & Jenrette Securities Corp.* [1986] Ch. 482.
[41] See *Société Eram Shipping Co. Ltd v Cie Internationale de Navigation* [2004] 1 AC 260, where the House of Lords refused to grant a third party debt order over foreign debts.
[42] *Derby & Co. Ltd v Weldon (No. 6)* [1990] 1 WLR 1139.   [43] See p. 215 below.

e. Worldwide freezing injunctions: foreign proceedings

Particular complexities have arisen in those cases where an applicant has sought a worldwide freezing order in support of proceedings overseas. Such cases raise both the questions over worldwide freezing orders and those in connection with granting orders in support of foreign proceedings. In the most extensive cases, a freezing injunction has been granted over assets abroad in support of foreign proceedings. In *Republic of Haiti v Duvalier*:

> The Republic of Haiti sought to cover US $120m which had been embezzled by the defendant respondents, the Duvalier family. Proceedings were continuing in France and the applicants asked the English court for a freezing injunction over their assets worldwide plus a disclosure order pending trial in France. The defendants did not appear before the court, but their solicitor in London had been found (by proceedings in the Jersey courts) to have control of some of the defendants' assets. The solicitors were named as third parties to the English order. Some banks with branches in London were also made defendants to the English proceedings. The order was in reality addressed to the solicitors and the banks.[44]

The Court of Appeal granted the order, saying that the case demanded international cooperation between courts and that if there was ever a case for the exercise of the court's powers, this must be it. *Republic of Haiti v Duvalier* is an extraordinary example, one right at the outer limit of the court's powers. The assets were not in England, neither was the respondent subject to the English court's jurisdiction (although its solicitors were), and the injunction was granted in aid of foreign proceedings. It is probably important that the injunction could be made effective by being addressed to the solicitors who had some control over the assets, even those located overseas. A slightly more limited but similar order was made in *Credit Suisse Fides Trust SA v Cuoghi*:

> The applicant had started proceedings in Switzerland against the respondent who was domiciled and resident in England. The applicant sought a worldwide freezing injunction from the English court in support of the Swiss proceedings. There was evidence that the Swiss court would not have been able to grant a similar provisional order.[45]

The Court of Appeal granted the worldwide freezing injunction. It did not hesitate to do so as it is sufficient that the respondent was subject to its jurisdiction *in personam* and it would have granted the order had proceedings been continuing in England on the substance. However, the Court did note

---

[44] *Republic of Haiti v Duvalier* [1990] 1 QB 202 (CA).   [45] [1998] QB 818 (CA).

that it would be inexpedient to grant the relief (i.e., that the injunction would be refused) if the injunction would 'obstruct or hamper the management of the case' in the foreign proceedings. Equally, if the foreign court has been requested to give similar relief and has refused to do so, it has been argued that the English court should not step in to fill the gap and grant a worldwide freezing injunction.[46] In *Motorola Credit Corp. v Uzan (No. 2)*,[47] the Court of Appeal left open the possibility of granting an injunction in those circumstances.

f. Protection of respondents and third parties: provisos

Worldwide freezing injunctions, especially those in support of foreign proceedings, raise particular difficulties. There is a risk that the applicant might misuse the information obtained and commence proceedings either on the substance of the dispute or to obtain assets in multiple other courts. The respondent may be harassed into settling at a disadvantage. The respondent's banks and other third parties may find themselves in a compromising position between the order of the English court and the demands of the respondent in other countries which do not recognise the English court's order. The freezing order is therefore made subject to undertakings and provisos which attempt to resolve those difficulties.[48] First, the respondent is given an undertaking in damages by the applicant to compensate if the order has been wrongfully made.[49] Secondly, the respondent must be appropriately protected from a multiplicity of proceedings in various jurisdictions where the applicant locates assets. The English court has made the order subject to a standard proviso. Its consent must be sought before proceedings can be launched in any other jurisdiction either on the substance of the dispute or to recover the assets.[50] Thirdly, the third party bank will not generally be in contempt of court if the order is breached by acts done outside the jurisdiction which comply with local law or the contractual law of the account.[51]

g. Concerns over human rights

If a respondent ignores the injunction and dissipates assets, the respondent will be in contempt of court. As we have seen, the consequences of being in contempt of court include being excluded from appearing to defend the

---

[46] See Millett LJ *obiter* in *Refco Inc. v Eastern Trading Co.* [1999] 1 Lloyd's LR 159 but cf. the view of Potter and Morritt LJJ in the same case.

[47] [2003] EWCA Civ 752, [2004] 1 WLR 113.

[48] See generally *Derby & Co. Ltd v Weldon* [1990] Ch. 48 (CA); *Baltic Shipping Co. v Transatlantic Shipping Ltd* [1995] 1 Lloyd's LR 673; *Bank of China v NBM LLC* [2001] EWCA Civ 844, [2002] 1 WLR 844 and the Annex to CPR PD 25.

[49] Though these orders appear to be very rarely made, see e.g., *Dadourian Group Inc. v Simms (Damages)* [2009] EWCA Civ 169, [2009] 1 Lloyd's LR 601.

[50] *Dadourian Group Inc. v Simms* [2006] EWCA Civ 399, [2006] 1 WLR 2499.

[51] *Babanaft International Co. SA v Bassatne* [1990] Ch. 13 (CA); *Bank of China v NBM LLC* [2001] EWCA Civ 844, [2002] 1 WLR 844.

substantive merits of the dispute. That may not be much of a problem for the respondent if there are no assets within the jurisdiction against which any judgment obtained by the applicant can be enforced. The applicant may seek to enforce the judgment against assets elsewhere but success will depend on the enforcement rules in place where the assets are found. Where a party has been excluded from participating in the proceedings leading to judgment, it is possible that such a judgment will not be enforced abroad. In addition, it has been suggested that Article 6 of the European Convention on Human Rights might limit the English court's power to exclude a respondent in contempt of court.[52] However, the English court has expressed the view that the right of access to a court is not absolute so that the court can legitimately restrict access so long as the sanction is appropriate and proportionate.[53] In *JSC BTA Bank v Ablyazov*, the Court of Appeal held that it would be disproportionate to prevent a contemnor from pursing the contemnor's appeal against committal for contempt.[54]

[52] See *Re Swaptronics Ltd* [1998] All ER (D) 407.
[53] See e.g., *Motorola Credit Corp. v Uzan (No. 2)* also known as *(No. 6)* [2004] 1 WLR 113 (CA).
[54] [2012] EWCA Civ 639.

8

Foreign judgments

1. Introduction

The availability of enforcement of any judgment awarded against a defendant is an important part of the decision whether and where to sue that defendant. A judgment which cannot be enforced against assets of the defendant is probably not worth the cost of obtaining it. Judgments may not only be enforceable in the state whose courts granted it. The enforcement mechanisms of other state's courts can be available to enforce not only that state's judgments but also foreign judgments. The English courts are particularly receptive to permitting an action to be brought on a foreign judgment as if it were a debt for which summary judgment is available. That is now the only avenue; a judgment creditor is no longer able to bring a fresh action in England on a claim which has been decided by another court.[1] If a judgment debtor has paid the foreign judgment then the debt is discharged.[2] Importantly, the decision of the foreign court is not re-opened, even if the English court would have come to a different decision.

Recognition of a foreign judgment can also be useful. Some judgments are incapable of enforcement, for example, because they are declaratory. A foreign judgment may have already been satisfied by the judgment debtor paying the sums due under the judgment. The judgment is then recognised as existence of a debt that has been discharged. The parties are bound by the decisions made by the foreign court if the judgment is recognisable. This means that the foreign judgment must satisfy the requirements under the relevant regime. It must also be between the same parties and on the merits.[3] A foreign judgment

---

[1] So long as the foreign judgment is recognisable in England: Civil Jurisdiction and Judgments Act (CJJA) 1982, s. 34. That has caught some claimants out. If the foreign court has made a much lower award of damages than the claimant was hoping for, the claimant cannot start again in England. See e.g., *Republic of India v India Steamship Co. Ltd (No. 2)* [1998] AC 878.

[2] *Black v Yates* [1992] 2 QB 246.

[3] I.e., the foreign judgment establishes that 'certain facts are proved or not in dispute; states what are the relevant principles of law applicable to such facts; and expresses a conclusion with regard to the effect of applying those principles to the factual situation concerned': Lord Brandon in *DSV Silo und Verwaltungsgesellschaft mbH v Owners of the Sennar (The Sennar) (No. 2)* [1985] 1 WLR 490 (HL) at 499.

can have three effects. First, the foreign judgment is treated as *res judicata* so that there is an end to litigation on the dispute. The English court applies *res judicata* to foreign judgments in the same way as the doctrine applies to English judgments. This is quite wide-ranging. Under the rule in *Henderson v Henderson*[4] an attempt to relitigate a question which has already been decided is regarded as an abuse of process. The rule goes further and treats all matters which could have been raised on a dispute as decided, whether in fact they were raised or not. Secondly, the foreign judgment may give rise to cause of action estoppel to prevent any party relitigating the same claim on liability. This is now on a statutory footing in Civil Jurisdiction and Judgments Act (CJJA) 1982, s. 34. Thirdly, a foreign judgment may produce an issue estoppel, by which a particular issue[5] is treated as having been decided by the foreign court and cannot now be re-opened in England.[6] For example, where the foreign court has decided that a machine was faulty, a party cannot deny that fact. In *Good Challenger Navegante SA v Metalexportimport SA*, the Court of Appeal laid down the four conditions for issue estoppels to arise from a foreign judgment: (1) the judgment must be given by a foreign court of competent jurisdiction; (2) the judgment must be final and conclusive and on the merits; (3) there must be identity of parties; and (4) there must be identity of subject matter, which means that the issue decided by the foreign court must be the same as that arising in the English proceedings.[7] In *Desert Sun Loan v Hill*,[8] the Court of Appeal accepted that it was possible for an issue estoppel to arise on an interlocutory decision on a question of fact to determine the foreign court's jurisdiction.

As with the rules of jurisdiction, there are two broad regimes covering the recognition and enforcement of foreign judgments. The original purpose of the Brussels I Regulation[9] was to provide for the easy recognition and enforcement of judgments in civil and commercial matters throughout the EU to support the internal market. It covers any decision of a court or tribunal of a Member State so long as the subject matter is within the scope of the Regulation. It does not matter whether the parties are domiciled in Member States or

---

[4] (1843) 3 Hare 100 (CA).　　[5] Which is narrower than a cause of action.

[6] There is an argument that the rules of the Brussels I Regulation only permit recognition as *res judicata* and cause of action estoppel as the Regulation provides for the recognition of final judgments on the merits (see R. Fentiman, *International Commercial Litigation* (Oxford University Press, 2010) para. 14.20).

[7] [2003] EWCA Civ 1668, [2004] 1 Lloyd's LR 67 at para. 50.

[8] [1997] 2 All ER 847.

[9] Regulation (EC) 44/2001 on jurisdiction and the recognition and enforcement of judgments in civil and commercial matters. See too the revised Lugano Convention on Jurisdiction and the Enforcement of Judgments in Civil and Commercial Matters concluded between the EU and EFTA in 2007, replacing the original 1988 Lugano Convention. It covers the EU countries (including Denmark), Iceland, Norway and Switzerland. On the history and interpretation of the Brussels I Regulation see further pp. 56–9 above.

not.[10] Nor is the basis on which the court of the other Member State took jurisdiction relevant. Therefore, a French judgment against a New York resident where the French court obtained jurisdiction on one of the grounds of jurisdiction outlawed in Article 3(2) and Annex I is recognisable and enforceable in England. Residually, the national law regime (also known as the common law regime) covers the recognition and enforcement of judgments from third states.[11] This is an ancient set of rules, with its foundations in the seventeenth century.

2. Theories of recognition and enforcement

Originally, the English courts viewed the basis for recognising or enforcing a foreign judgment to be a matter of comity or reciprocity. A foreign sovereign's court's decisions were to be accorded the same effect as an English decision because the law of nations required courts of each country to assist each other; or because English judgments would be more likely to be enforced abroad if foreign judgments were enforced here.[12] Those ideas were quickly supplanted with the theory of obligation.[13] The judgment debtor is considered to be under a duty or obligation created by the judgment of a court of competent jurisdiction to the judgment creditor. The decision of the foreign court is then treated as conclusive unless there is a defence. This theory is not particularly satisfying.[14] It does not explain the requirement for the judgment to be one from a court of competent jurisdiction. The Canadian courts, on the other hand, consider that foreign judgments should be enforced because of comity. This is seen not as a matter of obligation but a recognition of another sovereign's judicial acts 'having due regard both to international duty and convenience, and to the rights of its own citizens or of other persons who are under the protection of its laws'.[15] Thus, the Canadian courts recognise and enforce foreign judgments where the foreign court has exercised jurisdiction on an 'appropriate' basis, i.e., the similar basis to that used by the Canadian courts. This is close to reciprocity.

---

[10] This must follow from *Overseas Union Insurance Ltd v New Hampshire Insurance Co.* Case C-351/89 [1991] ECR I-3317.

[11] Two English statutes make particular countries' judgments recognisable and enforceable in England (Administration of Justice Act 1920 and Foreign Judgments (Reciprocal Enforcement) Act 1933). These substantially incorporate the common law rules and cover mainly the Commonwealth countries and countries which now are covered by the Brussels I Regulation. They will not be dealt with in any detail in this chapter.

[12] *Roach v Garvan* (1748) 1 Ves. Sen. 157 at 159; *Wright v Simpson* (1802) 6 Ves. 714 at 730; *Alves v Bunbury* (1814) 4 Camp. 28.

[13] *Williams v Jones* (1845) 13 M&W 628 at 633; *Godard v Gray* (1870) LR 6 QB 139 at 149–50: and *Schibsby v Westenholz* (1870) LR 6 QB 155.

[14] See H. Ho, 'Policy Underlying the Enforcement of Foreign Commercial Judgments' [1997] *ICLQ* 443.

[15] *Morguard Investments Ltd v De Savoye* (1991) 76 DLR (4th) 256 at 269.

The English court in *Adams v Cape Industries Plc*[16] used both a theory of obligation and one of comity to justify the possible recognition of a judgment from Texas.[17] The strongest justification was one of obligation based on territoriality. A foreign court is entitled to decide disputes against a person who is subject to that state's territorial jurisdiction. The court does not have jurisdiction over an absent foreigner unless that person has consented to the exercise of jurisdiction or otherwise voluntarily submitted.[18] These rules mirror the original bases of jurisdiction in the English court, although now so extended and altered via the service out rules and the doctrine of *forum conveniens* that the importance of presence-based jurisdiction is illusory. The continued insistence on presence within the foreign court's territorial jurisdiction does not sit well with the English court's own, more flexible, jurisdictional rules. As we shall see, the advantage of the more fixed rules on presence justifying recognition of a foreign court's judgment is that of certainty. Parties can predict and plan their activities so that they are not subject to likely foreign judgments. This is important in the commercial sphere, but permits multinational companies to hive off risky business ventures into local foreign subsidiaries and limit their exposure to harm to the capital sunk in that local company. That was the result in *Adams v Cape Industries Plc*[19] itself. It is interesting to compare this case with the later one of *Lubbe v Cape Plc*,[20] a case on the national rules of jurisdiction of the English court. The claimants in that case might not have been able to obtain full financial relief against a locally incorporated subsidiary, and were not able to enforce any South African judgment against the parent company. The claimants therefore tried a direct action against the parent in England and succeeded in the particular circumstances of the case. In a more straightforward case, the claimants would have failed in that attempt.

The justification for the Brussels I Regulation is more straightforward.[21] It is similar to that underpinning the 'full faith and credit' provision in the US Constitution. The purposes of the EU are promoted by the simple recognition and enforcement of Member State's judgments in other Member States. The objectives of the area of freedom, security and justice to ensure the freedom of movement of persons require easy recognition of judgments.[22] Differences between national rules on recognition and enforcement of judgments are said to hamper the sound operation of the internal market.[23] The CJEU has been interpreting the Brussels I Regulation and other instruments within the same

---

[16] [1990] Ch. 433 (CA).

[17] *Adams v Cape Industries Plc* [1990] Ch. 433 at 514 and 552. The case was complicated. The judgment was granted by the Texas federal courts but the judgment debtor was present, if at all, in Illinois. It was also *obiter* as the judgment was not enforced as the company was found not to be present in Illinois.

[18] *Adams v Cape Industries Plc* [1990] Ch. 433 at 514.   [19] [1990] Ch. 433.

[20] [2000] 1 WLR 1545.   [21] See further pp. 56–9 above.   [22] Recital 1.   [23] Recital 2.

field to promote the policies of further integration of procedural law[24] and unification of the rules of conflicts of jurisdiction.[25] Mutual trust and confidence in the decisions of other Member State's courts is paramount.[26] That justifies the fullest effect being given to a foreign judgment and the availability of very limited defences.

3. Recognition and enforcement under the Brussels I Regulation

As we have seen, the justifications for the recognition of judgments within the EU include supporting the internal market and other, wider, purposes of the EU. The Brussels I Regulation supplants the national rules on enforcement when it applies.[27] If a European enforcement order has been obtained[28] the judgment of the court of another Member State does not need to be registered under the Brussels I Regulation and the judgment need only be presented in England for enforcement.[29] Note that the other Member State's court may have taken jurisdiction under its national rules. Judgments given against defendants not domiciled in Member States are equally given automatic effect by recognition and enforcement in other Member States even though such defendants are not subject to the protection of the narrow bases of jurisdiction in the Regulation. However, a judgment of another Member State recognising a judgment from a third state[30] should not be given automatic effect in England.[31]

a. Judgments falling within the Brussels I Regulation

i. Scope of the Brussels I Regulation

Only judgments on matters that fall within the scope of the Brussels I Regulation are recognisable and enforceable.[32] As we have seen this means that the judgment must be on a 'civil and commercial matter' which has an autonomous meaning. It must not be on an excluded matter, such as a tax, fine or administrative decision. Note that damages awarded to a *partie civil* in a criminal case do come within the scope of the Regulation and can be enforced.

---

[24] *Götz Leffler v Berlin Chemie AG* Case C-443/03 [2005] ECR I-9611. Although this case was on Regulation (EC) 1348/2000 of 29 May 2000 on the service in the Member States of judicial and extrajudicial documents in civil or commercial matters and not a case on the Brussels I Regulation, it falls within the same area of freedom, justice and security (Art. 67(4) (ex Art. 61(c)) and Art. 81 (ex Art. 65) of the Treaty on the Functioning of the European Union.

[25] *Allianz SpA, Generali Assicurazioni Generali Spa v West Tankers Inc. (The Front Comor)* Case C-185/07 [2009] ECR I-663 at para. 24.

[26] See e.g., *Erich Gasser GmbH v MISAT srl* Case C-116/02 [2003] ECR-I 14693 and *Turner v Grovit* Case C-159/02 [2004] ECR I-3565.

[27] *De Wolf v Cox BV* Case C-42/76 [1976] ECR 1759.   [28] See p. 236 below.

[29] European Enforcement Order Regulation (EC) 1896/2006, Art. 5.

[30] I.e., a state which is not a Member State of the EU.

[31] *Owens Bank Ltd v Bracco* Case C-129/92 [1994] ECR I-117.   [32] See further pp. 59–68 above.

Importantly, a decision principally concerned with arbitration (such as an arbitration award) does not fall within the Regulation. These are recognised and enforced under the New York Convention as enacted in England in the Arbitration Act 1996. A judgment is not necessarily outside the recognition and enforcement provisions of the Regulation merely because a judgment decides some excluded matter, such as arbitration. In *National Navigacion Co. v Endesa*:[33]

> A dispute arose over the discharge of a cargo of coal. The Spanish cargo owners claimed damages in the Spanish court. It decided that an agreement for arbitration in England was not incorporated into the bill of lading from the charterparty. The English court had to recognise that decision, even though it would not have come to the same conclusion.

The Court of Appeal held that the Spanish court's decision on the arbitration clause was only a preliminary question in the Spanish proceedings. Those proceedings were on the substance of the dispute and therefore within the Brussels I Regulation. The judgment of the Spanish court on the incorporation of the clause therefore gave rise to an issue estoppel in England. The claimant ship-owners could not then in English proceedings dispute the finding of the Spanish court that the arbitration agreement was not incorporated into the bill of lading. This decision is surely correct. Nevertheless, it highlights some problems in the Brussels I Regulation. Any judgment on the substance of the dispute is recognisable and enforceable in England under the Regulation despite the other Member State's court failing to give effect to an arbitration agreement which the English court considers valid.[34] The English proceedings for a declaration of the incorporation of the arbitration agreement would be principally concerned with arbitration and so outside the Brussels I Regulation. This could lead to inconsistent judgments. Article 27 would not apply to stay the English proceedings. In the alternative where the English case was commenced first, proceedings in any other Member State's court would not be stayed under Article 27. The decision of the English court on the validity of the arbitration agreement would not be recognisable under the Regulation. However, if the Spanish proceedings were principally on the incorporation of the arbitration clause then those proceedings would have been outside the Regulation. All of which encourages prospective litigants to commence proceedings quickly in a preferred court as a matter of tactics.

---

[33] [2009] EWCA Civ 1397, [2010] 1 Lloyd's LR 193, noted R. Fentiman [2010] *CLJ* 242.

[34] This is also true of decisions in breach of jurisdiction agreements (see further p. 255 below) but compare with the opposite position under the national rules, CJJA 1982, ss. 32 and 33.

ii. Meaning of judgment

'Judgment' is widely defined in Article 32 of the Brussels I Regulation. Whatever the judgment is called, it includes decrees, orders, decisions, writs of execution, and the determination of costs or expenses by an officer of the court. The judgment need not be final or conclusive so orders for specific performance and injunctions are enforceable.[35] Judgments by consent are included but not judicially approved settlements which are essentially contractual.[36] Interim orders and those made under Article 31 are enforceable.[37] Courts are likewise broadly defined to include courts or tribunals of a Member State.[38] The judgments of private tribunals would not be recognised as they are not tribunals 'of a Member State'. The judgment must be enforceable in the Member State in which it was given.[39] The defendant must be allowed the opportunity to defend the defendant's case, so an order without notice to the defendant will not be recognised under the Brussels I Regulation.[40]

b. Recognition

The judgment of a court of another Member State is recognised in England without anything further than pleading and proving the existence of the judgment as a fact in the dispute; no special procedure is required.[41] Under no circumstances may a foreign judgment be reviewed as to its substance.[42] This is central to the principle of mutual trust and confidence. Articles 34 and 35 provide the only, limited, defences to recognition of a judgment given by a court of another Member State.[43] However, it is possible for the English courts to stay its proceedings if an 'ordinary appeal' has been lodged in the judgment granting court.[44] A judgment which is capable of recognition may then be enforced.

c. Enforcement

A party wanting to enforce a judgment from another Member State in England makes a without notice application to the English court and the judgment is then declared enforceable once certain formalities are completed.[45] After a declaration of enforceability is obtained it is then possible for a party to apply for protective measures immediately.[46] The other party is informed of the

---

[35] Cf. the national law approach, see further p. 236 et seq. below.

[36] *Solo Kleinmotoren GmbH v Boch* Case C-414/92 [1994] ECR I-2237.

[37] Note that English orders for freezing injunctions might not be enforceable in other Member States unless they were made with notice to the respondent. See further Chapter 8.

[38] Article 32.   [39] Article 38.

[40] *Denilauler v SNC Couchet Frères* Case C-125/79 [1980] ECR I-1553.

[41] Article 33(1).   [42] Article 36.   [43] See further p. 225 et seq. below.   [44] Article 37(1).

[45] Article 41.

[46] It is also possible to request protective measures at an earlier stage while the proceedings are continuing in the other Member State in support of those proceedings (Art. 31).

declaration of enforceability and has a right of appeal. The separation of the declaration of enforceability from the actual enforcement is understood as *exequatur* in many Continental Member States. At that point there is a hearing at which the defendant can raise one of the limited defences. These are the same defences as those for recognition.[47] A judgment which would be denied recognition under one of the defences will not be enforced, but there are no wider defences to enforcement. There is no review of the substance of judgment of the other Member State.[48] A judgment of a third state which has been recognised in another Member State is not enforceable in England using the Brussels I Regulation but has to be recognised and enforced via the traditional rules.[49] Under the proposed changes to the Brussels I Regulation this intermediate step of *exequatur* will be abolished.[50]

d. Effect

The Jenard Report notes that 'recognition must have the result of conferring on judgments the authority and effectiveness accorded to them in the State in which they were given'.[51] This might be greater or less than the effect given to a domestic judgment in England. An interlocutory decision of another Member State's court is not *res judicata* but is still to be given the similar effect in English proceedings as it has in the other Member State.[52] Therefore a provisional or protective order made under Article 31 of the Brussels I Regulation in another Member State (which has no jurisdiction over the substance of the proceedings) must be given effect to in England so long as it is not given without notice to the defendant. Also such decisions must be consistent with the requirement of a real connecting link between the subject matter of the provisional or protective measure and the territorial jurisdiction of the Member State whose courts made the decision to grant the measure.[53] Note, however, that a judgment which is unenforceable in the Member State in which it was given is not enforceable in other Member States.[54] The means of enforcement of a judgment of a court of another Member State is left to the

---

[47] Article 45(1).   [48] Article 45(2).

[49] *Owens Bank Ltd v Bracco* Case C-129/92 [1994] ECR I-117.

[50] Regulation (EU) 1215/2012 (Brussels I Regulation (recast)) [2012] OJ L351/1 will apply from 10 January 2015. The UK government has indicated that it will opt into any amended Regulation.

[51] *Jenard Report on the Convention on Jurisdiction and the Enforcement of Judgments in Civil and Commercial Matters* [1979] OJ C59/1 at 43 and *Hoffman v Krieg* Case C-145/86 [1988] ECR 645.

[52] There may be problems where the effect of a judgment is greater in another Member State than in England (see A. Briggs and P. Rees, *European Civil Practice* (2nd edn, Sweet & Maxwell, 2004) para. 24.009).

[53] *Van Uden Maritime BV v Kommanditgesellschaft in Firma Deco-Line* Case C-391/95 [1998] ECR I-7091.

[54] *Coursier v Fortis Bank* Case C-267/97 [1999] ECR I-2543 at para. 23.

national law.[55] The full panoply of English remedies is therefore available to aid the enforcement of a French judgment, such as third party debt orders, post-judgment freezing injunctions[56] and the use of bailiffs to obtain property of the judgment debtor.

e. Defences

The only possible defences are those which are listed in the Brussels I Regulation itself. These are to be narrowly interpreted.[57] The fact that the court of another Member State made an error applying the jurisdictional rules of the Regulation cannot be used as a reason to deny the judgment recognition and enforcement.[58] Therefore, if the court decided that an exclusive English jurisdiction agreement did not apply, the English court must enforce the judgment regardless of its own view that the jurisdiction agreement was operative. Note too that there can be no review of the substance of the decision of the court of another Member State. Even if that court mistakenly applied the wrong rules of law or misunderstood the facts there is no ground to refuse to recognise or enforce that judgment.

i. Manifestly contrary to public policy

Article 34(1) of the Brussels I Regulation permits the English court to refuse to recognise and enforce a judgment from another Member State's court if that judgment is manifestly contrary to English public policy. This, as with the other defences, is strictly and narrowly construed. The breach of public policy involves the recognition of the foreign judgment being 'at variance to an unacceptable degree of the [English] legal order inasmuch as it would infringe a fundamental principle'.[59] The court must find a fundamental principle which has been infringed. So in *Apostolides v Orams*:

> A judgment was given by the Republic of Cyprus court over the ownership of land in Northern Cyprus, which was part of the Turkish Republic of Cyprus. The defendants were the English owners of the land and the claimants had the benefit of the Cyprus judgment requiring the demolition of the property on the land and its return to them.[60]

As no fundamental principle of the English legal order could be identified as being infringed by the judgment, that judgment had to be recognised and enforced.

---

[55] *Hoffman v Krieg* Case C-145/86 [1988] ECR 645.
[56] Often known as *Mareva* injunctions.
[57] *Prism Investments BV v Jaap Anne van der Meer* Case C-139/10 [2012] ILPr. 13.
[58] *Krombach v Bamberski* Case C-7/98 [2000] ECR I-1935.
[59] *Apostolides v Orams* Case C-420/07 [2009] ECR I-3571.   [60] *Ibid.*

An example of where a fundamental principle was breached is *Krombach v Bamberski*:

> The German defendant was suspected by the French claimant of having killed the claimant's daughter in Germany. The claimant sued in France as a *partie civil* in criminal proceedings there. The German criminal proceedings had been dropped. The defendant did not appear in the French criminal proceedings (as he did not want to be present within the criminal jurisdiction of the French court) and therefore forfeited the right to be represented in the civil proceedings on appeal as a matter of French law. The claimant attempted to enforce the French judgment for damages in Germany. The defendant argued that it was contrary to public policy in Germany to enforce this judgment as he had not been permitted to defend himself in the French proceedings.[61]

The CJEU held that the defence of public policy was available. Although the definition of the content of public policy is for the judgment recognising Member State, the CJEU can review the limitations on that concept. Fundamental rights are protected by all Member States, especially those of the European Convention on Human Rights (ECHR). Therefore, a judgment in breach of one of the fundamental rights, such as the right to a fair legal process, would be contrary to public policy. The German court in this case could refuse to recognise and enforce the French judgment. The French judgment had been obtained without the defendant having access to a lawyer for the criminal case which infringed a right to fair trial which had been ruled on by the European Court of Human Rights (ECtHR).[62]

Some rights under the ECHR are not unfettered but may be subject to restriction if the infringement is not disproportionate; for example, many European legal systems impose some sort of sanction, such as disbarring a party, if prolonged and unnecessary delays occur. Is there an infringement such that it would be contrary to public policy to enforce a judgment if a party has been prevented from continuing proceedings because of some abuse of the court's procedures? In *Gambazzi v DaimlerChrysler Canada Inc.*:

> The claimant sought to enforce an English judgment in Italy. The defendant had been barred from defending the proceedings in England as he was in

---

[61] Case C-7/98 [2000] ECR I-1935. The dispute between Krombach and Bamberski was extremely acrimonious culminating in Dr Krombach being found tied up in a French street outside a courthouse in October 2009. In the subsequent criminal trial, Dr Krombach challenged the criminal jurisdiction of the French court on the ground that he had been kidnapped and brought to France. He failed in this and was sentenced to fifteen years in prison.

[62] For example, the early cases in the ECtHR, *Poitrimol v France*, judgment of 23 November 1993, Series A No. 277-A; *Pelladoah v Netherlands*, judgment of 22 September 1994, Series A No. 297-B.

breach of a freezing order and therefore in contempt of the English court. Until he had purged his contempt he was prevented from taking any further steps in the English action. After summary judgment was obtained, the defendant argued that that should not be enforced in Italy as he had not been able to participate in his defence.[63]

The CJEU held that it was for the Italian court to decide whether enforcing this judgment would be contrary to Italian public policy. Having noted that the right of defence may possibly be restricted the court held that any restriction on the right of defence must satisfy 'very exacting standards'. If the exclusion of the defendant from the proceedings was a manifest and disproportionate infringement of his right to be heard then the judgment might infringe the public policy of the Italian courts such that the judgment would not be recognised nor therefore enforced.

It is a little unclear whether the defence of public policy goes much beyond a breach of the fundamental rights in the ECHR. A misapplication of national or even European law by the Member State's court giving the judgment is insufficient to be contrary to public policy.[64] However, in *Maronier v Larmer*:

The claimant sought to enforce a Dutch judgment in England. The proceedings in Holland had been commenced some twelve years earlier and notice of those proceedings given to the defendant. The case was then stayed by the claimant when the defendant was found to be bankrupt, only to be reactivated after the defendant had left to become resident in England. No notice of the recommenced proceedings was given to the defendant who first heard of the action when served with the order for registration. By then it was too late for an appeal to be launched in Holland.[65]

The Court of Appeal refused to enforce the judgment. Although there was a strong presumption that the procedures of other Member State's courts were compliant with their obligations under the ECHR, so that the judgment was not in breach of public policy, this was rebuttable. In this case, the defendant had not been given a fair trial as he had not been informed of the reactivation of the proceedings nor had any notice of that until after the time for an appeal had passed.

Under the national rules, recognising a judgment obtained by fraud is contrary to English public policy. Fraud here could mean either that the court behaved fraudulently by being bribed, or that the proceedings were affected by

---

[63] Case C-394/07 [2009] ECR I-2563.
[64] *Apostolides v Orams* Case C-420/07 [2009] ECR I-3571.
[65] [2002] EWCA Civ 774, [2003] QB 620.

the fraudulent conduct of the parties by producing fake evidence, or that the merits of the case involve fraud.[66] There is no separate defence of fraud in the Brussels I Regulation. The Schlosser Report envisaged that fraud in the proceedings could bring the judgment within the public policy exception.[67] However, that probably does not cover a case in which fraud has been raised in the merits and either accepted or dismissed, as the substance of the decision cannot be reviewed.[68] If the issue of fraud could have been raised in the Member State's court (but was not) and the fraud may still be raised in that court, then it is better for the party to return to the Member State's court to argue the issue of fraud than to raise it as a defence to enforcement.[69] This should also cover the situation where a party has acted fraudulently during the course of proceedings. In *Societe d'Informatique Service Realisation Orga-nisation (SISRO) v Ampersand Software BV*,[70] the allegation that the court appointed expert had acted fraudulently in producing his report was dismissed by the French court. The English court did not accept the defence that to enforce this judgment would be contrary to public policy as this point could be appealed in France. However, where the court has itself acted fraudulently or if an appeal on this issue of fraud is not possible one can argue that the right to fair trial has been infringed.

Despite Waller J's obiter remarks in *Philip Alexander Futures and Securities Ltd v Bamberger*,[71] it is clear now that at least some aspects of a judgment of a Member State's court obtained in breach of an arbitration agreement must be recognised in England.[72] It is only if the principal question of the foreign proceedings concerns arbitration that recognition and enforcement can be denied, as the judgment would fall outside the scope of the Brussels I Regulation. In other cases, where the arbitration agreement is only a prelim-inary or ancillary matter to litigation on the substance of liability, the judg-ment must be recognised. That undermines the efficacy of arbitration agreements. The proposed reforms to the Brussels I Regulation attempt to resolve this but these are not completely satisfactory.

It is not possible to use the public policy defence as a general catch-all. If there is a specific defence available in the Brussels I Regulation, such as the way in which notice to defendants in a default judgment is to be treated in

---

[66] See further p. 254 *et seq.* below.

[67] *Schlosser Report on the Convention of 9 October 1978 on the Accession of the Kingdom of Denmark, Ireland and the United Kingdom of Great Britain and Northern Ireland to the Convention on Jurisdiction and the Enforcement of Judgments in Civil and Commercial Matters, and to the Protocol concerning its Interpretation by the Court of Justice* [1979] OJ C59/71 at 128.

[68] Brussels I Regulation, Art. 36.

[69] *Interdesco SA v Nullifire Ltd* [1992] 1 Lloyd's LR 180 approved in *Société d'Informatique Service Realisation Organisation (SISRO) v Ampersand Software BV* [1994] ILPr. 55.

[70] [1994] ILPr. 55.   [71] [1997] ILPr. 72.

[72] *National Navigation Co. v Endesa Generacion SA* [2009] EWCA Civ 1397, [2010] 1 Lloyd's LR 193, noted R. Fentiman [2010] *CLJ* 242, but compare with CJJA 1982, s. 32 (see further pp. 260–1 below).

Article 34(2), that provision must be complied with and recourse to public policy is not available.[73]

ii. Natural justice

Article 34(2) provides that a judgment shall not be recognised if it was given in default of the appearance of the defendant in some circumstances. The defendant must have been served with the document instituting proceedings in sufficient time and in such a way as to enable the defendant to arrange for a defence to the claim. If the defendant was not so served and then a judgment in default is given, the defendant can raise this defence against the recognition and enforcement of the judgment in another Member State. This is a protection for defendants from the generally easy and straightforward recognition and enforcement of judgments. It is a corollary to Article 26(1) which provides that if a defendant domiciled in a Member State is sued in a court of another state and does not enter an appearance the court shall of its own motion declare that it has no jurisdiction unless it has jurisdiction under the Regulation. The protection for defendants is continued in Article 26(2) which requires a court to stay its proceedings unless it is shown that the defendant has received the document instituting proceedings in time for the defendant to arrange the defence. It is central to the Brussels I Regulation that the judgment is properly adversarial and the defendant has been given an opportunity to defend the case. However, this defence is narrowly construed. If the defendant appeared, even to contest the jurisdiction of the judgment granting court, then the judgment is recognisable notwithstanding that an argument that insufficient time was given or that some defect in the service on the defendant is possible.[74] What amounts to an appearance is given an autonomous meaning.[75] At minimum, if a defendant has not lodged any formal document with the court nor was present during the proceedings the defendant cannot be taken to have submitted.[76] Also, the defendant loses the protection of Article 34(2) if the defendant failed to commence proceedings to challenge the judgment when it was possible for the defendant to do so.[77]

---

[73] *Hoffman v Krieg* Case C-145/86 [1988] ECR 645; *Hendrikman v Magenta Druck & Verlag GmbH* Case C-78/95 [1996] ECR I-4943; *TSN Kunststoffrecycling GmbH v Jurgens* [2002] EWCA Civ 11, [2002] 1 WLR 2459, but compare with *Maronier v Larmer* [2002] EWCA Civ 774, [2003] QB 620.

[74] *Sonntag v Waidmann* Case C-172/91 [1993] ECR I-1963.

[75] *Hendrikman v Magenta Druck & Verlag GmbH* Case C-78/95 [1996] ECR I-4943.

[76] *Tavoulareas v Tsavliris (No. 2)* [2006] EWCA Civ 1772, [2007] 1 WLR 1573 at paras 11–16.

[77] Compare with a case on the previous Brussels Convention *Klomps v Michel* Case C-166/80 [1981] ECR I-1593, in which an appearance after judgment was not found to be an appearance for this article (then Art. 27(2)) as the argument made was found to be inadmissible by the judgment granting court. It is possible that these rather special circumstances would result in the same decision.

At the stage of recognising the judgment of another Member State's court, the judgment creditor must produce evidence in a prescribed form[78] to the English court that the defendant has been served with notice of the original proceedings. Service no longer has to be 'duly' effected. The judgment will be recognisable notwithstanding that the notice was not properly translated, for example.[79] What is important is that the defendant knew about the proceedings in time to prepare a defence. Note that the CJEU has held that service need not be personal so that substituted service (by sending it to the last known address of the defendant, for example) is sufficient.[80] The judgment enforcing court may take account of all the circumstances 'including the means employed for effecting service, the relations between the plaintiff and the defendant or the nature of the steps which had to be taken in order to prevent judgment from being given in default'.[81] In *Orams v Apostolides*,[82] the English court was faced with a judgment from the Republic of Cyprus court over land in the Turkish Republic of Cyprus. Jack J held that what was sufficient time depended upon the circumstances, including any special difficulties that the defendant might face. He decided in this case that thirteen days including two weekends between the service of the document and the hearing was probably not enough time for the defendants to arrange their defence. They did not speak Greek or Turkish, and they would have had to find a Greek Cypriot lawyer from the Turkish Cypriot side of the border.

It is the enforcing court, England, that determines whether or not the service was effected and whether there was reasonable time for the defendant to arrange for the defence.[83] Any decision of the judgment granting court that sufficient time and notice was given is not binding on the English court when recognising or enforcing the judgment.[84] What is sufficient time is unclear, although the CJEU appears to consider it merely a factual matter.[85] This probably ought to have an autonomous definition. As we have seen, decisions of a court without notice are not recognisable under the Brussels I Regulation.

---

[78] Brussels I Regulation, Annex V, para. 4.4. As to the English procedure see CPR Part 74.

[79] *ASML Netherlands BV v Semiconductor Industry Services GmbH (SEMIS)* Case C-283/05 [2006] ECR I-12041.

[80] *Klomps v Michel* Case C-166/80 [1981] ECR I-1594 and *ASML Netherlands BV v Semiconductor Industry Services GmbH (SEMIS)* Case C-283/05 [2006] ECR I-12041. Note that the defendant did become aware of the proceedings in those cases.

[81] *Klomps v Michel* Case C-166/80 [1981] ECR I-1594 at para. 20.

[82] [2006] EWHC 2226 (QB), [2007] 1 WLR 241. This point was not part of the appeal to the CJEU.

[83] *Klomps v Michel* Case C-166/80 [1981] ECR I-1594.

[84] *Pendy Plastics v Pluspunkt* Case C-228/81 [1982] ECR 2723.

[85] *Klomps v Michel* Case C-166/80 [1981] ECR I-1594.

iii. Irreconcilable with an English judgment

A judgment from another Member State can be refused recognition and enforcement if it is 'irreconcilable with a judgment given in a dispute between the same parties in the Member State in which recognition is sought'.[86] Of course, avoiding irreconcilable judgments is an objective of the Brussels I Regulation. We have seen that Articles 6(1), 27 and 28 support that objective. In particular, Article 27 should have prevented two sets of proceedings continuing in two different Member States on the same cause of action between the same parties. However, conflicting decisions might still arise out of related actions or where the action has changed over the course of proceedings. Irreconcilable may well have a different meaning in each of these Articles. In the context of Article 6(1), the CJEU has held that irreconcilable decisions can occur even if the legal context and the factual situation were not identical.[87]

Irreconcilable judgments arise where (1) there is some divergence in the possible outcomes of the disputes which (2) arise out of the same situation of law and fact.[88] That relatively flexible interpretation[89] of irreconcilable judgments may be appropriate where the concept is used at an early stage of proceedings to avoid the final outcome of irreconcilable judgments. In the case of Article 34(3), the irreconcilability of the other Member State's judgment with an English judgment can be finally tested. Judgments include a wide range of decisions, so the CJEU held that an Italian decision on an interim measure ordering a party not to carry out certain acts was irreconcilable with a decision of the German court that there was no ground for interim relief to be granted.[90] As we can see, decisions of courts can conflict at different levels. The overall result may be different, one court finding that X is liable and another holding that X is not liable, or X is held liable for different amounts. The decisions of the two courts may be said to conflict if the legal rules for each decision might not be the same or if the courts take opposite views of the facts. It is also possible that the two courts have agreed on some legal issues and facts but not all. Alternatively, the two courts can come to the same decision on liability but using dissimilar legal rules or deciding differently on some of the facts.

The interpretation of irreconcilable judgments at this point probably depends on the effect that is being given to the other Member State's judgment. Where the judgment is being enforced arguably it is the outcome that is

---

[86] Brussels I Regulation, Art. 34(3).
[87] *Roche Nederland BV v Primus* Case C-539/03 [2006] ECR I-2535.
[88] *Ibid.* para. 26. Irreconcilable judgments were not a risk in this case as although the cases involved similar patents taken out under each national law, it was possible that the identical activity did not infringe the particular patent in dispute.
[89] Notwithstanding that, as a derogation from Art. 2, the CJEU recognises that Art. 6(1) should be narrowly interpreted, see *Painer v Standard VerlagsGmbH* Case C-145/10 [2011] ECDR 13.
[90] *Italian Leather SpA v WECO Polstermöbel GmbH & Co.* Case C-80/00 [2002] ECR I-4995.

central. If the English court has found that X is liable to pay £1,000,000 and the other Member State's court has found that X is not liable or liable for £500,000 or for £1,500,000, the two decisions are irreconcilable. This is probably irrespective of the rules and facts which underpin the two decisions. However, where some aspect of the judgment is being recognised, it is arguably only that aspect giving rise to issue estoppel[91] that must be irreconcilable. In that case, the legal rules and the facts underpinning the issue estoppel may have to be more closely aligned. In *Hoffman v Krieg*,[92] the CJEU said that the two judgments have to entail mutually exclusive legal consequences. Therefore, a German judgment which ordered a husband to pay maintenance which was part of his marital obligations was inconsistent with a Dutch judgment pronouncing the couple divorced.

The English judgment does not have to be prior in time to the judgment of the other Member State, but mere proceedings in England would be insufficient to refuse recognition and enforcement to the other Member State's judgment.[93]

iv. Irreconcilable with a judgment of another Member State or of a third state

A judgment of another Member State can be refused recognition if it conflicts with either a judgment of another Member State or with a judgment of a third state.[94] A judgment from France can be refused recognition in England if there is a conflicting judgment from either Germany or Utopia. This is more narrow in application than the previous provision. First, the judgment from the other Member State must be prior in time to the one to be recognised. Secondly, the judgments must be on the same cause of action and between the same parties. Thirdly, the judgment of the other Member State or the third state must be recognisable. The Utopian judgment would prevent recognition of the French judgment only if it is recognised under the English national common law rules.[95]

v. Conflicts with sections 3, 4, or 6 or Article 72

The Brussels I Regulation makes very limited provision for the enforcing court to examine the grounds on which the other Member State's court took jurisdiction in order to refuse recognition to its judgment. Another Member State's judgment may not be recognised if it conflicts with the jurisdictional provisions in insurance matters (section 3), consumer matters (section 4), or the exclusive jurisdictional provisions in Article 22.[96] Note that there is no defence for a judgment obtained in breach of the jurisdictional provisions of

---

[91] For example, in *National Navigation Co. v Endesa Generacion SA (The Wadi Sudr)* [2010] ILPr. 10, the English court recognised the issue of the non-applicability of the arbitration agreement decided by the Spanish court.

[92] Case C-145/86 [1988] ECR 645.

[93] *Landhurst Leasing plc v Marcq* [1998] ILPr. 822 (CA).   [94] Brussels I Regulation, Art. 34(4).

[95] See p. 236 *et seq.* below.   [96] Article 35(1).

Article 23 (jurisdiction agreements). This is different to the position under the national rules.[97] Nor is there a defence against a judgment obtained in breach of the employment provisions of section 5. Apart from the specified defences, the recognising court cannot review the jurisdiction of the judgment granting Member State's court.[98] In addition, in reviewing the grounds of jurisdiction in sections 3, 4 and 6 the judgment recognising court is bound by any decision on the facts of the judgment granting court.[99] An English court inspecting a French judgment which has taken jurisdiction improperly over what is allegedly a consumer contract will be bound by the French court's finding that it was not a consumer contract.

Article 72 provides a further defence to the recognition of a judgment from a Member State.[100] In the very rare cases that a Member State has entered into a treaty with a third state under Article 59 of the Brussels Convention before the Brussels I Regulation came into force, judgments of other Member States which conflict with the treaty can be denied recognition. It is possible to argue that the New York Convention on Arbitration[101] is protected by this Article so that an arbitration award from a third state is enforceable even if it conflicts with a judgment of a Member State. However, as we have seen, the relationship between arbitration and the Brussels I Regulation is complex. Unless the judgment of the Member State is primarily on the validity of the arbitration award it too is recognisable and enforceable. The United Kingdom has concluded treaties with Australia and Canada under Article 59 of the Brussels Convention. Concluding further treaties is within the competence of the EU and there is no equivalent provision to Article 59 in the Brussels I Regulation.

vi. No review of jurisdiction or substance

Other than the express provisions of the Brussels I Regulation, absolutely no review of either the other Member State's court's decision on jurisdiction[102] or of the substance of the decision[103] is possible. No matter whether the Member State's court improperly applied some rule of the Brussels I Regulation (such as ignoring Article 27) or of its own internal jurisdiction or came to a wrong decision on the law or facts of the dispute[104] the judgment must be recognised and enforced. The judgment is to be enforced even if the judgment granting court made an error in the application of EU law.[105] In particular, the defence of public policy cannot be used to review the jurisdiction of the judgment

---

[97] CJJA 1982, s. 32 does not apply to Brussels I Regulation judgments.

[98] Article 35(3).   [99] Article 35(2).   [100] Article 35(1).

[101] New York Convention on the Recognition and Enforcement of Foreign Arbitral Awards 1958. Enacted most recently by the Arbitration Act 1996, s. 100 et seq.

[102] Brussels I Regulation, Art. 35(3).   [103] Article 36.

[104] *Hengst Import BV v Campese* Case C-474/93 [1995] ECR I-2113.

[105] *Régie nationale des usines Renault SA v Maxicar Spa* Case C-38/98 [2000] ECR I-2973.

granting Member State.[106] In *Apostolides v Orams*,[107] the CJEU held that a judgment enforcing court cannot use a wider notion of public policy where there is a specific provision of the Brussels I Regulation providing a defence to recognition.[108]

vii. Appeals

If an 'ordinary appeal' is underway in the judgment granting Member State, the judgment recognising court may stay its proceedings to recognise the foreign judgment.[109] It is possible to appeal the declaration of enforceability and at the same time ask for a stay of the enforcement of the foreign judgment pending the expiration of the time for an 'ordinary appeal' in the judgment granting Member State.[110] English law does not have a distinction between ordinary and extraordinary appeals. The CJEU in *Industrial Diamond Supplies v Riva*[111] decided that an ordinary appeal must have an autonomous definition. An ordinary appeal is an appeal which (1) is 'any appeal which forms part of the normal course of an action and which, as such, constitutes a procedural development which any party must reasonably expect'; (2) may result in the amendment or annulment of the original judgment in the judgment granting Member State; and (3) has a specific period of time for the appeal which starts to run because of the granting of the judgment.[112] Extraordinary appeals therefore are those which may be dependent on events which are unforeseeable at the time of the original trial.

The power to stay proceedings is discretionary even in cases where an ordinary appeal has been lodged or in those when the time for appeal has not yet expired. The principles underlying the exercise of this discretion have not been fully worked out. The English court in *Petereit v Babcock International Holdings Ltd*[113] considered that as a general principle a foreign judgment from another Member State should be enforced. A defendant may be asked to provide security while the appeal is pending in order to protect the judgment creditor's position.

f. Reform of the Brussels I Regulation

We have already inspected the suggested reforms[114] of the jurisdictional rules of the Brussels I Regulation.[115]

---

[106] Article 35(3).   [107] Case C-420/07 [2009] ECR I-3571.   [108] *Ibid.* para. 100.
[109] Article 37(1).   [110] Articles 45 and 46.   [111] Case C-43/77 [1977] ECR 2175.
[112] *Ibid.* paras 27, 37, 38 and 42.   [113] [1990] 1 WLR 350.
[114] Regulation (EU) 1215/2012 on jurisdiction and the enforcement of judgments in civil and commercial matters (Brussels I Regulation (recast)) [2012] OJ L351/1 will apply from 10 January 2015. The UK government has indicated that it will opt into any amended Regulation.
[115] See further p. 133 *et seq.* above.

i. Abolition of *exequatur*

Despite the extensive criticisms of the European Commission's original proposals, the Brussels I Regulation (recast) abolishes the need for a declaration of enforceability before a judgment from another Member State is enforced. Instead all that will be required for the enforcement of a judgment from another Member State is the production of an authentic copy of the judgment and a certificate in the required form[116] issued by the judgment granting state. However, the judgment debtor will have advance notice of the enforcement proceedings.[117] The current defences to enforcement have been left relatively untouched in the recast Regulation. There were concerns about the previous proposals reform as the judgment debtor's assets could have been seised and disposed of without the debtor's knowledge. In addition, there was a possibility of fraud as the enforcement would have been effected without judicial scrutiny of the judgment from the other Member State, in particular, as 'judgments' were defined in the original proposals to include authentic instruments which, not being judicial determinations, are much more likely to be forged.

ii. Reduction of defences

Along with the abolition of *exequatur* the European Commission had proposed to reduce sharply the availability of defences to recognition and enforcement of judgments from other Member States.[118] The primary solution for a defendant is to challenge the judgment in the courts of the judgment granting Member State, rather than to defend enforcement proceedings in other Member States. However, the recast Brussels I Regulation retains the present defences.[119]

iii. Arbitration

As we have seen, as a result of the decision of the CJEU in *West Tankers*[120] decisions by other Member State's courts on the validity and scope of arbitration clauses may have to be recognised in England where those decisions were only a preliminary or ancillary part of the proceedings.[121] Ultimately, therefore, a decision in breach of an arbitration agreement must be enforced in England. However, if there is an English decision on the validity of the arbitration agreement and providing for enforcement of any award it should be possible to argue successfully that the other Member State's court's decision is irreconcilable with the English decision. That will result in a race to obtain a

---

[116] Articles 36 and 37 Brussels I Regulation (recast).
[117] Article 36(2) Brussels I Regulation (recast).
[118] A. Dickinson, 'Surveying the Proposed Brussels I bis Regulation: Solid Foundations but Renovation Needed' (2010) 12 *Yb Priv. Int. L* 247.
[119] Article 45 Brussels I Regulation (recast).
[120] *Allianz SpA, Generali Assicurazioni Generali Spa v West Tankers Inc. (The Front Comor)* Case C-185/07 [2009] ECR I-663.
[121] *National Navigacion v Endesa* [2010] 1 Lloyd's LR 193.

decision of the arbitrators and the English court, as well as the courts of a Member State which takes a more limited view of arbitration agreements.[122] The Brussels I Regulation (recast) strengthens the recitals to make the New York Convention on Arbitration take precedence over the Brussels I Regulation.[123]

4. Other European procedures

There are three other EU Regulations which may be useful to someone wishing to obtain easy satisfaction of a debt throughout Europe. These are the European Order for Payment Procedure Regulation,[124] the Regulation creating a European enforcement order for uncontested claims[125] and the Regulation establishing a European Small Claims Procedure.[126] The European Enforcement Order Regulation, like the others listed here, has no stage for *exequatur* unlike the present Brussels I Regulation. This means that a declaration of enforceability does not have to be obtained before the order is enforced.

5. Recognition and enforcement under national law rules

Judgments from courts outside the EU fall to be recognised and enforced under the traditional English rules. These are largely common law rules overlaid by statute. In addition, there are two specific regimes which apply to some Commonwealth countries and to states which largely fall in modern times into the Brussels I Regulation or into the Lugano Convention.[127] They will not be dealt with in any detail in this chapter. The statutory rules are substantially similar to those under national law.

A foreign judgment from a third state's court[128] can be recognised in England without any special action being taken so long as it fulfils the requirements for recognition. It is treated as *res judicata*, or as giving rise to cause of action estoppel or issue estoppels. Non-money judgments from a third state, for example, for an injunction, can be recognised as giving rise to

---

[122] The risk is recognised by the European Commission in its report on the proposed changes to the Brussels I Regulation (*Study on Data Collection and Impact Analysis of Certain Aspects of a Possible Revision of Council Regulation No 44/2001 on Jurisdiction and the Recognition and Enforcement of Judgments in Civil and Commercial Matters*, (2007) at 35, available at http://ec. europa.eu/justice/doc_centre/civil/studies/doc_civil_studies_en.htm).

[123] See Article 73(2) Brussels I Regulation (recast).

[124] Regulation (EC) 1896/2006.   [125] Regulation (EC) 805/2004.

[126] Regulation (EC) 861/2007.

[127] Administration of Justice Act 1920 and Foreign Judgments (Reciprocal Enforcement) Act 1933.

[128] I.e., one which is not a Member State of the EU, or one which is party to the Lugano Convention on Jurisdiction and Judgments in Civil and Commercial Matters 1990.

an issue estoppel but cannot be enforced.[129] A foreign judgment can also be enforced in England if it fulfils the requirements for enforcement under the national law. The foreign judgment is treated as if it were evidence of a debt which is outstanding to be paid immediately. It may therefore provide a basis for summary judgment in England unless the judgment debtor has a defence to the enforcement of that foreign judgment. The judgment creditor has to bring an action on the debt, using the CPR to provide a means of service of the claim form for the debt out of the jurisdiction on the judgment debtor if necessary.[130] It is no longer possible to commence an entirely fresh action on the claim in England.[131]

For ease of explanation, this chapter will focus largely on enforcement of the foreign judgment as a debt, rather than on recognition. The party seeking enforcement of the foreign judgment is called the judgment creditor and the party against whom enforcement is sought is called the judgment debtor. The rules on recognition are much the same. However, in order to be recognised, the foreign judgment does not have to be for a fixed sum.

Enforcing a foreign judgment can backfire on the unwary judgment creditor. In *AK Investment CJSC v Kyrgyz Mobil Tel Ltd*,[132] the judgment creditor sought to enforce a Kyrgyz judgment in the Isle of Man. The judgment debtor was able to defend the enforcement of the judgment and also to counterclaim in the enforcement action. The counterclaim covered many of the same issues as had been decided in the original dispute but included many more. Additionally, the Privy Council permitted the counterclaiming judgment debtor to bring the counterclaim against a number of other parties.

a. Jurisdiction of the foreign court

A judgment given against a judgment debtor determines the rights of the judgment creditor against that person.[133] In order for the debt created by the foreign judgment to be enforceable it is essential for the foreign court to have a special type of jurisdiction over the judgment debtor. It could be thought that the English court would accept foreign rules of jurisdiction which mirror the English traditional rules as a basis for recognition and enforcement (as the Canadian courts do)[134] but this is incorrect. The bases of jurisdiction accepted by the English court for the recognition and enforcement of a foreign judgment are much more limited. Buckley LJ laid out the rules in *Emanuel v Symon*: (1) where the judgment debtor is a subject of the foreign country in

---

[129] *Airbus Industrie v Patel* [1999] AC 19. cf. the position in Canada under *Pro Swing Inc. v Elta Golf Inc.* [2006] 2 SCR 612.
[130] CPR r. 6.36 and PD B para. 3.1(10).   [131] CJJA 1982, s. 34.
[132] [2011] UKPC 7, [2011] 4 All ER 1027.
[133] *Cambridge Gas Transportation Corp. v Official Committee of Unsecured Creditors of Navigator Holdings plc* [2006] UKPC 26, [2007] 1 AC 508 at para. 13.
[134] *Morguard Investments Ltd v De Savoye* [1990] 3 SCR 1077.

which the judgment has been obtained (this ground has been discredited)[135]; (2) where the judgment debtor was resident in the country when the action began (now replaced with presence); (3) where the judgment debtor was a plaintiff in the foreign court and the judgment debt arises out of a counter-claim; (4) where the judgment debtor voluntarily appeared in the foreign court; and (5) where the judgment debtor has contracted to submit to the foreign court in which the judgment was obtained.[136] These can be condensed into two rules. Only the presence or submission of the judgment debtor to the foreign court's jurisdiction is sufficient to found jurisdiction in the foreign court such that the foreign judgment will be enforced.

Over a hundred years ago, the English court rejected the argument that a cause of action which had arisen in the judgment granting state could be enforced when the judgment debtor had not been present in the territory of the foreign court at the time of the commencement of proceedings. In *Sirdar Gurdyal Singh v Rajah of Faridkote*:

> Singh had stolen money from the Rajah while he had been the Rajah's *bakshi* in Faridkote. Singh then fled to the nearby territory of Jhind. The Rajah obtained a Faridkote judgment and sought to enforce it in Jhind.[137]

The Privy Council refused to order the enforcement of the Faridkote judgment in Jhind. Although Singh had been resident in Faridkote at the time the cause of action arose, he was not present there at the point the proceedings were commenced. It was that latter time which is crucial for justifying the jurisdiction of the foreign court in order to enforce its judgment. This is a type of obligation theory much discredited elsewhere in the conflict of laws. The judgment debtor is obliged to pay the debt as the debtor is under an obligation to the foreign court by virtue of being present within its territory to be subject to its decisions. The rules are very similar to the national English rules by which the English court justifies taking jurisdiction over a defendant present within the territory.[138] A defendant who is not present within the territory is not subject to the jurisdiction of the court unless the defendant has other-wise submitted to that court's jurisdiction. Despite the extension of the national rules on domestic jurisdiction over the nineteenth and twentieth centuries in the *forum conveniens* doctrine, the rules on enforcement of foreign judgments have not been so expanded. As a corollary to the somewhat fixed view of the foreign court's jurisdiction, mere presence of the defendant within the territory of the foreign court at the time of the commencement of the proceedings (irrespective of little connection between the cause of action

---

[135] See *Blohn v Desser* [1962] 2 QB 116 and *Vogel v R and A Kohnstamm Ltd* [1973] QB 133.
[136] [1908] 1 KB 308 at 309.   [137] [1894] AC 670 (PC).   [138] See further pp. 139–46 above.

and that foreign state) is probably sufficient to make the foreign judgment enforceable in England.[139]

The advantage of the rules is that they are predictable, certain and defendants can order their business and travel arrangements to be sure which foreign judgments are enforceable and which will not be.[140]

i. Natural persons as judgment debtors

An individual judgment debtor is subject to the foreign court's jurisdiction such that that court's judgment can be enforced in England if the judgment debtor is present in that country. Residence would be a much stronger ground to justify the obligation created by the decision of the foreign court. However, it is likely that even temporary presence is sufficient. As the Court of Appeal in *Adams v Cape Industries Plc* explained:

> we would, on the basis of the authorities referred to above, regard the source of the territorial jurisdiction of the court of a foreign country to summon a defendant to appear before it as being his obligation for the time being to abide by its laws and accept the jurisdiction of its courts while present in its territory. So long as he remains physically present in that country, he has the benefit of its laws, and must take the rough with the smooth, by accepting his amenability to the process of its courts.[141]

This comment is technically *obiter* as the defendant in this case was a company but the point could not be more clearly made. By becoming present in the foreign country the judgment debtor has consented to the exercise of jurisdiction over the judgment debtor. Although it appears that the judgment debtor may only be present for a very short time the presence must be voluntary.[142] The justification for enforcing the obligation created by the judgment is that the judgment debtor accepted the territorial power of the foreign court. In the unlikely event that the judgment debtor had been tricked or kidnapped into setting foot on that territory the debtor's presence would not be voluntary. It is important to note that the judgment debtor must have been present at the time that proceedings were commenced. Presence at the point at which the cause of action arose is insufficient.[143] Unlike legal persons, a judgment debtor who is a natural person who did business in the foreign country but was not physically present there is not subject to the jurisdiction

---

[139] *Carrick v Hancock* (1895) 12 TLR 59. The case is not very good authority as it might be argued that the defendant submitted to the Swedish court.

[140] Editor's note: there was a rare occasion in my life when conflict of laws was personally rather useful. My husband was a possible defendant in an enormous US lawsuit against a firm in which he was a partner. We decided not to go to the United States on holiday until the case had settled to be sure that he could not be present in the United States!

[141] [1990] Ch. 433 at 519.   [142] *Adams v Cape Industries Plc* [1990] Ch. 433 at 517–18.

[143] *Sirdar Gurdyal Singh v Rajah of Faridkote* [1894] AC 670 (PC).

of the foreign court. A judgment given against that judgment debtor is therefore not enforceable in England. In *Lucasfilm Ltd v Ainsworth*:[144]

> The judgment debtor had been selling merchandise which he had made after his involvement with the Star Wars films via a website accessible from the United States. The judgment creditors obtained a judgment from the US courts for breach of copyright. The judgment debtor had taken no part in the US proceedings but challenged the enforcement of the judgment debt in England arguing that he was not present or resident in the United States.

The Court of Appeal held that the judgment debtor was not present in the United States by selling products there. Despite the fact that the website was accessible from the United States, and indeed the products were sold in US dollars to US residents via the website, the doing of business was insufficient to amount to presence. This is different to the rules on the presence of a company. A company can be present if it does business in the foreign country, so long as that business is done at a particular place.

ii. Legal persons as judgment debtors

Legal persons, such as companies, do not exist in a physical form. As Samuel Johnson's adage says a company has 'no soul to save and no bottom to kick'.[145] Legal persons come in many guises such as associations, corporations, societies and partnerships as well as companies. However, we will focus on companies in this chapter. Legal rules ascribe a physical location to a company and call it a company's presence or residence. The English law rules do not differentiate between the residence or presence of a company. It is resident or present in any country in which it carries on business from a fixed and reasonably permanent place for more than a minimum length of time. Companies do business in a number of ways. A company may itself open a branch office in a foreign country by renting premises in its own name, directly employing staff and doing its business from those premises using the staff to carry it out (the branch office example). A company could alternatively use a subsidiary company which is locally incorporated in the foreign country. The subsidiary rents the premises, employs the staff and does the business while the holding company directs operations of the subsidiary and takes the profit as the only shareholder (the subsidiary example). A company might enter into a joint venture with a local company, often through a separately locally incorporated vehicle company in which it and the local company share control

---

[144] *Lucasfilm Ltd v Ainsworth* [2009] EWCA Civ 1328, [2010] Ch. 503 at paras 189–95, point not taken on appeal to the House of Lords [2011] UKSC 39, [2011] 1 AC 208.

[145] Quoted in *JH Rayner (Mincing Lane) Ltd v Department of Trade and Industry* [1989] Ch. 72 at 211.

and profits (the joint venture example). A company could send some of its English employees out to the foreign country to drum up business on a temporary basis (as a travelling salesman or representative). A company could employ a local representative in the foreign country to do some business for it (the representative or agent example). The cases which have been used by the English courts to establish whether a foreign company has a presence in England for the national rules of jurisdiction are interchangeably used to determine if a judgment debtor has a presence in a foreign country.[146] One could criticise this as the purpose of the rules to take jurisdiction over a foreign company is not the same as those to enforce a foreign judgment despite their apparently similar foundations. There is a discretion in the first but not in the latter which may subtly overlay the application of the rules but which is complex to strip out. The application of the rules to these examples depends on whether the method of doing business fulfils the requirements that there is a fixed place at which the company's business is being done. Perhaps this is somewhat old-fashioned in the Internet age. It is now possible to do business very effectively around the world without having a fixed place in the foreign country at which business can be seen to be conducted.[147]

Where a company has established a branch in the foreign state, it clearly has a place of business in that state such that it is directly present there. Any judgment of that state's courts will be recognisable and enforceable in England. The cases do not appear to require that the judgment arises out of the business of the company done in that country although the reported cases all do so. The other ways of the company doing business in the foreign country are more difficult. These are forms of an indirect presence of a company in a state. It is doing business in the foreign country but via an agent or representative, which could include a subsidiary company, associated company or a joint venture established with another business. In order for a judgment debtor company to be present in the foreign country in these cases there must be a fixed and reasonably permanent place from which the company's business has been carried out for more than a minimal time. An example is *Adams v Cape Industries Plc*:

> Cape Plc is an English multinational company which has many subsidiaries incorporated around the world. Its major business includes the mining, processing and marketing of asbestos. It had two subsidiary companies active in the United States: NAAC (incorporated in Illinois) to market asbestos in the United States, and Capasco (incorporated in England) to market asbestos worldwide. Cape also had a factory in Texas. There had been a personal injury class action

---

[146] See *Adams v Cape Industries Plc* [1990] Ch. 433 at 467–72 but note Slade LJ's 'unease' at 471 and *SSL International plc v TTK LIG Ltd* [2011] EWCA Civ 1170, [2012] 1 All ER (Comm) 429 (CA) at paras 42–68.

[147] As in *Lucasfilm Ltd v Ainsworth* [2009] EWCA Civ 1328, [2010] 3 WLR 333, discussed above.

(*Tyler (No.1)*) in Texas by ex-employees who had suffered asbestosis against a range of defendants including Cape. That action was settled. A further class action involving 205 consolidated actions was brought in Texas against the same defendants (*Tyler (No.2)*). However, this time Cape and Capasco did not participate in the action and argued that the Texas court did not have jurisdiction over them. NAAC went into liquidation and ceased business. A new Illinois company associated with Cape was incorporated to undertake the marketing function of NAAC. The Texas court gave judgment in default of Cape's appearance. The judgment creditors sought to enforce the judgment in England.

Slade LJ gave the judgment of the Court of Appeal which held that Cape was not doing business in the United States at the time of the *Tyler (No.2)* actions which formed the basis for the judgment debt.[148] It had no place of business in the United States.

First, a fixed and reasonably permanent place of business must be identified. We have seen from the cases on the national rules of jurisdiction[149] that a place of business in England has been found where a foreign corporation set up a stall at an exhibition for nine days at which contracts were made.[150] However, some degree of identification with the foreign company's business at that place is necessary.[151] The application of these rules to judgment debtor companies establishing a place of business abroad provides quite wide jurisdiction on the foreign court. On the other hand, a judgment debtor has been found not to have established a place of business where a sales director was served with the writ in the foreign country but he was merely travelling around staying in hotels.[152]

Secondly, in order for the judgment debtor company to be present in the foreign country its agent, representative, subsidiary or joint venture company must be doing the judgment debtor company's business. In contradistinction, the agent, etc., could be doing its own business – which includes representing the judgment debtor company. Agency or representation of other companies is a well-known line of business. The line between these can be fuzzy, particularly in the subsidiary company example. The holding company in effect

[148] There was a complicated issue surrounding the overlaps between the US federal and state courts' jurisdiction. This action was not brought in the federal court in which it would have been relatively straightforward to accept that Cape's possible presence in Illinois could found jurisdiction in Texas (as federal jurisdiction is extensive over the whole of the United States rather than limited to the particular state). The action had been commenced in a state court. In that case there is an argument that the jurisdiction of the state court is only established by the judgment debtor company's presence in that state. The Court of Appeal found it unnecessary to decide this difficult question ([1990] Ch. 433 at 557).

[149] See further pp. 143–6 above.   [150] *Dunlop Ltd v Cudell & Co.* [1902] 1 KB 342.

[151] *Cleveland Museum of Art v Capricorn* [1990] 2 Lloyd's LR 166.

[152] *Littauer Glove Corp. v F W Millington* (1928) 44 TLR 746.

controls a wholly-owned subsidiary company despite the English company law rules of separate personality and the imposition of directors' duties on the subsidiary's directors independently of the parent company. Other countries take a more holistic view of groups of companies, treating them as one business. Part of the decision in *Adams v Cape Industries Plc* was taken up with an investigation of whether the corporate veil should be lifted to treat the subsidiary and associated companies in the United States as the parent company Cape Plc.[153] English company law[154] accepts that a subsidiary or associated company can be treated as the parent company in exceptional circumstances: first, where there is a façade, a sham or fraud in incorporating the company to disguise the real state of affairs,[155] however, as the subsidiaries here were independent and carrying on their own business under separate boards of directors, there was no façade or sham; secondly, if the subsidiary is the parent company's agent the parent can be treated as the principal and bound by the authorised acts of its agent. That requires agency to be proved as a matter of fact[156] and was not shown here. Merely being a wholly owned subsidiary of the parent company does not establish that the subsidiary is the parent's agent.

Nevertheless, without lifting the veil of incorporation it is possible that the agent, etc., is carrying on the judgment debtor company's business. What are the factors to take into account to make that determination? In *Adams v Cape Industries Plc*, Slade LJ held that it is necessary to investigate the relationship between the agent, etc., and the judgment debtor company to see:

(a) whether or not the fixed place of business from which the representative operates was originally acquired for the purpose of enabling him to act on behalf of the overseas corporation;

(b) whether the overseas corporation has directly reimbursed him for (i) the cost of his accommodation at the fixed place of business; (ii) the cost of his staff;

(c) what other contributions, if any, the overseas corporation makes to the financing of the business carried on by the representative;

(d) whether the representative is remunerated by reference to transactions, e.g., by commission, or by fixed regular payments or in some other way;

(e) what degree of control the overseas corporation exercises over the running of the business conducted by the representative;

---

[153] [1990] Ch. 433 at 531–45.

[154] Appropriately applied here as the parent company, Cape Plc, is incorporated in England. Were the judgment debtor company to be incorporated in another country there is a good argument that its relationship to its subsidiaries should be governed by that law.

[155] *Jones v Lipman* [1962] 1 WLR 832 and *Gilford Motor Co. Ltd v Horn* [1933] Ch. 935 (CA).

[156] As in *Rainham Chemical Works v Belvedere* [1921] 2 AC 465.

(f) whether the representative reserves (i) part of his accommodation, (ii) part of his staff for conducting business related to the overseas corporation;

(g) whether the representative displays the overseas corporation's name at his premises or on his stationery, and if so, whether he does so in such a way as to indicate that he is a representative of the overseas corporation;

(h) what business, if any, the representative transacts as principal exclusively on his own behalf;

(i) whether the representative makes contracts with customers or other third parties in the name of the overseas corporation, or otherwise in such manner as to bind it;

(j) if so, whether the representative requires specific authority in advance before binding the overseas corporation to contractual obligations.

It appears that the agent's power to contract on behalf of company may be a critical factor. In *Vogel v R and A Kohnstamm Ltd*,[157] the judgment debtor company was found not to be subject to the Israeli court's jurisdiction for enforcement of judgment. There was a representative of the company in Israel but he was not an agent as he had no authority to bind the defendants. It is therefore quite easy for a judgment debtor company to structure its operation of business to ensure that the agent, etc., does not have authority. The lack of a power to contract can apparently be overridden by other factors. In *Adams v Cape Industries Plc*, Slade LJ emphasised that the list is not exhaustive and that no factor is conclusive. He refused to accept the trial judge's proposition that in the absence of a power to contract the judgment debtor company could never be present in the foreign country unless it had established a branch office. However, he did not elaborate on this further.[158]

iii. Submission to the foreign court
1. By voluntary appearance

A foreign judgment is enforceable not only where the judgment debtor was present in the foreign country at the time of commencement of the proceedings in that country. Where a judgment debtor has voluntarily submitted the determination of the dispute to the foreign court it is obviously unjust for the judgment debtor then to re-open the dispute at the enforcement stage in England. This is an aspect of the principle that there should be an end to litigation. Having voluntarily participated in proceedings, the judgment debtor should not prolong the dispute in another forum. A judgment debtor will have submitted to the jurisdiction of the foreign court if the judgment debtor was a claimant in the foreign court,[159] or if the judgment debtor was a

---

[157] [1973] QB 133.   [158] [1990] Ch. 433 at 531.
[159] *Schibsby v Westenholz* (1870) LR 6 QB 155 at 161.

counterclaimant in a related matter in the foreign court.[160] It is for the English court to decide whether the judgment debtor was a claimant or whether the counterclaim was sufficiently related.[161]

A judgment debtor will have submitted to the foreign court if the judgment debtor appears voluntarily in that court to argue the merits of the dispute. In that case, the judgment debtor has had a chance at the determination of the litigation and cannot now fairly re-open the dispute. Appointing a lawyer who then appears in court to argue on the judgment debtor's behalf is appearance. It should not be a submission if the lawyer is not authorised by the judgment debtor to appear.[162] However, if the foreign court has decided that the lawyer is authorised to appear for the judgment debtor, the judgment debtor may be estopped from denying that fact in the English proceedings to enforce the judgment debt.[163]

Appearing to protest only the jurisdiction of the foreign court is not treated as a submission to argue the merits of the dispute. If a judgment debtor only questions the jurisdiction of the foreign court but does not go on to dispute the substance of the case, the judgment debtor has not submitted to the foreign court. Originally, the common law drew a distinction between an appearance to contest the existence of jurisdiction and an appearance to argue about the exercise of jurisdiction.[164] The latter was a submission to the foreign court while the former was not. However, CJJA 1982, s. 33(1) provides that several arguments are not to be treated as a submission. If the judgment debtor:

> by reason only of the fact that he appeared (conditionally or otherwise) in the proceedings for all or any one or more of the following purposes:
>
> (a) to contest the jurisdiction of the court;
> (b) to ask the court to dismiss or stay the proceedings on the ground that the dispute in question should be submitted to arbitration or to the determination of the courts of another country;
> (c) to protect, or obtain the release of, property seized or threatened with seizure in the proceedings;

then the judgment debtor is not treated as having submitted to the foreign court.[165] It is not entirely clear that s. 33(1) covers arguments of the judgment debtor against the exercise of jurisdiction of the foreign court based upon ideas of *forum conveniens*. It is better to give s. 33(1) a wide meaning so that this argument would fall into either (a) or (b).

---

[160] *Murthy v Sivajothi* [1999] 1 WLR 467.   [161] *Ibid.*
[162] By analogy with the Brussels Convention case *Hendrikman v Magenta Druck & Verlag GmbH* Case C-78/95 [1996] ECR I-4943.
[163] *Desert Sun Loan Corp. v Hill* [1996] 2 All ER 847 (CA).
[164] *Henry v Geoprosco International Ltd* [1976] QB 726 (CA).
[165] CJJA 1982, s. 33 does not apply to judgments of Member State's courts which are recognisable under the Brussels I Regulation.

Some foreign law requires a party who wishes to challenge the jurisdiction of the court also to make arguments as to the merits of the dispute. A party in that case could have to make a difficult decision. If the party does not dispute the jurisdiction of the court the judgment may be obtained by default, but if the party argues the merits of the case any judgment will be enforceable in England, as that party might be taken to have submitted to the foreign court. However, in *AES Ust-Kamenogorsk Hydropower Plant LLC v Ust-Kamenogorsk Hydropower Plant JSC*,[166] Rix LJ held that the judgment debtor had not submitted to the jurisdiction of the Kazakhstan court. The judgment debtor had appeared only for the purpose of challenging the jurisdiction of the Kazakhstan court. This was so despite that party having participated in the hearing on the merits of the dispute in the lower court where the matter had been fully aired and decided. The argument on the merits was only made in order to maintain the challenge to the Kazakhstan court's jurisdiction on appeal. The judgment debtor had expressly and clearly reserved its right to arbitrate. The older cases on submission make it clear that a judgment debtor's purpose in arguing the merits simply to make a challenge to jurisdiction must be unequivocal and obvious to all parties.[167] It is a mistake for the judgment debtor to argue the merits and jurisdiction in the alternative and then, having lost the argument on jurisdiction, to continue on the merits. That would be a submission and the judgment would be enforceable.[168]

A judgment debtor may consider whether to appeal against a judgment given in default of the judgment debtor's appearance. So long as the appeal is limited to challenging the jurisdiction of the original court, the judgment debtor does not appear.[169] However, if the appeal goes beyond that and becomes an appeal on the merits the judgment will be enforceable.

It is a little unclear exactly what amounts to a submission to the foreign court and by which law is submission to be determined. If the foreign court does not consider what the judgment debtor to have done to be a submission then neither should the English court.[170] On the other hand, it is for the English court applying English law to determine whether the judgment debtor's conduct is a sufficient submission to justify enforcing the foreign judgment. Even if the foreign court considers that the judgment debtor has submitted, that is not sufficient to be an appearance for this purpose.[171] The

---

[166] [2011] EWCA Civ 647, [2012] Bus. LR 330.
[167] *Marc Rich & Co. AG v Società Italiana Impianti PA (The Atlantic Emperor) (No. 2)* [1992] 1 Lloyd's LR 624.
[168] *De Cosse Brissac v Rathbone* (1861) 6 H&N 301.
[169] *AES Ust-Kamenogorsk Hydropower Plant LLC v Ust-Kamenogorsk Hydropower Plant JSC* [2011] EWCA Civ 647, [2012] Bus. LR 330.
[170] *Adams v Cape Industries Plc* [1990] Ch. 433 at 461.
[171] *Akande v Balfour Beatty Construction Ltd* [1998] ILPr. 110.

English court asks whether 'viewed objectively was [defendant's conduct] inconsistent with the continued challenge to the jurisdiction?'.[172]

2. By agreement

A judgment debtor has also submitted to the foreign court's jurisdiction such that the judgment of that court can be enforced, if the judgment debtor has entered into a valid jurisdiction agreement covering the dispute which confers jurisdiction on the foreign court.[173] Generally, such an agreement has to be express. So, in *Copin v Adamson*:[174]

> The articles of association of a French company contained a jurisdiction clause in favour of the French court which was found to be a submission by any shareholder to those courts. Therefore the French judgment in relation to debts owed by the English shareholder to the company was enforceable in England despite the shareholder not having appeared in the French proceedings.[175]

By taking shares in the company the shareholder had accepted the articles, including the jurisdiction clause. It appears from *Blohn v Desser*[176] that an implied jurisdiction agreement may suffice to found the jurisdiction of the foreign court. In that case, the judgment debtor had entered into a partnership in an Austrian firm and was held by Diplock J to have impliedly agreed to submit to the Austrian courts by having done so. In *New Hampshire v Strabag Bau*,[177] the Court of Appeal preferred the rejection of *Blohn v Desser* by Ashworth J in *Vogel v R and A Kohnstamm Ltd*.[178] An express agreement to submit is preferable as a clear justification for the judgment debtor's consent to the exercise of the foreign court's jurisdiction. Note that the jurisdiction agreement must be valid and cover the dispute in order to found jurisdiction in the foreign court. However, any question of the invalidity of the jurisdiction agreement should be raised in the foreign court. In *Israel Discount Bank of New York v Hadjipateras*, the judgment debtor could have raised the invalidity of the agreement in the foreign court but failed to do so.[179] He was then prevented from raising that defence again in England at the enforcement stage. That result is consistent with the general rule that a party must make all arguments possible in the court making the decision on the substance of the dispute rather than waiting until the stage of enforcement to raise the question.

---

[172] *Akai Pty Ltd v People's Insurance Co. Ltd* [1998] 1 Lloyd's LR 90 at 97.
[173] *Feyerick v Hubbard* (1907) 71 LJKB 509. [174] (1875–76) LR 1 Ex D 17.
[175] Indeed, the shareholder had not had actual knowledge of the French proceedings as the notice had been served in accordance with the articles on the French office of the company.
[176] [1962] 2 QB 116. [177] [1990] Ch. 433 at 463–7. [178] [1973] QB 133.
[179] [1984] 1 WLR 137.

iv. No other basis of jurisdiction

Other than the voluntary acceptance of the foreign court's jurisdiction through
the judgment debtor's presence or submission, no alternative ground of
jurisdiction in the foreign court will suffice for an English court to enforce
the judgment. It does not matter on what ground the foreign court established
its own jurisdiction nor that the foreign court is the *forum conveniens* in the
eyes of the English court. So it is irrelevant whether the judgment debtor was
domiciled in the foreign court, whether the dispute concerned a contract
governed by that court's law, whether the foreign claim form was served out
of the foreign court's jurisdiction on a similar ground to those contained in
CPR r. 6.36 and PD 6B, or that there is a real and substantial connection
between the parties, the events and the foreign court. Nor will the possession
of property in the territory of the foreign court found jurisdiction in that court.

In contrast, the Canadian courts, following *Morguard Investments Ltd v De
Savoye*,[180] have taken a different stance, first in relation to intra-Canadian but
later also for foreign judgments. So long as the foreign court took jurisdiction
'properly' (which initially meant in accordance with the Canadian Constitution) or 'appropriately' (equivalent to the rules on which the Canadian
courts themselves exercise jurisdiction) its judgment will be recognised and
enforced in Canada. The judgment debtor is protected from excesses of
jurisdiction by the foreign court as that court's judgment is only recognised
and enforced in Canada if there are the greatest or at least significant contacts
between the defendant or the subject matter and that foreign jurisdiction. This
'real and substantial' connection test of jurisdiction is different from, albeit
similar to, the English doctrine of *forum conveniens*. The Canadian approach
led to the interesting decision in *Beals v Saldanha*:[181]

> A judgment was granted by a Florida court over a disputed land sale in Florida.
> The defendants who were residents of Ontario did not defend the action in
> Florida[182] and a judgment for US$290,000 was given in default of their appear-
> ance in 1986. Some years later when the judgment creditors sought to enforce
> the judgment in Canada, the debt had grown to US$800,000 with interest. The
> trial judge in Canada refused to enforce the judgment, partly on the ground that
> there was an allegation of fraud in relation to the assessment of damages.[183]

The Canadian Supreme Court enforced the judgment. It had been given by a
court with a real and substantial connection with the dispute. Defences to the
enforcement of a foreign judgment remain. In this case, however, the defence

---

[180] [1990] 3 SCR 1077.   [181] [2003] 3 SCR 416.
[182] Having been given the perfectly sensible advice by an Ontario lawyer (at that time before
Morguard was decided) that the judgment would not be enforceable in Ontario.
[183] As to the effect of fraud on the enforcement of a foreign judgment see pp. 254–6 below.

of fraud was not made out. In addition, the Canadian courts have in principle accepted that foreign judgments other than debts can be enforced in *Pro Swing Inc. v Elta Golf Inc.*[184] On a bare majority, the Canadian Supreme Court considered that injunctions were an important remedy in modern commerce which should be supported when granted by a foreign court. So long as the foreign judgment was final and rendered by a court of competent jurisdiction it can be enforced.[185] However, the contempt order given by the US court after breach of the injunction could not be enforced in Canada as it was essentially penal. As in England, penal judgments are not enforceable.

Enforcing foreign judgments which have been obtained by virtue of jurisdictional rules which mirror the English rule on jurisdiction is attractive. As a matter of principle, if the jurisdictional rules are satisfactory for English courts they should be accepted as appropriate for other courts. An English defendant in a foreign court can hardly complain about the exercise of those jurisdictional rules. However, it is more difficult for a party to predict whether the foreign judgment is likely to be enforced in England and adjust its behaviour and business practices accordingly. There has been a good deal of expensive litigation in Canada while the courts have determined what is a 'real and substantial connection', which would undoubtedly also be the case in England. The increased importance of the defences to enforcement has additionally brought more uncertainty and more cases to the courts. There has been no move by the English courts to follow the Canadian approach.

b. Enforceable judgment

Not all judgments are enforceable. We have seen that, for example, a declaratory judgment is not capable of enforcement. There are other types of judgment which are capable of enforcement but are not enforceable in England. In order to be enforceable, a foreign judgment must be final, and for a fixed sum. It must not be for a tax, penalty or other public law enforcement, nor for a multiple of the original sum owing. Judgments against sovereigns may be refused enforcement.

i. Final and conclusive

A judgment which is not final and conclusive cannot be enforced in England. It must be *res judicata* and determine all the controversies between the parties. A judgment is final and conclusive if it cannot be re-opened in the court which granted it. Some judgments are only provisional, and so not final and conclusive. In *Nouvion v Freeman*:[186]

---

[184] [2006] 2 SCR 612.
[185] Note that the basis for the enforcement of judgments in Canada is founded more strongly in comity than is the case in England.
[186] (1889) 15 App. Cas. 1.

A preliminary judgment of the Spanish court was obtained. In that type of 'remate' action the defendant could only raise limited defences. Either the claimant or the defendant was able to bring another action on the same matter in which all defences could be raised and in which findings in the 'remate' action were not conclusive.

An interlocutory decision is not final and conclusive so cannot be enforced. So, for example, a decision of the foreign court that there is a good arguable case on a particular point is not sufficiently conclusive of that point. However, if an interlocutory decision decides a matter completely which cannot later be re-opened, it is possible for that part of the decision to give rise to an issue estoppel.[187] On the other hand, a judgment can be final and conclusive notwith-standing that an appeal is possible. If an appeal is pending, the English court may stay its proceedings for enforcement to await the outcome of the appeal.[188]

ii. Fixed sum

In addition to being final and conclusive, a foreign judgment debt must be for a fixed sum in order to be enforceable. This means that it should not be a sum which can be varied at some time in the future (such a judgment may not be final and conclusive either). This requirement has led to difficulties over the enforcement of maintenance awards from foreign courts.[189] Likewise, damages which are liable for later assessment are not enforceable before that assessment. So in *Sadler v Robins*:

A court in Jamaica had awarded the judgment creditor a specified sum but first deducting from that amount the defendant's costs which were to be taxed by the court.[190]

Until taxation was carried out, the judgment was not enforceable as the sum was not sufficiently fixed. It is possible for a sum to be fixed if it can be arrived at by a straightforward arithmetical process.[191]

iii. Taxes, penalties or other public law judgments

There is a general rule of conflict of laws by which the courts will not enforce foreign taxes, penalties or other public laws.[192] Specifically in regard to foreign judgments, this means that a judgment which directly or indirectly collects

---

[187] *Desert Sun Loan Corp. v Hill* [1996] 2 All ER 847.

[188] *Colt Industries Inc. v Sarlie (No. 2)* [1966] 1 WLR 1287.

[189] See e.g., *Harrop v Harrop* [1920] 3 KB 386 and *Re Macartney* [1921] Ch. 522. Maintenance orders may now be enforced via the Maintenance Orders (Facilities for Enforcement) Act 1920 and the Maintenance Orders (Reciprocal Enforcement) Act 1972.

[190] (1808) 1 Camp. 253.   [191] *Beatty v Beatty* [1924] 1 KB 807.

[192] See further pp. 424–33 below.

revenue for the foreign state is for a criminal fine or otherwise enforces a public law of the foreign state, is not enforceable in England. It would be recognisable as having determined some issue of fact, however. English law determines whether the judgment is for a tax, penalty or other public law. In *Huntingdon v Attrill*:

> The judgment creditor sought to enforce a judgment of the New York courts in Canada. The judgment was against some directors of a company for the way in which they had run the company into debt in New York. The New York statute described their liability as penal.[193]

The Privy Council held that however the foreign court viewed the liability it imposed under its own law, English law determined whether this was a penalty such that it could not be enforced in England. A penalty must (a) be payable to the state or some officer of the state, and (b) for some criminal offence or an offence of public disorder. So in *Raulin v Fischer*:

> An American recklessly galloped her horse down the Champs Elysées and injured the judgment creditor. An action was brought in the criminal courts in France and the judgment creditor joined in that action as a *partie civil*. The judgment in the *action civile* was held to be private and not a public penalty. It was therefore enforceable.[194]

If the debt is to some private individual, even if it somehow can be seen as enforcing a foreign public law, it has been found not to be a penalty.[195] Punitive or exemplary damages are therefore enforceable at common law.

Some foreign laws are so objectionable as to be refused recognition (as well as enforcement) in England. So judgment which discriminates on the grounds of race or religion,[196] or which is founded on slavery, will not be enforced in England. Others, while not so objectionable, have been recently regarded as public laws not to be enforced outside the territory of the foreign state.[197] The extent of these public laws is not entirely clear.[198] However, it is possible to argue that judgments enforcing such laws may not be enforceable.

iv. Multiple damages: Protection of Trading Interests Act 1980

US courts started granting punitive damage awards with more frequency during the 1970s which we have seen are generally enforceable in England. In response, the Protection of Trading Interests Act was passed in 1980.

---

[193] [1893] AC 150 (PC).   [194] [1911] 2 KB 93.
[195] *SA Consortium General Textiles v Sun and Sand Agencies* [1978] QB 279 (CA).
[196] *Oppenheimer v Cattermole* [1976] AC 249.   [197] See further pp. 424–33 below.
[198] Laws on export controls, securities regulation and for the protection of cultural heritage are probably included, see further Chapters 12 and 13.

A foreign judgment sum which has been arrived at by 'doubling, trebling or otherwise multiplying a sum assessed as compensation for the loss or damage sustained by the person in whose favour the judgment is given'[199] is not enforceable in England.[200] Assessing the manner in which the final sum was arrived at can be difficult. The compensatory part of the award can be enforced where it is severable from the non-compensatory part.[201] That appears to be inconsistent with the wording of s. 5 of the 1980 Act which refers to the non-enforcement of 'the judgment' rather than just the non-compensatory part. However, there is no policy reason not to enforce the compensatory part of the damages. On the other hand, a judgment which arrives at one final amount by multiplying, without the compensatory part being severable, is unenforceable as to the whole. The 1980 Act is incompatible with the Brussels I Regulation as no question of the substance of the foreign judgment can be re-opened in the judgment enforcing court.[202] However, as the laws of many Member States consider multiple damages contrary to public policy, the question is unlikely to arise.

v. Sovereign immunity

A judgment given in a matter in which the judgment debtor is immune by reason of sovereign immunity cannot be enforced in England.[203] In order for a judgment against a foreign state to be enforceable, the foreign court would have had jurisdiction as if it had applied rules corresponding to those in ss. 2–11 of the State Immunity Act 1978. The judgment can be enforced if the foreign state had submitted to the foreign court's jurisdiction or if the basis of the claim is a commercial transaction which could be pursued in the English courts.[204]

c. Effect of foreign judgments

A foreign judgment is conclusive of the facts that it decides. It is not possible to re-open a foreign judgment. Whether or not the foreign court accurately decided a matter of substance is irrelevant. Generally, a party who is aggrieved at the decision of the foreign court must make an appeal in that court[205] and cannot challenge the decision in England except if one of the defences to recognition and enforcement apply. Therefore, it is not possible to argue in England that the foreign court made a mistake about its procedure or jurisdiction,[206] was in error

---

[199] Protection of Trading Interests Act 1980, s. 5(3).   [200] *Ibid.* s. 5(1).
[201] *Lewis v Eliades (No. 3)* [2004] 1 WLR 693 (CA) at para. 51.
[202] Brussels I Regulation, Art. 36.   [203] CJJA 1982, s. 31.
[204] *NML Capital Ltd v Republic of Argentina* [2011] UKSC 31, [2011] 2 AC 495.
[205] *Ellis v M'Henry* (1871) 6 CP 228; *Israel Discount Bank of New York v Hadjipateras* [1984] 1 WLR 137 (CA).
[206] *Pemberton v Hughes* [1899] 1 Ch. 781 at 790.

in applying English law[207] or did not properly find a matter of fact. Exceptionally, a mistake on the foreign court's own jurisdiction which made the foreign judgment null and void under the law of the country of the judgment granting court may be a successful defence to the recognition and enforcement of the foreign judgment.[208] Usually, because under the foreign law the matter can be raised on appeal abroad, this argument is no defence at the enforcement stage in England. The English court may also strike out a defence to the enforcement of a foreign judgment on the grounds that the defence is an abuse of process of the English court. In *Owens Bank Ltd v Étoile Commerciale Ltd*,[209] the Privy Council found raising an unfounded defence in the enforcement proceedings to be an abuse of process of the English court. Once the defence is struck out as an abuse of process, the enforcement can go ahead. It is not sufficient merely to allege the existence of a defence, some evidence to sustain it is necessary.

d. Defences

In some sense many of the defences can be described as aspects of public policy. It is contrary to public policy to enforce a judgment obtained by fraud, or one which is contrary to natural justice, or which is contrary to a previous English judgment, as well as those which are discussed under the specific public policy heading below.[210]

i. Public policy

Public policy is a residual category which covers a number of reasons not to enforce a foreign judgment. A foreign judgment which enforces a foreign law which is discriminatory on the grounds of race or religion will not be enforced;[211] nor will one which prejudices the national interest, such as a judgment enforcing a contract for trading with the enemy in times of war.[212] A judgment which enforces a contract which furthers an act to be performed which is illegal under the law of the place where it is to be performed may not be enforced.[213] The judgment debtor should raise fresh evidence of the illegality which was not brought before the foreign court in order to use this defence.[214] Otherwise the principle of finality would be abridged. A judgment which is contrary to established principles of international law (such as one infringing human rights) may not be

---

[207] *Castrique v Imrie* (1870) LR 4 HL 414 and *Godard v Gray* (1870) LR 6 QB 139.
[208] *Papadopoulos v Papadopoulos* [1930] P 55.   [209] [1995] 1 WLR 44 (PC).
[210] Enforcing judgments for taxes, penalties or enforcing other public laws would also be contrary to public policy, which is why some textbooks consider them in this heading.
[211] *Oppenheimer v Cattermole* [1976] AC 249.
[212] *Dynamit AG v Rio Tinto Co.* [1918] AC 260.
[213] *Soleimany v Soleimany* [1999] QB 785 (CA).
[214] See Fentiman, *International Commercial Litigation*, para. 18.37 *et seq.*

enforced.[215] A foreign judgment in breach of an English injunction restraining the proceedings in that foreign court will not be enforced as the judgment creditor would be in contempt of court for breaching the injunction.[216] Somewhat controversially, a judgment ordering the perpetual maintenance of an illegitimate daughter has been refused enforcement in England. The judgment was contrary to public policy as no equivalent cause of action was available in England.[217] This must be wrong as otherwise any foreign order without an equivalent English cause of action would be refused enforcement. The court in *Phrantzes v Argenti*[218] made a better decision. So long as the judgment was for a fixed sum it would be enforceable even if the cause of action was unknown in England.

ii. Fraud

Under domestic English law a judgment 'tainted by fraud' may be impeached.[219] A new action can be brought to set aside the original judgment rather than an appeal. The claimant bears a heavy burden in such cases to allege and prove new facts. This is also the case with a foreign judgment which has been tainted by fraud.[220] However, there is also no recognition or enforcement of a foreign judgment which is impeachable by fraud. The maxim that 'fraud unravels all' applies and no *res judicata* or issue estoppel operates from the foreign judgment. 'Fraud' here bears a rather wide meaning. It 'includes every variety of *mala fides* and *mala praxis* whereby one of the parties misleads and deceives a judicial tribunal'.[221] A judgment which has been obtained by tricking the foreign court, for example, by perjury or bribing a witness, is not recognisable due to the fraud ('a fraud on the court').[222] Nor is the judgment recognisable or enforceable if the foreign court itself acted fraudulently, for example, if the judge was biased ('a fraud by the court').[223] However, fraud goes further than these clear examples. If the substantive case in the foreign court raises an allegation of fraud, a judgment on that matter may not be recognised or enforced ('fraud on the merits').[224] A foreign judgment will not be recognised or enforced if the judgment debtor was coerced or threatened with violence in the course of the case ('collateral fraud').[225] In any of these

---

[215] *Al Jedda v Secretary of State for Defence* [2009] EWHC 397 at paras 68–73. See also discussion on Article 6 of the ECHR pp. 259–60 below.

[216] *Philip Alexander Securities & Futures Ltd v Bamberger* [1997] ILPr. 73 (affirmed by Court of Appeal at [1997] ILPr. 104).

[217] *Re Macartney* [1921] 1 Ch. 522.   [218] [1960] 2 QB 19.

[219] *R v Humphrys* [1977] AC 1 at 21.   [220] *Vadala v Lawes* (1890) 25 QBD 310.

[221] *Jet Holdings Inc. and others v Patel* [1990] QB 335.

[222] *Ochsenbein v Papelier* (1873) 8 Ch. App. 695.

[223] *Price v Dewhurst* (1837) 8 Sim. 279; more recently *Korea National Insurance Corp. v Allianz Global Corporate & Specialty AG* [2008] EWCA Civ 1355, [2008] 2 CLC 837 and *AK Investment CJSC v Kyrgyz Mobil Tel Ltd* [2011] UKPC 7, [2011] 4 All ER 1027.

[224] *Vadala v Lawes* (1890) 25 QBD 310.   [225] *Jet Holdings Inc. v Patel* [1990] 1 QB 335.

cases, it does not generally matter that the foreign court investigated the possibility of fraud and rejected it. In *Abouloff v Oppenheimer*:

> The claimant brought an action in Russia alleging that goods had been unlawfully detained by the defendant. Judgment was obtained in Russia and an action brought to enforce the judgment in England. The judgment debtor had alleged in the Russian court that the claimant had falsely represented that the judgment debtor was in possession of the goods as the claimant had been in possession of them all along. This was rejected by the Russian court. The same argument was made before the English court at the enforcement stage.[226]

Lord Esher in the Court of Appeal held that the allegation of fraud could be re-opened in the English court despite the fact that it had been raised and rejected abroad and that no new evidence was forthcoming. The Russian judgment was not recognisable or enforceable though the claimant could bring a new trial on the merits in England. The English court would then decide the matter afresh.[227] The judgment debtor may raise the defence of fraud in cases where the fraud could have been but was not in fact raised in the foreign court.[228]

There has been some criticism of the use of all types of fraud as a defence to enforcement of a foreign judgment. It appears very chauvinist to believe that only the English court can properly understand and decide an issue of fraud. However, the House of Lords in *Owens Bank Ltd v Bracco*[229] (which is a case on one of the statutes which mirror the position at common law) affirmed the common law rule in the strongest terms. The defence is a serious inroad to the principle of finality of judgments. So, in the slightly later case of *Owens Bank Ltd v Étoile Commerciale SA*,[230] the Privy Council accepted that there are strong policy arguments in favour of that principle. One can see that a case of fraud by the foreign court could justifiably raise uncertainties about the whole process abroad. These might not be settled by further decision of that court. Nevertheless, why should an allegation of fraud which has already been investigated by the foreign court and rejected be permitted to be raised again at the enforcement stage? Any concerns in a case of fraud on the foreign court or of collateral fraud might be answered by a new action in the foreign court. There also seems little good reason not to require a party to raise the argument of fraud abroad, at least in cases where there is no suggestion of fraud by the court. In the analogous area of a judgment on a contract allegedly entered into

---

[226] (1882–83) LR 10 QBD 295 (CA).
[227] CJJA 1982, s. 34 does not apply to prevent a new action where the foreign judgment is not enforceable.
[228] *Syal v Heyward* [1948] 2 KB 443.   [229] [1992] 2 AC 443.
[230] [1995] 1 WLR 44 at 50 (PC).

under undue influence, the English court refused to allow a retrial of that issue. It could have been and should have been raised in the New York courts and not at the stage of enforcement.[231]

It is possible to avoid the effect of the judgment in *Abouloff v Oppenheimer*. First, there must be prima facie evidence of the fraud. Otherwise to relitigate the matter could be an abuse of process of the English court.[232] Secondly, in the (admittedly rare) case that the issue of fraud has been litigated in the foreign court in separate actions, it would be an abuse of process of the English court to raise the matter a third time at the point of enforcement of the first foreign judgment. So in *House of Spring Gardens Ltd v Waite*:

> The claimants in Ireland had obtained a judgment for £3 million for misuse of confidential information and breach of copyright. The judgment debtors appealed to the Supreme Court in Ireland and lost. They then brought an action to set aside that judgment in Ireland, alleging it had been obtained by fraud. That action was also dismissed. In the action in England to enforce the £3 million judgment, the judgment debtors again raised the question of fraud.[233]

The English Court of Appeal enforced the Irish judgment.[234] Unless the second Irish judgment was itself somehow affected by fraud, the second judgment was capable of creating an issue estoppel on that matter. This is a little odd. It is not very clear what the justification for accepting issue estoppel from the second judgment but not the first judgment might be. The case is better explained either as an example of an abuse of process of the English court by raising the matter for the third time; alternatively, the fact that the judgment debtor had itself brought and lost the second action makes the further appeal in England unjustifiable.

The Canadian court in *Beals v Saldanha*[235] has adopted a more sensible rule that a foreign judgment can be challenged on the ground of fraud only where the allegations are fresh and have not been adjudicated on by the foreign court.

iii. Judgments contrary to natural justice

A judgment in which the defendant was denied a fair trial will not be enforced. Normally, the English court will not investigate the propriety of the foreign proceedings at the enforcement stage. However, there are exceptions to this general rule. The foreign judgment will not be enforced if the judgment debtor has not had due notice of the proceedings; or has not been given a proper right

---

[231] *Israel Discount Bank of New York v Hadjipateras* [1984] 1 WLR 137.
[232] *Owens Bank Ltd v Étoile Commerciale SA* [1995] 1 WLR 44 at 50 (PC).
[233] [1991] 1 QB 241.
[234] This was before the Brussels Convention provided automatic enforcement of Irish judgments.
[235] [2003] SCC 72.

to be heard; or there is a wider issue with the substantial justice; or a breach of Article 6 of the ECHR. In *Jacobson v Frachon*, Atkin LJ noted that natural justice seems to involve 'first of all that the court being a court of competent jurisdiction, has given notice to the litigant that they are about to proceed to determine the rights between him and the other litigant; the other is that having given him that notice, it does afford him an opportunity of substantially presenting his case before the court.'[236]

1. Notice of the proceedings

In order for the foreign judgment to be enforceable, the judgment debtor must have been given notice of the proceedings. So in *Buchanan v Rucker*[237] notice of the proceedings nailed to the courthouse door was found to be insufficient. However, in that case the judgment debtor had never been present in the foreign country so the case is explicable on the grounds that the foreign court lacked sufficient jurisdiction. Usually, English courts are reluctant to criticise foreign courts' procedures where it is considered that the foreign court has sufficient jurisdiction; for example, there is no defence to the foreign judgment even if the foreign court made a mistake in its own jurisdiction.[238] Therefore, the fact that the foreign procedure permits notice to be served in a way that is different to English procedures is not enough to prevent the enforcement of the foreign judgment. In *Jeannot v Fuerst*,[239] lack of notice of the proceedings was not a denial of justice. But in that case the judgment debtor had agreed to submit to the jurisdiction of the foreign court and was taken to know of the French court's rules as to service. Moreover, the judgment debtor had had the right, which the judgment debtor had not taken up, to defend the proceedings before and after execution of the judgment.

2. Right to be heard

For the foreign judgment to be enforced, the judgment debtor must also have been given a proper opportunity to participate in the hearing. No defence has been successful on this ground but it must be right. In *Jacobson v Frachon*:

> Evidence was given to the French court by an expert nominated by the French seller who was the defendant in those French proceedings. The expert, who was also a relative of the defendant, did not examine the matter properly and refused to hear the evidence of the English buyer. The French court was not bound to accept that evidence but it did so and gave judgment against the buyer. The buyer sought to start a new action in England and the seller pleaded the French judgment as a bar to the action.

---

[236] (1927) 138 LT 386 at 392 (CA).   [237] (1808) 9 East 192.
[238] *Pemberton v Hughes* [1899] 1 Ch. 781 at 790.   [239] (1909) 25 TLR 424.

The Court of Appeal held that the judgment did not infringe natural justice. The French court could have rejected the evidence of the expert and the buyer was able to make (and had made) representations as to the accuracy of the report. In modern times, this defence is probably subsumed into the defence where the judgment of the foreign court is in breach of Article 6 of the ECHR.[240]

3. 'Substantial justice'

The Court of Appeal in *Adams v Cape Industries Plc*[241] said *obiter* that in addition to the defences discussed above, a foreign judgment would not be recognised or enforced if it was contrary to English concepts of 'substantial justice':

> The judgment debtor Cape Industries had had notice of the Texas proceedings and had an opportunity to be heard. However, Cape Industries had not participated in the *Tyler (No. 2)* action. The Texas court had agreed with the claimants' allegations and assessed damages by fixing an average per claimant and multiplying that by the total claimants. The claimants' lawyers then divided up the total sum for each claimant. This method was not strictly in accordance with the procedure required of the Texas court by its own federal rules.

Slade LJ in the Court of Appeal regarded this as an infringement of substantial justice. In the case of unliquidated damages[242] the extent of the judgment debtor's obligation to pay the default judgment must be assessed objectively by a judge.[243] This is a little dubious as any irregularity in the foreign court's procedure is not generally a defence to enforcement. Also, in principle there should be no investigation as to the manner in which a competent foreign court deals with cases. Note that if the foreign judgment was for a liquidated sum, apparent on the face of the claim of which the judgment debtor had been given notice, it would not be contrary to substantial justice to enforce the debt unless it was somehow fraudulently inflated or 'irrational'. However, the dictum in *Adams v Cape Industries Plc* was applied by the Court of Appeal in *Masters v Leaver*,[244] which was another case of a default judgment. Here, the unliquidated damages were assessed by a jury which did not independently consider the evidence contrary to the procedure required by the foreign court. The Texas judgment was again not enforced.

---

[240] See pp. 259–60 below.   [241] [1990] Ch. 433 (CA).
[242] Where the total amount cannot be fixed objectively, for example, a debt under a contract.
[243] [1990] Ch. 433 at 567.   [244] [2000] ILPr. 387.

iv. Article 6 of the European Convention on Human Rights

Article 6 of the ECHR provides that everyone is entitled 'to a fair and public hearing within a reasonable time by an independent and impartial tribunal established by law' in the determination of a person's civil rights and obligations.[245] Generally, the ECHR applies to domestic cases but it can have an indirect effect in the enforcement of foreign judgments. An English court must refuse to enforce a judgment which has been obtained in proceedings which involve a 'flagrant breach' of Article 6.[246] It is irrelevant that the judgment has been obtained from a state which is not party to the ECHR.[247] The UK government may be in breach of its own obligation to enforce compliance with the ECHR if the English courts permitted enforcement of a judgment which does not conform to Article 6.[248] In *Pellegrini v Italy*,[249] the obligation appeared to extend to a 'review' of the manner of the foreign proceedings to ensure that those proceedings were compliant with Article 6. In *Merchant International Co. Ltd v Natsionalna Aktsionerna Kompaniya Naftogaz Ukrayiny*:

> A judgment had been obtained from the Ukrainian courts against a Ukrainian energy company. It could not enforce the judgment in the Ukraine as a law had been passed suspending enforcement against energy companies there. The judgment creditor therefore sought to enforce the judgment in England. Before the hearing in England the judgment debtor had obtained an order of the Ukrainian court setting aside its original judgment on the basis of allegedly new information. This information was in fact easily discoverable at the time of the original trial. The judgment debtor resisted the summary enforcement of the judgment debt, arguing that there was no debt to enforce. The judgment creditor argued that the proceedings in the Ukraine were contrary to Article 6. The setting aside of the original judgment infringed the principle of legal certainty relating to final judgments. The judgment creditor also argued that the Ukraine proceedings setting aside the original judgment deprived the creditor of its possessions contrary to Article 1 of Protocol 1 to the ECHR.[250]

The Court of Appeal refused to set aside the summary English judgment providing enforcement of the original Ukrainian judgment. The second judgment of the Ukrainian court invalidating its original judgment was in flagrant

---

[245] See J. Fawcett, 'The Impact of Article 6(1) of the ECHR on Private International Law' [2007] *ICLQ* 1.

[246] *Al Bassam v Al Bassam* [2004] EWCA Civ 857.

[247] *Drozd and Janousek v France and Spain* (1992) 14 EHRR 745 at 749.

[248] *Government of the United States v Montgomery (No. 2)* [2004] 1 WLR 2241. However, in that case the House of Lords distinguished *Pellegrini v Italy* (2001) 35 EHRR 44 and enforced the US judgment finding that the rights under Art. 6 had not been infringed.

[249] (2001) 35 EHRR 44.   [250] [2012] EWCA Civ 196, [2012] 2 All ER (Comm) 1.

breach of Article 6 and so provided no defence to enforcement. The principle of legal certainty permits final judgments (such as the original one of the Ukrainian court) to be set aside only on the basis of evidence which could not have been reasonably discoverable at the time of the original trial.[251] Setting aside a judgment which has been properly obtained is also depriving the judgment creditor of an asset. As there had been an English summary judgment this case could be narrowly confined to English judgments. However, it is of wider application. A foreign judgment which has been obtained in a manner which breaches Article 6 rights probably cannot be enforced. The development of the European Court of Human Rights' jurisprudence on Article 6 is therefore of increasing interest to private international lawyers.

v. Conflicting English or foreign judgment

A foreign judgment will not be recognised or enforced where it conflicts with an English judgment on the same matter.[252] If there is a foreign judgment which is already in existence and capable of recognition and enforcement, the first judgment in time should be recognised and enforced.[253]

e. Civil Jurisdiction and Judgments Act 1982, s. 32

A foreign judgment which has been obtained in breach of an agreement to settle the dispute otherwise than by proceedings in that country will not be recognised or enforced in England.[254] Therefore, a Ruritanian judgment given over a dispute in a contract which contains an arbitration clause in favour of arbitration in England will not be recognised or enforced. Nor will such a judgment be enforced if the contract contained an exclusive jurisdiction clause in favour of France. The jurisdiction or arbitration agreement must not have been illegal, void or unenforceable or incapable of being performed for reasons which were not the fault of the party commencing the foreign proceedings.[255] The protection of the section is lost if the judgment debtor submitted to the proceedings in the foreign country, or agreed to them, or waived the jurisdiction or arbitration agreement. It is also lost if the judgment debtor is the claimant or counterclaimant in the foreign court. The English court is not bound by any judgment made by the foreign court as to the validity of the arbitration agreement or the submission of a party.[256] As we have seen, more

---

[251] ECtHR cases of *Pravednaya v Russia, Lizanets v Ukraine* and *Agrokompleks v Ukraine*, Application no. 23465/03, 6 October 2011.

[252] *Vervaeke v Smith* [1983] 1 AC 145.   [253] *Showlag v Mansour* [1995] 1 AC 431 (PC).

[254] CJJA 1982, s. 32.

[255] This latter provision is to prevent a party from preventing the jurisdiction or arbitration agreement from being performed and then commencing foreign proceedings. However, if the agreement cannot be performed, for example because of civil unrest in the country, then the protection of s. 32 falls away.

[256] CJJA 1982, s. 32(3).

generally, the CJJA 1982 provides that a person is not considered to have submitted to the foreign jurisdiction if that person had appeared in the foreign proceedings only to contest the jurisdiction of the court or ask that the proceedings be dismissed or stayed in favour of proceedings elsewhere or be submitted to arbitration.[257] In *AES Ust-Kamenogorsk Hydropower Plant LLC v Ust-Kamenogorsk Hydropower Plant JSC*:[258]

> The heart of the case was the enforceability of an English arbitration clause in a contract between two Kazakhstani companies to operate hydroelectric facilities in Kazakhstan. The contract was expressly governed (apart from the arbitration clause) by Kazakhstan law. The Kazakhstan court had ruled that the arbitration clause was void as contrary to Kazakhstani public policy. The parties had both actively participated in this decision. Did the judgment have to be recognised in England?

Rix LJ in the Court of Appeal held that it did not have to be recognised. So long as the English court considered that the arbitration agreement is valid and enforceable, that was sufficient. Note that this defence is not possible under the Brussels I Regulation as no review of the substance of the judgment (which would include any decision on the validity of a jurisdiction clause) is possible.[259]

6. Hague Convention on Choice of Court Agreements

In 2005, the Hague Convention on Choice of Court Agreements was signed. It was the only successful negotiation from a more wide-ranging original project by the Hague Conference on Private International Law for a worldwide multilateral convention on jurisdiction, and on recognition and enforcement of judgments in civil and commercial matters. The name is perhaps misleading as the Convention applies largely to exclusive jurisdiction agreements.[260] An exclusive agreement is one which designates the courts of one contracting state to the exclusion of others.[261] There are also reasonably extensive exclusions from the scope of the Convention, such as contracts of employment and the carriage of goods, which further narrow its operation.[262] The EU became a member of the Hague Conference and ratification of the Convention is to be done by the Union rather than by the individual states.[263] As we have

---

[257] *Ibid.* s. 33(1)(c).   [258] [2011] EWCA Civ 647, [2012] Bus. LR 330.

[259] Brussels I Regulation, Art. 36.

[260] Hague Convention, Art. 1(1). A contracting state may declare that it will recognise and enforce judgments of another contracting state which have been given pursuant to a non-exclusive jurisdiction agreement under Art. 22 but this is optional.

[261] Article 3.   [262] Article 2.

[263] After Lugano Opinion (Opinion 1/03) [2006] ECR I-1145, it is clear that the EU has external competence over matters which affect its internal competence, such as jurisdiction in civil and

seen,[264] the purpose of the Convention is to enhance the effectiveness of jurisdiction agreements. The Convention provides rules to grant jurisdiction to the designated court, which cannot stay its proceedings pending the decision of a different court, as to that court's jurisdiction. Generally, courts other than that designated must decline to exercise jurisdiction over the dispute.[265]

For our present purposes it is important to note that a judgment given by the courts of the designated contracting state will be recognised in other contracting states so long as it is effective in the designated state and enforced so long as it is enforceable in the designated state.[266] Review of the designated state's decisions is limited to what is necessary for the application of Chapter III of the Convention.[267] The enforcing court is bound by the findings of fact of the designated court as to its own jurisdiction[268] other than in cases of default judgments. However, it is possible to refuse to recognise and enforce the nominated court's decision. Articles 9, 10 and 11 provide the only[269] grounds for refusal. Recognition or enforcement of the judgment may be refused:

(1) if the jurisdiction agreement was null and void under the law of the designated court;[270]
(2) if a party lacked capacity to conclude the agreement under the law of the enforcing state;
(3) if the document instituting proceedings or an equivalent document was not notified to the defendant in time to enable the defendant to arrange the defence[271] or was notified but in a manner which is incompatible with the fundamental principles of the enforcing state on the service of documents;[272]
(4) if the judgment was obtained by fraud in procedure;[273]
(5) if the recognition or enforcement is manifestly contrary to the public policy of the enforcing state;[274]
(6) if the judgment is inconsistent with a judgment of the enforcing state or of a recognisable prior judgment of another state;[275]

---

commercial matters. See A. Schulz, 'The Accession of the European Community to the Hague Conference on Private International Law' [2007] *ICLQ* 915.

[264] See further pp. 186–8 above.   [265] Hague Convention, Art. 6.   [266] Article 8.

[267] Article 8(2).

[268] There are complicated carve-outs; for example, a decision of the designated court on the scope of the Hague Convention is generally not binding (Art. 10(1)) except in some cases on copyright or other related rights (Art. 10(3)).

[269] Article 8(1).

[270] Unless the designated court has determined that the agreement is valid (Art. 9(a)).

[271] Unless the defendant appeared and presented a case without contesting the service of the documents (where such contest is permissible, if it is not the defendant's appearance will not 'cure' the defect of lack of notification) (Art. 9(c)(i)).

[272] Article 9(c)(ii).   [273] Article 9(d).

[274] Article 9(e). This includes where the procedures of the designated state are 'incompatible with the fundamental principles of procedural fairness' of the enforcing state.

[275] Article 9(f) and (g).

(7) if the enforcing state has made a declaration under Article 21 in respect of a strong interest in not applying the Convention to a specific matter[276] and the judgment falls within this matter;[277]

(8) if (and to the extent that) the judgment awards non-compensatory damages; the enforcing court is to take into account to what extent the damage award is to cover costs and expenses of the proceedings.[278]

In addition, the designated court's decision on the scope of the Convention itself may be refused recognition.[279] The enforcing court can make its own decision on the application of the Convention and refuse to enforce a judgment which it considers falls outside the scope.[280] As one can see, this Convention will not make much difference to the existing English national rules on recognising and enforcing judgments which involve an exclusive jurisdiction agreement. However, they will alter some of the effects of the rules of the Brussels I Regulation such as the consequences of *Erich Gasser v MISAT srl*.[281]

---

[276] Article 21.   [277] Article 10(4).   [278] Article 11.   [279] Article 10(1).
[280] Article 10(2). However, there are limits to this (see Art. 10(3)).
[281] Case C-116/02 [2003] ECR I-14693.

9

Choice of law rules

1. Introduction

As we have seen, conflict of laws deals with cases which involve a foreign element in a number of ways. First, there are rules which decide whether the English court can and should hear a particular dispute. Secondly, there are rules by which the English court will recognise or enforce a foreign judgment. Thirdly, there are choice of law rules by which the English court identifies a system of applicable rules under which the substantive result of the case is determined. These rules may be ones of English law or of a foreign law. In the American case of *Loucks v Standard Oil Co. of New Jersey*, Cardozo CJ eloquently put it 'We are not so provincial as to say that every solution of a problem is wrong because we deal with it otherwise at home'.[1] Choice of law rules are not generally determinative of themselves, they point to substantive rules which are so determinative. Some domestic English rules are unilaterally applied because their territorial scope requires their application to particular circumstances, even if there is a foreign element to the facts or the parties. These unilateral rules are not generally recognised as choice of law rules but the interpretation of the territorial scope of English rules often requires rather similar techniques to multilateral choice of law rules. It is clear that choice of law rules themselves are rules of English law and the English court in applying foreign law does so in the context of English procedure.

2. Analysis

The conflict of laws, in so far as it is concerned with the choice of applicable law, consists only of a relatively small number of rules; the problems tend to arise, as in most areas of law, with the exceptions. But, for the moment we will stay with the general rules. These can all be stated in the same simple form, for example:

---

[1] 224 NY 99 (1918).

(a) the formal validity of a marriage is governed by the law of the place of celebration;

(b) capacity to marry is governed by the law of the parties' domiciles;

(c) title to movable property is governed by the *lex situs*[2] at the time of the transaction;

(d) succession to movable property is governed by the law of the domicile of the deceased at the date of death;

(e) succession to immovable property is governed by the *lex situs*;

(f) procedure is governed by the *lex fori*;[3]

(g) liability in contract is governed by the applicable law of the contract;[4]

(h) liability in tort is generally governed by the law of the country in which the damage occurred.[5]

It is possible for some issues to be governed by more than one system of law. These may be applied cumulatively as, for example, liability for defamation committed abroad arises only if liability is established both by the law of the place where the events took place *and* by English law as the *lex fori*.[6] Or the laws may be applied alternatively as, for example, a contract is formally valid if it is valid either by the law applicable to the contract or by the law of the place where the parties were when it was concluded.[7]

These rules can all be analysed in the same manner. First, the legal category or issue is to be identified. For example, in (c) the legal category is a question of title to movable property. This is a pigeon-hole into which the legal issue disclosed by the facts of cases may be placed. Secondly, the connecting factor is to be identified, so-called as they connect legal categories to the applicable law. In (c) it is the *situs* of the property, i.e., its location. There are not many legal categories; they may be ascertained by looking at the headings and subheadings of most of the chapters of this book; similarly there are not many connecting factors.

This may all seem very straightforward, but there are disguised difficulties about it. Problems may occur in a number of ways.

(1) The case may fall into one legal category in the view of the *lex fori* (English law) but into another in the view of the foreign law which is alleged to be the *lex causae* (applicable law). Thus, English law may regard the case as being concerned with formalities of marriage, but French law may regard it as raising the question of capacity to marry. To put it another way, how is the issue to be characterised?

---

[2] The law of the place where the property is situated.

[3] The law of the forum or court, i.e., English law as far as this work is concerned.

[4] As determined by the Rome I Regulation (Regulation (EC) 593/2008 on the law applicable to contractual obligations [2008] OJ L177/6), see further Chapter 10.

[5] Rome II Regulation, Art. 4(1) (Regulation (EC) 864/2007 on the law applicable to non-contractual obligations [2007] OJ L199/40), see further Chapter 11.

[6] The double-actionability test, see further Chapter 11.

[7] Rome I Regulation, Art. 11(1), see further Chapter 10.

(2) English law and the foreign law may agree on the legal category but disagree on the connecting factor to be employed, as where English law regards succession to movables to be governed by the law of the domicile, whereas by the foreign law it is governed by the law of nationality. This raises a question of *renvoi*. What is meant by a reference to the 'applicable law'? Is it the law as would be decided exactly by a judge of the foreign court, including some reference to the international elements of the case, i.e., together with the private international law of the foreign law? Or is it merely a reference to the domestic rules of the foreign court?

(3) English law and the foreign law may agree on the legal category and even on the connecting factor. However, this conceals a latent conflict, because the two laws mean something different by the connecting factor. Thus, under both laws succession to movables is governed by the law of the last domicile of the deceased. But, by the English law of domicile the deceased died domiciled in France; under French law the deceased died domiciled in England. This is also a question of *renvoi*.

(4) The issues might fall into two different legal categories, each having a different choice of law rule. So a wife may claim a right of intestate succession to her husband's immovable property. The property is situated in Italy, therefore the choice of law rule says that Italian law applies. However, if there is also a question whether the wife is married to the husband, a separate choice of law issue also arises. This is termed an 'incidental question'.

3. Connecting factors

The connecting factors employed by the conflict of laws are not especially numerous. They include the personal law (domicile, habitual residence and, rarely, nationality); the place where the transaction takes place (as place of celebration of marriage); the intention of the parties (as expressed by a choice of law clause in a contract); the place of the seller's residence (as in contracts for the sale of goods); the place of the damage (as in torts); the *situs* (the location of property); and the place where the court is hearing the case.

Since the conflict of laws forms part of English law, English law alone can determine when a foreign law is to be applied. It follows from this that English law must not only select the connecting factor, it must also say what it means. This is clear in respect of domicile and, for jurisdictional purposes, the place of contracting.[8]

Thus, if both English and French law use domicile as a connecting factor, but by English law a person is domiciled in France and by French law in England, he will be regarded by an English court as domiciled in France. In *Re Annesley*.[9]

---

[8] *Entores v Miles Far East Corp.* [1955] 2 QB 327; *Brinkibon v Stahag Stahl GmbH* [1982] 2 AC 34; but cf. *Apple Corp. Ltd v Apple Computer Inc.* [2004] 2 CLC 720. See pp. 154–5 above.

[9] [1926] Ch. 692. The case was complicated by *renvoi*. See p. 280 *et seq.* below. See also *Re Martin* [1900] P 211.

> Mrs A died domiciled in France according to English law. By French law she had
> never acquired a domicile there. Russell J held that Mrs A died domiciled in France.

This question also arose in relation to the *situs* of property, which is the
connecting factor for proprietary interests. In *Dornoch Ltd v Westminster
International BV*:[10]

> The matter concerned the *situs* of the ship; in this case its physical location was
> Thailand. However, the ownership of ships and aircraft is generally registered
> on a registry recording sales and some other proprietary interests; this ship was
> registered in the Netherlands. There was evidence that the law of Thailand
> would refer to Dutch law to determine title. Tomlinson J determined the *situs* of
> the ship for the choice of law rule at the physical location of the ship not the
> place of the registry.

There can be no doubt that if it should be necessary to determine the *situs* of
intangible property, for example, a bank account at a New York bank's English
branch, English law would apply, and the *situs* would be England, even if by
New York law it would be New York.[11]

There are two exceptions to this general rule. These are: (i) nationality – this
can only be determined by French law if a person is alleged to be a French
national; (ii) for jurisdictional purposes, some statutes provide that in certain
cases, domicile shall be as determined by the foreign law in question.[12]

There is also a quasi-exception. If, as in *Re Annesley*,[13] the English court
decides that a person died domiciled in France, but continues by applying
renvoi,[14] and pretends that it is a French court, it is then applying French
conflict rules and not those of English law. This will entail the determination
that the deceased died domiciled in England.

4. Characterisation

We have seen that the process known as 'characterisation' is sometimes
necessary because English law may regard the case as falling into one legal
category but the relevant foreign law believes it to belong to a different one.
This process is undertaken also in cases which do not contain a foreign
element; a court may be called upon to determine whether the issue sounds

---

[10] [2009] EWHC 889. This case was also complicated by *renvoi*.
[11] *X A/G v A Bank* [1983] 2 All ER 464.
[12] See Family Law Act 1986, s. 46(5) and Civil Partnership Act 2004, s. 237; Brussels I Regulation,
Art. 59 (Regulation (EC) 44/2001 on jurisdiction and the enforcement of judgments in civil
and commercial matters).
[13] [1926] Ch. 692.   [14] See further pp. 280–8 below.

in contract or tort, or whether property is realty or personalty, but it is obviously more difficult where a foreign element is present.

Examples of characterisation are to be found throughout this book, where they are discussed in some detail. They include questions such as whether a rule of English law which required that in order for an action to be brought on a contract there must be written evidence thereof, was a rule of evidence and thus procedural, so that it applied by virtue of the *lex fori* to a contract governed by French law. It was held that it was procedural and applied.[15] In several cases the question was whether a rule of a foreign law requiring an action to be brought within a certain period of time was substantive and applicable or procedural and irrelevant. The courts held that it was procedural[16] although that has now been overturned by statute.[17] The question has arisen whether a sum awarded as part of a judgment by a foreign court and described by the foreign law as a penalty, though it was not so regarded by English law, should be characterised as a penalty or not. It was held that English law governed the matter and it was not a penalty.[18]

It will be observed from these examples that the English courts have generally characterised the issue before them according to their own notions; this will be illustrated further.[19]

The problem of characterisation is one of the most difficult in the conflict of laws, and it has generated an enormous amount of writing in many languages. It might well be thought that its difficulties and obscurities increase in direct proportion to the amount of juristic discussion of it.[20] There has been considerable difference of opinion as to how the problem should be solved. The courts are usually criticised for solving it the wrong way and nearly all the cases referred to above have been the subject of severe criticism. It is true that the solutions arrived at have caused, or are capable of causing, considerable difficulties. This is so much so that in some areas, legislation has been used to turn the law around.[21] It is not sought to add to the confusion here, it is merely desired to state the problem, illustrate it, discuss briefly the chief methods which writers have suggested as solutions for it, and to exemplify the whole matter by giving some English cases.

---

[15] *Leroux v Brown* (1852) 12 CB 801; this problem of characterisation does not now arise in the same manner as it is resolved by Art. 12(1)(c) of the Rome I Regulation, [2008] see pp. 319–20 below.

[16] See e.g., *Huber v Steiner* (1835) Bing. NC 202; *Harris v Quine* (1869) LR 4 QB 653.

[17] See Foreign Limitation Periods Act 1984.

[18] *Huntingdon v Attrill* [1893] AC 150 (PC) (on appeal from Ontario). The English courts will not enforce a judgment for a sum that they view as a penalty. For a more recent example, see *Republic of Iran v Barakat Galleries Ltd* [2007] EWCA Civ 1374, [2009] QB 22 at para. 106.

[19] See pp. 271–80 below.

[20] There are some clear accounts of the issues: *Dicey, Morris and Collins, Conflict of Laws* (14th edn, Sweet & Maxwell, 2006) ch. 2; J. Harris, 'Does Choice of Law Make Any Sense?' [2004] *Current Legal Problems* 305; C. Forsyth, 'Mind the Gap: A Practical Example of the Characterisation of Prescription/Limitation Rules' [2006] *Jo. Priv. Int. Law* 169.

[21] As with limitation, see Foreign Limitation Periods Act 1984.

Before proceeding further it has to be said that there has been very great debate and confusion right at the start of the inquiry as to what it is that is characterised. Is it a 'legal issue', a 'legal relation', 'a legal claim', 'a legal question', 'a factual situation', the 'facts of a case', or 'the rule of English (or foreign) laws'? The real question is whether it is the facts or factual situation or a legal question. Since some aspects of characterisation clearly do not involve the facts this leads to the conclusion that it is a legal question. It is generally accepted that legal issues are characterised for the purposes of the choice of law rule,[22] rather than particular legal rules. There is one exception to this rule: the case of classifying foreign penal, revenue and other public laws. Here, it is the foreign rule which is classified for the very particular reason that such rules are not applied even if they are part of the governing law. English law as the *lex fori* appears to adopt its own classification of the foreign law.[23]

Legal issues are characterised rather than facts because although any case involves the facts, of course, what the choice of law rule points to is the legal rules of some system. The facts are those data which enable the judge to formulate, as he must always do, a legal issue which leads to the application of the legal rule. A judge or lawyer is not interested in the facts in some sort of vacuum and they cannot be characterised in the abstract, but only by formulating legal categories; these are categories of legal questions. In addition, the manner in which the claim is put to the court for decision inevitably involves some prior classification of the facts into legal issues by the parties.

Various solutions to the problem of characterisation have been put forward; five will be mentioned.

a. The *lex fori* theory

This was proposed by the German and French writers, Kahn[24] and Bartin,[25] who 'discovered' the problem in the 1890s. It has been the prevailing theory in continental Europe, and by and large, has been adopted in practice by the English courts. According to this theory the court should characterise the issue in accordance with the categories of its own domestic law, and foreign rules of law in accordance with their nearest analogy in the court's domestic law. Thus, a French rule requiring

---

[22] By the English courts at least: *Macmillan Inc. v Bishopsgate Investment Trust Plc (No. 3)* [1996] 1 WLR 387 and *Maher v Groupama Grand Est* [2009] EWCA Civ 1191, [2010] 1 WLR 1564.

[23] *Huntingdon v Atrill* [1893] AC 150. As to which see further pp. 271–80 below.

[24] F Kahn, 'Gesetzkelten' in (1891) 30 *Jehrings Jahrbucher* 1.

[25] F Bartin, *De l'impossibilité d'arriver à la suppression definitive des Conflits des Lois* (Clunet, Paris, 1897) pp. 225–55, 466–95, 720–38. The most comprehensive discussion of this topic in English is that by A. H. Robertson, *Characterisation in the Conflict of Laws* (Harvard University Press, Cambridge, MA, 1940). It was introduced to English-speaking lawyers by E. G. Lorenzen in 1920. His article, published in that year, is reproduced in his *Selected Articles on the Conflict of Laws* (Yale University Press, New Haven, CT, 1947). The best discussion is that of Prof. Lipstein's Chapter 5 on 'Characterization' in the *International Encyclopaedia of Comparative Law* (Mohr Seibeck, Tubingen, 1999) vol. III.

parental consent to marriage should be characterised as pertaining to formalities, since English law so regards its own rules regarding parental consent.

Objections raised to the *lex fori* theory are that its application may result in a distortion of the foreign rule and render it inapplicable in cases in which the foreign law would apply it, and vice versa. Moreover, if there is no close analogy in the domestic law (as there is no analogy in English law to the matrimonial property regime known to foreign laws) the theory does not work. Lastly, proponents sometimes seem to suggest that it is facts alone which have to be classified, but this is not so; it is facts which are presented as issues in the light of a foreign law.

b. The *lex causae* theory

According to this theory, characterisation should be effected by adopting the categories of the governing law. It is sometimes suggested that at least one English decision is based on this method, though this is perhaps doubtful.[26] There are two serious objections to this theory. First, the whole purpose of characterisation is to discover what law governs the issue. To say that the governing law dictates the process of characterisation is to argue in a circle, for how can we know what the governing law is until the process of characterisation is completed.[27] Secondly, if there are two possible foreign laws to govern the matter, and they characterise the issue differently, which is to be adopted by the English court? It may be added that the adoption of this theory could compel the adoption of idiosyncratic foreign characterisation, such as a rule of Utopian law that a Utopian person can only be validly married if he or she goes through the ceremony before a Utopian shaman, wherever in the world the ceremony takes place. A court may have to resort to public policy to avoid the consequence of an invalid marriage if a Utopian person marries in England without a shaman. As public policy should be very sparingly used in conflict of laws,[28] the theory can be criticised for requiring such an exception.

c. Analytical jurisprudence and comparative law

This theory was espoused by the author of the encyclopaedia of comparative conflict of laws, Ernst Rabel,[29] and views similar to his were advanced in England by W. E. Beckett,[30] who said that conflicts rules should use 'conceptions of absolutely general character', and that:

---

[26] *Re Maldonado* [1954] P 233.

[27] M. Wolff denied that circularity was necessarily involved: *Private International Law* (2nd edn, Oxford University Press, 1950) p. 156, but his arguments are not entirely convincing.

[28] See further Chapter 13.

[29] E. Rabel, *The Conflict of Laws, a Comparative Study* (2nd edn, University of Michigan, Ann Arbor, MI, 1968) vol. I.

[30] W. Beckett, 'The Question of Classification ("Qualifications") in Private International Law' (1934) 15 *BYIL* 46. Beckett was then Assistant Legal Advisor and later Legal Advisor to the Foreign Office.

> These conceptions are borrowed from analytical jurisprudence, that general science of law, based on the results of the study of comparative law, which extracts from this study essential general principles of professedly universal application – not principles based on, or applicable to, the legal system of one country only.

This is at first sight attractive, but it has its drawbacks. First, few universal principles are disclosed by analytical jurisprudence and comparative law which would be of assistance in this area. Secondly, though comparative law may disclose similarities between legal systems, it may also disclose differences, which it is hardly capable of resolving; thus, it may show that requirements of parental consent to marriage pertain to formalities in some systems or to capacity in others, but this does not tell us how in the case before us these differences are to be settled. Thirdly, it is rather impractical; it would be asking too much of legal advisors and judges to undertake the exercise involved and the results would be unpredictable.[31] This method would certainly add to the length and cost of litigation. However, a variant of this theory has found some favour with the English court which has said that characterisation must be done with a 'broad internationalist spirit'.[32]

d. Falconbridge's views

The Canadian lawyer, Falconbridge, proposed a two-stage process.[33] The first stage, a task for the *lex fori*, is to define the scope of the legal category, the categories not being those of the domestic law system but of its private international law; and the second to examine the relevant legal rule in its own context to see whether it can be fitted into the legal category in question.

e. English courts and characterisation

The English courts have not consciously adopted any one doctrine or theory. Indeed, the question of characterisation has been referred to in the cases in the most general form. For example, in *Wight v Eckhardt Marine GmbH*,[34] Lord Hoffmann approved of the argument made by the defendants, noting 'the purpose of the conflicts taxonomy is to identify the most appropriate law. This meant that one has to look at the substance of the issue rather than the formal clothes in which it may be dressed.' It is to be remembered that characterisation is done for the purpose of identifying the choice of law rule. Choice of law

---

[31] An analogy could be drawn with the pleading and proof of foreign law. See further pp. 46–52 above.

[32] *Raiffeisen Zentralbank Österreich AG v Five Star General Trading LLC* [2001] QB 825 at 840.

[33] J. D. Falconbridge, *Selected Essays in the Conflict of Laws* (2nd edn, Canada Law Book Co., Toronto, 1954) p. 50. Similar views were expressed earlier by L. Raape (1934 IV) 50 *Hague Recueil des Cours* 477.

[34] [2003] UKPC 37, [2004] 1 AC 147.

rules are developed in order to achieve just results in particular cases in which a foreign element is present. Justice is a broad concept but in this area it has been focused largely on fulfilling parties' expectations. Also, choice of law rules limit the role of domestic law because the foreign elements make unrestricted application of that law unjust.[35] Looked at in this way, characterisation is necessarily part of a process of the *lex fori*. Indeed, the *lex fori* theory, modified in some cases so as to approximate to Falconbridge's view, represents the actual method employed by the courts. The foreign classification is not adopted as such except in deciding whether foreign property is immovable or movable.[36] This is not to say that the foreign law is completely ignored as irrelevant, as it may be considered both to identify the issue and to determine the choice of law rule 'in a broad internationalist spirit'.[37] So the concept embraced in the choice of law rule is given a wider interpretation than it would be for domestic law. In *De Nichols v Curlier*,[38] the English court accepted a claim based upon the French community property regime despite there being no exact equivalent in England.[39] Likewise at common law the 'contract' choice of law rules cover agreements not supported by consideration.[40]

In practice, the English courts formulate the issue and define the ambit of the legal category for themselves, and then they determine whether a question posed by a foreign rule comes into that category. An example of this is *Re Cohn*:[41]

> A mother and her daughter, domiciled in Germany, were killed by the same bomb in an air-raid on London. It could not be shown which died first and which survived the other.

The choice of law rule for succession issues is that of the law of the domicile, here German law. By that law the daughter's estate could only succeed under her mother's will if she survived the mother. There is an English rule by which a younger person is presumed to have survived the older where they die together.[42] Uthwatt J held that this rule was not one of evidence but of substance and so did not apply as English law was not the applicable law. The corresponding provision of German law, by which the two were deemed to have died simultaneously, he held part of the law of inheritance and so applicable by the choice of law rule. Thus, he categorised the issue as one

---

[35] See J. Harris, 'Does Choice of Law Make Any Sense' [2004] *Current Legal Problems* 305.

[36] See further p. 379 below.

[37] As we have seen, characterisation of the legal issues means that the facts cannot be considered in abstract.

[38] [1900] AC 21.

[39] It did so by the device of implying a contract between the husband and wife on marriage adopting the community property regime.

[40] *Re Bonacina* [1912] 2 Ch. 394.   [41] [1945] Ch. 5.   [42] Law of Property Act 1925, s. 184.

of succession and then held that the question presented by German law came within that category.

Another way of looking at the matter is to ask whether the German rule came within the scope of the English conflict of laws rule. One way of determining the scope of the conflict of laws rule is to identify its purpose and then inspect whether the foreign rule in question falls within or without the policy of and reasons for that choice of law rule. It may well be that choice of law rules need to be further refined to take account of this process. However, in *Re Cohn* it might be argued that the purpose behind the choice of law rule referring matters of succession to the law of the domicile is to identify a law which the deceased person is personally connected to and which that person and their relatives would expect to govern questions of title to property on death. Further, the deceased could then be forewarned to make a will consistent with their wishes under that law. Here, there was little connection with England so that was not a system of law that fulfils that purpose. In this case Uthwatt J was trying to avoid a characterisation of the English rule as one of evidence which would then have applied as part of the choice of law rule relating to procedure. However, once that was decided, he did not need to go further and classify the German law, it applied merely by reason of the choice of law rule.

In *Macmillan Inc. v Bishopsgate Investment Trust Plc (No 3)*:[43]

> The claimant company sought return of shares it owned in another company which its own controlling director, Robert Maxwell, had fraudulently pledged to a third party. The defendant claimed ownership of the shares as a bona fide purchaser. The exact meaning of bona fide depended on whether English law or New York law applied.

The Court of Appeal classified the issue as one of title to intangible property, rejecting the claimant's argument that the claim sounded in restitution. Once the issue was identified as that of title to intangible property, the choice of law rule was that of the *lex situs* of the shares. This was New York law which the claimants had wanted to avoid in favour of English law, which might have governed a restitutionary claim. It is not exactly clear why a proprietary rather than a restitutionary classification was adopted. It can be argued that a proprietary characterisation led to a law which was more consistent with what all parties interested in the possible ownership of the shares could have expected to apply. However, an appeal to the parties' expectations may disguise the reasons why particular parties' expectations are preferred. In this case 'parties' means more than the parties to the case but all those who might have an interest in the property under dispute.

---

[43] [1996] 1 WLR 387.

We have seen that English choice of law rules may have to take account of unknown foreign concepts. It is also the case that peculiarly English concepts are not given a solely English characterisation. An example is the claim which pleaded entirely in equity, say the ancillary liability of someone who has dishonestly assisted in a breach of trust. As this concept might be unknown to a foreign law, the temptation is to consider the liability and any defences wholly under English law. But this would be wrong, especially where there is no connection with England other than the case being brought here. Equitable claims for choice of law purposes can be characterised more properly as proprietary,[44] tortious,[45] restitutionary[46] or as matters of company law.[47]

Although the area is fraught with theoretical difficulty, the English court has not found it hard to arrive at pragmatic solutions. As Mance LJ has said in *Raiffeisen Zentralbank Österreich AG v Five Star General Trading LLC*:

> the identification of the appropriate law may be viewed as involving a three-stage process: (1) characterisation of the relevant issue; (2) selection of the rule of conflict of laws which lays down a connecting factor for that issue; and (3) identification of the system of law which is tied by that connecting factor to that issue: see *Macmillan Inc. v Bishopsgate Investment Trust plc (No. 3)* [1996] 1 WLR 387, 391–392 per Staughton LJ. The process falls to be undertaken in a broad internationalist spirit in accordance with the principles of conflict of laws of the forum, here England.
>
> While it is convenient to identify this three-stage process, it does not follow that courts, at the first stage, can or should ignore the effect at the second stage of characterising an issue in a particular way. The overall aim is to identify the most appropriate law to govern a particular issue. The classes or categories of issue which the law recognises at the first stage are man-made, not natural. They have no inherent value, beyond their purpose in assisting to select the most appropriate law. A mechanistic application, without regard to the consequences, would conflict with the purpose for which they were conceived. They may require redefinition or modification, or new categories may have to be recognised accompanied by new rules.[48]

Characterisation of the issue is resolved in a slightly different way by the Rome I and Rome II Regulations.[49] Contractual obligations are given an autonomous meaning which probably includes gifts. An autonomous

---

[44] *Macmillan Inc. v Bishopsgate Investment Trust Plc (No. 3)* [1996] 1 WLR 387.

[45] As argued by the editors of *Dicey, Morris and Collins* para. 35–023.

[46] See *ibid.* para. 34–032.

[47] See *Base Metal Trading Ltd v Shamurin* [2005] 1 WLR 1157, which referred matters of the duties of the directors to the law of incorporation of the company.

[48] [2001] QB 825 at paras 26–7.

[49] Regulation (EC) 593/2008 on the law applicable to contractual obligations [2008] OJ L177/6 and Regulation (EC) 864/2007 on the law applicable to non-contractual obligations [2007] OJ L199/40.

definition of contractual obligations is not very difficult as the CJEU appears to prefer to use 'general principles of law' to guide it and many Member States agree on the characteristics of a contract. On the other hand, an autonomous definition of non-contractual obligations by reference to 'general principles' is much less straightforward given the divergence of laws of Member States. Many equitable claims (if they are to be considered obligations) should fall within the Rome II Regulation.[50]

f. A special case: substance and procedure

Matters of procedure are governed by the *lex fori* (*i.e.*, English law) whatever be the *lex causae*, for example, the Utopian applicable law of a contract. Whether a question is procedural or substantive has presented particular difficulties of characterisation, as has the question of whether a foreign rule of law affects procedure or substance. It is easy enough to state that the substantive issues are those which concern the existence of a right, whereas procedural issues are those which concern the method and means of enforcement of a right; but acute difficulties may be encountered in deciding whether even an English rule is procedural or substantive. Thus, in *Harding v Wealands*[51] the English court was faced with an issue concerning damages for an accident in New South Wales, Australia. The applicable law determining liability was that of New South Wales and that law contained various rules calculating the sums payable as a result of accidents on the road. However, their Lordships followed the earlier case of *Boys v Chaplin*[52] to hold that the issue of quantification of damages was procedural and thus for English law as the *lex fori*. Therefore, these rules of New South Wales law did not apply to limit the claimant's damages. Whether the events gave rise to liability was a question for the applicable law, but the extent of the remedy in terms of money damages was procedural. This result has been criticised and will be discussed further in Chapter 13. If one is to look at the purpose for the rule that procedural matters are decided by the *lex fori*, it can be concluded that procedural matters should be limited to those relating to the administration of the court proceedings, such as what language is spoken, which party is to make their case first and what advocates are permitted. In addition, as the purpose of a substantive choice of law rule is often to conform to the parties' expectations, the applicable law should be given a broad scope which could include the manner of assessment of damages. Although this is the better view, it has not found complete acceptance in England.

An example of a pragmatic approach which appears to take account of both the *lex fori* and the substantive law can be seen in the more recent case of *Maher v Groupama Grand Est*:

---

[50] See further Chapter 11.   [51] [2007] 2 AC 1.   [52] [1971] AC 356.

> The claimant had been injured in a road accident in France by a French driver insured by the French defendant. Liability was accepted but quantum was disputed. The claimant brought an action in damages directly against the insurer in England.[53] The dispute centred on the issue whether the award of pre-judgment interest on the damages was to be determined under English or French law. Was the liability to pay interest before judgment substantive or procedural? Senior Courts Act 1981, s. 35A, gives the court power to award such interest 'as it thinks fit'. A further complication was that the insurer's liability sounded in contract but the tort victim's claim was in tort. Fortunately, the applicable law of both tort and contract was French law. The *lex fori*, obviously, was English law.[54]

The Court of Appeal decided that individual issues were characterised rather than whole claims. In this case, therefore, the issue to be characterised was what damages the claimant should receive to compensate the claimant for the injury suffered by the action of the tortfeasor. This sounded in tort and was substantive. It was referred to French law. The insurer was liable for damages under that law. The liability to pay interest was also to be determined by French law. However, Moore-Bick LJ held that Senior Courts Act 1981, s. 35A (which is a rule of English law) creates a remedy which was to be characterised as procedural. The section therefore applied so long as French law imposed liability for interest. As it is a discretionary remedy, the exercise of discretion should take into account the relevant provisions of French law on the recovery of interest. Note that this case was decided before the Rome II Regulation[55] was applicable.[56] After the entry into force of that Regulation, the assessment of damages is generally for the applicable law.[57]

g. Limitation of actions

Rules governing the period of time during which an action must be brought are, in legal systems generally, of two kinds; first, those which merely bar the action, which are considered procedural; secondly, those which extinguish the claimant's rights, which are substantive. Most English rules are of the first type.[58] Moreover, the English courts have almost always regarded a rule of

---

[53] As is possible under the Fourth Motor Insurance Directive, Parliament and Council Directive 2000/26/EC of 16 May 2000 [2000] OJ L181/65.

[54] [2009] EWCA Civ 1191, [2010] 1 WLR 1564.

[55] Regulation (EC) 864/2007 on the law applicable to non-contractual obligations [2007] OJ L199/40.

[56] See further the discussion at pp. 338–9 below.

[57] But see further pp. 344–5 below.

[58] See Limitation Act 1980. Exceptions are s. 3 (conversion of goods) and s. 17 (land) where title is extinguished.

foreign law in the same light, usually in reliance on its literal wording.[59] The result has been that the English rule almost always applied. Many foreign systems regard their own limitation rules as substantive, and the conflict of characterisation can lead to undesirable results, especially where an action abroad has been dismissed on the ground that a limitation period has expired, but an English action is allowed to continue.[60]

The Law Commission criticised the existing law in 1982[61] and its recommendations were enacted in the Foreign Limitation Periods Act 1984. The matter is also dealt with as regards contracts in the Rome I Regulation[62] and for torts in the Rome II Regulation.[63] These state that prescription and limitation are governed by the relevant applicable law. The Act provides that all limitation periods,[64] both English and foreign, should be classified as substantive so that the foreign rule would be applied.[65] This is so whether the foreign rules are classified as substantive or procedural by the foreign courts. Any extension of the limitation period allowed under the foreign law is to be given effect except where it is extended because of either parties' absence from the jurisdiction;[66] otherwise, if a party were to stay out of the jurisdiction permanently, the case would never be decided. A foreign judgment on a limitation point is now regarded as a judgment on the merits and so provides a good defence to a further action here on the same cause of action.[67] The court may refuse in its discretion to apply the foreign rule on the ground of public policy,[68] or where its application would cause undue hardship.[69] 'Undue hardship' has been found to be caused where the foreign limitation period was 12 months or less and the claimant had been somehow led into missing the limitation period.[70] But undue hardship is not caused merely by the foreign limitation period being shorter than the equivalent English one.

5. The incidental question

The problem of the so-called incidental question arises when, in the course of deciding a case, an issue which is subsidiary to the actual issue to be decided occurs. Thus, entitlement to share in the estate of a deceased person may

---

[59] See e.g., *Huber v Steiner* (1835) 2 Bing. NC 202.
[60] See *Harris v Quine* (1869) LR 4 QB 653 and *Black-Clawson International Ltd v Papierwerke-Waldhof Aschafffenburg A/G* [1975] AC 591; the effect of these cases has been overturned by Foreign Limitation Periods Act 1984, s. 3.
[61] Report No. 114 (1982).   [62] Article 12(1)(d).   [63] Article 15(a).
[64] As defined in Foreign Limitation Periods Act 1984, s. 4.
[65] *Ibid.* s. 1(1). *Renvoi* is excluded: s. 1(5). The Law Commission also recommended that the effect given by our courts to the foreign rule should be that given to it by the foreign courts, i.e., whether it bars the remedy or extinguishes the right. This is not mentioned in the Act.
[66] *Ibid.* s. 2(3).   [67] *Ibid.* s. 3.   [68] *Ibid.* s. 2(1) and (2).   [69] *Ibid.* s. 2(2).
[70] *Jones v Trollop Colls Cementation Overseas Ltd, The Times*, 26 January 1990 (in which the defendants misled the claimant), and *Harley v Smith* [2009] 1 Lloyd's LR 359 (in which circumstances forced the claimants into overlooking the limitation period).

depend on whether the person in question is legitimate or illegitimate, and this in turn depends on the validity of his parent's marriage as in *Shaw v Gould*.[71]

For the problem to arise there must be (1) a principal or main question governed by English conflict rules by the law of country A; and (2) a subsidiary or incidental question in the same case, which could arise on its own and is governed by the law of country B. Also (3) the application of the law of A must produce a result different from that which would follow from the application of the law of B.

In only a very few cases has this situation arisen. It did not in the event arise in *Shaw v Gould*, since all the issues involved were governed by the same law.[72]

Writers express different views on whether the answer to the subsidiary issue should, when the problem arises, decide the case (in which event the law governing the principal issue should not be given its normal effect), or whether the latter law should be applied so that international harmony as to the result might be more easily achieved.

The problem arose in one Canadian case and in two English cases. In all three the principal question concerned capacity to marry or remarry and in all three the subsidiary issue was the recognition of a foreign divorce decree. In the Canadian case and the first of the English cases, the court applied the law governing the principal issue and effectively excluded the law which would have governed the subsidiary issue had it arisen on its own. In the second English case, the court allowed the main question to be determined by the answer to the subsidiary question.

In the Canadian case of *Schwebel v Ungar*:[73]

> H1 and W were Jews domiciled in Hungary. They both left Hungary for Israel but *en route* obtained a divorce in Italy. They both arrived in Israel where W acquired a domicile. She then went to Ontario and there married H2 who was domiciled in Ontario.

Under Ontario conflict rules W had capacity to marry H2 since her capacity to marry was governed by Israeli law at the time of the marriage. Since Israeli law recognised the Italian divorce, it regarded her as a single woman. But by Ontario conflict rules that divorce was not recognised since at the time it was obtained the parties were still domiciled in Hungary, whose courts had not granted it and did not recognise it. Therefore, in the eyes of the Ontario court W was still married to H1 and H2 under the law of his domicile, Ontario, had

---

[71] (1886) LR 3 HL 55.

[72] I.e., English law. Nor did it arise in *Perrini v Perrini* [1979] Fam. 84, since the main question (capacity to marry) and the subsidiary question (recognition of a foreign nullity decree) were both governed by English law. It did arise in the US case of *Meisenhelder v Chicago & NW Railway*, 170 Minn. 317 (1927) and an Australian one *Haque v Haque* (1962) 108 CLR 230.

[73] (1962) 42 DLR (2d) 622, affd (1964) 48 DLR (2d) 644.

no capacity to marry her. The court, applying Israeli law (governing the principal issue) and ignoring Ontario law (governing the subsidiary issue) held the marriage valid.

The converse situation arose in England in the *Brentwood Marriage case*:[74]

> H and W were domiciled in Switzerland, where a divorce was obtained. This was recognised in England. H was an Italian national and by Swiss law his capacity to marry was governed by Italian law as his national law. By Italian law the Swiss divorce was not recognised so that under Italian and Swiss law he could not marry.

The English court, like the Canadian court, concentrated on the issue of H's capacity to marry to the exclusion of the recognition of the foreign divorce, applied the law of his domicile[75] and held that he could not remarry in England, though in the eyes of English law he was an unmarried man.

In one sense *Schwebel v Ungar* might be regarded as satisfactory, but the *Brentwood Marriage* case as unsatisfactory, since the former promoted freedom to marry and the latter denied it. Indeed the *Brentwood Marriage* case has since been reversed by statute, in that H's incapacity would now be disregarded.[76]

From another point of view *Schwebel v Ungar* is equally unsatisfactory. If it represented English law it would mean that a person who is domiciled here could marry someone who, in the eyes of English law, is a married person, that is to say, contract a bigamous union and in so doing commit a crime here. It is not clear that *Schwebel v Ungar* would be followed in England, but it is thought it would not.

In the second English case *Lawrence v Lawrence*,[77] the facts were basically the same as the *Brentwood Marriage* case except that the remarriage had taken place abroad. This being so, and the legislative provision which reversed the latter case being inapplicable where the marriage takes place outside the United Kingdom, one would have expected the decision to have been the same and the remarriage to have been held invalid.

But the Court of Appeal, without saying that the *Brentwood Marriage* case was wrong, held that because the court must recognise the foreign divorce the wife was free to remarry, though she had no capacity to do so under the law of her domicile.[78] It thus made the incidental question effectively determine the main question. Indeed, the majority specifically said that the question of

---

[74] *R v Brentwood Superintendent Registrar of Marriages, ex parte Arias* [1968] 2 QB 956.
[75] This is an example of *renvoi* by transmission.
[76] Family Law Act 1986, s. 50.   [77] [1985] Fam. 106.
[78] The court thus extended Recognition of Divorces, etc. Act 1971, s. 7, to remarriages outside the United Kingdom in spite of the limiting words therein and achieved a reform proposed by the Law Commission in Report No. 137 (1984) and enacted by the Family Law Act 1986, s. 50.

capacity to marry in the usual sense did not arise. It is submitted that this was highly dubious at common law.[79] However, it was enacted in law by the Family Law Act 1986, s. 50.

Another version of the incidental question can arise when a defendant claims that a contract between the defendant and the claimant contains a defence to what would otherwise amount to tortious liability; for example, the tort claim is governed by one law, say Utopian, and the contractual defence is governed by another law, say Ruritanian. Ruritanian law allows the defence even though the claimant is a consumer, whereas Utopian law would invalidate this contractual provision. Which law is to govern whether the defendant is liable? The tort issue might be argued to be the principal one and the contractual issue subsidiary, so that although the contractual defence is valid by its own applicable law, it is ineffective as a defence to the tortious liability. This argument suggests that it is the law of the principal issue which governs the matter, but the law of the incidental issue must also be inspected. Where Ruritanian law would invalidate the contractual defence, it should not be given effect even where Utopian law applicable to the tort would – if the contract had been governed by Utopian law – have denied liability.[80]

6. *Renvoi*

a. Meaning

The doctrine of *renvoi* is deployed as a way of deciding a case when referred to a foreign law by a choice of law rule. What 'law' is meant? Merely domestic law rules of that law? Or, the rules of that law including its choice of law rules? Where the conflict of laws rules of the foreign law are included in 'law', a *renvoi* (passing on or passing back) to another law may occur. *Renvoi* is therefore a technique for solving problems which arise out of differences between the connecting factor used by English law and that of the law to which the English connecting factor leads. Such differences may be either (i) that English law and the applicable law, say Utopian law, use the same connecting factor for a legal category such as domicile, but mean different things by it;[81] or (ii) English law and the applicable law, say Ruritanian law, use different connecting factors for the legal category – domicile and nationality respectively.

---

[79] Purchas LJ expressly dissented from this view; he held that the remarriage was valid on another ground which is even more dubious. Anthony Lincoln J had decided that the remarriage was valid on another ground which is perhaps slightly less dubious, since he regarded the question in the same light as the court in the *Brentwood Marriage* case.

[80] Surprisingly, this question has not properly been raised or answered in the English courts; and cf. *Sayers v International Drilling Co. NV* [1971] 1 WLR 1176; *Coupland v Arabian Gulf Petroleum Co.* [1983] 3 All ER 226. See further pp. 364–5 below.

[81] See e.g., *Re Annesley* [1926] Ch. 692.

The English court might in such cases apply English law on the ground that the Utopian court would decide the case in accordance with English law following Utopian conflict of laws rules (this is called remission). On the other hand, an English court might apply a different law on the ground than a Ruritanian court would apply that other law following Ruritanian conflict of laws rules (this is called transmission).

The topic has been bedevilled by rather intemperate academic discussion; most writers are, in general, hostile to *renvoi*,[82] but many courts in many states have adopted it, at least for some choice of law rules.[83] It is perhaps fair to say that it got a bad reputation internationally from the case which was its *fons et origo*, the decision of the Court of Cassation in France in *Forgo's* case in 1883:[84]

> Forgo, an illegitimate Bavarian national, was born with a domicile in Bavaria, but lived most of his life in France without ever acquiring a 'domicil' in French law. He left movable property in France but no relatives except for some remote collateral relatives of his mother. These could not succeed him under French law, and under French law the property, being ownerless, would go to the French state. Under Bavarian law they could succeed. The French courts would determine the question by applying Bavarian law but the state argued that the Bavarian courts would apply French law, and the French courts should do likewise.

The court held in favour of the French state's arguments. The result was that the French treasury got its hands on the property to the exclusion of the collateral relatives.

The real question is: what does the English court mean by the 'foreign law' it is proposing to apply? As Maugham J put it in *Re Askew*,[85] 'when the English courts refer the matter to the law of Utopia as the *lex domicilii*,[86] do they mean the whole of that law or do they mean the local or municipal law which in Utopia would apply to Utopian subjects?'. This poses the problem neatly, though it needs further elucidation.

There are, in fact, three possibilities. The first is that by the law of Utopia is meant Utopian law without its conflict of laws rules, so that we apply Utopian domestic law of succession as if the case had no connection with any country

---

[82] But see A. Briggs, 'In Praise and Defence of Renvoi' [1998] *ICLQ* 878.

[83] See e.g., for Australia in the case of torts *Neilson v Overseas Projects Corporation of Victoria Ltd* [2005] HCA 54, 223 CLA 331.

[84] 10 Clunet 64; see also *L'Affaire Soulié* (1910) Clunet 888. In fact, the real and earlier originator was an English judge, Sir Herbert Jenner, in *Collier v Rivaz* (1841) 2 Curt. 855, though he did not use the French term *renvoi*.

[85] [1930] 2 Ch. 259.

[86] This is only an example; the same issue can arise if the courts refer the matter to the law of Utopia as the *lex situs*.

other than Utopia. This has been done in many cases without question and is expressly required in cases of contract, tort and trusts.[87]

The second is that by the law of Utopia is meant its law including its conflicts rules but not those conflicts rules applying *renvoi*, if it has any. This is sometimes called 'single' or 'partial' *renvoi* or *renvoi simpliciter*. Thus, if the Utopian courts would apply English or Ruritanian law to decide the case, so will the English courts. This is what happened in *Forgo's* case, and what, in part, Sir Herbert Jenner did in *Collier v Rivaz*,[88] when he applied English law to uphold the validity of four codicils to a will made in Belgium by an Englishman domiciled there. The codicils were formally valid under English but not Belgian law. But the Belgian courts would, if they had had to decide the case, have applied English law as the law of the nationality of the testator.[89]

The third meaning of the 'law of Utopia' is all the relevant law of Utopia including both its conflicts rules and *renvoi* where they include it. This is sometimes called 'double' or total *renvoi*.[90] Another name for it is the 'foreign court' doctrine since the English court first decides by its own conflict rules to apply Utopian law and then pretends to be the Utopian court or, more plausibly, asks how that court would decide the case. If it would apply English law and by English law mean simply English law including its conflicts rules without *renvoi*, then the Utopian court would apply Utopian law. So then, will the English court do the same. There are difficulties when the Utopian court would apply English law including its conflicts rules as well as *renvoi*, which in theory is possible but in practice can lead to endless complicating *renvoi*.

The third meaning was first adopted by Russell J in *Re Annesley*,[91] a case which concerned the material or essential validity of the terms of a will:

> An English testatrix had lived in France for fifty-six years. She died leaving a will of movable property. The English court held that she died domiciled in France, so that French law governed the validity of her will. By French law it was partly invalid because she was not free to dispose of all her property in the way she had done, since she had not provided for certain persons who were entitled by law to a share. By French law also the validity of the will was governed by the law of Mrs Annesley's last domicile, but by French law she died domiciled in England. So English law would be applied by a French court. However, by means of *renvoi* it would apply the English conflict rule, so that it would (as in *Forgo's* case) apply the French law of succession.

---

[87] Rome I Regulation, Art. 20; Rome II Regulation, Art. 24; and Recognition of Trusts Act 1987, enacting the Convention on the Law Applicable to Trusts and their Recognition, Art. 17.

[88] (1841) 2 Curt. 855. This meaning of 'foreign law' was applied in *Re Johnson* [1903] 1 Ch. 821, a case of transmission. See also *Re Trufort* (1887) 36 Ch. D 600.

[89] The wills and two other codicils were admitted to probate on the ground that they were valid by Belgian law, that is, by the first possibility. The judge was being pragmatic rather than doctrinaire, and was evidently trying to fulfil the testator's intentions.

[90] Or even 'English *renvoi*' since it appears to be peculiar to English law.   [91] [1926] Ch. 692.

The court applied the French law of succession and held the will partly invalid. On the other hand, in *Re Ross*:[92]

> An English testatrix died domiciled in Italy leaving movable property in England and Italy and immovable property in Italy. Succession to all her property was, therefore, governed by Italian law as the *lex domicilii* and the *lex situs*. The will was partly invalid by Italian law. But the Italian court would apply English law as her national law, but not apply *renvoi*.

Therefore, Luxmoore J applied English domestic law and held the will valid.

In two cases which involved German law, which in this respect was like French law but unlike Italian law, the English court applied German law. These were *Re Askew*[93] which concerned legitimation by subsequent marriage, and *Re Fuld (No. 3)*[94] which concerned the formal validity of a will of movable property.

This perhaps eccentric technique is certainly under attack in the English courts. There has been no approval of the doctrine by an appeal court.[95] Recent cases have shown a distinct unwillingness to adopt *renvoi*.[96] The applicability of *renvoi* was squarely questioned in *Dornoch Ltd v Westminster International BV* and, a little tentatively, rejected by Tomlinson J. He followed the previous first instance decisions to find no requirement of principle or policy to include *renvoi* in questions relating to title to movable property where it had only been used in the non-cognate areas of succession and legitimation. He noted that there may be policy reasons of the English conflict of law rule which make *renvoi* a better solution. One asks whether the purpose of the conflict of laws rule is furthered more by including the conflict of laws rules, i.e., deciding as the foreign court would decide, in each particular case. Tomlinson J did see a justification for *renvoi* in the case of title to immovable property. However, that inquiry can only be undertaken when the foreign law is known and its rules of conflict of laws identified, which had not happened at this stage of this case. That use of *renvoi* can be criticised as requiring expensive and possibly futile investigation of the foreign laws by the parties. Beatson J rejected *renvoi* more definitively in *Blue Sky One Ltd v Mahan Air*:

---

[92] [1930] 1 Ch. 377.   [93] [1930] 2 Ch. 259.   [94] [1968] P 675.

[95] However, *renvoi* (in its 'single' form) was stated by the Privy Council in *Kotia v Nahas* [1941] AC 403, but its application in that case was prescribed by a local Palestinian law.

[96] *Macmillan v Bishopsgate Investment Trust (No. 3)* [1995] 1 WLR 978 (this point not appealed); *Glencore International AG v Metro Trading Inc.* [2001] All ER (Comm) 103; *Republic of Iran v Berend* [2007] 2 All ER (Comm) 132; and *Dornoch Ltd v Westminster International BV* [2009] EWHC 889 (Admlty).

The main issues in this extremely complicated case concerned the validity of mortgages over aircraft and the effect of apparent sales of the aircraft. Both were to be characterised as property questions to be determined by the *lex situs* of the aircraft at the time the mortgages and sales were executed. However, the parties disagreed as to whether the *lex situs* included the private international law rules of that law or merely the rules which applied in wholly domestic cases. There was evidence that Dutch law, the location of one of the aircraft at the time the mortgage was created, would apply the law of the register, which was Armenian law. Armenian law would apply English law as the governing law of the contracts of mortgage.[97]

Beatson J considered the cases carefully to decide that *renvoi* should not operate and applied Dutch domestic law. He favoured the commercial certainty which resulted from a simple application of the domestic law, even if a Dutch court would have decided the matter differently. Fentiman has pointed out that that 'strict compliance with the governing law is a chimera' and that the application of a foreign law inevitably compromises it because of the difficulties of pleading and proof.[98] The arguments against *renvoi* are powerful.

b. Arguments against *renvoi*

Several arguments have been advanced against *renvoi* by writers.

(a) It is often difficult to ascertain whether the foreign system of law does or does not apply *renvoi*. This reflects the almost lachrymose remarks of Wynn Parry J in *Re Duke of Wellington*[99] when faced with deciding whether Spanish law did or did not adopt it.

This difficulty may be thought no greater than that of ascertaining any other rule of foreign law, such as whether consideration is necessary, and could be done in the usual ways.[100] It might be said that the attitude of many foreign systems to *renvoi* is well known. However, that does not seem to be borne out by the cases, which indicate enormous difficulties with the particular question of whether *renvoi* is available in foreign law.[101]

(b) It is claimed that by applying *renvoi* an English court is surrendering to a foreign court, in that instead of applying the English choice of law rule it is effectively applying the Utopian or Ruritanian choice of law.

---

[97] [2010] EWHC 631 (Comm), this issue not affected by appeal [2011] EWCA Civ 544; C. Knight, '*Blue Sky One Ltd v Mahan Air*: Renvoi and Moveable Property – Another Nail in the Coffin' [2010] *Conveyancer and Property Lawyer* 331.

[98] R. Fentiman, *International Commercial Litigation* (Oxford University Press, 2010) para. 5.46.

[99] [1947] Ch. 506, affd without reference to this point [1948] Ch. 118.

[100] For proof of foreign law, see further pp. 46–51 above.

[101] See, for example, the first instance cases mentioned above.

This is true, but only occurs because our choice of law rule leads to the application of Utopian or Ruritanian law. This process is undertaken because our courts consider that the most appropriate law will be identified in accordance with the purpose of the particular choice of law rule. Moreover, as we have seen, the question (to quote Maugham J) is: what do the English courts mean by the law of Utopia? This surely cannot be described as an abdication in favour of Utopian conflict of laws.

(c) A difficulty arises if the foreign court, should it be seised of the case, would apply the person's nationality. If a person is a national of a federal state or one which, like the United Kingdom, contains several territories each possessing its own system of law, reference to his or her national law is meaningless, since it could be one of several laws. *Re O'Keefe*[102] is usually held up to ridicule in this context:

> A woman of British nationality died intestate in Italy, leaving movable property. By English conflict of laws succession was governed by Italian law since she died domiciled there. By Italian law it was governed by her national law and Italian courts reject *renvoi*. Though she was born in India, her domicile of origin was Ireland,[103] where her father had his domicile at the time of her birth. She had only paid one short visit to Ireland, she had stayed rather longer in England, but the only country in which she had settled was Italy.

Crossman J held that, in these circumstances, the law of her nationality should be taken to mean that part of the British Empire to which she 'belonged' and that this was the southern part of Ireland, then (1940) Eire, now the Irish Republic.[104]

This does seem odd in a way since she had hardly ever been to Ireland and Eire did not exist when she was born or went to Ireland, but what else was the court to do? Eire was a more realistic choice than any other part of the British Isles or Commonwealth.[105] In any case, the objection misses the target; it was not *renvoi* but the use by Italian law of nationality as a connecting factor, added to there being no one system of law throughout the British Isles, which caused the trouble. If further inquiries had been made as to how the Italian courts would have decided the actual case, a different and perhaps more realistic answer might have been forthcoming. Italian jurists have suggested that Italian domestic law might have been applied.

---

[102] [1940] Ch. 124.   [103] As to domicile, see further pp. 12–27 above.

[104] It should be noted carefully that this was not, as many students seem to think, a case of the revival of the domicile of origin (see further p. 14 above). Mrs O'Keefe died domiciled in Italy.

[105] It is curious that *Re Ross* [1930] 1 Ch. 377 comes in for no similar criticism.

(d) There is no logical reason why the process should ever stop. Moreover, the English 'double *renvoi*' only operates at all because the courts of other countries reject it. Thus, if French courts adopted our method, in *Re Annesley*[106] the English court would apply French law, the French court English law and so on *ad infinitum*. This is, of course, true. But if some foreign law (as for example, New South Wales) also used the double *renvoi* method, and these horrendous consequences would ensue, one cannot help thinking that the courts would put a stop to it out of pragmatism.[107] In more recent cases, it appears that the pragmatic needs of commercial reality have won to defeat *renvoi*.

(e) *Re Annesley*[108] would have to be decided the same way if Russell J had simply applied French domestic law. This is correct, but not true of, for example, *Re Ross*,[109] *Re O'Keefe*[110] or *Collier v Rivaz*.[111]

c. Arguments in favour of *renvoi*

(a) Professor Briggs and others are much in favour of *renvoi*,[112] particularly for the sophistication the doctrine can bring to otherwise blunt choice of law rules, especially when these are added to fixed rules of jurisdiction. Choice of law rules have some role in preventing unwarranted forum shopping but where *renvoi* is unavailable, that role is curtailed. It is also clear that *renvoi* is a way of avoiding an unattractive and unjust result.[113]

(b) Though *renvoi* does not necessarily achieve uniformity of decision, which its opponents say it does not and the proponents claim it does,[114] it tends towards it, as in *Re Ross*. If it is not employed, determination of rights is more than likely to depend on where the action is brought. If one action is brought in England and the other in Ruritania, conflicting decisions of the English and Ruritanian court might well result.

(c) The use of *renvoi* might achieve the legitimate expectation of a person as it did in *Collier v Rivaz*, *Re Ross* or *Re O'Keefe*. This, of course, does not always ensue; in one or two cases such as *Re Annesley* or *Re Fuld (No. 3)*[115] the intention of the deceased was to some extent upset. But in *Re Askew*[116] a person was held to have been legitimated who would, without *renvoi* being employed, have been held to have been a bastard by reason of what was then a gap in English domestic law.[117]

---

[106] [1926] Ch. 692.   [107] It would be better not to plead *renvoi* at all, and this is the usual case.
[108] [1926] Ch. 692.   [109] [1930] 1 Ch. 377.   [110] [1940] Ch. 124.   [111] (1841) 2 Curt. 855.
[112] See A. Briggs, 'In Praise and Defence of Renvoi' [1998] *ICLQ* 877 and 'Decisions of the British Courts in 2007' [2007] *BYIL* 626.
[113] See further pp. 423–4 below.
[114] Not even complete elimination of differences between choice of law rules of various conflicts systems would do this; it could only be done by all legal systems having identical rules for each legal question.
[115] [1968] P 675.   [116] [1930] 2 Ch. 259.
[117] The Legitimacy Act 1926 did not allow a child born of an adulterous liaison to be legitimated.

(d) It appears to have been agreed on all sides, or at any rate conceded, that if the choice of law rule requires the application of the *lex situs* to questions concerning immovable property, *renvoi* should be applied. For if Utopian law says that the person entitled to Utopian land is the one who is entitled to succeed by English law, it would be pointless for the English court to insist that it should be whoever is so entitled under Utopian law of succession. It could do nothing to enforce that English view.

d. Summary

So there are respectable arguments both for and against the application of *renvoi*. But it is suggested that the matter is not as important in practice as the writing about it might suggest. It has not been applied uniformly in respect of many English choice of law rules, nor in respect of any one of them. In some decided cases, no resort has been made to *renvoi*, presumably because neither party, in proving the relevant foreign law, proved also the rules of its conflict of laws. Moreover, as we have seen, the English courts do not apply *renvoi* in connection with some of their choice of law rules. 'Utopian law' is generally taken to mean only Utopian domestic law without its conflict rules, and, because of certain legislation, it is not nowadays nearly as important as it was in areas to which it has in the past been applied.

e. Areas of application

English courts have employed *renvoi* in one form or another in respect of:

(a) formal validity of wills of movables (and immovables):[118] see *Collier v Rivaz*;[119] *Re Fuld (No. 3)*;[120] but now the Wills Act 1963, s. 1 provides seven systems of law (and eight in the case of immovables) by any one of which a will can be formally valid, the rules are the domestic rules thereof;[121]

(b) essential or material validity of wills of movables: see *Re Trufort*;[122] *Re Annesley*;[123] *Re Ross*;[124]

(c) succession to movables on intestacy: see *Re O'Keefe*;[125]

(d) essential validity of wills of movables: see *Re Ross*;[126]

(e) almost certainly, succession to immovables on intestacy;

(f) possibly, title to movables by transfer *inter vivos*. This was suggested by Slade J in *Winkworth v Christie, Manson and Woods Ltd*,[127] however, it was not adopted in the more recent cases culminating in *Blue Sky Ltd v Mahan Air*[128] and *Dornoch Ltd v Westminster International BV*;[129]

(g) almost certainly, title to immovables *inter vivos*.

---

[118] There is no actual decision regarding a will of immovables.   [119] (1841) 2 Curt. 855.
[120] [1968] P 675.   [121] Wills Act 1963, s. 3.   [122] (1887) 36 Ch. D 600.
[123] [1926] Ch. 692.   [124] [1930] 1 Ch. 377.   [125] [1940] Ch. 124.   [126] [1930] 1 Ch. 377.
[127] [1980] Ch. 496.   [128] [2010] EWHC 631 (Comm).
[129] [2009] EWHC 889 (Admlty), [2009] 2 Lloyd's LR 191.

Importantly, *renvoi* plays no part at all in choice of law in contract,[130] tort[131] and trusts falling within the Hague Convention.[132] It goes without saying that *renvoi* cannot be applicable except in connection with choice of law, so there is no role for the doctrine in questions of the jurisdiction of the English court nor in the recognition and enforcement of foreign judgments.

7. Time factor

Problems may sometimes arise in the conflict of laws because over a period of time changes take place in the law. A change may take place in a conflict rule of the *forum*. This occurred with the Wills Act 1963, and in *Chaplin v Boys*.[133] Here, the questions which may arise are whether the new rule affects transactions or relationships already entered into or a status already acquired, and whether the new rule entirely supersedes the old one.[134] Or a change may take place in the connecting factor, for example a change in a person's domicile or in the *situs* of movable property. Some connecting factors, such as the *situs* of immovable property or the place of the events making up a tort, cannot change – though the law might. Changes in connecting factor will not be considered further; it is a factual matter which once determined merely requires the identification of the content of the applicable law at that time.

The more difficult problems arise in respect of changes in the *lex causae*; for example, Utopian law, the law governing a subsisting contract, is altered by legislation, or a marriage which was formerly formally invalid by the law of the place of celebration is subsequently validated by or under that law. The problem has always existed, but did not attract much learned or judicial attention.[135]

Examples concern the following:

(a) in tort: in *Phillips v Eyre*,[136] an act which was a tort in Jamaica was later justified by Jamaican legislation, thus making the act not actionable as a tort in England;

(b) in contract: in *R v International Trustee for the Protection of Bondholders A/G*,[137] a provision of New York law, the applicable law, which rendered a gold clause in a contract void, and in *Re Helbert Wagg & Co. Ltd's*

---

[130] Rome I Regulation, Art. 20.   [131] Rome II Regulation, Art. 24.

[132] Recognition of Trusts Act 1987, enacting the Convention on the Law Applicable to Trusts and their Recognition, Art. 17.

[133] [1971] AC 356.

[134] For example, the Companies Act 2006 in relation to directors' duties does supersede the previous law but must be interpreted and applied in the same way as the common law rules (s. 170(3) and (4)).

[135] Two important articles by F.A. Mann, 'The Time Element in the Conflict of Laws' (1954) 31 *BYIL* 217, and J. K. Grodecki, 'Conflicts of Laws in Time' (1959) 35 *BYIL* 58, were published after the decision in *Starkowski v AG* [1954] AC 155.

[136] (1870) LR 6 QB 1.   [137] [1937] AC 500.

Claim,[138] a moratorium imposed by a German law which had the effect of discharging the debtor from liability under a contract which was governed by German law, were given effect;

(c) formal validity of a marriage: in *Starkowski v AG*,[139] a marriage which was formally invalid under Austrian law when it was celebrated in that country was held to have been validated by its registration under the provisions of a later Austrian law;

(d) succession to immovables: in *Nelson v Bridport*,[140] the *lex situs* (law of Sicily) was changed after the death of the testator so as to invalidate interests created by his will in land in Sicily.

It will be observed that in all these cases effect was apparently given to the change in the *lex causae*,[141] but in two cases it was not.[142] They concerned succession to movables. In *Lynch v Provisional Government of Paraguay*,[143] a law of Paraguay which purported to invalidate the will of a testator who had died domiciled there was denied effect, and the will was held valid as regards property in England. This was followed in *Re Aganoor's Trusts*,[144] where interests in movable property in England bequeathed by the will of a person who died domiciled in Padua were held not to have been invalidated when, later, the Austrian law was supplanted by Italian law upon Italy succeeding to the territory of Padua, Italian law regarding the interests as invalid.

It should be added that, as regards the formal validity of wills, provision is made in the Wills Act 1963[145] whereby a change in one of the applicable laws after the will is made or after the testator's death is to be given effect if it validates the will, but not if it invalidates it.

The general view of the cases mentioned appears to be that a reference to the *lex causae* should be a reference to that law in its entirety, including any changes in it between the relevant event and the date of its application. On this view the cases in (a) to (d) are correct and *Lynch's* case and *Re Aganoor's Trusts* wrong.[146]

But a more subtle analysis suggests that they are all correct. Lipstein[147] has drawn attention to the need to distinguish between 'once and for all' acts or events which are over and done with and those which form part of a

---

[138] [1956] Ch. 323.

[139] [1954] AC 155. It was distinguished in *Ambrose v Ambrose* (1961) 25 DLR (2d) 1, a Canadian case on capacity to marry.

[140] (1845) 8 Beav. 527.

[141] This was done in a South African case concerning laws governing matrimonial property: *Sperling v Sperling* (1975) (3) SA 707, and in a Canadian case on the same matter, *Topolski v The Queen* (1978) 90 DLR (3d) 66.

[142] Three if one includes *Ambrose v Ambrose* (1961) 25 DLR (2d) 1.

[143] (1871) LR 2 P&D 268.   [144] (1895) 64 LJ Ch. 521.

[145] Wills Act 1963, s. 6(3). The Act applies to wills of immovables as well as movables.

[146] In *Starkowski v AG* [1954] AC 155, the House of Lords rather feebly tried to distinguish *Lynch's* case.

[147] K. Lipstein, 'Conflict of Laws 1921–71: the Way Ahead' [1972B] 67 *CLJ* 96.

continuing relationship. Thus, the death of a testator is a 'once and for all' event, but the entry into a contract is not, for the contractual relationship may continue for many years. *Lynch's* case[148] is an example of the former, *R v International Trustee for the Protection of Bondholders A/G*[149] of the latter. A law enacted subsequent to the death of a testator cannot affect the succession to the testator's property, as the succession has taken place at death, but it can affect the contractual relationship which is still subsisting. Further, one must characterise the rule of the *lex causae* to determine what it is concerned with and whether it is in fact applicable at all.[150]

Examined thus, *Nelson v Bridport*[151] and *Re Aganoor's Trusts*[152] which, prima facie, appear quite incompatible, are reconcilable (and *Re Aganoor's Trusts* carried *Lynch's* case with it). Thus, Sicilian law in the former case did not invalidate the will, but was concerned with the invalidity of subsisting interests in immovable property in Sicily and thus was correctly applied as the *lex situs*. The Italian law in *Re Aganoor's Trusts* likewise purported to invalidate subsisting interests in property but since the property was in England, it was not part of the *lex situs*, which was English law. By English law those interests were valid. It may be added that, as Diplock J observed in *Adams v National Bank of Greece and Athens SA*,[153] the Paraguayan law in *Lynch's* case was not really concerned to invalidate the will, but to expropriate to that state the property bequeathed to it. But again, the *lex situs* of the property was English law, and Paraguayan law did not govern title to it.

At first sight, the two cases *Phillips v Eyre*[154] and *Starkowski v AG*,[155] did not fit with this explanation, since the act had taken place and was 'over and done with' when the tort was committed and the ceremony of marriage performed. But this is not really so. In *Phillips v Eyre*, the *lex causae* governing tort liability was English law, and the result reflected a rule of that law which gave justificatory effect to the conduct in question if it was justified where it was done. In *Starkowski v AG* it is arguable that the parties remained subject to their Austrian law after they were 'married', by reason of their domicile there. The Austrian validating law was passed in June 1945, the month after the wedding, and they only left Austria for England in July 1945.

---

[148] (1871) LR 2 P&D 268.   [149] [1937] AC 500.
[150] Its scope must also be inspected to be sure that it has retrospective effect.
[151] (1845) 8 Beav. 527.   [152] (1895) 64 LJ Ch. 521.   [153] [1958] 2 QB 59 at 76, 77.
[154] (1970) LR 6 QB 1.
[155] [1954] AC 155. On the analysis reproduced here, the Austrian law should have had no effect, had it been enacted after the parties had acquired a domicile in England. (However, this was not the view adopted in the South African case of *Sperling v Sperling* (1975) 3 SA 707.)

10

Contractual obligations

1. Introduction

As we have seen, choice of law rules are rules of English law which identify the substantive law to determine a dispute between litigants. Choice of law rules have the general form of a legal category and a connecting factor. This chapter will be concerned with the legal category of contract. Which system of legal rules is to apply to resolve the issue which has arisen? For example, the litigants may be disputing whether one has properly performed the contract, or whether that party has a sufficient excuse for non-performance. The litigants may contest whether there is a contract at all, or what the terms of the contract might be. A party to the contract may argue that it was not properly entered into in writing, or that the party lacks capacity to conclude such a contract. The term of the contract relied upon might be a term which is ineffective as being unfair to a consumer or employee. All these issues are clearly contractual for choice of law purposes, although there may be some characterisation difficulties with rules which might be categorised as evidentiary (such as presumptions when a contract is signed) or non-contractual (such as rules requiring contracting in good faith).[1] The contractual choice of law rule is generally multilateral and jurisdiction selecting. Therefore, the applicable law identified is a system of domestic law rules of contract which could be of any national legal system[2] and does not directly take account of the policy interests underlying the particular rules to be applied.[3]

Originally, the law of the place of contracting[4] was the choice of law rule for contracts. In times when merchants travelled long distances and met physically to trade, the place of contracting held obvious advantages. It was certain,

---

[1] See further pp. 361–2 below on *culpa in contrahendo* and the Rome II Regulation on the law applicable to non-contractual obligations (Regulation (EC) 864/2007 [2007] OJ L199/40).

[2] Under English law the system identified does have to be a country's legal system of contract, rather than a set of rules in a treaty or more generally *lex mercatoria*, Jewish law or Sharia law (*Beximco Pharmaceuticals Ltd v Shamil Bank of Bahrain* [2004] EWCA Civ 19, [2004] 1 WLR 1784).

[3] Unlike some of the choice of law rules in the United States (see e.g., American Restatement, (Third), Art. 6).

[4] *Lex loci contractus.*

predictable and connected with the parties. However, with increasing international trade which did not require face-to-face meetings, the place of
contracting became difficult to locate and may have lacked real connection
with the parties and the dispute. A rising interest in promoting party autonomy as the best principle underlying contractual rules also led to an emphasis
in choice of law on the parties' expressed preference as to the domestic law to
govern their contractual relations.[5] Problems remained where the parties had
not expressed a choice of law. The place of performance[6] may well provide a
more substantial connecting factor for the choice of law rule in contract.
However, identifying whether the place of delivery or that of payment was
the place of performance led to difficulties.[7] Choice of law rules work most
satisfactorily when a single law is identified, otherwise there are possible
conflicts between the two laws, overlaps and gaps. In the absence of a choice
of law by the parties, the courts in England attempted to find an implied
choice or one which could be inferred from the surrounding circumstances.[8]
If that was unsuccessful the court determined the law governing the contract
objectively. That was the law with the closest and most substantial connection
with the contract. This is known as the 'proper law' rule.[9] The proper law
approach can be criticised for being too unpredictable and uncertain, albeit
that it only applies when the parties have been unable or unwilling to agree on
a law to govern their contract and is therefore residual.

The common law rules dealing with choice of law in contractual matters
have largely been replaced by two European instruments. The first was the
Rome Convention 1980.[10] As a Convention and not a Regulation it had to be
ratified and subsequently enacted to have force in England. This was done by
the Contracts (Applicable Law) Act 1990 for contracts concluded after 1 April
1992. It is said that harmonising choice of law rules (as well as jurisdictional
rules) will support the free movement of persons, goods, services and capital
within the Member States. Such harmonisation will also reduce the incentive
to forum shop within the EU (as the substantive law applied in a dispute
should be the same wherever the case is brought) and will increase legal
certainty and predictability. The Rome Convention was followed by the
Rome I Regulation.[11]

---

[5] See *Robinson v Bland* (1760) 2 Burr. 1077.   [6] *Lex solutionis.*

[7] Some of these difficulties remain after the Rome I Regulation (Regulation (EC) 593/2008 on the
law applicable to contractual obligations [2008] OJ L177/6) where the 'characteristic
performance' of the contract may have to be determined in order to identify the applicable law.

[8] See *The Assunzione* [1954] P 150 (CA) and *Coast Lines Ltd v Hudig & Veder Charterparty NV*
[1972] QB 34 (CA) for discussion on the differences between an inferred choice and an
objectively determined proper law.

[9] Which reached its zenith in *Amin Rasheed Corp. v Kuwait Insurance Co.* [1984] AC 50 (HL).

[10] Rome Convention on the law applicable to contractual obligations 1980; the consolidated text is
at [1998] OJ C027/34.

[11] Regulation (EC) 593/2008 [2008] OJ L177/6, preceded by a Green Paper COM(2002)654 final.

A Regulation has several advantages over a Convention. It applies directly to all Member States (including automatically to new Member States as part of the *acquis communitaire*) and referrals to the CJEU of questions of interpretation are achieved through the general power of Article 267 of the Treaty on the Functioning of the European Union. There are considerable differences between the two instruments but also some similarities. The Rome I Regulation applies to all contracts litigated before the English court, wherever made and wherever the parties come from. It is not limited to contracts between parties domiciled in the EU. The rules of the Regulation apply whether the applicable law is that of a Member State or of a third state.[12] It is therefore both universal and exclusive. The Rome Convention will continue to be of importance to cases coming through the English courts but this chapter will concentrate on the Rome I Regulation rules. There are very few cases on that Regulation so previous case law, both on the Rome Convention and the common law, will also be discussed, where appropriate.

Very often questions of the law applicable to a contract arise at the stage when the court is determining its own jurisdiction. In fact, surprisingly few reported cases ever turn on the applicable law at the stage when the substantive dispute is heard. The applicable law may need investigation when the court is deciding jurisdiction in a number of instances. Under the national rules, a claimant may wish to use various gateways in CPR PD 6B which require the applicable law to be determined, for example, the gateway that the applicable law of the contract is English law.[13] Or the claimant might allege that the contract was to be performed in England,[14] and the defendant argues there is no contract or that it was not to be performed in England. The applicable law may need to be identified and its content determined in order to decide whether the claimant's claim has a 'reasonable prospect of success' necessary for the court to give permission to serve the claim form out of the jurisdiction.[15] Under the Brussels I Regulation,[16] the applicable law of the contract may, exceptionally under Article 5(1)(a), have to be determined to identify the place of performance. It is that court which has jurisdiction as well as the court of the defendant's domicile.[17] Using the cases which determined the applicable law for the purpose of jurisdiction as source of doctrine for choice of law may be misleading. That is particularly so when the jurisdiction

---

[12] Rome I Regulation, Art. 2.

[13] CPR r. 6.36 and PD 6 B para. 3.1(6)(c) and *Bank of Baroda v Vysya Bank* [1994] 2 Lloyd's LR 87.

[14] CPR r. 6.36 and PD 6 B para. 3.1(7).

[15] *Seaconsar Far East Ltd v Bank Markazi Iran* [1994] 1 AC 438 (HL).

[16] Regulation (EC) 44/2001 on jurisdiction and the recognition and enforcement of judgments in civil and commercial matters ([2001] OJ L12/1).

[17] See e.g., *Definitely Maybe (Touring) Ltd v Marek Lieberberg Konzertagentur GmbH* [2001] 1 WLR 1745. This particular provision has been much narrowed by the amendments to Art. 5(1) and the decision in *Color Drack GmbH v Lexx International Vertriebs GmbH* Case C-386/05 [2007] ECR I-3699.

is being established under the national rules. The decision on the applicable law is not as carefully undertaken as it would be at a trial of the substance of the dispute. First, the determination of the applicable law is done without full disclosure of the evidence and without a full determination of the facts. Secondly, the exercise of discretion and the overriding importance of the proper place to hear the dispute can mask the decision on the applicable law.

It is often useful to note that several words are used to describe the same concept in choice of law. The law applicable to the contract, the law governing the contract and the proper law of the contract all mean the same thing. That law is the one the domestic rules of which will be applied to answer the particular issue in dispute. It might also be called the *lex causae* or the substantive law. In contradistinction, the *lex fori* or the procedural law is the law which governs matters of procedure and, for our purposes, will be English law as the law of the court in which the dispute is being heard.

2. Background to Rome I Regulation

The legal basis for the Rome I Regulation is found in Article 61(c) and Article 65 of the Treaty on the European Union[18] authorising measures in the field of judicial co-operation in judicial matters having cross-border implications. Choice of law rules for contractual obligations are arguably 'necessary for the proper functioning of the internal market' as required by Article 65. Article 81, the replacement for Article 65, uses more limited language when referring to the proper functioning of the internal market. The Preamble to the Rome I Regulation states that in order to maintain an area of freedom, security and justice 'the Community is to adopt measures relating to judicial co-operation in civil matters with a cross-border impact to the extent necessary for the proper functioning of the internal market'.[19] The proper functioning of the internal market therefore creates a need to harmonise choice of law rules in order 'to improve the predictability of the outcome of litigation, certainty as to the law applicable and the free movement of judgments'.[20] The British government had the option of opting out of the Rome I Regulation but decided eventually to opt in.[21]

3. Temporal scope and interpretation

The Rome I Regulation applies to all contracts falling within its scope which were entered into after 17 December 2009.[22] As it is a Regulation, questions on the interpretation of it can be referred to the CJEU from any court. Article 267

---

[18] Now Art. 81 of the Treaty on the Functioning of the European Union.
[19] Recital 1.   [20] Recital 6.
[21] EC Commission Decision 2009/29 [2009] OJ L10/22 accepting the British government's request.
[22] Articles 28 and 29.

of the Treaty on the Functioning of the European Union permits *any* court of a Member State to seek a ruling from the CJEU if the court considers 'that a decision on the question is necessary to enable it to give judgment'.[23] The recitals refer in various places to the Rome Convention, generally to make clear that the Rome I Regulation is intended to be interpreted in those instances in the same way as the Rome Convention.[24] Although that Convention had the benefit of a preliminary report by Professors Giuliano and Lagarde,[25] the Rome I Regulation does not have the equivalent scholarly report to which to refer as an aid to interpretation. Given the substantial changes made to the Convention by the Regulation, it is probably unwise to rely too heavily directly on decisions on the Rome Convention. However, where the wording or concepts are substantially similar there is less risk.

4. Material scope and exceptions

Article 1 lays out the material scope of the Rome I Regulation. First the Regulation applies only to contractual obligations in civil and commercial matters in situations which involve a conflict of laws. Contractual obligations must have an autonomous meaning but the term is not defined in the Regulation. Therefore, local domestic rules such as the necessity for consideration or concerns about privity should not narrow the conception of a contractual obligation[26] for this Regulation. In a case on the same wording in the Rome Convention, the Court of Appeal had to characterise an assignment of an insurance policy and the consequences for the insurer. The court considered that the process of characterisation had to be guided by the wording and purpose of the Rome Convention and held that the matter was contractual rather than proprietary.[27] The CJEU is likely to decide that the meaning of contractual obligations is probably to be interpreted in a similar way to a matter related to a contract in Article 5(1) of the Brussels I Regulation. Recital 7 of the Rome I Regulation requires that the substantive scope and provisions of the Regulation should be consistent with the Brussels I Regulation and the Rome II Regulation. A matter relating to a contract in accordance with principles accepted in all Member States[28] appears to require at least some relationship freely entered into.[29]

---

[23] Courts from which there is no further judicial remedy *must* seek rulings from the CJEU, i.e., the Supreme Court (previously the House of Lords) or the Court of Appeal in some circumstances, but lower courts may also do so. The previous limitation on references to the CJEU contained in old Art. 68(1) EC has gone.

[24] For example, on contracts for the carriage of goods (recital 22).   [25] [1980] OJ C282.

[26] Even before the Rome Convention the English courts accepted that for choice of law purposes a contract did not require consideration (*Re Bonacina* [1912] 2 Ch. 394).

[27] *Raiffeisen Zentralbank Osterreich AG v Five Star Trading LLC* [2001] EWCA Civ 68, [2001] QB 825.

[28] *Jacob Handte v Traitements Mechano Chimiques* Case C-26/91 [1992] ECR I-3967.

[29] *Réunion Européenne SA v Spliethoff's Bevrachtingskantoor BV* Case C-51/97 [1998] ECR I-6511; *Peters v ZNAV* Case C-34/82 [1983] ECR 987, but cf. *Engler v Janus Versand* Case C-27/02

The meaning of civil and commercial matters is expressed in the same manner as in the Brussels I Regulation (the Rome I Regulation does not apply to revenue, customs or administrative matters) and is to be interpreted consistently with that Regulation. The list of exclusions is much longer, however. These include questions involving the status or legal capacity of natural persons.[30] Questions governed by the law of companies and other legal persons are excluded.[31] Obligations arising out of family relationships and maintenance obligations, matrimonial property regimes, wills and succession are also excluded,[32] as are bills of exchange, cheques, etc.[33]

Importantly, jurisdiction and arbitration agreements are excluded from the Rome I Regulation.[34] It might be considered that the Brussels I Regulation exclusively deals with jurisdiction agreements and the New York Convention with arbitration agreements. That would be naïve. There may well be questions of the applicable law pertaining to the validity and interpretation of such agreements which are not covered by those other instruments. Fentiman argues that this exception reflects the procedural character of arbitration and jurisdiction agreements.[35] However, such agreements do not merely have procedural effect on the jurisdiction of the court but also have contractual characteristics which should be answered by the contractual law governing them. It is very likely that the applicable law of the jurisdiction agreement or arbitration agreement will be determined using the same rules as the Rome I Regulation. It would be impractical to have to fashion completely separate choice of law rules for these agreements. Broadly, where the agreement expresses a choice of applicable law (whether of the court or seat of the arbitration or of another law) that choice should be given effect. If there is no express choice, it is very likely that the applicable law will be that of the chosen court or of the seat of the arbitration. Difficulties arise when there is more than one court chosen or if the seat of the arbitration is not identified.

Questions of authority, such as whether an agent can bind a principal or whether an organ of a company can bind the company to an agreement, are excluded from the Rome I Regulation.[36] Likewise the constitution of trusts and the relationship between settlors, trustees and beneficiaries are excluded.[37] Critically, obligations arising out of dealings prior to the conclusion of the contract are excluded from this Regulation.[38] Many questions of precontractual liability therefore fall within the scope of the Rome II Regulation[39] on the

---

[2005] ECR I-481 – there could still be a contract where the contract is imposed by law even though one party did not intend to create a contract. See further pp. 77–9 above.

[30] Without prejudice to the limited rule dealing with capacity of natural persons in Rome I Regulation, Art. 13.

[31] Article 1(2)(f).   [32] Article 1(2)(b) and (c).   [33] Article 1(2)(d).   [34] Article 1(2)(e).

[35] R. Fentiman, *International Commercial Litigation* (Oxford University Press, 2010) para. 4.04.

[36] Article 1(2)(g).   [37] Article 1(2)(h).   [38] Article 1(2)(i).

[39] Regulation (EC) 864/2007 [2007] OJ L199/40.

applicable law for non-contractual obligations.[40] Indeed, liability for negligent misrepresentation has been considered tortious rather than contractual at common law.[41] The Rome II Regulation also covers liability for unjust enrichment following a failed contract.[42] Some insurance contracts are excluded.[43] In many of these cases, agreement between all Member States on the rules to apply may have been impossible to obtain.

The Rome I Regulation does not apply to evidence and procedure.[44] We have seen that procedure is a matter for the forum applying its own law. The delineation of procedure from substance is not always clear.[45] The Rome I Regulation itself makes some provision for matters of presumptions, burden and modes of proof in Article 18. Note that Article 12 subjects the matter of the assessment of damages to the applicable law. The common law position to the contrary[46] no longer applies to the assessment of damages for breach of contractual obligations. The English law rule which permits a party not to rely on an express choice of law but instead to default back to English law if no other law is pleaded or proved might be regarded as procedural, in which case the rule is unaffected by this Regulation. Some argue that this is wrong and that Article 4 has a more mandatory effect which cannot be evaded by this English procedural rule.[47] Although jurisdictional rules are procedural, the applicable law for the purposes of determining the jurisdiction of the English court will be identified using the rules of the Rome I Regulation rather than the pre-existing common law rules.[48]

5. Effect of applicable law

Most issues which can arise in a contractual dispute will be resolved by the application of the domestic rules of the applicable law. Articles 10 and 12 of the Rome I Regulation provide that all matters of the existence and enforcement of contractual obligations are governed by the applicable law.

(1) Questions of interpretation, such as the meaning of express terms of the contract, or what terms can be implied into the contract, are resolved by

---

[40] Such as Rome II Regulation, Art. 12 for *culpa in contrahendo* (duty to negotiate in good faith) and Rome II Regulation, Art. 11 for *negotiorum gestio* (liability for unauthorised contracts).

[41] Falling within the pre-Rome II Regulation statute, Private International Law (Miscellaneous Provisions) Act 1995.

[42] Rome II Regulation, Art. 10. But compare Rome I Regulation, Art. 12(1)(e) which expressly refers the consequences of nullity of the contract to the applicable law of the contract.

[43] Rome I Regulation, Art. 1(2)(j).   [44] Article 1(3).

[45] See further Chapter 9 and Chapter 13.

[46] See *Harding v Wealands* [2006] UKHL 32, [2007] 2 AC 1.

[47] See Fentiman, *International Commercial Litigation*, para. 4.89 *et seq.* He argues that a failure to plead and prove a foreign law in the face of an express choice of law is more properly treated as a choice under Rome I Regulation, Art. 3(2) by both parties to subject the contract to a different law.

[48] *Bank of Baroda v Vysya Bank* [1994] 2 Lloyd's LR 87 applying the Rome Convention. The position must be the same under the Rome I Regulation.

the applicable law (Article 12(1)(a)). When this matter, as any other regarding the application of foreign law, comes before the English court the content of the foreign law has to be proved by expert evidence.

(2) It is central to the proper operation of the Rome I Regulation that the important question of the system of law to determine the performance of the contract (payment, delivery, and so on) can be easily identified and applied with certainty. Article 12(1)(b) of the Regulation provides that matters of the performance of the contract are for the applicable law; for example, whether a party has done what is required of the contract is answered by the domestic contract rules of the applicable law. Therefore, questions such as whether payment has been made, or the application of *de minimis* rules, or the possibility of substitute performance of the contract, are referred to the applicable law. Also within this category would be rules implying a place of performance where none is specified in the contract. All these questions of performance are referred to the applicable law.

However, the Rome I Regulation makes special provision for matters of the manner of performance. Article 12(2) provides that 'in relation to the manner of performance and the steps to be taken in the event of defective performance regard shall be had to the law of the country in which performance takes place'. In many international contracts the applicable law is not that of the place where performance is to be carried out. That can cause difficulties where the contract provides, for example, for delivery 'on a working day' and the definition of that varies between the applicable law and the place of performance. What is a question of the manner of performance is to be answered by the *lex fori*. Under the old common law cases, questions such as the hours during which delivery was to be effected were referred to the law of the place of performance.[49] The provision is intended to deal with minor practical matters of performance but not the major issues, which should be referred to the applicable law. Article 12(2) is flexible, merely permitting the court to 'have regard to' the law of the place of performance rather than requiring application of that law. The operation of this discretion may lead to a lack of uniformity in the application of the Rome I Regulation. However, it is not a matter of enormous concern to the English courts which have historically taken a pragmatic and sensible view.

(3) The consequences of breach of contract, including the assessment of damages, are referred to the applicable law by Article 12(1)(c). This is also very important in practice and critical to the proper operation of the Rome I Regulation. The liability of the defaulting party, including what heads of damage are available, issues of causation and forseeability are all questions which are answered by the rules of the applicable law. The remedies available are to be determined by the applicable law. So whether specific enforcement is possible is a matter which the applicable law will govern. The provision is

---

[49] See *Cheshire, North and Fawcett, Private International Law* (14th edn, Oxford University Press, 2008) p. 755.

hedged at the beginning with the phrase 'within the limits of the powers conferred on the court by its procedural law'. This might permit the English court to refuse to order specific performance of a contract where it would under its own law be unwilling to do so, such as a contract for services, whatever the applicable law requires.[50] A further limitation is found at the end of the Article. The assessment of damages is referred to the applicable law 'in so far as it is governed by rules of law'.[51] Where the assessment of damage is a matter of fact, such as how to arrive at the sterling cost of a replacement item, then it is a matter for the procedural law of the court to determine. However, if the assessment is a matter of law it is now for the applicable law to determine. Under the common law the whole manner of quantifying the damage was for the *lex fori*, although the liability and heads of damage were for the applicable law.

(4) Article 12(1)(d) refers issues of extinguishing obligations and the prescription and limitation of actions to the applicable law. Under English contract law contractual obligations can be extinguished, for example, by performance or by legislation such as a moratorium or by novation by which new parties become subject to the obligations of the contract. Prescription and limitation of actions on the contract were at one time seen as a procedural matter. The English law on limitation of actions was applied to all cases brought before the English court. It is clear from the Rome I Regulation that prescription and limitation is to be referred to the applicable law and not the *lex fori*. The English law on limitation was changed in the Foreign Limitation Periods Act 1984 to make this a substantive matter such that the applicable law governs it.

(5) The consequences of nullity of the contract are a matter for the applicable law (Article 12(1)(e)).[52] It is a little unclear exactly how this provision interacts with the exclusion of liability for precontractual dealings from the Rome I Regulation. Liability for unjust enrichment is referred to the law closely connected to the relationship which existed between the parties by Article 10(1) of the Rome II Regulation; this may be the same law as that of the putative applicable law under Article 10 of the Rome I Regulation but possibly may not be.

(6) The applicable law also applies 'to the extent that it contains rules which raise presumptions of law or determine the burden of proof' in matters of contract (Article 18). Therefore rules such as the English law presumption that a signed contract contains all the parties' agreement shall apply to contracts where English law is the applicable law, but not to contracts governed by a different law.

---

[50] See the domestic case of *Co-operative Insurance Society Ltd v Argyll Stores Ltd* [1998] AC 1 (HL), for an example of a case in which the English court refused an order for performance as it would be unable to supervise the order.

[51] Rome I Regulation, Art. 12(1)(c).

[52] The United Kingdom had entered a reservation from the equivalent provision of the Rome Convention.

(7) If there is a question raised regarding the material or essential validity of the contract the identification of the applicable law is difficult, for example, an argument that a party lacked consent to enter into the contract or that the contract is invalid because it was intended from the outset by the parties to perform some illegal act or that the contract was entered into under duress. All these arguments raise the fundamental question of whether there is a contract or not. If there is no contract then how is the law to govern the question to be identified? The Rome I Regulation, Article 10(1) takes the pragmatic approach to assume that the contract is valid, identify the applicable law using the usual rules of the Regulation and then apply that law to determine whether indeed there is a contract. This is called a putative applicable law approach. Note that both Articles 3 and 4 of the Rome I Regulation will apply. Therefore, the domestic law rules of a legal system identified in an express choice of law expressed in the 'contract' will operate to determine whether there is a contract. It is unfair to foist a choice of applicable law on a party who has not consented to it. Therefore, a party who needs to establish that such party did not consent to the contract 'may rely upon the law of the country in which he has his habitual residence if it appears from the circumstances that it would not be reasonable to determine the effect of his conduct in accordance' with the putative applicable law.[53] It is unclear whether what would or would not be considered reasonable is autonomously defined or whether it is a matter for the *lex fori*. However, this protection is limited to the issue of lack of consent rather than, for example, the effect of initial illegality on the contract. Consent could be broadly interpreted to cover the effect of duress, fraud and misrepresentation on the alleged contract. It does not cover the effect of an incapacity which is excluded from the Rome I Regulation apart from Article 13.[54]

6. General rules

a. Introduction

We have seen that the applicable law of the contract is important as it resolves many of the issues which might be raised in a dispute about the contract. The applicable law has to be a system of domestic contract law, not of general principles of law such as *lex mercatoria*, Jewish law or Sharia law.[55] Article 22(1)

---

[53] Article 10(2).   [54] Article 1(2)(a).

[55] The Rome I Regulation refers in Art. 3(3) to 'the *country* whose law has been chosen' (emphasis added) and see *Beximco Pharmaceuticals Ltd v Shamil Bank of Bahrain* [2004] EWCA Civ 19, [2004] 1 WLR 1784 (a case on the Rome Convention). Note that some states have incorporated conventions which provide contractual rules into their domestic law of contract; for example, the Geneva Convention on the Contract for the International Carriage of Goods by Road 1956 is part of French domestic contract law. An issue on a contract which is governed by French law may therefore be resolved by application of those rules.

defines 'country' in cases where a state has more than one legal system as a territorial unit which has its own rules of law in respect of contractual obligations.[56] The parties to a contract may incorporate directly into their contract some non-municipal law either by setting out the provisions explicitly or referring expressly in the contract to the body of law by name, making it clear that those rules are also to apply.[57] Any conflict between those rules and the domestic contract law of the applicable law is for the applicable law to determine. It is possible under English law for the *interpretation* of a contract's terms to be done by reference to a non-municipal law as evidence of the parties' intentions.[58] However, this rule should only operate where English law is the applicable law.

b. *Renvoi* is excluded

Renvoi is excluded from the Rome I Regulation[59] so there is no application of the choice of law rules of the system of law chosen. The European Commission considered that *renvoi* undermines certainty.[60]

c. Method to follow in matters of contract

Faced with an issue of contract, it is best to commence by identifying the applicable law. First, is there an express choice of the law to govern the contract?[61] Beyond the importance of uniformity, legal certainty and predictability of outcome (which are the general objectives of the Rome I Regulation) the central principle of the Regulation is to give effect to the parties' choice of law. Therefore, where the parties to a contract have expressed their agreement as to the law to govern their relationship, the agreed law is the applicable law and will apply to most issues. The parties may vary the applicable law by agreement after the contract was concluded.[62] It is this rule which facilitates the argument that the English procedural rule applying English law where no foreign law is pleaded and proved is allowed under the Rome I Regulation as a post-contractual choice of law. Many contracts have some provision, even orally agreed, that the contract should be governed by the law of, say, England. This is the best course of action.

---

[56] Where the case solely concerns conflicts between territorial units of a single Member State, that state need not apply the Rome I Regulation (Art. 22(2)).

[57] As suggested by recital 13.

[58] As Jewish law principles were taken into account in *Halpern v Halpern* [2007] EWCA Civ 291, [2008] QB 195.

[59] Article 20.

[60] See Proposal for a Regulation of the European Parliament and the Council on the law applicable to non-contractual obligations (Rome II) referring to Article 15 of the Rome Convertion, COM(2003)0427 final.

[61] Article 3(1).   [62] Article 3(2).

Secondly, if there is no express choice, can a choice by the parties be inferred from the terms of the contract or the circumstances of the case?[63] Thirdly, if no choice can be inferred, then the rules identifying the applicable law where there has been no choice apply. These are found in Article 4 of the Rome I Regulation.

d. Parties' choice of law

i. Express choice

Where the parties to a contract have made an express choice of a law to govern it, Article 3 gives that choice full effect providing 'A contract shall be governed by the law chosen by the parties'. The choice may be made orally and generally can be of a law completely unconnected with the parties and their contract. Some contracts, such as those for the carriage of passengers[64] and insurance,[65] have limited the range of laws which the parties can choose to govern their contracts to protect the weaker party.[66] There is also a limited exception to the absolute freedom of choice in the case where all the elements of the contract other than the express choice of law are connected to a country other than the one chosen.[67]

An express choice of law can be made by reference to some factor external to the contract, for example, to one of the parties' place of business or the flag of a ship.[68] Choice of law clauses, on the other hand, should not be directly incorporated from one contract into another without an express reference to that other contract. The argument that an express choice of law in another contract is applied to the contract in question pulls itself up by its own bootstraps. The Rome I Regulation makes provision for an inferred choice of law, so the better view is that a choice of law clause in a related contract may be used as evidence of that inferred choice.[69] Alternatively, the express choice of law in a related contract which is insufficient to evidence an inferred choice is a factor to take into account in determining the applicable law in Article 4. However, a different solution applies to a contract which has express words of reference to another contract (which contains an express choice of law), for example, a reinsurance contract which provides that it should be 'as per' the underlying insurance contract. In this case, the focus could be on the 'as per' clause itself but the choice of law rule is not apparent from the Rome I Regulation. It has been suggested that the scope of the 'as per' clause is to be referred to English domestic law as the *lex fori*.[70] That argument deals with the

---

[63] Article 3(1).   [64] Article 5(2).   [65] Article 7(3).

[66] However, there is no such protection in employment contracts, see Art. 8.

[67] Article 3(3). See further pp. 306–7 below.

[68] See e.g., *Compagnie Tunisienne de Navigation SA v Compagnie d'Armement Maritime SA* [1971] AC 572.

[69] Article 3(1).

[70] *The Heidberg* [1994] 2 Lloyd's LR 287 and *Dornoch Ltd and others v Mauritius Union Assurance Company Ltd and another* [2006] EWCA Civ 386, [2006] 1 CLC 714.

incorporation of a choice of law clause as a question of fact prior to the choice of law inquiry.[71] Under English law, general words of incorporation do not incorporate choice of law and jurisdiction agreements, something more precise is needed as evidence of the parties' intentions.[72] Clarke J in *Kingspan Environmental Ltd v Borealis A/S*[73] adopted the alternative solution of using the putative applicable law to decide whether terms were incorporated:

> The defendant sellers had supplied a polymer to the claimant purchasers which the claimants used to manufacture oil tanks. The oil tanks failed due to the alleged inadequacy of the defendant's polymer. The parties had dealt with each other over a few years and the claimants had never objected to the terms and conditions. Indeed, there was no evidence that the claimants had read and understood the terms. The invoices made it clear that the contracts of supply were subject to the defendant's general terms and conditions. Those terms and conditions contained an express choice of law of the seller's domicile. As a matter of fact, the court held that the seller was domiciled in Denmark.

Clarke J commenced by finding that English law would incorporate the terms. However, he considered that the matter of incorporation was for the putative applicable law. This was Danish law as the terms and conditions identified Danish law as the choice of the parties, albeit by reference to the factor of the seller's domicile. Under Danish law, the term on choice of law would only be incorporated if the party accepting it was aware of the term or if the term was reasonably expected. Clarke J found that the choice of law term was one which could reasonably be expected. The criticism of using the putative applicable law is that it permits a party (here the defendant sellers) to foist the applicable law by a choice made in general terms and conditions onto the other party. As it happens, English law would have incorporated the terms, including the choice of law clause, on these facts.

If one party alleges that the choice of law clause itself is materially or essentially invalid, or formally invalid, or affected by incapacity, there is a logical conundrum. Article 3(5) refers the question of material or essential validity to the putative applicable law (Article 10), the question of formality to the provisions of Article 11 and any question of incapacity covered by the Regulation to Article 13. The solution of the putative applicable law has been criticised as permitting one party to choose the law to validate the contract and then foist it on the other party. An alternative solution as suggested in *Iran Continental Shelf Oil Co. v IRI International Corp.*[74] is preferred.

---

[71] Fentiman, *International Commercial Litigation*, para. 4.78.
[72] *Dornoch Ltd and others v Mauritius Union Assurance Company Ltd and another* [2006] EWCA Civ 386, [2006] 1 CLC 714.
[73] [2012] EWHC 1147 (Comm).   [74] [2002] EWCA Civ 1024, [2004] 2 CLC 696.

Where there is no evidence of agreement to the particular choice of law clause itself, the court must identify the applicable law in another way. In *Iran Continental Shelf Oil Co v IRI International Corp.*, each party had apparently contracted on its own terms:

> Each party's draft contractual documentation included an express choice of law provision. The defendant had provided for the law of Texas and the claimant for the law of Iran.[75]

The Court of Appeal held that the contract was found to be most closely connected with English law by operation of Article 4 of the Rome I Regulation. The different choice of law provisions in each party's draft documentation meant that they had not come to an unequivocal conclusion on choice of law so there was no express choice. In these cases the court should apply the rules identifying the applicable law in the absence of choice to these cases, i.e., to omit Article 3 and merely apply Article 4.

Impossible or meaningless choices of law have been ignored by the English courts under the common law and the Rome Convention. This will continue under the Rome I Regulation. A choice of Sharia law may be meaningless as it is not a single legal system.[76] Also the choice of two inconsistent laws for the same obligation will be ignored.[77] However, it is possible under the Rome I Regulation to sever two obligations and make each of them subject to a different law, so long as there is no conflict between them.[78] A floating choice of law, i.e., one which is not identifiable at the start of the contract, will not be given effect to. This was also the position at common law. So long as a law is applicable from the commencement of the contract, it may later be changed by agreement between the parties.[79]

ii. Inferred choice

Where the parties have not expressly identified a choice of law to govern their contract by explicit words, the Rome I Regulation recognises a choice of law if it can be 'clearly demonstrated by the terms of the contract or the circumstances of the case'.[80] It is different from the common law cases on 'implied' choice. The parties' inferred choice is to be determined from the surrounding circumstances, not an implied choice objectively imposed by the court. The test is quite strict: the parties must have chosen the particular law to govern their contract, despite the lack of articulation of that choice in

---

[75] *Ibid.*

[76] *Beximco Pharmaceuticals Ltd v Shamil Bank of Bahrain* [2004] EWCA Civ 19, [2004] 1 WLR 1784.

[77] *Centrax v Citibank NA* [1999] 1 All ER (Comm) 557 (CA) at 562 and 569.

[78] *Ibid.*   [79] Rome I Regulation, Art. 3(2).   [80] Article 3(1).

the contract. The Guiliano and Lagarde Report to the Rome Convention described this as 'a real choice of law'.[81] Several factors have indicated such an intention to choose an applicable law in the past, but these are not presumptions. Either the parties have chosen a law or they have not. If the parties' choice cannot be clearly demonstrated, Article 4 applies to determine the applicable law. The Report lists examples from which the inference of the parties' choice can be drawn. These include standard form contracts which are generally known to be drawn up under a system of law (such as Lloyd's marine insurance policies),[82] a choice of court agreement[83] (where the general inference is that the parties intended to subject the contract to the same law, for efficiency and convenience reasons), or a reference to specific articles of a system of law (such as the French *Code Civil*). A reference to arbitration in England with some indication that the arbitrator should apply local law may also provide an inference that English law should govern the contract.

The parties' choice can also be inferred from the circumstances of the case, for example, where there is a choice of law in a related contract which is part of a long-term relationship between the parties.[84] This could be a more wide-ranging exercise looking at all the circumstances and weighing various factors.[85] However, that is an exercise that is more properly done under Article 4. It is unlikely that the parties' choice of a particular law can be seen clearly in this way. It may be the case that the circumstances of the case reject the inference drawn from the contract's terms. For example, no clear evidence of the parties' choice was found in *Samcrete Egypt Engineers and Contractors SAE v Land Rover Exports Ltd*,[86] as one party had deleted the reference to the choice of law in the draft contract of guarantee. Had that circumstance not been taken into account, the inference of the parties' choice of law might have been drawn from the choice of the applicable law of the underlying contract which was being guaranteed. If the inferences drawn from the contract conflict with one another there is no clear demonstration of the parties' choice of an applicable law.[87]

---

[81] A. Guiliano and C. Lagarde, *Report on the Convention on the Law Applicable to Contractual Obligations* (1980) [1980] OJ C282/1 at 15–17. The wording of Art. 3(1) in the Rome I Regulation has changed a little from the equivalent in the Rome Convention. The choice must now be 'clearly demonstrated' rather than 'demonstrated with reasonable certainty'. The factors to consider probably remain the same, but the inference must be more clearly drawn.

[82] See e.g., *Oldendorff v Libera Corp.* [1996] 1 Lloyd's LR 380 (QBD).

[83] This factor is specifically mentioned in recital 12 if the choice of court agreement exclusively refers disputes to a single court.

[84] See e.g., *Marubeni Hong Kong and South China Ltd* [2002] 2 All ER (Comm) 873.

[85] See the Rome Convention case *American Motorists Insurance Co. v Cellstar Corp.* [2003] EWCA Civ 206, [2003] ILPr. 22.

[86] [2001] EWCA Civ 2019, [2002] CLC 533.

[87] *Dornoch Ltd and others v Mauritius Union Assurance Company Ltd and another* [2006] EWCA Civ 386, [2006] 1 CLC 714.

iii. *Dépeçage*

The parties to a contract are permitted by the Rome I Convention to subject parts of their contract to different laws (Article 3(1)). However, such choice must be logically consistent. There is a real risk of the chosen laws having contradictory effects and being impossible to apply. The English court has held that a contract cannot be subject to two different laws in its entirety.[88]

iv. Limitations on parties' choice

Article 3(3) provides a limit on the application of the chosen applicable law where all the elements relevant to the situation of the contract are connected with one country but the parties have chosen the law of another country to govern their contract. Essentially, the contract is a domestic contract in which the parties and facts are connected to a single country but the parties have chosen a different law. In that case, the provisions of law which cannot be derogated from by agreement (non-derogable provisions) of the country with which all the relevant elements are connected cannot be evaded by the application of the chosen law. The chosen law would apply except in so far as the non-derogable provisions require a different result. So, if the English court has to decide a dispute on a contract made between two Ruritanian parties for performance in Ruritania in which the parties had expressly chosen Utopian law, the non-derogable rules of Ruritanian law would apply.

Non-derogable provisions used to be called 'mandatory rules' in the Rome Convention but this term is reserved for specific use elsewhere in the Rome I Regulation. Here, non-derogable provisions are those rules of domestic contract law which either cannot be contracted away by that domestic law or cannot be avoided by choice of another law. This involves a wider range of rules than the overriding mandatory rules protected in Article 9.[89] Examples of non-derogable rules would include the right to cancel consumer contracts, maximum interest rates, the right to particular information, unfair dismissal rights and other employment protection legislation, exchange controls, price controls, rules on cartels or monopolies, and so on. It is a matter of the interpretation and scope of the domestic law provision to decide whether the provision cannot be contracted out of or cannot be avoided by the choice of a different applicable law. Few English statutes are explicit about their territorial scope or their application if another law has been chosen by the parties. Section 27 of the Unfair Contract Terms Act 1977 is a rare example of one which does address this point.

Article 3(3) of the Rome I Regulation only applies where all the relevant elements connect the contract to one country. What are the relevant elements? If one of the parties is incorporated in a different country is that not a relevant

---

[88] *Beximco Pharmaceuticals Ltd v Shamil Bank of Bahrain* [2004] EWCA Civ 19, [2004] 1 WLR 1784.

[89] See further p. 232 *et seq.* above.

element?[90] In *Caterpillar Financial Services Corp. v SNC Passion*,[91] although almost all of the connections were with France, the facts that one of the parties was not French and the loan was given for a ship being built in Singapore were sufficient to prevent the operation of Article 3(3). Note too that most rules of the applicable law will apply. It is only the effect of those particular domestic rules of the other law (with which all the elements are connected) which cannot be prejudiced.

Article 3(4) provides that Community laws which are not permitted to be derogated from by agreement[92] cannot be evaded by the parties' choice of an applicable law which is not the law of a Member State. Therefore, the parties cannot avoid the application of EU law by choosing the law of a third state to apply. Article 3(4), rightly, only applies where all the relevant elements are located in one or more Member States.

e. Absence of choice: Article 4

The parties may not have agreed on a law to govern their contract.[93] The Rome I Regulation provides a failsafe objective rule to determine the applicable law for contracts in this case. Article 4 of the Regulation differs substantially from Article 4 of the Rome Convention, although some of the same terms are used. The Regulation provides fixed rules for particular types of contracts where the parties have not chosen a law to govern their contract.

i. Specific contracts

Under the Rome I Regulation:

(a) contracts 'for the sale of goods shall be governed by the law of the country where the seller has his habitual residence' (Article 4(1)(a));

(b) contracts 'for the provision of services shall be governed by the law of the country where the service provider has his habitual residence' (Article 4(1)(b)).

These two provisions give the person who is to achieve what is considered to be the more complex part of a contract the benefit of that party's own law. The Rome I Regulation defines habitual residence for the purposes of the Regulation and we shall discuss this below;

---

[90] See e.g., the Australian case *Golden Acres Ltd v Queensland Estates Pty Ltd* [1969] Qd R 378.

[91] [2004] EWHC 569 (Comm).

[92] For example, the Commercial Agents Directive (Directive 86/653/EC [1986] OJ L352/17).

[93] It is good practice, particularly for lawyers who have had the benefit of studying conflict of laws, to ensure that any contract contains a choice of law clause. However, many contracts are negotiated without expensive lawyers on hand. In addition, the reality of most commercial contracts is not in these 'boilerplate' clauses, but in the quantity, specification and price of the product and payment for it. In focussing on agreeing these more important matters, the choice of law issue is justifiably overlooked, especially if it is likely to be a deal-breaker.

(c) contracts 'relating to a right *in rem* in immovable property or to a tenancy of immovable property shall be governed by the law of the country where the property is located' (Article 4(1)(c)). This is a commonsense rule and widely accepted in legal systems. The best law to govern any contract over land and proprietary rights in land is that of the law of the place where the land is situated. That law will certainly govern the proprietary effect of the contract and so confusion and conflict between the laws is reduced.[94] Note that it is possible to choose another law to apply to the contract, however;

(d) temporary tenancies for private use shall be governed by the law of the landlord's habitual residence (Article 4(1)(d)).[95] After the experience of holiday lets in the Brussels I Regulation, it is clear that a carve-out from the usual rule is appropriate in cases where a holiday-maker rents a vacation property from a landlord from the holiday-maker's state;

(e) a franchise contract shall be governed by the law of the franchisee's habitual residence (Article 4(1)(e));

(f) a distribution contract shall be governed by the law of the distributor's habitual residence (Article 4(1)(f)).

It was difficult to identify a law to govern franchise and distribution contracts under the previous rule in the Rome Convention of the habitual residence of the characteristic performer. These two provisions make the applicable law clear in the absence of a choice of law by the parties;

(g) a contract for the sale of goods by auction shall be governed by the law of the place of the auction, if it is possible to determine that place (Article 4(1)(g)). This is again a pragmatic solution to a complex choice of law question. However, it may well be impossible to determine the place of, for example, an Internet-based auction. A solution could be to refer to the law of the company providing the auction services, such as eBay. However, that is not straightforward either. Would that reference be to the law where the computer servers are located (which could be relatively easily moved), or where eBay is incorporated, or where its central administration is found?

(h) a contract concluded in a market in financial instruments shall be governed by the law of the market (i.e., where trading is conducted) where that market is regulated by non-discretionary rules and governed by a single law (Article 4(1)(h)).[96] This rule is to provide some certainty as to the law governing the contractual aspects of trading in securities. There are difficult questions in relation to such trading matters, for example, whether the Rome I Regulation applies to proprietary issues arising therefrom.

---

[94] See further pp. 383–5 below.

[95] So long as the tenancy is for less than six months and the tenant is a natural person who has the same habitual residence as the landlord.

[96] Financial instruments are defined in Art. 4(1)(17) of Directive 2004/39/EC of the European Parliament and of the Council on markets in financial instruments [2004] OJ L145/1.

ii. Residual rule for other contracts

Article 4(1) does not cover all contracts. Article 4(2) therefore provides that contracts not covered by the specific rules in Article 4(1) shall be governed by the law of the habitual residence of the party which has to perform the obligation characteristic of the contract. Likewise, the law of the habitual residence of the characteristic performer will apply if the contract has elements which fall into more than one provision of Article 4(1). Note that the law to apply in the absence of choice is not that of the characteristic performance but a law related to the characteristic performer of the contract.

The concept of a performance which is characteristic of a contract was first mooted in Switzerland but was more enthusiastically adopted in the Rome Convention. It was found to be too uncertain in application for many contracts. The Rome I Regulation therefore provides for more certain rules for specific contracts, relegating this to a residual rule. First, the characteristic performance has to be identified. Secondly, the party to perform that obligation must be found. Lastly, the habitual residence of that party must be located. It is only that last law which is applied in the absence of the parties' choice of law. Generally, contracts are bilateral so that one party performs an obligation for which the other party pays. In such contracts, the characteristic performance is the non-payment obligation, i.e., the one for which payment is to be made. In a more complex contract (such as those with continuing and alternative obligations, 'swap' contracts or those for barter or joint venture arrangements) the characteristic performance is more difficult to identify. The English court has held that it is the repayment which is characteristic of a contract of loan.[97] In *Print Concept GmbH v GEW (EC) Ltd*,[98] the Court of Appeal searched for the 'real meat' of the contract to find its characteristic performance. In that case the distribution of the goods manufactured by the seller was held to be the characteristic performance. That particular case would now fall within Article 4(1)(f). As we have seen, most of the more straightforward contracts have been given specific choice of law rules.[99] This residual rule is left for the more complex contracts in which the characteristic performance is inherently difficult to identify. Once the characteristic performance has been found, the applicable law is that of the habitual residence of the party whose obligation is to make that performance.

iii. Habitual residence

Habitual residence is an important concept throughout the Rome I Regulation. It is defined for some parties in Article 19. Companies and other incorporated or unincorporated bodies have their habitual residence at the place of their

---

[97] *Sierra Leone Telecommunications Co. Ltd v Barclays Bank Plc* [1998] 2 All ER 820.
[98] [2001] EWCA Civ 352, [2002] CLC 352.
[99] For example, Art. 4(1)(a) which provides that the applicable law of a contract for the sale of goods (in which the characteristic performance is the provision of the goods) is the law of the seller's habitual residence.

central administration.[100] Natural persons acting in the course of the natural person's business activity have their habitual residence at the natural person's principal place of business.[101] However, if the contract is concluded 'in the course of the operations of a branch, agency or any other establishment' the place where the branch, etc. is located is treated as the habitual residence. Likewise if the performance of the contract 'is the responsibility' of a branch, etc., the habitual residence is at the place where the branch, etc. is located.[102] It is possible for a natural person to act in the course of the natural person's business through a branch, etc., but this provision is more likely to apply to companies and other legal persons. It therefore becomes important to establish whether the performance of the contract is either concluded in the course of the operations of the branch, etc. or to be the responsibility of the branch, etc.

Article 5(5) of the Brussels I Regulation uses the similar concept of a dispute 'arising out of the operations' of a branch, etc. It is likely those cases will be followed both in identifying what relationship suffices for a branch, etc. and for determining whether the contract is concluded in the course of the operations of the branch, etc.[103] Determining whether the performance of the contract is 'the responsibility of' the branch, etc. could be difficult. This issue is a mixture of fact and law. The contract may expressly state the place of performance in which case the office of the party to perform it should be identifiable as a matter of fact. Then the applicable law can be determined. However, if no place of performance is specified then some implied term is necessary and that implication is a question of law. In *Ennstone Building Products Ltd v Stanger Ltd*[104] (a case under the Rome Convention which had a similar provision), the Court of Appeal held that the obligation to perform through a particular branch, etc. must be a term (express or implied) of the contract such that a party which did not perform the obligation there would be in breach. This approach is difficult. At this stage we do not know what the law is to govern the contract so how can a term be implied? In *Iran Continental Shelf Oil Co. v IRI International Corp.*[105] (also under the Rome Convention), the Court of Appeal decided, apparently as a matter of fact, that the contract was to be performed through the UK office. Therefore English law applied to that contract.[106]

---

[100] Article 19(1), first indent.   [101] Article 19(1), second indent.   [102] Article 19(2).

[103] See e.g., *De Bloos SPRL v Société en Commandite par Actions Bouyer* Case C-14/76 [1976] ECR 1497; *Somafer SA v Saar Ferngas AG* Case-33/78 [1978] ECR 2183; *SAR Schotte GmbH v Parfums Rothschild SARL* Case 218/86 [1987] ECR 4905 and *Lloyd's Register of Shipping v Société Campenon Bernard* Case C-439/93 [1995] ECR I-961. All discussed at pp. 94–6 above.

[104] [2002] EWCA Civ 916, [2002] 1 WLR 3059.

[105] [2002] EWCA Civ 1024, [2004] 2 CLC. 696.

[106] Likewise in *Sierra Leone Telecommunications Co. Ltd v Barclays Bank Plc* [1998] 2 All ER 820 and *Bank of Baroda v Vysya Bank Ltd* [1994] 2 Lloyd's LR 87, the English court found that contracts were to be effected through branches of banks by looking at the contract to glean the parties' intentions. In both cases it appears that English law views were adopted.

If it is necessary to determine the habitual residence of a natural person not acting in the course of the natural person's business then the national rules identifying that person's habitual residence will apply. These are quite complicated in English law.[107] An autonomous EU definition of habitual residence is preferable to ensure predictability and certainty. However, there are few CJEU cases on habitual residence[108] and these have been decided for EU legislation with very different purposes to that of choice of law. They may therefore not be reliable as indicators of a definition of habitual residence for the Rome I Regulation.

iv. Exceptional rule: close connection

Article 4(3) of the Rome I Regulation provides a rule which is an exception both to the specific rules in Article 4(1) and to the residual rule of the habitual residence of the characteristic performer in Article 4(2). 'Where it is clear from all the circumstances of the case that the contract is manifestly more closely connected' with a country other than that indicated in the specific rules or the residual rule, the law of the country which is most closely connected applies instead. Article 4(4) also provides that the law of the country which is most closely connected with the contract applies if it is not possible to determine the applicable law under the specific rules or the residual rule.

The application of the law of the closest connection was the primary rule in the absence of the parties' choice at common law. We shall look at the way in which the courts have identified the law of the country with which the contract is most closely connected below.

v. Deconstructing Article 4

Article 4 of the Rome I Regulation is different from the Rome Convention and from the previous common law. The common law rules identified the law with the most close and substantial connection with the parties and the contract. Many factors were taken into account, and a sophisticated decision was made depending upon the weight to be given to various factors. Occasionally, presumptions were relied upon but these were generally rebuttable by other circumstances. Sometimes the closest connection was determined subjectively by looking for the intentions of the parties. For example, in *Amin Rasheed Shipping Corp. v Kuwait Insurance Co.*:[109]

A Liberian incorporated shipping company had a head office in Dubai and insured its ship with a Kuwaiti insurance company. The contract was entered into with the London office of the insurance company through London-based brokers. The policies were issued in Kuwait and the policy expressed that claims were to be payable in Kuwait. In practice claims were settled in London. In order for the case to be heard in England the proper law of the contract had to be English law.

---

[107] See further pp. 32–7 above.   [108] See further pp. 36–7 above.   [109] [1984] AC 50.

Lord Diplock considered that the parties intended that English law was to govern their contract as the law with the closest connection to the contract. This was largely due to the negotiations of the parties in London through London brokers, and the terms of the contract using the language of Lloyd's of London. Alternatively, in other cases the law with the closest connection was objectively ascertained. That required collecting the various factors, determining their significance and then weighing the factors to conclude which law was most closely connected. Factors which could be important in some cases, such as the currency of the payment, might be unimportant in others: for example, expressing the currency of payment in US dollars may be irrelevant as US dollars are an internationally accepted payment; but suppose the currency was South African rand, the choice of that currency may be significant. Likewise expressing the contract in the English language did not necessarily carry weight. That factor might nonetheless be important if one of the parties was English. The test was criticised for being uncertain and unpredictable. However, it is always open to parties who wish certainty to choose a law applicable to the contract.

The Rome Convention used a mixture of a general objectively determined proper law and also a presumption of the applicable law. However, it was unclear exactly how these elements related to each other. Therefore, the structure of Article 4 of the Rome I Regulation dealing with the applicable law in the absence of choice was altered from the same Article in the Rome Convention. This alteration was intended to make Article 4 more predictable and more uniformly applied throughout the EU.

Article 4 of the Rome Convention commenced with a provision that the contract was to be governed by the law with which it had its most close connection. Then, there was a presumption that the most closely connected law was that of the habitual residence of the party to perform characteristic performance.[110] As with the Rome I Regulation this was not the law of the place of characteristic performance but of the party to perform the characteristic obligation. However, the presumption was subject to the final provision which enabled the presumption to be disregarded if it appeared from the circumstances as a whole that the contract was more closely connected with another country.[111] The relationship between the general rule of close connection and the presumption vexed courts and commentators. The English courts tended to depart from the presumption and follow the proper law approach if there was some closer connection with a law other than that of the performer of the characteristic obligation. The connection had to be 'clearly' closer to another law but it was relatively easy to rebut the presumption.[112] The continental courts preferred applying the presumption unless there was *no* connection with that law; this left the general rule of close connection with

---

[110] Rome Convention, Art. 4(2).   [111] *Ibid.* Art. 4(5).
[112] See e.g., *Cecil v Bayat* [2010] EWHC 641.

very little application.[113] This is known as the 'strong model', i.e., that the presumption is strongly applied. In contrast, the English approach is a version of the 'weak model'. The presumption could be rebutted but only in clear cases.[114] It could be described as a middle way. The weakest model would be only to follow the presumption if there is some connection with that law, such as performance there. This model has not found favour with the courts.

The English courts were most likely to rebut the presumption where the place of performance differed from the law of the performer of the characteristic obligation. An example is *Definitely Maybe (Touring) Ltd v Marek Lieberberg Konzertagentur GmbH (No. 2)*:

> The defendants wanted the pop group Oasis to perform a series of concerts in Germany. The claimants had agreed with the defendants to provide Oasis for the concerts but then the lead singer refused to perform. As the defendants refused to pay the full amount the claimants sued for the balance in England. Whether the English court had jurisdiction depended upon Article 5(1) of the Brussels Convention.[115] Was the contractual obligation to pay to be performed in England? As the contract was silent on this point,[116] the applicable law had to be determined. The rules of that law would then identify where the obligation to pay was to be performed. Under English law it would be payable in England, under German law it would be payable in Germany. The characteristic performance of the contract was agreed to be the provision of the services of Oasis in Germany. The providers of the obligation were the English claimants. Therefore under the presumption English law applied.

The Court of Appeal held that the presumption was rebutted.[117] There was a clear preponderance of factors in favour of Germany. That was where the concerts were to be performed, that was where the arrangements had to be made and the defendants were German. Although the band and the claimants were English, the more important connections were with Germany.

That case can be contrasted with the decision in *Ennstone Building Products Ltd v Stanger Ltd*:[118]

---

[113] *Nouvelle des Papeteries de L'Aa SA v BV Machinefabriek BOA* 1992 Nederlands Jurisprudentie 750.

[114] *Definitely Maybe (Touring) Ltd v Marek Lieberberg Konzertagentur GmbH (No. 2)* [2001] 1 WLR 1745.

[115] The case predates the Brussels I Regulation.

[116] Note that this was before the changes to Art. 5(1) in the Brussels I Regulation.

[117] Compare with the position in Scotland: *Caledonia Subsea Ltd v Microperi SRL* 2003 SC 70, in which Lord President Cullen refused to accept that there was an easy rebuttal of the presumption where the place of performance differed from the law of the characteristic performer.

[118] [2002] EWCA Civ 916, [2002] 1 WLR 3059.

> The parties were both English companies, one of which had a Scottish office. The claimants contracted with the defendants to investigate the staining of some stone that the claimants had supplied to a building in Scotland. The defendants inspected the stone in Scotland. A report was drawn up on the causes of the staining and the remedial work which was sent to the claimants in England. The defendants were allegedly negligent in that report and the claimants sued both in contract and in tort.

The Court of Appeal held that the contract was not clearly more closely connected with Scotland and therefore the presumption that English law (as the law of the characteristic performer) applied was not displaced. Although some performance of the contract was to be effected in Scotland, much of it was done in England. There was sufficient connection with the country of the characteristic performance.

The CJEU first inspected the relationship between the presumption and the close connection in Article 4 of the Rome Convention in *Intercontainer Interfrigo SC (ICF) v Balkenende*:

> The Belgian claimants sued two Dutch companies in the Netherlands for unpaid invoices. The claimants agreed in the charterparty to make railway wagons available to the defendants between the Netherlands and Germany. If the law applicable was that of the Netherlands, the claim was time-barred, but if the law applicable was Belgian the claim could continue.[119]

The CJEU held that the primary objective of Article 4 of the Rome Convention was to identify the law with the most close connection. The most closely connected law identified by the presumptions should be adopted except where it is clear from the circumstances as a whole that the contract was more closely connected with another country. This merely repeats the wording of Article 4 and does not give clear guidance as to the weight to be given to the presumptions. However, the CJEU rejected the strong model which had been advocated by the Commission. It is probable that the weakest model does not reflect the requirement of certainty in the operation of the Regulation. Therefore, both the English courts and the CJEU use some middle way.

As we have seen, the Rome I Regulation provisions for identifying the applicable law in the absence of the parties' choice of law have a different structure. Article 4(1) commences by providing specific rules for particular contracts, such as contracts for the sale of goods or provision of services.[120] Article 4(2) then provides a residual rule for those not covered by the specific

---

[119] Case C-133/08 [2009] ECR I-9687.   [120] Article 4(1)(a).

rules, which is based on identifying the habitual residence of the party to effect characteristic performance of the contract.[121] Article 4(3) then follows this with an exceptional rule. The law of the manifestly more closely connected country will apply instead of the law chosen by the previous two rules.[122] Under Article 4(4), finally, where the applicable law cannot be determined by either of the first two rules the contract is governed by the law with which it is most closely connected.[123]

The changes to the structure and terms of Article 4 probably make it even clearer that the specific rules are more than presumptions. Article 4(1) uses the terms 'the law governing the contract *shall* be determined as follows'[124] and the word 'shall' is repeated in each of the specific rules. The word 'manifestly' has been added to 'more closely connected' in Article 4(3). Those both imply that the specific rules are only very exceptionally to be displaced by the more closely connected law. However, it is not clear that this goes as far as the strongest model under which the specific rules are only displaced where there is no connection with the law identified by them.

vi. Manifestly more close connection

Determining the law of the country which is more closely connected with the contract is a complex exercise. Although the English courts have some cases to draw upon, both under the previous common law and the Rome Convention, the position under the Rome I Regulation is different. We have seen that the structure of Article 4 has changed. Presumptions are not used and the close connection test has been clearly relegated to an exceptional role. Article 4 is notably different from the common law in specifying that the close connection has to be with a country rather than a law. This might reduce the importance of such factors as the parties using a form of contract common in English commercial practice.[125] However, in common with the common law approach, it is clear that there must be some evaluation of the weight to be attached to each factor, i.e., that the significance of the factor must be shown. Identifying the country with the closest connection therefore requires more than a mere counting of contacts with various countries. An assessment of their relevance must be undertaken.[126] However, no method to assess the significance or relevance of the factors or contacts is given in the Rome I Regulation. The court can consider all the circumstances of the case.[127]

Under the common law the most significant factors included the party's places of business or residence; the language of the contract; its currency of payment; the place(s) of performance; the place where the contract was made;

---

[121] Article 4(2).   [122] Article 4(3).   [123] Article 4(4).   [124] Emphasis added.

[125] However, it is possible that those factors have been elevated in importance if they suffice to clearly demonstrate a choice of law by the parties under Art. 3(1).

[126] See Fentiman, *International Commercial Litigation*, paras 4.107–9.

[127] *Apple Corp. Ltd. v Apple Computer Inc.* [2004] EWHC 768 (Ch), [2004] ILPr. 34, a case on the Rome Convention.

the subject matter of the contract; and other connected contracts. If a jurisdiction or arbitration clause is insufficiently clear to show a choice of law by the parties it may nevertheless be useful as a factor determining the closest connection. These would still be important factors under the Rome I Regulation, but others can also be taken into account. Fentiman argues that 'the significance of the relevant connecting factors should be assessed in commercial terms',[128] for example, the applicable law of a letter of credit should take account of the fact that it is more commercially convenient to have the various contracts governed by the same law. This approach has not yet been adjudicated by the CJEU but recital 21 does require account to be taken of whether the contract in question has a close relationship with other contracts. An example of the way in which the closest connection was identified under the Rome Convention is *Samcrete Egypt Engineers and Contractors SAE v Land Rover Exports Ltd*:[129]

> Samcrete had given the Land Rover parent company a guarantee of the performance of Technotrade. This was an Egyptian company in which Samcrete held 20 per cent of the shares and through which Samcrete distributed Land Rovers in Egypt. On the termination of the distributorship, Land Rover claimed against Samcrete under the guarantee. There was no choice of law and the presumption under Article 4(2) of the Rome Convention made Egyptian law the governing law. The payment obligation was expressed in the contract to be performed in England. One of the parties was Egyptian, the other English. The products supplied in the distributorship contract were to be delivered 'ex works' from England and the currency of payment was sterling.

Potter LJ held that the 'centre of gravity' of the guarantee was in England. The factors were fairly evenly balanced, but the place of performance of the guarantee was in England and this appears to have been the most significant matter.

Sometimes, it is extremely difficult to decide on the closest connection. In *Apple Corp. Ltd v Apple Computer Inc.*:[130]

> The parties had entered into an agreement to control the use of their respective trademarks. The action arose out of an alleged breach of that agreement. Each party had agreed not to carry out certain activities in relation to worldwide intellectual property rights. One party was from California, one from England. Each controlled the performance of the contract not to compete from their respective states.

---

[128] Fentiman, *International Commercial Litigation*, para. 4.110 *et seq.*
[129] [2001] EWCA Civ 2019, [2002] CLC 533.   [130] [2004] EWHC 768 (Ch), [2004] ILPr. 34.

The factors were therefore very evenly balanced. Some factors were given no weight, such as the place of contracting, as it was probably fortuitous. So were the currency of payment (US dollars are an internationally accepted currency) and the language of the contract (English is used in both California and England). The London trademark agents used to negotiate the agreement could have been from anywhere. In conclusion, Mann J reluctantly decided that because the contract was to settle a previous dispute in England that factor just tipped the balance in favour of English law.

7. Special rules

Particular types of contracts have special rules for determining the applicable law. Some rules are to protect the party considered the weaker in the bargain,[131] such as consumers[132] or employees.[133] Some rules are to deal with specialist concerns, such as insurance or carriage of goods.

a. Contracts of carriage of goods

Where the parties have not chosen the law applicable to their contract, Article 5(1) provides that the law of the country of the habitual residence of the carrier is the applicable law, however, only if that country is the same country as the place of receipt or delivery or the habitual residence of the consignor. In other cases, the law of the country of the agreed place of delivery applies. There is an exception to these rules where the contract is manifestly more closely connected with another country, in which case the law of that other country applies.

b. Carriage of passengers

The parties' choice of the applicable law of a contract for the carriage of passengers is restricted. Article 5(2) second indent limits the parties' choice of law under Article 3 to the law of the country where (a) the passenger or carrier has his habitual residence; or (b) where the place of departure or destination is situated; or (c) where the carrier has his place of central administration. If the parties have not chosen an applicable law, the law of the country of the habitual residence of the passenger is the applicable law, however, only if that country is the same country as the place of departure or destination. In other cases, the law of the carrier's habitual residence applies. There is an exception to these rules where the contract is manifestly more closely connected with another country, in which case the law of that other country applies.

---

[131] Rome I Regulation, recital 23.   [132] Recitals 24 and 25.   [133] Recitals 34 to 36.

c. Consumer contracts

Consumers may well need protecting from the stronger party to their contract. The consumer is not in a position to bargain away from an express choice of an applicable law which could be detrimental to the consumer or at least more favourable to the stronger party. Often laws which protect consumers are mandatory, i.e., such laws are considered so important by a legal system that they cannot be contracted away, or cannot be evaded by the choice of a different applicable law. Article 6 provides that without prejudice to the articles on carriage and on insurance, consumer contracts shall be governed by the law of the consumer's habitual residence. A consumer contract is one which is concluded 'by a natural person for a purpose which can be regarded as being outside his trade or profession' with another person 'acting in the exercise of his trade or profession', so long as the professional pursues his commercial or professional activities in the country of the consumer's habitual residence or by any means directs the professional's activities to that country.[134] Therefore, a sale of a doll to a father living in England buying the toy for his daughter from a company incorporated and operating in France but offering its goods for sale over the Internet will be governed by English law.

d. Insurance contracts

Insurance contracts for 'large risks'[135] are governed by the law chosen by the parties. If no law has been chosen such contracts are governed by the law of the country where the insurer has his habitual residence. There is the usual exception for a more closely connected law.[136] Other than large risk insurance, the parties may choose a law to govern their contract only from a limited list of possibilities.[137] In the absence of choice the contract is governed by the law of the Member State in which the risk is situated.[138] Reinsurance contracts are not covered by these provisions.[139]

---

[134] Or several countries which include the consumer's habitual residence.
[135] As defined in Art. 5(d) of Directive 73/239/EEC on the co-ordination of laws, regulations and administrative provisions relating to the taking up and pursuit of the business of direct insurance other than life assurance.
[136] Article 7(2).   [137] Article 7(3).
[138] The country in which the risk is situated is determined according to Art. 2(d) of the Second Council Directive 88/357/EEC of 22 June 1988 on the co-ordination of laws, regulations and administrative provisions relating to direct insurance other than life assurance; and, in the case of life assurance, the country in which the risk is situated will be the country of the commitment within the meaning of Art. 1(1)(g) of Directive 2002/83/EC (Rome I Regulation, Art. 7(6)).
[139] Article 7(1).

e. Individual employment contracts

The parties can choose the law to govern an individual employment contract using Article 3. However, the choice cannot deprive the employee of the protection of some rules[140] of the law which would have governed the contract in the absence of choice. Where the law has not been chosen by the parties, the contract is governed by the law of the country in which[141] the employee habitually carries out his work in performance of the contract.[142] If that country cannot be identified, in the absence of a choice of law, the contract is governed by the law of the country where the place of business through which the employee was engaged is situated. There is the usual exception that if the contract is more closely connected with another country, that country's law will apply.[143]

8. Formal validity

A contract will be formally valid if it has complied with the formal requirements of any one of a number of laws. Although English law has remarkably few formal requirements,[144] other systems of law may impose formalities such as the need for writing, signatures, notarisation or registration. It may be difficult to distinguish between a formality and a requirement which has more substantive effect. Article 11 provides that a contract is formally valid if it satisfies the formal requirements of:

(1) the applicable law; or
(2) the law of the country in which the parties are present at the time the contract was concluded or, if the parties were in different countries, the law of either of the countries; or
(3) the law of either of the parties' habitual residence.

These enabling rules do not apply to consumer contracts which are governed by Article 6. Such contracts are formally valid only if they comply with the formal requirements of the law of the habitual residence of the consumer.[145] Likewise, contracts over immovable property[146] and rights therein are generally subject to the formal requirements of the law of the country in which the property is situated.[147] However, the formal requirements of that law only apply if they are mandatory under that law.[148]

---

[140] Those which cannot be derogated from by agreement (Art. 8(1)).
[141] Or if that place cannot be found the contract is governed by the law of the country from which the employee habitually carries out the employee's work.
[142] Article 8(2). If the employee is temporarily employed in another country that does not change the applicable law.
[143] Article 8(4).
[144] Other than contracts for the creation, sale or transfer of an interest in land, the only contracts which require writing are contracts of guarantee.
[145] Article 11(4).   [146] I.e., land.   [147] Article 11(5).
[148] I.e., that the formal requirements apply irrespective of the place of contracting, irrespective of the law governing the contract, and cannot be derogated from by agreement (Art. 11(5)(a) and (b)).

9. Capacity

The status and legal capacity of natural persons to contract is generally excluded from the Rome I Regulation[149] but Article 13 provides a direct rule. It limits the possibility of a natural person invoking his or her own incapacity. If the contract is concluded with both parties in the same country, a natural person cannot invoke his or her incapacity under the law of any other country unless the other party was aware of the incapacity or was only not aware of it as a result of negligence. Therefore, if X sells a horse in England to a Ruritanian woman who came to England to inspect the horse, X can assume that the buyer has capacity to conclude and be bound by the contract even though under Ruritanian law she is incapable of contracting. However, X would have to be careful. Note that X could not invoke the buyer's lack of capacity in order to avoid delivering the horse. This provision has changed somewhat since the Rome Convention and is probably more protective of the party who lacks capacity.

At common law what law governs the capacity of a natural person to conclude a commercial contract is a matter for some speculation, for there is a dearth of English authority on the point. The question is of comparatively little practical importance, perhaps, since large commercial concerns are companies whose capacity is governed by the law of the place of their incorporation.[150] With respect to individuals, in the English context few problems can occur, since the only categories of person whose contractual capacity may be limited are minors, intoxicated persons and mental patients.[151]

There are several possibilities. The governing law may be (1) that of the domicile of the person alleged to be under the incapacity; (2) that of the place of contracting; (3) the law applicable to the contract. Application of the first could work unjustly towards the other party[152] and the second is unsatisfactory if the place of contracting is 'fortuitous'.[153]

Only two English cases touch on the point. In the early case, *Male v Roberts*,[154] the decision appears to be equally consistent with the law of the place of contracting and with what would now be called the applicable law.[155] The issue was probably quasi-contractual rather than contractual

---

[149] Article 1(2)(a).

[150] *Haugesund Kommune v Depfa ACS Bank* [2010] EWCA Civ 579, [2011] 1 All ER 190.

[151] See e.g., *Chitty on Contracts* (30th edn, Sweet & Maxwell, 2008) ch. 8.

[152] It finds support in the dicta in cases concerning marriage and matrimonial property settlements: e.g., *Sottomayor v de Barros (No. 1)* (1877) 3 PD 1 (CA); *Baindail v Baindail* [1946] P 122. These seem to have little relevance to commercial contracts. But the US Supreme Court has favoured the law of the domicile: *Union Trust Co. v Grosman*, 245 US 412 (1918).

[153] It is supported, however, by *McFeetridge v Stewarts & Lloyds Ltd* 1913 SC 773 (Scotland); *Bondholders Securities v Manville* (1933) 4 DLR 699 (Canada); *Milliken v Pratt*, 125 Mass. 374 (1878) (US Massachusetts).

[154] (1800) 3 Esp. 163.

[155] Lord Eldon LC used the words 'the law of the country where the contract arose must govern the contract'. At that time the *lex loci contractus* governed all contractual issues.

and it was not shown that the law of Scotland, where the defendant (an infant circus performer), had incurred a debt for 'liquors of various sorts', differed from English law. In the much more modern case of *Bodley Head Ltd v Flegon*,[156] which concerned the copyright in Alexander Solzhenitsyn's novel, *August 1914*, the author had signed in Moscow a power of attorney authorising a Swiss lawyer to deal in the author's works outside the Soviet Union. It was argued that the author had no capacity under Soviet law, the law of the place of contracting and of his domicile, to contract with the lawyer. The argument was rejected on the ground that Russian law had not been shown to have the effect contended for, though the court suggested that Swiss law as the applicable law of the contract possibly governed the question.

In this state of the authorities, the writer favours the applicable law of the contract. This should be the putative applicable law,[157] which here should mean the applicable law ascertained by looking for the system of law with which the transaction has its closest and most significant connection. Any express choice of law should be ignored, at any rate if that law was chosen in order to confer capacity which otherwise would not exist.

10. Exceptions to the applicable law

As we have seen the applicable law, once determined, generally governs most issues which arise on a contract. However, there are exceptions. We have seen that the applicable law has limited application where all the elements relevant to the situation (other than the choice of law) are connected with one country.[158] The applicable law is also limited with respect to consumer and employment contracts.[159] In those cases, an express choice of law does not prevent the application of rules of law which cannot be derogated from by contract. The rules which cannot be derogated from by contract can be considered domestic mandatory rules. These rules are usually statutory in origin and are imposed generally to protect the weaker party. Examples include rules which oust unfair contract terms or those which outlaw unfair competition. The scope of the rules which cannot be derogated from by contract has to be determined. It may help understanding to consider the following questions:

(1) Do the rules apply to all contracts? Sometimes such rules only apply to a specified class of contracts or only to particular types of parties, in which case the rule might not apply unless the contract under consideration falls within the class.

---

[156] [1972] 1 WLR 680.

[157] Since if the contract is void for incapacity (or any other means) it cannot have an applicable law.

[158] Rome I Regulation, Art. 3(3) and (4).   [159] Articles 6 and 8.

(2) Do the rules only apply to contracts which are governed by the law of that country? In which case they apply when the applicable law is the law of that country but not to contracts governed by a foreign law. These are domestic mandatory rules.

If the rules apply to all contracts whatever the applicable law the rules are not merely domestically mandatory but internationally mandatory. There are then three further questions:

(3) Does there have to be some territorial connection with the country? For example, does the employee have to be working in that country to be able to claim the protection of those rules? Such a rule may be an example of a unilateral rule.[160]

(4) Do the rules apply to contracts in which the parties have expressly chosen another law to govern their contract, perhaps in order to evade the domestic rule?[161]

(5) Do the rules also apply when the applicable law is determined not by the parties' choice but by some objective rule such as those in Article 4?[162]

Internationally mandatory rules have more narrow operation and apply to oust the applicable law either when expressly chosen or even when it has been objectively determined according to Article 4. It is possible that a mandatory rule can apply when the parties have expressly chosen a different law but not if the law is objectively chosen by a choice of law rule such as Article 4. It is a matter of interpreting the mandatory rule in question to determine its precise scope and effect. In either case, the rule is an example of what English law calls an 'overriding' law. For the present purpose the rules override the usual choice of law rules, rather than merely the terms of the parties' contract.

The Rome Convention did not make the distinction between domestic mandatory rules and international mandatory rules very clearly. The Rome I Regulation does not call the first type mandatory but 'rules which cannot be derogated from by contract'. The designation 'overriding mandatory rules' is restricted to internationally mandatory rules in Article 9. Often, mandatory rules are a specification of an aspect of the public policy of the country. However, public policy may be much more generally defined to cover not just rules but also the effects of applying them.

---

[160] See p. 333 below.

[161] Fentiman calls these 'inalienable overriding rules' (*International Commercial Litigation*, para. 4.45).

[162] Fentiman calls these 'indefeasible overriding rules' (*International Commercial Litigation*, para. 4.45).

11. Public policy and mandatory rules

a. Article 9

Article 9 of the Rome I Regulation provides that mandatory rules of a law other than that usually applicable may exceptionally be applied. Article 9(1) gives a definition of overriding mandatory provisions. These are rules which are regarded as 'crucial by a country for safeguarding its public interests, such as its political, social or economic organisation, to such an extent that they are applicable to any situation falling within their scope, irrespective of the law otherwise applicable to the contract'.[163] The reference to political, social or economic organisation comes from the decision of the CJEU in *Arblade*,[164] which was not a conflict of laws case but one in which the relationship between national mandatory rules and EU legislation was determined:

> Belgian rules requiring an employer to pay some dues and maintain certain records were mandatory with respect to employees working in Belgium. The French employers had complied with French law but were prosecuted in Belgium for failing to comply with Belgian law where the work was carried out. They argued that the Belgian law was incompatible with (then) Articles 59 and 60 of the EU Treaty on freedom of movement. Those articles could only be restricted by rules justified by overriding reasons relating to the public interest.

The result is that mandatory rules in the Rome I Regulation are restricted to rules which protect public interests of the state concerned, such as its political, social or economic organisation. These rules must also be 'crucial'. They could include laws protecting consumers, employees or trade unions, cultural heritage,[165] or those which render contracts to perform some activities illegal.[166] It could be a matter of the law of the state whose rules are under consideration to determine whether the rules are in the public interest and also whether they are crucial. Clearly, the actual scope and interpretation of the law must be determined according to the legal system from which it derives. However, it is possible that that system considers the rule internationally mandatory but that it would not be sufficiently crucial to protect the political, social or economic organisation of the state in the view of English courts.[167] Alternatively, it might be argued that whether the rules are in the public interest and whether

---

[163] The definition of overriding mandatory rules being those which apply 'irrespective of the law otherwise applicable' is also used in Art. 16 of the Rome II Regulation (Regulation (EC) 864/2007).

[164] Cases C-369/96 and C-374/96 [1999] ECR I-8453 at para. 30.

[165] For example, export controls making contracts for the export of antiques illegal.

[166] Such as laws preventing contracts for the sale of drugs, prostitution and gambling.

[167] For example, English law would enforce a contract for the assignment of a cause of action, but the foreign law may not do so.

they are crucial must be ascertained objectively. In the cases following *Arblade* the CJEU has adjudicated on Member States' national rules to hold that some are not sufficiently overriding to justify a restriction on the fundamental freedoms.[168] That might suggest that an objective assessment is appropriate, at least within the EU. After *Ingmar GB Ltd v Eaton Leonard Technologies Inc.*[169] it is likely that rules which derive from EU legislation will be considered internationally mandatory even if they are not made so expressly in the legislation. Therefore, it would not be possible to evade EU objectives by choosing another law to apply to the contract. Applying an autonomous definition to mandatory rules of third states could be less easy than deciding on rules of other Member States.

Article 9(2) clearly provides that internationally overriding mandatory rules of the forum will apply irrespective of the applicable law. Of course, if the applicable law is English law, all English mandatory rules apply to that contract, whether the rule is domestically or internationally mandatory. Internationally mandatory rules could be argued to include English public policy rules which prevent the enforcement of a contract which from its outset the parties intended to perform an act which is illegal under the law of a friendly foreign state.[170] This suggestion may be unlikely to find favour as the traditionally mandatory rules are considered to require some statutory basis. Note, however, the relatively narrow way in which such rules have been interpreted in the English courts. Often a territorial connection is required before the apparently mandatory rule applies. There are rather few internationally mandatory rules of English law.[171] Traditionally, this matter has been answered via the application of public policy, which is dealt with under Article 21 rather than Article 9.

The Guiliano and Lagarde Report on the Rome Convention suggested that rules on cartels, competition and restrictive practices, along with some rules on carriage, would fall into the category of internationally overriding mandatory rules.[172] In the Scots case *English v Donnelly*:

> The Scots defender had contracted with the English pursuer (claimant) under a hire-purchase arrangement which had not complied with the requirement under a Scots statute to provide a copy of the agreement. The agreement contained an express choice of English law. When the pursuer sued in Scotland, the defender sought to rely on the statute as a defence.

---

[168] Such as *Commission of the European Communities v Luxembourg* Case C-319/06 [2008] ECR I-4323, in which Luxembourg rules were inspected through the prism of other EU legislation to determine whether the rules were compliant with the fundamental freedoms.

[169] Case C-381/98 [2000] ECR I-9305.   [170] See further p. 329 *et seq.* below.

[171] An example is the forerunner of the now repealed Exchange Control Act 1947, which was held to apply to a contract under Monégasque law (*Boissevain v Weil* [1950] AC 327). Others include the Unfair Contract Terms Act 1977 and the Carriage of Goods by Sea Act 1971.

[172] Guiliano and Lagarde Report [1980] OJ C282/1 at 28.

The Scots court held that he could do so. The Scots statute overrode the choice of English law.

More controversially, Article 9(3) permits the English court to give effect to the internationally overriding mandatory rules of a country the law of which is not the applicable law. This was included in the Rome I Regulation in a more narrow form than the equivalent provision in the Rome Convention.[173] The United Kingdom had derogated from that provision and might have used the opt-out from the Rome I Regulation in its entirety had Article 9(3) not been restricted.[174] Article 9(3) provides:

> Effect may be given to the overriding mandatory provisions of the law of the country where the obligations arising out of the contract have to be or have been performed, in so far as those overriding mandatory provisions render the performance of the contract unlawful.

Therefore the English court can take into account a law which is not that of the *lex fori* (English law) or the applicable law but some other law, that of the place where the contract is to be performed, where that law makes performance of the contract unlawful.

Four matters need consideration. First, Article 9(3) is discretionary. The English courts are permitted to give effect to the mandatory rule of the other law but are not required to do so. Flexibility is unusual in choice of law rules and it is unclear how the discretion is to be exercised. Article 9(3) specifies that in considering whether to give effect to the internationally mandatory provisions of the other law 'regard shall be had to their nature and purpose and to the consequences of their application or non-application'. That does not give much more clarity. It appears that the English court is to undertake some sort of evaluative exercise, looking at the context and effect of the third law's rule to decide whether it should apply to the particular case under consideration. For example, it might be concluded that the other law is not intended under its own system to apply to the particular conduct in question. This method is more common in US choice of law cases.[175] Secondly, it is also unclear what 'effect' is to be given to the provision. Either it applies and alters the parties' obligations and liabilities or it does not. Thirdly, the other law is limited to that of the country in which the obligations have to be or have been performed. That country must be ascertained. The place of performance is clear enough where the obligations have been performed or where the contract expressly states where performance is to take place. It is more complicated where the

---

[173] Article 7(1) of the Rome Convention permitted effect to be given to the mandatory rules of a country with which the 'situation has a close connection'.

[174] The original wide draft provision for Art. 9(3) was the main reason that the UK government withdrew from the negotiations over the Rome I Regulation (Ministry of Justice Report, *Rome I – Should the UK Opt In?*, Consultation Paper CP05/08, (2nd April 2008) para. 77).

[175] Although there was a similar exercise undertaken in the English case on the common law choice of law rules in tort, *Johnson v Coventry Churchill International Ltd* [1992] 3 All ER 14.

contract is silent and performance has not yet occurred. A party may wish to know whether it remains under an obligation to perform, where that performance has become unlawful under the law of a country. The party cannot be sure that any excuse is available. Partly that is due to the discretionary element of Article 9(3) but it is also due to the difficulty of identifying the place of performance where the contract is silent.[176] Fourthly, Article 9(3) will cover both initial and supervening illegality in the place of performance where the applicable law is not English law. Where the applicable law is English law, then English domestic contract law rules will apply.

Article 9(3) will only have purpose when the applicable law does not provide some acceptable domestic contract law solution to the issue of performance of an obligation where it is unlawful under the law where performance is to occur. The English domestic contract law rules to deal with initial and supervening illegality in the place of performance will be discussed below. Where English law is the applicable law of the contract, then those rules will apply. Where the applicable foreign law has rules excusing performance or replacing the obligation with a different lawful one, then those rules will apply.[177] Obviously, any mandatory rules of the applicable law will apply to the contract.

b. Article 21

There is a general rule in conflicts of law which enables the English court to refuse to apply a foreign law where to do so would be contrary to English public policy.[178] Note that the public policy in question is not a purely domestic notion which would apply to domestic contracts but public policy which applies at the international level. On the one hand, English public policy should not be evaded by the parties choosing another law. On the other hand, where English public policy was not directly engaged (as the facts display no connection with England or the contract is not governed by English law) purely domestic English public policy may be inappropriate. English courts at common law are careful about this distinction.

There are some contracts which have been refused enforcement at common law. Often the contracts have been governed by English law and therefore the result is better explained as a rule of domestic English law of contract. However, the judgments may have been couched in such wide terms as to

---

[176] J. Hill and A. Chong suggest that the place of performance must be identified by the *lex fori* as it is a connecting factor (*International Commercial Disputes* (Hart, Oxford, 2010) para. 14.3.13). If the CJEU follows its own jurisprudence on Art. 5(1) of the Brussels I Regulation, it is likely to decide that the place of performance is either a factual matter or one to be decided by choice of law rules. Given that the place of performance is needed in order to identify a law which decides on a matter of performance, using choice of law rules would be circular.
[177] See F. Reynolds, 'Illegality by *lex loci solutions*' (1992) 108 *LQR* 470.
[178] See further pp. 424–33 below.

suggest that, whatever the law applicable to the contract, contracts in the following list would not be enforced in England where non-enforcement of the contract whatever the applicable law has been expressed is indicated:

(a) contracts in restraint of trade in England;[179]
(b) contracts entered into under duress have been denied enforcement, even if they would be enforceable by the applicable law of the contract;[180]
(c) contracts with the enemy;[181]
(d) contracts to prejudice interests of the United Kingdom with a friendly foreign country;[182]
(e) contracts infringing English conceptions of morality, such as contracts for prostitution[183] or slavery, even if the applicable law permits enforcement of such contracts;[184]
(f) contracts intended to deceive a third party;[185]
(g) contracts to stifle a prosecution in England;[186]
(h) contracts requiring the performance of an illegal act in a friendly foreign country[187] (including contracts to defraud the foreign revenue authority)[188] whatever the applicable law.

The rule on public policy is reflected in Article 21 of the Rome I Regulation. It provides that the court can only refuse the application of a rule of law which is specified by the Regulation if it would be manifestly incompatible with the public policy of the forum. That would include the applicable law and any other law which might have to be applied under the Regulation, such as the mandatory provision of a place of performance or the formal rules of the place of contracting.[189] As we shall see, the English courts are rather reluctant to use public policy to avoid choice of law rules and so public policy is narrowly defined.[190] Some civilian systems of law use public policy more widely, hence the use of 'manifestly' in Article 21. At common law, the English courts refused to apply foreign rules of the applicable law which, for example, permitted a contract of slavery, contrary to English notions of law. Such contracts would not be enforced, nor would damages be awarded for their breach. Article 21 permits the English court to continue to do so.

---

[179] *Rousillon v Rousillon* (1880) 14 Ch. D 351.
[180] *Kaufman v Gerson* [1904] 1 KB 591 (CA); *Royal Boskalis Westminster NV v Mountain* [1999] QB 674 at 729.
[181] *Dynamit A/G v Rio Tinto Co.* [1918] AC 292 (HL).
[182] *De Wütz v Hendricks* (1824) 2 Bing. 314.
[183] See e.g., *Pearce v Brooks* (1865–6) LR 1 Ex. 213.
[184] *Robinson v Bland* (1760) 2 Burr. 1077 at 1084.
[185] *Mitsubishi Corp. v Alafouzos* [1988] 1 Lloyd's LR 191.
[186] *Kaufman v Gerson* [1904] 1 KB 591 (CA).
[187] *Foster v Driscoll* [1929] 1 KB 470 (CA); *Regazzoni v KC Sethia (1944) Ltd* [1958] AC 301 (HL).
[188] *Re Emery's Investment Trust* [1959] Ch. 410.
[189] It is a little hard to envisage formality rules which would contravene public policy.
[190] See generally pp. 424–33 below.

Note that Article 21 is negative; it permits the English court to refuse to apply a foreign law only when the effect of the applicable law is manifestly incompatible with its public policy. It does not permit the application of a particular law which may, for example, make a contract illegal.[191] Therefore, faced with a foreign rule which is objectionable, the English court should disapply that rule but not the entire law applicable to the contract. Article 21 does not say what should happen in place of the disapplied rule. At common law, generally the English court denied enforcement to contracts where the contract infringed English public policy. The English courts have also disapplied a foreign rule which altered the performance of a contract on the grounds that the foreign rule was discriminatory or oppressive. In *Frankfurther v WL Exner Ltd*:

> The claimant, an Austrian Jew, and an English company entered into a contract under which the claimant was paid commission on business he had done for the defendants in Austria. Just before the Second World War a decree was passed making it unlawful to deal with Jewish businesses. As a result the claimant was forced to write a letter to the defendants informing them that the balance on the commission was to be paid to the Austrian commissar. Relying on that letter the defendants had set off amounts owing to them from the commissar against amounts owed to the claimant. The claimant escaped to England and wanted to recover the commission already earned. The defendants relied on the Austrian decree.[192]

Romer J held that English law applied and the contract was enforced. The Austrian decree was contrary to public policy and not given effect. It is not clear what was the applicable law of the contract and the case was expressly decided on the ground that foreign penal laws cannot have extraterritorial effect. However, the principle of not giving recognition to a foreign law which is discriminatory was broadly stated.

In many of these cases, the contracts were governed by English law, so it is difficult to be sure the same rules would necessarily apply to contracts governed by foreign law. However, the courts often used the broadest language to refuse enforcement of a contract, whatever the governing law, which infringed English public policy. In *Royal Boskalis Westminster NV v Mountain*:[193]

> The claimants had entered into a joint venture agreement with the Iraqi port authorities to dredge an Iraqi port. The agreement was expressly governed by Iraqi law. When Iraq invaded Kuwait the claimants were forced (by threats of violence against their employees) to agree to a 'finalisation' agreement under which they waived all their rights under the joint venture arrangement. That agreement was governed by French law.

---

[191] That is done in Art. 9(3) for a more limited range of rules than those of public policy.
[192] [1947] Ch. 629.   [193] [1999] QB 674 (CA).

The Court of Appeal refused to give effect to the finalisation agreement on the grounds that it contravened English public policy because of the degree of coercion applied to make the claimants agree.[194] The court noted that no civilised tribunal would have enforced the contract.[195]

It is possible that the CJEU will lay down principles of public policy in the same way as it has done under the Brussels I Regulation.[196] It would be for each Member State to decide what infringes its own public policy but within limits set by the CJEU. However, public policy in this context goes beyond fundamental rights of procedure for a fair trial. Public policy probably also is wider than the boundaries established by the European Convention on Human Rights.

12. Effect of illegality on a contract

The way in which illegality affects a contract is a particularly vexing example of public policy.[197] It can be dealt with under the Rome I Regulation by Article 9(1) and (3), Article 10, Article 12 and Article 21. The parties, or one of the parties, may intend to do something illegal either in England or abroad. That is a question of initial illegality. That intention to do something illegally may affect the material validity of the contract which is a question to be referred to the putative applicable law under Article 10.[198] Alternatively, the illegality may affect the performance of the contract, or the discharge of the obligation, or the remedy for non-performance, which are all questions to be referred to the applicable law under Article 12. Where the performance of the contract was lawful at its conclusion but later becomes unlawful where it has to be performed (supervening illegality), that too is a matter for the applicable law under Article 12. Therefore, in principle, the answer to a question on the effect of illegality on a contract is found in the domestic contract law rules of the applicable law. That is certainly the better solution.

However, the English common law cases have shown that illegality can affect a contract in a manner which raises wider concerns of public policy. This is obvious in the case that the parties contract to do something unlawful in England, irrespective of the applicable law of the contract.[199] English public policy is engaged to prevent enforcement of that contract. But public policy

---

[194] Following *Kaufman v Gerson* [1904] 1 KB 591.   [195] [1999] QB 674 at 689.

[196] See *Krombach v Bamberski* Case C-7/98 [2000] ECR I-1935; *Gambazzi v DaimlerChrysler Canada Inc.* Case C-394/07 [2009] ECR I-2563 discussed at p. 225 *et seq.* above.

[197] See A. Chong, 'The Public Policy and Mandatory Rules of Third Countries in International Contracts' (2006) 2 *Jo. Priv. Int. Law* 27; A. Dickinson, 'Third-Country Mandatory Rules in the Law Applicable to Contractual Obligations: So Long, Farewell, Auf wiedersehen, Adieu?' (2007) 3 *Jo. Priv. Int. Law* 53; and M. Hellner, 'Third Country Overiding Mandatory Rules in the Rome I Regulation: Old Wine in New Bottles' (2009) 5 *Jo. Priv. Int. Law* 447.

[198] See e.g., under the Rome Convention, *Continental Enterprises Ltd v Shandong Zhucheng Foreign Trade Group Co.* [2005] EWHC 92 (Comm) at para. 49.

[199] *Clugas v Penaluna* (1791) 4 Term. Rep. 466.

has a wider effect and can include a contract to perform an illegal act abroad. An example is *Foster v Driscoll*, which was a case on initial illegality:

> The parties wanted to load a ship with whisky and smuggle it into the United States in violation of the laws prohibiting the sale of alcohol in the United States at that time. The whisky was never delivered to the loading port and one of the parties sued in England for rescission of the contract.[200]

The majority of the Court of Appeal held the whole venture illegal and refused to entertain the claim. It is notable that the applicable law in this case was English law. In English domestic contract law the intention to perform an illegal act in a friendly foreign country makes the contract void and unenforceable. However, if the putative applicable law is not English law, in principle as a matter of conflict of laws the effect of the illegality should be a question that the putative applicable law must answer. Nevertheless, the statements of the court in *Foster v Driscoll* are so wide as to make the rule of non-enforcement one of public policy.[201] This means that the effect of public policy may go further and a contract with a foreign applicable law by which the parties intend to perform an illegal act in a foreign state may also be unenforceable. There is no case that goes quite this far, as in all the decided cases either the applicable law was English law or the illegal act was to be done in England. However, the dicta in the cases are wide enough to cover that situation. The extension of domestic public policy to foreign conduct and foreign law may be justifiable by reason of international comity. The English court should not sanction the doing of an illegal act in a foreign state any more than it would permit such an act in England, whatever the applicable law. So in *Regazzoni v KC Sethia*:

> The defendants repudiated a contract by which they had agreed to sell and deliver jute bags to the claimants. English law was the applicable law of the contract. Both parties contemplated that the bags were to be shipped from India to Italy for resale in South Africa. Indian law prohibited the export of jute from India to South Africa. The claimants sued for damages.[202]

The claimants lost. An English court would not enforce a contract or award damages for its breach if the performance would involve the doing of an act in a friendly foreign state that violated the law of that state. This stance is said to encourage friendly relations with foreign states.[203] More obvious perhaps is *De Wutz v Hendricks*,[204] in which the English court refused to enforce a contract to raise money to assist a rebellion in Crete.

---

[200] [1929] 1 KB 470 (CA).   [201] *Ibid.* 496 (Scrutton LJ).   [202] [1958] AC 301.
[203] *Foster v Driscoll* [1929] 1 KB 470 at 518.   [204] (1824) 2 Bing. 314.

It might be argued that Article 21 could be used to give the same effect where the applicable law is a foreign law. Note that because Article 21 is negative, the English court should first apply the applicable law and only if that law apparently would enforce the contract or would award damages for its non-performance should English public policy require the applicable law to be disapplied. If public policy is very narrowly confined to prevent application only of discriminatory or oppressive laws, Article 21 could not be used to resolve an illegality in the place of performance. However, it might be argued that the rule of English public policy under which the courts will not assist a party in an illegal act is fundamental to English law and therefore within Article 21.[205]

In the case of supervening illegality, the parties may have entered into the contract intending to perform it lawfully and then matters change so that performance by one or both parties becomes illegal. For example, in *Ralli Bros v Compañia Naviera Sota Y Aznar*:

> English charterers chartered a Spanish ship from her Spanish owners to carry jute from Calcutta to Barcelona at a specified freight, half to be paid on sailing and half to be paid in Spain on discharge of the cargo. Before the ship reached her destination, the Spanish government decreed that freight on jute was not to exceed certain price. This charterparty exceeded that sum. The charterers offered to pay only the decreed rate and the ship-owners sued in London for the balance. The applicable law of the charterparty was English.[206]

The Court of Appeal held that it was illegal under the law of Spain to pay more than the decreed rate for freight on jute, so the extra required under the contract could not be enforced. The effect of a supervening illegality on the performance and discharge of a contract should be a question for the applicable law. Where the applicable law is English law, as in *Ralli Bros*, there are extensive rules in domestic contract law to deal with the effect of illegality, which apply even if the performance is illegal under the law of some foreign country where the contract is to be performed.[207] There are also English domestic law of contract rules which permit 'innocent' parties to enforce the contract, notwithstanding the illegality.[208] Where English law is not the applicable law of the contract, the effect of a supervening illegality is a question for the applicable law under Article 12. It may remain possible that English public policy requires the disapplication of a rule of the applicable law in

---

[205] See Fentiman, *International Commercial Litigation*, para. 3.128.

[206] [1910] 2 KB 287.   [207] See Fentiman, *International Commercial Litigation*, para. 3.86 *et seq.*

[208] See e.g., *Fielding and Platt Ltd v Najjar* [1969] 1 WLR 357 – can sue for payment; *Clay v Yates* (1856) 1 H&N 73 – can sue on a *quantum meruit* or *quantum valebant*; *Oom v Bruce* (1810) 12 East 225 – can sue for return of property.

which case Article 21 could be used. However, as we have seen Article 21 is negative and also could be narrowly confined. It probably goes too far to argue that the English domestic contract rules on illegality should apply as a matter of public policy to every contract, whatever the applicable law and wherever the contract is to be performed. Alternatively, where the foreign law in the place of performance is a mandatory rule which falls within Article 9(3), the English court is permitted to 'give effect to' that rule of foreign law which is not the applicable law. That would be the right solution to the problem within the Rome I Regulation. The European Commission argued that this provision would give the same result as in *Ralli Bros.*

Two further matters should be borne in mind. Not all arguments about illegality will affect a contract. First, the performance of the obligation must be performance which is required by the contract. In *Libyan Arab Foreign Bank v Bankers Trust Co.*:

> The claimants, a Libyan bank, sued the defendants, an American bank for US $131 million which was the credit balance on its account at the London branch of the defendants. The defendants argued that it was contrary to a Presidential decree freezing all Libyan property in the United States or in the possession or control of US persons and therefore illegal to pay the claimants. The bank account was governed by English law.[209]

Staughton J found that the US decree could not affect the English performance of an English contract. Even though it was difficult to perform the contract by paying US $131 million physically in London, English law applied to make London the required place of payment. Secondly, the English court will interpret a contract governed by English law so that it can be performed lawfully if possible. So in *Kleinwort, Sons and Company v Ungarische Baumwolle Industrie Aktiengesellschaft*:[210]

> The claimants had accepted three bills of exchange drawn by a Hungarian company, which were guaranteed by a Hungarian bank. The Hungarian bank argued it was unable to pay under the guarantee as it was illegal under Hungarian law for Hungarians to pay money outside Hungary without the consent of the Hungarian National Bank. The contract was governed by English law.

The Court of Appeal interpreted the contract to hold that it was to be performed in England, where the guarantee was payable and therefore there was no illegal performance. The defendants could have performed the contract without taking money from Hungary but from their assets elsewhere. Merely contemplating that

---

[209] [1989] QB 728.   [210] [1939] 2 KB 678.

the performance of the contract might be achieved in a manner which would be illegal where performance could be done is insufficient.[211]

13. Unilateral rules

Some rules of English law apply to situations which fall within their scope, whatever the parties have said about the law to apply to their contract. Such rules can be categorised as unilateral rules. There is no choice of law question as such and the issue is only about their scope. These rules could also be described as overriding mandatory rules. They occur most frequently in employment law. Examples could include the right not to be unfairly dismissed in Part X of the Employment Rights Act 1996, the right not to be discriminated against now contained in the Equality Act 2010, and the National Minimum Wage Act 1998. Some Acts make the overriding nature of their provisions explicit. For example, s. 204 of the Employment Rights Act 1996 provides that it is immaterial whether the law governing the contract is English or not. Other provisions make no express reference to the applicable law. Where English law is the applicable law the English rules apply. Nevertheless, English law might apply in these unilateral cases even if English law is not the applicable law. What is interesting about the English cases on the application of employment legislation is that the discussion tends to focus solely on the territorial scope of the legislation.[212] If the employment falls within the territorial scope then the legislation applies.[213] Generally the dispute is over the jurisdiction of the employment tribunal, but once jurisdiction is established the English legislation then applies. Note that the various statutes do not all have exactly the same territorial scope.[214]

14. Liability in both contract and tort

In domestic law a claim in the English courts can be pleaded in any manner the claimant wishes. The claim may omit possible claims, or the possible claims can be pleaded alternatively or concurrently. If the claims are pleaded in the alternative, the claimant may succeed on one or the other, or both. If the latter, then the claimant can only recover one set of damages as the judgment is then satisfied. However, as a matter of choice of law, the picture is probably different. If a claim is made in contract, the contractual choice of law rules in this chapter apply to that claim. If a claim is made in tort (which is a non-

---

[211] *Toprak v Finagrain* [1979] 2 Lloyd's LR 98.

[212] See e.g., *Williams v University of Nottingham* [2007] IRLR 660; *Lawson v Serco Ltd* [2006] UKHL 3, [2006] ICR 250; *Ministry of Defence v Wallis* [2011] EWCA Civ 231; *Ravat v Halliburton* [2012] UKSC 1, [2012] ICR 389.

[213] There may also be other requirements such as a qualifying length of employment to satisfy.

[214] See generally on employment issues and private international law L. Merrett, *Employment Contracts in Private International Law* (Oxford University Press, 2011).

contractual obligation), the choice of law rules from the following chapter apply to that claim. What if the claim is concurrently in contract and tort, for example, where the duty to take reasonable care is implied into a contract? As the meaning of a contractual claim or a non-contractual claim is autonomously defined and the CJEU considers a claim can fall only into one category or another, the claimant does not have a free choice. If the liability is concurrent, the English courts for jurisdictional purposes have categorised the claim as contractual.[215] The editors of *Cheshire, North and Fawcett* argue that this is unlikely to be the correct solution after the Rome I and Rome II Regulations.[216] If the claim sounds in a non-contractual obligation, the Rome II Regulation applies. In *Sayers v International Drilling Co. Ltd NV*[217] (a common law case), the Court of Appeal applied a wholly contractual analysis to accept the contractual exemption clause as a defence to a claim that could have been made in tort. The majority[218] of the court ignored the tortious aspects of the case and only applied the contractual choice of law. The clause and defence were valid under the applicable law of the contract and that was enough. This remains possible after the Rome I Regulation if no question of a non-contractual obligation is raised by either party or where the claims arise from separate lines of argument rather than being concurrent.[219]

---

[215] *Source Ltd v TUV Rheinland Holding AG* [1998] QB 54.
[216] See further pp. 363–5 below.   [217] [1971] 1 WLR 1176.
[218] Cf. Lord Denning, who regarded the claim as tortious and the defence as contractual. He adopted a novel 'proper law of the issue' approach which combined both tort and contract.
[219] Such as *Domicrest v Swiss Bank Corp.* [1999] QB 548.

11

Non-contractual obligations

1. Introduction

As we have seen, choice of law rules are rules of English law which identify the substantive law to determine a dispute between litigants. Choice of law rules have the general form of a legal category and a connecting factor. This chapter will be concerned with a broad legal category of non-contractual obligations. This category includes what in English domestic law we consider tortious liability; the duty to make restitution in cases of unjust enrichment; liability for precontractual negotiations; infringement of intellectual property rights; liability for unfair competition and defamation. It probably also includes equitable obligations. Which system of legal rules is to apply to resolve an issue which has arisen? For example, the litigants may be disputing whether X is liable in negligence or whether no duty arose or the line of causation was broken. What about the effect of contributory negligence? What if the various laws which could apply differ in the way in which accidents are dealt with? Some systems have a no-fault scheme and some cap the level of damages. How are joint tortfeasors to be dealt with? What is the effect of insurance? These questions are frequent in motor accident claims, which also are the most common source of cases in conflict of laws. Other tort issues could include the question of whether an employer is vicariously liable for the employee's action. What is the effect of a failure of precontractual negotiations? What happens to the claim if the victim dies? Or the tortfeasor? What if the tortfeasor acts in one country and the victim is damaged in another? What if there is a contract which excludes or caps the liability of the tortfeasor?

We can see, therefore, that choice of law issues relating to non-contractual obligations are much more complex than those relating to contractual obligations. The US experience over the last fifty years has been dominated by choice of law concerns over tortious liability.[1] These concerns have led US courts into very sophisticated and complex methods of choice of law, including investigating the purpose of the domestic law rules in question and evaluating the interest of a state in having its rules apply to the case at hand. Huge criticism

---

[1] See e.g., S. Symeonides, 'The American Choice-of-Law Revolution' (2002) 298 *Hague Recueil*.

has been levelled at those methods, largely because they are considered too uncertain and unpredictable and because there is a definite trend to applying the *lex fori* which might encourage abusive forum shopping. On the other hand, if the choice of law rule is too strict and inflexible, there appears to be a temptation for the courts to avoid the choice of law result by adopting *renvoi* or utilising public policy. For example, the Australian choice of law rule for tort is that of the *lex loci delicti commissi*. The law of the place where the accident occurred is applied to determine questions of liability, causation, heads of damage and quantification of damage. This is a strict rule without any exception for the rare cases when another law is more closely connected with the parties or the tort.[2] In the Australian case of *Neilson v Overseas Projects Corporation of Victoria Ltd*:

> The claimant sued her husband's Australian employer for damages for personal injury. She had fallen down the stairs in the house rented for the couple by the employer in China while her husband was working there. Under Chinese law her claim was barred as being out of time. However, there was evidence that in these circumstances the Chinese court would exceptionally apply the law of Australia as both parties were nationals of Australia.[3]

The Australian High Court applied a partial *renvoi* which had the effect of permitting the application of Australian law.[4] There has been criticism of the way in which *renvoi* can be justified,[5] and whether or not a total or partial *renvoi* is preferable.[6] However, it would have been better to accept the need for a flexible exception to the choice of law rule in cases like these.[7]

It may be surprising that there are so few English cases on choice of law in tortious liability given the rise in international travel. However, one might suggest that the parties to litigation usually choose not to plead and prove foreign law or that, in the event, the result under the foreign law is not so different to English law.

At common law the English choice of law rule for torts was a double actionability rule together with flexible exceptions to that rule.[8] The claimant only recovered damages for actions which took place abroad if the acts gave rise to liability of the defendant both under the law of the place where the acts

---

[2] *Regie Nationale des Usines Renault SA v Zhang* (2002) 210 CLR 491.

[3] [2005] HCA 54.

[4] There was a further difficulty as to the law of which State of Australia then applied.

[5] See further p. 280 *et seq.* above.

[6] R. Mortensen, '"Troublesome and Obscure": The Renewal of Renvoi in Australia' [2006] *Jo. Priv. Int. L* 1; A. Lu and L. Carroll, 'Ignored No More: Renvoi and International Torts Litigated in Australia' [2005] *Jo. Priv. Int. L* 35.

[7] A. Mills, 'Renvoi and the Proof of Foreign Law in Australia' [2006] *CLJ* 37.

[8] *Phillips v Eyre* (1870) LR 6 QB 1; *Boys v Chaplin* [1971] AC 356; and *Red Sea Insurance Co. Ltd v Bouygues SA* [1995] 1 AC 190.

were done (the *lex loci*) and under English law as the *lex fori*. There was a flexible exception under which a claimant could recover even if the *lex loci* or the *lex fori* denied recovery. That rule and exception remains for defamation and libel.[9] It was abolished for most torts in the Private International Law (Miscellaneous Provisions) Act 1995. The Act generally provided that the law of the country in which the events constituting the tort occurred was to apply. If the events happened in more than one country there were various rules to identify the applicable law. For example, in personal injury the applicable law was that of the country where the victim sustained the injury. There was also a flexible exception where it was substantially more appropriate for the applicable law for determining the issues to be the law of another country.

The Rome II Regulation on the law applicable to non-contractual obligations[10] applies to all Member States except for Denmark, which has opted out. It was the result of long negotiations from 1996 onwards between the European Commission and the Parliament before being adopted in 2007. Like the Rome I Regulation,[11] the legal basis for the Rome II Regulation is found in Article 61(c) and Article 65 TEU[12] authorising measures in the field of judicial co-operation in judicial matters having cross-border implications. It is not absolutely clear that choice of law rules for non-contractual obligations are 'necessary for the proper functioning of the internal market' as required by Article 65.[13] However, they could fall within the general objective of establishing an area of freedom, security and justice in which the free movement of persons is ensured.[14]

As with choice of law in contract several words are used to describe the same concept in choice of law in non-contractual obligations. The law applicable to the tort and the law governing the non-contractual obligation mean the same thing. 'The proper law of the tort' has tended to mean a choice of law rule under which the law of the closest or most significant relationship with the tort applies. The applicable law might also be called the *lex causae* or the substantive law. In contradistinction, the *lex fori* or the procedural law is the law which governs matters of procedure and, for our purposes, will be English law as the law of the court in which the dispute is being heard.

2. Universal application and interpretation

The Rome II Regulation applies irrespective of the location of the events or the residence of the parties. The law specified by the Regulation applies whether or not that law is the law of a Member State.[15] Therefore, the choice of law rules

---

[9] See further p. 366 *et seq.* below.

[10] Regulation (EC) 864/2007 on the law applicable to non-contractual obligations [2007] OJ L199/40.

[11] Regulation (EC) 593/2008 on the law applicable to contractual obligations [2008] OJ L177/6.

[12] Now Art. 81 of the Treaty on the Functioning of the European Union.

[13] Article 81 TFEU does not refer to the internal market.

[14] Article 2 of the Treaty on European Union (ex Art. 2 TEU).   [15] Article 3.

in the Regulation will apply Ruritanian law to damage done by a Utopian resident to property in Ruritania owned by a Lilliputian resident.[16] As it is a Regulation, questions on the interpretation of it can be referred to the CJEU from any court. Article 267 of the Treaty on Functioning of the European Union permits any court of a Member State to seek a ruling from the CJEU if the court considers 'that a decision on the question is necessary to enable it to give judgment'.[17] The extensive recitals to the Rome II Regulation can aid in interpretation of it, especially in identifying the objectives of the rules. These include the importance of certainty; of predictability of the outcome of litigation;[18] of the free movement of judgments; of the need to do justice in individual cases and 'ensuring a reasonable balance between the interests of the person claimed to be liable and the person who has sustained the damage'.[19] There are also some *travaux préparatoires* which can be used as an aid to interpretation.[20]

3. Temporal scope

The date from which the rules in the Rome II Regulation apply is not obvious. Article 31 provides that the Regulation 'shall apply to events giving rise to damage which occur after its entry into force'. Under EU law,[21] a Regulation enters into force on the twentieth day following that of its publication (which would be 20 August 2007). That appears to contradict Article 32 which says that the Regulation 'shall apply' from 11 January 2009. Arguments were raised as to whether the Regulation applied to events happening after the first date but to litigation commencing after the other.[22] The CJEU has now held in *Homawoo v GMF Assurances*[23] that Article 32 is determinative so that the Rome II Regulation applies to events which give rise to damage only when the events occurred after 11 January 2009. It may therefore take a little time before cases on the Rome II Regulation are regularly heard in the English courts.

---

[16] Whether the English court would take jurisdiction over such a case is a different matter, see Chapter 5.

[17] Courts from which there is no further judicial remedy *must* seek rulings from the CJEU, i.e., the Supreme Court (previously the House of Lords) or the Court of Appeal in some circumstances, but lower courts may also do so. The previous limitation on references to the CJEU contained in ex Art. 68(1) EC has gone.

[18] Recitals 6 and 16.   [19] Recital 14.

[20] Explanatory Memorandum from the Commission on the Proposal for a Rome II Regulation COM(2003)427 final (22 June 2003) [2004] OJ C96/8; Commission's Amended Proposal COM (2006) 83 final; Common Position of the Council adopted 25 September 2006 [2006] OJ C289/68; M. Giuliano, P. Lagarde and C. Van Sasse van Ysselt Report to the Draft Convention on the Law Applicable to Contractual and Non-Contractual Obligations, Doc. XIV/408/72-E.

[21] Article 297(1) TFEU.

[22] See *Homawoo v GMF Assurances* [2010] EWHC 1941 (QB), [2011] ILPr. 12.

[23] Case C-142/10 [2010] EWHC 1941 (QB).

4. 'Non-contractual obligation'

The Rome II Regulation does not provide a definition of a non-contractual obligation. However, Dickinson[24] confidently states that the category of 'non-contractual obligation' is to be defined negatively, by excluding contractual obligations and covering all other types of obligation. It is clear that 'non-contractual obligation' has an autonomous meaning.[25]

a. Non-contractual or contractual obligation?

Consistency with the Rome I Regulation[26] and the Brussels I Regulation[27] would suggest that the delineation between contract and non-contractual obligations will be determined in a similar way to that between Article 5(1) and Article 5(3) of the Brussels I Regulation.[28] Note that the wording of these Articles is not an exact match with the Rome I and Rome II Regulations.[29] There should be no overlap between the Rome I Regulation and the Rome II Regulation but also there should be no gap between them. In *Kalfelis v Schroder*, the CJEU noted that in order to ensure uniformity, matters relating to a tort, delict and quasi-delict fall into Article 5(3) of the Brussels I Regulation. That Article covers '*all* actions which seek to establish the liability of a defendant and which are not related to a "contract" within the meaning of Article 5(1)'.[30] If a contractual obligation is 'by its very nature one which is voluntarily assumed by agreement'[31] and a non-contractual obligation is any other liability, the category of non-contractual obligations is extremely wide. It would cover restitutionary and equitable obligations as well as those which English domestic law considers tortious. The cases on Article 5 of the Brussels I Regulation indicate that a matter relating to a contract 'presupposes the establishment of a legal obligation freely consented to by one person towards another'.[32] Also, as Dickinson notes, there should be some reciprocal voluntary act by the other person which combines to form the contractual obligation.[33] In contrast, a non-contractual obligation is 'imposed by law independently of any agreement between the parties'.[34]

---

[24] A. Dickinson, *The Rome II Regulation: the Law Applicable to Non-contractual Obligations* (Oxford University Press, 2008) para. 3.104.

[25] Recital 11.   [26] Regulation (EC) 593/2008 [2008] OJ L177/6.

[27] Regulation (EC) 44/2001 on jurisdiction and the recognition and enforcement of judgments in civil and commercial matters [2001] OJ L12/1.

[28] See recitals 7 and 11 of the Rome II Regulation and recital 7 of the Rome I Regulation, As to the delineation between Art. 5(1) and (3) of the Brussels I Regulation, see further pp. 77–8, 87–9 above.

[29] Article 5(1) refers to 'matters relating to a contract' not 'contractual obligations'. Article 5(3) refers to 'matters relating to tort, delict or quasi-delict' rather than 'non-contractual obligations'.

[30] Case C-189/87 [1988] ECR 5565 at para. 17 (emphasis added).

[31] *Base Metal Trading Ltd v Shamurin* [2004] EWCA Civ 1316, [2005] 1 WLR 1157 at para. 28.

[32] *Engler v Janus Versand GmbH* Case C-27/02 [2005] ECR I-1481.

[33] Dickinson, *The Rome II Regulation*, para. 3.121.

[34] AG Jacobs in *Jacob Handte and Co. GmbH v Traitements Mecano-chemiques* Case C-26/91 [1992] ECR I-3967, Opinion at para. 16.

Note that some obligations which English law would not consider contract-ual fall within the Rome I Regulation and not the Rome II Regulation, such as the consequences of nullity of a contract.[35] That might include the conse-quences of a contract set aside for misrepresentation or duress. Dickinson argues that perhaps also a claim for damages in lieu of rescission under s. 2(2) of the Misrepresentation Act 1967 should fall within the Rome I Regulation. On the other hand, claims under s. 2(1) of the Misrepresentation Act 1967 fall within the scope of Article 12 of the Rome II Regulation.[36] Some other obligations which English law might consider quasi-contractual, such as unjust enrichment, are explicitly dealt with by the Rome II Regulation.[37] The equitable obligation arising out of dishonest assistance is a non-contractual obligation in domestic law,[38] and it is likely that other equitable obligations will fall within the Rome II Regulation.

b. Non-contractual obligation or property?

There may also be difficulties delineating non-contractual obligations from property obligations, for example, the rules on conversion are considered tortious in English domestic law but may be dealt with in a civilian system by way of *actio rei vindicatio* which is an aspect of property law. Dickinson suggests three factors which may be relevant to consider in order to decide whether the claim is for a non-contractual obligation or a property right, which are drawn from cases on the determination of property for Article 22 of the Brussels I Regulation.[39] In addition, fiduciary obligations, based on a relationship of trust and confidence,[40] may be contractual if they are based upon some contractual relationship such as those of bankers and solicitors.[41]

c. Excluded matters

As with the Rome I Regulation, the Rome II Regulation applies to civil and commercial matters.[42] This will be interpreted in the same way as that concept is used in the Brussels I Regulation. Likewise, revenue, customs and adminis-trative matters are excluded.[43] Liability for *acta de jure imperii* (the exercise of state authority) is expressly excluded. Therefore, an action by Greek residents

---

[35] Rome I Regulation, Art. 12(1)(e).   [36] Dickinson, *The Rome II Regulation*, para. 3.123.
[37] In modern times English domestic law has rejected the theory that a claim to recover payments made under a mistake was based on an implied contract (*Westdeutsche Landesbank Girozentrale v Islington LBC* [1996] AC 669).
[38] *OJSC Oil Company Yugraneft v Abramovich* [2008] EWHC 2613 (Comm).
[39] Dickinson, *The Rome II Regulation*, paras 3.99–3.100.
[40] *Bristol and West Building Society v Mothew* [1998] Ch. 1 at 18.
[41] See Dickinson, *The Rome II Regulation*, para. 3.142.
[42] Article 1(1).   [43] Article 1(1).

to recover damages from Germans after the Second World War would not fall within this Regulation.[44]

Note that the Rome II Regulation expressly excludes non-contractual obligations:

(a) arising out of family relationships (and relationships with comparable effects including maintenance obligations);[45] therefore an action to recover unpaid maintenance does not fall within this Regulation;[46]

(b) arising out of matrimonial property regimes and property regimes of relationships with similar effects, and wills and succession;[47] there is a proposal for a new Regulation to deal with succession issues;[48]

(c) arising under bills of exchange, cheques, promissory notes and negotiable instruments 'to the extent that the obligations under such negotiable instruments arise out of their negotiable character';[49] these issues are also excluded from the Rome I Regulation;

(d) arising out of the law of companies and other incorporated or unincorporated bodies, for example, the personal liability of the officers or members for the obligations of the company. Notably, the personal liability of auditors *to the* company or its members is also excluded for liability arising in the statutory auditing of the accounts;[50]

(e) arising out of the relations between the settlors, trustees and beneficiaries of a trust created voluntarily;[51] express trusts are therefore excluded;[52]

(f) arising out of nuclear damage;[53]

(g) arising out of violations of privacy and rights relating to personality, including defamation.[54] Importantly, therefore, actions in libel and slander against newspapers fall to be determined under the common law rules. These actions were also excluded from the Private International Law (Miscellaneous Provisions) Act 1995 so they fall under the double actionability test.[55]

---

[44] Such an action is excluded from the Brussels I Regulation as well (*Lechouritou v Germany* Case C-292/05 [2007] ECR I-1519).

[45] Article 1(2)(a).

[46] English courts do not consider there to be a choice of law issue in such an action in any event as English law would be applied.

[47] Article 1(2)(b).

[48] Proposal for a Regulation of the European Parliament and of the Council on jurisdiction, applicable law, recognition and enforcement of decisions and authentic instruments in matters of succession and the creation of a European Certificate of Succession (COM/2009/0154 final – COD 2009/0157).

[49] Article 1(2)(c).   [50] Article 1(2)(d).

[51] The 1985 Hague Convention on the Law Applicable to Trusts and their Recognition, implemented by the Recognition of Trusts Act 1987, covers some of these issues. The relationship between the Rome II Regulation and this Hague Convention may be problematic (see Dickinson, *The Rome II Regulation*, paras 3.173–3.207).

[52] Article 1(2)(e).   [53] Article 1(2)(f).

[54] Article 1(2)(g).   [55] See further p. 366 *et seq.* below.

As with the Rome I Regulation, matters of evidence and procedure are excluded.[56]

We shall deal with trusts and defamation later in this chapter but will first focus on what English law categorises as torts, along with some other specific non-contractual obligations covered by the Rome II Regulation.

5. Exclusion of *renvoi*

As with the Rome I Regulation, the Rome II Regulation excludes the operation of *renvoi*.[57] Therefore the law which is applied by the choice of law rule determined by the Rome II Regulation is that of the domestic law without the choice of law rules identified. Excluding *renvoi* is a way of increasing the certainty of the choice of law rules.[58]

6. Habitual residence

Habitual residence is an important concept in the Rome II Regulation, as with the Rome I Regulation, and the definition is similar. Companies and other incorporated or unincorporated bodies have their habitual residence at the place of their central administration.[59] The location of a company's central administration should be identified in the same way as in the Brussels I Regulation and the Rome I Regulation. However, if 'the event giving rise to the damage occurs, or the damage arises, in the course of the operations of a branch, agency or any other establishment' the place where the branch, etc. is located is treated as the habitual residence.[60] The meaning of branch, agency or other establishment, as well as what are the operations of the branch, etc., should be the same as under Article 5(5) of the Brussels I Regulation.[61] Natural persons acting in the course of the natural person's business activity have their habitual residence at the natural person's principal place of business.[62] There is no definition of habitual residence for a natural person who is not acting in the course of the natural person's business activity. In such cases, the habitual residence of the natural person has to be determined. There are extensive English cases determining habitual residence of natural persons.[63] Caution must be exercised with those cases. It is probable that only those rules on habitual residence for other EU legislation should be used, rather than

---

[56] Article 1(3) apart from the limited effect of Arts 21 and 22.   [57] Article 24.

[58] The Australian courts have applied *renvoi* to the choice of law rules in tort, see *Neilson v Overseas Projects Corp. of Victoria Ltd* [2005] HCA 54.

[59] Article 23(1) first indent.   [60] Article 23(1) second indent.

[61] See e.g., *De Bloos SPRL v Société en Commandite par Actions Bouyer* Case C-14/76 [1976] ECR 1497; *Somafer SA v Saar Ferngas AG* Case C-33/78 [1978] ECR 2183; *SAR Schotte GmbH v Parfums Rothschild SARL* Case C-218/86 [1987] ECR 4905; and *Lloyd's Register of Shipping v Société Campenon Bernard* Case C-439/93 [1995] ECR I-961, all discussed pp. 94–6 above.

[62] Article 23(2).   [63] See further Chapter 3.

those for English domestic legislation. Although the rules for identifying habitual residence might be argued to be autonomously defined, it is not necessarily the case that they must be uniform whatever EU legislation is being applied. Many of the EU Directives and Regulations in which habitual residence is an important concept relate to social security and employment matters. It is not obvious that those rules are apt for choice of law. In particular, for choice of law purposes it is necessary for the rules to identify a single habitual residence.

7. Damage

Damage covers any consequence arising out of tort/delict, unjust enrichment, *negotiorum gestio* or *culpa in contrahendo*.[64] The consequences of a event giving rise to damage should be broadly interpreted. In the context of Article 5(3) of the Brussels I Regulation, the CJEU has held that damage is capable of covering 'the undermining of legal stability by the use of unfair terms'.[65] In that case a consumer organisation was bringing an action against a trader to prevent the breach of unfair contract terms legislation. The action could not be brought in contract, as the consumer organisation was not party to any contract but the legislation provided a cause of action. Non-contractual obligations which are likely to arise are also covered by the Rome II Regulation.[66]

8. Effect of the applicable law

The applicable law identified by the choice of law rules discussed below determines all matters of substance[67] which arise in connection with non-contractual obligations. Article 15 provides that the applicable law shall govern 'in particular':

(a) the basis and extent of liability, including who may be held liable.

Any question whether an actor is liable is to be referred to the domestic law of the applicable law. Likewise, issues of liability for what damage as a consequence of events are also to be referred to the domestic law of the applicable law. For example, the applicable law will determine the existence of a duty, whether that duty has been breached, whether the damage was caused by the events, questions of foreseeability, issues of remoteness, and the contribution of joint tortfeasors or indemnity between them. Whether fault has to be shown or if there is strict liability is a question for the applicable law;

---

[64] Article 2(1).
[65] *Verein für Konsumenteninformation v Henkel* Case C-167/00 [2002] ECR I-8111.
[66] Article 2(2).
[67] We have seen that questions of procedure are generally excluded from the Rome II Regulation.

(b) the 'grounds for exemption from liability, any limitation of liability and
    any division of liability'.

These exonerations from liability will also be referred to the applicable law,
such as *force majeure*, necessity, and contributory negligence (both where the
accident is the entire fault of the victim and where the liability is reduced as a
result of the victim's own negligence). Liability for maritime claims which is
apparently limited under an international convention would be determined by
the applicable law as well.

(c) the 'existence, nature and assessment of damage or the remedy claimed'.

The applicable law would cover, for example, what is the maximum level of
damages (where a rule provides for that), what heads of damage are available
(such as pain and suffering), whether loss of profits or mere financial loss can
be recovered, and whether punitive damages are available. The assessment of
damage is also a matter for the applicable law. Although traditionally the
English court considered the quantification of damages to be a matter of
procedure,[68] Article 15(c) makes it clear that this issue is now to be referred
to the applicable law. The editors of *Cheshire, North and Fawcett* note[69] that
although the words 'in so far as prescribed by law' have been omitted from the
Rome II Regulation unlike the equivalent in the Rome I Regulation,[70] these
should be implied into the operation of Article 15(c). Often the assessment of
damage involves matters of fact, such as the value of a particular item. That is a
question better determined by the *lex fori*, as it would be nearly impossible for
a court to apply a different law to such questions of fact. Statutory ceilings on
damages are very likely to be a question of law, but characterising other issues
is not so straightforward. English courts may have special difficulty if the
applicable law determines damages by means of a jury in tort cases.

The remedy given by the court is a matter for the applicable law. The
applicable law therefore determines whether only compensation is required
or whether the property must be returned.

Traffic accident cases raise particular concerns. A victim may be injured in
one country and that country's law is then applied via the general rule. In
consequence, the damage is assessed according to that law. However, the
victim will live out a life that has been damaged in the country of the victim's
habitual residence where the medical expenses and costs of after-care may be
very different. Recital 33 provides that a court seised of the action can 'take
into account all the relevant actual circumstances of the specific victim,
including in particular the actual losses and costs of after-care and medical
attention' where the victim has his or her habitual residence in a state other

---

[68] See, in particular, *Harding v Wealands* [2006] UKHL 32, [2007] 2 AC 1.
[69] J. Fawcett and J. Carruthers, *Cheshire, North and Fawcett, Private International Law* (14th edn,
     Oxford University Press, 2008) pp. 844–5.
[70] Rome I Regulation, Art. 12(1)(c).

than where the accident takes place.[71] This was a compromise between the European Parliament and the European Commission. Beyond a general exhortation to judges to assess the actual position of the victim it is quite unclear exactly what effect the recital is supposed to have.

(d) 'within the limits of the powers conferred on the court by its procedural law, the measures which a court may take to prevent or terminate injury or damage or to ensure the provision of compensation'.

The applicable law will determine whether an injunction is available either as an interlocutory matter or a final injunction or whether compensation by way of payment of damages is the only remedy. Also the applicable law determines whether a lump sum or periodical payments are to be awarded. The court does not have to provide remedies which are unknown to its own procedural law but, according to Dickinson, should find the 'best fit' to reflect the remedial framework of the applicable law.[72]

(e) the transfer of a remedy or damages, including by inheritance.

In some systems of law the right to damages terminated on death and in others the victim's claim cannot be transferred. Either matter is for the applicable law under the Rome II Regulation.

(f) 'persons entitled to compensation for damage sustained personally'.

This is intended to cover the question whether someone can recover for damage suffered by reason of injury to another person. An example might be the claim that a widow can make for the financial loss to her after the death of her husband in an accident caused by the tortfeasor. It would also cover the issue of recovery for psychological distress caused by seeing another person injured.

(g) 'liability for acts of another person'.

Vicarious liability (such as the liability of an employer for an employee's activities), the liability of parents for their children's acts and the liability of principals for the acts of their agents are matters for the applicable law.

(h) extinguishing obligations, and prescription and limitation.

The applicable law will determine if a claim for a non-contractual obligation has to be brought within a specific time. This was also the case under the Foreign Limitation Periods Act 1984. However, that Act excludes the foreign

---

[71] Sometimes this concern is illustrated in the court finding the law applicable to the tort being that of the victim's habitual residence. See e.g., the pre-Rome II Regulation case of *Edmunds v Simmonds* [2001] 1 WLR 1003, in which the accident happened in Spain but both drivers were from England and England was the place where the victim suffered the costs of extra care and loss of earnings.

[72] Dickinson, *The Rome II Regulation*, para. 14.34.

limitation period in so far as its application would cause 'undue hardship'.[73] That exclusion is probably now incompatible with the Rome II Regulation which makes specific and narrow provision for the non-application of the applicable law on the grounds of public policy in Article 26.

9. Applicable law of non-contractual obligations arising out of a tort/delict

The general rules in Chapter II of the Rome II Regulation apply to tort/delict but not to unjust enrichment, *negotiorum gestio* or *culpa in contrahendo* which have specific rules. Delineating tort from unjust enrichment may not be easy. Equitable obligations other than unjust enrichment (such as a breach of fiduciary duty) should fall within the general rule in Article 4. However, the remedy for these claims is often a disgorgement or an account of profits which could be treated as an unjust enrichment. In English domestic law there is considerable discussion as to whether restitution for wrongdoing is part of obligations or unjust enrichment. Dickinson argues that these equitable claims should fall within Article 4,[74] *Cheshire, North and Fawcett*[75] that they fall within Article 10. The better view is probably the latter. Article 10 makes specific rules in relation to unjust enrichment which also envisage unjust enrichment arising outside a contract. In any event in a difficult case, it is likely that the displacement rule permitting the law of the closest connection will apply. This displacement rule is available in both Article 4 and Article 10. Delineating tort from *culpa in contrahendo* may also raise difficulties. It is clear that a violation of the duty to disclose information (such as the *uberimae fidei* rule in insurance contracts) and any obligations arising out of a breakdown of contractual negotiations fall within *culpa in contrahendo*.[76] The applicable law is determined in accordance with Article 12. Note that if the liability for misrepresentation before the contract is concluded has become a contractual misrepresentation, the applicable law is determined by the Rome I Regulation as the obligation is contractual. It is not so easy to characterise liability for negligent or fraudulent misstatements that are made prior to a contract. However, it is likely that the same law will be applied whether under Article 4 or Article 12 as both permit the law of the contract to apply. Note that precontractual obligations imposed on a third party to the contract fall within Article 4, for example, a claim for negligent misrepresentation by a purchaser against the vendor's surveyor for inflating the value of an asset. There is, in that case, no contract between the surveyor and the purchaser.

---

[73] See s. 2(2).   [74] Dickinson, *The Rome II Regulation*, para. 4.13.
[75] *Cheshire, North and Fawcett*, p. 825. As does R. Fentiman, *International Commercial Litigation* (Oxford University Press, 2010) para. 16.66.
[76] Recital 30.

The general rule in Article 4 does not apply to unfair competition, to product liability, to environmental damage, to infringements of intellectual property rights or to liability which may arise from industrial actions. These torts also have specific rules. However, Article 4 does apply to many torts such as negligence resulting in personal injury, occupier's liability, damage to goods, and the inducement to breach a contract.

a. General rule: Article 4

Article 4 of the Rome II Regulation provides a choice of law rule for many torts. It has three components: (1) the *lex loci damni* applies unless (2) the person damaged and the person allegedly liable both have a habitual residence in the same country, in which case that country's law applies (components (1) and (2) are alternatives);[77] but (3) if it is clear from all the circumstances that the tort is manifestly more closely connected with the law of a country other than (1) or (2) then the most closely connected country will apply. This structure is not dissimilar to that of the Rome I Regulation and also to that of the Private International Law (Miscellaneous Provisions) Act 1995. The relationship between the first two components and the third will require some determination from the CJEU. However, given the similarity of language with Article 4 of the Rome I Regulation, it is not unlikely that the court will undertake a similar evaluation of factors to assess the closest connection in order to displace the general rule.[78]

i. *Lex loci damni*

Article 4(1) provides that 'the applicable law of a non-contractual obligation arising out of a tort/delict shall be the law of the country in which the damage occurs'. This is a *lex loci damni* rule. The justification for applying the law of the place where the damage occurs is because it accords with the parties' expectations. In some fundamental way tort is closer to crime than to contract. As an obligation imposed because of the behaviour of the defendant in causing the injury to the claimant, the law of that place is the obvious law which the parties should have expected. Note that the *lex loci damni* rule differs from the *lex loci delicti* rule which was a part of the English common law of double actionability. The *lex loci delicti* was the law of the place where the tort occurred. That rule then required several subrules to identify that place, which could be particularly difficult if the events which made up the tort occurred in more than one country. Often a choice has to be made between the place where the events which give rise to the tort occurred and the place where the damage was suffered. For example, in *Bier v Mines de Potasse d'Alsace SA* which was a case on jurisdiction under Article 5(3) of the Brussels I Regulation:

---

[77] They are also mutually exclusive.   [78] See Chapter 10 and further p. 311 *et seq.* above.

> Activities of the defendant's factory in France polluted the waters of the Rhine. The claimants grew flowers in the Netherlands which were poisoned and they suffered loss.[79]

The CJEU held that the harmful event occurred in either place. The identification of two places is not problematic in the context of allocating jurisdiction where there is a *lis pendens* rule. However, choice of law rules work best if a single law is identified, as otherwise gaps, overlaps and contradictions between two laws cause difficulties. Article 4(1) of the Rome I Regulation adopts the law of the place where the damage occurs rather than where the events happened. This is because it is said to strike 'a fair balance between the interests of the person claimed to be liable and the person sustaining the damage'[80] and it reflects 'the modern approach to civil liability and the development of systems of strict liability'.[81] Article 4(1) explicitly denies any relevance to the country in which the event giving rise to the damage occurred. So, in a case where the defendant acts in one place and the claimant is injured in another, it is the latter law which is applicable. Therefore, the rule prioritises ideas that the law of tort is about compensating loss, rather than focussing on the wrongdoer and the risk-spreading and behaviour-controlling functions of the law of tort.

Where the damage occurs physically or all the damage is suffered in one place, the law of that place is the *lex loci damni*. So, the damage of personal injury occurs where the person was when injured. Damage to property occurs where it was located at the time of damage.[82] An example of this is *Anton Durbeck GmbH v Den Norske Bank ASA*, which is a case on jurisdiction:

> The claimants were suing for damage to a cargo of bananas carried on a ship. The cargo was found to be damaged due to being held up when the ship was arrested in Panama by the defendant mortgagee bank. The instructions for the arrest were given in London, where the loan had been negotiated. The cause of action was the wrongful interference with the contract in the bill of lading.[83]

Where was the damage suffered? At first instance this was held to be in Panama where the bananas were found to be damaged.[84]

It is more difficult to identify the *lex loci damni* if the damage is suffered indirectly or financially. The damage must be the direct consequence of the tort/delict, as Article 4(1) expressly provides that the *lex loci damni* is 'irrespective of

---

[79] Case C-21/76 [1976] ECR 1735.   [80] Recital 16.   [81] *Ibid.*
[82] If the damage occurs in several countries which can be identified on a distributive basis, a different law can be applied to each individual tort. This is known as the 'mosaic principle' in Germany. This is similar to the approach taken in Art. 5(3) of the Brussels I Regulation, see *Shevill v Presse Alliance SA* Case C-68/93 [1995] ECR I-415.
[83] [2003] EWCA Civ 147, [2003] QB 1160.   [84] The point was not appealed.

the country or countries in which the indirect consequences' of the event giving rise to the damage occurred. Limiting the damage to direct loss is consistent with Article 5(3) of the Brussels I Regulation. In its Proposal for the Regulation, the European Commission argued that in the case of traffic accident the law of the place of the physical injury must apply under the general rule 'irrespective of the financial or non-material damage sustained in another country'.[85] It cited *Marinari v Lloyds Bank*,[86] which is a jurisdiction case:

> The Manchester branch of Lloyds Bank refused to return some promissory notes to Mr Marinari which had been sequestered after the bank had notified the police that they were possibly stolen. He wanted compensation for the damage which he had allegedly suffered financially and to his reputation in Italy.

The CJEU held that the place where the harmful event occurred could not extend to any place where adverse consequences of the acts of the defendants had taken place. The initial damage had taken place in Manchester where the notes were sequestered and the later losses were indirect. Therefore, the loss of earnings following personal injury would also be indirect damage.

Financial loss, particularly from economic torts, can be especially difficult to locate. One might consider that any financial loss is suffered in the residence or principal place of business of the victim. The English case *ABCI v Banque Franco-Tunisienne*[87] was concerned with locating a tort for the purpose of determining the English court's jurisdiction under the national rules. The Court of Appeal held that the damage was suffered where the money was debited from the claimant's account. However, it is not necessarily the case that financial damage is suffered at the victim's residence. In *Kronhofer v Maier*, another case on Article 5(3) of the Brussels I Regulation:

> An Austrian claimant was persuaded by the German defendants to invest speculatively in call options in various companies, largely on the London Stock Exchange. The defendants had telephoned the claimant and he had transferred the money to Germany.[88] Austria was the country where his assets were concentrated. He argued that the harmful event had occurred in Austria where he was domiciled and presumably from where the money had been sent.

The CJEU held that the harmful event had not occurred in Austria. It appears that it was conceded that the damage was suffered in Germany[89] and also that the event giving rise to the damage occurred in Germany. So too in *Dumez*

---

[85] Commission Proposal COM(2003)427 final, 2003/0168 (COD) p. 11.
[86] Case C-364/93 [1995] ECR I-2719.   [87] [2003] EWCA Civ 205, [2003] 2 Lloyd's LR 146.
[88] Case C-168/02 [2004] ECR I-6009.   [89] *Ibid.* para. 17.

France SA and Tracoba SARL v Hessische Landesbank,[90] the French parent company did not suffer the loss due to the liquidation of a German subsidiary in Germany on its balance sheet in France. The harmful event occurred in Germany. This case can also be explained as an example of indirect damage.

It is possible that the place where the damage occurs may be fortuitous, in which case there would be very little connection with that place and its law. For example, a car accident in Ruritania in which an English woman is injured by the fault of her English husband could have happened anywhere. That is the archetypal case for an exception to the general rule. In other cases, the law of the place where the events occurred may have a stronger connection than the place of the damage. For example, a misrepresentation is made in a report compiled in Ruritania by a Ruritanian surveyor on the value of assets in Ruritania. The report is emailed to the purchaser, a Utopian company, which relies on the report to release moneys from a bank account in London to the vendor. The loss is arguably suffered in London but the events largely occurred in Ruritania. Again, those facts show the necessity for an exception to a strict rule based on the *lex loci damni.*

Article 4(1) is expressly subject to other provisions in the Regulation, such as Article 4(2); the specific rules for other torts;[91] the parties' right to choose the applicable law;[92] public policy;[93] and mandatory rules.[94]

ii. Common habitual residence

Where both the person suffering the damage and the party allegedly liable for the tort both have their habitual residence in the same country at the time the damage occurs, Article 4(2) provides that the law of their common habitual residence shall be the applicable law.[95] The language of Article 4(2) is surprisingly strict. It appears to apply the law of the common habitual residence despite any lack of connection with that country. For example, if X drives into Y, a pedestrian in Utopia, but both happened to be habitually resident in Ruritania, Ruritanian law applies even though there is no previous connection between the parties. It was often a pre-existing relationship founded in the common habitual residence which justified the application of the law of the common habitual residence.[96] For example, in the Canadian case of *McLean v Pettigrew*:

> Both the claimant and the defendant lived in Quebec. The defendant had offered the claimant a lift to Ottawa and they had an accident in Ontario caused by the defendant's driving. The claimant sued the defendant in Quebec. Under Quebec law the defendant was liable but under the law of Ontario the claimant was a 'guest' in the defendant's car and liability did not arise.

---

[90] Case C-220/88 [1990] ECR I-49.   [91] Articles 5 to 9.   [92] Article 14.
[93] Article 26.   [94] Article 16.   [95] Article 4(2).
[96] This was not so in the seminal case of *Boys v Chaplin* [1971] AC 356, in which English law was applied to a road accident in Malta as both parties came from England. However, they had no pre-existing relationship.

The Supreme Court of Canada held that the defendant was liable. The pre-existing relationship and common habitual residence made Quebec law more appropriate.[97] It does not appear to be straightforward that the *lex loci damni* can be applied instead of the law of the common habitual residence even using the displacement rule in Article 4(3). Article 4(3) seems to rule out the application of Article 4(1) as the more closely connected law. This means that even if the *lex loci damni* is more closely connected than the law of the common habitual residence, the law of the common habitual residence must apply.

Note that the habitual residence of the persons concerned will probably not fall within the definition in Article 23 as they are very likely to be natural persons not acting in the course of business. The English court faced with this problem may well fall back on the common law rules determining habitual residence discussed in Chapter 3. That practice can be criticised. First, because those rules have been developed for various purposes many of which are not the same nor even analogous to the purposes of this Regulation.[98] Secondly, in order for uniformity of application of this Regulation, an autonomous definition of habitual residence needs to be developed. This will need determination from the CJEU. There are a very few cases in which the CJEU has considered the meaning of habitual residence in EU legislation. One is *Mercredi v Chaffe*,[99] which is a case on the Brussels II *bis* Regulation.[100] There, the CJEU held that habitual residence of a child must correspond to the place which reflects some degree of integration by the child in a social and family environment. This is not particularly helpful in relation to adults. Inevitably there will be difficult cases, such as determining the habitual residence of the person who moves to another country to live during the week but returns 'home' for holidays or weekends; or locating the habitual residence of the itinerant worker. For choice of law purposes a single habitual residence must be identified.

b. Displacement

The applicable law identified by either Article 4(1) or (2) can be displaced if 'it is clear from all the circumstances of the case that the tort/delict is manifestly more closely connected with' another country.[101] An escape from the general

---

[97] The case has been overruled in Canada: *Tolofson v Jensen* [1994] 3 SCR 1022. A similar result was reached in the Scottish case of *M'Elroy v M'Allister* 1949 SC 110 and the English case of *Edmunds v Simmonds* [2001] 1 WLR 1003, albeit in the context of assessing damages.

[98] For example, habitual residence is critical to Council Regulation (EC) 2201/2003 concerning jurisdiction and the recognition and enforcement of judgments in matrimonial matters and the matters of parental responsibility [2003] OJ L338/1 (Brussels II*bis* Regulation). Residence, meaning habitual residence, is also regularly used in EU legislation on social security, see Regulation 1408/71, Art. 1. Habitual residence is also used for domestic taxation purposes. These are all very different to choice of law.

[99] Case C-497/10 [2011] 3 WLR 1229.   [100] Council Regulation (EC) 2201/2003.

[101] See also recital 18.

rule is needed especially where the connections between the parties, the events and the place of the damage are fortuitous or slight, particularly where there is a stronger connection with another country.[102] The wording is similar to that in the Rome I Regulation and raises similar questions. First, what is the relationship between the general rule and the exception? We have seen in the previous chapter that the CJEU favoured a middle way in deciding between the presumption and exception in Article 4 of the Rome Convention. In *Intercontainer Interfrigo SC (ICF) v Balkenende*,[103] the court rejected a strong model in which the rule was to be given effect unless there was *no* connection between the events and that law. The CJEU appeared to prefer some middle way between a strong presumption (i.e., applying the rules in Article 4(1) or (2) in the context of the Rome II Regulation) and the weakest model in which the presumption would be given effect only if there was some other connection with that country. The wording of Article 4 of both the Rome I Regulation and the Rome II Regulation make the rule clearer and the displacement weaker than the wording of the Rome Convention. Nevertheless, it is not clear that the changes go as far as to require the strong model which would prevent displacement of the general rules in Article 4(1) and (2) except in very rare cases.

Where the place of the accident is gratuitous, the rule of the *lex loci damni* is more easily displaced as there is no real connection with it.[104]

Note that Article 4(3) itself expresses that a pre-existing relationship, such as a contract, can form a manifestly closer connection. Therefore, if two friends who were sharing a flat together in England went to Australia on holiday where one caused an accident driving a car in which the other was injured, their pre-existing friendship may make English law applicable instead of that of New South Wales where the accident occurred.[105] Or if a solicitor was sued in negligence by her client the applicable law of the contract between them might be applied instead of the *lex loci damni*. The existence of a pre-existing relationship such as a contract does not require the application of the law applicable to the contract or relationship but exemplifies possible circumstances for displacement of the general rules in Article 4(1) and (2). It can be difficult to determine the law applicable to the pre-existing relationship if it is not a contract. For example, what law should be applicable to two friends who holiday together? In any event, the pre-existing relationship must be connected to the tort.

Secondly, what factors are to be taken into account in determining the closer connection? Closely related to that is the weight and significance to be

---

[102] See Explanatory Memorandum from the Commission on the Proposal for a Rome II Regulation, COM (2003)427 final (22 July 2003) [2004] OJ C96/8 at 12.

[103] Case C-133/08 [2009] ECR I-9687.

[104] See e.g., the pre-Rome II Regulation case of *Edmunds v Simmonds* [2001] 1 WLR 1003.

[105] See the facts of the pre-Rome II Regulation case *Harding v Wealands* [2006] UKHL 32, [2007] 2 AC 1.

attached to particular factors.[106] It is difficult to hypothesise precisely what will be the relevant factors and how to weigh their significance in displacing the rules in Article 4(1) and (2). All circumstances can be taken into account. These must include the connections between the parties and countries (such as their residence), and the connections between the events and countries (such as where the elements which make up the tort occurred, where direct and indirect harm was caused and suffered, and possibly where insurance was taken out).[107]

The pre-Rome II Regulation English law in the Private International Law (Miscellaneous Provisions) Act 1995 had a rule and exception structure and also required evaluation of the significance of factors connecting the tort to different countries. It might therefore be instructive to look at cases under that legislation. *Harding v Wealands*[108] is an interesting example:

> An Australian woman met an Englishman at a wedding in Australia and three months later moved to England to live with him. They had been sharing a flat in England for eight months before returning to Australia to holiday with her family. She drove her vehicle, insured in New South Wales, over some potholes and the claimant was very badly injured when the car turned over. They both returned to England but the relationship broke down. The claimant sued for his injuries as he needed a specially adapted bungalow and would not work again.

Under the Private International Law (Miscellaneous Provisions) Act 1984, the general rule was to apply the place where the events occurred (here New South Wales). There was an exception if it was 'substantially more appropriate' for another law to apply. At first instance, English law was applied by way of exception to the general rule.[109] Elias J noted the factors which connected the tort with New South Wales were that the accident occurred there; the defendant was an Australian national from New South Wales; she was driving on a New South Wales driving licence with New South Wales insurance; and the injuries were suffered there. He went on to list the factors connecting the tort with England. The claimant was British (*sic*); he had always lived and worked in England; he was domiciled in England at the relevant time; he and the

---

[106] In *Trafigura Beheer BV v Kookmin Bank Co.* [2006] EWHC 1450 (Comm), [2006] 2 Lloyd's LR 455 at para. 79, Aikens J noted that, in assessing the significance of various factors, he had to make a 'value judgement' about them. Although this was to be done in the context of the Private International Law (Miscellaneous Provisions) Act 1995, it is likely that a similar exercise must be undertaken to assess the country with which the tort is 'manifestly more closely connected' for Art. 4(3).

[107] The use of insurance as a factor is complicated. On the one hand, by taking out insurance a party has considered the risk and has some expectation that the party will be protected from liability under a particular law. On the other hand, insurance is an extrinsic factor that should not be allowed to determine whether liability exists.

[108] [2006] UKHL 32, [2007] 2 AC 1.   [109] [2004] EWHC 1957 (QB).

defendant were both resident in England and living together in a settled manner; and they were only in Australia for the purposes of a holiday. The consequences of the injury would be suffered by the claimant in England and the cost of dealing with the special care required in the future would have to be borne in England. The Court of Appeal disagreed and applied the general rule of the law of the place where the personal injury was suffered. Waller LJ held that it should be difficult to displace the law of the place where the injury was suffered when it was also the law of one of the parties. The defendant's link with New South Wales was no less significant than the claimant's link with England. He saw the parties' pre-existing relationship not as exclusively located in England as had Elias J at first instance.[110] A similar conclusion could be reached under the Rome II Regulation. The *lex loci damni* of New South Wales may be displaced by the manifestly closer connection with England, arising from the pre-existing relationship. The difference of opinion between Elias J and Waller LJ over the evaulation and significance of the pre-existing relationship would also remain.

An example which was decided under the old common law is *Johnson v Coventry Churchill International Ltd*. The double actionability test was subject to a flexible exception whereby a claimant could recover under the law with the closest connection to the tort:

> The claimant was an English joiner recruited by the defendant English employment agency to work on building sites in Germany. In the course of his work the claimant suffered injuries so he sought to recover damages from the defendants in England. The German state provided a type of no-fault compensation scheme under social security legislation but the scheme was not available to the claimant as he had not been employed for a sufficient time. He was also unable to claim redress directly from his employers under West German law as they were not in wilful breach of their duty.[111]

What was the law with the closest connection to the case? The employer defendant was English, as was the claimant. However, he was working in Germany and that was where the accident occurred. The factors appeared to be fairly evenly split between Germany and England. Nevertheless, the judge adopted a type of interest analysis often used in the US cases on choice of law in tort. He decided (after hearing expert evidence on German law) that the German rule was not intended to have application to foreign workmen working for foreigners. On the other hand, the English rules on protecting workers from the

---

[110] This conclusion was not appealed and the House of Lords judgment is confined to what was then a difficult question of the law to determine the assessment of damages. That is now a matter for the applicable law.

[111] [1993] 3 All ER 14.

negligence of their employers were intended to cover these circumstances, even though the worker was working abroad. Both parties probably expected that English law would govern their relationship and liability. Although not directly relevant in determining the close connection under the Rome II Regulation, a consideration of the significance of the various rules can be aided by questioning whether the rule is intended to apply in the particular circumstances where there is a foreign element. Applying a rule to circumstances which it was not intended to cover is obviously wrong. Interest analysis is of less help where both countries' laws are intended to cover the circumstances and they both conflict. English law could be applied in this case under the Rome II Regulation due to the pre-existing relationship which was centred in England.

Note that Article 4 identifies a law to govern the whole tort, rather than a particular issue in tort which is different from the approach under the Private International Law (Miscellaneous Provisions) Act 1995.

10. Rules of safety and conduct

Article 17 of the Rome II Regulation requires account to be taken 'as a matter of fact and so far as is appropriate' of the rules of safety and conduct in force at the place and time of the event giving rise to liability. It is rather unclear how this provision interacts with Article 4. Recital 34 explains that this provision is required to 'strike a reasonable balance between the parties'. The rules of safety and conduct include the road safety rules in the case of an accident. Article 17 was inspired by the Hague Traffic Accidents Convention[112] and the Hague Products Liability Convention.[113] It is clear that a driver has to follow the rules of the road where he or she is driving. So, for example, if there is a road accident in Ruritania for which a Utopian driver is liable to a Utopian victim under Article 4(2), Utopian law would be applicable. However, whether the driver was under the legal limit for alcohol or was above the speed limit should be a question for Ruritanian law. An English court would probably consider those examples as matters of fact rather than of law, so they would be determined as part of the context in which liability is to be established by Utopian law. Article 17 does not permit the direct application of the law of the place of the events, merely that account should be taken of it.

11. Particular non-contractual obligations

a. Product liability

A non-contractual obligation arising out of damage caused by a product has its own choice of law rule. Article 5 has a cascading structure. First, the law of the country of the habitual residence of the person damaged applies if the product

---

[112] Hague Convention of 1971 on the Law Applicable to Traffic Accidents.
[113] Hague Convention of 1973 on the Law Applicable to Products Liability.

was marketed in that country.[114] Failing that, next the law of the country in which the product was acquired applies, if the product was marketed in that country.[115] Failing that, next the law of the country in which the damage occurred applies if the product was marketed in that country.[116] However, in any event if the person allegedly liable could not reasonably foresee the marketing of the product in the country of the law which is applicable under the previous rules, then the law of the habitual residence of the person allegedly liable applies. If both parties have their habitual residence in the same country then the law of that country applies.[117] So, where a defective hairdryer purchased in Venusia causes damage to a Utopian resident on holiday in Ruritania, Utopian law applies if it was marketed in Utopia. If it was not marketed in Utopia, Venusian law applies and if it was not marketed in Venusia, then Ruritanian law applies. If it was not marketed in Ruritania, the general rules on product liability do not seem to apply and either the applicable law is determined by the general rule in Article 4 or perhaps the displacement rule in Article 5(2) applies. The displacement rule in Article 5(2) provides that the law of the country which is manifestly more closely connected with the tort applies. The important concept of 'marketed' is not defined but must include selling products through some type of sales network; maybe even advertising a product using the Internet might suffice so long as there is some direction of the advertising towards the consumers in that country.[118] Article 5 is not restricted to consumers but will extend to businesses sustaining damage. 'Product' is likely to be widely defined to include all movables and electricity.[119]

b. Unfair competition and restricting free competition

Article 6(1) and (2) of the Rome II Regulation cover the tort of unfair competition. It is difficult to define unfair competition exactly, especially because English domestic law contains no such tort. Clearly, it must have an autonomous definition. The Explanatory Memorandum notes that substantive rules of domestic law protecting unfair competition have three dimensions: protecting competitors, consumers and the public at large.[120] It says that unfair competition covers rules which 'outlaw acts calculated to influence demand (misleading advertising, forced sales, etc.), acts that impede competing supplies (disruption of deliveries by competitors, enticing away a competitor's staff, boycotts), and acts that exploit a competitor's value (passing off and the like)' as well as industrial espionage, disclosure of business secrets and

---

[114] Rome II Regulation, Art. 5(1)(a).　　[115] Article 5(1)(b).　　[116] Article 5(1)(c).

[117] Article 5 is expressly subject to Art. 4(2).

[118] See Dickinson, *The Rome II Regulation*, para. 5.20.

[119] Consistent with the definition in the Product Liability Directive (EC) 85/374 as amended by Directive 1999/34/EC.

[120] Explanatory Memorandum from the Commission on the Proposal for a Rome II Regulation, COM (2003)427 final (22 July 2003) [2004] OJ C96/8 at 15.

inducing breach of contract.[121] Although English law does not have a tort of unfair competition it does have torts of passing off, malicious falsehood and defamation against a competitor's goods. These fall within Article 6.

Article 6(2) provides that if the act of unfair competition 'affects exclusively the interests of a specific competitor, Article 4 shall apply'. In such a case, only a particular competitor is targeted. The editors of *Cheshire, North and Fawcett* say that this provision covers enticing away a competitor's staff, corruption, industrial espionage, intimidation, conspiracy, disclosure of business secrets or inducing breach of contract.[122] In other cases, the applicable law is the law of the country where competitive relations or the collective interests of consumers are affected. The Explanatory Memorandum informs us that this place is the market where the competitors are seeking their customers' favour.[123] The rule has two advantages: it protects the consumers as victims of the unfair competition and also promotes a level playing field for all competitors.

Article 6(3) deals with the distinct tort of restricting free competition. There are substantive domestic and EU rules dealing with competition law. Free competition can be impaired in a number of ways, including agreements between businesses to fix prices, abuse of a dominant position, erecting barriers to entry, and so on.[124] A breach of EU law which gives rise to a claim in damages which can be brought in the domestic courts is a tort within this provision. However, most actions would be brought by the European Commission and the Commission's action may not be characterised as a civil and commercial matter. If the market is or is likely to be affected in just one country, the law of that country applies.[125] Determining the market affected is a complex matter involving both law and economics.[126] If the market is or is likely to be affected in more than one country the applicable law can be allocated between the countries affected on a distributative basis. Alternatively, the claimant is given a possible choice of the law of the forum if (a) that country's market is 'amongst those directly and substantially affected' and (b) is the defendant's domicile.[127]

The applicable law under Article 6(1) or (3) cannot be derogated from by agreement.[128]

c. Environmental damage

The law applicable to non-contractual obligations arising out of acts causing environmental damage is the *lex loci damni*, i.e., the law of the place where the damage was sustained.[129] However, the claimant may choose to base the claim

---

[121] *Ibid.* pp. 15–16.   [122] *Cheshire, North and Fawcett*, p. 810.
[123] Explanatory Memorandum from the Commission on the Proposal for a Rome II Regulation, p. 16.
[124] See recital 23 and Arts 101 and 102 TFEU.   [125] Rome II Regulation, Art. 6(3)(a).
[126] See Dickinson, *The Rome II Regulation*, paras 6.63–6.64.   [127] Article 6(3)(b).
[128] Article 6(4).   [129] Article 7 refers the question to the law determined pursuant to Art. 4(1).

on the law of the country in which the event giving rise to the damage occurred.[130] Recital 24 gives the definition of environmental damage as 'adverse change in a natural resource such as water, land or air, impairment of a function performed by that resource for the benefit of another natural resource or the public, or impairment of the variability among living organisms'. This can be compared with the more detailed definition in the Environmental Liability Directive.[131] That Directive gives no right of compensation to the person damaged, although national law may do so.

d. Infringements of intellectual property rights

Infringements of intellectual property rights are considered special torts requiring specific rules. The two international Conventions[132] emphasise the primacy of the law of the country in which protection is claimed but do not give clear choice of law rules. Recital 26 provides 'the term "intellectual property rights" should be interpreted as meaning, for instance, copyright, related rights, the *sui generis* right for the protection of databases and industrial property rights'. Patents, trademarks and registered designs would be included but other rights such as plant rights could also be brought within Article 8.[133] Article 8 lays down two choice of law rules. First, where the intellectual property right is conferred under national legislation or an international convention, Article 8(1) makes the applicable law that of the country for which protection is claimed, which for a registered right is where it is registered. So a case for the infringement of a patent registered in England would be determined according to English law; that law requires the infringement also to have taken place in England. For copyright, that country would be where the infringement is committed. Secondly, where the infringement concerns a unitary Community intellectual property right, Article 8(2) provides that the applicable law shall be the law of the country in which the infringement was committed unless the question is governed by the relevant Community instrument[134] (in which case the Community instrument applies). There is no exception to Article 8 for common habitual residence or more close connection or choice of law by the parties.

---

[130] Article 7.

[131] Article 2 of Directive 2004/35/EC on environmental liability with regard to the prevention and remedying of environmental damage [2004] OJ L143/56, as amended [2006] OJ L102/15.

[132] The 1886 Berne Convention for the Protection of Literary and Artistic Works and the 1883 Paris Convention for the Protection of Industrial Property, both of which have been subsequently revised and amended.

[133] *Cheshire, North and Fawcett*, p. 815.

[134] For example, the Community Trademarks Regulation (EC) 40/1994, see Dickinson, *The Rome II Regulation*, para. 8.31.

e. Industrial action

Non-contractual action arising from industrial action includes the liability of individuals for strikes and lock-outs.[135] It is not clear from recital 27 whether non-contractual obligations in respect of industrial action are to be given an autonomous meaning. English law does not have a tort of industrial action although actions for inducement to breach of contract, for intimidation and for unlawful conspiracy can arise out of strikes. Article 9 provides that the applicable law 'in respect of the liability of a person in the capacity of a worker or an employer or the organisations representing their professional interests for damages caused by an industrial action, pending or carried out, shall be the law of the country where the action is to be, or has been, taken'. Workers acting lawfully according to the law of the place where they act are thereby protected. The rule in Article 9 is subject to the displacement rule in Article 4(2) where the parties share a common habitual residence. There is no exception for a more close connection. Recital 28 makes Article 9 'without prejudice to the conditions relating to the exercise of such action in accordance with national law and without prejudice to the legal status of trade unions or of the representative organisations of workers as provided for in the law of the Member States'.

f. Unjust enrichment

As we have seen earlier in this chapter, there are difficulties separating unjust enrichment from tort. Unjust enrichment will have an autonomous meaning, probably drawn from the principles common to the laws of the Member States. In *Masdar (UK) Ltd v Commission of the European Communities*,[136] the CJEU drew upon these principles in a different context.[137] The court noted that 'a person who has suffered a loss which increases the wealth of another person without there being any legal basis for that enrichment has the right, as a general rule, to restitution from the person enriched, up to the amount of the loss'.[138] An action for unjust enrichment in English domestic law can lie in property,[139] contract, tort or equity. If the claim falls into the latter two domestic classifications, the applicable law is determined by the Rome II Regulation. If it is a tort, the applicable law is determined by Article 4; if it is an obligation arising out of unjust enrichment it falls under Article 10.

---

[135] Recital 27.   [136] Case C-47/07P [2008] ECR I-9761.

[137] The claimant was suing the European Commission under Art. 288 of the EC Treaty (now Art. 340 TFEU).

[138] Case C-47/07P [2008] ECR I-9761 at para. 1.

[139] In which case the correct choice of law rule is one in property, see *Macmillan Inc. v Bishopsgate Investment Trust plc (No. 3)* [1996] 1 WLR 387 (CA). In that case a claimant alleged it was beneficially entitled to shares which had been held on trust and wrongfully assigned by the trustee. The claim sought their return or compensation for their loss.

Delineating contract from unjust enrichment is not straightforward, neither is separating tort or equity from unjust enrichment a clearcut matter. The consequences of nullity of a contract are expressly included in the Rome I Regulation and so must be considered contractual.[140] However, Article 10(1) of the Rome II Regulation specifically mentions payment of amounts wrongfully received. The editors of *Cheshire, North and Fawcett* argue that it is likely that other restitutionary claims, such as restitution for wrongdoing[141] as well as unjust enrichment by subtraction, should be determined under Article 10 rather than Article 4.[142]

Article 10(1) provides that the obligation arising out of unjust enrichment which concerns a relationship existing between the parties such as a contract or tort shall be governed by the law which governs the relationship. This is an example of a secondary connection principle. It generally aligns the applicable law with that which would determine the liability if it were to be characterised as contractual[143] or tortious.[144] The obligation arising out of the unjust enrichment must be separate from the relationship in contract or tort which would have its own governing law. The obligation must be closely connected with the relationship. Therefore, if the claimant sues the defendant for the value of the goods wrongfully sold by the defendant although belonging to the claimant (which is the tort of conversion), the law which governs the tort under Article 4 also covers the unjust enrichment claim.[145] However, where the applicable law cannot be determined under Article 10(1) *and* the parties have a common habitual residence, Article 10(2) makes the law of the country of the common habitual residence apply. Article 10(3) applies the law of the country in which the unjust enrichment took place if the applicable law cannot be determined under Article 10(1) or (2). Finally, if it is clear from all the circumstances of the case that the unjust enrichment is manifestly more closely connected with a country other than that already indicated in Article 10, Article 10(4) makes the law of the more closely connected country apply instead. It is quite likely that this escape provision will permit national courts to continue to apply their pre-existing choice of law rules where they desire to do so, either by using the general rule or the exception. That would lead to a lack of uniformity throughout the EU.

---

[140] Rome I Regulation, Art. 12(1)(e).

[141] So long as this was not restitution for a contractual wrongdoing, which would fall within the Rome I Regulation.

[142] *Cheshire, North and Fawcett*, p. 825. Both Dickinson, *The Rome II Regulation*, para. 10.16 and the editors of *Dicey, Morris and Collins, The Conflict of Laws* (14th edn, Sweet & Maxwell, London, 4th cumulative supplement 2011) p. 433) are much less certain of this.

[143] I.e., Rome I Regulation, Art. 4.   [144] I.e., Rome II Regulation, Art. 4.

[145] The claimant could sue for the value of the sale, which would be a claim in tort and fall directly within Art. 4.

g. *Negotiorum gestio*

Liability for *negotiorum gestio* is not known in English domestic law. It can be described as liability arising between an agent and a principal when the agent acts without the authority of the principal.[146] Note that *negotiorum gestio* does not apply between the third party and the agent or the third party and the principal.[147] It must have an autonomous meaning. Article 11 refers to 'a non-contractual obligation arising out of an act performed without due authority in connection with the affairs of another person'. As with Article 10, Article 11(1) applies the law governing the relationship where the non-contractual obligation concerns a relationship existing between the parties such as one in contract or tort which is closely connected to the non-contractual obligation. Therefore, where a principal is suing an agent for damage suffered when the agent entered into a contract on the principal's behalf but without authority and there is a contract of agency, the law applicable to the contract of agency will determine if liability arises. Where the parties have a common habitual residence *and* the applicable law cannot be determined by Article 11(1), Article 11(2) makes the law of the common habitual residence apply. Then, if the applicable law cannot be determined by Article 11(1) or (2), the law of the country in which the act was performed will apply.[148] As with Article 4 and Article 10, exceptionally the law of the more closely connected country will apply.[149]

h. *Culpa in contrahendo*

Culpa in contrahendo is to have an autonomous meaning.[150] It includes 'the violation of the duty of disclosure and the breakdown of contractual negotiations'. Liability for precontractual negotiations which are converted into contractual obligations at the conclusion of the contract (such as warranties based upon assumptions made during negotiations) are enforced by suing on the contract. Those obligations fall within the Rome I Regulation even if the contract is vitiated.[151] Nevertheless, the Rome I Regulation does not apply to 'obligations arising out of dealings prior to the conclusion of a contract'.[152] The Rome II Regulation is concerned with distinct obligations which are not contractual but which may arise in the parties' precontractual relationship. Some precontractual obligations derive from tort and would fall within Article 4, others are concerned with the duty to negotiate in good faith. It is these latter obligations which form the basis of Article 12. However, Article 12 'covers only non-contractual obligations presenting a direct link with the

---

[146] Explanatory Memorandum from the Commission on the Proposal for a Rome II Regulation, p. 21.
[147] See Dickinson, *The Rome II Regulation*, para. 11.05.   [148] Article 11(3).
[149] Article 11(4).   [150] Recital 30.   [151] See Rome I Regulation, Arts 10, 12.
[152] *Ibid.* Art. 1(2)(i).

dealings prior to the conclusion of a contract'.[153] Article 12 applies regardless of whether the contract was concluded or not.[154] Article 12(1) makes the applicable law of a non-contractual obligation arising out of dealings prior to the conclusion of a contract the same law as the applicable law of the contract or which would have been applicable had the contract been entered into. That has the effect that the parties can choose the law to govern their non-contractual obligation arising out of dealings prior to the conclusion of their contract. It is a rigid rule without the possibility of displacement. However, if the applicable law cannot be determined on the basis of Article 12(1), the applicable law is either (a) the law of the country in which the damage occurs;[155] or (b) if the parties have a common habitual residence, that law; or (c) if it is manifestly more closely connected with a country other than that in (a) or (b), that law.[156]

12. Parties' choice of law

By Article 14(1)(a) of the Rome II Regulation the parties may choose the law applicable to a non-contractual obligation. This can be done after the event giving rise to the damage. Alternatively, it can be done by an agreement freely negotiated before the event giving rise to the damage if the parties are 'pursuing a commercial activity'. Article 14(1)(a) is a novel provision. Possibly, it permits the application of the English rule allowing parties to refrain from pleading and proving foreign law and just relying on English law to apply to determine a non-contractual obligation.[157] Alternatively, the English court may decide that the rule is one of procedure and excluded from the Rome II Regulation by Article 1(3). However, if all the elements relevant to the situation are located within country X and the parties had chosen the law of country Y, the choice cannot prejudice the application of the rules of country X which cannot be derogated from by contract.[158] The choice of law to govern the non-contractual obligation must be express or demonstrated with reasonable certainty. Third party rights cannot be prejudiced by the choice of law. This is explained in the Explanatory Memorandum as '[t]he typical example is the insurer's obligation to reimburse damages payable by the insured'.[159]

---

[153] Rome II Regulation, recital 30.   [154] Article 12(1).

[155] This can be especially difficult to determine in the case of negligent or fraudulent misrepresentation, see e.g., the jurisdiction case of *Raiffeisen Zentral Bank Osterreich AG v Alexander Tranos* [2001] ILPr. 85.

[156] Article 12(2).

[157] The English rule was upheld in a case on the Private International Law (Miscellaneous Provisions) Act 1995 in *Parker v Tui UK Ltd* [2009] EWCA Civ 1261.

[158] Article 14(2). The freedom of choice does not apply to infringements of intellectual property rights (Art. 8(3)) or unfair competition claims (Art. 6(4)). If all the elements occur within the EU and the parties have chosen a third state's law, the provisions of Community law which cannot be derogated from by contract will apply (Art. 14(3)).

[159] Explanatory Memorandum from the Commission on the Proposal for a Rome II Regulation, p. 22.

13. Liability in both contract and tort

In domestic law a claim in the English courts can be pleaded in any manner the claimant wishes. The claim may omit possible claims, or the possible claims can be pleaded alternatively or concurrently. If the claims are pleaded in the alternative, the claimant may succeed on one or the other, or both.[160] If the latter, then the claimant can only recover one set of damages as the judgment is then satisfied. However, as a matter of choice of law, the picture is more complicated. In theory, if a claim is made in contract, the contractual choice of law rules in the previous chapter apply to that claim. Alternatively, if a claim is made for a non-contractual obligation, the choice of law rules from this chapter apply to that claim. Some causes of action in English law do give rise to alternative and separate possible claims. It can be argued that as the meaning of a contractual claim or a non-contractual claim is autonomously defined and the CJEU considers a claim can fall only into one category or another, the claimant no longer has a totally free choice. If the liability is concurrent, for example, where the duty to take reasonable care is implied into a contract, the problem is difficult. Is this to be categorised as contractual or non-contractual? The duty to take care is a non-contractual imposition of liability but clearly that duty is being implied into a contract. The problem is obviously acute when the contractual and non-contractual aspects are subject to different applicable laws. Before both Rome I and Rome II Regulations, the English courts have categorised that type of claim as contractual for jurisdictional purposes.[161] The editors of *Cheshire, North and Fawcett* argue that this is unlikely to be the correct solution after the Rome I and Rome II Regulations.[162] The Rome II Regulation itself envisages the situations where there is a pre-existing contractual relationship between the parties to a tortious claim.[163] Those issues at least are to be resolved by application of the Rome II Regulation. The contract is a factor to take into account in determining the applicable law of the particular question, rather than the final determination of that applicable law. So, for example, the employer's duty of care to employees should be dealt with under the Rome II Regulation despite a contract of employment.[164]

---

[160] For example, see *Base Metal Trading Ltd v Shamurin* [2004] EWCA Civ 1316, [2005] 1 WLR 1157.

[161] *Source Ltd v TUV Rheinland Holding AG* [1998] QB 54.

[162] *Cheshire, North and Fawcett*, p. 779.

[163] Rome II Regulation, Arts 4(3), 5(2), 10(1) and 11(1).

[164] In practice, the applicable law is unlikely to differ from that of the contract. In *Base Metal Trading Ltd v Shamurin* [2004] EWCA Civ 1316, [2005] 1 WLR 1157, the directors' tortious duty of care was considered non-contractual despite a contract between the directors and the company. Nevertheless, both the contract and the duty of care were governed by Russian law under which no liability arose.

14. Effect of a contract limiting liability

The effect of a contractual defence excluding, limiting or exempting an apparent liability in tort raises difficult questions in conflict of laws. This is a different problem to the one just discussed of concurrent liability. Here, the issue is which law should apply to determine the validity and effect of the defence? Is it a contractual or tortious matter for choice of law? There are several options: the contractual exemption clause is valid under the contract's applicable law and effective as a defence in tort under the law applicable to the tort. Or, the contractual exemption clause is invalid under the applicable law of the contract but effective as a defence to the tortious liability under the tort's applicable law. Or the contractual exemption clause is valid under the law of the contract but ineffective as a defence under the law of the tort. Or, lastly, the contractual exemption clause is invalid under the law of the contract and ineffective as a defence to the tort under the applicable law of the tort. The last is the most straightforward, the contractual defence fails. The other three possibilities raise the issue of characterisation.

There is often a concern that the stronger party to a contract imposes an exemption clause on the weaker party and deliberately chooses a contractual applicable law to give effect to the clause. A choice of a law to govern tortious liability and any defence is permitted by Article 14 of the Rome II Regulation only if all the parties are pursuing a commercial activity. In any event, where such exemption clauses are invalidated by the mandatory overriding rules of the forum (i.e., English law), the exemption clause will be denied effect.[165] The problem is illustrated by the common law case of *Sayers v International Drilling Co. NV*:

> The claimant was an English oil rig worker and was engaged by a Netherlands company under a contract which contained no express choice of the applicable law. However, it did contain limited compensation in the event of accidents and excluded liability beyond that. Such clauses are invalid under English law but are valid under Dutch law. He was injured on a rig off the coast of Nigeria and claimed against the Netherlands defendants for his injuries. The company pleaded as a defence to liability that it had paid the limited compensation provided for in the contract.[166]

The correct approach[167] is to decide as follows. (1) What is the contractual applicable law? If the clause is invalid under that law it should not be allowed

---

[165] Article 16.

[166] [1971] 1 WLR 1176; L. Collins, 'Exemption Clauses, Employment Contracts and the Conflict of Laws' (1972) 21 *ICLQ* 320; P. Carter, 'Renvoi and the Proof of Foreign Law in Australia' (1971) 45 *BYBIL* 404.

[167] Fentiman, *International Commercial Litigation*, para. 16.75, advocates this for pre-Rome II Regulation cases.

to operate as a defence by recharacterising it as tortious. If it is valid, then (2) is the clause effective to provide a defence to liability under the law applicable to the tort? Article 15(b) of the Rome II Regulation provides that the law applicable to the tort governs the grounds for exemption from liability and any exemption from liability. Note (3) there may be overriding mandatory rules of English law which avoid even a valid and effective clause from preventing liability.[168] The editors of *Cheshire, North and Fawcett* prefer to apply the Rome II Regulation exclusively[169] but the danger is that a clause invalid under the law which governs the contract is given greater effect than is possible by the law which governs the contract. Dickinson looks to the tortious applicable law first and then whether that law requires a contract to exclude or limit liability to determine the effect of the contractual clause according to the Rome I Convention.[170] It can be difficult to draw a distinction between the validity of the exemption clause (a matter of contract) and its effectiveness (a matter of tort). In practice, it is quite likely that the law governing the contract also is the applicable law of the tort as there is a relationship between the parties which can be given weight in determining a manifestly closer connection. In any event, the forum's mandatory rules will be applied which may prevent the effectiveness of the most egregious exemption clauses.

15. Mandatory rules and public policy

As one might expect, the rules of the forum which are mandatory 'irrespective of the law otherwise applicable to non-contractual obligations' override the applicable law. These are internationally mandatory rules.[171] Such rules are likely to be concerned with the prevention of any limitation or exclusion of liability and would raise the question of the relationship between non-contractual obligations and contractual obligations discussed in the previous heading. Domestic mandatory rules are applicable in the case in which the parties have chosen a law to govern their non-contractual obligation but where all the elements relevant to the situation are located in one country.[172] Also, Article 26 of the Rome II Regulation preserves the public policy of the forum. The English court is permitted to refuse to apply a provision of law if the application of that law is manifestly incompatible with the public policy of the forum. An example of this can be found in *Kuwait Airways Corp. v Iraqi Airways Co. (Nos 4 and 5)*:

---

[168] *Ibid.* para. 16.75 cites the example of Misrepresentation Act 1967, s. 3.
[169] *Cheshire, North and Fawcett*, p. 865.
[170] Dickinson, *The Rome II Regulation*, para. 14.15.
[171] See the discussion at p. 321 *et seq.* above.   [172] Article 14(2).

The Republic of Iraq had confiscated six aircraft belonging to the claimants Kuwait Airways during the Gulf War of 1990. The aircraft had been transferred to the defendants and largely destroyed by the action of the United States and their allies liberating Kuwait. The claimants sued the defendants in conversion and applied for damages. The defendants argued that liability did not exist due to a Resolution of the Iraqi government giving title to the aircraft to the defendants.[173]

The House of Lords accepted that Iraqi law was applicable. However, the Resolution was not given effect to as it infringed English public policy. It was in flagrant breach of clearly established principles of public international law of a particular kind. The invasion of Kuwait had been condemned by the UN Security Council and a resolution of the Security Council had in terms exhorted no recognition to be given to the Iraqi invasion.[174] With the Iraqi government's Resolution excised, Iraqi law applied to leave title with the claimants, who then were able to claim damages for the tort of conversion. It is an open question whether a cause of action would lie in respect of torture committed by a foreign state official in a foreign country where torture does not give rise to liability as a matter of the foreign law. The foreign law condoning torture may well be contrary to established principles of public international law. Up until the present the claims have mostly fallen at the jurisdictional stage as being non-justiciable or contrary to the act of state doctrine.[175] The Rome II Regulation does not apply to the liability of a state for acts and omissions in the exercise of state authority[176] but if a claimant is suing an individual torturer, it might be argued that the liability is not that of the state.

16. Defamation, etc. (the common law rule of double actionability)

The Rome II Regulation does not presently apply to claims for 'non-contractual obligations arising out of violations of privacy and rights relating to personality including defamation'.[177] Proposals to include those non-contractual obligations have been suggested by the Committee on Legal Affairs of the European Parliament[178] but these have not been developed

---

[173] [2002] UKHL 19, [2002] 2 AC 883; P. Rogerson, 'Kuwait Airways Corp. v Iraqi Airways Corp.: The Territoriality Principle in Private International Law: Vice or Virtue' (2003) 56 CLP 265.

[174] UN Security Council Resolutions 661 and 662.

[175] As for example in Jones v Saudi Arabia [2006] UKHL 26, [2007] 1 AC 270. However, claims for torture were settled without admitting liability in Al Rawi and others v Security Service and others [2011] UKSC 34, [2012] 1 AC 531.

[176] Article 1(1).   [177] Article 1(2)(g).

[178] Working Document on the amendment of Regulation (EC) 864/2007 on the law applicable to non-contractual obligations (23 May 2011).

further.[179] Neither did these claims fall within the Private International Law (Miscellaneous Provisions) Act 1995. These therefore fall to be considered under the traditional common law rules. In English domestic law these would cover the torts of malicious falsehood, slander and libel, often called collectively defamation. If a coherent tort of breach of privacy were to be developed that would also be determined by the common law. If the tort of defamation was committed in England, then English domestic law would apply.[180] In order to be committed in England both the publication of the defamatory statement and the reputation damaged must be in England. However, where the tort has occurred via acts in more than one country, say the publication of the defamatory statement in a newspaper in France but the claimant was only known in England, matters become more complicated.

The common law cases developed in relation to torts arising out of physical injury. The general rule was one of double actionability. In order to recover in England the tort had to be actionable (i.e., giving rise to a claim) under both the law of England[181] and the law of the place where it was done.[182] The double actionability test derives from two cases. The first was *The Halley*[183] which required the act to give rise to a claim in England. A ship-owner was found not liable for the actions of a pilot causing damage in Belgium. The act did not give rise to liability in the ship-owner under English law, even though there was liability under Belgian law where the accident happened. The second was *Phillips v Eyre*,[184] by which the governor of Jamaica escaped liability for the tort of battery as his conduct had been excused by legislation in Jamaica where the tort was committed despite the act being tortious in English law.

The double actionability rule was subject to a flexible exception by which a more closely connected law would be applied instead, despite the claim not giving rise to a tort under the law of the place where the tort occurred. So in *Boys v Chaplin*,[185] where the act of the defendant gave rise to a claim for pain and suffering under English law but not under the law of Malta where the accident happened, the claimant could recover. This exception was extended in *Red Sea Insurance Co. v Bouygues SA*,[186] in which the claimant was permitted to recover damages where these were available under the law of

---

[179] The conclusion was only tentative, and adopted a position suggested by Prof. Jan von Hein. He proposed that the applicable law for violations of privacy and rights relating to personality should be 'the law of the country where the rights of the person seeking compensation for damage are, or are likely to be, directly and substantially affected. However, the law applicable shall be the law of the country in which the person claimed to be liable is habitually resident if he or she could not reasonably foresee substantial consequences of his or her act occurring in the country designated by the first sentence.'

[180] *Szalatny-Stacho v Fink* [1947] KB 1; *Jameel v Dow Jones & Co. Inc.* [2005] EWCA Civ 75, [2005] QB 946.

[181] The *lex fori*.   [182] The *lex loci delicti commissi*.

[183] *Liverpool, Brazil and River Plate Steam Navigation Co. Ltd v Benham* (1867–69) LR 2 PC 193 (PC).

[184] (1870–71) LR 6 QB 1 (QB).   [185] [1971] AC 356.   [186] [1994] 3 WLR 926 (PC).

the place where the tort was committed but not under English law. The rule can now be stated that claimant can only recover for an act of defamation if:

> it is both (a) actionable as such according to English law (or, in other words, is an act which, if done in England, would give rise to such a claim) *and* (b) actionable according to the law of the foreign country where it was done ... By way of exception ... a particular issue between the parties which arises in a defamation claim may be governed by the law of the country which, with respect to that issue, has the most significant relationship with the occurrence and the parties.[187]

The choice of law rule is not commonly raised in defamation cases. In practice the case will not be heard in England unless the defamation happens here. If the case falls into the national rules on jurisdiction the English court will stay the action at the jurisdictional stage, unless the publication was substantially done in England.[188] If the case falls into the Brussels I Regulation, the CJEU has held that the place where the harmful event occurred in defamation is where the publication was distributed and where the claimant suffered damage to the claimant's reputation.[189]

If the case is exceptionally heard in England, the English court will have to determine where the tort of defamation was committed. In *Church of Scientology of California v Metropolitan Police Commissioner*,[190] the defamation was committed in Germany where the report was published by being sent to the Berlin police but not in England where the report was prepared. The place where the tort was committed being the place of publication can be unsatisfactory for cases of defamation over the Internet.[191] The defamation must be actionable according to that law and also according to English law (i.e., there must be no defence of justification, for example). If the tort is not actionable by one or other law then it is possible that the flexible exception applies to provide a remedy. So, if the defamation was published in Ruritania where truth is not a defence to the tort it would be actionable under Ruritanian law but not English law. In theory, the English court should then identify which law has the most significant and close connection with the issue of the availability of the defence. That law should then be applied to determine whether liability is established. It is somewhat unlikely that an English court would decide that the closest connection or most significant relationship is with Ruritania and thus permit a defamation action in England upon a true statement. It is also somewhat unlikely that any law other than the law of the place of publication will have the most significant relationship with the tort of

---

[187] Rule 235 in *Dicey, Morris and Collins*, p. 1957 (emphasis added).
[188] *Berezovsky v Michaels* [2000] 1 WLR 1004 (HL).
[189] *Shevill v Presse Alliance* Case C-68/93 [1995] ECR I-41.   [190] (1976) 120 Sol. Jo. 690.
[191] See the Australian case of *Dow Jones & Co. Inc. v Gutnick* [2002] HCA 56, which decided that the place of publication is where the material was downloaded, if the claimant has a reputation which is damaged in that place.

defamation. A possible example is where the claimant and defendant have a common habitual residence and the place of publication is fortuitous, such as one friend slandering another on holiday. Even in that case, damage to reputation is necessary in order to complete the tort and that place is unlikely to be fortuitous.

17. Trusts

The 1986 Hague Convention on the law applicable to trusts has been enacted in the Recognition of Trusts Act 1987. Although the Convention does not create trusts in the substantive law of contracting states which do not have such a concept, those states are required to recognise trusts for the purposes of private international law. Most of the rules in the Convention deal with laying down the choice of law rules to govern trusts and only a few articles deal with their recognition. The main interest of the United Kingdom in the conclusion of the Convention was not so much in laying down choice of law rules but in securing the recognition of English trusts by other countries' courts.

a. Application of the Hague Convention

The Convention[192] applies to trusts created voluntarily and evidenced in writing.[193] Purely oral trusts, for example, are not within it directly. However, in England both oral trusts and other types of trust (such as those created by judicial decisions) can be recognised according to the same provisions.[194] Article 3 also excludes trusts created by judicial decision, though Article 20 allows contracting states to extend the Convention to such trusts, and this was done in s. 1(2) of the Recognition of Trusts Act 1987.

The Hague Convention provides that 'the term "trust" refers to the legal relationships created – *inter vivos* or on death – by a person, the settlor, when assets have been placed under the control of a trustee for the benefit of a beneficiary or for a specified purpose'.[195] The Convention covers both charitable and commercial trusts. The personal liability to account as a constructive trustee is therefore excluded from the Convention and falls within the Rome II Regulation on non-contractual obligations. Resulting trusts are also excluded as they are not generally in writing. Constructive trusts which are evidenced in writing (such as those arising from mutual wills) will fall within the Convention but most will not. The editors of *Dicey, Morris and Collins* argue that a claim to recover assets of an express written trust which have been wrongfully

---

[192] 1986 Hague Convention on the Law Applicable to Trusts and on their Recognition; the Explanatory Report by Prof. von Overbeck can be found at www.hcch.net/upload/expl30.pdf.

[193] Article 3.

[194] Recognition of Trusts Act 1987 s. 1(2); see *Berezovsky v Abramovich* [2011] EWCA Civ 153, [2011] 1 WLR 2290.

[195] Article 2.

dissipated such that the third party holds the assets on constructive trust falls within the Convention.[196] The Convention lays out the characteristics of a trust which conform to the characteristics of an English trust, such as the assets constituting a separate fund and not being part of the trustee's estate.[197]

The Convention does not apply to what Article 4 calls 'preliminary issues' but only to questions concerning the validity and operation of the trust provisions themselves. This means that it does not deal with questions which relate to the validity of the instrument which creates the trust. This is governed by the law which governs the validity of wills or contracts generally.[198] Nor does it govern the valid transfer of property into the trust. That is governed by the law which governs the transfer of property, which is the *lex situs* for tangible and immovable property and the law of the underlying obligation for intangible property.[199] It can be difficult to draw a distinction between preliminary issues and the ability to create a trust, which is within the Convention.[200] For example, the rule against perpetuities could be argued to be a rule relating to the transfer of property or equally as a rule on the creation of a trust.[201] The law governing the capacity of the settlor, beneficiary and trustee all fall to be determined by the common law rules outside the Convention as they are preliminary issues.

The Convention applies whatever the governing law of the trust might be. It applies to recognition of all trusts and not only where the governing law is that of a contracting state. It is irrelevant that the trust is established under the law of a contracting or non-contracting state.[202]

b. Choice of law rules: the governing law

Article 6 of the Hague Convention provides that the trust is to be governed by the law chosen by the settlor. The settlor's choice may be *express* or *implied* from the terms of the instrument which creates or the writing which evidences the trust, interpreted in the light of the circumstances of the case.[203] No further assistance is given as to how the implication is to be made.[204]

The settlor's freedom of choice may be limited to some extent at least by the application of mandatory rules of English law or by the requirements of English public policy.[205]

---

[196] *Dicey, Morris and Collins*, para. 29–007.   [197] Article 2(a).

[198] The Rome I Regulation does not apply to many aspects of trusts (Art. 1(2)(h)). Likewise, the Rome II Regulation has excluded many aspects of trust (Art. 1(2)(e)).

[199] See further Chapter 12.   [200] *Re Barton's Estate, Tod v Barton* [2002] EWCH 264 (Ch).

[201] See D. Hayton, P. Matthews and C. Mitchell, *Underhill and Hayton's Law of Trusts and Trustees* (18th edn, Sweet & Maxwell, London, 2010) para. 100.107.

[202] Recognition of Trusts Act 1987, s. 1(4).   [203] Article 6.

[204] Perhaps implications can be drawn from such factors as the *situs* of the property and the presumed intention of the settlor that the governing law should be one under which the trust is valid.

[205] Articles 15, 16 and 18 and Art. 13.

Article 7 states that, in the absence of an express or implied choice of law, a trust is governed by the law with which it is most closely connected. This is to be ascertained by reference, in particular, to (a) the place of administration designated by the settlor; (b) the *situs* of the assets; (c) the trustee's place of residence or business; and (d) the objects of the trust and places where those are to be fulfilled.[206] These considerations are not exclusive of others. It might be possible to refer to the settlor's domicile, as was done in *Iveagh v IRC*.[207] Jacob J had to decide the governing law of a trust under Article 7 in *The Armenian Patriarch of Jerusalem v Sonsino*:

> The claimant had an interest in the income arising from the capital of the settlement. The defendant was the residuary beneficiary who would gain if the trusts failed as not being charitable. There was no express choice of law in the settlement. The settlor was originally from Iraq, married a Scot and acquired British citizenship. She then divorced, remarried an Indian and lived in Italy and India but often visited London. The assets had been removed (with permission of the Indian government) from India to control of the professional bank trustee based in London. The settlement provided for the income to be paid to the Armenian Patriarchate of Jerusalem.[208]

Jacob J considered that the possibilities were the laws of England, Jerusalem or India. As the parties were not prepared to argue that the law of Jerusalem applied,[209] the choice was between India and England. He held that the closest connection was with England: the assets were under the control of an English professional trustee, the settlor was resident in England at the time of making the settlement and there was a particular direction about investment in English property (though the trustees could invest elsewhere). It appears he also thought this was the intention of the settlor.[210]

If under the chosen law, trusts are not provided for or the category of trust involved in the instrument are not provided for, the choice of law is ineffective. In that case Article 7 determines the applicable law. Therefore, such a trust is governed by the law with which it is most closely connected.

Article 8 of the Hague Convention provides that the applicable law specified by Articles 6 or 7 shall govern the validity, construction, effects and administration of the trust. Article 8 then continues with particular examples of matters which the applicable law governs:

(a) the appointment, resignation and removal of trustees, the capacity to act as a trustee and the devolution of the office of trustee;

---

[206] *Chellaram v Chellaram* [1985] Ch. 409.   [207] [1954] Ch. 364.
[208] [2002] EWHC 1304 (Ch).
[209] It was not clear whether that would be Israeli law or that of Jordan.
[210] [2002] EWHC 1304 (Ch) at para. 13.

(b) the rights and duties of the trustees among themselves;

(c) their right to delegate in whole or in part the discharge of their duties or the exercise of their powers;

(d) their powers to administer, dispose of, create security interests in or to acquire new trust assets;

(e) trustees, powers of investment;

(f) restrictions on the duration of the trust and on accumulation of its income;

(g) the relationship between the trustees and beneficiaries, including the former's personal liability to the latter;

(h) variation and termination of the trust;

(i) distribution of the trust's assets; and

(j) the trustees' liability to account.

Other issues are not excluded and would also be governed by the applicable law in-so-far as the issue is not excluded from the Convention or covered by another article.

Article 9 states that a severable aspect of a trust, in particular its administration, may be governed by a different law from that governing other aspects.[211] The law which governs the validity of the trust determines whether that law itself or the law governing a severable aspect may be replaced by another law.[212]

The operation of *renvoi* is excluded throughout the Convention.[213]

c. Recognition of trusts

Article 11 of the Hague Convention provides that 'a trust created in accordance with the law specified in this Convention must be recognised as a trust'. In order to indicate what recognition will consist of and what its effects will be, it is further provided that recognition implies, as a minimum, the following consequences: that the trust property is a separate fund, that the trustee may sue and be sued in his capacity as such and may appear or act in this capacity before a notary or any person acting in an official capacity. Moreover, if the trust's applicable law so provides, recognition implies (a) that the trustee's personal creditors have no recourse against trust assets; (b) that trust assets form no part of the trustee's estate on insolvency; (c) that trust assets form no part of the trustee's or the trustee's spouse's matrimonial property or estate on death; and (d) that trust assets may be recovered when the trustee has in breach of trust mingled assets with the trustee's own property or has alienated

---

[211] So the construction of the terms of the trust instrument might be governed by a law different from that which governs the trust, such as the law of the settlor's domicile, even if the settlor has not expressly stipulated this. Cf. *Philipson-Stow v IRC* [1961] AC 727.

[212] Article 10.   [213] Article 17.

them.[214] An example of the operation of Article 11 is *Dornoch Ltd v Westminster International BV*:

> A ship was damaged in a collision off China and became a constructive total loss. The claimants had issued a policy covering the excess and eventually accepted the notice of abandonment. The ship was towed to Thailand where the claimants and most of the other underwriters took over the ship. A dispute arose over the residual value of the wreck. The claimants alleged they had acquired an interest in the ship by means of a beneficial interest under a trust.[215]

Tomlinson J applied the law of Thailand as the law of the *situs* of the ship at the time to determine whether the claimants had a beneficial interest under a trust in the ship. Article 11(d) of the Hague Convention would then apply that law to govern the question whether the claimants had a right to claim against the defendants for breach of trust. In the event, Thai law did not give the claimants a proprietary interest.

If the trustee desires to register assets or documents of title to them, the trustee may do so in the capacity of a trustee or in such a way that the existence of the trust is disclosed, provided that this is not prohibited by or inconsistent with the law of the state where recognition is sought.[216] So, for example, a trustee could not register as a trustee of shares in an English company. English company law does not permit registration as a trustee.[217]

The least satisfactory aspect of these provisions is that they concentrate almost entirely on the position of the trustee and deal not very satisfactorily with the beneficiary's position.

The effect of recognition is, of course, subject to the provisions on mandatory rules and public policy of the forum.

d. Restrictions: mandatory rules and public policy

The application of a law selected by a settlor to govern the trust and the recognition by an English court of a foreign trust may both be restricted by the application of mandatory rules and of English public policy.

Article 13 of the Hague Convention provides that the English courts need not recognise a trust if its significant elements are (but for the choice of the applicable law, the place of administration and the habitual residence of the trustee) more closely connected with a state or states which do not have

---

[214] Article 11. However, the rights and obligations of any third party holder of the assets will remain subject to the law determined by the choice of law rules of the forum.
[215] [2009] EWHC 1782 (Admlty), [2009] 2 CLC 226.
[216] Article 12.   [217] Companies Act 2005, s. 126.

the institution of the trust or the category of trust involved. This possibility of non-recognition might inhibit a settlor in exercising a freedom to choose the governing law.

The English courts may continue to apply the mandatory rules of English law, described in Article 16 as 'provisions of the law of the forum which must be applied even in international situations'. This is slightly different in terminology to the Rome I and Rome II Regulations[218] but is probably intended to cover those internationally mandatory rules of the forum which cannot be derogated from by choice of another law. Article 15 also preserves the application of other mandatory rules. The Convention 'does not prevent' the English court applying provisions of a law designated by its own conflict rules in so far as such provisions cannot be derogated from by voluntary act, relating to certain matters 'in particular'. These are (a) the protection of minors and incapable parties; (b) the personal and proprietary effects of marriage; (c) succession rights; (d) transfer of title to property and security interests therein; (e) protection of creditors on insolvency; and (f) protection of third parties acting in good faith. If recognition of a trust is thereby prevented, the court must try to give effect to the objects of the trust by other means.[219]

The mandatory rules referred to in Article 15 are not English mandatory rules but those of a system of law other than that which governs the trust, whose application is determined by the English conflict of laws rules. Moreover, the English conflict rules are rules other than those contained in the Convention; i.e., as the list set out in the last paragraph demonstrates, the rules are those which apply to issues which are not concerned with the validity of a trust itself, or its recognition.

Article 18 provides that the Convention's provisions may be disregarded if their application would be 'manifestly incompatible' with public policy.

e. Variation of trusts

The Variation of Trusts Act 1958 gives the English courts the power to vary the terms of the trust in certain circumstances.[220] This power extends to trusts of both movable and immovable property.

In the case of an *English* settlement by way of trust, s. 1(1) allows the court to approve an arrangement revoking the settlement and substituting for it a foreign settlement and foreign trustees. In *Re Seale's Marriage Settlement*,[221] a settlement governed by Quebec law was substituted. But the court will not approve a substitution if it does not consider the proposed arrangement a proper one. Thus, in *Re Weston's Settlements*,[222] the settlor and two of his sons who were beneficiaries emigrated to Jersey before the application was made to

---

[218] See pp. 323–6 and 365 above.
[219] By Recognition of Trusts Act 1987, s. 1(3), the English court must apply any such rules.
[220] Variation of Trusts Act 1958, s. 1.   [221] [1969] Ch. 574.   [222] [1969] 1 Ch. 223 (CA).

the court. The parties' uncontradicted evidence was that they intended to remain there permanently, but the Court of Appeal did not believe this. It was convinced that, even though a substitution of a settlement governed by Jersey law would benefit the beneficiaries, the object of the arrangement was solely to avoid taxation, and refused to approve it. On the other hand, in *Re Windeatt's Will Trusts*,[223] the substitution of a Jersey settlement was approved. The life tenant had lived in Jersey for nineteen years and was probably domiciled there and her children had been born there.

As to a *foreign* settlement, in *Re Ker's Settlement Trusts*,[224] Ungoed Thomas J held that the court had power under the 1958 Act to approve a variation of a trust governed by a foreign law. In that case he approved an arrangement which involved a Northern Irish trust. He said that s. 2(2), which states that the Act does not extend to Scotland or Northern Ireland, means only that the courts of those countries have no jurisdiction to approve a variation. In *Re Paget's Settlement*,[225] Cross J accepted this, but having assumed that the settlement was governed by New York law, warned that where there are substantial foreign elements involved, the court must consider carefully whether it is proper to exercise its jurisdiction.

Before a case on a foreign trust can be heard on its merits in England, there may be a challenge to the jurisdiction of the court. In *Chellaram v Chellaram*,[226] the English court held that it had jurisdiction to hear a case to remove old trustees and appoint new ones as some of the defendant trustees could be served in London. This was so even over a trust the proper law of which was probably Indian law, with Indian trustees and assets which were held out of the jurisdiction. In that case the court refused to exercise its discretion to decline jurisdiction. However, when the case returned to the English court after substantial litigation in London, Bermuda, Bombay and Singapore, Lawrence Collins J held that because the governing law of the trust was not English law the English court did not have jurisdiction to determine the issues under CPR r. 6.36 and Practice Direction 6B.[227]

This power to vary the terms of a foreign trust seems to be unaffected by the Recognition of Trusts Act 1987, but in exercising the jurisdiction, Cross J's caution should be heeded by the court. Moreover, it should only exercise that jurisdiction and vary the terms of the trust if the law governing the trust allows it to be varied, since the Hague Convention, by Article 8(2)(h), provides that the variation of a trust is a matter which is regulated by that law.

By s. 24 of the Matrimonial Causes Act 1973, the court can, on granting a decree of divorce, nullity or judicial separation, vary any ante- or post-nuptial settlement made between the parties to the marriage. This power is exercisable though the settlement is governed by foreign law and the property is abroad.[228] But any order will only be made in such a case if it would be

---

[223] [1969] 1 WLR 692.   [224] [1963] Ch. 553.   [225] [1965] 1 WLR 1046.
[226] [1985] Ch. 409.   [227] Then CPR r. 6.20.   [228] *Nunneley v Nunneley* (1890) 15 PD 186.

effective in the foreign country.[229] It seems that the ability of the court to exercise this power is not restricted by the Recognition of Trusts Act 1987. Article 15 of the Hague Convention allows the English court to apply its conflict rules (here, leading to the application of English law) to the 'personal and proprietary effects of marriage'. Therefore, in *C v C (Ancillary Relief: Nuptial Settlement)*:

> The husband and wife had been among the beneficiaries of a discretionary trust. The trust deed provided that it was expressly governed by Jersey law and subject to the exclusive jurisdiction of the Jersey courts. Using a power in the deed, the trustees had removed both parties as beneficiaries. They later divorced in England. The wife then sought a variation of the trust as ancillary relief under s. 24 of the Matrimonial Causes Act 1974 before the English courts. She argued the trust was a post-nuptial settlement. The husband argued that the English court did not have power to hear the case because of the express provisions of the deed.[230]

The Court of Appeal held that the English court had jurisdiction to vary the settlement using s. 24. Article 15 of the Hague Convention permitted the English court to apply the forum's provisions on the personal and proprietary effects of marriage so long as those provisions could not be derogated from and s. 24 was such a provision. The wife's claim for ancillary relief was governed by English law as it was a question of the jurisdiction which determined the marital status. The provisions of the trust deed were therefore overridden.

---

[229] *Tallack v Tallack* [1927] P 211, see also *Goff v Goff* [1934] P 107.
[230] [2004] EWCA Civ 1030, [2005] 2 WLR 241.

12

Property

1. Introduction

Issues concerning property are often fascinating, if difficult, and even more so in conflict of laws than in domestic law.[1] Whether one has a right to occupy a house and keep other people out of it, or whether the bicycle you have just bought is likely to be taken back as it has been stolen, or how one might use shares in a company as security for a loan all raise questions of property. This chapter will not cover questions of succession (transfer of assets on death of the owner) or marriage (some legal systems have a community property regime) or insolvency (what is to happen to a bankrupt's property).

2. Characterisation

As this chapter is concerned with choice of law the first matter to resolve is the characterisation of the issue. To take the simplest example of the sale of a bicycle by A to B, this transaction has both contractual elements and proprietary ones. The choice of law rules are different for the contractual and proprietary issues. Also the choice of law rules are different for movable and immovable property, for voluntary and involuntary transfers of property, and for intangible and tangible property.

a. Contract, tort or property?

We have already seen the choice of law rules which apply to the contractual issues which may arise on the sale of the bicycle by A to B. So questions whether B has paid or whether the bicycle is suitable for its purpose are referred to those rules.[2] One of the terms implied into the contract by English domestic law is that the seller owns the bicycle.[3] If the buyer wishes to sue in contract on that term,

---

[1] See generally J. M. Carruthers, *The Transfer of Property in the Conflict of Laws* (Oxford University Press, 2005).

[2] See generally, Rome I Regulation (Regulation (EC) 593/2008 on the law applicable to contractual obligations [2008] OJ L177/6) and Chapter 10.

[3] Sale of Goods Act 1979, s. 12.

that would be a contractual issue referred to the contractual applicable law. However, where the buyer is asserting that because of the sale to the buyer the seller had no title to transfer to anyone else (i.e., the buyer is claiming the bicycle itself), that is a proprietary question referred to the law chosen by the property choice of law rule. Sometimes, therefore, the property choice of law rule becomes important in what appears, at first sight, to be a tort or contract question. In *Kuwait Airways Corp. v Iraqi Airways Co. (Nos 5 and 6)*:

> The defendants had had possession of ten civil aircraft which had been taken from the claimants by the Iraqi forces during the first Gulf War. The Iraqi government had given the aircraft to the defendants under a Resolution of the Iraqi Council. Some of the aircraft had been destroyed and some were damaged when they were returned. The claimants wanted delivery up of their aircraft, or in the alternative to recover damages in tort for wrongful interference with the claimants' property, or in the alternative damages of the value of the aircraft. Under the tort choice of law rules applicable at the time, in order to recover damages the claimant had to show that the events gave rise to a claim in tort both under English law and under the law of the place where the tort was committed. The defendants relied on Iraqi law as giving them good title to the aircraft, i.e., that by virtue of the Resolution of the Iraqi Council the claimants did not own the aircraft and so could not claim in tort for damage to them.[4]

Despite the claim being in tort, the central issue for determination was a matter of property: did the Iraqi Resolution apply to give title to the aircraft to the defendant thereby defeating the claim in tort?

The claimant in English procedural law generally has the right to choose to frame the claim in whatever manner the claimant considers most advantageous to the claimant. Where the claimant is suing a defendant seller, often damages are a sufficient remedy and the claim can be made in contract. However, if the claimant wishes to assert rights against someone who is not a party to the contract, or to claim a right to the property itself, then the claim will be a proprietary one. If the question before the court concerns title to the property or concerns an interest in the property, that question is proprietary whoever is the defendant. The contractual applicable law is not applied to these questions.

b. Voluntary or involuntary?

The choice of law rule may appear to be the same for voluntary and some involuntary transfers of the property, i.e., that of the *lex situs* for immovable and tangible property. In cases where the property has been requisitioned or

---

[4] [2002] UKHL 19, [2002] 2 AC 883.

nationalised by a state or dealt with by a court as part of the execution of a judgment (which are involuntary transfers) different factors come into play, in particular the application of public policy becomes prominent. Note that where the property has been subject to insolvency rules on the bankruptcy of its owner or is being transferred automatically on the death of its owner, the choice of law rules are different. These latter areas are not covered in this book.

c. Immovable or movable?

In English domestic law, property is divided into personalty and realty. Nevertheless, as a matter of conflict of laws, the distinction is between immovables and movables and not the same distinction as in domestic law. The categorisation of property into movables and immovables largely depends on the physical characteristics of the property. There is rarely much dispute over the category into which the property is placed. However, any borderline case is decided according to the law of the country where the property is located, i.e., the *lex situs*.[5] So whether a key to the door of a flat is treated as a movable or immovable is decided according to the law of the place where the key is located. That is an exception to the usual rule on characterisation.[6] Land in England and all interests in that land, such as leases, are treated as immovable even though leases are considered personalty in domestic law.[7] However, property which is abroad must be characterised as immovable or movable according to its *lex situs*. Therefore, in an old case, the slaves on the land in Antigua were considered part of the land in Antiguan law and therefore included in the equitable mortgage of that land.[8]

d. Tangible or intangible?

Again, this distinction is essentially factual: either property has a tangible form or not. A bicycle or a painting is tangible and a sum in credit in a bank account is intangible, as are other debts, patents, shares, copyrights, trademarks and goodwill. The English domestic classification is that of choses in possession and choses in action and this mirrors the conflict of laws divide. However, some choses in action have a tangible form. For example, old-fashioned bearer share certificates are evidence of the ownership of the share itself and physical possession of the certificate is sufficient to have complete title to the share.[9] The same is true of promissory notes (such as bank notes). Share certificates in English companies are more commonly evidence of the existence of the share but not proof of ownership. The ownership of the interest in the share is

---

[5] *Re Berchtold* [1923] 1 Ch. 192 and *Re Cutcliffe's WT* [1940] Ch. 565.
[6] See further Chapter 9.   [7] *Freke v Lord Carbery* (1873) LR 16 Eq. 461.
[8] *Ex p Rucker* (1834) 3 Dea. & Ch. 704.
[9] Bearer shares have not been popular in England for many decades.

proved by entry on the share register as a matter of English company law. In *Williams v Colonial Bank*, the Court of Appeal noted that a distinction be drawn between the possession of the certificates and the ownership of the shares.[10] The law of England (where the certificates were at the time) determined the ownership of the physical share certificates in a New York company. However, it did not determine the effect of possessing the certificates as a matter of any rights against the company. It was for the law governing the existence of the share or debt to determine whether the mere possession of certificates was enough to entitle the holder to full membership of the company or if more was needed (such as registration of the transfer). Therefore, the law of incorporation of the company determines questions of membership of a company, what rights are given to members and how title to membership can pass.

3. Immovables

a. Jurisdiction

Before deciding what the choice of law rule for property questions over foreign immovable property might be, the court must decide if it has jurisdiction. Under Article 22 of the Brussels I Regulation,[11] the English court cannot take jurisdiction over proceedings which have as their object a right *in rem* in immovable property located in another Member State.[12] Under the national rules too, the English court does not generally have jurisdiction over a question of title to foreign immovable property located in a third state. This appears to be a very strong rule.[13] In *British South Africa Co. v Companhia de Moçambique*, the House of Lords held that it did not have jurisdiction in an action for trespass to land in Africa. It can decide neither an action for title nor one for possession of foreign land. So in *Hesperides Hotels v Aegean Turkish Holidays*,[14] the House of Lords refused to hear an action in respect of an alleged conspiracy made in England to trespass upon a hotel in Cyprus. There is little justification for the rule as the English court will usually apply the *lex situs* to decide the question and therefore would come to the same decision as the court of the location of the property. However, it remains powerful. There are limited exceptions to the rule.

(1) Civil Jurisdiction and Judgments Act 1982, s.30, has modified the *Moçambique* rule and reversed *Hesperides Hotels*. Actions for trespass to

---

[10] (1888) 38 Ch. D 388.
[11] Regulation (EC) 44/2001 on jurisdiction and the recognition and enforcement of judgments in civil and commercial matters [2001] (OJ L12/1).
[12] See further Chapter 5.
[13] It was reiterated in the strongest terms in *Lucasfilm Ltd v Ainsworth* [2011] UKSC 39, [2012] 1 AC 208 at para. 54.
[14] [1979] AC 508.

or any other tort affecting immovable property situated outside England and outside the EU can now be heard in the English court. However, it is only in rare cases that the English court will exercise its discretion to decide the dispute. The applicable law will be foreign, specific enforcement will be difficult and the evidence is likely to be abroad.

(2) An exception applies where the English court is exercising jurisdiction or administering an English trust or will which consists in whole or in part of foreign land and the question of title thereto arises incidentally.[15] In so far as the general principle rests on the basis of effectiveness, in that an English court could not make a determination effective in the face of a contrary decision by a local court, this does not apply in such a case as this. The English court can act upon the person of the trustee or personal representative.

(3) Equitable jurisdiction *in personam*: this is a somewhat ill-defined exception based on the principle that the English courts can act *in personam* upon a defendant within the jurisdiction to enforce a personal obligation incumbent upon the defendant when the subject matter is land abroad, by making a decree of specific performance against the defendant and dealing with the defendant as being in contempt of court if the order is disobeyed. The basic requirements are:

(a) that the defendant is within the jurisdiction;[16]

(b) that the subject matter of the action arises out of a contract between the parties, or concerns the defendant's fraudulent or other unconscionable conduct, or arises from an equitable or fiduciary relationship; and

(c) that the act the defendant is ordered to do must not be illegal or impossible by the *lex situs*.[17]

The cases in which the English court has operated in this way are few; this is understandable as it is effectively doing by a roundabout route what they disclaim a right to do directly. Moreover, it may be doubtful whether the court would itself, as the courts of the *situs* of English land, take a similar foreign decree into account.[18]

---

[15] See, e.g., cases on *renvoi* such as *Re Ross* [1930] 1 Ch. 377; *Re Duke of Wellington* [1947] Ch. 501 discussed p. 283 above; and *Nelson v Lord Bridport* (1845) 8 Beav. 527.

[16] Or in principle if the defendant can be served with permission outside the jurisdiction under CPR r. 6.36 and PD 6B, see further p. 147 above. It is a little difficult to envisage circumstances in which permission to serve out would be granted as England is unlikely to be the proper forum in which to hear the case as required by CPR r. 6.37.

[17] The equitable jurisdiction is not curtailed only by reason of the fact that by the transaction sought to be enforced no interest subsists under the *lex situs*. See *Re Courtney, ex parte Pollard* (1840) Mont. & Ch. 239. It suffices that by that law the defendant can carry out the order of the court. If the defendant cannot, the court can only award, e.g., damages for breach of contract.

[18] In *Duke v Andler* [1932] SCR 734, the Canadian Supreme Court refused to recognise such a decree of the Californian court; however, in *Shami v Shami* [2012] EWHC 664 (Ch), David Donaldson QC sitting as a Deputy High Court Judge doubted that decision. He recognised a

Requirement (b) needs further elaboration.

Contract: this is the clearest case. In *Penn v Lord Baltimore* a decree of specific performance was made to enforce a contract to fix the boundaries of Pennsylvania and Maryland.[19] The court has also ordered the creation of a legal or equitable mortgage of foreign land in pursuance of an agreement to do so,[20] and in *West (Richard) & Partners (Inverness) Ltd v Dick* specific performance was ordered of a contract of sale of land in Scotland.[21]

Fraud: in *Cranstown v Johnston*,[22] a creditor, ostensibly in order to recoup money owed to him, refused the debtor's tender of payment and put up the debtor's land in St Christophe at public sale but bought it himself at a low price. He was ordered to reconvey the land on payment of the debt, otherwise a gross injustice would be perpetrated and perpetuated. The case was followed in *Masri v Consolidated Contractors International Co. SAL*.[23] The Court of Appeal appointed a receiver to collect in oil revenues over a concession in Yemen belonging to a judgment debtor company. Oil and revenues from its sale are not immovables but the dicta in the judgment were broadly stated. The company was subject to execution of an English judgment which it had resisted all over the world. The court had jurisdiction over the judgment debtor *in personam* and therefore Arden and Rimer LJJ held that it could appoint a receiver over foreign assets, including the oil located abroad. The order had no *in rem* effect, i.e., it did not of itself alter title to the property and the receiver's success in obtaining actual title to the property depended upon the law of the country where the oil was located. Toulson LJ dissented, holding that the court should not act extraterritorially as to do so was an infringement of comity. This view applies *a fortiori* to acts over foreign land. However, he accepted that there might be circumstances in which it was acceptable to infringe comity and act over property abroad though he did not give examples.

Any other equity or fiduciary relationship: the difficulty is to determine when this arises in cases other than outright fraud.[24] It requires a privity of obligation between the parties but it is no easier to determine when this exists. Thus, if A agrees to sell foreign land to B, A is under the necessary obligation to B, but if A then sells to C, there is no privity of obligation between C and B.[25] In the absence of privity, knowledge by C of the preceding transaction between A and B is not sufficient for the exercise of this jurisdiction against C. Thus, in *Norris v Chambres*:

---

decision of the Israeli court in divorce proceedings which dealt with ownership of a flat in London.

[19] (1750) 1 Ves. & Sen. 444.

[20] *Re Smith* [1916] 2 Ch. 206 (legal mortgage of land in Dominica); *Re Courtney, ex parte Pollard* (1840) Mont. & Ch. 239 (equitable mortgage of land in Scotland).

[21] [1969] Ch. 424.   [22] (1796) 3 Ves. Jnr 170.

[23] Also known as *Joujou v Masri* [2011] EWCA Civ 746, [2011] 2 CLC 566.

[24] See *Cook Industries v Galliher* [1979] Ch. 439.

[25] *Re Hawthorne* (1883) 23 Ch. D 743; *Deschamps v Miller* [1908] 1 Ch. 856.

> The chairman of a company agreed to buy mines in Prussia for the company and paid part of the price to the vendor. He then committed suicide, whereupon the vendor repudiated the agreement and conveyed the mines to trustees for another company, who knew of the payments made by the chairman. The latter's administrators brought the action against the trustees who were in England, claiming a lien on the mine for the amount of the payments. Neither the original company nor the vendor were parties to the action.[26]

It was held that the court had no jurisdiction to determine the matter.

The case is difficult to reconcile with *Mercantile Investment & General Trust Co. v River Plate Co.*, where:

> An American company issued debentures to the claimants secured by an equitable charge on land in Mexico. It then transferred the land to the defendant company, the transfer deed stating that the defendant was to hold the land subject to the charge, but the registration needed to make this condition binding under Mexican law was not effected.[27]

The court held that it had jurisdiction to enforce the charge since the defendants had expressly agreed to respect the claimant's rights when taking a transfer of the land. It is not easy to distinguish this case from *Norris v Chambres*,[28] since the difference between buying a mine with notice of a previous contract and taking property subject to notice of a charge, even when expressly agreeing to be bound by it, seems somewhat tenuous. The *River Plate* case can better be distinguished as a case in which the defendant was accused of fraud or other unconscionable conduct.[29]

b. Choice of law

The choice of law rule for proprietary questions in relation to immovable property is very clearly that of the *lex situs*. Even in those rare cases that the English court will hear a matter of title to foreign land it will apply the law of that country to determine the substantive dispute. This is also the rule in most other countries, for very good reason. Any enforcement of a decision in relation to the property rights in land requires local action. If the English court decided that A took ownership of land in Ruritania there would be a risk that unless the law of Ruritania also considered A the owner to that land that

---

[26] (1861) 3 De GF & J 583.   [27] [1892] 2 Ch. 303.   [28] (1861) 3 De GF & J 583.
[29] The same is certainly true of *Cook Industries v Galliher* [1979] Ch. 439. Moreover, in that case, the third person acted in collusion with the original party. They were in fact co-defendants.

the English judgment would be a *brutum fulmen*.[30] The transfer, the extinction of interests in immovables, and the formal and essential validity of transfers are all governed by the *lex situs*. There are no examples of exception to this rule.[31] Thus, in *Adams v Clutterbuck*:

> Two domiciled Englishmen in England entered into a lease of land in Scotland. The lease was not under seal and it was argued that the shooting rights were not appurtenant to the land, as was true under English law.

It was held that Scots law determined the issue, and since under that law no seal was required, the rights were appurtenant to the land.

The application of the *lex situs* includes *renvoi*. So where Ruritanian law would apply Utopian law to determine the rights and interests in land in Ruritania, the English court should also apply Utopian law. It is argued that in disputes over immovable property the English court should strive to decide the matter (in the rare cases in which it will do so) as closely as possible to the way in which the courts of the country where the property is located would do so.

It seems that capacity to convey or take conveyance of foreign land is governed also by the *lex situs*. In *Bank of Africa v Cohen*:

> A married woman domiciled in England, by a deed executed here, agreed to make a mortgage to a bank in England of her land in South Africa to secure her husband's debts. Under South African law she had no capacity to do so. She was sued for breach of contract.[32]

Even though it was clear that she knew what she was doing, it was held that she could not be liable since she had no capacity to enter into the agreement.

It may be true that any conveyance she might have executed would have been void. That only means that Mrs Cohen could not have been compelled to execute the mortgage.[33] There is no reason why she should not have been liable in damages for breach of contract.[34] The case principally concerned the contract to convey, which has its own applicable law determined according to the Rome I Regulation.[35] In the absence of choice the applicable law will be the

---

[30] Literally a futile threat.

[31] The only case in which the *lex situs* was not applied to a foreign land is *Earl of Nelson v Lord Bridport* (1845) 8 Beav. 527, which is a case on succession not on property.

[32] [1909] 2 Ch. 129 (CA).

[33] Thus distinguishing the case from *Re Courtney, ex parte Pollard* (1840) Mont. & Ch. 239 and *Re Smith* [1916] 2 Ch. 206.

[34] See the contractual characterisation of a similar issue concerning foreign land in *Re Smith* [1916] 2 Ch. 206.

[35] Regulation (EC) 593/2008 [2008] OJ L177/6.

lex situs[36] subject to an exception where it is clear from all the circumstances that the contract is manifestly more closely connected with another law.[37] In *British South Africa Co. v de Beers Consolidated Mines*,[38] a contract concerned with land in Northern and Southern Rhodesia was held to be governed by English law. Arguably, the contract which Mrs Cohen entered into was governed by English law. Although questions of capacity do not fall directly within the Rome I Regulation, it is possible to argue that the applicable law determined by that Regulation also determines questions of capacity falling outside its scope. Alternatively, the question of capacity could be a matter for the *lex domicilii*. Under English law she had capacity, so should have been bound by the contract. An alternative criticism would be that the purpose of the South African law may well have been to protect South African married women from unwarranted pressure to support their husbands financially. There appears to be no such policy in England. In that case, an American choice of law analysis would not apply the South African law (but would apply the English law) which was not intended to apply to English women.[39] However, it is clear that the property effects (if any) created by the mortgage must be referred to the *lex situs*.

The formal validity of a contract concerning immovable property is determined according to the Rome I Regulation. This has considerably freed contracts from formal requirements. A contract will be formally valid if it complies with the formal requirements of the place where it is made or with those of the applicable law.[40] However, if the subject matter of the contract is a right *in rem* in immovable property, the contract is:

> subject to the requirements of form of the law of the country where the property is situated if by that law:
>
> (a) those requirements are imposed irrespective of the country where the contract is concluded and irrespective of the law governing the contract; and
> (b) those requirements cannot be derogated from by agreement.[41] Again the proprietary effects of the valid contract on the land must be determined according to the *lex situs*.

4. Tangible movables

a. Jurisdiction

The Brussels I Regulation presently contains no ground of jurisdiction based upon the presence of property in the territory of the English court. However, the proposals for a recast Brussels I Regulation contained provision for the courts of the location of the movable property to have jurisdiction over rights *in rem* in

---

[36] Article 4(1)(c).   [37] Article 4(3). See further Chapter 10.   [38] [1910] 2 Ch. 502 (CA).
[39] See e.g., *Proctor v Frost* 89 NH 304, 197 A 813 (1938).
[40] Rome I Regulation, Art. 11(1) and (2).   [41] *Ibid.* Art. 11(5).

that property.[42] The usual rules based on the domicile of the defendant in England also apply. Under its national rules the English court can assert jurisdiction *in rem* for a claim for ownership, possession, mortgage or condemnation of a ship if the claim is served on the ship physically.[43] There is no *in rem* jurisdiction for other forms of tangible property. *In personam* jurisdiction can also be exercised in the usual way by serving the claim form on the defendant either within the jurisdiction or out of the jurisdiction with the permission of the court.[44] CPR PD 6B r. 3(11) permits service of the claim form out of the jurisdiction if 'the whole subject matter of the claim relates to property located within the jurisdiction'.

b. General rule: *lex situs*

As we have seen, proprietary questions relating to tangible movables include the effect of a transfer on the original owner's title; whether the purchaser acquires good title; what is the effect of a theft of the property; can a partial property interest be created in the property (for example, a lien, pledge, or charge); what is the effect of a gift of the property, and so on. Very often there may be layers of different issues arising out of the facts, some of which may be contractual and some proprietary. Questions are also complicated by the fact that tangible movable property changes location. The law in one place may well be different from the law of the different location in which the property is now found.

If the tangible movable has remained in one country, that country's law will determine title to the asset.[45] Where the *situs* has changed by the asset being moved from one country to another the problem is slightly more complicated:

(1) If X acquired title by the law of Utopia when the goods were there, X's title will be recognised in England unless when they are subsequently in Ruritania a transaction takes place there which by the law of Ruritania gives title to Y. In that case, Y's title will prevail over X's.

(2) If the facts are the same but no transaction takes place in Ruritania, or if one does take place there which does not give Y title under Ruritanian law, then X's title will continue to be recognised.

---

[42] New Art. 5(3) of the Proposal for a Regulation of the European Parliament and of the Council on jurisdiction and enforcement of judgments in civil and commercial matters (Recast) COM (2010)748 final. This amendment has been omitted from the Brussels I Regulation (recast) 1215/2012 [2012] OJ L351/1.

[43] *Castrique v Imrie* (1870) LR 4 HL 414 at 448; Senior Courts Act 1981, ss. 20 and 21; CPR PD 61 r. 3.6. There is provision for some more limited claims against aircraft.

[44] CPR r. 6.36 and PD 6B, see Chapter 5.

[45] *Inglis v Usherwood* (1801) 1 East. 515 (Russian law determined the effect of a stoppage in transit when the goods were there); *Inglis v Robertson* [1898] AC 616 (HL) (validity of a pledge in England of goods in Scotland determined by Scots law).

An example is the early case of *Cammell v Sewell*:

> X owned a cargo of timber, title to which he had acquired by Russian law when it was in Russia. It was shipped from Russia to England on a Prussian ship which was wrecked on the coast of Norway. The ship's master sold the timber to Y in Norway. This sale gave Y title under Norwegian law but not under English law. Y brought the timber to England and X sued Y in England claiming title to it.[46]

The court held that Y's title acquired by Norwegian law when the timber was in Norway prevailed over that of X. Note that merely moving the property to another country with different rules does not change the title, it is the transaction in the new location which affects the title.[47]

Another example is the first instance decision of *Winkworth v Christie, Manson and Woods Ltd*:

> Some paintings owned by the claimant were stolen in England and then taken to Italy where they were sold to the second defendants. The paintings were returned to England and accepted for auction by the first defendant auctioneers. The claimant sought a declaration that the paintings were his property.[48]

Under English law a thief can give no better title than he has (the *nemo dat* rule) so the second defendants could not have acquired good title to the paintings which remained the property of the claimants. Under Italian law the second defendants acquired good title to the paintings by sale to them so long as they had acted in good faith. Under Italian law the claimants had no longer any property in the paintings. The property issues are a matter for the *lex situs* of the property at the time of the transaction. Italian law was applied and the claimant failed to recover the paintings. Note that any contractual issues are a matter for the contractual applicable law to answer.

By Sale of Goods Act 1979, s. 18 rule 1, there is a presumption that, in the absence of any contrary intention, where there is an unconditional contract for the sale of specific goods in a deliverable state, property (i.e., ownership) passes at the time the contract is made and not at the time of delivery or payment or both, if these take place later. Suppose that X sells a car to Y by a contract and its applicable law is English but the car is then in Utopia. Suppose, further, that by Utopian law property passes only on the delivery of the goods to the buyer.

---

[46] (1860) 5 H&N 728.   [47] *Winkworth v Christie, Manson and Woods Ltd* [1980] Ch. 496.
[48] *Ibid.*

English law will govern the contractual issues, such as whether X was in breach of contract or of a term of the contract. But Utopian law determines whether title has passed to Y. If the car has not been delivered to Y then title has not passed and X is still the owner.

Choice of law rules other than the *lex situs* have been suggested: first, the law of the domicile of the owner which is now limited to questions of succession to movables;[49] secondly, the law of the place of acting which probably applies to bills of exchange.[50] Neither are satisfactory. The *lex situs* is the best rule as it gives effect to the expectations of those who may have an interest in the property or who wish to acquire an interest. In the past the rule was also justified as being consistent with the control of the sovereign over assets in the sovereign's territory. However, that does not entirely explain the rule, which does not refer the issue to the law of the present location of the property but to the law of its location at the time of the transaction allegedly affecting the property. Therefore, in *Winkworth v Christie, Manson and Woods Ltd*, Slade J applied Italian law to decide whether the claimant had ownership of the paintings as that was the law of the country where the transaction allegedly affecting the claimant's title had taken place. Despite the fact that the paintings had come back to England, the second defendants had bought them in Italy, under which law they acquired good title and defeated the claimant's title.[51]

The consequences of the *lex situs* rule can be harsh on the original owner of the tangible movable. If the goods are moved abroad without the owner's knowledge and consent, even in breach of an express provision that they remain in England, the owner's title can be defeated by a transfer of property abroad. The rule can also be criticised for encouraging the taking of property to countries with rules which prefer the title of purchasers and transferees over those of the original owner in order to 'clean up' the title. However, as Slade J noted in *Winkworth v Christie, Manson and Woods Ltd*, security of title is as important to the innocent purchaser as it is to the original owner.[52] It is a function of the characterisation of the issue as property that only one party will succeed in claiming ownership, leaving the other with nothing. However, other countries strike the balance differently between those interested in the property. Commercial convenience requires predictable rules and clear rules,

---

[49] *Provincial Treasurer of Alberta v Kerr* [1933] AC 710 (PC) at 721.

[50] *Alcock v Smith* [1892] 1 Ch. 238 (CA) and *Embiricos v Anglo-Austrian Bank* [1905] 1 KB 677 (CA). The *lex situs* of the bill and the place of acting will coincide.

[51] See too *Hardwick Game Farm v Suffolk Agricultural Poultry Producers Association* [1966] 1 WLR 287 at 330 (affirmed [1969] 2 AC 31); *Bank voor Handel en Scheepvart NV v Slatford* [1953] 1 QB 248 at 257; *Kuwait Airways Corp. v Iraqi Airways Co. (Nos 5 and 6)* [2002] UKHL 19, [2002] 2 AC 883; *Iran v Barakat* [2007] EWCA Civ 1374, [2009] QB 22 (CA) at para. 132; *Iran v Berend* [2007] EWHC 132 (QB).

[52] [1980] Ch. 496 at 512.

obvious to all who might be interested in the property. The *lex situs* rule performs this function for tangible property. A would-be purchaser of the property knows to inquire about title under the law of the country where the tangible is located.[53]

c. Security interests, conditional sales, reservations of title, etc.

In modern times, the methods of financing transactions have become complex. In order to be able to use a large piece of equipment such as an oil rig, the purchaser may agree to pay for it over a period and only take legal ownership at the end of that period (hire purchase). Alternatively, the asset can be sold to a bank and leased by the bank to the user (sale and leaseback). A seller can give the purchaser possession of the equipment but retain title until it is paid for in full (reservation of title). The equipment can be made the subject of a charge, either legal or equitable, to a financier. Property can be bailed or made the subject of a lien or pledge, which may give the person holding the lien or possessing the property a right of sale if the owner does not pay. There are many variations on these and other finance arrangements. In a sense, the property is being used as a type of security. The financier rarely has a use for the property itself, but wants to be able to assert a property interest in it if the other party is unable to pay. Some legal systems do not recognise partial property interests at all and deal with any question only as a matter of contract between the original owner and the chargee. Others have different ways of protecting third parties who may have acquired some interest in the property as against the original owner. In principle, the *lex situs* of the property at the time of each transaction governs the determination of the respective rights of the original owner and the third party.

In addition, some legal systems require registration of property interests that are anything less than full ownership and possession. The requirement of registration is often to enable a purchaser from a person in possession of the property to check that there are no other interests in the property. Non-registration may make the partial property interest (such as a charge) ineffective against some or all persons interested in the property (such as creditors of or other purchasers from the chargor). Alternatively, a non-registered charge may be entirely void. The effect of such rules of registration and the effect of non-registration on property transactions is complicated. Again, in principle, the *lex situs* applies. Consider the following examples:

---

[53] See *Macmillan Inc. v Bishopsgate Investments plc* [1996] 1 WLR 387 at 400 and *Glencore Intl AG v Metro Trading Inc.* [2001] 1 Lloyd's LR 284 at para. 28.

> (1) X sells a machine to Y in a contract governed by English law which contains a reservation of title to X until the machine is paid for in full. The machine is in Ruritania at the time of sale. Suppose the contract and the reservation of title is valid in English law. Suppose further that under the law of Ruritania the reservation of title clause must be registered at a public registry. The machine has been brought to England and X wishes to recover it.

The effect of the reservation of title clause is a matter to be determined by Ruritanian law, the *lex situs* at the time. If that law makes the reservation of title clause invalid and ineffective (even against Y) due to lack of registration, X cannot recover the machine. It is more likely that as a matter of Ruritanian law X has good title as against Y despite the lack of registration. As there is no further transaction in England to divest X of title, X should recover the property even though it is now in England.[54] However, say Y had sold the machine to Z while the machine was in Ruritania. X would then be unable to claim good title (and therefore the machine) against Z where Ruritanian law gives Z better title than X due to the lack of registration. If Y is a company and instead of a reservation of title clause, Y has created a charge over the machine in favour of X, the charge must be registered in England in order to bind the liquidator of the company, administrator or any creditor of the company.[55]

> (2) X sells a machine to Y in a contract governed by English law which contains a reservation of title to X until the machine is paid for in full. The machine is in Ruritania at the time of sale. Before Y has completely paid for the machine, Y takes it to Utopia and sells it to Z. Suppose the contract and the reservation of title is valid in English law. Suppose further that under the law of Ruritania the reservation of title clause must be registered at a public registry. Suppose finally that in Utopia no registration of the reservation of title clause is necessary to protect X's interest. The machine is now in Z's factory in England and X wants to recover it.

In this example, X has done what is necessary under Ruritanian law (the *lex situs* at the time) to ensure that X kept good title to the machine as against everyone. When the machine was moved to Utopia, merely crossing the border does not affect that title. The transaction in Utopia did not divest X of title (as no registration was necessary) nor did it give Z title as against X. Although the machine is now in England, English law recognises X's title under Ruritanian law which was unaffected by the transaction in Utopia.

---

[54] The Scottish cases on this often dealt with this question under Scots law (which also happened to be the *situs* at the time of the appointment of a receiver). However, by the time of the hearing the parties had agreed not to prove the foreign law; see e.g., *Armour v Thyssen Edelstahlwerke AG* [1991] 2 AG 339.

[55] Companies Act 2006, s. 874.

(3) X sells a machine to Y in a contract governed by English law which contains a reservation of title to X until the machine is paid for in full. The machine is in Ruritania at the time of sale. Before Y has completely paid for the machine, Y takes it to Utopia and sells it to Z. Suppose the contract and the reservation of title is valid in English law. Suppose further that under the law of Ruritania the reservation of title clause need not be registered at a public registry. Suppose finally that in Utopia registration of the reservation of title clause is not necessary to protect X's interest. The machine is now in Z's factory in England and X wants to recover it.

In this example, X can retain the machine against Z. X did not have to register the reservation of title clause in Ruritania to have good title and the sale to Z under Utopian law did not divest X of title. Z has taken the risk of qualified title under Utopian law.

(4) X sells a machine to Y in a contract governed by English law which contains a reservation of title to X until the machine is paid for in full. The machine is in Ruritania at the time of sale. Before Y has completely paid for the machine, Y takes it to Utopia and sells it to Z. Suppose the contract and the reservation of title is valid in English law. Suppose further that in Ruritania no registration of reservation of title clauses is necessary. Suppose finally that under the law of Utopia the reservation of title clause must be registered at a public registry (which obviously it has not been) to bind a purchaser such as Z. The machine is now in Z's factory in England and X wants to recover it.

In this example, X has not needed to do anything in Ruritania so X had a valid title as against Y and anyone else at that time. However, it is argued that the effect of the sale in Utopia is to divest X of title and give good title to Z.[56] In contradiction to this conclusion, the New York case of *Goetschius v Brightman*[57] recognised the title of X reserved in California (equivalent to the law of Ruritania) and returned the property (a car) to X despite the sale to Z in New York (equivalent to the law of Utopia). One explanation is that the New York *lex situs* did not require registration of out-of-state reservation of title clauses.[58] Another could be a *renvoi* to the law of California. Fentiman argues that the law of the second *situs* is irrelevant as it cannot have extraterritorial

---

[56] See the Canadian case of *Century Credit Corp. v Richard* (1962) 34 DLR (2d) 291.

[57] (1927) 245 NY 186.

[58] Much was made in the New York court of the Californian licence plates and registration document of the car, putting the buyer on some sort of notice that merely inspecting the New York register would not reveal the whole story of the car's title.

effect.[59] This is not entirely convincing. The purpose of registration requirements is to ensure that a purchaser in the second *situs* can obtain good title
under that law if the purchaser has inspected the local register. The registration rule is no different from a good faith requirement. However, as argued
above, it is possible that the registration requirement of the *lex situs* may be
interpreted as not applying to prior out-of-state transactions.

> (5) X sells a machine to Y in a contract governed by English law which contains
> a reservation of title to X until the machine is paid for in full. The machine is in
> Ruritania at the time of sale. Before Y has completely paid for the machine,
> Y takes it to Utopia and sells it to Z. Suppose the contract and the reservation of
> title is valid in English law. Suppose further that the law of Ruritania requires
> registration of reservation of title clauses. Suppose finally that under the law of
> Utopia the reservation of title clause must be registered at a public registry
> (which obviously it has not been) to bind a purchaser such as Z. The machine is
> now in Z's factory in England and X wants to recover it.

This example leads to the same result as (4) if X had registered the reservation
of title in Ruritania. However, if X had *not* registered the reservation of X's
title, in principle X does not retain good title under the original *lex situs*, the
law of Ruritania. In which case, there is a difficulty. Under Ruritanian law
Z has good title, but under Utopian law X retains good title. The better
solution to this example is to recognise Z's title. X has not taken sufficient
care to protect X's title in the appropriate *lex situs*, therefore Y has good title
which Z will acquire in Utopia.

One can see that it is important to consider the rules of the various *leges
situs* extremely carefully, first to discover whether the rules apply to the
particular circumstances (especially what is the effect of the law on X's title
and whether Y and Z obtain better title), and next to determine exactly the
consequences of the transaction to Z.

d. Exceptions

i. Goods in transit

Goods in transit or those with an unknown or casual location may not be
subject to the *lex situs* rule. The merchant community has developed practical
solutions to dealing with goods in transit, through bills of lading, and so on.
The law governing the bill of lading may be applied to determine ownership to
a cargo on the high seas.

---

[59] R. Fentiman, *International Commercial Litigation* (Oxford University Press, 2010) para. 4.152,
citing *Lecouturier v Rey* [1910] AC 262, which was a case concerning the alleged expropriation
of assets located in England by French legislation. It is well established that foreign sovereigns
cannot act extraterritorially. This is very different from what is under discussion here.

ii. Public policy, mandatory rules and fraud

As with all choice of law rules, the *lex situs* is subject to the exceptional application of mandatory rules of English law. Also, the application of the *lex situs* may be denied on the grounds of public policy.[60] These cases arise more commonly when the property has been nationalised or requisitioned by a foreign state.[61] In *Winkworth v Christie, Manson and Woods Ltd*, Slade J said *obiter* that there should be a further exception to the *lex situs* in the case of a purchaser claiming title who had not acted bona fide. This is unsound.[62] There is no good reason for English notions of good faith to override the *lex situs* except in truly exceptional circumstances in which the lack of good faith is totally unacceptable to English public policy. Possibly this would include seriously fraudulent behaviour which borders on theft.

iii. Insolvency and succession

General assignments of property on bankruptcy or death are dealt with by different choice of law rules.

iv. Cultural heritage

The *lex situs* rule can operate harshly against states seeking to protect their cultural heritage from unscrupulous removal from their territory. In *AG for New Zealand v Ortiz*:

> The Attorney General for New Zealand brought an action to restrain the sale in London of a Maori artefact and asked the court to order that it should be returned to New Zealand. It had been illegally exported from New Zealand in violation of local legislation which provided for forfeiture to the Crown of historic articles which were or were sought to be illegally exported from New Zealand.[63]

The first question before the courts and the only one argued before the House of Lords, was whether the legislation provided for automatic forfeiture of such articles, or merely that the Crown could take proceedings to forfeit them. If it meant the former, title had passed to the Crown when the article was in New Zealand. If the latter, the Attorney General had to rely on the legislation in order to recover the artefact when it was in England. Staughton J, the Court of Appeal and the House of Lords held that the legislation meant the latter.

---

[60] *Glencore Intl AG v Metro Trading Inc.* [2001] 1 Lloyd's LR 284 at para. 33.

[61] Such as *Peer International Corp. v Termidor Music Publishers Ltd (No. 1)* [2003] EWCA Civ 1156, [2004] Ch. 212. See further p. 405 *et seq.* below.

[62] Even in English domestic law it is possible for a purchaser who has not acted in good faith to obtain good title (Sale of Goods Act 1979, s. 48).

[63] [1984] AC 1 (HL).

Likewise in *Iran v Berend*:

> The defendant had acquired an ancient fragment of limestone relief discovered
> in the 1930s in Iran (then Persia). It was not disputed that the fragment had
> been the property of the State of Iran before it was exported. The defendant had
> acquired the fragment in France some thirty years before this case was brought.
> Under French law she had good title, having acted in good faith.[64]

French law was applied as the *lex situs* of the transaction under which the
defendant acquired title and the claimant lost. The claimant was more successful in *Iran v Barakat*:

> Other antiquities had been removed from Iran unlawfully, having allegedly
> been recently unlawfully excavated there. The claimant made a claim in con-
> version and sought the return of the antiquities from a gallery in London.[65] An
> Iranian Act of 1979 provided among other things that it was a criminal offence
> to unlawfully excavate antiquities and that a finder of antiquities must hand
> them to the authorities otherwise a penalty applied.

The Court of Appeal held that the claimant could rely on Iranian law to show
that it had title to the antiquities. The Court disagreed with the first instance
judge to hold that the content of Iranian law vested ownership in the claimant.
The antiquities had been in Iran and despite the claimant never having had
possession of them, Iranian law as the *lex situs* applied to give the claimant an
immediate right to possession.

There are various EU rules and international conventions dealing with the
protection of cultural property. None are entirely satisfactory. The EU Regulation on the export of cultural goods protects 'cultural goods'[66] from unlawful
removal from the territory of the EU. Before removal from the EU, an export
licence is required from the Member State in whose territory the cultural
object was located on 1 January 1993.[67] Member States are permitted to refuse
an export licence in some circumstances.[68] A linked Directive deals with the
return of cultural objects which have been unlawfully removed from the

---

[64] [2007] EWHC 132 (QB), [2007] 2 All ER (Comm) 132.
[65] [2007] EWCA Civ 1374, [2009] QB 22.
[66] As defined in Annex 1 to Council Regulation (EC) 116/2009 [2009] OJ L39.
[67] Council Regulation (EC) 116/2009 (codifying Regulation (EC) 3911/92) and Commission
Regulation (EC) 792/93 laying down provisions for the implementation of Council Regulation
(EC) 3911/92 on the export of cultural goods [1993] OJ L201.
[68] 'Where the cultural goods in question are covered by legislation protecting national treasures of
artistic, historical or archaeological value in the Member State concerned' (Regulation 116/
2009, Art. 2).

territory of a Member State.[69] A Member State has the right to take proceedings against the possessor of the cultural object, or the holder, for the return of a cultural object which has been unlawfully removed from its territory.[70] The court may order the requesting Member State to pay compensation.[71] However, that EU legislation does not protect cultural objects from outside the EU. The United Kingdom has not ratified the 1995 Unidroit Convention on Stolen or Illegally Exported Cultural Objects. Under that Convention illegally excavated cultural objects are considered stolen. In 2002, the United Kingdom ratified the 1970 UNESCO Convention on the Means of Prohibiting and Preventing the Illicit Import, Export and Transfer of Ownership of Cultural Property, but it does not directly apply to individuals. Under English criminal law it is an offence to deal dishonestly in cultural property.[72] The offence applies to activity done abroad. However, the Act does not provide for property rights to be affected which are governed by the *lex situs*.

The salutary effect of the *lex situs* can be seen in *R Cruickshank Ltd v Chief Constable of Kent County Constabulary*:

> The claimant sued the defendant police force for misfeasance in public office. The police had impounded various luxury cars found on the claimant's premises. The police believed the cars had been stolen in Japan to order. Had the cars been stolen property, the police had power to impound them. However, the claimants argued that they had imported the cars from Dubai. Under the law of Dubai, the original owner of a stolen car can only recover it by paying the innocent purchaser the price the innocent purchaser paid for it, meanwhile the purchaser obtained good title. Their argument was that the police were negligent in impounding cars to which the claimants had good title.[73]

The Court of Appeal allowed the claim for misfeasance in public office to go to trial. The police should not have turned a blind eye to the complications which arose when the cars were transferred in a third jurisdiction.

e. *Renvoi*

There have been suggestions[74] that when applying the *lex situs*, the conflict of laws rules of that country are also applied, i.e., a *renvoi*.[75] So, if the law of Ruritania is applied to determine ownership of a piece of property and

---

[69] Directive 93/7/EC on the return of cultural objects unlawfully removed from the territory of a Member State implemented by Return of Cultural Objects Regulations 1994, SI 1994/501, as amended.

[70] *Ibid.* reg. 3(1).   [71] *Ibid.* reg. 7(1).   [72] Dealing in Cultural Objects (Offences) Act 2003.

[73] [2002] EWCA Civ 1840, [2002] All ER (D) 215 (Dec).   [74] See further p. 280 *et seq.* above.

[75] Implicit in *Winkworth v Christie, Manson and Woods Ltd*, also mentioned in *Glencore International AG v Metro Trading International Inc. (No. 2)* [2001] 1 Lloyd's LR 284.

Ruritanian law would apply Utopian law in those circumstances (for example, because that is the law of the contract of sale), the English court should apply Utopian law. The *renvoi* is justified on the ground that it more completely conforms to the decision of the courts of the *lex situs*. *Renvoi* has fallen out of favour and the more recent cases reject the application of *renvoi* to questions of tangible property.[76] In *Blue Sky One Ltd v Mahan Air*,[77] Beatson J refused to apply *renvoi*, preferring the commercial certainty afforded by the application of the domestic law rules of the *lex situs*. In property cases, certainty and predictability can be said to be more important than a theoretically attractive but complicated and unpredictable result.

5. Intangible property

Intangible property is increasingly valuable, often forming the bulk of a person's assets. It is a very broad category indeed and includes intellectual property in all its forms,[78] debts,[79] insurance policies, shares in companies and rights to pension funds or unit trusts. The law relating to intangible property is also very complicated,[80] even before one considers aspects of conflict of laws.[81] This work will concentrate on the more straightforward types of intangible property, leaving aside intellectual property (which raises particular territorial issues).[82]

a. Assignment of debts

i. Introduction

The assignment of obligations (commonly debts) is the basis of many types of financing arrangements, including factoring and securitisation.[83] Figure 12.1 gives the following example: the debtor owes an obligation to pay to the creditor created by a contract of loan governed by Ruritanian law. Suppose the creditor assigns the right to the debt to the assignee by way of a contract governed by Utopian law. It is clear that as between the creditor and the debtor

---

[76] *Dornoch Ltd v Westminster International BV (The WD Fairway)* [2009] EWHC 1782 (Admlty), [2009] 2 Lloyd's LR 420 and *Blue Sky One Ltd v Mahan Air* [2010] EWHC 631 (Comm), this issue not affected by appeal [2011] EWCA Civ 544. See further p. 283 *et seq.* above.

[77] [2010] EWHG 631 (Comm).

[78] Copyrights, trademarks, patents, design rights, goodwill, and so on.

[79] Including bank accounts, bonds, letters of credit and other securities (those which are not shares in companies).

[80] Consider the practices of the financial markets in securitisation, collateralisation, 'swaps' and tiered holdings of dematerialised securities.

[81] In the 1930s, Foster said 'The decisions on the subject are conflicting, indecisive and obscure, and the writings of the leading authors are equally contradictory and certainly more obscure' (1935) J. Foster, 'Some Defects in the English Rules of Conflict of Laws' 16 *BYIL* 84 at 94.

[82] See J. Fawcett and P. Torremans, *Intellectual Property and Private International Law* (Oxford University Press, 2011).

[83] See Fentiman, *International Commercial Litigation*, para. 4.154.

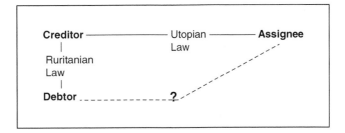

Figure 12.1 A simple assignment of a debt.

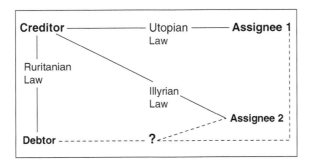

Figure 12.2 Competing assignments of a debt.

Ruritanian law will determine any contractual question that arises, such as the interpretation of the terms of the contract. Likewise, the law of Utopia will govern contractual questions between the creditor and the assignee, such as whether the contract of assignment is materially valid.[84] What law should govern such questions as the assignability of the debt? Whether the debtor is discharged by paying the debt to the creditor? or the assignor? Any requirement for notice to be given to the debtor? Can the debtor set off against the debt any sums owing to the creditor? Just like the transfer of tangible property by contract, these issues in relation to the intangible property of the debt must all be characterised as something other than merely contractual. They relate not simply to the individual contracts of the debt or the assignment but to the effect and conditions of the assignment on parties outside those individual contracts. The best analysis is that these issues are *sui generis* for choice of law purposes, but mostly they are characterised as proprietary.

    Figure 12.2 gives a different example raising choice of law questions in what we have just called property. Again, the debtor owes an obligation to pay to the creditor created by a contract of loan governed by Ruritanian law. Suppose the creditor assigns the right to the debt to assignee 1 by way of a contract governed by Utopian law and then to assignee 2 by way of a contract governed

---

[84] Rome I Regulation, Art. 10(1).

by Illyrian law. The second assignment may be fraudulent or because the first assignment was initially partial (such as an assignment for a specific amount combined with a floating charge over future proceeds). Similar questions to those above may need to be answered. But also, what law should govern questions of priority between assignee 1 and assignee 2?

ii. Possible applicable laws to determine property issues

Originally, it was thought that the choice of law rule for intangible property – like tangible property – should be that of the *lex situs*.[85] Alternative choice of law rules are the law of the contract of assignment or the law of the contract between the debtor and the creditor.

1. *Situs* of intangible property

English law does ascribe a *situs* to intangible property, often for the purposes of taxation and occasionally when a foreign state attempts to take over the property[86] or a foreign court attaches it to enforce a judgment of that court.[87] This requires rules to identify the *situs* or location of the intangible asset. Thus, intellectual property rights like patents, copyrights and trademarks have their *situs* where, by the law which governs their creation, they can be effectively transferred, and if they are assigned, where their holder is. A share or security issued by a company is, if transferable by an entry in the company's share register and represented by a share certificate, situated where the register is kept. If a register is kept in two or more countries, the *situs* of a share is the place where the register is kept in which the shares can be effectively dealt with or would usually be dealt with. Thus, in *Standard Chartered Bank Ltd v IRC*:

> Shares in certain South African companies were inscribed in registers kept there and in England. But for the refusal of consent by the Treasury they would have been dealt with in the register kept in South Africa.[88]

It was held that they were situated outside the United Kingdom for taxation purposes. If, on the other hand, the share or security is a bearer document, payable to the holder, its *situs* is where the document is kept.[89]

The simple case is a contract debt which generally has its *situs* where it is properly recoverable and can be enforced. This is where the debtor resides. If X owes a debt under a contract governed by the law of Ruritania but resides in Utopia, the applicable law of the debt is Ruritanian but its *situs* is Utopia.

---

[85] See the previous edition of this work, J. G. Collier, *Conflict of Laws* (3rd edn, Cambridge University Press, 2001) pp. 251–2.

[86] See further p. 405 *et seq.* below.   [87] See further p. 409 *et seq.* below.

[88] [1978] 1 WLR 1160.   [89] *AG v Bouwens* (1838) 4 M&W 171.

If a debtor has two or more residences,[90] the *situs* is where payment is expressly or implicitly stipulated for in the contract creating the debt. So in *Kwok v Estate Duty Commissioners*[91] it was held that when a Liberian company which did business in Hong Kong gave a promissory note (a debt) to a Hong Kong resident, the debt was situated in Liberia where it was stipulated in the contract to be payable. Where there is no stipulation, then the debt's *situs* is the place where it would be paid in the ordinary course of business. Thus, a debt arising under a bank's documentary letter of credit is situated not where the issuing bank is located but where the monies are payable or drafts can be drawn against the documents.[92]

These rules have been developed for particular purposes such as taxation and expropriation of the property. However, there is no need to ascribe a *situs* to intangible property to provide a connecting factor for a choice of law rule for voluntary assignments.[93] The connecting factor would be more transparent if it were framed as the residence of the debtor. That would not be an attractive choice of law rule for property issues. The debt may be enforceable at the residence of the debtor or it may not (as where the contract contains an exclusive jurisdiction agreement for a court elsewhere). The debt may also be enforceable in many places at once, even in the case where it is expressed to be payable only in one country. That is particularly true for companies which are resident in many places. The residence of an individual debtor may change. Therefore, the *situs* of the debt based upon the residence of the debtor is unpredictable and may not lead to a single applicable law but many possible laws. It is not a satisfactory choice of law rule for property issues in intangible property.

Likewise, the law of the creditor's residence would be an unsatisfactory connecting factor. That could be suggested as a suitable choice of law rule, particularly when the issue is the priority between two assignees or to provide an obvious law for the creditor's own creditors to check in the case of potential insolvency. However, the creditor's residence may also be unpredictable and changeable.

2. Law of the contract of assignment

It has been suggested that the law of the contract of assignment should govern the property issues relating to intangible property. This is attractive in cases where many debts have been parcelled up and assigned in a bundle, as with factoring. Both the creditor and the assignee can identify and indeed choose the law to govern the property aspects of the transfer of the debts. However, it is not an entirely satisfactory choice of law rule. First, if there is more than one

---

[90] If the debtor is a company, its residence is its place of business, so a company may have many residences.

[91] [1988] 1 WLR 1035 (PC).

[92] *Power Curber International Ltd v National Bank of Kuwait* [1981] 1 WLR 1233 (CA).

[93] See P. Rogerson, 'Situs of Debts in the Conflict of Laws: Illogical, Unnecessary and Misleading' [1990] *CLJ* 441.

assignment, each with its own governing law (see Figure 12.2), why should one law have application and not the other? Secondly, the purposes of the choice of law rule include that parties (other than those to the assignment) can investigate the assignor's title to the intangible property, and also that the debtor can know how to obtain discharge of the debt. Neither of these purposes is fulfilled by a law which is known only to the creditor and the assignee. That is not to say that the law governing the contract of assignment has no role to play. Obviously, where the issue relates to the assignment and is contractual, the applicable law of that contract will determine the dispute. So, for example, if there is a question of the meaning of any warranty in the contract or a claim for non-payment of consideration by the assignee, those matters are to be referred to the applicable law of the contract of assignment.[94]

3. Law of the contract between the debtor and creditor

See Figure 12.2. This is the only sensible connecting factor for the choice of law rule to apply to property matters over a debt.[95] The law governing that contract clearly governs any contractual question arising between the debtor and the creditor in the usual way. The meaning of terms relating to payment, for example, would be referred to that law.[96] The debtor's obligations to the creditor are defined by the applicable law of their contract. Therefore, in principle that law must govern such questions as whether the debt is capable of assignment (assignability) and whether the debtor has done what is necessary to discharge the debt. That would include the conditions under which the debtor makes payment to the creditor or the assignee(s). The law of the contract between the debtor and creditor is obvious to the debtor and can be investigated by other persons who may become interested in the property in the debt. It is fixed at the commencement of the contract so does not change as the debtor's residence might. It is also a single law. However, it is less attractive as a choice of law rule for factoring, where many debts (possibly created under different laws) are subject to one assignment, for the practical reason that investigating many individual contracts is impossible.

iii. Capacity to assign or take an assignment

Whether intangible property can be assigned at all is sometimes viewed as a question of the capacity of the assignor to assign it. The capacity of a natural person to assign or to receive an assignment of an intangible is not within the scope of the Rome I Regulation. Unfortunately, the common law decisions on this matter are remarkable for their lack of clarity. In an old case, *Lee v Abdy*,[97] an assignment between a South African husband and his wife in South Africa of the benefit of an insurance policy taken out there with an English insurer was held void because of their lack of capacity to give or take the assignment by South

---

[94] Rome I Regulation, Art. 14(1).   [95] In Figure 12.2 that law is Ruritanian law.
[96] Rome I Regulation, Art. 12.   [97] (1886) 17 QBD 309.

African law. The grounds for the decision were that South Africa was the place of their domicile and of the place of contracting. The question was discussed in the confused and indeterminate case of *Republica de Guatemala v Nunez*:[98]

> In 1906, Cabrera, President of Guatemala, deposited sums of money with Lazards Bank in England. By an assignment executed in 1919 in Guatemala and sent to Lazards, he asked the bank to transfer the sums to his illegitimate son, Nunez. In 1920 he was deposed and in 1921 under duress assigned the sums to the Republic. Nunez's claim under the assignment of 1919 was valid by English law but invalid by Guatemalan law for two reasons: (1) being a minor he lacked capacity to accept otherwise than through a legal representative; (2) being unsupported by consideration and not effectuated in notarial form it was formally void. Both Nunez and the Republic claimed the debt and Lazards interpleaded, wanting a declaration as to who the bank should pay.

English law was both the *lex situs* and the applicable law of the debt. Guatemalan law was the *lex loci actus* and almost certainly the applicable law of the assignment,[99] and the law of the domicile of the parties. The Republic's claim was dismissed, as was its appeal against this dismissal. Nunez's claim was also dismissed. With respect to capacity, Scrutton and Lawrence LJJ both held that this was governed by the law of the domicile or the *lex loci actus*,[100] but since these were both Guatemalan law there was no need to decide between them.[101] It is not very helpful that the only possible *ratio decidendi* of this case is that capacity to take (and presumably to give) an assignment is governed either by the law of the domicile or the *lex loci actus*. It is submitted that capacity should be governed by the applicable law of the assignment. Since this was almost certainly Guatemalan law in the case of *Republica de Guatemala v Nunez*,[102] the assignment was void for that reason.

iv. Article 14 of the Rome I Regulation
1. Application: contract or property?

Article 14 of the Rome I Regulation applies to voluntary assignments and to contractual subrogation of a claim against another person.[103] It has been suggested that the property aspects of assignment are not governed by the

---

[98] [1927] 1 KB 669 (CA).

[99] Lawrence LJ seems to have thought that English law governed the assignment. This cannot be right.

[100] The place of acting, i.e., the place where the contract of assignment was entered into. In more modern times, this concept arguably translates to the applicable law of the contract.

[101] Formal validity is now governed by Art. 11 of the Rome I Regulation.

[102] [1927] 1 KB 669 (CA).

[103] This is the right, often of the insurer under an insurance contract, of one party to recover 'in subrogation' from the tortfeasor (the debtor) what that party has paid out already to the victim.

Rome I Regulation but by the common law.[104] The common law rule applied could be that of the *lex situs* or the proper law of the contract between the debtor and the creditor. Although the Guiliano and Lagarde Report to the Rome Convention said that that Convention only applied to contractual rights and not property rights, neither the Rome Convention nor the Rome I Regulation expressly excludes issues of property. In *Raiffeisen Zentralbank Österreich AG v Five Star General Trading (The Mount I)*:

> The owners of *The Mount* had assigned the insurance policies issued by a French insurer over the ship to the claimant Austrian bank. The policies were governed by English law. The bank gave notice of the assignment according to English law which also governed the assignment. However, under French law (the *lex situs*) the notice was ineffective. *The Mount* had collided with another ship which then sank off Malaysia. The owners of the other ship obtained attachment orders over the insurance policies. The bank sought declarations that it was entitled to the insurance policies under the assignment.[105]

Mance LJ concluded that the effect of the assignment was governed by Article 14 of the Rome I Regulation. The concept of 'contractual obligations' was to be determined autonomously. He viewed the issue as substantially whether the obligor was bound to pay the assignee rather than the assignor-creditor. Or put another way, which of the assignee or creditor was entitled to claim as against the debtor?[106] In any event, as Article 14(2)[107] explicitly embraces the issues of the assignability, 'the conditions under which the assignment can be invoked against the debtor' and the discharge of the debtor, it must cover those questions. To make other similar matters subject to another rule is to add unnecessary complexity.

2. Article 14(1)

Article 14(1) applies the law of the contract of assignment to the intrinsic validity of the assignment. Thus, the interpretation, material validity and legality of that contract are determined by its proper law and its formal validity, generally speaking, by either its applicable law or the law of the place of contracting.[108] The Dutch Supreme Court has held that Article 14(1)[109] applies to the proprietary aspects of an assignment as well.[110] This case

---

[104] R. Goode, *Commercial Law* (4th edn, Penguin, 2009) p. 1126 and M. Moshinsky, 'The Assignment of Debts in the Conflict of Laws' (1992) 108 *LQR* 591 at 613. Both suggest that the *lex situs* should be applied as the common law rule.

[105] [2001] EWCA CIV 68, [2001] QB 825.   [106] *Ibid.* 842.

[107] Then Art. 12(2) of the Rome Convention.   [108] See Chapter 10.

[109] In its previous form of Art. 12(1) of the Rome Convention.

[110] *Brandsma qq v Hansa Chemie AG* Hoge Raad, 16 May 1997, noted T. Struycken, 'The Proprietary Aspects of International Assignment of Debts and the Rome Convention, Article 12' [1998] *LMCLQ* 345.

concerned an assignment which was invalid by Dutch law because it purported to assign an undifferentiated parcel of debts by way of security only. The court saw the question as one between the assignee and the creditor. No third party to the contract of assignment (such as the debtor or a further assignee) was involved. Recital 38 of the Rome I Regulation notes that the property aspects of the assignment between assignor and assignee are within Article 14(1) but it is unclear exactly what effect that recital is to have. If the assignment is invalid under its own applicable law, that may affect the assignee's relationship with the debtor.[111] As a matter of principle that remains a question for the applicable law of the contract of assignment to decide. Only if that contract is valid should it have any possible effect on the debtor.

3. Article 14(2)

Article 14(2) of the Rome I Regulation provides that the law governing the claim between the debtor and the creditor determines the assignability of the debt and also 'the conditions under which the assignment or subrogation can be invoked against the debtor' as well as any question 'whether the debtor's obligations have been discharged'. This should cover most questions which could be considered proprietary in relation to intangible property, for example, any question of whether the debtor has paid the debt; whether a clause preventing assignment is effective; and who can claim payment from the debtor. The latter question was referred to the law governing the contract between the debtor insurer and the creditor insured in *Raiffeisen Zentralbank Österreich AG v Five Star General Trading (The Mount I)*.[112] It probably also answers such questions as whether the assignment has to be perfected by giving notice to the debtor. In English domestic law an assignment must be made in writing and notice in writing has to be given to the debtor by the assignee in order that the assignee can sue directly on the contract without joining the assignor.[113] If the contract assigned is governed by English law then an assignee who wishes to be sure that the assignment is effective to give the assignee rights to sue and obtain the payment without the assignor must comply with those rules.[114] Also, the question whether the debtor has paid the debt and is discharged from any obligation to pay again is to be referred to the law of the contract between the debtor and the creditor by Article 14(2). If there are provisions in the contract between the debtor and creditor which the debtor wishes to rely on to excuse performance, the effect of those provisions on the assignee should also be referred to the applicable law of the contract

---

[111] A matter referred to the law of the contract between the debtor and the creditor by Rome I Regulation, Art. 14(2).

[112] [2001] QB 825.   [113] Law of Property Act 1925, s. 136.

[114] However, partial assignments and those for which notice is not given to the debtor can take effect as equitable assignments in English law.

between the debtor and creditor and not to the applicable law of the contract of assignment. It is important in principle that the debtor's obligations are clear and not imposed by some event (assignment) over which the debtor has no control. Of course, where there is no express governing law clause the identity of the law of the debtor-creditor contract may be unclear. However, it is a law which is determined according to the debtor's relationship with the creditor and therefore more closely connected to the debtor than any law of the assignment.

v. Priority and security interests

It could be argued that questions of priority between competing assignments[115] and whether security interests can be created in intangible property[116] are not matters within the Rome I Regulation. They do not fall squarely within the wording of Article 14. Nevertheless, the German Federal Supreme Court has held that claims of priority between successive assignees fall within Article 14(2).[117] The question of priority is close to the question whether the debtor is discharged by making payment because the debtor will wish to be clear which of the competing assignees should be paid. It is also close to the question of the conditions under which the assignment or subrogation can be invoked against the debtor – by one assignee or the other. In domestic English law priority between competing assignments is determined by the rule in *Dearle v Hall.*[118] The first assignee to give notice to the debtor will obtain priority provided that when he took his assignment he knew of none preceding it. Other systems of law may have different rules, such as, for example, giving the first assignee in time priority.

The English common law authorities on priority between assignees are inconclusive, mainly favouring the *lex situs*[119] but also the *lex fori.*[120] In principle these questions should be referred to the same choice of law rule, that of the law of the claim between the debtor and the creditor. It has also been suggested that in the case of assignment of parcelled up debts the law governing the assignment should be the law in force at the assignor's place of business.[121]

---

[115] See Figure 12.2.

[116] Some systems of law do not allow the creation of partial interests in intangible property by way of security, some systems do not allow assignment of future property (debts to be paid in the future), and so on.

[117] VIII ZR 158/89 (1990) RIW 670; see *Raiffeisen Zentralbank Österreich AG v Five Star General Trading LLC (The Mount I)* [2001] 1 QB 825 at 846, para. 49.

[118] (1828) 3 Russ. 1 and Law of Property Act 1925, s. 137.

[119] *Le Feuvre v Sullivan* (1855) 10 Moo. PC 1, which is also consistent with the applicable law of the debt.

[120] *Kelly v Selwyn* (1905) 2 Ch. 117.

[121] UNCITRAL Convention on the Assignment of Receivables in Trade Finance 2001 which has not been ratified by the United Kingdom.

vi. Set off

Article 17 of the Rome I Regulation provides that the right to set-off between the parties 'shall be governed by the law applicable to the claim against which the right to set-off is asserted' (where the right to set-off has not been agreed). This is complicated. Suppose X is owed a debt by Y governed by Utopian law and X also owes Y a debt governed by Ruritanian law. If X wishes to set off the debt X owes to Y against the amount Y is claiming from X, Utopian law governs the question.

b. Reform

Article 27(2) of the Rome I Regulation provides for a review of Article 14 which is underway at the time of writing.[122] The original European Commission proposal for Article 14 in the Rome I Regulation provided for the law of the assignor's habitual residence to determine the question whether the assignment can be relied on against third parties. This was heavily criticized in the United Kingdom. The most recent BIICL report for the EU[123] suggests three possible alternatives, including the law of the creditor-assignor's habitual residence; a restricted application of the law applicable to the contract between the creditor-assignor and the assignee; and the law governing the assigned claim (debt).

6. Involuntary transfers

a. Nationalisation or requisition of tangible property

A great deal of unnecessary difficulty or confusion has been generated when the English court has been called upon to consider the applicability, effectiveness or enforcement of laws which purport to confiscate property. The basic issues involved, which have sometimes been obfuscated by the use of words like 'confiscatory' or 'penal', are proprietary and so, in principle, governed by the *lex situs*, which is the usual rule, as discussed above. Further discussion may be divided into two parts: (a) cases in which the property is situated outside the foreign country whose laws are in issue (usually in England); and (b) cases where it is in that foreign country at the time the law is enacted or enforced.

i. Where the property is in England

If the property is in England at the relevant time and the foreign law does not purport to apply extraterritorially, that law is obviously irrelevant. The fact that it is confiscatory may induce the English court to hold that it was

---

[122] R. Fentiman, 'Assignment and Rome I: Towards a Principled Solution' [2010] *L&FMR* 405; 'Trading Debts Across Borders: A European Solution' [2010] *Indiana Jo. Global Legal Studies* 245.

[123] *Study on the Question of Effectiveness of an Assignment or Subrogation of a Claim Against Third Parties and the Priority of the Assigned or Subrogated Claim over a Right of Another Person, Final Report* (British Institute of International and Comparative Law, 2012), available at http://ec.europa.eu/justice/civil/files/report_assignment_en.pdf.

not intended to affect property outside the foreign country. This was the reasoning in *Lecouturier v Rey*[124] which concerned a French law which purported to expropriate the property of the expelled monks of the Carthusian order, including the patent (registered in England) of making Chartreuse.

Even if the foreign rule does purport to have extraterritorial effect, then it has been held that it should not be enforced because it was confiscatory and penal since it intended to discriminate against one person or class of persons. So, in *Banco de Vizcaya v don Alfonso de Borbon y Austria*,[125] a law of the Spanish Republic confiscating the property of the ex King Alfonso XIII was refused recognition in relation to a bank account with an English bank. In *Frankfurthner v WL Exner Ltd*,[126] Nazi laws confiscating the property of Austrian Jews were refused recognition where the debt was situated in England. However, the terms 'confiscatory', 'penal' and 'discriminatory' seem to be otiose in this context.[127] Since the property was here, the *lex situs* was English law and no foreign law could affect the owner's continued title to the property.

That this is the case is confirmed by the English court's refusal also to enforce a foreign law which was not only penal, but meritorious, in English eyes. In *Bank voor Handel en Scheepvaart NV v Slatford*,[128] Devlin J decided that a decree of the Dutch government in exile in London in 1940 requisitioning the property of Dutch residents in the Netherlands to prevent it falling into the hands of the German occupying forces did not affect title to gold deposited in London.

ii. Where the property is in the foreign country

If the foreign country enacts a law which deprives the owner of title to the property which is in the foreign country at the time, that effect will be recognised in England, even if the law is confiscatory, provided that the foreign government is recognised by the Crown.[129] This effect follows from principle and it is once again simply an application of the *lex situs* rule.[130] The effect of the foreign decree will also be recognised so that if the property is brought into England by a purchaser from the foreign state, the original owner will not be able to recover the property. In *Princess Paley Olga v Weisz*:

---

[124] [1910] AC 262 (HL).   [125] [1935] 1 KB 140.   [126] [1947] Ch. 629.

[127] Foreign laws which are applicable may be recognised so long as the laws do not offend against English public policy. See further p. 405 above.

[128] [1951] 2 All ER 779.

[129] A decree of an unrecognised government was denied effect in *Luther v Sagor* [1921] 1 KB 436 and see *Carl Zeiss Stiftung v Rayner & Keeler Ltd (No. 2)* [1965] Ch. 525 (CA) reversed [1967] 1 AC 853 (HL).

[130] *Luther v Sagor* [1921] 1 KB 436; *Princess Paley Olga v Weisz* [1929] 1 KB 718; *Jabbour v Custodian of Israeli Absentee Property* [1954] 1 WLR 139 (insurance policy); *Bank Saderat Iran v Farsneshani* (1982) Com. LR 111 (shares).

> Some paintings and other *objets d'art* had been taken from her Russian house by Soviet revolutionaries. The title of the revolutionaries was confirmed by the Soviet government (which was eventually recognised by the UK government). The defendant had bought some of the articles in the Soviet state and brought them to England for sale. The claimant sought to recover them.[131]

The Court of Appeal recognised the Soviet decree which had taken the title of the property away from the claimant.

There are two cases in which a foreign law which affected property in the relevant state at the time it was enacted was not applied (in time of peace). The first was *The Rose Mary*,[132] in which the Supreme Court of Aden refused to give effect to an Iranian law which deprived the Anglo-Iranian Oil Company, an English company, of its title to oil in Iran by nationalising its concession. This was because it was held that the Iranian law was contrary to public international law, which distinguished it from laws in earlier cases,[133] where the property belonged to nationals of the confiscating state. This reason was doubted by Upjohn J in *Re Helbert Wagg & Co. Ltd's Claim*.[134] He explained *The Rose Mary* on the ground that the decree was penal, as discriminating against one company – that is not very satisfactory either.

The other case is *Kuwait Airways Corp. v Iraqi Airways Co. (Nos 4 and 5)*:

> Iraq had invaded Kuwait and appropriated several aircraft belonging to the claimants. The aircraft were taken to Iraq and handed over to the defendants. A resolution of the Iraqi government purported to transfer title to the aircraft to the defendants. There had been resolutions of the Security Council of the United Nations sanctioning the invasion of Kuwait and in particular calling upon all states not to recognise the annexation of Kuwait by Iraq. The claimants sought return of the aircraft in the English court or alternatively damages for their wrongful detention. The defendants argued that they had ownership of the aircraft by application of Iraqi law, the *lex situs*, at the time.[135]

The House of Lords refused to recognise the Iraqi law as giving title to the aircraft to the defendants. It was manifestly contrary to English public policy to give effect to such a gross breach of international law. The court held that the United Kingdom was bound by the resolutions of the Security Council.

---

[131] [1929] 1 KB 718.

[132] *Anglo Iranian Oil Co. v Jaffrate* [1953] 1 WLR 246. In time of war such a law enacted by an enemy state will not be recognised: *Wolff v Oxholm* (1817) 6 M&S 92.

[133] For example, *Luther v Sagor* [1921] 1 KB 436; *Princess Paley Olga v Weisz* [1929] 1 KB 18.

[134] [1956] Ch. 323.   [135] [2002] UKHL 19, [2002] 2 AC 883.

b. Expropriation of intangible property

In relation to the expropriation of intangible property by the foreign state, the *lex situs* rule is also applied. So, if the intangible property is located within the territory of the foreign state which expropriates the property, the foreign rule transferring ownership of the property will be recognised. In *Williams & Humbert Ltd v W and H Trademarks (Jersey) Ltd*:

> The Spanish state had confiscated a Spanish company, Rumasa, by expropriating all its shares and the shares in its subsidiaries, which included the claimants (Rumasa itself was claimant in a second action, together with two other subsidiaries). The claimants sued to recover assets in the form of trademarks and property allegedly misappropriated in breach of fiduciary duty by the controller. This was done at the instigation of the Spanish state, the shareholder.

The defendants sought to argue that the proceedings were an attempt indirectly to enforce Spanish penal or other public laws, which should not be recognised as being contrary to public policy.[136] The House of Lords disagreed. The shares in the Spanish companies were located in Spain. All that was needed was for the English court to recognise the Spanish law which applied as the *lex situs*. The rights asserted by the claimants were independent rights to recover their own assets which arose before the Spanish laws came into effect. Moreover, the object of those laws was to acquire ownership and control of the companies and this had been attained by the perfection of the Spanish state's title to the shares in Rumasa in Spain.

If, on the other hand, the intangible property is situated in England, then no effect will be given to the foreign law purporting to transfer title to it.[137] So in *Peer International Corp. v Thermidor Music Publishers Ltd*,[138] a copyright situated in England where the copyright was protected against unauthorised copying was not subject to a confiscation order by the Cuban state. The Court of Appeal held that the Cuban law could not have extraterritorial effect over property situated in England.

Where the intangible property is a debt, one could argue that the applicable law of the contract should apply. If the state whose law applies to the contract alters the law to discharge the contract, or make it payable to another person, that could have the same effect as a confiscation of the

---

[136] See further Chapter 13.

[137] *Lecouturier v Rey* [1910] AC 262 (HL); *Frankfurthner v WL Exner Ltd* [1947] Ch. 629; *Banco de Vizcaya v don Alfonso de Borbon y Austria* [1935] 1 KB 140; *Jabbour v Custodian of Israeli Absentee Property* [1954] 1 WLR 139; *Bank Saderat Iran v Farsneshani* (1982) Com. LR 111.

[138] [2003] EWCA Civ 1156, [2004] Ch. 212.

debt. Applying the contractual applicable law in this way can be achieved by adopting a contractual rather than a proprietary characterisation of the issue.[139]

c. Third party debt orders

Third party debt orders used to be known as garnishee orders. A third party debt order is a method of execution of a judgment, by way of attachment of a debt owing to the judgment debtor.[140] If A owes a debt to B and C obtains judgment against B, C may obtain an order from the court addressed to A telling A to pay C rather than B. It is important to the debtor (A) that by paying C rather than B, A's obligation is discharged. Clearly, if A, B and C are all in England and the applicable law of A's contract with B is English law, the order of the English court has the effect of discharging A. It is more complicated when the applicable law is not English or the parties are not English. The making of an order is in the court's discretion, which will only usually be exercised if A (the debtor) is 'within the jurisdiction'.[141] B (A's creditor, who is in turn C's judgment debtor) should also be subject to the jurisdiction, so that B is bound by the order. If B is not, there is a danger that A will have to pay B again abroad, having paid C in England, should the foreign courts not recognise the third party debt order. But even if B is not within the jurisdiction it may suffice that A is subject to the jurisdiction. In the older cases, this was explained as the debt being located here and therefore within the control of the English court. Thus, in *Swiss Bank Corporation v Boehmische Industrial Bank*:

> Swiss Bank sued Boehmische, a Czech bank, to judgment. Boehmische had submitted to the jurisdiction. Swiss Bank obtained a third party debt order and attached a debt due to Boehmische from two English banks. They asked for it to be set aside, arguing that if they paid Swiss Bank they might be liable to pay the debt again to Boehmische in Prague.[142]

It was held that since the debt was situated here, and Boehmische had submitted to the jurisdiction, there was no more than a theoretical risk that it would have to pay twice over and the third party debt order was made absolute. If the debt was not situated here, as in *Martin v Nadel*,[143] where the debtor was a bank's German branch, the order was refused. There appeared to be a real risk that it would have to pay the debt in Germany to the judgment debtor.[144]

---

[139] See e.g., *Wight v Eckhardt Marine GmbH* [2003] UKPC 37, [2004] 1 AC 47.   [140] CPR r. 72.
[141] CPR r. 72.1(1).   [142] [1923] 1 KB 673 (CA).   [143] [1906] 2 KB 26 (CA).
[144] Note that the result would be different now following the Brussels I Regulation, see further p. 221 *et seq.* above.

In more modern times, the emphasis has moved away from the *situs* of the debt and more to a practical assessment of the risk of the debtor having to pay twice. So, in *Zoneheath Associates Ltd v China Tianjin International and Technical Cooperative*,[145] the English court refused to grant a third party debt order over the account of the debtor at a branch in China of a Chinese bank merely because it also had a branch in England, there being evidence that the English order would not be recognised in China. In that case the debt could not easily be said to be located in England as the account was held in China.[146] There has been a case in which the debt is situated in England and governed by English law but the third party debt order was refused as there was a real risk that the debtor would have to pay again. In *DST v Rakoil*,[147] the foreign court which would require the debt to be paid again was exercising over the debtor what the House of Lords regarded as exorbitant jurisdiction and indulging in what was looked upon as judicial extortion. Nonetheless, the risk to the debtor was too great to make the granting of the order just.

If the debt is governed by a foreign law, under which the English order would not be recognised, the English court has held that it does not have power to make the order at all. In *Société Eram Shipping Co. Ltd v Compagnie Internationale de Navigation*:

> A judgment creditor sought to enforce a judgment of the French court in England against moneys to the judgment creditor's credit in a Hong Kong Bank which had a branch in England. The account in Hong Kong was governed by Hong Kong law. There was evidence that the Hong Kong law would not recognise the English third party debt order.[148]

Because the English third party debt order did not provide a discharge to the debt under the applicable law, the House of Lords held that no third party debt order should be made. The focus on the applicable law is much more attractive in principle than relying on the artificial *situs* of the debt.

There are few reported cases on the recognition of foreign third party debt orders.[149] If the English court were to give no effect to such an order, then the debtor might have to pay twice, first to the person ordered by the foreign court and then again to the original creditor (the foreign judgment debtor) in England. The crucial question appears to be whether or not the

---

[145] [1994] CLC 348.

[146] In theory the debt could be argued to be situated here as the branch of the bank in England could be sued for it here. The applicable law of the account was Chinese law.

[147] *Deutsche Schachtbau- und Tiefborhgesellschaft mbH v Ras A- Khaimah National Oil Co.* [1990] 1 AC 295.

[148] [2003] UKHL 30, [2004] 1 AC 260.

[149] *Re Queensland Mercantile Agency Co. Ltd* [1891] 1 Ch 536 (CA); *Rossano v Manufacturer's Life Insurance Co.* [1963] 2 QB 352; *Power Curber International Ltd v National Bank of Kuwait* [1981] 1 WLR 1233 (CA).

debt is situated in the country where the order was made. In *Rossano v Manufacturers Life Insurance Co.*:

> An Egyptian order was served in England by the Egyptian revenue authorities. It was in respect of Egyptian taxes due. The debt, which consisted of moneys due under maturing insurance policies, was not situated in Egypt, but in Ontario, at the head office of the insurers.[150]

The English court refused to give effect to this order. However, it is not very strong authority as other reasons for the court's decision were (i) the debtor was not subject to the jurisdiction of the Egyptian courts; (ii) the claim was for taxes; (iii) the order was an administrative and not a judicial one.

The rules above would now only apply to the risk of non-recognition of the English order in third states.[151] Within the EU, the Brussels I Regulation would apply so that any other Member State would recognise the order of the English courts as discharging the debt. This would be irrespective of the *situs* of the debt or its applicable law.[152] Therefore, the English court can easily grant a third party debt order in cases where the debtor is only likely to be sued again on the debt in another EU Member State. There would be no risk of a successful suit against the debtor irrespective of the ground of jurisdiction exercised by the English court. Also, the English court would have to recognise the judgment of any Member State's court granting an equivalent order, again irrespective of the applicable law, the *situs* of the debt or the jurisdiction taken by the other Member State's court.

---

[150] [1963] 2 QB 352, especially at 374–83.
[151] I.e., those which are not Member States of the EU.   [152] See further p. 221 above.

13

Avoiding the results of the choice of law process

1. Introduction

We have seen that the choice of law process is intended to identify the most appropriate and just law whose rules will determine the outcome of a particular case. More than any other set of rules, choice of law rules have to cover widely differing circumstances and as a result are often elucidated in a less specific, more flexible way than domestic law rules. This can make their application uncertain or unpredictable. Even where the choice of law rule is clearly applicable, the courts appear willing to use a number of avoidance techniques to achieve a different result. The most obvious exception to a choice of law rule is that of public policy. Where the application of a foreign law leads to a result which is contrary to English public policy, the foreign law will not be applied.[1] It is not always clear what law is applied instead; sometimes the claim relying on foreign law fails, sometimes the defence based on foreign law fails and sometimes English law is applied to determine the case.[2] Resort to public policy should be relatively rare as it frustrates the purposes of choice of law. In particular the courts need to be careful to recognise the international character of the case and be wary of relying on merely domestic public policy concerns. Few cases should need the blunt instrument of public policy to achieve justice. The other, more fine-textured, methods of avoiding or steering the choice of law process include a characterisation of a matter as one of procedure rather than substance, or adopting a *renvoi* to English law, or applying a mandatory rule of another law than that which would otherwise be applicable. These are part of the choice of law process rather than true exceptions.

2. Substance and procedure

Procedural issues are determined by English law as the *lex fori*, whatever the applicable law (*lex causae*) may be. This has raised complex problems of characterisation: is it the rule of foreign law that is characterised or the issue

---

[1] In *Re Fuld's Estate (No. 3)* [1968] P 675, the court said that it would not apply a law which 'outrages its sense of decency or justice'.

[2] *Kuwait Airways v Iraqi Airways (Nos 4 and 5)* [2002] 2 AC 883.

before the court, or something else? In *Boys v Chaplin*,[3] the majority of the House of Lords regarded the question whether a victim of the tort of negligence could recover damages for pain and suffering as concerned with remoteness of damage, whereas the minority appeared to think it was a question of quantification of damages. Remoteness is a question of substance but quantification is traditionally seen as a matter of procedure. In *Harding v Wealands*,[4] the House of Lords held that the matter of quantification of the damages was procedural, but along the way characterised the rules of New South Wales legislation laying down the manner of quantification also as ones of procedure (and so inapplicable to a case in England). The better view of the distinction between substance and procedure is that adopted by the Australian courts[5] and adopted by the Court of Appeal in *Harding v Wealands*,[6] although overruled by the House of Lords on a matter of statutory interpretation. This limits rules of procedure to those 'directed at governing or regulating the mode of conduct of court proceedings' whereas 'laws that bear on the existence, extent or enforceability of remedies, rights and obligations should be characterised as procedural'.[7] Otherwise there is a risk of the procedural category encompassing important matters of substance and denaturing the purposes of choice of law. Any application of the *lex fori* may tend to encourage forum shopping and so should be subject to limitations.

In the Privy Council case of *AK Investment CJSC v Kyrgyz Mobil Tel Ltd*,[8] Lord Collins gave the opinion of the Board. He had to characterise a foreign rule of law which allegedly gave rise to the cause of action governed by that foreign law. He seemed to agree with the parties that 'In deciding whether a foreign rule is procedural, the court examines the foreign law in order to determine whether the rule is of such a nature as to be procedural in the English sense'.[9] This may explain *Harding v Wealands*. The rule on quantification of damages would be procedural in English law and so was treated as such even though it was part of New South Wales law. Other matters raising similar questions include issues of evidence, priorities, set-off and who may be party to the dispute.

a. Evidence

Questions of evidence, such as what has to be proved, how it may be proved, and the sufficiency of proof, are clearly procedural. The same is true of burdens of proof. In *Re Fuld (No. 3)*,[10] three codicils to a will executed by a

---

[3] [1971] AC 356.   [4] [2007] 2 AC 1.

[5] *John Pfeiffer Pty Ltd v Rogerson* (2000) 203 CLR 503.

[6] [2004] EWCA Civ 1735, [2005] 1 WLR 1539; noted P. Rogerson, 'Conflict of Laws, Tort, Quantification of Damages: Substance or Procedure?' [2005] *CLJ* 305. Note that the common law rule has been overturned by the Rome I and Rome II Regulations.

[7] Mason J, cited in *Harding v Wealands* [2004] EWCA Civ 1735, [2005] 1 WLR 1539 at para. 54.

[8] [2011] UKPC 7.

[9] *AK Investment CJSC v Kyrgyz Mobil Tel Ltd* [2011] UKPC 7 at para. 105.   [10] [1968] P 675.

testator who died domiciled in Germany were challenged on the ground that
he lacked testamentary capacity because of illness, and that he did not 'know
and approve' of their contents. Scarman J held that whether illness affected
capacity was a matter for German law, the *lex causae*, but that the burden of
proof being a procedural matter, the English rule to the effect that in cases of
doubt 'knowledge and approval' must be affirmatively demonstrated to have
existed must be applied.

But this question is complicated by the existence of presumptions in English
and foreign laws. These may be presumptions of law, which are either irre-
buttable, as until 1993 that a boy under the age of fourteen is incapable of
sexual intercourse,[11] or rebuttable, as is that of legitimacy; or they may be
presumptions of fact, such as the presumption of sanity. It is obvious that
some presumptions, such as the one concerning a boy under fourteen, are
substantive in effect since their application determines the outcome of the
case. In one case this view led to conflicting English and German presumptions both being classified as substantive and the latter, which formed part of
the *lex causae*, was applied. In *Re Cohn*:[12]

> A mother and daughter, both domiciled in Germany, were killed together in an
> air raid on London and it was impossible to determine for the purpose of
> deciding a question of entitlement to the mother's estate which died first. By
> English law[13] the mother, being older, was presumed to have died first; by
> German law they were presumed to have died simultaneously.

It was held that, though the method of proof was a matter of procedure, this
was of no use when it was impossible to decide who died first. The issue was
really substantive, and German law as the *lex causae*, was applied.

The Rome I Regulation[14] does not apply to evidence (Article 1(3)) but this is
subject to exceptions. In relation to evidence, Article 18 makes specific provision for rules of the applicable law which raise presumptions of law or
determine the burden of proof in contractual matters. Though some foreign
laws of contract may contain such rules, there appear to be none in the English
law of contract.

As respects the manner of proof, such as whether written evidence is
required,[15] this was held in the old and much criticised decision in *Leroux v
Brown*[16] to be a question of procedure and so governed by English law:

---

[11] This was only true of criminal law, it did not apply in civil cases.
[12] [1945] Ch. 5.   [13] Law of Property Act 1925, s. 184.
[14] Regulation (EC) 593/2008 on the law applicable to contractual obligations [2008] OJ L177/6.
[15] This is of much less importance than it used to be in English law since written evidence is now
only required of declaration of trusts of land, creation or alienation of interests of land (Law of
Property Act 1925, s. 53) and contracts of guarantee (Statute of Frauds 1677, s. 4).
[16] (1852) 12 CB 801.

> By an oral agreement made in France an English resident agreed to employ the plaintiff, a French resident, in France for more than a year. The contract was valid and enforceable by its French applicable law, but though valid was not enforceable by English law as it was not evidenced by writing as required by the Statute of Frauds 1677 which then applied to all contracts.[17]

The court, influenced by the fact that the relevant English statutory provision began with the words, 'no action shall be brought', held that the issue and the English rule were procedural, that the latter applied and that the contract could not be enforced. This decision has been attacked[18] on the grounds that the issue was effectively one of substance since it made no difference whether the contract was invalid or unenforceable – the claimant lost either way – and that the English rule could have been outflanked if the claimant had either done some act or part performance of the contract or recovered judgment in France and then enforced that judgment in England. The case was not followed in California.[19]

Leroux v Brown would now be decided differently in respect to the formal validity of a contract. The Rome I Regulation[20] by Article 18(2) provides that a contract may be proved by the methods of English law or by those of the applicable law or by those of the law of the place of contracting. It needs only to apply the last two types of rule if it can administer them. Suppose that the guarantee is governed by Utopian law or was given in Utopia, and that Utopian law treats a verbal guarantee as valid and allows it to be proved by oral evidence. Since English courts can obviously hear oral evidence, they must admit such testimony of the guarantee.

Whether particular evidence is admissible, as, for example, an unstamped document,[21] or a copy of a foreign document,[22] or whether oral evidence may be introduced to vary, add to or contradict a written document,[23] is a question

---

[17] Since the Law Reform (Enforcement of Contracts) Act 1954, such a contract is no longer required to be in writing.

[18] It was criticised by Willes J in two cases, but apparently approved by the House of Lords in *Morris v Baron & Co.* [1918] AC 1. It was approved by the Court of Appeal in *Irvani v G and H Montage GmbH* [1990] 1 WLR 667. In *Mahadervan v Mahadervan* [1964] P 233, the conclusiveness of a foreign certificate of marriage was treated as a question of substance. In *Monterosso Co. Ltd v International Transport Workers' Federation* [1982] 3 All ER 841, it was held that a requirement of the Trade Union and Labour Relations Act 1974, s. 18, that a collective agreement should be conclusively presumed not to have been intended to be a legally enforceable contract unless it stated that the parties intended it to be so was a matter of substance and, since the agreement in question was not governed by English law, the requirements did not apply.

[19] *Bernkrant v Fowler*, 55 Cal. 2d 588 (1961).   [20] Regulation (EC) 593/2008 [2008] OJ L177/6.

[21] *Bristow v Sequeville* (1850) 5 Exch. 275. It is otherwise if the foreign law renders an unstamped document a nullity: *Alves v Hodgson* (1797) 7 TR 241.

[22] *Brown v Thornton* (1827) 6 Ad & E 185.

[23] *Korner v Witkowitzer* [1950] 2 KB 128 (this type of evidence is usually inadmissible in an English court by virtue of the so-called parol evidence rule).

of procedure. But whether oral evidence is admissible in order to interpret a written document is a matter of substance and so governed by the *lex causae*.[24] The interpretation of a document or term is clearly a matter of substance.

The Rome II Regulation[25] also specifically excludes evidence by Article 1(3). However, it also provides that rules of the applicable law which raise presumptions of law or determine the burden of proof in non-contractual matters shall apply.[26] In addition, a unilateral act which is intended to have legal effect in relation to the non-contractual obligation may be formally valid either by the law of the non-contractual obligation or the law of the place where the act was done.

b. Limitation of actions

Rules governing the period of time during which an action must be brought are, in legal systems generally, of two kinds: first, those which merely bar the action, which are procedural; secondly, those which extinguish the claimant's rights, which are substantive. Most English rules are of the first type.[27] Moreover, the English courts have almost always regarded a rule of foreign law in the same light, usually in reliance upon its literal wording.[28] The result has been that the English rule has almost always been applied. Many foreign systems regard their own limitation rules as substantive, and the conflict of characterisation can lead to undesirable results, especially where an action abroad has been dismissed on the ground that a limitation period has expired, but an English action is allowed to continue.[29]

The Law Commission criticised the existing law in 1982[30] and its recommendations were enacted in the Foreign Limitation Periods Act 1984. The matter is also dealt with as regards actions on contractual[31] and non-contractual obligations[32] via the Rome I and Rome II Regulations. In those cases, the Act is probably superseded by the express provisions of the Regulations. The Foreign Limitation Periods Act 1984 provides that all limitation periods,[33] both English and foreign, and whether the latter are classified as substantive or procedural by the foreign courts, should be classified as substantive so that the foreign rule would be applied.[34] But this would not prevent

---

[24] *St Pierre v South American Stores Ltd* [1937] 1 All ER 206, [1937] 3 All ER 349.
[25] Regulation (EC) 864/2007 on the law applicable to non-contractual obligations Art. 15(a) [2007] OJ L199/40.
[26] Article 22(1).
[27] See Limitation Act 1980. Exceptions are s. 3 (conversion of goods) and s. 17 (land) where title is extinguished.
[28] See, e.g., *Huber v Steiner* (1835) 2 Bing. NC 202.
[29] See *Harris v Quine* (1869) LR 4 QB 653 and *Black-Clawson International Ltd v Papierwerke-Waldhof Aschaffenburg A/G* [1975] AC 591 (HL), where the German court regarded the German rule as one of substance.
[30] Report No. 114 (1982).   [31] Rome I Regulation, Art. 12.   [32] Rome II Regulation, Art. 15.
[33] As defined in s. 4.   [34] See s. 1(1). *Renvoi* is excluded (s. 1(5)).

the court refusing in its discretion to apply the foreign rule on the ground of public policy,[35] or where its application would cause undue hardship.[36] What might be contrary to public policy or causing undue hardship? In *Harvey v Smith*, the Court of Appeal applied a foreign limitation period of twelve months which was considerably shorter than the English period of three years. In deciding whether there was undue hardship, the Court noted that it was important to look at the application of the limitation period rather than, as in this case, the hardship resulting from the wrong advice on that limitation period.[37] A much longer period than in English law was applied in *Arab Monetary Fund v Hashim (No. 9)*.[38] In *Gotha City v Sotheby's (No. 2)*,[39] the German limitation period was some thirty years which commenced again every time the stolen property was transferred. This too was applied. However, had the German limitation period not been so long, Moses J said that he would have disapplied the German limitation rule as against public policy. In his view the English limitation rule that did not permit time to run in favour of a thief or a transferee from a thief would have to be applied instead. This result is barely justifiable on the ground that English law applied as well as German law to determine the title of the holder of paintings stolen by the Nazi regime in this case. It is an example of a tendency to prefer English public policy.

Any extension of the limitation period allowed under the foreign law is to be given effect except where it is extended because of either party's absence from the jurisdiction;[40] otherwise, if a party were to stay out of that jurisdiction permanently, the case would never be decided. A foreign judgment on a limitation point is now regarded as a judgment on the merits and so provides a good defence to a further action here on the same cause of action.[41]

c. Remedies

A claimant can only obtain English remedies and so cannot obtain a remedy which exists by the *lex causae* but not in English law. The claimant can, however, obtain a remedy available under English law but not by the *lex causae*. Thus, a decree of specific performance might be awarded though this is not obtainable in the courts of the country whose law governs the contract. But the claimant will not be granted an English remedy if this would effectively alter the right the claimant has acquired by the foreign law. In *Phrantzes v Argenti*:[42]

---

[35] See s. 2(1) and (2).   [36] See s. 2(2).

[37] [2010] EWCA Civ. 78. The claimant's lawyer had been misinformed and so let time run too long.

[38] [1996] 1 Lloyd's LR 589.   [39] *The Times* 8 October 1988.

[40] Foreign Limitation Periods Act 1984, s. 2(3).

[41] See s. 3. Thus, *Harris v Quine* (1869) LR 4 QB 653 and *Black-Clawson International Ltd v Papierwerke-Waldhof Aschaffenburg A/G* [1975] AC 591 (HL) are no longer good law. The Act also applies to arbitrations (see Arbitration Act 1996, ss. 5–13) and to the Crown (s. 6).

[42] *Phrantzes v Argenti* [1960] 2 QB 19.

the claim related to an obligation under Greek law that a father establish a dowry for his daughter and if he failed to do so the daughter had a right to compel him. All the parties were Greek but the daughter sought an action in England. The action failed not because the claim was unknown in English law but because there was no appropriate remedy.

Article 12 of the Rome I Regulation[43] states that the applicable law governs the consequences of breach of a contract, but within the limits of the powers conferred on the court by English procedural law. This may ensure that the applicable law decides, for example, whether the innocent party can rescind the contract on account of its breach. It may also encourage the court to refer the availability of a remedy such as specific performance to that law.

The existence, nature and assessment of damage or the remedy claimed are matters for the applicable law by Article 15(b) of the Rome II Regulation.[44] Article 15(c) of that Regulation provides that the applicable law also governs the measures which a court may take to prevent or terminate injury or damage or to ensure provision of compensation. Both provisions are aimed at ensuring that, so far as possible, the remedies available for damages suffered are the same whatever court is hearing the dispute.

d. Damages

The question of damages poses a particular issue within remedies. Here, two questions must be distinguished. These are (i) remoteness of damage, or for what types of damage can the claimant recover,[45] which are both substantive matters; and (ii) measurement or quantification of damages, which is a procedural matter under the traditional English view. At common law, the former is governed by the *lex causae*, the latter by the *lex fori*. In contract, the position can be illustrated by subcontract losses; in general these are not recoverable under English law.[46] This is a matter of remoteness of damage and if, as in *D'Almeida Araujo v Sir Frederick Becker & Co. Ltd,*[47] damages are recoverable under the Portuguese applicable law, they will be awarded in an English court. How much money the claimant will receive in respect of such contractual losses depends on English law exclusively under the common law. The same is true of damages in tort at common law. So, whether damages for

---

[43] Regulation (EC) 593/2008 [2008] OJ L177/6.
[44] Regulation (EC) 864/2007 [2007] OJ L199/40.
[45] I.e., the heads of damage claimed for by the claimant.
[46] *Williams Bros v ET Agius Ltd* [1914] AC 510. But if the subsale was in the contemplation of the parties it may be taken into account: *Re Hall (R&H) v WH Pim Jr* (1928) 139 LT 50.
[47] [1953] 2 QB 329.

pain and suffering[48] or pre-judgment interest[49] or damages for loss of expectation of life[50] are recoverable is for the *lex causae* to determine. How much can be awarded for these is a matter for the *lex fori*.[51] This has been the subject of criticism. A claimant wants recompense for losses, and drawing a distinction between the availability of a right and the amount of the remedy seems legalistic. The House of Lords in *Harding v Wealands*[52] reiterated the traditional view, overturning the Court of Appeal's decision that New South Wales rules of assessment of damages were applicable in relation to a motor accident which had occurred in New South Wales. The House of Lords applied English rules for assessment of the damages payable to the claimant. The Court of Appeal in *Harding v Wealands*[53] had taken a much narrower view of the role of procedure, limiting it to those rules which deal with the mode or conduct of proceedings. This definition would include rules on how evidence should be given, for example, but not those on quantification of damages. It is submitted that this is a much better conclusion, more fitted to the objectives of private international law. Giving the *lex fori* anything but the narrowest of scope would mean that the result in a case differs depending on where it is litigated.[54] English law also determines whether any deduction should be made for social security payments.[55]

However, Article 12(1)(c) of the Rome I Regulation[56] provides that the applicable law determines the *assessment of damages for breach of contract* so far as it is governed by rules of law which, of course, it is. Likewise, Article 15 of the Rome II Regulation[57] also provides that the applicable law governs 'the *assessment of damage* or the remedy claimed'. Thus, the assessment of damage is a substantive matter once these provisions are in force. Particularly the latter piece of European legislation will change the common law to align with continental European rules. It has merit in preventing forum shopping within the EU, especially for tort claims.[58]

Whether a claimant has been contributorily negligent such that the right to a remedy is altered is a matter of substance; it goes beyond merely quantifying the amount payable.[59]

---

[48] See *Chaplin v Boys* [1971] AC 356.

[49] *Maher v Groupama Grand Est* [2009] EWCA Civ 1191, [2010] 1 WLR 1564.

[50] These were abolished in English law by the Administration of Justice Act 1982.

[51] See *Kohnke v Karger* [1951] 2 KB 670; *Harding v Wealands* [2007] 2 AC 1.

[52] [2007] 2 AC 1.   [53] [2005] 1 WLR 1355.

[54] Von Savigny was the greatest advocate for ensuring uniformity of result. Although it is not always possible, it remains a worthy objective of conflict of laws.

[55] *Roerig v Valiant Trawlers Ltd* [2002] 1 WLR 2304, although English law was also the applicable law in this case.

[56] Regulation (EC) 593/2008 [2008] OJ L177/6.

[57] Regulation (EC) 864/2007 [2007] OJ L199/40.   [58] See further Chapter 11.

[59] *Dawson v Broughton*, County Court Manchester, 31 July 2007 (unreported but cited in J. Fawcett and J. Carruthers, *Cheshire, North and Fawcett, Private International Law* (14th edn, Oxford University Press, 2008) p. 99 n. 191.

e. Interest on damages and currency of damages

Whether interest is payable on the damages and at what rate is confusing. With a claim on a debt for contractual interest, the common law determined that both whether interest was payable and the rate at which it was payable was a matter of the applicable law. This remains the position after the Rome I Regulation.[60] Whether interest is payable on a claim in damages for breach of contract or in tort[61] is also a matter for the relevant applicable law. However, the rate at which interest is payable is a question for the applicable law in a claim for damages for a contractual debt[62] but not so clearly where damages are claimed in tort. It may be regarded as a procedural matter and so referred to the *lex fori*.[63] Surprisingly, this may well be the best result. In England the rate of interest is discretionary.[64] The court is permitted to take into account the rules of the foreign substantive law on awarding interest, what currency the award is to be made in and the prevailing interest rate in that currency.

Until 1975, the English courts could only award damages in sterling,[65] and even if the applicable law of the contract was foreign and the money of account and the money of payment were in a foreign currency, the damages had to be converted into sterling. The rate of conversion was the exchange rate at the date of breach of contract or when the debt was payable or when a loss suffered by means of a tort being committed.[66] This 'breach date' rule, as opposed to the 'judgment date' rule, resulted in injustice to foreign creditors when sterling went through periods of severe devaluation. A revolution was engineered mainly by Lord Denning MR[67] in a case in which the Court of Appeal disregarded the precedents,[68] for which it was castigated by the House of Lords. However, in *Miliangos v George Frank*,[69] the House of Lords itself reversed the old law and held that in certain cases the English courts could give judgments in foreign currency, here Swiss francs. In this case the difference in value between the breach date and the judgment date was almost 50 per cent. The debt arose out of a contract governed by Swiss law and denominated in Swiss francs. It was further extended to cases of contract where the governing law was English law,[70] and to tort.[71] In times of wildly fluctuating exchange

---

[60] Rome I Regulation, Art. 12(1)(c).　　[61] Rome II Regulation, Art. 15(c).

[62] The contract may specifically provide for a rate of interest.

[63] See *Maher v Groupama Grand Est* [2009] EWCA Civ 1191, [2010] 1 WLR 1564.

[64] Supreme Court Act 1981, s. 35A.

[65] *Manners v Pearson* [1898] 1 Ch. 581 at 593; *Tompkinson v First Pennsylvania Banking & Trust Co.* [1961] AC 1007.

[66] See e.g., *SS Celia v SS Volturno* [1921] 2 AC 544.

[67] The first shots were fired when the Court of Appeal held in 1973 that an arbitrator could make an award in foreign currency; *Jugoslavenska Oceanska Plovidba v Castle Investment Co. (The Kezara)* [1974] QB 292 (CA).

[68] *Schorsch Meier GmbH v Hennin* [1975] QB 416.　　[69] [1976] AC 443.

[70] *Services Europe Atlantiques Sud v Stockholms Rederiaktiebolag SVEA (The Folias)* and *Owners of the Elftherotria v Despina R (The Despina R)* [1979] AC 685 (conjoined appeals).

[71] *Ibid.*

rates and allied interest rates, the matter has become important to claimants and defendants. The rule appears to be one of procedure, independent of the substantive law of the claim. The court decides which currency truly reflects the claimant's loss, having regard to the currency in which the claimant normally operates or with which the claimant has the closest connection. If there is no evidence of the latter, then the currency in which the loss is incurred reflects the claimants' loss. However, in contractual damages the court will often refer to the applicable law of the contract to decide the currency in which damages are payable, especially if there is an express term.[72] The rule has been applied, for example, to third party debt orders,[73] claims against a company in liquidation,[74] and claims for restitution.[75]

The method of execution, for example, whether attachment of a debt or execution on land or on goods is available, is determined by the *lex fori*.[76]

f. Priorities and set-off

The question of what law governs the priority of assignments of single debts or other interests was discussed earlier.[77] In the case of priority of claims against funds administered by an English court, such as winding up, bankruptcy and administration of insolvent estates, it is clear that English law as the *lex fori* orders priorities.[78] The same is true of claims against a ship when the court is exercising its Admiralty jurisdiction.[79] Thus, in *The Tagus*:

> Claims were brought against an Argentine ship. The master claimed a lien for wages and disbursements on several voyages. Under Argentine law he only had priority for the lien of the last voyage; under English law this extended to all voyages.

It was held that the English rule applied.

In this case and *The Zigurds*,[80] the interest which arose under the foreign law was one with which English law was familiar. If it is not, the foreign law governing the transaction under which one of the competing interests arose

---

[72] *Ibid.*

[73] *Choice Investments v Jeromnimon* [1981] QB 149. Third party debt orders were previously known as garnishee orders.

[74] Converted as at the date of the winding-up order: *Re Dynamics Corporation of America* [1976] 1 WLR 757.

[75] *BP Exploration Co. (Libya) Ltd v Hunt (No. 2)* [1979] 1 WLR 783 at 840–1.

[76] See *de la Vega v Vianna* (1830) 1 B&Ad. 284.

[77] See Chapter 12 on assignments and priorities of intangible property.

[78] *Re Kloebe* (1884) 28 Ch.D 175; *Bankers Trust International Ltd v Todd Shipyard Corp. (The Halcyon Isle)* [1981] AC 221.

[79] *The Milford* (1858) Swa. 362.   [80] [1932] P 113.

will have to be consulted to ascertain what the interest amounts to, but English law will determine whether it amounts to a lien and what its priority will be. Thus, in *The Halcyon Isle*:

> An English bank was the mortgagee of a ship which was repaired in New York. By New York law the repairer had a maritime lien for the price of the repairs. The ship left New York and arrived in Singapore where the mortgagees arrested the ship, which was sold by court order.

The Privy Council, on appeal from Singapore, held that the mortgagees had priority over the New York repairers or 'necessaries men'. These may have had a maritime lien under New York law but none by the *lex fori* (Singapore) which determined what classes of events gave rise to a maritime lien and priority between such liens.[81] In principle, the validity and effect in substance of the repairer's lien should be determined by its own governing law, which was New York law, where the ship was when the lien was established. The lien's rank with other competing claims may then be determined according to the *lex fori* which is also the present location of the ship.

Priority of claims against foreign land is presumably governed by the *lex situs*.[82]

g. Parties

A question may arise as to whether a party is a proper claimant in, or a proper defendant to, an action. Is this procedural or substantive?

An example of this is to be found in the law of assignments of intangible property. In English law an equitable assignor or assignee must join the other as a party but a legal assignor or assignee need not do so. In the case of an equitable assignee is this a procedural requirement? If so, the English rule applies even though it is not required by the *lex causae*. If it is a substantive rule, it does not apply unless English law is the substantive law. In one early case,[83] the question seems to have been governed by the *lex fori*, but this was also the *lex causae*. In another, which concerned an assignment of an Irish judgment debt, it was held to be substantive and the claimant could sue in his own name as Irish law allowed this.[84]

---

[81] The majority (Lords Diplock, Elwyn-Jones and Lane) said that the decision of the Supreme Court of Canada to the contrary in *The Ioannis Daskalelis* [1974] 1 Lloyd's LR 174 was based on a misunderstanding of *The Colorado* [1923] P 102. Lords Salmon and Scarman supported the Supreme Court's understanding of *The Colorado* and effectively described the judgment of the majority as a breach of the comity of nations and natural justice and a denial of private international law.

[82] *Norton v Florence Land and Public Works Co.* (1877) 7 Ch. D 332.

[83] *Wolff v Oxholm* (1817) 6 M&S 92.   [84] *O'Callaghan v Thomond* (1810) 3 Taunt. 82.

Another example is the requirement of some systems that if X is a member of a firm, the firm's creditors cannot sue X without having sued the firm first, and that a surety or guarantor cannot be sued before the principal debtor. (This is the converse of English law.) If (a) the *lex causae* regards X as under no liability until the firm or principal is sued, this is substantive and its rule applies; if (b) X is liable thereunder but can only be sued after all the other remedies have been exhausted, this is procedural and ignored. This distinction was drawn in *General Steam Navigation v Goulliou*,[85] but the court was equally divided as to whether the French law was of type (a) or (b).

In principle, it is important to decide whether a foreign rule creates or delimits a substantive right within its own context; if so, the matter is substantive and to be referred to the *lex causae*. If the foreign rule is only dealing with the way in which the right is to be enforced in the foreign court then it is procedural and can be overlooked in favour of the English rules as the *lex fori*. On the other hand, English rules of procedure should not be given greater scope than is necessary to regulate the court's proceedings and administration. The English court has taken a broad view of who can sue and be sued in England, even permitting a Hindu Temple to make a claim to recover property here.[86]

3. *Renvoi*

It may be controversial to characterise *renvoi*[87] as a method of avoiding choice of law rules, but on occasion the use of *renvoi* achieves a similar purpose of avoiding the rules of domestic law identified by the choice of law rule.[88] For example, in the Australian case of *Neilson v Overseas Projects Corporation of Victoria Ltd*:

> The claimant sued her husband's Australian employer for damages for personal injury. She had fallen down the stairs in the house rented for the couple by the employer in China while her husband was working there. Under Chinese law her claim was barred as being out of time. However, there was evidence that in these circumstances the Chinese court would exceptionally apply the law of Australia as both parties were nationals of Australia.[89]

The choice of law rule for tort in Australia is that of the *lex loci delicti commissi*. This is a strict rule without any exception for the rare cases when

---

[85] (1843) 11 M&W 877. A Spanish rule was held to be of type (b) and inapplicable in *Re Deutsch* [1896] 2 Ch. 836.

[86] *Bumper Development Corp. v Metropolitan Police Commissioner* [1991] 1 WLR 1362.

[87] See further p. 280 *et seq.* above.

[88] As notably in *Re Ross* [1930] 1 Ch. 377; *Collier v Rivaz* (1841) 2 Curt. 855 but not in *Re Annesley* [1926] Ch. 692.

[89] [2005] HCA 54.

another law is more closely connected with the parties or the tort.[90] The Australian High Court applied a partial *renvoi* which had the effect of permitting the application of Australian law.[91] *Renvoi* is expressly excluded in many areas of choice of law in England. It plays no part at all in choice of law in contract,[92] tort[93] and trusts falling within the Hague Convention.[94] It is rarely used in choice of law in movable property but is almost certainly applicable to questions of choice of law to title to immovable property.

4. Public policy

We have seen that resort to public policy[95] to avoid the normal result of the choice of law process should be rare. Otherwise the wider purposes of choice of law are circumvented. As Cardozo J noted in the US case of *Loucks v Standard Oil Co. of New York*:

> The courts are not free to refuse to enforce a foreign right at the pleasure of the judges, to suit the individual notion of expediency or fairness. They do not close their doors, unless help would violate some fundamental principle of justice, some prevalent conception of good morals, some deep-rooted tradition of the common weal.[96]

Nevertheless, there is undoubtedly a doctrine that the English court will not recognise (or will not apply or will not enforce) foreign rules which are repugnant to English public policy. This use of public policy includes the more specific rules that English courts will not enforce foreign penal, revenue or other public laws. Such laws may nevertheless be recognised and given some effect. The courts relatively rarely have to adopt a public policy justification to exclude the effect of a foreign law as many areas in which public policy looms large in other legal systems are resolved by using English law. So, for example, in matters of divorce, maintenance, adoption and guardianship of children, English law applies so long as the English court has jurisdiction.[97] It should always be remembered that any avoidance of the choice of law rule should be truly exceptional and any recourse to English public policy justified on grounds that recognise the international character of the case. As Lord Steyn has noted in *Kuwait Airways v Iraqi Airways (Nos 4 and 5)*:

---

[90] *Regie Nationale des Usines Renault SA v Zhang* (2002) 210 CLR 491.
[91] There was a further difficulty as to the law of which State of Australia then applied.
[92] Rome I Regulation, Art. 20.   [93] Rome II Regulation, Art. 24.
[94] Recognition of Trusts Act 1987, enacting the Convention on the Law Applicable to Trusts and their Recognition, Art. 17.
[95] A. Mills, 'The Dimensions of Public Policy in Private International Law' (2008) 4 *Jo. Priv. Int. Law* 201.
[96] 120 NE 198, 202 (1918).   [97] Which are beyond the scope of this book.

> The conception of public policy is, and should be, narrower and more limited in private international law [citing *Cheshire and North*] ... Local values ought not lightly to be elevated into public policy on the transnational level.[98]

Public policy in the conflict of laws must therefore have a special meaning, reflecting its context. We are not here looking to domestic public policy to justify a result as that would be too parochial given the international elements of the case. Merely because the result in a particular case differs from that which would have happened had all the connections been to England, that does not justify utilising some exception to the choice of law rule. The case may have no connection with England and merely have been litigated here due to some accident of jurisdiction.

Where the result is manifestly incompatible with international public policy,[99] then the resort to the public policy exception can be argued to achieve a result which would occur in most countries in which the claim could have been raised.[100] International public policy includes rules which infringe fundamental human rights, for example, by being discriminatory on the grounds of race, religion, or the like. The use of public policy in these cases to prevent the application of the foreign law would be unobjectionable internationally.

Traditionally, public policy only operates negatively; it prevents the law which would otherwise apply from taking effect. It is the application of the foreign law which must be contrary to English public policy, as there is an understandable reluctance by the courts to find that a foreign law of itself is contrary to public policy.[101] In every case in which the court resorts to public policy it must remember that this is an exception to a choice of law process. That process has a purpose which is to achieve a just result taking account of the international elements.

It is also true to say that public policy in the conflict of laws may have a smaller role than it appears to have. This is particularly true of the rules in relation to title to property which has been purportedly confiscated by a foreign state.[102] The *lex situs* rule is applied, which is a sufficient answer even though the court may make reference to public policy to explain its decision.

a. Penal laws

A penal law, strictly defined, is one which is intended to have a punitive effect. A penalty, including a penal sum of money or a fine, is therefore imposed by way of punishment.[103] The adjective 'penal' is also applied to legal disabilities

---

[98] [2002] 2 AC 883 at para. 114.

[99] *Kuwait Airways v Iraqi Airways (Nos 4 and 5)* [2002] 2 AC 883, and see further below.

[100] Though presumably not in that country whose law is being made inapplicable through the use of the public policy exception.

[101] See e.g., *Oppenheimer v Cattermole* [1976] AC 249 at 277–8.   [102] See further pp. 408–9 above.

[103] See Lord Denning MR in *SA Consortium General Textiles v Sun and Sand Agencies* [1978] 2 QB 279 (CA).

or incapacities which are imposed on someone, not in order to punish the person for a criminal offence, but because they are imposed upon a few persons, or upon a group of people merely because they form a distinct group such as slaves or Jews or gypsies. This rather loose usage of the term 'penal' is really employed when what is meant is discriminatory. The usage may be justified on the ground that the person who is subjected to the disability is in effect being punished for being the sort of person that person is.

The English courts will not enforce penalties such as fines for criminal offences,[104] nor will they enforce foreign judgments for sums imposed by way of penalty.[105] Note that the meaning of a penalty in relation to foreign judgments does not depend on how the foreign law characterises the term. English law considers that a penalty must (a) be payable to the state or some officer of the state; and (b) for some criminal offence or an offence of public disorder.[106] A judgment for non-compensatory damages is not considered penal and it is not therefore contrary to public policy to enforce such a judgment.[107] The English court has justified the non-enforcement of foreign penal laws by noting that crimes are 'only cognisable and punishable in the country in which they were committed'.[108] Along with revenue and other public laws, penal laws are not enforced outwith the territory of the foreign state because they are seen as promoting a governmental interest or the assertion of a sovereign right. As such those laws operate intra-territorially only.[109] The different view of the non-enforcement of such rules is that they are not a matter for the judges but for the executive branch of government or the legislature. In *Equatorial Guinea v Royal Bank of Scotland International*,[110] the Privy Council, on appeal from the courts of Guernsey, opined that there were sound policy reasons why the courts should not involve themselves in questions of sovereign authority. But that international co-operation can be achieved by way of government to government relationships.[111]

Penal laws will not be enforced, even indirectly. Therefore in *United States v Inkley*:

---

[104] See *Folliott v Ogden* (1790) 3 Term. Rep. 726 (HL).　　[105] See p. 251 above.

[106] *Huntingdon v Attrill* [1893] AC 150 (PC) and *Raulin v Fischer* [1911] 2 KB 93.

[107] *SA Consortium General Textiles v Sun and Sand Agencies* [1978] 2 QB 279 (CA).

[108] *Republic of Iran v Barakat Galleries Ltd* [2007] EWCA Civ 1374, [2009] QB 22.

[109] See the Australian cases *Attorney General in and for the United Kingdom v Heinemann Publishers Australia Pty Ltd* (1988) 165 CLR 30; *Robb Evans of Robb Evans Associates v European Bank Ltd* [2004] NSWCA 82; followed in *Republic of Iran v Barakat Galleries Ltd* [2007] EWCA Civ 1374, [2009] QB 22 and *United States Securities and Exchange Commission v Manterfield* [2009] EWCA Civ 27, [2010] 1 WLR 172.

[110] [2006] UKPC 7.

[111] Citing two UN Conventions which were appropriate to this case, the Convention on the Prevention and Punishment of Crimes Against Internationally Protected Persons (1035 UNTS 167) which entered into force on 20 February 1977 and the Convention for the Suppression of the Financing of Terrorism (UN Doc. A/54/49 (Vol 1) (1999)), which entered into force on 10 April 2002.

> A sum of money had been given under a bail bond by the defendant in criminal proceedings in the United States. The bail bond was recoverable by way of civil suit in the United States and the United States sought to bring a civil action for its recovery in England.[112]

The claim was rejected by the English court. This was a penalty and not enforceable indirectly by way of a civil action.

Penal laws of foreign states can be recognised, however. They are not treated as having no effect whatsoever – unlike laws which are denied even recognition. The law can be relied upon, for example, as a defence to an action for enforcement of a contract. In *The Playa Larga*:

> Contracts to sell sugar by C, a Cuban state trading enterprise with separate legal personality and not part of the Cuban state, were entered into with I, a Chilean corporation, a majority of whose shares were held by a Chilean state trading concern. C failed to deliver parts of the cargoes of sugar. I claimed in arbitration in England damages for non-delivery. C's defence was that the contracts were frustrated by the enactment by Cuba twelve days after the coup against President Allende in Chile in 1973, of a law purporting to freeze all property of or demandable or claimable by Chilean bodies such as I.

The arbitrators found that the enactment of the law rendered further performance illegal under Cuban law. They, Mustill J and the Court of Appeal all held that the Chilean law constituted a frustrating event and a defence for C. I contended that the Chilean law was penal and discriminatory. The arbitrators and Mustill J agreed, but thought that since the law did not require enforcement, it could not be disregarded even though it was penal. Ackner LJ, who gave the judgment of the Court of Appeal, seemed to believe the law was not penal, since it was not intended to punish anyone, but was meant to be a means of helping to secure compensation from Chile for Cuban property damaged in the coup.[113] He thought the law did not contravene public policy. This, with respect, seems the more correct approach. Likewise, in *Republic of Iran v Barakat Galleries Ltd*, the Iranian law which gave title to antiquities unlawfully excavated in Iran to the Republic of Iran also made unlawful excavation criminal and imposed criminal penalties. However, the Court of Appeal held that the provisions as to title were not penal.[114]

---

[112] [1989] QB 255.

[113] Compare his analysis of the New Zealand legislation in *AG for New Zealand v Ortiz* [1984] AC 1 discussed further pp. 429–30 above.

[114] [2007] EWCA Civ 1374, [2009] QB 22, discussed P. Rogerson, 'Public Policy and Cultural Objects' [2008] *CLJ* 246.

Where the foreign claim or judgment is composed of two parts, one for civil recovery of damages and one for a penalty imposed by the state, the English court has severed the penalty and enforced the remainder of the judgment.[115]

b. Revenue laws

The English court will not enforce claims which are based on foreign revenue laws, and will not act as tax collectors for foreign governments and public authorities.[116] This principle was clearly reaffirmed by the House of Lords in *Government of India v Taylor*,[117] where it held that the rejection of a claim by the Indian government to prove in an English bankruptcy as a creditor for unpaid tax was correct. Nor will the courts enforce such claims indirectly, as when a liquidator of a company sues to enforce debts due to the company, but it is shown that the liquidator will have to pay all the proceeds of the action to a foreign revenue authority.[118] A foreign judgment for a claim for taxes will not be enforced in England.[119] A foreign government cannot evade this principle by claiming under some other law if it is really claiming to recover taxes.[120] If the foreign revenue authority makes a claim for possession of goods in order to enforce its claim for payment of tax, then it will also fail. So, in *Brokaw v Seatrain UK Ltd*,[121] the US government served notice of a levy in respect of unpaid taxes on goods aboard a ship when it was on its way to England. Lord Denning MR pointed out that had the US government reduced the goods into its actual possession in a warehouse or had the matter of the ship attorned in respect of the goods to an officer of that government, the latter would have obtained possessory title to them. If it had then lost possession of them, it could have claimed the goods in reliance on its possessory title. It would not need to have recourse for this purpose to its revenue laws.

This is correct, but one might argue that such technicalities and distinctions cast doubt upon the merits of the rule which, in fact, countenances the avoidance of payment of a non-penal tax lawfully imposed. No real reason for the existence of the rule (and the House of Lords in *Government of India v Taylor*[122] gave none beyond the statement that the English courts will not sit as tax collectors for foreign countries) has been given except that a foreign revenue law is a public law. It could be argued that the rule hardly serves the interests of international comity.[123] However, this can also be said of penal and other public laws. It appears from the recent decisions that the court is willing

---

[115] *United States Securities and Exchange Commission v Manterfield* [2009] EWCA Civ 27, [2010] 1 WLR 172.
[116] *Municipal Council of Sydney v Bull* [1909] 1 KB 7.   [117] [1955] AC 491.
[118] *Peter Buchanan Ltd v McVey* [1955] AC 516n, Supreme Court of Ireland, approved in *Government of India v Taylor* [1955] AC 491 and applied in *QRS 1 Aps v Frandsen* [1999] 1 WLR 2159 (CA).
[119] *Rossano v Manufacturer's Life Insurance Co.* [1963] 2 QB 352.
[120] *Re Lord Cable* [1977] 1 WLR 7.   [121] [1971] 2 QB 476.   [122] [1955] AC 491.
[123] See J. G. Collier, *The Conflict of Laws* (3rd edn, Cambridge University Press, 2001) p. 369.

to take some cognisance of such foreign laws but not to enforce them extra-territorially. For example, the House of Lords very sensibly held in *Re State of Norway's Application (Nos 1 and 2)*[124] that a request for evidence to be taken in England for use in tax proceedings in Norway was not an attempt to enforce that country's tax laws either directly or indirectly. Their only enforcement would take place in Norway. There is nothing wrong in principle with helping a country enforce its own tax laws within its own territory. In any case, a further limitation on the ambit of the rule is that, although Lord Mansfield once said that 'no country ever takes notice of the revenue laws of another',[125] the English court will recognise such a law by declining to enforce an agreement designed to avoid its incidence.[126]

Note that not every sum payable to a foreign state or public authority is payable by way of tax. If it is owed for particular services rendered, such as airport landing charges or a contribution to the state legal aid fund,[127] it is enforceable as not being a tax.

c. Public laws

'Public laws' are generally recognised but not enforced. For some time there was doubt that there was such a further category of law, beyond penal laws and revenue laws, which the English court would not enforce extraterritorially because the public law was said to be a matter of sovereign power.

In *AG for New Zealand v Ortiz*:

> A Maori artefact had been illegally exported from New Zealand in violation of a New Zealand law which provided for forfeiture to the Crown of historic articles which were, or were sought to be, illegally exported from New Zealand. The Attorney General for New Zealand sought to recover the property which had been brought to England.

The first question was the interpretation of the New Zealand law which the House of Lords decided did not mean that the title had passed to the Crown before the artefact left New Zealand. The second question, whether the New Zealand legislation could be enforced here as a public law, was not before the House of Lords. Staughton J had held that it could be enforced. Though it was a public law it was not penal. Therefore, public policy and comity required its application.[128] This argument had been rejected previously by Devlin J in *Bank voor Handel en Scheepvaart NV v Slatford*[129] as violating the *lex situs*

---

[124] [1990] 1 AC 723.   [125] *Holman v Johnson* (1775) 1 Cowp. 341 at 343.
[126] *Re Emery's Investment Trusts* [1959] Ch. 410.
[127] See the New Zealand case of *Connor v Connor* [1974] 1 NZLR 632.
[128] [1982] QB 349.   [129] [1953] 1 QB 248.

rule. The Court of Appeal reversed the judgment of Staughton J, partly on the ground that the statute was a public law and not enforceable.[130]

However, in *Republic of Iran v Barakat*,[131] the Court of Appeal held that there was a category of 'other public law' which would be recognised but not enforced extraterritorially.[132] This category includes claims which 'involve the exercise or assertion of a sovereign right or seek to enforce governmental interests'.[133] The court did not expand on what these laws might be beyond remarking that they are acts *de jure imperii*, which takes us no further. It gave examples of exchange control legislation, defence of citizens and possibly export restrictions. The editors of *Dicey, Morris and Collins* suggest also trading with the enemy legislation, and anti-trust legislation.[134] Protection of cultural heritage laws by compulsory acquisition could be included as well. However, there seems little reason to complicate the matter. The *lex situs* rule operates to denote the applicable law. If the *lex situs* determines that the artefact is the property of the foreign state (or someone holding from that state), that should be the answer without further investigation into the public law nature of the legal rule in question. In the event, this was the method adopted by the Court of Appeal.

Laws which promote the security of the state, such as the imposition of security measures and the apprehension and trial of suspects, are aspects of sovereign authority which will not be enforced by the English courts. Traditionally, the non-enforcement of such rules has formed part of the act of state doctrine, by which reliance on them is non-justiciable in the English courts.[135] This 'hands off' approach to matters of sovereign authority can be criticised as operating unfairly and not in the best interests of the UK government. Nevertheless, it remains powerful. Recently, in *Equatorial Guinea v Royal Bank of Scotland International*,[136] the Privy Council, on appeal from the courts of Guernsey, refused to grant a *Norwich Pharmacal* order[137] against the respondent. The order would have aided the government of Equatorial Guinea in its action against some alleged mercenaries who were British nationals taking part in an unsuccessful coup against the government. The action was held to be an exercise of sovereign authority and not justiciable in the English courts.

---

[130] Per Lord Denning MR. Ackner and O'Connor LJJ held that the law was penal and therefore unenforceable.

[131] [2007] EWCA Civ 1374, [2009] QB 22.

[132] Following the Australian cases *Attorney General in and for the United Kingdom v Heinemann Publishers Australia Pty Ltd* (1988) 165 CLR 30, *Robb Evans of Robb Evans Associates v European Bank Ltd* [2004] NSWCA 82; as interpreted in *Mbasogo v Logo Ltd (No. 1)* [2006] EWCA Civ 1370, [2007] QB 846.

[133] [2007] EWCA Civ 1374, [2009] QB 22 at para. 126.

[134] Dicey, Morris and Collins, *Conflict of Laws* (14th edn, Sweet & Maxwell, London, 2006) Rule 210, i.e., rules protecting against anti-competitive behaviour.

[135] *Mbasogo v Logo Ltd* [2007] QB 846.   [136] [2006] UKPC 7.

[137] These are orders by which claimants can discover the whereabouts of assets from a person who is mixed up in the wrongdoing of another.

Therefore, the Guernsey court just did not have power to make such an order. A claim which has to rely on this type of public law will fail.

d. Laws which grossly infringe human rights

Laws which grossly infringe human rights will not be treated as laws at all and are not recognised. A German decree was refused recognition in *Oppenheimer v Cattermole*.[138] The decree deprived Jewish émigrés of their German nationality which had the effect of confiscating their property. Such a rule cannot therefore be enforced either. Likewise, slavery laws have been denied recognition.[139] Human rights are now protected under the European Convention on Human Rights (ECHR) of 1950[140] and one can expect a more frequent application of this rule. It has been used to prevent enforcement of foreign judgments which have been obtained in breach of Article 6 of the ECHR.[141]

e. Laws which fundamentally breach public international law

Laws which fundamentally breach public international law have been denied recognition (and so enforcement). These laws are more extensive than those which grossly infringe human rights but the extent of the category is difficult to determine. In *Kuwait Airways v Iraqi Airways (Nos 4 and 5)*:[142]

After the invasion of Kuwait by Iraq there had been resolutions of the Security Council of the United Nations sanctioning the invasion of Kuwait and in particular calling upon all states not to recognise the annexation of Kuwait by Iraq. The claimants sought return of aircraft taken by the Iraqi forces and transferred to the defendants or alternatively damages for their wrongful detention. The defendants argued that they had ownership of the aircraft by application of Iraqi law, the *lex situs*, at the time. The Iraqi government had passed a resolution confirming that the aircraft were the property of Iraq.

The House of Lords refused to recognise the Iraqi law transferring property in the aircraft to the defendants. The law was a fundamental breach of international law. Therefore, it was not recognised and not applied. However, the remainder of Iraqi law operated to give the claimants a right to the return of

---

[138] [1976] AC 249 (HL).

[139] *Sommersett's Case* (1772) 20 State Trials 1, also reported as *Somerset v Stewart* (1772) Lofft. 1.

[140] Enacted in England by the Human Rights Act 1998.

[141] Under the Brussels I Regulation: *Krombach v Bamberski* Case C-7/98 [2000] ECR I-1935; under national rules: *Al Jedda v Secretary of State for Defence* [2009] EWHC 397 at paras 68–73; *Merchant International Co. Ltd v Natsionalna Aktsionerna Kompaniya Naftogaz Ukrayiny* [2012] EWCA Civ 196.

[142] [2002] 2 AC 883.

the aircraft. It is unclear beyond the specific resolution of the Security Council in this case what amounts to a fundamental breach of public international law, in particular, whether a law which requisitions or nationalises property within the territory of the state whose law is in question would be unrecognisable on the basis that adequate compensation was not paid.

f. Laws which infringe basic principles of justice or morality

This, too, is an unclear category of laws. Lord Nicholls in *Kuwait Airways v Iraqi Airways (Nos 4 and 5)*[143] opined that:

> the courts of this country must have a residual power, to be exercised exception-ally and with the greatest circumspection, to disregard a provision in the foreign law when to do otherwise would affront basic principles of justice and fairness which the courts seek to apply in the administration of justice in this country. Gross infringements of human rights are one instance, and an important instance, of such a provision. But the principle cannot be confined to one particular category of unacceptable laws. That would be neither sensible nor logical. Laws may be fundamentally unacceptable for reasons other than human rights violations.[144]

Examples include some of the list below in relation to contracts (such as those entered into under duress),[145] and laws contrary to human rights (such as those which deny a proper trial).

g. Contracts contrary to public policy

There are a wide range of contracts which have been refused enforcement at common law.[146] Often the contracts have been governed by English law and therefore the result is better explained as a rule of domestic English law of contract. However, some of the judgments have been couched in such wide terms as to suggest that, whatever the law applicable to the contract, contracts in the following list would not be enforced in England. Where non-enforcement of the contract whatever the applicable law has been expressed, this is indicated:

(a) contracts in restraint of trade in England;[147]
(b) contracts entered into under duress have been denied enforcement, even if they would be enforceable by the applicable law of the contract;[148]

---

[143] *Ibid.*   [144] *Ibid.* at 1077–8.

[145] *Royal Boskalis Westminster NV v Mountain* [1999] QB 674 at 729.

[146] These contracts would now be subject to the Rome I Regulation which provides an exception to the application of the applicable law where it would be manifestly contrary to English public policy (Art. 21). See further Chapter 10.

[147] *Rousillon v Rousillon* (1880) 14 Ch. D 351.

[148] *Kaufman v Gerson* [1904] 1 KB 591 (CA); *Royal Boskalis Westminster NV v Mountain* [1999] QB 674 at 729.

(c) contracts with the enemy;[149]

(d) contracts to prejudice interests of the United Kingdom with a friendly foreign country;[150]

(e) contracts infringing English conceptions of morality, such as contracts for prostitution,[151] even if the applicable law permits enforcement of such contracts;[152]

(f) contracts to stifle a prosecution in England;[153]

(g) contracts requiring the performance of an illegal act in a friendly foreign country[154] (including contracts to defraud the foreign revenue authority)[155] whatever the applicable law.

5. Unilateral choice of law rules

Although not always obvious in English law, unilateral choice of law rules are found here as well as in other legal systems. These make a particular law apply in given circumstances (sometimes at one party's choice) so that one law is identified at the outset rather than a possible number of rules with the more traditional common law multilateral approach. Such rules can also be described as internationally mandatory rules, certainly they have that effect. An example would be the rule of English law that a spouse can make an application for financial provision from a deceased's estate if the deceased was domiciled in England.[156] Another example is the Employment Rights Act (ERA) 1996 which imposes English rules relating to unfair dismissal irrespective of the law governing the contract of employment. The House of Lords in *Lawson v Serco* held that the provisions of the ERA 1996 apply even if an employee is working outside Great Britain in some cases, such as when the employee is working in a 'British enclave'. Unilateral choice of law rules often favour a consumer or an employee. For example, the Rome II Regulation provides that the law of the consumer's habitual residence applies in relation to questions of liability for defective manufacture.[157] That can be seen as a unilateral rule although it does not conform to the classical unilateralist view that such rules only delimit the scope of application of domestic forum law.

---

[149] *Dynamit A/G v Rio Tinto Co.* [1918] AC 292 (HL).

[150] *De Wütz v Hendricks* (1824) 2 Bing. 314.

[151] See e.g., *Pearce v Brooks* (1865–66) LR 1 Ex. 213.

[152] *Robinson v Bland* (1760) 2 Burr. 1077 at 1084.

[153] *Kaufman v Gerson* [1904] 1 KB 591 (CA).

[154] *Foster v Driscoll* [1929] 1 KB 470 (CA); and *Regazzoni v KC Sethia (1944) Ltd* [1958] AC 301 (HL).

[155] *Re Emery's Investment Trust* [1959] Ch. 410.

[156] Inheritance (Provision for Family and Dependants) Act 1975, s. 1(1).

[157] Rome II Regulation, Art. 5(1)(a).

6. Mandatory rules

Mandatory rules are those which apply to a case irrespective of the parties' wishes either as to the terms of the contract or as to the applicable law (which may or may not have been expressly chosen). They may be rules of English domestic or of foreign law and override the result of the normal choice of law process. They come in several forms: first, English domestic mandatory rules which apply to contracts governed by English law and override the contract's provisions. These are not uncommon, an example being the prohibitions on contractual terms which attempt to circumvent consumer protection. Domestic mandatory rules would apply even when the parties have not expressly chosen English law, so long as English law governs the contract. There are also internationally mandatory rules. These come in two types. Some apply to override the parties' choice of another law; for example, Article 3(3) of the Rome I Regulation[158] which provides that where all the elements of a contract are connected with one country but the parties have chosen the law of another country, the mandatory rules (in the domestic sense) of the first country will apply. The second type is those rules of English law which would apply to the case even where the normal English choice of law rule would apply a different law. At their strongest, such rules apply irrespective of a lack of connection with England and also disregarding the parties' express choice of another law. These rules would be truly internationally mandatory rules. These are relatively rare in English law. However, a similar effect can be achieved through unilateral choice of law rules or, in some cases, by the application of public policy.

---

[158] Regulation (EC) 593/2008 [2008] OJ L177/6.

Index